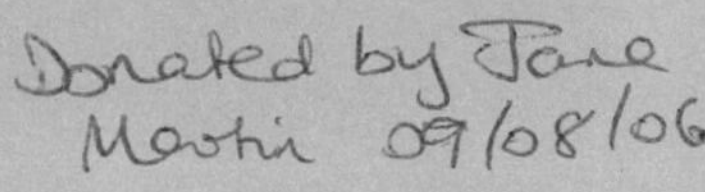
Donated by Jane
Martin 09/08/06.

D0674168

Donation
LIBRARY
ACC. No.
01140924
DEPT.
pbs
3wk
CLASS No.
658.8 BER
UNIVERSITY OF CHESTER
WARRINGTON CAMPUS
09/08/06.

MARKETING

MARKETING

SECOND EDITION

ERIC N. BERKOWITZ
UNIVERSITY OF MASSACHUSETTS

ROGER A. KERIN
SOUTHERN METHODIST UNIVERSITY

WILLIAM RUDELIUS
UNIVERSITY OF MINNESOTA

with 456 illustrations

1989

HOMEWOOD, IL 60430
BOSTON, MA 02116

SPONSORING EDITOR Elizabeth J. Schilling
DEVELOPMENTAL EDITOR Alice E. Fugate
PROJECT MANAGER Mark Spann
PRODUCTION EDITOR Donna L. Walls
ART DIRECTOR Kay Michael Kramer
DESIGNER Diane M. Beasley
COVER ILLUSTRATOR Kristen Throop
PHOTO RESEARCHERS Rhonda Fowler, Laura Wolff

LIBRARY OF CONGRESS CATALOGING-IN-PUBLICATION DATA

Berkowitz, Eric N.
Marketing/Eric N. Berkowitz, Roger A. Kerin, William Rudelius.—
—2nd ed.
p. cm.
Bibliography: p.
Includes indexes.
ISBN 0-256-07513-1 ISBN 0-256-07515-8 (Int'l. ed.)
1. Marketing. I. Kerin, Roger A. II. Rudelius, William.
III. Title.
HF5415.B44113 1989
658.8—dc19 88-27583
CIP

Printed in the United States of America
1234567890 GW/VH/VH 54321098

PREFACE

What makes marketing unique? Perhaps it is the blend of people and organizations, science and art, conscious decisions and blind chance. A textbook must recognize the challenges, controversies, and constraints that marketing professionals encounter. Like our first edition of *Marketing,* this new edition tries to capture the vitality of marketing for you, the reader.

We are delighted by the success of the first edition of *Marketing*. To date, over 150,000 students and 1,000 instructors have used it, and we value highly both the positive comments and the suggestions for improvement we've received from both groups. In this edition we have tried to build on the strengths of the original book while adding new material that reflects the latest developments in this dynamic field.

NEW IN THIS EDITION

- We have expanded coverage of ethical, legal, and regulatory issues to attempt to demonstrate how they affect marketing. We've added new material in "Promotional Process, Sales Promotion, and Publicity" (Chapter 16), discussing possible abuses of promotion and its ethical and social dimensions. In other chapters we discuss laws and regulatory trends that affect pricing, advertising, and packaging decisions.

• Significant new marketing topics have also been added, such as hypermarkets, single-source data, the "people meter," and just-in-time inventory. We also analyze current trends in the field, including the move toward "lean" management structures, regional and ethnic market segmentation, entrepreneurial startup businesses and the resurrection of old stand-bys as new stars in many companies' product lines.

• Finally, significant recent research related to marketing is utilized. We believe that students must be aware of important research that analyzes and explains consumer behavior and the success or failure of marketing programs. This edition features an in-depth treatment of consumer behavior (Chapter 4) that examines both classic research and the latest studies on psychographics, demographics, and psychology. In addition, Marketing Research Reports throughout the book relate research findings to important issues facing marketing managers.

As in the first edition, we want to move you out of the role of bystander and to involve you in the role of the marketing decision maker. We introduce you to contemporary people and organizations that have made both brilliant and disastrous marketing decisions. These extended examples appear both in the text and in the Marketing Action Memos found throughout the book, which apply marketing principles to actual situations.

Our innovative pedagogical approach was overwhelmingly endorsed in the first edition, and we utilize it again in this edition. The book reinforces major concepts as they are introduced in each chapter to stimulate your understanding of them and foster your ability to apply them appropriately. At the end of every major section, Concept Checks pose 2 to 3 questions to test your recall. The Learning Objectives at the beginning of each chapter and the Key Terms and Concepts and Summary at the close provide further reinforcement. We also include Suggested Readings, which are annotated to help you decide which source would be most useful to investigate for further information. We believe these features are a giant stride toward capturing on paper the dynamic nature of marketing.

Marketing, Second Edition, is divided into six main parts. Part One, Initiating the Marketing Process, looks first at what marketing is and how it identifies and satisfies consumer needs (Chapter 1). Then Chapter 2 provides an overview of the strategic marketing process that occurs in an organization—planning, implementation, and control—which provides a structure for the text. Chapter 3 analyzes the five major environmental factors in our changing marketing environment.

Part Two, Understanding Buyers and Markets, first describes, in Chapter 4, how ultimate consumers reach buying decisions. Next, because of their important differences from ultimate consumers, industrial and organizational buyers and how they make purchase decisions are covered in Chapter 5.

In Part Three, Targeting Marketing Opportunities, the marketing research function is divided into two important parts: collecting (Chapter 6) and using

(Chapter 7) marketing information. Chapter 7 also describes how today's marketing managers use marketing decision support systems and make market and sales forecasts. The process of segmenting and targeting markets and positioning products appears in Chapter 8.

Part Four, Satisfying Marketing Opportunities, covers the four *P*'s—the marketing mix elements. Unlike most competitive textbooks, the product element is divided into the natural chronological sequence of first developing new products (Chapter 9) and then managing the existing products (Chapter 10). Pricing is covered in terms of underlying pricing analysis (Chapter 11), followed by actual price setting (Chapter 12) and the related Appendix A, "Financial Aspects of Marketing." Three chapters address the place (distribution) aspects of marketing: "Marketing Channels and Wholesaling" (Chapter 13), "Physical Distribution" (Chapter 14), and "Retailing" (Chapter 15). Retailing is a separate chapter because of its importance and interest as a career for many of today's students. Promotion is also covered in three chapters. Chapter 16 discusses marketing communications in general and presents an in-depth treatment of sales promotion, an activity that often exceeds advertising in the promotional budgets of many firms but receives minimal coverage in many current textbooks. "Advertising" (Chapter 17) and "Personal Selling and Sales Management" (Chapter 18) complete the coverage of promotional activities.

Part Five, Managing the Marketing Process, expands on Chapter 2 to show how the four marketing mix elements are blended to plan (Chapter 19) and implement and control (Chapter 20) marketing programs. Because these topics can become very abstract, both chapters close with an example of how Yoplait Yogurt's marketing program is planned, implemented, and controlled.

Part Six, Expanding Marketing Settings, devotes separate chapters to two marketing topics of increasing importance in today's world: international marketing (Chapter 21) and marketing of services (Chapter 22). The part closes with Appendix B, "Career Planning in Marketing," which discusses the marketing jobs themselves and how to get them.

Cases from actual organizations, a detailed glossary, and three indexes (brand, product, and firm; author; and subject) complete the book.

As we observe in Chapter 1, we genuinely hope that somewhere in *Marketing* the reader will discover not only the challenge and excitement of marketing, but possibly a career as well.

Supplements

Producing supplements of extraordinary quality and utility to complement the text itself was, from the onset, a primary objective of the authors and publisher. Too often, emphasis and investment in these key components are based on quantity, not utility. All supplements accompanying this text that are to be used with students, from the test items to the study guide, have been reviewed by many of the same instructors who critiqued various drafts of the text. Additionally, much attention has been given throughout to providing elements and features in these supplements that were requested by both inexperienced and experienced instructors. As a result, each component contains several features not offered with any other marketing text.

Instructor's Manual

The Instructor's Manual includes conversion notes, lecture outlines, transparencies and transparency masters, and answers to text questions. Supplementary Marketing Action Memos and Marketing Research Reports are also provided.

Transparency Acetates

A set of 200 overhead transparency acetates in both two and four colors is available free to adopters. More than two-thirds of these have been developed from outside the text.

Test Bank

Our Test Bank has been reviewed to ensure clarity, accuracy, and an appropriate range and level of difficulty. It contains more than 2,000 questions, categorized by chapter, by subject area within the chapter, and by level of difficulty. With this edition, the bank also includes approximately 20 applications questions, 5 essay questions, and approximately 75 to 100 multiple choice questions per chapter, making it one of the most comprehensive test packages on the market.

Computest II Microcomputer Testing System

In addition to the printed format, the computerized test bank is also available free to adopters. The easy-to-use test bank includes all the questions in the printed version. Additional benefits include the ability to:

- Add or delete individual test items.
- Personalize individual questions.
- Generate several versions of the same exam.
- Maintain class files and test scores on disk.

Videotape Case Studies

A unique series of contemporary marketing programs is available on a videotape cassette. Subjects range from the conception and launching of new products to strategies used in designing advertising programs.

Study Guide

Coauthored by an educational consultant, the Study Guide enables the student to learn and apply marketing instead of simply memorizing facts for an examination. New case problems and five types of exercises are used to accomplish this goal: (1) application exercises, (2) matching terms to definitions, (3) matching concepts to examples, (4) recognition and identification exercises, and (5) chapter recall.

Computer Problem Software

This software features short cases and problems that allow students to make marketing decisions and see the results.

Newsletter

An annual newsletter will update the text with supplemental Marketing Research Reports, Marketing Action Memos, transparency masters, and reprints of pertinent magazine and newspaper articles.

DEVELOPMENT OF THIS BOOK

As with any new product, developing a good textbook requires extensive market research and comparative analysis of the competition. We were fortunate in having the developmental resources of Times Mirror/Mosby and Richard D. Irwin to support this effort. To guide the basic focus of the book, we conducted focus groups, group discussions, and reviews of the manuscript, as well as class-testing the manuscript in actual teaching situations. Additionally, photo researchers worked closely with us to select illustrations that would effectively reinforce the textual narrative.

In creating the second edition, we drew on multiple sources. In addition to another focus group, we commissioned faculty who were using the first edition to keep regular "diaries" documenting their classroom experiences. We also commissioned instructors who were familiar with other textbooks to do comparative reviews that told us how our book could be improved. The wealth of information that resulted from these reviews enabled us to determine which features of the manuscript were most effective and revise those which needed more work.

Finally, faculty from various schools nationwide were commissioned to review our first and second drafts, on a chapter-by-chapter basis. Our textbook cases, test bank, software, and study guide also underwent this painstaking attention and concern for quality.

ACKNOWLEDGMENTS

Writing and publishing a major textbook and supplements package are beyond the capacity of one author—or even three! The preceding section demonstrates the amount of reviewing that went into this project, and we are deeply grateful to the numerous people who have shared their ideas with us. Reviewing a book or supplement takes an incredible amount of energy and attention, and we are glad that the people listed below took the time to do it. Their comments have inspired us to do our best.

Reviewers who contributed to the first edition and basic focus of this book include:

William D. Ash
California State University, Long Beach

Thomas Bertsch
James Madison University

William Brown
University of Nebraska, Omaha

William G. Browne
Oregon State University

Stephen Calcich
Norfolk State University

Gerald Cavallo
Fairfield University

S. Tamer Cavusgil
Michigan State University

Ken Crocker
Bowling Green State University

Joe Cronin
University of Kentucky

Lowell E. Crow
Western Michigan University

Bill Curtis
University of Nebraska, Lincoln

Dan Darrow
Ferris State University

Martin Decatur
Suffolk County Community College

Francis DeFea
El Camino College

Bill Dodds
Boston College

James Donnelly
University of Kentucky

Roger W. Egerton
Southwestern Oklahoma State University

Charles Ford
Arkansas State University

Leslie A. Goldgehn
California State, Hayward

James Grimm
Illinois State University

Al Holden
St. John's University

Jarrett Hudnall
Stephen F. Austin State University

Mike Hyman
University of Houston

Kenneth Jameson
California State University, Dominguez Hills

Jim Johnson
Saint Cloud State University

Mary Joyce
University of Central Florida

Herb Katzenstein
St. John's University

Roy Klages
State University of New York at Albany

Priscilla LaBarbera
New York University

Ed Laube
Macomb Community College

Karen LeMasters
University of Arizona

Richard Leventhal
Metropolitan State College

Lynn Loudenback
New Mexico State University

Robert Luke
Southwest Missouri State University

Bart Macchiette
Plymouth State University

James McAlexander
Iowa State University

Peter McClure
University of Massachusetts, Boston

Jim McHugh
St. Louis Community College at Forest Park

Gary McKinnon
Brigham Young University

Lee Meadow
Bentley College

Ron Michaels
University of Kansas

Stephen W. Miller
St. Louis University

Donald F. Mulvihill
Virginia Commonwealth University

Joseph Myslivec
Central Michigan University

Carl Obermiller
University of Washington

Allan Palmer
University of North Carolina, Charlotte

Dennis Pappas
Columbus Technical Institute

William Perttula
San Francisco State University

Michael Peters
Boston College

Bob Ruekert
University of Minnesota

Starr Schlobohm
University of New Hampshire

Stan Scott
Boise State University

Bob Smiley
Indiana State University

Robert Swerdlow
Lamar University

Clint Tankersley
Syracuse University

Andy Thacker
California State Polytechnic University, Pomona

Fred Trawick
University of Alabama at Birmingham

Ottilia Voegtli
University of Missouri, St. Louis

Gerald Waddle
Clemson University

Randall E. Wade
Rogue Community College

Kaylene Williams
University of Delaware

Wilton Lelund Wilson
Southwest Texas State University

Robert Witherspoon
Triton College

Van R. Wood
Texas Tech University

William R. Wynd
Eastern Washington University

Reviewers who helped us create this new edition include:

Siva Balasubramanian
University of Iowa

A. Diane Barlar
University of West Florida

James Barnes
University of Mississippi

S. Tamer Cavusgil
Michigan State University

Clark Compton
University of Missouri, St. Louis

Ken Crocker
Bowling Green State University

John H. Cunningham
University of Oregon

Dexter Dalton
St. Louis Community College at Meramec

Martin Decatur
Suffolk County Community College

Barbara Evans
University of Melbourne (Australia)

Donald Fuller
University of Central Florida

Kenneth Goodenday
University of Toledo

Richard Hill
University of Illinois

Mike Hyman
University of Houston

James C. Johnson
St. Cloud State University

Herbert Katzenstein
St. John's University

Irene Lange
California State University, Fullerton

Kenneth Maricle
Virginia Commonwealth University

Elena Martinez
University of Puerto Rico

James Meszaros
County College of Morris

Fred Morgan
Wayne State University

Keith Murray
Northeastern University

Allan Palmer
University of North Carolina, Charlotte

Richard Penn
University of Northern Iowa

John Penrose
University of Texas, Austin

Joe Puri
Florida Atlantic University

James Rakowski
Memphis State University

Heikki Rinne
Brigham Young University

Eberhard Scheuing
St. John's University

Stan Scott
Boise State University

Allen Smith
Florida Atlantic University

Robert Swerdlow
Lamar University

Andrew Thacker
California State Polytechnic University, Pomona

Thomas Trittipo
Central State University, Oklahoma

Sue Umashankar
University of Arizona

Harlan Wallingford
Pace University

James Wilkins
University of Southwestern Louisiana

We were also fortunate to be able to call on the special expertise of individuals who reviewed and revised parts of the text and supplements. Attorney Robert J. Dockery of Becton Dickinson reviewed and corrected legal topics in the book, and Finance Professor James M. Gahlon reviewed Appendix A, "Financial Aspects of Marketing." James C. Cross of the University of Minnesota revised Chapter 14, "Physical Distribution"; Robert W. Ruekert of the University of Minnesota revised Chapter 16, "Promotional Process, Sales Promotion, and Publicity" and Chapter 17, "Advertising"; and Steven W. Hartley of the University of Denver revised Chapter 22, "Marketing of Services" and Appendix B, "Career Planning in Marketing." Lee Meadow of Bentley College provided helpful advice on the Test Bank, and educational consultant Erica Michaels, assisted by Ron Michaels of the University of Kansas, wrote the Study Guide and coauthored the Test Bank. Carl Obermiller of the University of Washington also contributed to the Test Bank.

The business community also provided great help in making available cases and information that appear in the text and supplements—much of it for the first time in college materials. Thanks are due to Earl Bakken of Medtronics, Fernando Garcia of Garid, Susan Narayan of 3M, Roy D. Adler of Pepperdine University, George B. Glison of Southern Illinois University, and James E. Nelson of the University of Colorado. We also acknowledge the help of Craig Britton and Jan Tritsch of Pillsbury, Ed Johnson of Minnesota Color Envelope, Kristi Rudelius, Scott Tonneslan, Steven Rothschild of General Mills, Roger K. Thompson of The Olive Garden, Wanda Truxillo of IBM, and James Watkins of Golden Valley Microwave Foods.

Staff support from the University of Massachusetts, the Southern Methodist University, and the University of Minnesota was essential.

Finally, staff members and consultants at Richard D. Irwin and Times Mirror/Mosby have been invaluable in helping us get this text into your hands. We thank Elizabeth Schilling for managing the project, setting high standards, and bringing all the pieces together. Her broad knowledge of the marketing field and the academic marketplace was a valuable guide in building a cohesive package that we confidently feel is the best available. Alice Fugate read the manuscript closely, managed the review process, and provided valuable comments on style, content, and illustrations—not to mention deadlines! But no matter how tight the schedule, she retained both her tact and her sense of humor. We would also like to thank Diane Beasley for designing a visually exciting textbook, and Mark Spann and Donna Walls for helping us meet tight production schedules.

We thank all these people and organizations for their contributions. We feel that together we have provided you with the second edition of an educationally vital yet immensely readable book.

ERIC N. BERKOWITZ
ROGER A. KERIN
WILLIAM RUDELIUS

Contents In Brief

CONTENTS

PART ONE
INITIATING THE MARKETING PROCESS

PART TWO
UNDERSTANDING BUYERS AND MARKETS

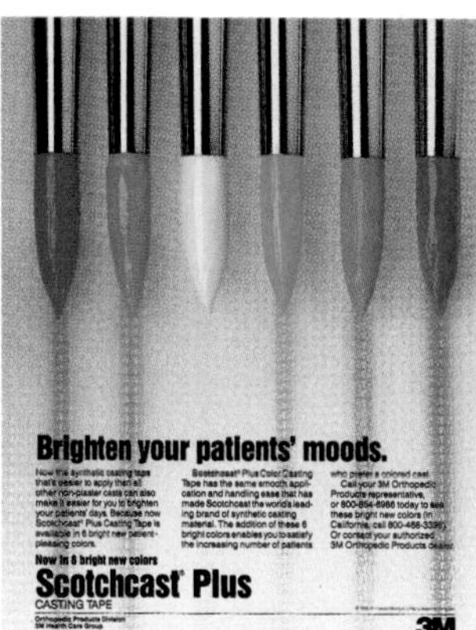
Brighten your patients' moods.
Now in 6 bright new colors
Scotchcast Plus
CASTING TAPE
3M

PART THREE

TARGETING MARKETING OPPORTUNITIES

DIGITS
FINGER WATCHES
bloomingdale's

6002009

Sunkist
Fun Fruits
DINOSAURS
Dinersaurs
PRONTOSAURUS

True Courage.
Show Your True Colors.
Kodacolor

PART FIVE

MANAGING THE MARKETING PROCESS

PART SIX
EXPANDING MARKETING SETTINGS

Sometimes the best way to stand out is to blend in.
It's a very important lesson we learned early in our 65-year history.
Leadership in the worldwide insurance industry isn't won by imposing our corporate culture on local operations. It's won by becoming part of the social, cultural and moral fabric of the countries in which we do business. That idea is one reason for our current success in providing a broad range of commercial and personal insurance to businesses and individuals around the world. To learn more, contact AIG, Dept. A, 70 Pine St., New York, N.Y. 10270.
Thinking more like our customers than other insurance companies is how we won our stripes.
Insurance Companies That Don't Think Like Insurance Companies.
AIG

CASES 643

MARKETING

PART ONE

INITIATING THE MARKETING PROCESS

A PRODUCT OF
GOLDEN VALLEY MICROWAVE FOODS, INC.
Heat this side down
ACT II

1

MARKETING: A FOCUS ON THE CONSUMER

After reading this chapter you should be able to:

Define marketing and explain the importance of (1) assessing and (2) satisfying consumer needs and wants.

•

Distinguish between marketing mix elements and environmental factors.

•

Describe how today's marketing concept era differs from prior eras oriented to production and selling.

•

Know what is required for marketing to occur.

•

Describe how marketing creates utilities for consumers.

Getting the Product, Market, and Timing Right

Jim Watkins still wonders if timing is his big problem.

He knows that business success lies in getting the right product to the right market at the right time. Today Watkins' timing problem involves microwave popcorn (opposite page), but it wasn't always that way. Still, he does seem to make a habit of developing products ahead of their time.

While in college, Watkins spent all of his student-loan money developing a "waterbike," a kind of aquatic motorcycle. It had only one major flaw: when Watkins rode it on its first test, it sank.[1] Today, about 20 years later, a dozen brands of self-powered water-sleds, which are cousins to his original design, are skimming across lakes around the country. His waterbike was ahead of its time.

After college in the early 1970's, Watkins joined the Pillsbury Company and worked with a team developing a family of 30 new food products to be cooked in microwave ovens.[2] The problem: at the time only about 10 percent of American households owned microwave ovens, so sales never took off. It was the problem of bad timing all over again.

In 1978, Watkins left Pillsbury and started his own business. Watkins named his firm Golden Valley Microwave Foods, Inc., (Golden Valley) and focused it on the research-and-development and marketing of microwave foods, leaving production and quality control to others. The first products were a line of single-portion frozen soups and entreés. The products had quality-control problems and fizzled.

DISCOVERING WHAT CONSUMERS WANT

Going back to basics, Watkins concentrated on frozen popcorn and pancakes for vending machines. He produced them in his own plant so he could control quality. He became convinced that the secret to success lay in developing food products and the necessary packaging targeted specifically for microwave ovens—not in simply adding new microwave cooking instructions to the labels of existing food products.

By the mid-1980's, Watkins concluded Golden Valley should not rely exclusively on sales through vending machines but should market microwave popcorn for home use, where the average American was eating over 28 quarts a year.[3] His marketing research found two key benefits people wanted in their microwave popcorn: (1) fewer unpopped kernels and (2) good popping results in even low-powered microwave ovens. His research-and-development staff successfully addressed these wants by finding better strains of popcorn and by developing new, patented packages to produce high-quality popped corn regardless of the power of the ovens.

A challenge? By 1985, Watkins and Golden Valley had developed what they thought was a better microwave popcorn. They accomplished this by following an almost classic textbook approach to marketing: (1) assessing buyers' needs and wants, and (2) satisfying them with a quality product. They introduced the Act I brand of microwave frozen popcorn, which was soon followed by the shelf-stable, microwave, nonfrozen Act II brand.

Watkins then decided to take Golden Valley's microwave popcorn into the fiercely competitive retail market, even though it would involve fighting for shelf space with 70 popcorn producers—some with nationally distributed products, such as the Orville Redenbacher brand. Considering this decision and Golden Valley's puny size, one experienced food-industry executive told Watkins, "Jimmy, my boy, you're going after an elephant with a .22."

MICROWAVE POPCORN, MARKETING, AND YOU

Can Golden Valley get retail shelf space and enough consumer sales to succeed while competing with some firms dozens of times its size? By the time you reach the end of this chapter, you will know the outcome of Jim Watkins' entry into the retail microwave popcorn business.

Answer the questions below. The correct answers are given later in the text.

1. In a nationally televised public hearing, a U.S. senator referred to "Xeroxing some reports." What was the Xerox Corporation's reaction? (a) delighted, (b) upset, or (c) somewhere in between. Why?
2. What is "Polavision"? (a) a new breathable contact lens, (b) a TV network that competes with Home Box Office, (c) special bifocal glasses, (d) instant movies, or (e) a political newspaper.
3. Right after World War II, International Business Machines Corporation (IBM) commissioned a study to estimate the *total* market for electronic computers. The study's results were (a) less that 10, (b) 1000, (c) 10,000, (d) 100,000 or (e) 1 million or more.
4. How should Jim Watkins and "puny" Golden Valley try to gain retail shelf space for its line of shelf-stable microwave popcorn?
5. Jim Watkins knows that the top seven microwave foods in the United States in order are coffee, vegetables, hot dishes / casseroles, potatoes, hot dogs / sandwiches, tea, and red meats.[5] What new product should he add to his present lines of popcorn and pancakes? Why?

FIGURE 1-1
The see-if-you're-really-a-marketing expert test

One key to that result lies in the subject of this book: marketing. In this chapter and in the rest of the book we'll introduce you to the people, organizations, ideas, activities, and jobs in marketing that have spawned the products and services that have been towering successes, shattering failures, or something in between. The successes we see, buy, and use every day. The failures fade from sight.

Where will Golden Valley be in 1992? Prospective buyers will decide. Later in this chapter you can observe and participate in some critical marketing decisions made by Watkins. Decide for yourself—probably before the market does—whether these decisions were the right ones.

In this chapter and in the ones that follow, you will feel the excitement of marketing. You will see both successes and disasters. You will also meet many very human, ordinary men and women whose marketing creatively sometimes achieved brilliant, extraordinary results. And who knows? Somewhere in these pages you may find a career.

WHAT IS MARKETING?

BEING A MARKETING EXPERT: GOOD NEWS—BAD NEWS

In many respects you are a marketing expert already. But just to test your expertise, try the "marketing expert" questions in Figure 1-1. These questions—some of them easy, others mind boggling—show the diverse problems marketing exectives grapple with every day. You'll find the answers in the next few pages.

Xerox ran this ad to communicate a specific message. What is that message? For the answer and why it is important, see the text.

The Good News: You Already have Marketing Experience You are somewhat of an expert because you do many marketing activities every day. You already know many marketing terms, concepts, and principles. For example, would you sell more Sony Walkmans at $500 or $50 each? The answer is $50, of course, so your experience in shopping for products—and maybe even selling them—already gives you great insights into the world of marketing. As a consumer, you've already been involved in thousands of marketing decisions, but mainly on the buying, not the marketing, side.

The Bad News: Surprises About the Obvious Unfortunately, common sense doesn't always explain some marketing decisions and actions.

A U.S. senator's reference to "Xeroxing some reports" in a nationally televised public hearing (Question 1, Figure 1-1) sounds like great publicity for the Xerox Corporation, right? But Xerox was upset. After seeing the hearing on TV, a Xerox attorney contacted the senator the next day to remind him of his misuse of the trademarked name *Xerox*. Legally, Xerox is a registered trademark of Xerox Corporation and, as a brand name, should be used only to identify its products and services. With this reminder and other advertisements (like that shown in the accompanying ad), Xerox is trying to protect a precious asset: its own name.

Under American trademark law, if consumers generally start using a brand name as the basic word to describe an entire class of products, then the company loses its exclusive rights to the name. "Xerox" would become "xerox"—just another English word to describe all kinds of photocopying. That fate has already befallen some famous American products such as linoleum, aspirin, cellophane, escalator, and yo-yo.

Today American firms are spending millions of dollars both in advertising and in court cases to protect their important brand names. Examples are Kimberly-Clark's Kleenex and 3M's Scotch tape. Coca-Cola takes dozens of restaurants to court every year for serving another cola drink when the patron asks for a Coca-Cola or even a Coke. Because legal and ethical issues such as the Xerox trademark problem are so central to many marketing decisions, they are addressed throughout the book.

The point here is that although your common sense usually helps you in analyzing marketing problems, sometimes it can mislead you. This book's in-depth study of marketing augments your common sense with an understanding of marketing concepts to help you assess and make marketing decisions more effectively.

MARKETING: USING EXCHANGES TO SATISFY NEEDS

The American Marketing Association, representing marketing professionals in the United States and Canada, states that "**marketing** is the process of planning and executing the conception, pricing, promotion, and distribution of ideas, goods, and services to create exchanges that satisfy individual and organizational objectives."[6] This definition stresses the importance of beneficial exchanges that satisfy the objectives of both those who buy and those who sell an array of ideas, goods, and services—whether they be individuals or organizations.

To serve both buyers and sellers, marketing seeks (1) to assess the needs and wants of prospective customers and (2) to satisfy them. These prospective customers include both individuals buying for themselves and their households and organizations that buy for their own use (such as manufacturers) or for resale (such as wholesalers and retailers). The key to achieving these two objectives is the idea of **exchange,** which is the trade of things of value between buyer and seller so that each is better off after the trade. This vital concept of exchange in marketing is covered below in more detail.

THE DIVERSE FACTORS INFLUENCING MARKETING ACTIVITIES

Although an organization's marketing activity focuses on assessing and satisfying consumer needs, countless other people, groups, and forces interact to shape the nature of its activities (Figure 1-2). Foremost is the organization itself, whose mission and objectives determine what business it is in and what goals it seeks. Within the organization, top management is responsible for achieving these goals. The marketing department works closely with other departments and employees to help provide the customer-satisfying products required for the organization to survive and prosper.[7]

FIGURE 1-2
An organization's marketing department relates to many people, groups, and forces

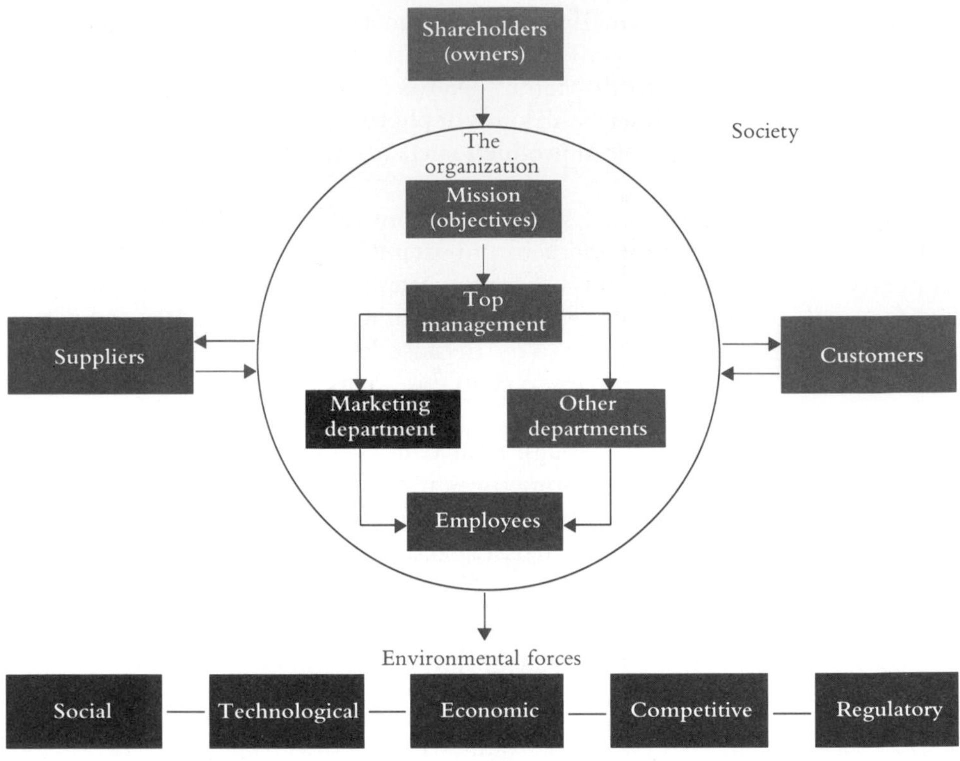

Figure 1-2 also shows the key people, groups, and forces outside the organization that influence marketing activities. In addition to the customers, two groups with an important stake in the organization's success are the shareholders of a business firm (or often representatives of groups served by a nonprofit organization) and its suppliers. Environmental forces such as social, technological, economic, competitive, and regulatory factors also shape an organization's marketing activities. Finally, an organization's marketing decisions are affected by and in turn often have an important impact on society as a whole.

The organization must strike a continual balance among these individuals and groups, whose objectives sometimes conflict. For example, it is not possible to simultaneously provide the lowest-priced and highest-quality products to customers and pay the highest prices to suppliers, highest wages to employees, and maximum dividends to shareholders.

REQUIREMENTS FOR MARKETING TO OCCUR

For marketing to occur, at least four factors are required: (1) two or more parties (individuals or organizations) with unsatisfied needs, (2) a desire and ability on their part to satisfy them, (3) a way for the parties to communicate, and (4) something to exchange.

Two or More Parties with Unsatisfied Needs Suppose several years ago you had an unmet need—a desire for a diet, sugar-free soft drink that tasted like

Drawing by Richter; © 1988, The New Yorker Magazine, Inc.

Coca-Cola—but you didn't yet know that Diet Coke existed. Also unknown to you, several dozen six-packs of Diet Coke were sitting on your nearest supermarket's shelf, waiting to be bought. This is an example of two parties with unmet needs: you, with a need for a Cokelike diet drink, and your supermarket owner, needing someone to buy the Diet Coke.

Desire and Ability to Satisfy These Needs Both you and the supermarket owner want to satisfy these unmet needs. Furthermore, you have the money to buy the item and the time to get to the supermarket. The store's owner has not only the desire to sell Diet Coke but also the ability to do so, since it's stocked on the shelves.

A Way for the Parties to Communicate The marketing transaction of buying the Diet Coke will never occur unless you know the product exists and its location. Similarly, the store owner won't stock Diet Coke unless there's a market or potential consumers near the supermarket who are likely to buy.

How does your search for a diet cola show what is needed for marketing to occur? The answer appears in the text

Photo by Ray Marklin

When you see your supermarket's newspaper ad for half-price off on Diet Coke, this communications barrier between you (the buyer) and your supermarket (the seller) is overcome.

Something to Exchange Marketing occurs when the transaction takes place and both the buyer and seller exchange something of value. In this case you exchange your money for the supermarket's Diet Coke. Both of you have gained something and also given up something, but you are both better off because you have each satisfied your unmet needs. You have the opportunity to drink Diet Coke, but you gave up some money; the store gave up the Diet Coke but received money, which enables it to remain in business. This exchange process is central to marketing.[8]

CONCEPT CHECK

1 **What is marketing?**

2 **Marketing focuses on ______________ and ______________ consumer needs.**

3 **What four factors are needed for marketing to occur?**

HOW MARKETING ASSESSES AND SATISFIES CONSUMER NEEDS

The importance of assessing and satisfying consumer needs is so critical to understanding marketing that we look at each of these two steps in detail below.

ASSESSING CONSUMER NEEDS

The first objective in marketing is assessing the needs of prospective consumers. Sound simple? Well, it's not. In the abstract, assessing needs looks easy, but when you get down to the specifics of marketing, problems crop up.

Some Product Disasters With much fanfare, Radio Corporation of America (RCA) introduced its SelectaVision Videodisc player to the world in the late 1970's. Polaroid, flushed with the success of its instant still-photography business, introduced Polavision (Question 2, Figure 1-1) as the first instant home movie in 1978. Similarly, Federal Express first ballyhooed its ZapMail, a 2-hour electronic mail service available throughout the United States, in 1984.

All these firms quietly dropped or redirected these products a short time after their introduction, with RCA losing over $600 million on its venture, Polaroid losing $170 million, and Federal Express losing $200 million.

These are three of the best-known product disasters in recent U.S. history, but thousands of lesser-known products fail in the marketplace every year. One major reason is that in each case the firm miscalculates consumers' wants and

RCA's SelectaVision videodisc player was soon replaced by VCRs

needs for these products. In the RCA Videodisc case, American consumers wanted to record TV programs, something videocassette recorders (VCRs) could do but Videodisc machines could not. They didn't want instant movies as much as they wanted instant still pictures, and Polavision failed in the consumer market. Today, of course, consumers are showing their "electric home movies" on their VCRs. ZapMail failed because of lack of demand, at least partly because major potential customers were buying their own facsimile machines.

The solution to preventing such product failures seems embarrassingly obvious. First, find out what consumers need and want. Second, produce what they do need and want and don't produce what they don't need and want. This is much more difficult than it sounds, as shown by Kenner Parker Toys, Inc. Many of its "consumers" are 6 years old, so Kenner Parker marketing researchers are sent to observe unobtrusively how children play with toys and see what they like and don't like about them. As shown in the Marketing Action Memo, this research has helped spawn some tremendously successful toys: Play-Doh, Care Bears, and X-Wing Fighters. Research on Strawberry Shortcake (shown at right), one of Kenner Parker's products, uncovered a difficult request: a special fragrance for the doll that would last for years without being hazardous to the children playing with it. Kenner Parker marketing executives asked their chemists to solve the problem, which required mixing 2000 ingredients that were nontoxic both separately and in combination.[9]

It's frequently very difficult to get a precise reading on what consumers want and need when they are confronted with revolutionary ideas for new products. Right after World War II, International Business Machines (IBM) asked one of the most prestigious management consulting firms in the United States to estimate the total future market for *all* electronic computers for *all* business, scientific, engineering, and government uses (Question 3, Figure 1-1). The answer was less than 10! Fortunately, key IBM executives disagreed, so IBM started building electronic computers anyway. Where would IBM be today if it had assumed the market estimate was correct? Most of the firms that bought computers 5 years after the market study had not actually recognized they were

MARKETING · ACTION · MEMO

CONSUMERS SPEAK EVEN WHEN THEY ARE ONLY 6 YEARS OLD AND DON'T SAY ANYTHING

In a school classroom outside Cincinnati, four 6-year-olds are playing with Play-Doh at a long wooden table. Two children are playing at one end of the table with a Play-Doh Fun Factory, making clay "spaghetti" and "worms." The other two are making clay Care Bears using the plastic molds in the Play-Doh Care Bears Playset. Four adults are scattered around the table, observing the action intently and asking an occasional question. Parent-child fun time? Not at all. This is serious business, and the four adults are marketing researchers from Kenner Parker Toys, Inc. They are searching for ideas for new toys and improvements on existing ones. During this field work the researchers see how the children play with toys, sit on toys, and drop toys on the floor. The goal is to discover what children want and don't want in toys, a task that requires an annual marketing research budget of $2 million. This research, coupled with the good judgment of marketing executives who work to stay in touch with their market, has resulted in some incredibly popular toys:

- Play-Doh: the 40-year-old veteran in Kenner's toy line
- The Care Bears: including Grumpy Bear, Friend Bear, and, of course, Funshine Bear
- The Star Wars toys: X-Wing Fighters, Millenium Falcons, and Jabba the Hutt
- Real Ghostbusters and Silverhawks, hot new lines of toys

The demands of children are intense. One hard-to-handle request was a special fragrance for Strawberry Shortcake, who almost was named "Sweet Pickles" until cooler heads prevailed. To understand the special efforts taken to obtain this fragrance, see the text.

Source: Based on D.J. Tice, "Toy Wars," *Twin Cities* (December 1983), pp. 96-107; Josephine Marcotty, "Creating Successful Toys is not Child's Play," *Minneapolis Star and Tribune* (October 14, 1985), pp. 1M, 8M; "Can Monopoly Find Success in Spiderman's Arms?" *Business Week* (August 3, 1987), p. 34.

prospective buyers because they had no understanding of what computers could do for them: they didn't recognize their own need for faster information processing.

Consumer Needs and Consumer Wants Should marketing try to satisfy consumer needs or consumer wants? The answer is both! Heated debates rage over

The job of assessing needs of consumers in the marketplace is like putting those needs under a microscope to understand them in detail.

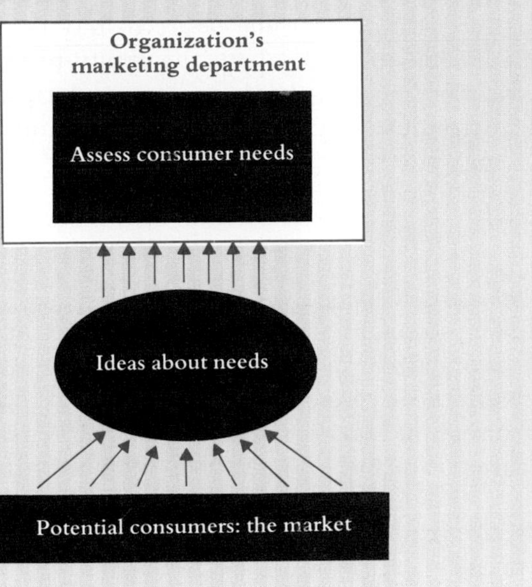

FIGURE 1-3
Marketing's first task: assess consumer needs

this question, and a person's position in the debate usually depends on the definitions of needs and wants and the amount of freedom given to prospective customers to make their own buying decisions.

A *need* occurs when a person feels physiologically deprived of basic necessities like food, clothing, and shelter. A *want* is a felt need that is shaped by a person's knowledge, culture, and personality. So if you feel hungry, you have developed a basic need and desire to eat something. Let's say you then want to eat an apple or a candy bar because, based on your past experience and personality, you know these will satisfy your hunger need. Effective marketing, in the form of creating an awareness of good products at convenient locations, can clearly shape a person's wants.

At issue is whether marketing manipulates prospective customers to buy the "wrong" things—say a "bad" candy bar rather than a "good" apple to satisfy hunger pangs. This does occur in a free society, and marketing tries to influence what we buy. The question which then arises is: At what point do we want government and society to step in to protect consumers? Most Americans would say they want government to protect us from harmful drugs and unsafe cars, but not from candy bars and soft drinks. The issue is not clearcut, which is why legal and social issues are central to marketing. Because even psychologists and economists still debate the exact meanings of *need* and *want,* we shall avoid the semantic arguments and use the terms interchangeably in the rest of the book.

As shown in Figure 1-3, assessing needs involves looking carefully at prospective customers, whether they are children buying M & M's candy, adults buying Calvin Klein jeans, or firms buying Xerox photocopying machines. The principal activity of a firm's marketing department is to carefully scrutinize the consumers to understand what they need.

What a Market is Potential consumers make up a **market,** which is (1) people (2) with the desire and (3) with the ability to buy a specific product. All markets ultimately are people. Even when we say a firm bought a Xerox copier, we mean one or several people in the firm decided to buy it. People who are aware of their unmet needs may have the desire to buy the product, but that alone isn't sufficient. People must also have the ability to buy, such as the time and money. As we saw earlier in the definition of marketing, people may "buy," or accept, more than just goods or services. For example, they may buy an idea that results in an action, such as having their blood pressure checked annually or turning down their thermostat to save energy.

SATISFYING CONSUMER NEEDS

Marketing doesn't stop with the ideas obtained from the assessment of consumer needs. Since the organization obviously can't satisfy all consumer needs, it must concentrate its efforts on certain needs of a specific group of potential consumers. This is the organization's **target market,** one or more specific groups of potential consumers toward which it will direct its marketing program.

The Four P's: Controllable Marketing Mix Factors Having selected the target market consumers, the firm must take steps to satisfy their needs. Someone in the organization's marketing department, often the marketing manager, must take action and develop a complete marketing program to reach consumers by pulling a combination of four levers, often called the four *P's*—a useful short-hand reference to them first published by Professor E. Jerome McCarthy[10]:

- Product: a good, service, or idea to satisfy the consumer's needs
- Price: what is exchanged for the product
- Promotion: a means of communication between the seller and buyer
- Place: a means of getting the product into the consumer's hands

We'll define each of the four *P's* more carefully later in the book, but for now it's important to remember that they are the elements of the marketing mix, or simply the **marketing mix.** These are the marketing manager's **controllable factors,** the marketing actions he or she can take in specific circumstances. The marketing mix elements are called controllable factors because they are under the control of the marketing department in an organization.

The Uncontrollable, Environmental Factors There are a host of factors largely beyond the control of the marketing department and its organization. These factors can be placed into five groups (Figure 1-2): social, technological, economic, competitive, and regulatory forces. Examples are what consumers themselves want and need, changing technology, the state of the economy in terms of whether it is expanding or contracting, actions that competitors take, and government restrictions. These **uncontrollable** or **environmental factors** in a marketing decision may serve as an accelerator or a brake on marketing, sometimes expanding an organization's marketing opportunities and other times restricting them. These five environmental factors are covered in Chapter 3.

Traditionally, many marketing executives have treated these environmental

After first assessing consumer needs, the marketing department must satisfy them by developing a marketing program consisting of the four marketing mix elements: product, price, promotion, and place.

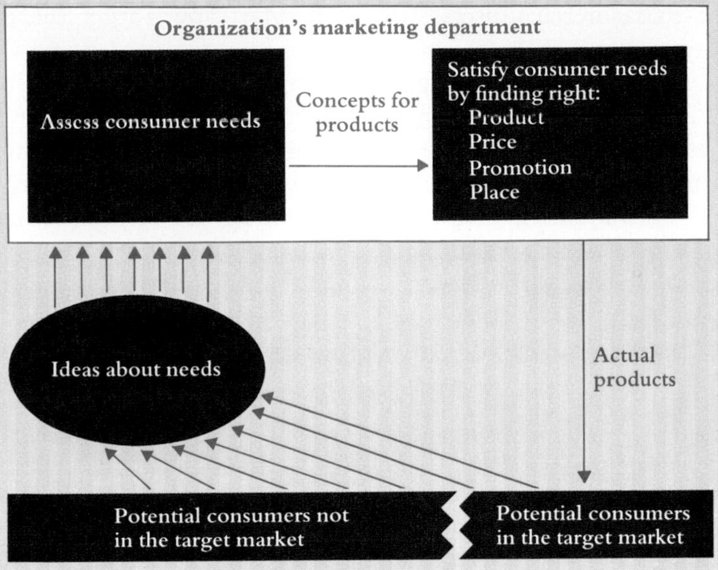

FIGURE 1-4
Marketing's second task: satisfy consumer needs

factors as rigid, absolute constraints that are entirely outside their influence.[11]

However, recent studies and marketing successes have shown that a forward-looking, action-oriented firm can often affect some environmental factors. IBM's technical and marketing breakthroughs generated the entire electronic digital computer industry, even though initially consumers were apathetic. Apple did the same for personal computers. H.J. Heinz received permission to buy a controlling interest in a Zimbabwe food company to produce and sell Heinz products there. These consumer and political factors might have forestalled productive marketing actions had they been seen as rigid and uncontrollable.[12]

The Marketing Program After assessment the marketing manager must translate the ideas from consumers into some concepts for products the firm might develop (Figure 1-4). These ideas must then be converted into a tangible **marketing program**—a plan that integrates the marketing mix to provide a product, service, or idea to prospective consumers. These prospects then react to the offering favorably (by buying) or unfavorably (by not buying), and the process is repeated. In an effective organization this process is continuous: consumer needs trigger product concepts that are translated into actual products that stimulate further assessment of consumer needs.

A Marketing Program for Golden Valley Microwave Foods To see the specifics of a marketing program, let's return to the earlier example of Jim Watkins, Golden Valley Microwave Foods, and their microwave popcorn.

Watkins knew that he and Golden Valley had a huge problem: finding ways to get their microwave popcorn onto shelves of retail stores. The company didn't have the money to hire its own sales force and establish its own distribution system for sales to various types of retail outlets across the United States. So Watkins devised a marketing program for Golden Valley's microwave popcorn with two key elements (Question 4, Figure 1-1). One element was a program in which the firm would market its popcorn under the brand name "Act II" to mass merchandisers such as K Mart and Target throughout the United States.

Reprinted with permission of General Mills, Inc.

The second element was to gain space on supermarket and grocery store shelves across the country by granting an exclusive license to General Mills to market shelf-stable microwave popcorn using Golden Valley's patented process and packaging technology. General Mills now sells microwave popcorn nationwide under the trademarked "Betty Crocker Pop Secret® brand name, using its own sales force and distribution system.[13]

Watkins, working with General Mills, combined these two elements into two marketing programs for two different target markets: (1) mass merchandisers and (2) supermarkets. The two programs have these main features:

MARKETING MIX ELEMENT	MARKETING PROGRAM FOR MASS MERCHANDISERS	MARKETING PROGRAM FOR SUPERMARKETS
• Product	3½ ounces of popcorn in an Act II package that serves as the microwave cooking unit.	3½ ounces of popcorn in a Betty Crocker Pop Secret package that serves as the microwave cooking unit.
• Price	59¢ for a package, or $2.99 for a "six-pack."	$2.09 for a "three-pack."
• Promotion	Sold direct to mass-merchandiser chain accounts. Advertising in local newspapers in ads run by mass merchandisers.	Sold by General Mills sales force to supermarkets. Advertising in national TV commercials.
• Place	Consumers can buy popcorn on snack shelves of mass merchandisers throughout the United States.	Consumers can buy popcorn on snack shelves of supermarkets throughout the United States.

Current Golden Valley products are shown in Figure 1-5.

And how has the Golden Valley marketing program for its microwave popcorn turned out? So far, extremely well. By 1988, its regional brand—Act II—had 20 percent of all retail microwave popcorn sales throughout the United States. The Betty Crocker Pop Secret® brand of General Mills—which entered the market later than Act II—had another large share of the total U.S. market. Golden Valley's "Microwave Morning" brand of microwave pancakes, which represented about 10 percent of its total sales revenue, was also doing well. So far, so good!

With things going so well, what concerns do Watkins and his firm have? Concerns center on both controllable marketing mix variables and uncontrollable environmental variables. Concerning the former, Golden Valley's phenomenal growth—from annual sales of $8 million to $100 million in 4 years—possess serious challenges. For example, how do you grow from 20 to 400 employees in 4 years and ensure that high-quality products and on-time deliv-

FIGURE 1-5
The product line of Golden Valley Microwave Foods, Inc.

Courtesy of Golden Valley Microwave Foods, Inc.

eries are maintained? To continue growing, Watkins knows that he must broaden his product line. In 1988, after spending several million scarce dollars on research, Golden Valley introduced Act II microwave french fries (Question 5, Figure 1-1)—an example of its company mission "of harnessing microwave energy to heat, brown, or crisp products using inexpensive, flexible packaging materials."[14]

Although Watkins can't anticipate all the uncontrollable factors facing his company, he has taken steps to minimize many threats. For example, Golden Valley has developed special hybrid popcorns that require 3 years of development to reach the consumer's microwave. The company oversees all aspects of the popcorn growing process, even to contracting with Iowa and Nebraska farmers who use irrigated land to reduce the risk of drought. And Golden Valley has recently added highly automated production equipment—much of it designed by company engineers—to provide the large volume of packaged popcorn required by the market.

Jim Watkins remains optimistic and realistic. This is shown by his firm's low overhead and lean operating style. "We make stuff and we sell stuff, and we don't have a lot of nonsense in between. We focus on only one thing—microwave food—and we're *very* competitive."[15] As a reminder of timing lessons from his past, Watkins still keeps a picture of his failed waterbike in his billfold.

CONCEPT CHECK

1 **Because an organization can't attempt to satisfy the needs of all consumers, it must select one or more subgroups on which to concentrate, which are its ________.**

2 **What are the four marketing mix elements that make up the organization's marketing program?**

3 **What are uncontrollable variables?**

FIGURE 1-6
Three different orientations in the history of American business

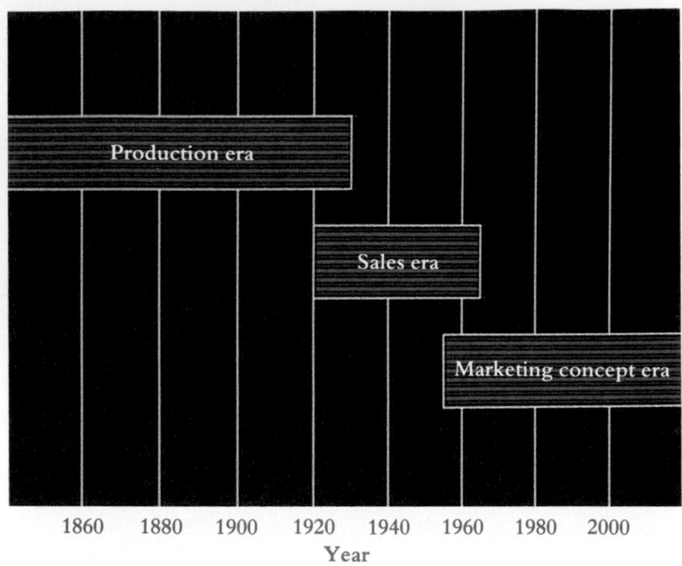

How Marketing Became so Important

Marketing is a driving force in the modern American economy. Two of the key reasons for this are (1) the evolution of the marketing concept and (2) the breadth and depth of marketing activities.

EVOLUTION OF THE MARKETING CONCEPT

Executives in the Pillsbury Company point to different stages in the life of their firm. Using Pillsbury as an example, we can identify three distinct stages experienced by many consumer-oriented manufacturing firms in the United States.

Production Era Goods were scarce in the early years of the United States, so buyers were willing to accept virtually any goods that were produced and make do with them as best they could. French economist J.B. Say developed his law in the nineteenth century that described the prevailing business theory of the period: "Production creates its own demand." The central notion was that products would sell themselves, so the major concern of business firms was production, not marketing.[16]

In 1869, Charles Pillsbury founded his company on the basis of high-quality wheat and the accessibility of cheap water power. Robert Keith, a Pillsbury president, described his company at this stage: "We are professional flour millers. Blessed with a supply of the finest North American wheat, plenty of water power, and excellent milling machinery, we produce flour of the highest quality. Our basic function is to mill quality flour." As shown in Figure 1-6, this **production era** generally continued in America through the 1920's.

Sales Era About that time, many firms discovered that they could produce more goods than their regular buyers could consume. Competition became more

FIRM	PRODUCTION-ORIENTED VIEW	MARKETING CONCEPT-ORIENTED VIEW
United Airlines	We run an airline.	We offer transportation services for people and things.
Honeywell	We make thermostats and temperature control devices.	We provide a comfortable climate in your home.
IBM	We make computers.	We offer solutions to your information problems.
20th Century Fox Studios	We produce movies.	We offer entertainment.

FIGURE 1-7
Two views of a business

significant, and the problems of reaching the market became more complex. The usual solution was to hire more salespeople to find new markets and consumers. Pillsbury's philosophy at this stage was summed up simply by Keith: "We must hire salespersons to sell it [the flour] just as we hire accountants to keep our books." The role of the Pillsbury sales force, in simplified terms, was to find consumers for the goods that the firm found it could produce best, given its existing resources. This **sales era** continued into the 1950's for Pillsbury and into the 1960's for many other American firms (Figure 1-6).

Today: The Marketing Concept Era In the 1960's, marketing became the motivating force in Pillsbury. Since then its policy can be stated as, "We are in the business of satisfying needs and wants of consumers." This is really a brief statement of what has come to be known as the **marketing concept.** This consumer-oriented idea is that an organization should (1) strive to satisfy the wants of consumers (2) while also trying to achieve the organization's goals.

Probably the best-known statement of a firm's commitment to satisfying consumer wants and needs is that appearing in a 1952 annual report of General Electric Company[18]:

> The concept introduces . . . marketing . . . at the beginning rather than the end of the production cycle and integrates marketing into each phase of the business. Thus, marketing, through its studies and research, will establish for the engineer . . . what the customer wants in a given product, what price he is willing to pay, and where and when it will be wanted. Marketing will have authority in product planning . . . as well as sales, distribution, and servicing of the product.

This statement has two important points. First, it recognized that sales is just one element of marketing—that marketing includes a much broader range of activities. Second, it changed the point at which marketing ideas are fed into the production cycle to *before* the item is designed rather than *after* it is produced. Clearly the marketing concept is a focus on the consumer.

Figure 1-7 shows the difference in emphasis for companies having a production versus a marketing concept orientation. In today's **marketing concept era,** a firm stresses solving the consumer's problems, not its own problems.

Executives have discovered that applying the marketing concept in practice is not always easy, but it serves as a guideline for their decisions. Even sophisticated firms such as Pillsbury occasionally stub their toes and fail to recognize consumer trends: one reason Jim Watkins left Pillsbury was because he didn't think the company recognized the importance of microwave foods in the future. Pillsbury has now changed its thinking and is investing $30 million annually in developing microwave food.

The **consumerism** movement started in the 1960's because the marketing concept was being overlooked by sellers. American consumers sought to obtain a greater say in the quality of products they buy and the information they receive from sellers. Although both the marketing concept and consumerism are constant reminders that "the customer is king," with today's competition, firms must also have efficient production and sales operations—carryovers from earlier eras.

BUSINESS ETHICS: BALANCING CONFLICTING GOALS OF DIFFERENT GROUPS

Should a customer's complaint and request for satisfaction always be honored? Of course not. Legitimate complaints should be dealt with fairly by the seller to satisfy the customer, but excessive demands by a complaining customer should not be honored because the costs of doing so are eventually passed to other customers in the form of higher prices.

These issues relate to **business ethics,** which are guidelines that indicate how to act rightly and justly in a business situation. The Marketing Research Report illustrates the ethical questions that arise when interests of customers must be balanced against those of sellers. After reading the two complaints and evaluation reports and answering the questions in the box, you can see how difficult it is to decide what is ethical and fair.

Researchers Resnik and Harmon[19] showed 122 consumers and 40 branch managers the letters and evaluations and found close agreement between the two groups, which believed the first complaint is legitimate and the second is not. The study also showed that the branch managers preferred personal contact to a letter to address the complaint, whereas more consumers would be satisfied with just a letter rather than personal contact.

Fair responses by the manager were judged to be replacement of the four panels in the first complaint and explanation of how the consumer misused the panels in the second. Yet inconsistencies in actions proposed by the managers show the difficulty in giving ethically consistent and fair treatment. In both instances, managers offered at least what was required rather than falling short. They were also likely to offer far more than required when the complaint was seen as legitimate (61 percent gave more than the replacement of the four panels for complaint 1) rather than not legitimate (24 percent gave more than merely an explanation of the misuse for complaint 2).

To survive, an organization must achieve an ethical balance between the interests of other groups such as its employees, shareholders, and suppliers and those of its consumers. American business firms must achieve this ethical balance

MARKETING · RESEARCH · REPORT

CUSTOMER COMPLAINTS: BALANCING THE INTERESTS OF CUSTOMERS AND SELLERS

In addressing a consumer complaint, what is fair and equitable for both the consumer and the seller? Assume you are a branch manager of a store that sells wood paneling. You get the two pairs of customer letters and evaluations from your assistant, shown below.

Read each pair carefully and answer the following questions: (1) Is the complaint legitimate or not? (2) Is a letter or personal contact (in person or by telephone) in order? (3) What action should the branch manager take from among five options: explanation, apology, replacement, repair, and no response? For the results of this study by Resnick and Harmon and their marketing implications, see the text.

Complaint 1

Dear Sir:

We purchased about 20 sheets of your prefinished paneling, and the veneer is coming off 6 or 8 sheets. They said the salesman would call us, but so far we have heard nothing. Could you please tell us who to contact?

Complaint 2

Dear Sir:

I purchased 40 sheets of your paneling at a cost of approximately $125.00. A week later, I paid $40.00 to have the paneling hung in my garage. Yesterday, I inspected it and noticed all the paneling had warped severely. I know it wasn't your top grade merchandise, but I thought it would last longer than two weeks. I hope you have some kind of guarantee and will refund my $165.00 for cost and labor charges.

Thank you.

Evaluation Report 1

Inspection indicated 4 pieces of paneling had some minor face veneer separation from backing. It was first grade paneling and guaranteed against separation (delamination). Retail value of paneling is $8 per sheet.

Evaluation Report 2

Inspection revealed paneling had a sticker on the back of each sheet warning against use in areas exposed to extreme moisture. It also said to use the panel only over gypsym wallboard or plywood on interior of house in areas not subject to extreme moisture.

Paneling was installed in an open garage directly over studs with no backing. It was subjected to alternate extremes of very high moisture to very dry conditions.

Source: Based on Alan J. Resnik and Robert R. Harmon, "Consumer Complaints and Managerial Response: A Holistic Approach," *Journal of Marketing* (Winter 1983), pp. 86-97; by permission of the American Marketing Association.

today under the most intense pressure from competitors throughout the world that they have known this century. Because of the importance of ethical issues in marketing today, they—and related legal and regulatory actions—are discussed throughout the book.

The well-being of society at large should also be recognized in an organization's marketing decisions.[20] In fact, some marketing experts see the field as moving toward the **societal marketing concept,** which holds that an organization should assess and satisfy the needs of its consumers while also providing for society's welfare. Products such as soft drinks in disposable cans and

Today's Cleveland Clinic is increasingly sensitive to patient needs

Courtesy of The Cleveland Clinic Foundation

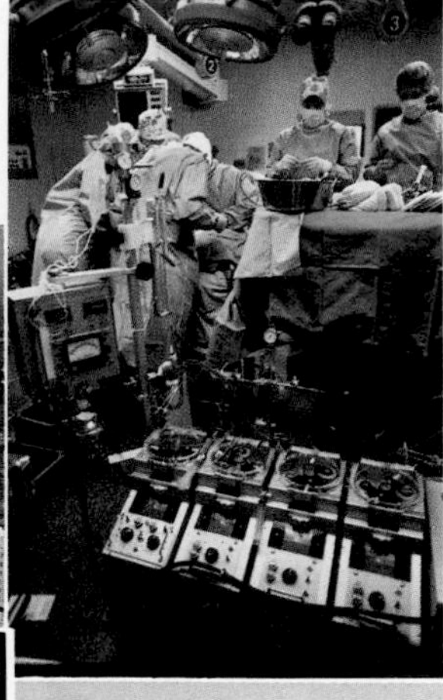

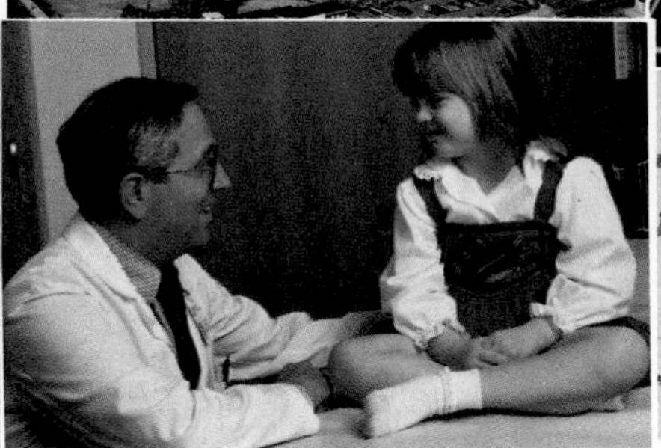

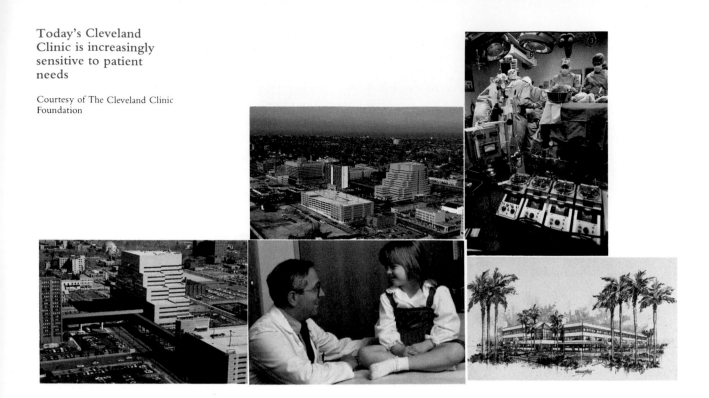

cigarettes have important side effects in terms of dollar and health costs for all of us in society—not just the manufacturer and consumer of the specific product.

This book focuses on how an individual organization uses the strategic marketing process (an overview of which appears in Chapter 2) to direct its marketing activities and allocate its resources. Occasionally this process is called **micromarketing** to contrast it with **macromarketing,** which looks at the aggregate flow of a nation's goods and services to benefit society.[21] Macromarketing addresses broader issues such as whether marketing costs too much, whether advertising is wasteful, and what resource scarcities and pollution side effects result from the marketing system. Macromarketing issues relate directly to the societal marketing concept and are addressed briefly in this book. The book's main focus is on an organization's marketing activities, or micromarketing.

THE BREADTH AND DEPTH OF MARKETING

Marketing today affects every person and organization. To understand this, let's analyze (1) who markets, (2) what they market, (3) who buys and uses what is marketed, (4) who benefits from these marketing activities, and (5) how they benefit.

Who Markets? Every organization markets! It's obvious that business firms in manufacturing (Xerox, Heinz, Puma), retailing (Sears, K Mart, J.C. Penney), and providing services (Merrill Lynch, National Broadcasting Corporation, 20th

Century Fox) market their offerings. And so do colleges and universities (to attract good students and faculty members and donations) and government agencies (to encourage Americans to quit smoking or obtain annual health check-ups). Individuals such as entertainers or politicians market themselves. Nonprofit business firms (San Francisco Ballet, New York Metropolitan Opera, Museum of Modern Art, your local hospital) also engage in marketing.[22]

Recent decisions of a world-renowned medical facility, the Cleveland Clinic Foundation, illustrate the diverse marketing-related activities of today's non-profit organizations. The Clinic operates an expanded 1,250-bed hospital in Cleveland and—to respond to growing health care needs in the Southeast—a new facility in Fort Lauderdale, Florida. It has programs to serve the specialized needs of low-income and kidney dialysis patients, and it even operates its own 300-room hotel in Cleveland to serve the needs of patients from throughout the United States and the world. To try to improve its patient services, the Clinic conducts programs in marketing research, consumer affairs, and physician liaison.

What is Marketed? Goods, services, and ideas are marketed. Goods are physical objects, such as toothpaste, cameras, or computers, that satisfy consumer needs. Services are intangible items such as airline trips, financial advice, or telephone calls. Ideas are intangibles such as thoughts about actions or causes. Some of these—such as lawn mowers, dry cleaning, and annual physical examinations—may be bought or accepted by individuals for their own use. Others, such as office copiers and vending machine repair services, are bought by organizations. Finally, the products marketed in today's shrinking globe are increasingly likely to cross a nation's boundaries and involve exports, imports, and international marketing (covered in Chapter 21).

Who Buys and Uses What is Marketed? Both individuals and organizations buy and use the goods and services that are marketed. **Ultimate consumers** are the individuals—whether 80 years or 8 months old—who use the goods and services purchased for a household. A household may consist of one person or ten. The way one or more of the people in the household buys for it is the topic of consumer behavior in Chapter 4. In contrast, **organizational buyers** such as manufacturers, retailers, or government agencies buy for their own use or for resale. Industrial and organizational buyer behavior is covered in Chapter 5. Although the terms *buyers* and *customers* are sometimes used for both ultimate consumers and organizations, there is no consistency on this. In this book you will be able to tell from the example whether the buyers are ultimate consumers, organizations, or both.

Who Benefits? In our free-enterprise society there are three specific groups that benefit from effective marketing: consumers who buy, organizations that sell, and society as a whole. True competition between products and services in the marketplace ensures that we consumers can obtain (1) the best products and services available (2) at the lowest price. Providing the maximum number of choices leads to the consumer satisfaction and quality of life that we have come to expect from our economic system.

Organizations that provide need-satisfying products with effective marketing programs—for example, McDonald's, IBM, Avon, and Merrill Lynch—have blossomed, but this competition creates problems for the ineffective competitors. For example, Osborne Computers, DeLorean cars, and W.T. Grant retail stores were well-known names a few years back, but may now be unknown to you. Effective marketing actions result in rewards for organizations that serve consumers and result in millions of marketing jobs such as those described in Appendix B.

Finally, effective marketing benefits the whole country. It enhances competition, which in turn improves both the quantity of products and services and lowers their prices. This makes the country more competitive in world markets and provides jobs and a higher standard of living for its citizens.

How do Consumers Benefit? Marketing creates **utility,** or value, for consumers using the product. There are four different utilities: form, place, time, and possession. The production of the good or service constitutes *form utility*. *Place utility* means having the offering available where consumers need it, whereas *time utility* means having it available when needed. *Possession utility* is getting the product to consumers so they can use it.

Thus marketing provides consumers with place, time, and possession utilities by making the good or service available at the right place and right time for the right consumer. Although form utility usually arises in manufacturing activity and could be seen as outside the scope of marketing, an organization's marketing activities influence the product features and packaging. Marketing creates its utilities by bridging space (place utility) and hours (time utility) to provide products (form utility) for consumers to own and use (possession utility).

CONCEPT CHECK

1 **Like Pillsbury, many firms have gone through three distinct orientations for their business: from the production to the ____________ to the ____________ eras.**

2 **What are the two key characteristics of the marketing concept?**

3 **What three things are included in this book under the term *product?***

SUMMARY

1 Our daily exposure to the diverse marketing activities around us has already given us some marketing expertise. Combining this experience with more formal marketing knowledge will enable us to identify and solve important marketing problems.

2 Marketing is the process of planning and executing the conception, pricing, promotion, and distribution of ideas, goods, and services to create exchanges that satisfy individual and organizational objectives. This definition relates to two primary goals of marketing: (1) assessing the needs of consumers and (b) satisfying them.

3 For marketing to occur, it is necessary to have (a) two or more parties with unmet needs, (b) a desire and ability to satisfy them, (c) communication between the parties, and (d) something to exchange.

4 Because an organization doesn't have the resources to satisfy the needs of all consumers, it selects a target market of potential customers—a subset of the entire market—on which to focus its marketing program.

5 Four elements in a marketing program designed to satisfy customer needs are product, price, promotion, and place. These elements are called the marketing mix, the four *P*'s, or the controllable variables because they are under the general control of the marketing department.

6 Environmental factors, also called uncontrollable variables, are largely beyond the organization's control. These include social, technological, economic, competitive, and regulatory forces.

7 In marketing terms, U.S. business history is divided into three periods: the production era, the sales era, and the modern marketing concept era.

8 An organization using the marketing concept tries to satisfy the needs of consumers at a profit (if a business firm) or more efficiently (if a nonprofit agency). However, consumer and organizational needs must be balanced against needs of employees, shareholders, suppliers, and society as a whole.

9 Most organizations perform marketing activities, whether they are profit-making business firms or nonprofit organizations. They market products, services, and ideas that benefit all consumers, the organization, and the entire nation. Marketing creates utilities that benefit customers.

KEY TERMS AND CONCEPTS

marketing p. 7
exchange p. 7
market p. 14
target market p. 14
marketing mix p. 14
controllable factors p. 14
uncontrollable factors p. 14
environmental factors p. 14
marketing program p. 15
production era p. 18
sales era p. 19
marketing concept p. 19
marketing concept era p. 19
consumerism p. 20
business ethics p. 20
societal marketing concept p. 21
micromarketing p. 22
macromarketing p. 22
ultimate consumers p. 23
organizational buyers p. 23
utility p. 24

CHAPTER PROBLEMS AND APPLICATIONS

1 What consumer wants (or benefits) are met by the following products or stores? (a) Carnation Instant Breakfast, (b) Adidas running shoes, (c) Hertz Rent-A-Car, and (d) catalog showroom retail stores.

2 Each of the four products or stores in Question 1 have substitutes. Respective examples are (a) ham and egg breakfast, (b) regular tennis shoes, (c) taking a bus, and (d) a department store. What consumer benefits might these substitutes have in each case that some consumers might value more highly than those products mentioned in Question 1?

3 What are the characteristics (for example, age, income, education) of the target market customers for the following products or services? (a) *National Geographic* magazine, (b) *Playboy* magazine, (c) New York Giants football team, and (d) the U.S. Open tennis tournament.

4 A college in a metropolitan area wishes to increase its evening-school offerings of business-related courses such as marketing, accounting, finance, and management. Who are the target market customers (students) for these courses?

5 What actions on the four marketing mix elements might be used to reach the target market in Question 4?

6 What environmental factors (uncontrollable variables) must the college in Question 4 consider in designing its marketing program?

7 Polaroid introduced instant still photography that proved to be a tremendous success. Yet Polavision, its instant movie system, was a total disaster. (a) What wants and benefits does each provide to users? (b) Which of these do you think contributed to Polavision's failure? (c) What research could have been undertaken that might have revealed Polavision's drawbacks?

8 Jim Watkins has chosen to focus the efforts of Golden Valley Microwave Foods, Inc. on—just what its name suggests—microwave foods. What are the advantages and disadvantages of this strategy?

9 No firm can rest comfortably on its current product line; it must look for new products. What criteria—some suggested by its company mission statement—should Golden Valley use in deciding what new products to add to its line of microwave foods?

10 Consider the uncontrollable environmental factors that might affect Golden Valley during the coming 5 years. Which will work in its favor? Which will work against it?

11 Does a firm have the right to "create" wants and try to persuade consumers to buy goods and services they didn't know about earlier? What are examples of "good" and "bad" want creation? Who should decide what is "good" and "bad?"

SUGGESTED READINGS

Richard P. Bagozzi, "Marketing as Exchange," *Journal of Marketing* (October 1975), pp. 32-39. *Bagozzi describes exchange relationships that help explain the expanded role of marketing in society.*

John F. Gaski and Michael J. Etzel, "The Index of Consumer Sentiment Toward Marketing," *Journal of Marketing* (July 1986), pp. 71-81. *Gaski and Etzel propose an index that measures a national consumer sentiment toward marketing's perceived performance on product quality, prices, advertising, and retailing/selling activities.*

Franklin S. Houston, "The Marketing Concept: What It Is and What It Is Not," *Journal of Marketing* (April 1986), pp. 81-87. *Houston gives a realistic assessment of the marketing concept and restates it to put it in perspective for marketers.*

Shelby D. Hunt, "The Nature and Scope of Marketing," *Journal of Marketing* (July 1976), pp. 17-28. *By looking at three pairs of dimensions (micromarketing versus macromarketing, profit versus nonprofit sector, and descriptive versus prescriptive), Hunt structures the field of marketing.*

Philip Kotler and Sidney I. Levy, "Broadening the Concept of Marketing," *Journal of Marketing* (January 1969), pp. 10-15. *Kotler and Levy argue that marketing applies to organizations such as nonprofit organizations, government agencies, and colleges, as well as to traditional manufacturing businesses.*

How to move a paragraph.

For memos or manuscripts, sales reports or book reports, a person could use the IBM Personal Computer.

Because, with the EasyWriter* software program, creating, revising and storing text is just that. Easy.

With ten function keys that help save time on repetitious tasks and "menus" that guide you along, the IBM Personal Computer can insert a clause. Delete a line. Move a paragraph from one page to another. Transfer text from file to file. Even merge words from your EasyWriter program with numbers generated by your VisiCalc† program.

And when you're done, a copy of the finished product can be printed out at 80 characters a second.

So if you do any kind of writing, try it on the IBM Personal Computer at your nearest authorized dealer. You'll see that the performance, quality and price are really something to write home about.

IBM

The IBM Personal Computer
A tool for modern times

Introducing the IBM Personal System/2

2

MARKETING IN THE ORGANIZATION: AN OVERVIEW

After reading this chapter you should be able to:

Describe the strategic management process and how it relates to an organization's business (or mission) and objectives.

•

Describe the strategic marketing process and its three key phases: planning, implementation, and control.

•

Understand how organizations search for new marketing opportunities and select target markets.

•

Explain how the marketing mix elements are blended into a cohesive marketing program.

•

Describe how marketing control compares actual results with planned objectives and acts on deviations from the plan.

"Big Blue's" Search for an Encore

The year was 1981, and Big Blue had never produced or marketed a personal computer.

So "Big Blue"—the nickname given IBM because of the color of many of its large computers—unveiled the most unlikely of advertising campaigns to annoucc its ncw IBM Personal Computer (PC): a little mustachioed man in a black bowler hat. He used an IBM PC not simply to control inventory and move paragraphs (see ads at top of opposite page) but also to save his "Hat of the Month Club" business.

It was a controversial advertising campaign. Some IBM employees were concerned that potential PC buyers might see the ad's Little Tramp—a take-off on the Charlie Chaplin silent-movie role—as "nonprofessional." But the campaign was a smash and did just what it was intended to do: attract attention and inform prospective PC users, the target market, in a nonthreatening way about the benefits of an IBM PC. The result was astounding. IBM's share of the PC market grew from nothing in 1981 to 40 percent in 1985.

By 1986, however, IBM saw its share of the total PC market falling, partly because of IBM "clones," PCs compatible with IBM PCs. John F. Akers, IBM's new president, declared that IBM had lost touch with its customers[1] and shared their concern that IBM PCs didn't "network" or communicate easily with each other.[2]

IBM's answer was a new family of PCs, the Personal System/2 (PS/2), introduced in 1987. The advertising campaign to support the introduction of the PS/2 used a group of people that IBM hoped American buyers could relate to as they had to the Little Tramp. This group is shown in the ad at the bottom of page 28. Who are these people? Who is missing from the group? Why did IBM select a group rather than one person? Think about these questions as you read the next pages. We'll answer them and describe some details of IBM's marketing strategy for its PS/2 later in the chapter.

This chapter gives an overview of how organizations plan, implement, and control successful marketing strategies. In essence, this chapter describes how an organization tries to put the marketing concept into action to serve its customers.

THE STRATEGIC MANAGEMENT PROCESS

Key marketing decisions are made within limits set by the organization. The **strategic management process** involves the steps taken at an organization's corporate and divisional levels to develop long-run master strategies for survival and growth. In contrast, the **strategic marketing process** involves the steps taken at the product and market levels to allocate its marketing resources to viable marketing positions and programs.[3] Key steps in each of these two processes are shown in Figure 2-1. Note that other units in the organization—assumed here to be a manufacturing firm—develop detailed plans based on directions from the strategic management process.

DEFINING THE ORGANIZATION'S BUSINESS (MISSION)

Organizations such as the San Francisco Ballet, Dallas Cowboys, Disneyland, Mayo Clinic, Procter & Gamble, Sears Roebuck, and 3M often ask themselves what "business"—in its broadest sense—they are in. The answer can dramatically narrow or broaden the range of marketing opportunities available.

Railroads may have let other forms of transportation take business away from them because they saw themselves in "the railroad business" rather than "the transportation business."[4] This narrow definition hurt railroads because they failed to design effective marketing strategies to compete with a broad range of modes of transportation, including airlines, trucks, bus lines, and cars.

Focusing the Business with the Three C's Business theorists point out that three *C's*—the customers, the competitors, and the company itself—interrelate

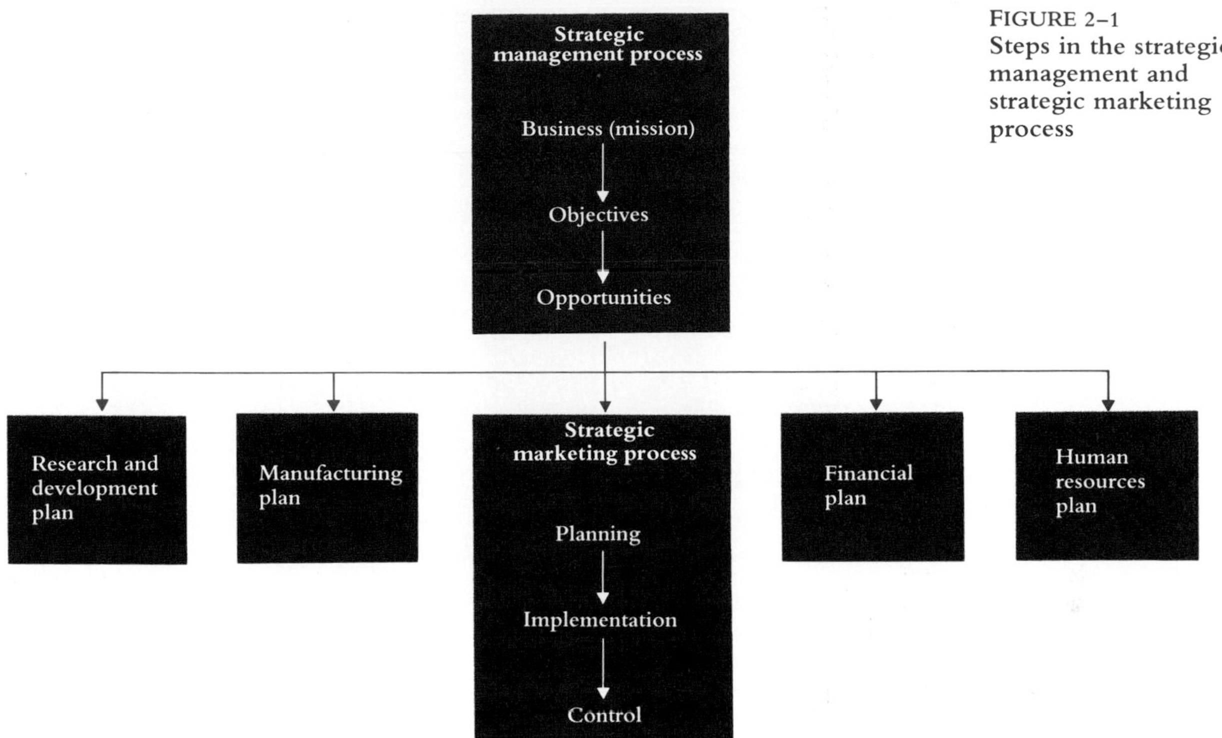

FIGURE 2–1
Steps in the strategic management and strategic marketing process

to establish the basic character of an organization's business.[5] An **organizational business (mission)** is a statement about the type of customer it wishes to serve, the specific needs of these customers, and the means or technology by which it will serve these needs. This definition affects the company's growth prospects by establishing guidelines for selecting opportunities in light of customer needs, competitors' actions, the organization's resources, and changes in environmental factors.

Sears's Business In the early 1980's, Sears Roebuck & Company discovered that discounters and specialty stores were winning over more and more of its traditional middle-class customers. This left Sears scrambling to find a market niche. First, it tried promoting itself as a fashion-oriented department store for higher-income customers. Failing at that, Sears experimented with budget products and price slashing. These efforts were also unsuccessful.

Today Sears has tried to "become itself" again by selling functional, rather than fashionable, goods and services that offer value to middle-class, home-owning families. This definition of its business has permitted Sears (the company) to adapt to changing consumer tastes (the customer) in light of actions of other catalog and chain-store retailers (the competitors). Recently Sears has entered the service business in a big way: appliance installation, financial services through Dean Witter, real estate through Coldwell Banker, and even dental and optometry services. Perhaps Sears' biggest gamble for the 1990's is the development of an interactive computer system linked by telephone to Sears stores

Prodigy; a $450 million joint effort of Sears and IBM

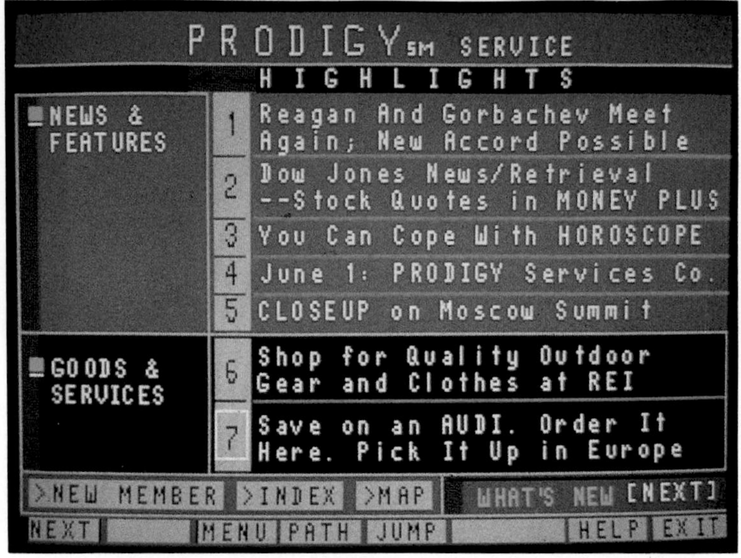

in which consumers can buy products they see advertised. Sears and IBM invested more than $450 million in the system, called "Prodigy," before it provided its first sales dollar. Sears obviously runs a diverse set of businesses, but all of them tie into its existing, tremendously strong distribution system.[6] All these businesses can also use the Discover credit card, which was Sears' biggest gamble for the 1980's. The Discover card had lost $400 million by early 1988.[7]

SPECIFYING THE ORGANIZATION'S GOALS

An organization must translate the broad statement of its business into its **organizational goals,** specific objectives it seeks to achieve and by which it can measure its performance. For our purposes, the terms *goals* and *objectives* mean the same thing.

How an Organization's Goals Relate to its Business An example of a precise policy statement of an organization's business and goals is that of the Sara Lee Corporation (Figure 2-2). Note that the goals are specific targets that flow directly from the broader statement about Sara Lee Corporation's businesss. In fact, the business statement is broad enough to cover five business segments. These segments and some of their better-known brand names include:

- U.S. consumer foods: Chef Pierre, Jimmy Dean Meats, Popsicle, Kitchens of Sara Lee
- International consumer foods: Douwe Egberts coffee (Europe), Hearty Fruit Muffins (Australia)
- Food service distribution: Booth Fisheries, PYA/Monarch, Lyon's Restaurants
- Consumer personal products: Bali, Hanes Hosiery, L'eggs Products
- Consumer household products: Electrolux, Fuller Brush, Kiwi

FIGURE 2–2
Mission and goals of Sara Lee Corporation

Source: 1987 *Annual Report* (Chicago: Sara Lee Corporation, 1987), pp. 5-6. Reprinted courtesy of Sara Lee Corporation, 1988.

Business (mission)
To be a leading consumer marketing company worldwide in manufacturing, marketing, and distributing:

- Branded food products, and household and personal consumer packaged goods through retail outlets
- Branded consumer products through distribution channels direct to the consumer
- New consumer branded products and services to exploit changing trends and serve consumer needs
- Food products and services for the foodservice industry

Goals
To maximize the long-term financial performance of the corporation enabling us to better serve our stockholders, customers, employees, and the communities in which we do business. Specifically:

- To maintain a return on stockholders' equity to a minimum of at least 20 percent
- To achieve a real annual growth rate in earnings of at least 6 percent

In relative terms, to rank continuously among the leaders of the best managed, high-performance, high-quality consumer marketing-oriented companies with which we compete.

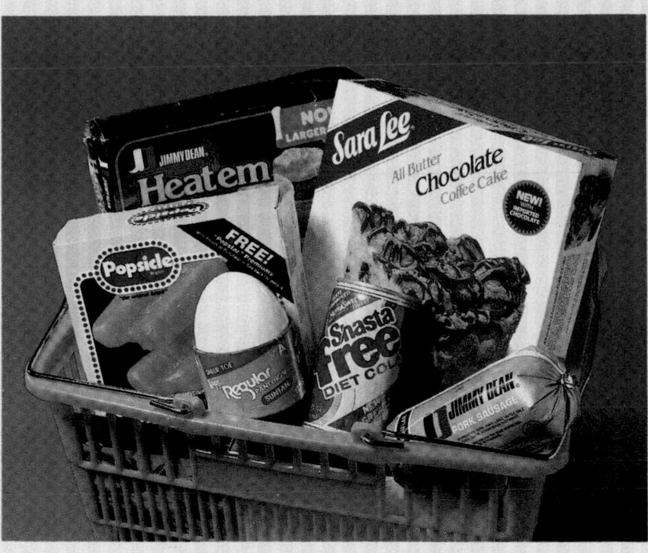

Even with this diversity of products and services, Sara Lee Corporation's policy statement about its business and goals gives direction to the entire organization and its divisions.

All organizations, both profit and nonprofit, require some kind of goals. A **business firm** is an organization that carries on economic activity to earn a profit. In contrast, a **nonprofit organization** carries on economic activity to serve the needs of special segments of the public. Goals of these two different kinds of organizations are discussed separately in the following sections. For simplicity in the rest of the book, however, the terms *firm, company,* and *organization* are used to cover both business and nonprofit operations.

Goals of Business Firms Business firms, with some exceptions cited later, must earn profits to survive. **Profit** is the reward to a business firm for the risk it undertakes in offering a product for sale: the money left over after a firm's total expenses are subtracted from its total revenues. As long as profits are earned fairly—and not through collusion, monopoly power, or other unfair business practices—they represent a reward for good performance. Thousands of firms fail every year because they are not run well enough and do not serve consumers well enough to make profits and continue operations. The profit of a business firm may be expressed in actual money earned during a time period ("an after-tax profit of $5 million") or in terms of the money earned as a percentage of invested capital ("an after-tax profit of 15-percent return on investment [ROI]").

Several different objectives have been identified that business firms can pursue, each of which has some limitations:

- Profit. Classic economic theory assumes a firm seeks to maximize long-run profit, achieving as high a financial return on its investment as possible. One difficulty with this is what is meant by long run. A year? Five years? Twenty years?
- Sales revenue. If profits are acceptable, a firm may elect to maintain or increase its sales level, even though profitability may not be maximized. The increased sales revenue may result in promotions sought by executives.
- Market share. A firm may choose to maintain or increase its market share, sometimes at the expense of greater profits if industry status or prestige is at stake. **Market share** is the ratio of sales revenue of the firm to the total sales revenue of all firms in the industry, including the firm itself.
- Unit sales. Sales revenue may be deceiving because of the effects of inflation, so a firm may choose to maintain or increase the number of units it sells, such as cars, cases of breakfast cereal, or TV sets.
- Survival. A firm may choose a safe action with reasonable payoff instead of one with large return that might endanger its future. It must survive today to be in business tomorrow.
- Social responsibility. A firm may respond to advocates of corporate responsibility and seek to balance conflicting goals of consumers, employees, and stockholders to promote overall welfare of all these groups, even at the expense of profits.

Whatever its primary goal, a business firm must achieve a profit level that is high enough for it to remain in operation. Satisfactory profits are possible only if consumer needs are identified and satisfied. Procter & Gamble (P&G) is a good example. For its corporate objectives, it seeks a 10 percent after-tax profit

An example of General Electric's search for growth opportunities in high technology

(twice the average for U.S. manufacturing firms) and a doubling of the sales revenue from a product every 5 years. To help achieve these objectives, it uncovers needs and manufactures products that have developed tremendous consumer loyalty in the marketplace. Its high-visibility brands introduced decades ago and still dominant are cases in point: Ivory Soap (introduced in 1879), Crisco (1912), Tide (1947), Pampers (1956), and Crest (1966). The long market lives of these products are proof of their continuing ability to satisfy consumer needs, a basic corporate objective of P&G.

Goals of Nonprofit Organizations Many private organizations that do not seek profits also exist in the United States. Examples are museums, symphony orchestras, operas, private hospitals, and research institutes. These organizations strive to provide goods or services to consumers with the greatest efficiency and the least cost. The nonprofit organization's survival depends on its meeting the needs of the consumers it serves. Government agencies have "serving the public good" as their primary goal. Such organizations include all levels of federal, state, and local government, as well as special groups such as city schools, state universities, and public hospitals. As discussed later, marketing is an important acitivity for nonprofit firms and government agencies, just as it is for profit-making businesses.

IDENTIFYING THE ORGANIZATION'S OPPORTUNITIES

To achieve growth, an organization tries to find the right match between the market opportunities in its environment and its own capabilities and resources. Answers to three questions help an organization focus on choice opportunities[3]:

1. *What might we do,* in terms of environmental opportunities we foresee?

2. *What do we do best,* in terms of our capabilities, resources, and distinctive competencies?
3. *What must we do,* in terms of achieving success in a market or with a product?

General Electric's Opportunities Search The search for growth opportunities by General Electric (GE) shows how these questions apply. GE started at the turn of the century with a narrow definition of its business: the generation of electricity. With this definition, GE's focus was on turbines, generators, and transformers. GE initially got into the home appliance business with its General Electric and Hotpoint brand names and into the electric light business to stimulate the demand for electricity. Through the first half of this century these divisions provided tremendous growth for the company.

In the early 1980's GE's performance was lackluster, and it was looking for new business opportunities. In 1981 John F. Welch, Jr. took over as GE's chief executive officer with the charge to get the company moving again. Welch needed to assess where GE stood—an ideal time for a SWOT analysis.

SWOT Analysis The acronym *SWOT* refers to a simple, effective technique a firm can use to appraise in detail its internal **s**trengths and **w**eaknesses and external **o**pportunities and **t**hreats. The goal of a SWOT analysis is to help a firm identify the strategy-related factors that can have a major effect on it. However, all factors in such an analysis are not of equal value, so the goal is to identify those *critical* factors that can have a major effect on the firm and then build on vital strengths, correct glaring weaknesses, exploit significant opportunities, and avoid disaster-laden threats.[9] That is a big order.

A SWOT analysis of GE's situation in 1981 would have revealed the factors shown in the Marketing Action Memo. From this kind of analysis, Welch concluded that two opportunities that answered the question "What might we do?" were providing services and high-technology products. In terms of "What do we do best?" he concluded that GE should find markets that could exploit its technological leadership and avoid competing with low-cost producers in the Far East in small consumer appliances.[10]

In the process Welch answered the third question: "What must we do to achieve success in our businesses?" by providing a strategic focus that stressed growth from GE business sectors that were or could be number 1 or number 2 in market share and profits in their markets.[11] This strategy targeted growth in service and high-technology areas by creating a streamlined organization with fewer layers of management that would not attempt to compete in mass-produced, small consumer appliances. As a result, GE first sold its small-appliance business to Black and Decker[12] and its consumer-electronics business (TV, radios) to a French firm.[13]

This means that American consumers will no longer see the GE brand on toasters, mixers, and TV sets, but only on large appliances (dishwashers, refrigerators, and dryers) and light bulbs. And GE will be far stronger in industrial segments such as jet engines, aerospace, plastics, electrical apparatus, and medical electronics and in services such as insurance and finance.

MARKETING · ACTION · MEMO

GENERAL ELECTRIC: A "SWOT" TO GET IT MOVING AGAIN

Concerned about its slow growth, in 1981 General Electric (GE) selected John F. Welch, Jr., to head the company and get it moving forward again. A SWOT analysis (described in the text) of GE at that time might have looked as shown below.

Sources: Peter Petre, "What Welch Has Wrought at GE," *Fortune* (July 7, 1986), pp. 43-47; "Can Jack Welch Reinvent GE," *Business Week* (June 30, 1986), pp. 62-67; "Jumping Jack Strikes Again," *Time* (August 3, 1987), p. 44.

LOCATION OF FACTOR	TYPE OF FACTOR	
	FAVORABLE	UNFAVORABLE
INTERNAL	*Strengths:* • Quality products in many consumer and industrial markets • Respected name among buyers of its products • Financial power • Technical leadership in many sectors	*Weaknesses:* • No clear strategic direction • Bureaucracy and many layers of management • High costs of production • Stable annual sales • Deteriorating competitive position in many markets
EXTERNAL	*Opportunities:* • High-technology and service sectors growing rapidly • International markets growing • U.S. government more lenient in cooperative joint ventures • Company technologies can provide new products for new markets	*Threats:* • Existing markets facing many changes • Foreign firms have lower production costs • Sales gains by competitors in its established markets • Many products no longer competitive

An Organization's Distinctive Competency In assessing organizational opportunities, a firm objectively evaluates its **distinctive competency**—its principal competitive strengths and advantages in terms of marketing, technological, and financial resources. In the strategic management process all three of these areas must be thoroughly assessed or there may be problems: for example, Welch concluded that all of GE's resources weren't enough to overcome its lack of distinctive competency in competing with high-quality, low-cost electronics manufactured in the Far East. So it left this business.

CONCEPT CHECK

1 **What are the three steps in the strategic management process?**

2 **Which is more specific, an organization's business, or its goals?**

3 **What is an organization's distinctive competency?**

FIGURE 2-3
The strategic marketing process

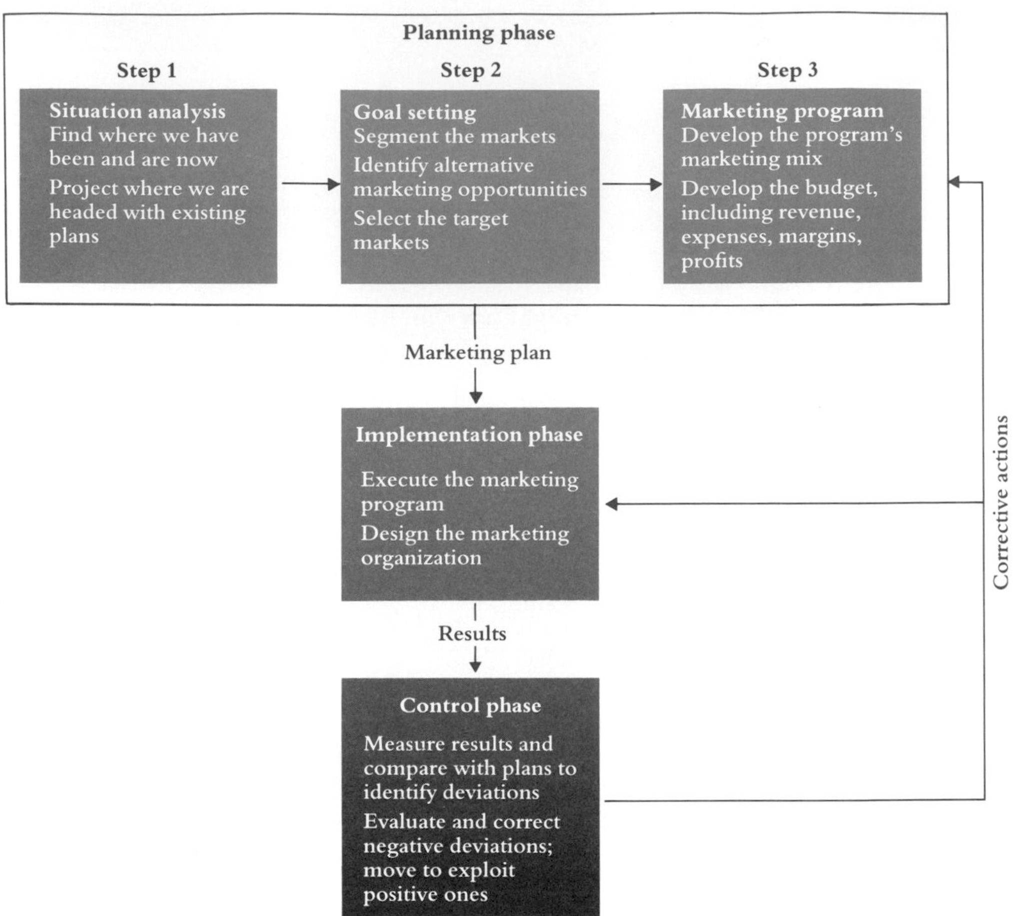

THE STRATEGIC MARKETING PROCESS: PLANNING PHASE

All approaches to planning will incorporate procedures to find answers to these key questions:

1. Where have we been, where are we now, and where are we headed with our existing plans?
2. Where do we want to go?
3. How do we allocate our resources to get where we want to go?
4. How do we convert our plans into actions?
5. How do our results compare with our plans, and do deviations require new plans and actions?

This same approach is used in the strategic marketing process, whereby an organization allocates its marketing mix resources to reach its target markets. This process is divided into three phases: planning, implementation, and control (Figure 2-3). This section covers the planning phase; the last two phases are discussed afterward.

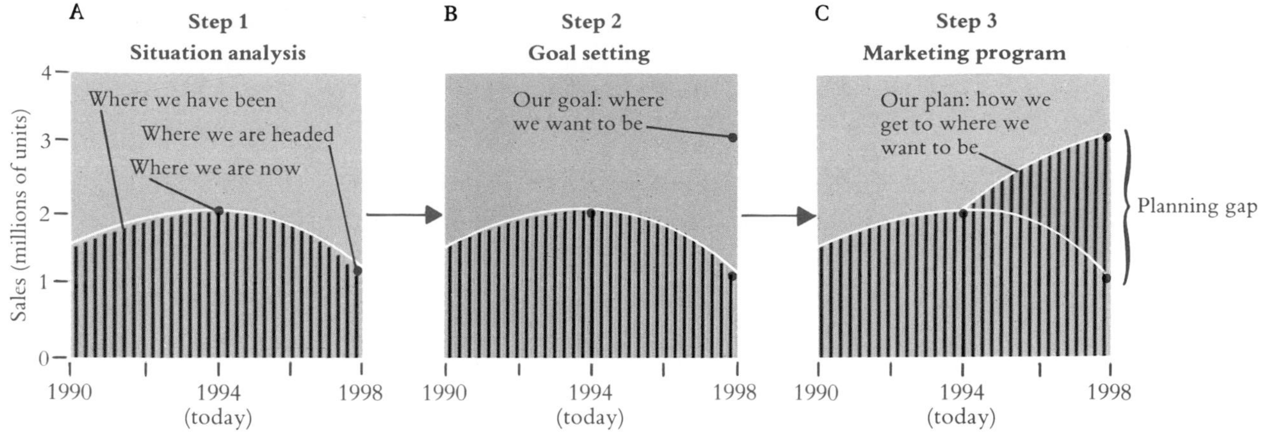

FIGURE 2-4
The planning phase of the strategic marketing process

HOW THE PLANNING STEPS TIE TOGETHER

Before details of the planning phase of the strategic marketing process are discussed, it is important to understand how the three steps of the process interrelate. The IBM PC provides an example.

Step 1: Situation Analysis Suppose it is December 1994 and you are IBM's marketing vice-president responsible for marketing its line of PCs. You want to look at the current picture, which is Step 1, or the situation analysis, in your marketing strategy process. As shown in Figure 2-4, *A,* you have shipped 2 million PCs during 1994, up from 1.5 million in 1990. But competition is heating up, and, with your present product and marketing strategy, you can see unit sales falling to 1 million in 1998.

This is the essence of the **situation analysis**—taking stock of where you've been recently, where you are now, and where you are likely to end up, following your present plans. Situation analysis requires that you assess the current strengths and weaknesses of your PC and the markets in which it competes. You then must analyze the factors both inside and outside IBM to project their effect on your future sales. These steps result in your estimate of 1 million units in 1998, a projection neither you nor your boss is very happy about.

Step 2: Goal Setting Not satisfied with a drop-off in sales for 1998, you set a target of selling 3 million units (Figure 2-4, *B*). This goal isn't pulled out of a hat. **Goal setting,** Step 2 in the strategic marketing process, is setting measurable marketing objectives to be achieved. This is the result of a careful analysis of the goals for all of IBM, as well as for your PC division, and assessment of alternative marketing opportunities—in terms of both old and new products *and* old and new markets. This ultimately results in selecting specific target markets to achieve the goal of 3 million units in 1998.

Step 3: Marketing Program The upper dotted line in Figure 2-4, *C,* shows the path you want to follow to sell 3 million units in 1998. The difference between this line and the lower one (the projection of what will happen if you only follow through with current plans) is often called the **planning gap.** Your task in Step 3 is to organize IBM's potential resources into a coherent marketing program that uses the four marketing mix elements (product, price, promotion, and place) to reach the targeted goal of 3 million units in 1998.

Plans don't automatically become reality. The implementation and control phases of the strategic marketing process (discussed later) are attempts to convert plans into actions and results.

STEP 1: SITUATION ANALYSIS

There are two steps in the situation analysis of the strategic marketing process.

Finding Where the Organization has Been and is Now Discovering where a company has been and is at present involves taking a careful inventory of the strengths and weaknesses of both the markets it serves and the array of competing products in those markets (Figure 2-4). Two important considerations in this inventory are (1) the industry growth (growth of sales of all the firms competing in that market) and (2) the competitive position of the firm's products relative to those of other businesses in the market.

High profits on a new product soon attract competitors. For example, GE had almost 2 dozen competitors within 2 years of introducing its electric carving

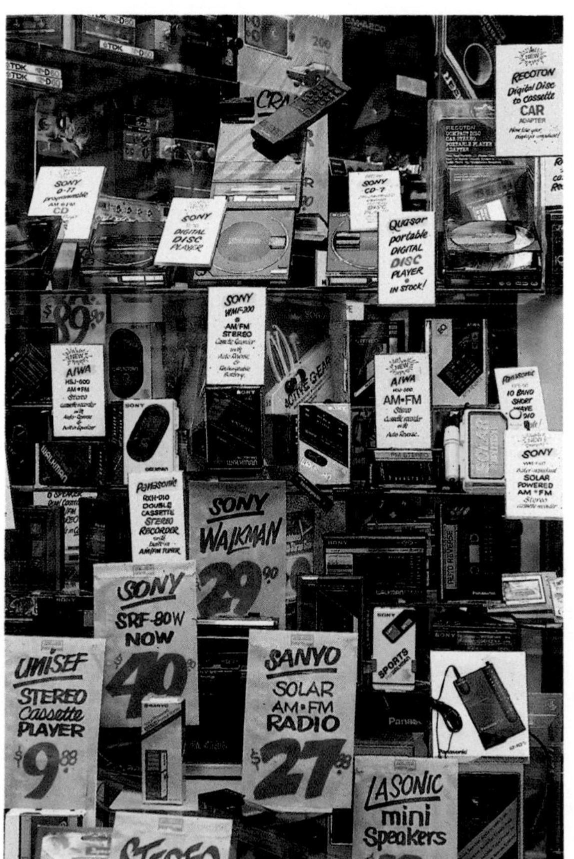

Sony's Walkman stimulated many high-quality competitors

knife. Similarly, Sony's Walkman, Apple's PC, and Prince's large-head tennis racket stimulated countless high-quality imitators who often leapfrogged the original innovation with improved models.

Projecting Where the Firm is Headed with Existing Plans When the firm knows where it is now with its present products and markets, it must project future sales and profits on the basis of its existing plans. This requires that the firm assess the impact of both internal and external factors on its products. Both can either constrain or enhance opportunities, as illustrated by IBM's introduction of its PS/2.

Internal factors include departmental objectives and resources, as well as organizational strengths and weaknesses as identified by the SWOT analysis. The marketing manager must consider all of these in assessing the future.

By the mid-1980's IBM's overall market share in PCs had fallen, and it knew action was required. It decided to design a new line of PCs. Internal factors had a major effect on IBM's decision:

- Departmental goal. The goal of the department was to develop and market a successful line of new PCs by mid-1987.
- Resources. IBM provided almost unlimited financial, technological, and marketing resources to its new PS/2 team.
- Strengths. In designing the PS/2, IBM's special strengths were its name, the strength of its original PC, and its outstanding sales and customer service personnel.
- Weaknesses. IBM PCs did not have the ability to "network," or "speak" to each other.

Hush Puppies takes market "segmentation" one step further . . .

Thus internal factors can have both positive and negative effects on marketing decisions.

External factors in a SWOT analysis cover consumer demand and competitive, economic, political, legal, and technological issues. All these affected IBM's decision to introduce its PS/2:

- Consumer demand considerations. IBM research showed that consumers wanted PCs that were fast and user-friendly and could communicate with each other and large systems.
- Competitive considerations. Apple, Tandy, Compaq, and other IBM clones were already producing high-quality PCs.
- Economic considerations. The dollar was weakening against foreign currencies, especially the Japanese yen, making foreign PCs more expensive than American-built PCs for U.S. buyers.
- Political and legal considerations. With the number of IBM clones in existence, a critical issue was whether competitors could legally "clone" its new PS/2.
- Technological considerations. Designing a technologically complex PS/2 line of PCs that could network with all sizes of IBM computers was a task that would tax even IBM's resources. Could it be done at a cost that would eventually make the PS/2 profitable?

IBM added up the internal and external factors in the mid-1980's and committed itself to the PS/2 project.

STEP 2: GOAL SETTING

An effective marketing program requires a focus—a specific group of target market customers toward which it is directed. This requires that the marketing manager (1) segment the firm's markets, (2) identify alternative marketing opportunities, and (3) actually select target markets. Note that there is a hierarchy of goals in an organization. For example, marketing objectives must flow directly from goals set by top management in the strategic management process.

Segmenting the Market The process of **marketing segmentation** involves dividing a large market with diverse needs into submarkets, or segments, of prospective buyers that (1) have common needs and (2) will respond similarly to a marketing action. Ideally, each segment can be reached by a specific marketing program targeted to its needs. The Coca-Cola Company now offers four different Coca-Colas to reach market segments that want or don't want sugar and want or don't want caffeine. It also offers new-formula Coca-Cola for those wanting a sweeter taste and Cherry Coke for those wanting that flavor. The decision to target soft drinks to these segments was a major one because, until 1982, the name "Coca-Cola" was never allowed on any drink but original-formula Coca-Cola—now "Coca-Cola Classic."

Identifying Alternative Market Opportunities One way for a marketing manager to identify alternative market opportunities is by analyzing various market-producing strategies.

Movies and TV programs are part of the diversification strategy of the Coca-Cola Company

As Coca-Cola attempts to increase sales and profits, there are four combinations of present and new markets and present and new products.[14] For example, the Coca-Cola marketing manager can try to achieve deeper **market penetration,** which is selling more of a firm's present products to existing customers, by increasing sales of Coca-Cola to ultimate consumers. There is no change in the product line, but increased sales are possible through actions such as better advertising, more retail outlets, or lower prices. In fact, to strengthen its network of retail outlets, Coca-Cola bought some of its biggest bottlers, made them a separate company (Coca-Cola Enterprises, Inc.), and sold it to the public.[15]

Market development, which means taking present products to new customers, has been undertaken by selling Coca-Cola to a new market—such as China—that had not been reached before by the company. Coca-Cola believes opportunities for increased soft drink sales are greater in international markets than in the United States.[16]

An expansion strategy using **product development** requires changing the product itself but selling it to existing markets. Coca-Cola has exploited numerous other new product opportunities: Fresca (1966), Diet Coke (1982), Cherry Coke (1986), and Diet Cherry Coke (1986).

Diversification involves developing new products and selling them in new markets. This is a potentially high-risk strategy for Coca-Cola because the company has neither previous production experience nor marketing experience on which to draw. In the early 1980's, Coca-Cola acquired Columbia Pictures Industries, a producer of movies and TV programs for U.S. and foreign markets. This acquisition represents diversification strategy far different from selling soft drinks to American consumers.

As often occurs, Coca-Cola has used all four strategies shown in Figure 2-5 to arrive at its present line of products serving today's diverse markets.

FIGURE 2–5
Four market-product strategies: alternative ways to expand marketing opportunities, using Coca-Cola Company products as examples

MARKETS	PRODUCTS PRESENT	PRODUCTS NEW
Present	**Market penetration** Selling more Coca-Cola to Americans	**Product development** Selling a new product like Cherry Coke to Americans
New	**Market development** Selling Coca-Cola to Chinese for the first time	**Diversification** Selling a new product like movies and home videos to Europeans

Selecting the Target Markets Having considered a number of alternative marketing opportunities, the organization must select the one or more target markets for which it will develop its marketing program. An important strategic issue for firms to use in selecting target markets is to balance the increased expenses (such as research and development [R&D] and production) against increased revenues (such as expected sales revenue).

Diet Coke—a sugar-free, caffeinated soft drink—is an example of the difficult choices an organization faces in deciding to introduce a new product. In this case Coca-Cola was especially concerned about **product cannibalism**—a new product gaining sales merely by stealing them from the company's other products. Coca-Cola managers were worried that Diet Coke would make money at the expense of Tab and not by reaching new customers. This is exactly what has happened. The even more controversial Coca-Cola decision on new-formula Coca-Cola and Coca-Cola Classic is discussed in Chapter 6.

STEP 3: THE MARKETING PROGRAM

Selecting the target markets tells the marketing manager which consumers to focus on and what needs to try to satisfy—the *who* aspect of the strategic marketing process. The *how* part involves (1) developing the proper marketing mix and (2) developing the budget. Figure 2-6 shows components of each marketing mix element that are combined to provide a cohesive marketing program.

Developing the Marketing Mix In the 1950's a doting grandfather was babysitting his first grandchild. Called on to change the baby's diapers, he was certain there must be something better than cloth diapers or the poor-quality disposable diapers then on the market. The grandfather, a P&G engineer, did something about this unsatisfied need and convinced the firm to develop a better product. Was the U.S. market large enough to warrant this new product development effort? P&G market researchers estimated that in the United States at that time there were 15 billion diaper changes a year, so the market *was* big enough to justify a closer look.

After several redesigns, many trials with babies, countless interviews with

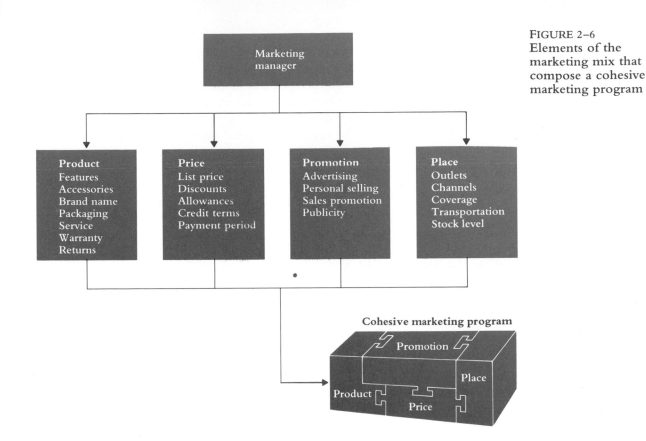

FIGURE 2–6
Elements of the marketing mix that compose a cohesive marketing program

Marketing manager

Product
Features
Accessories
Brand name
Packaging
Service
Warranty
Returns

Price
List price
Discounts
Allowances
Credit terms
Payment period

Promotion
Advertising
Personal selling
Sales promotion
Publicity

Place
Outlets
Channels
Coverage
Transportation
Stock level

Cohesive marketing program

Promotion
Place
Product
Price

parents, and four trial introductions, a product was found that satisfied consumers' expectations of quality for the price paid. Pampers disposable diapers were the result.

From its introduction in 1956 until the early 1980's, Pampers dominated the disposable diaper market. But in 1982 Kimberly-Clark's Huggies disposable diaper went into national distribution, and P&G's share of the disposable diaper market fell about 20 percent during the next 2 years.

If you were P&G and lost 20 percent of a $3 billion a year market, what would you do? Its answer was to counterattack! In 1986 P&G introduced an improved Pampers using a new marketing program:

Diaper wars: new Huggies versus Ultra Pampers

- Product. The new, thinner diaper is better fitting. Even more important is a cross-linked polyacrylate material that can absorb 700 to 800 times its own weight in fluid. The new name: Ultra Pampers.
- Price. It was comparable to the price of the old Pampers.
- Promotion. A major advertising program informed buyers of the improved product features.
- Place. P&G fought for space on retailers' shelves by stressing that a 24-count box of the new Ultra Pampers is about half the size of other boxes of disposable diapers.

P&G's diaper war with Kimberly-Clark continues. A big problem for P&G is educating buyers, many of whom can't believe the new, thinner diaper is as absorbent as the old Pampers.[17]

Developing the Budget A P&G marketing executive responsible for introducing Ultra Pampers had to develop a budget to ensure that revenues would exceed expenses and result in a profit. To project the budget's sales revenue, he first had to answer some key questions:

- Will national sales for Ultra Pampers jump 25 percent to 35 percent, as they did in a sales test of the product in Wichita?
- When Kimberly-Clark introduces its own super-absorbent disposable diaper (a product it shelved when market research incorrectly said buyers didn't want it) what will the effect be?[18]
- If Ultra Pampers is a success, will it cannibalize sales of P&G's Luvs, its premium-priced brand?

Answering such questions is the first step in developing a realistic budget for the marketing program. The planning phase of the strategic marketing process is discussed in greater detail in Chapter 19.

CONCEPT CHECK

1 **What is situation analysis?**

2 **What is market segmentation?**

3 **When Coca-Cola decided to produce Fresca and Tab and sell them to its existing customers, which kind of market-product strategy was it following?**

THE STRATEGIC MARKETING PROCESS: IMPLEMENTATION PHASE

As shown in Figure 2-3, the result of the tens or hundreds of hours in the planning phase of the strategic marketing process is a **marketing plan**—a written statement that identifies the target market; specific marketing goals such as units sold, sales revenue, and profit; and the budget and timing for the marketing mix elements that make up the marketing program.

Implementation, the second phase of the strategic marketing process, involves carrying out the marketing plan that emerged from the planning phase. Two key elements in the implementation phase are (1) executing the program described in the marketing plan and (2) designing the marketing organization needed.

EXECUTING THE MARKETING PROGRAM

Marketing plans are meaningless pieces of paper without effective execution of those plans.

Marketing Strategies and Marketing Tactics Effective execution requires attention to detail for both marketing strategies and marketing tactics. Two factors characterize a **marketing strategy:** (1) a specified target market and (2) a marketing program to reach it. Although the term *strategy* is often used loosely, it implies both the end sought (target market) and the means to achieve it (marketing program), such as a pricing or promotional strategy.

To implement a marketing program successfully, hundreds of detailed decisions are often required, such as writing advertising copy or selecting the amount for temporary price reductions. These decisions, called **marketing tactics,** are detailed day-to-day operational decisions essential to the overall success of marketing strategies. Compared with marketing strategies, marketing tactics generally involve actions that must be taken right away. We cannot cover many aspects of marketing tactics in detail in a book of this size, and the emphasis here is on marketing strategy—the strategic marketing process. However, examples of marketing tactics are occasionally described to show the concern for detail present in effective marketing programs.

Strategies and Tactics for Introducing IBM's PS/2 IBM president John F. Akers concluded that IBM's problems in 1986 (see beginning of chapter) oc-

IBM's PS/2: a new personal computer to get it "in touch with its customers" again curred because "IBM got out of touch with its customers." Akers believed that IBM had persisted in selling computers when customers actually wanted "solutions" on how to get their dozens of computers to "talk" to each other to improve productivity.[19] The strategy was to return IBM to what its distinctive competency had traditionally been—"solving customer problems"—as opposed to selling products. So when IBM launched its family of PCs named the Personal System/2 in 1987, IBM believed it was critical to have a cohesive marketing program to meet the needs of its target market customers. This required effective planning and implementation of countless strategic issues for all four marketing mix elements, as follows:

- Product. IBM introduced four models of the PS/2 with far more speed and memory than earlier IBM PCs had but capable of running their software. In addition, PS/2 offered easier-to-use software, colorful graphics, and better links with all sizes of other computers.[20]
- Price. The initial prices ranged from $1,695 for the desktop model to $10,995 for the high-end, fully-equipped version. This was accompanied by price reductions of up to 35 percent on older IBM PC models.[21]
- Promotion. The PS/2 introduction got buyers' attention: The kickoff included a Beach Boys concert in Miami Beach for 2,000 key computer dealers from across the United States and an elaborate TV presentation beamed live to 20,000 customers, employees, reporters, and analysts nationwide.[22]
- Place. IBM restricted the number of dealers authorized to sell the entire PS/2 line and required them to take 5 days, and service technicians 8 days, of special IBM training at the dealers' expense.[23]

IBM even undertook an aggressive information campaign warning competitors they could not build legal clones without obtaining patent licenses from IBM for its mysterious "Micro Channel."[24]

Having resolved these strategic issues, IBM turned to the tactical problem of finding a group of people that would be attention-getting, believable, and effective in presenting the PS/2 line of products to prospective buyers. Another problem was whether all the group members could be put under contract to be in the ads. Look at the ad in the Marketing Action Memo and try to identify the people and the characters they played on a major TV series. Who is missing and why? The answers appear at the end of the box.

IBM and its advertising agency decided that the actors from the M★A★S★H television series were ideal spokespeople for the PS/2 family. Your ability to identify and relate to the actors in the ad is a good indicator of the likely success of IBM's advertising campaign.

The concern for tactical details in marketing programs shows why Jamie Farr almost wasn't selected for IBM's M★A★S★H team. According to *Advertising Age* magazine, "there was a question of the appropriateness of Mr. Farr as a spokesman for Big Blue because his appearance might conjure up memories of his M★A★S★H character—the cross-dressing Corporal Max Klinger."[25] Regardless, the vital point is that IBM's successful introduction of its PS/2 reflects attention to the details of marketing strategies and tactics that combine to become a cohesive marketing program.

MARKETING · ACTION · MEMO

IBM'S TACTICS FOR AN ADVERTISING ENCORE: M★A★S★H

IBM's first PC in 1981 was essentially a one-product line, and the lonely, nonthreatening Little Tramp was a good spokesman for it. However, in 1987 the new Personal System/2 consisted of dozens of products, and IBM's advertising agency searched for another slice of Americana that could present an entire product line to potential buyers of the PS/2. The solution: the M★A★S★H group of characters who are intended to represent "a new generation of IBM team work."

The ad at the bottom of page 28 is the cover of a 24-page insert used in many business magazines to introduce the PS/2 in 1987.

The people in that ad are shown again here. From left to right in the ad you might recognize the actors whose contracts to appear for IBM were negotiated with their agents: William Christopher (Father Mulcahy), Harry Morgan (Colonel Potter), Jamie Farr (Klinger), Gary Burghoff (Radar), Wayne Rogers (Trapper John), Loretta Swit (Hot Lips Houlihan), and Larry Linville (Major Frank Burns).

Conspicuously absent are Alan Alda as Hawkeye (he had one year left on an Atari contract, but he was added to the IBM team in 1988), David Ogden Stiers as Major Charles Emerson Winchester III, and Mike Farrell as Captain B.J. Hunnicutt (whose agents couldn't agree on contracts with IBM).

Will the M★A★S★H characters be as effective in representing the PS/2 as the Little Tramp was for the original IBM PC? Time—and target market customers—will tell.

Sources: Patricia Winters, "Little Tramp Ends Stint as IBM Front Man," *Advertising Age* (April 6, 1987), p. 80; Cleveland Horton, "Stars Drafted to Revive IBM," *Advertising Age* (April 6, 1987), p. 80; Cleveland Horton, "M★A★S★H' Stars Enjoy Reunion," *Advertising Age* (April 20, 1987), p. 78; Gary Levin, "Alda Joins IBM Campaigns," *Advertising Age* (February 28, 1988), p. 4.

DESIGNING THE MARKETING ORGANIZATION

To execute the marketing program effectively, a marketing organization must be developed.

General Motors' Reorganization In the mid-1980's General Motors (GM) announced a total reorganization of the company that was prompted by increased competition from Japanese and European imports.

As shown in Figure 2-7, reporting to the president are two group vice-

FIGURE 2–7
Organization of the automobile operations of General Motors Corporation

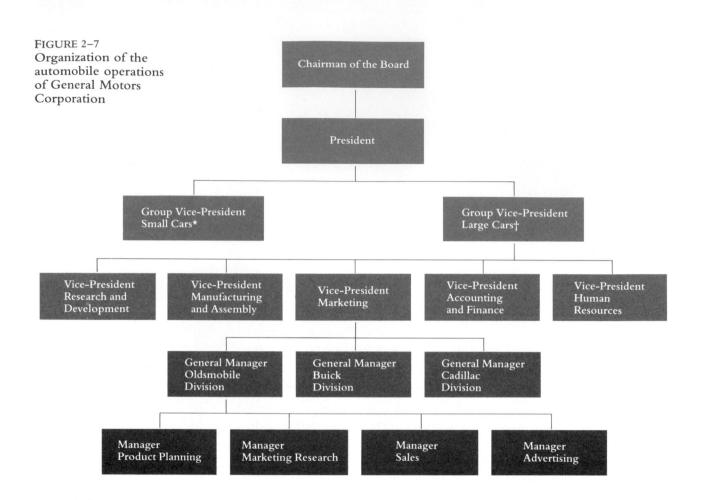

presidents—one for small cars (Chevrolet, Pontiac, and General Motors of Canada) and the other for large cars (Oldsmobile, Buick, and Cadillac). Under the new organization both the Large Car and Small Car groups are divided into five main departments: R&D (including parts of the old Fisher Body Division), manufacturing and assembly (including parts of the old Assembly Division), marketing, accounting and finance, and human resources.

General Motors' Marketing Organization One reason for GM's restructuring is to enable it to respond more quickly to changes in the market.[26] Another reason is the growth in overlapping brands of GM cars that aren't targeted to specific market segments but have similar designs, thus confusing buyers.[27] Thirty years ago consumers saw Chevrolet as a reliable, low-priced smaller car and Cadillac as a large luxury car. These distinctions have blurred because GM's centralized design group was producing blueprints for what competitors called "look-alike" brands of GM cars. This caused special problems such as that experienced by Cadillac, whose upscale buyers couldn't understand why their high-priced cars looked like cheaper GM brands.[28]

GM hopes its new organization will change all that. Three general managers from the Oldsmobile, Buick, and Cadillac Divisions report to the vice-president

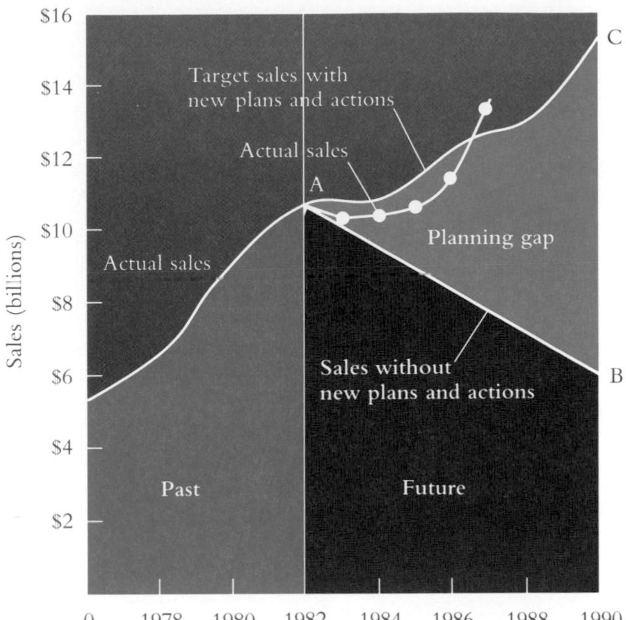

FIGURE 2–8
Evaluation and control of Kodak's marketing program

of marketing for the Large Cars group. These divisions are now marketing and sales organizations designed to develop and sell more distinctive cars to different market segments.

To achieve this, the Oldsmobile Division, for example, has product planning, marketing research, sales, and advertising units reporting to the general manager. Product planning and marketing research translate consumer preferences into product features, which will appear in designs drawn by R&D. The advertising unit develops promotional campaigns, and the sales unit is responsible for selling Oldsmobiles through GM's complex dealer network.

THE STRATEGIC MARKETING PROCESS: CONTROL PHASE

The control phase of the strategic marketing process seeks to keep the marketing program moving in the direction set for it (Figure 2-4). Accomplishing this requires the marketing manager (1) to compare the results of the marketing program with the goals in the written plans to identify deviations and (2) to act on these deviations—correcting negative deviations and exploiting positive ones.

COMPARING RESULTS WITH PLANS TO IDENTIFY DEVIATIONS

In 1981 Eastman Kodak saw its sales start to plateau from the high growth it had experienced from 1975 to 1980 (Figure 2-8). The year 1982 also produced flat sales and a dramatic drop in profits. The outlook was grim at the end of 1982. Technological innovations were redefining the entire amateur photo-

New Kodak 35mm cameras help fill in its planning gap

Reprinted courtesy of Eastman Kodak Company

graphic market, and several of Kodak's product lines were faltering. A decreasing market share for instant cameras, declining sales of movie films, and greater competition from Fuji in the traditional film and photographic paper markets necessitated drastic action.

To equal its late-1970's sales growth, Kodak would have to follow line AC in Figure 2-8, which could fill in its large, wedge-shaped planning gap. But continued competition and a slowdown in sales of its Disc cameras, introduced in 1982, resulted in actual 1983 sales being far less than the targeted level. This is the essence of *evaluation*—comparing actual results with planned objectives.

ACTING ON DEVIATIONS

When the evaluation shows that actual performance is not up to expectations, a corrective action is usually needed to adjust and improve the program and help it achieve the planned objective. In contrast, comparing results with plans may sometimes reveal that actual performance is far better than the plan called for. In this case the marketing manager wants to uncover the reason for the good performance and act to exploit it.

Kodak's evaluation of its 1983 performance showed that it fell short of its plans, so the company initiated a drastic new action program that involved developing and marketing hundreds of new products it manufactured and distributing dozens of products produced by others. Targeted at consumers are new automatic "point-and-shoot" 35 mm cameras, "throwaway" cameras, faster film, and a complete line of batteries—all manufactured by Kodak. Pointed at industrial and medical consumers are new 1-hour photoprocessing minilabs, optical-data storage systems, blood-analysis tests, and pharmaceuticals.[29]

This action program helped sales to rise again, thereby helping to close the planning gap shown in Figure 2-8. Although Kodak's profit has not increased as rapidly as has sales revenue, it is also improving. Kodak's corrective actions to bring its marketing program under control illustrate the final phase in the strategic marketing process.

The implementation and control phases of the strategic marketing process are discussed in greater detail in Chapter 20.

CONCEPT CHECK

1 **What is the control phase of the strategic marketing process?**

2 **How do the objectives set for a marketing program in the planning phase relate to the control phase of the strategic marketing process?**

SUMMARY

1 The strategic management process involves the steps taken at an organization's corporate and divisional levels to develop long-run master strategies for survival and growth. Three key steps in this process are (a) defining the organization's business (or mission), (b) specifying its goals, and (c) identifying its opportunities.

2 The strategic marketing process, using objectives and limits set by the strategic management process, involves the steps taken at market and product levels to allocate a firm's marketing resources to viable marketing positions and programs. It has three phases: planning, implementation, and control.

3 The planning phase of the strategic marketing process involves three steps: (a) the situation analysis (where are we now, how did we get here, and where are we headed with present plans?), (b) goal setting (where do we want to go?), and (c) designing a marketing program in the form of a marketing plan that blends the elements of the marketing mix (how do we allocate our marketing resources to get where we want to go?).

4 The task of identifying marketing opportunities can be facilitated by looking at the four combinations of present and new markets and present and new products.

5 The implementation phase of the strategic marketing process involves executing the marketing plan and designing the marketing organization needed.

6 Marketing strategies involve specifying a target market and a marketing program to reach it. Marketing tactics are the detailed, day-to-day operational decisions essential to the overall success of marketing strategies.

7 The control phase of the strategic marketing process involves (a) comparing results with the goals established in the marketing plan to identify deviations from plan and (b) taking action to correct negative deviations or exploit positive ones.

KEY TERMS AND CONCEPTS

strategic management process p. 30
strategic marketing process p. 30
organizational business (mission) p. 31
organizational goals p. 32
business firm p. 34
nonprofit organization p. 34
profit p. 34
market share p. 34
distinctive competency p. 37
situation analysis p. 39
goal setting p. 39
planning gap p. 40
market segmentation p. 42
market penetration p. 43
market development p. 43
product development p. 43
diversification p. 43
product cannibalism p. 44
marketing plan p. 46
marketing strategy p. 47
marketing tactics p. 47

CHAPTER PROBLEMS AND APPLICATIONS

1 Look again at IBM's PS/2 ad at the start of the chapter. Recognizing that the ad is targeted at businesses, what are (a) good features of the ad and (b) the concerns that IBM might have had in running this advertising campaign?

2 How did the three *C*'s—company, customer, and competitor—lead IBM to conclude it should introduce its new PS/2?

3 Sara Lee Corporation produces a variety of products and services that fall into the five divisions cited in the chapter: (a) consumer foods, (b) international consumer foods, (c) food service distribution, (d) consumer personal products, and (e) consumer household products. Where are each of these "businesses" included in its business (mission) statement in Figure 2-2?

4 What is the main result of each of the three phases of the strategic marketing process? (a) planning, (b) implementation, or (c) control.

5 Many American liberal arts colleges traditionally have offered an undergraduate degree in liberal arts (the product) to full-time 18-year-old to 22-year-old students (the market). How might such a college use the four market-product expansion strategies shown in Figure 2-5 to compete in the 1990's?

6 Today many Americans are concerned about the volume of their salt intake. Coca-Cola might (a) add salt and no-salt combinations to its existing (b) sugar and no-sugar and (c) caffeine and no-caffeine brands. How many combinations would Coca-Cola have to offer to hit all these combinations? What are the strengths and weaknesses of such a product strategy?

7 There are both advantages and disadvantages to introducing a new, improved version of an existing brand. What are examples of each for P&G in choosing (a) not to introduce and (b) to introduce its improved, high-absorbency Ultra Pampers disposable diaper?

8 The goal-setting step in the planning phase of the strategic marketing process sets quantified objectives for use in the control phase. What actions are suggested for a marketing manager if measured results are below objectives? Above objectives?

9 Suppose you headed up General Motors today. Develop a simple SWOT analysis for the company based on what you know about its cars and environmental factors.

SUGGESTED READINGS

Derek F. Abell, *Defining the Business* (Englewood Cliffs, NJ: Prentice-Hall, Inc., 1982). *Using existing management theory, Abell identifies ways to help organizations answer the question of "what business are we in?"*

Nancy Giges, "Adam of the Year: Coca-Cola's Roberto Goizueta Engineers Startling Comeback," *Advertising Age* (December 29, 1986), pp. 1, 26, 27. *The article describes how the Cuban-born head of Coca-Cola developed and executed a series of marketing strategies that gave new life to this century-old firm.*

"The Greatest Capitalist in History," *Fortune* (August 31, 1987), pp. 24-35. *This is a personal memoir of Thomas J. Watson, Jr., who led IBM during its years of greatest growth and points out that marketing—not technological innovation—was the key to IBM's tremendous success.*

"GM Faces Reality," *Business Week* (May 9, 1988), pp. 114-122. *This article describes how General Motors is responding to the world it foresees in the 1990's.*

Theodore Levitt, "Marketing Myopia," *Harvard Business Review* (July-August 1960), pp. 45-56. *This is probably the most frequently quoted marketing article ever published and describes how growth industries decline by being product oriented rather than customer oriented.*

3

THE CHANGING MARKETING ENVIRONMENT

After reading this chapter you should be able to:

Understand how environmental scanning studies social, economic, technological, competitive, and regulatory forces.

•

Explain how social forces like demographics and culture and economic forces like macroeconomic conditions and consumer income affect marketing.

•

Describe how technological changes and their ecological impacts can affect marketing.

•

Understand the competitive structures that exist in a market, the role of marketing within each, and key components of competition.

•

Explain the major legislation to ensure competition and to regulate the elements of the marketing mix.

You're Invited to a Birthday Party: White Tie and Tails, Please!

You turn on the T.V. set and see a commercial. A person reaches into the closet and pulls out a well-pressed black tuxedo. The screen shows a leg slipping into the pants, then a shirt with pearl buttons, and finally the cumberbund. Ah, but without seeing the face of the person, you can tell that he is having trouble with the bow tie. In walks an attractive woman in an evening dress to help. She stoops down and says, "Let me do it, son. Daddy is in the car waiting for us." "Thanks, Mommy," says the smiling 5-year-old boy.

Wait a minute—tuxedos for kids? Yes, it's the latest trend, along with $90 suits and Nike sneakers. Benetton, Laura Ashley, Esprit, and even Land's End are just some of the formerly adult-only clothing retailers that have discovered kids.

Why now, you might ask. The answer: the environment is changing. A combination of demographics and economics has led to the greater interest in fashion and children's wear. On average, 3.4 million babies are expected to be born each year in the United States through the year 2000—a baby boom the likes of which has not been seen since the 1950's. And an unusually high number of these children, 45 percent, are the firstborn of their parents. Combine this figure with the rise in two-income families and their larger earnings, and the price of clothing is no longer the obstacle it was in past days. Some clothing industry people believe that because many parents both work, guilt is also spurring them to spend more on their children. In August, 1987, Laura Ashley, a retailer of classic women's clothing, opened its first five Mother and Child stores. Quality party dresses for little girls retail for between $54 and $100.[1]

Trends in the environment can create new marketing opportunities. So don't be surprised if the next invitation to your nephew's or niece's birthday party reads "Formal Dress Only, Please!"

How Marketing Uses Environmental Scanning

The change in the age distribution and birth trends in the United States represents an opportunity for companies such as Benetton, Laura Ashley, and even Sears with its line of McDonald's children's clothes.

THE MEANING OF ENVIRONMENTAL SCANNING

Like these companies, people in many firms continually acquire information on events occurring outside their organization to identify and interpret potential trends—a process called **environmental scanning.** The objective of environmental scanning is to spot the trends and determine if they pose specific op-

FIGURE 3-1
How environmental scanning reveals marketing opportunities and threats

An organization's very existence often depends on its ability to spot trends in its environment and turn these to its advantage. For each of the three questions below, estimate (1) what percentage of Americans have that characteristic, (2) what type of firm could use this fact as an opportunity, and (3) what type of firm could view it as a threat.

1. What percentage of Americans love Mexican food?
2. What percentage of American women wear size 14 or larger?
3. What percentage of Americans cook for fun?

The percentages, along with some opportunities and threats, are described below.

portunities or threats to the firm, as described in SWOT analysis in Chapter 2. This understanding leads to marketing actions.

Surprisingly, a trend that represents an important opportunity for one firm may be a major threat to another and vice versa. To understand environmental scanning and its importance, read Figure 3-1 and try to estimate the percentage of Americans with those characteristics and how such facts pose both opportunities and threats for different firms.

Concerning Mexican food, 23 percent of all Americans say they love it. This suggests a marketing opportunity as seen in the growth of Mexican restaurant chains (such as Chi-Chi's, Guadalaharry's, and Taco Bell) and a threat to more traditional chains such as McDonald's and Kentucky Fried Chicken. Concerning Question 2, nearly half of all American women wear size 14 or larger, a segment targeted by the Limited Stores. In 1982, the Limited, Inc., bought Lane Bryant, the first U.S. chain to specialize in large sizes for women. And from 1982 to 1987 the number of Lane Bryant stores grew from 214 to almost 800, which might threaten the sales in traditional department stores. About 20 percent of Americans cook for fun—a boon to firms selling gourmet cookbooks and spices, but a threat to restaurant chains if the percentage increases significantly.[2]

AN ENVIRONMENTAL SCAN OF THE 1990'S

Every organization exists as part of a larger environment in which continuous changes provide both marketing opportunities and threats. This chapter examines five broad, uncontrollable factors in a company's environment: social, economic, technological, competitive, and regulatory forces. As shown in Figure 3-2, these factors are the environmental forces that affect the marketing activities of a firm.

A firm conducting an environmental scan of the United States in the 1990's might uncover key trends such as those listed in Figure 3-3 for each of the five environmental forces. Although the list of trends is far from complete, it reveals

FIGURE 3-2
Environmental forces affecting the organization, as well as its suppliers and customers

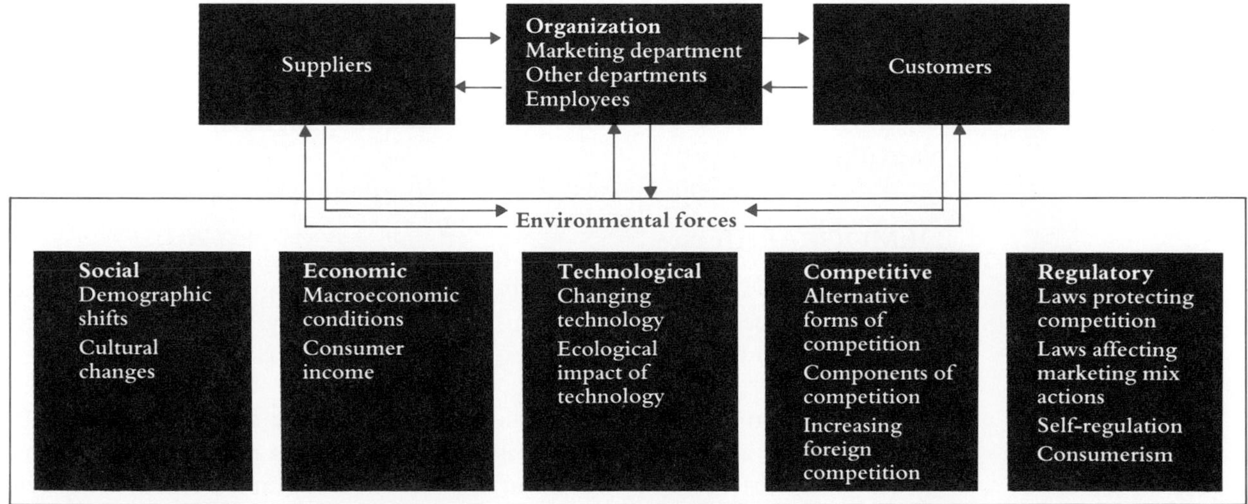

ENVIRONMENTAL FORCE	TREND IDENTIFIED BY AN ENVIRONMENTAL SCAN
Social	• Growing number and importance of older Americans • Continuing U.S. population shifts to South and West • Desire for "high-tech and high touch": gadgets plus human interaction • Greater desire for product quality, customer service • Greater role for women in jobs, purchase decisions
Economic	• Concern that U.S. budget and trade deficits can trigger inflation • More U.S. firms will look to foreign markets for growth • Continuing decline in real per capita income of Americans • Greater consumer acceptance of debt
Technological	• Increased use of massive computer data bases and networks • Major breakthroughs in biotechnology, superconductivity • More problems with pollution and solid and nuclear wastes
Competitive	• More employment in small, innovative firms • Downsizing, restructuring of many corporations • Flexible manufacturing will reduce economies of scale • More international competition from Europe and Asia
Regulatory	• Less regulation of U.S. firms competing in international markets • More protection for those owning patents • Greater concern for ethics in business • Renewed emphasis on self-regulation

FIGURE 3-3
An environmental scan of the United States of the 1990's

the breadth of an environmental scan—from identifying changing consumer tastes such as "high-tech and high touch" and the desire for improved product quality and customer service to technological breakthroughs in biotechnology and competitive challenges in restructuring American corporations. These trends affect all Americans and the businesses and nonprofit organizations that serve them. Trends such as these are covered as the five environmental forces are described in the following pages.

SOCIAL FORCES

The **social forces** of the environment include the characteristics of the population, its income, and its values. Changes in these can have a dramatic impact on marketing strategy.

DEMOGRAPHICS

Describing the distribution of the population according to selected characteristics—where people are, their numbers, and who they are, such as their age, sex, income, and occupation—is referred to as **demographics.**

The Population Trend In 1987 the population of the United States was 244 million people, an 11 percent increase over 1975.[3] This represents a continued decline in the birth rate and signals an important demographic trend: the graying of America. The American population is aging as birth rates decline and life

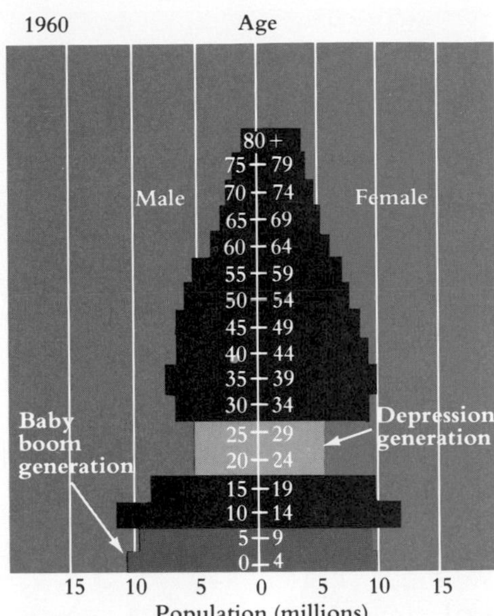

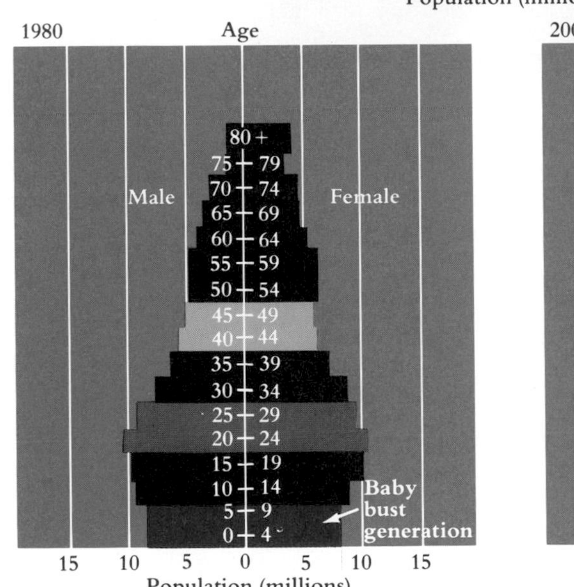

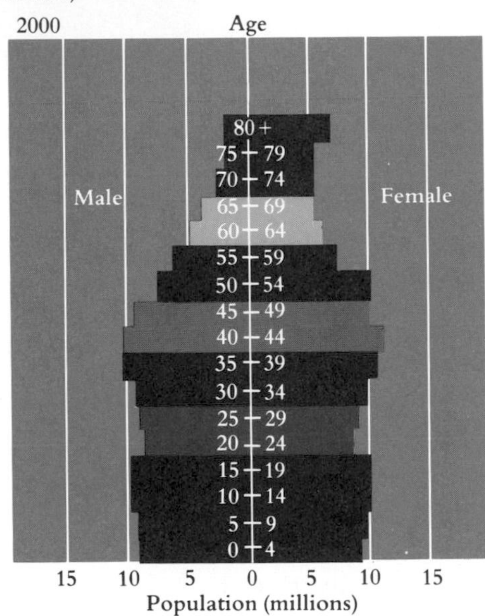

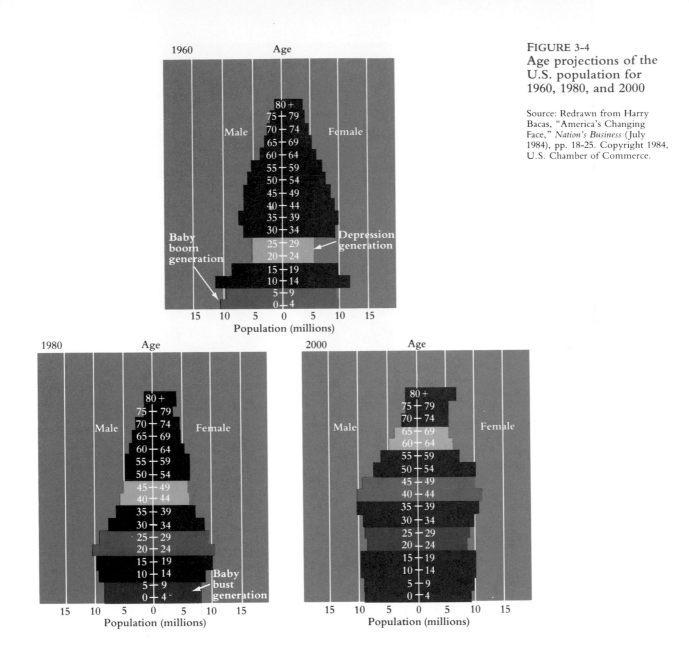

FIGURE 3-4
Age projections of the U.S. population for 1960, 1980, and 2000

Source: Redrawn from Harry Bacas, "America's Changing Face," *Nation's Business* (July 1984), pp. 18-25. Copyright 1984, U.S. Chamber of Commerce.

expectancies increase. In 1960 only 9 percent of the population was over 65 years of age, but by the year 2000 the number of people over 65 is expected to be close to 22 percent of the population.[4] A careful look at Figure 3-4 reveals that by the year 2000, the over-65 age group will almost double in number compared with the 1980 level. There will be a significant increase in the number of women over age 70 years. Companies are beginning to notice this aging market. As shown on the following page, the advertising focus for Silk & Silver, a coloring mousse, was changed from a product that helps ward off the effects of old age to a product that enhances the beauty of age.

In recent years, a greater marketing attention is being focused on the

A product directed at the over-50 segment of women

Nothing is more flattering than Silk & Silver.
The coloring mousse that creates silvery highlights with body and shine.
Silk & Silver works ever so gently, bringing out highlights and body where dull, lifeless yellow used to be. All without peroxide or ammonia.
Just mousse it in. And you'll keep on shining through eight shampoos. Of course, if you prefer, Clairol also makes Silk & Silver lotion. Either way you get a very flattering look. And a lot of looks.

mature household. Such households are headed by people over 50 years in age, who represent the fastest growing age segment in America. In the next 15 years, the adult population will grow by 14 percent, but the number of people over age 50 will increase by 23 percent.[5] People over 50 control nearly 70 percent of the net worth of U.S. households, and the over-50 category includes the period (between ages 55 and 60) when a person's per capita income peaks.

Environmental scanning of demographic trends clearly will affect the marketing future of some companies. Columbia Records must identify musical stars who will appeal to an older age segment. Humana Corporation, a large health care firm, runs nursing homes, which are promising businesses in light of present demographic trends.

The Baby Boom A large reason for the graying of America is that baby boomers are growing up. According to Figure 3-4, the largest 10-year age group in 1960 was the 0 to 9 category. This group is included in the **baby boomers,** the generation of children born between 1946 and 1964. Because they account for nearly a third of the population, baby boomers are becoming more and more important to marketers.[6]

This generation has a distinct profile compared with that of other age groups. Baby boomers have the highest education level, with a fourth of those between the ages of 25 and 35 having college degrees, and their income is significant. The median income of baby boomers should rise by 20 percent from $32,110 in 1986 to $38,410 by the year 2000, adjusted for inflation.[7]

The American Family Although dramatic changes exist in terms of age and birth rate, marketers are also monitoring a changing American family. In the 1950's, 70 percent of U.S. households consisted of a stay-at-home mother, working father, and 1 or more children, whereas only 15 percent of today's households do so.[8]

About 50 percent of all first marriages now end in divorce. The majority of divorced people eventually remarry, which has given rise to the **blended family,** one formed by the merging into a single household of two previously separated units. In scanning this environment, Levitz, a furniture retailer, found blended families prefer rectangular tables—his kids on one side, hers on the other.[9]

The Geographical Shifts The major regional shift in the population has been to the Western and Sunbelt states. The 4 states that had the highest growth rates from 1980 to 1987 were Nevada, Arizona, Utah, and Florida.[10] As consumers shift their locations and the demographic profiles of states change, new opportunities will open for distribution centers, retail outlets, and products. States in the West now have a younger population than 20 years ago.

In recent decades, people have also moved from rural areas to major cities and their suburbs. So marketers focus on population centers, where about three fourths of the population lives. To assist marketers in gathering data on population centers, the government has a three-level classification system that reflects their degree of urbanization. From largest to smallest, these three areas are the consolidated metropolitan statistical area (CMSA), primary metropolitan statistical area (PMSA), and metropolitan statistical area (MSA), as described below:

- *Consolidated metropolitan statistical area (CMSA)* is the largest designation in terms of geographical area and market size and is made up of component PMSAs, defined below, that total at least 1 million people.
- *Primary metropolitan statistical area (PMSA)* is an area that is part of a larger CMSA that has a total population of 1 million or more. It must also contain counties that conform to the following standards: (1) a total population of at least 100,000, (2) a population that is at least 60 percent urban, and (3) fewer than 50 percent of the resident workers commute to jobs outside the county.
- *Metropolitan statistical area (MSA)* is (1) a city having a population of at least 50,000 or (2) an urbanized area with a population in excess of 50,000, with a total metropolitan population of at least 100,000. An MSA may include counties that have close economic and social ties to the central county.

Regional Marketing A new trend within marketing focuses not only on the shifting of consumers geographically, but also on the differences in their product preferences based on where they live. This concept has been referred to as **regional marketing,** which is developing marketing plans to reflect specific area differences in taste preferences, perceived needs, or interests. The Marketing Action Memo on p. 64 shows how some companies are beginning to deal with this changing view of a regional America.

Technology has aided marketers to begin to understand the variations of regional preferences. Computerized cash registers have allowed companies to coordinate and analyze a large amount of sales data for geographical units as small as neighborhoods. Scott Paper found that their paper towels had a 47.7 percent

MARKETING · ACTION · MEMO

"ONE NATION UNDER ALL . . .? THAT'S A BUNCH OF BEANS!"

For marketers today, such as Campbell's and Chevrolet, regional marketing is the key to successful strategy. This concept recognizes that pronounced differences may be reflected in the products people buy and how products are promoted. People in the Southwest buy more pickup trucks, whereas people in the Northeast purchase more vans.

The shift in strategy for companies is significant. Often, a marketing program is put together with the idea of the product being sold nationally. But now, several firms such as Campbell's and Con Agra (makers of Banquet, Morton, and Armour frozen foods) have divided the country into several sales regions. Strategies and plans may change for the *same* brand across regions. Campbell's, for example, found that its pork and beans did not sell well in the Southwest. The company cut out the pork, added some chili pepper, and called the result Ranchero beans. Taste preferences for spicier foods exist in the Southwest. Campbell's sales went from hardly anything to 75,000 cases in 1984. Con Agra anticipates marketing catfish as a delicacy in the East and as a traditional food in the Mississippi region.

What does this new regional strategy mean for marketers? Hopefully, more profits. Yet there are still questions to be answered. Will the consumer be confused, for example, by seeing the Chevy Cavalier sold as a family car in the Midwest and as an exciting car in California? Will it raise marketing costs as companies need to use more specialized ways to reach specific regions, or will greater marketing successes result?

Source: Rebecca Fannin, "Hit the Road, Jack," *Marketing and Media Decisions* (July 1987), pp. 118-124; Carol Hall, "In First Gear," *Marketing and Media Decisions* (July 1987), pp. 126-129; Thomas Moore, "Different Folks, Different Strokes," *Fortune* (Sept. 16, 1985), pp. 65-68.

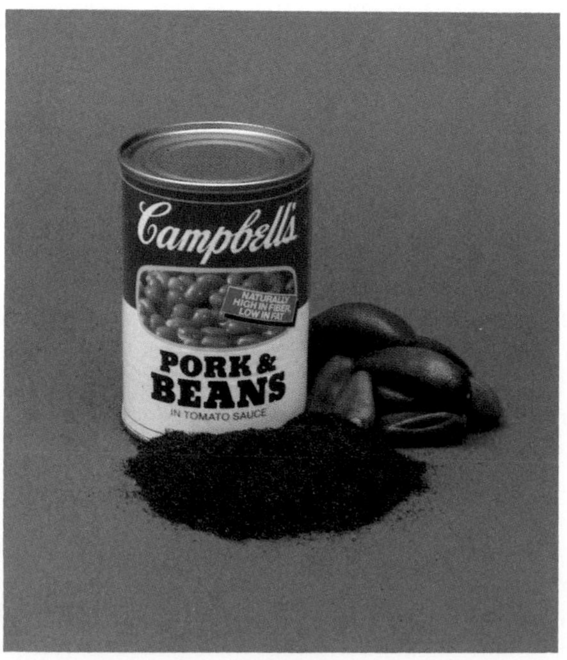

Campbell's caters to regional tastes

share in Chicago, yet only a 2.5 percent share in Los Angeles.[11] And, with more local TV stations coming into being, this focus on regional marketing allows a better targeting of ads and products. Ideally, Scott Paper can now create a specific campaign for their heavy buyers in Chicago and develop a marketing strategy to encourage new purchases in Los Angeles.

The future of regional marketing depends on the cost of these localized efforts. General Foods, in sponsoring a series of regional events such as a rodeo in Texas and a show at Radio City Music Hall to promote a new Maxwell House coffee, found the costs of specialized events to be two to three times the cost of a single national promotion.[12]

CULTURE

A second social force, **culture,** incorporates the set of values, ideas, and attitudes of a homogeneous group of people that are transmitted from one generation to the next. Culture includes both material and abstract elements, so monitoring cultural trends is difficult but important for marketing.

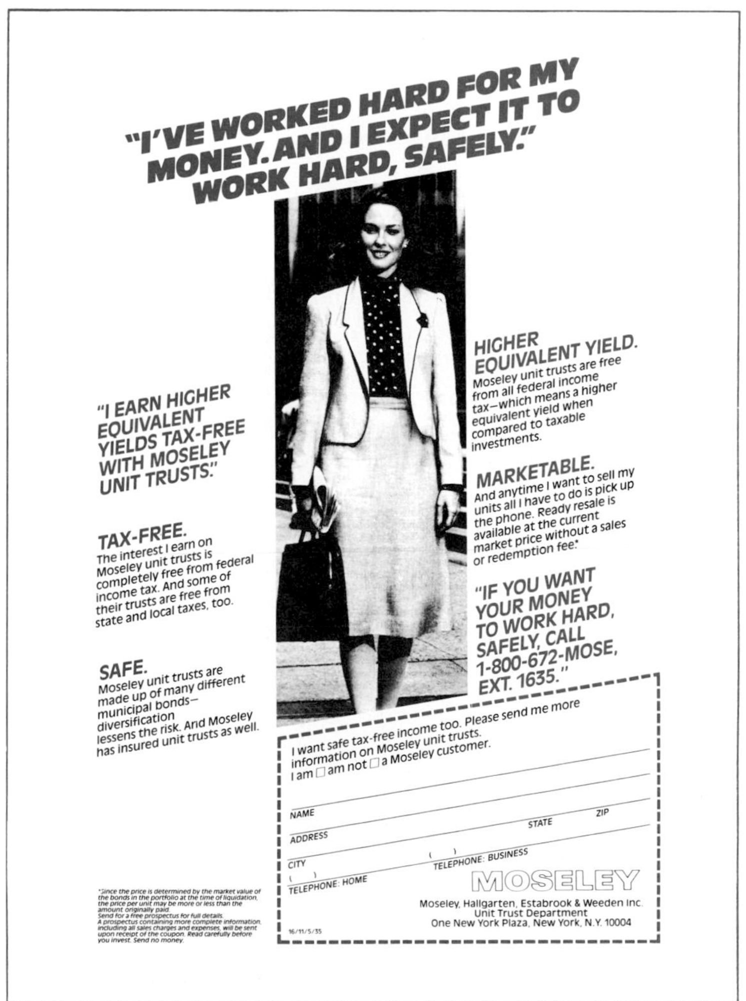

Investment ad oriented to women

MARKETING · RESEARCH · REPORT

MEN AND WOMEN SHOPPERS: ARE THEY REALLY DIFFERENT?

The changing roles of men and women are important to marketers in suggesting new product opportunities or new ways to meet consumer needs. The growing presence of males in supermarkets has been noted by every company and all those who shop. In 1986, *Progressive Grocer,* a trade publication of the grocery industry, found that 25 percent of all men report shopping alone or with a woman and that men now account for 40 percent of all food shopping dollars.

With the growing presence of men in supermarkets, a key question remains—are male shoppers different from female shoppers? Evidence gathered from several research studies suggests a surprising answer. The composite results from the 1984 USC Food Industry Management Program Study and a 1986 Campbell's/*People* magazine study on the male food shopper are given below.

	PERCENT SAYING "YES"	
QUESTION: DO YOU . . .	MEN	WOMEN
Normally buy products you don't plan to?	67%	76%
Use a shopping list?	67	75
Use coupons?	25	25
Buy national brands?	98	99
Buy store brands?	87	88
Buy generic (no-name) products?	42	46

Are men different from women? Look one more time at the comparisons, and then read the text for some interesting observations.

The Changing Role of Women Women's role in the work force has changed significantly in the past few decades. Only 17 million women were in the work force in 1947, but there were 49 million in 1982, an increase of 180 percent.[13]

One impact of this trend has been seen in the marketing of life insurance. Metropolitan Life, an insurance company, developed a series of print ads aimed at women. In 1986, Met sales to women represented 42 percent of total sales, versus 32 percent in previous years.[14] Advertisements such as that on p. 65 are being directed to women and placed in publications with female readers. The higher number of working women has led to changes in the marketing strategies of many companies. Retailers such as Elizabeth Arden Salons, for instance, have extended their hours to 8:00 PM on Thursday, and they will open early on request. Both Chrysler and Ford have set up internal committees to study the women's automobile market.[15]

The Changing Role of Men The changing role of women has affected the marketing of products to men as well. A cooperative study by Campbell's and *People* magazine found that the influence of men on food purchases compared with that of women has risen from a ratio as low as 10:90 to as much as 50:50 in households where both partners are working.[16] Responding to growing male influence, Fisher peanuts has changed its advertising strategy. It used to advertise in *Sports Illustrated* only during major sports events, but now it advertises throughout the year in this magazine.

Safeway Stores, trying to attract the male shopper, has shifted advertisements to *Newsweek* and *Sports Illustrated* and away from women's publications. As the roles of men and women change, marketers must become sensitive to the differences of the sexes in terms of how they shop.

Are the differences between men and women real or imagined? Well, the Marketing Research Report shows that differences between men and women with regard to their shopping behavior are not that great. Both sexes rate about the same in using coupons and in the brands they buy. However, women are more likely to buy products they didn't plan to buy and also to use shopping lists than are men. Over the next few years, however, as more research takes place on this environmental trend, companies may have to alter their marketing strategies to reflect possible differences.

Changing Attitudes As noted earlier, culture also includes attitudes and values. In recent years some major attitudinal changes have occurred toward work and life-styles. Recent study has shown a decrease in the value of the work ethic and the belief that hard work will pay off. There is a growing sense that the Puritan ethic of "I live to work" may be redefined as "I work to live." Work is seen as a means to an end—recreation, leisure, and entertainment—which has contributed to a growth in sales of products such as videocassette recorders, sports equipment, and easily prepared meals. So as attitudes toward work change, consumers are placing increased importance on quality of life.

There is greater concern for health and well-being as evidenced by the level

Nike products appeal to health-conscious consumers

of sports participation in the United States and increased interests in diet. Sears fitness products, Nike workout clothes, and Lean Cuisine dinners are but a few products developed in response to and profiting from this trend. P&G may have developed the biggest health-related breakthrough with *olestra,* a fat substitute that gives the flavor, but not calories, to food. Olestra could lead to fat-free ice cream, cake, and even french fries.[17]

CONCEPT CHECK

1 **Explain the term *regional marketing.***

2 **What are the marketing implications of blended families?**

3 **The work ethic of today may best be stated as "I work ____________."**

ECONOMIC FORCES

The third component of the environmental scan, the **economy,** pertains to the income, expenditures, and resources that affect the cost of running a business and household. We'll consider two aspects of these economic forces: a macroeconomic view and a microeconomic perspective of individual income.

MACROECONOMIC CONDITIONS

Of particular concern at a societal level is the state of the economy, whether it is inflationary or recessionary. For the consumer the impact of inflation is felt in escalating prices. In 1975 the cost of a Volkswagen Rabbit was $2,599. In 1987, largely because of inflation, the cost of a Golf (the model that replaced the Rabbit) was $10,645, which made it less competitive in the small-car market against the Korean-made Hyundai and Yugoslavian Yugo. A Big Mac at McDonald's was 69 cents in 1975; in 1987 it was averaging $1.60. Inflation reduces the number of items a consumer can buy and affects companies in similar ways.

To manufacture and deliver products, companies borrow money from banks. The rate of interest charged by banks to their largest customers (usually corporations) is called the *prime rate,* which rises during inflationary times and increases the cost of doing business. As the prime rate increases significantly, so does the number of business failures. Within that fact is shown the fate of some large retailers that are no longer in business, such as W.T. Grant (1906 to 1976) and Robert Hall (1940 to 1977), whose deaths were somewhat affected by the prime rate. Companies must react to rising interest rates, as auto manufacturers found when the price of car loans severely cut demand. A solution was to allow the consumer to extend the payment from 36 to 60 months so the higher interest charge would not be felt in the size of the monthly payment.

Whereas inflation is a period of rapid price increase, recession is a time of slow economic activity, so businesses decrease production, and unemployment

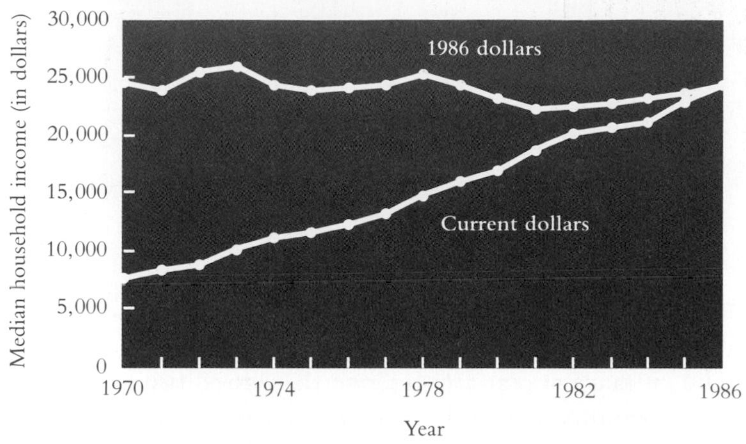

FIGURE 3-5
Trends in median family income from 1970 to 1986

rises. Consumers have less money to spend, so marketers need to focus on the function and value of their products. Department stores such as Woodward & Lothrop in Washington, D.C., and Bloomingdale's in New York find that consumers focus on value during recessions and buy more moderately priced lines than normally.

CONSUMER INCOME

The microeconomic trends in terms of consumer income are important issues for marketers. Having a product that meets the needs of consumers may be of little value if they are unable to purchase it. A consumer's ability to buy is related to income, which consists of gross, disposable, and discretionary components.

Gross Income The total amount of money made in 1 year by a person, household, or family unit is referred to as **gross income.** Figure 3-5 shows the median family income from 1970 to 1986 for households in the United States in terms of current dollars and 1986 dollars (income adjusted for inflation). The figure shows that while the typical U.S. household earned only about $8,700 of income in current dollars in 1970, it earned about $24,900 in 1986. In 1986 dollars, however, income of that typical U.S. household was relatively stable from 1970 to 1986.[18]

In conducting an environmental scan, marketers often focus their efforts on upscale households—those with incomes significantly higher than the typical household. Mazda introduced a $20,000 luxury sedan, the 929, targeted to the baby boomer segment with upscale incomes. Levi Strauss is branching into nondenim clothing. Even Merrill Lynch has put together a mutual fund of companies and products that appeal to baby boomers, called the Fund for Tomorrow. Figure 3-6 shows the age and income profile of the baby boomers who purchase four brands of products. After looking at this profile, the BMW ads on TV may make more sense. The people in the commercials look like the upscale yuppie (young, urban professionals) "boomers" targeted by the firms selling the products in Figure 3-6.

FIGURE 3-6
Who is that yuppie and what does she buy?

INDUSTRY	MEDIAN AGE	MEDIAN INCOME
BMW car	38	$73,800
Club Med vacation	37	50,000
Jacuzzi	38	40,000
Cartier Tank watch	38	40,000

Source: *Forbes* (February 25, 1985), p. 135.

Disposable Income The second income component, **disposable income,** is the money a consumer has left after paying taxes to use for food, shelter, and clothing. Thus if taxes rise at a faster rate than does disposable income, consumers must economize. In recent years consumers' allocation of income has shifted. Compared with a decade ago, consumers devote a higher proportion to energy for homes as its cost rises, and the percentage of disposable income spent on food away from home has risen to about one third of the total food budget.[19] The impact of this can be seen in marketing with the growth of family restaurant chains such as Red Lobster and Denny's.

Discretionary Income The third component of income is **discretionary income,** the money that remains after paying for taxes and necessities. Discretionary income is used for luxury items. An obvious problem in defining discretionary versus disposable income is determining what is a luxury and what is a necessity.

The Department of Labor has calculated a budget for a household of four persons. Using these budget amounts, the Census Bureau defines a household as having discretionary income if its spendable income exceeds that of an average, similarly sized family by 30 percent or more. Based on this definition, 31 percent of U.S. households (26 million families) have some discretionary income, and 57 million households have none.[20] The importance of two-income couples is

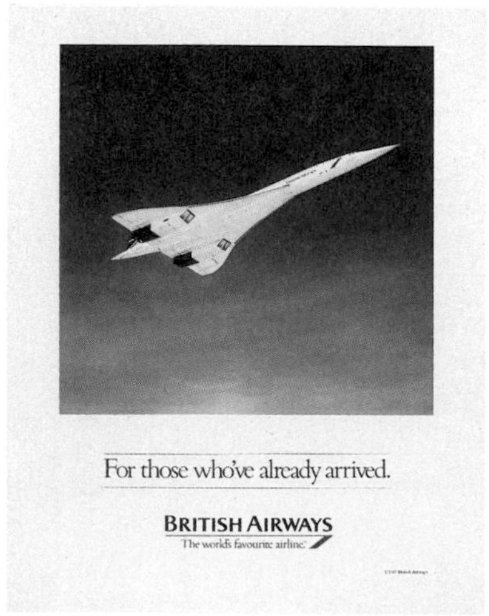

For those who've already arrived.
BRITISH AIRWAYS
The world's favourite airline

As a household's discretionary income increases, so does its pleasure travel

seen by the fact that 46 percent of these couples have discretionary income, as compared with 33 percent of couples in which one spouse works and the other stays at home. Royal Doulton china, Rolex watches, and O'Day yachts all might identify as a possible market the two-person household of professionals, 35 to 54 years old, with incomes over $50,000.[21]

TECHNOLOGICAL FORCES

Our society is in the age of technological change. **Technology,** a major environmental force, refers to inventions or innovations from applied science or engineering research. Each new wave of technological innovation can replace existing products and companies. Do you recognize the items pictured below and what they have replaced in the last 2 decades?

Technology continually makes products obsolete

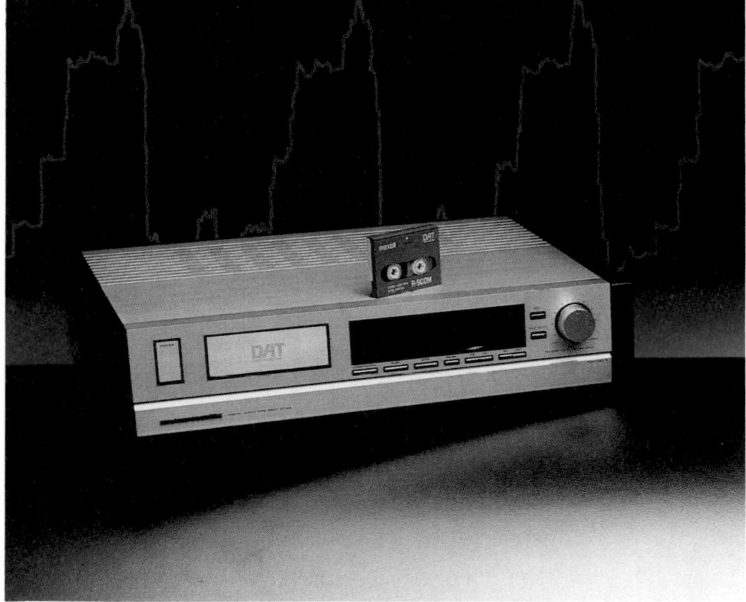

THE FUTURE OF TECHNOLOGY

Technological change is the result of research, so it is difficult to predict the timing of new developments. The Battelle Corporation, an internationally recognized research and consulting company, has made the following projections regarding technological change to the year 2000[22]:

1. Continued advancement in development and refinement of microprocessors
2. Advanced telecommunications systems and techniques
3. Greater use and refinement of robots
4. Improvement in materials technology, resulting in greater strength-to-weight ratios

These trends in technology are seen in today's marketplace. The digital audio tape player on the previous page may soon replace the compact-disc player, which has only recently entered the market. Advanced communications systems have spawned a growing industry in cellular radio telephones, and companies compete aggressively to get their phone in every car, as shown in the accompanying ad.

TECHNOLOGY'S IMPACT ON MARKETING

Advanced technology such as the continuing development of computers has a dramatic impact on marketing. Computerized checkout lanes allow supermarkets to monitor daily consumer demand for products. The future of buying and selling products will change with further developments in interactive home shopping in front of the consumer's TV screen. Chemical Bank, Merrill Lynch, Dow Jones, and American Airlines are some of the companies considering new ways to offer their services through home computer linkages.[23]

Technology spawns new products. Two promising areas are biotechnology and advanced materials. Biotechnology brings together technology with the science of the living cells. Applications in this area are leading to revolutionary new drugs that include Genentech's t-PA to dissolve blood clots, which cause

New technology in telecommunications

Toxic waste is a growing ecological concern

Newsweek—John Ficara

heart attacks; Merck's Meracor, which lowers cholesterol levels in people; and Amgen's new medicine to cure anemia. Merck, in a humanitarian gesture, is giving free to Third World countries a drug that prevents river blindness, which disfigures and blinds up to 15 percent of some villages. This good-will gift will cost Merck millions of dollars in lost profits.[24]

Similar advances are being attempted through advanced materials. Superconductors, materials that allow electricity to be transmitted with great efficiency, are being developed by IBM, Corning Glass, and GTE. In theory, these materials will shrink the size of the fastest computers to that of a shoe box and allow trains to travel 300 miles per hour on a cushion of magnetism. Optoelectronics, which merges electronics and optics, is leading to discs that will make the relatively recent CD as antiquated as 78 RPM's, records from the 1950's. Keeping pace with the potential applications of this new technology is the growing challenge for marketing managers at companies such as GE, Westinghouse, and AT&T.[25]

ECOLOGICAL IMPACT OF TECHNOLOGY

Technology has affected society in the development of products and in the ecological balance of the world's resources. **Ecology** refers to the relationship of physical resources in the environment. There is growing recognition that decisions today on use of the earth's resources have long-term consequences to society.

A growing problem in the United States is the disposal of waste. America is rapidly running out of places to dump the 1,100 pounds of packaging and other solid waste thrown away each year by the typical American. The problem is so severe that in 1987 a garbage barge crew from Long Island, N.Y., searched for several months for a place to deposit the waste. Cleanup of toxic wastes in the United States alone is estimated to cost $100 billion. The growing ecological problem of waste management has led to forecasts of a doubling of the $10 billion waste management industry by the mid-1990's.[26] Advances in technology may also revolutionize how products are packaged. In recent years, concern has grown about the proliferation of plastic waste and disposal. New technology developed by Belland's, a Swiss company, has led to a plastic that dissolves into environmentally acceptable residues.[27]

Also of concern is the discovery that chlorofluorocarbons (CFCs) are eating away at the earth's ozone layer. The ozone barrier in the stratosphere filters the rays, thereby reducing skin cancer and cataracts. If CFCs are not eliminated, there is danger that the earth's surface will warm, meaning that the Midwest could become a dust bowl and the East and Gulf coasts could be flooded in 60 years. Companies are now spending millions of dollars on research to find substitutes for CFCs, which are used for aerosol sprays (now banned in the United States) and in the manufacture of foam coffee cups and egg cartons.[28]

COMPETITIVE FORCES

The fourth component of the environmental scan, **competition,** refers to the alternative firms that could provide a product to satisfy a specific market's needs. There are various forms of competition, and each company must consider its present and potential competitors in designing its marketing strategy.

ALTERNATIVE FORMS OF COMPETITION

There are four basic forms of competition that form a continuum from pure competition to monopolistic competition to oligopoly to monopoly. Chapter 11 contains further discussions on pricing practices under these four forms of competition.

At one end of the continuum is *pure competition,* in which every company has a similar product. Companies that deal in commodities common to agribusiness (for example, wheat, rice, and grain) often are in a pure competition position in which distribution (in the sense of shipping products) is important but other elements of marketing have little impact.

In the second point on the continuum, *monopolistic competition,* the many sellers compete with their products on a substitutable basis. For example, if the price of coffee rises too much, consumers may switch to tea. Coupons or sales are frequently used marketing tactics.

Oligopoly, a common industry structure, occurs when a few companies control the majority of industry sales. For example, in the airline industry over the past few years, 5 carriers (American, Delta, United, Northwest, Texas Air) have gained control of 70 percent of all sales.[29] Because there are few sellers, price competition among firms is not desirable because it leads to reduced revenue for all producers. In 1987, these 5 airlines hiked prices to recoup the costs of the earlier airline wars.

The final point on the continuum, *monopoly,* occurs when only one firm sells the product. It has been common for producers of goods considered essential to a community: water, electricity, and telephone service. Typically, marketing plays a small role in a monopolistic setting because it is regulated by the state or federal government. Government control usually seeks to ensure price pro-

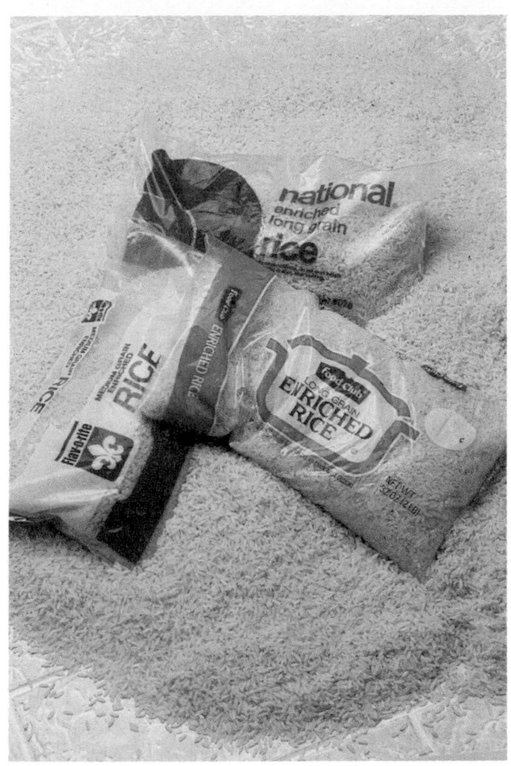

Rice: a commodity representative of pure competition

tection for the buyer. The major change in recent years has been the AT&T shift from a monopoly to a monopolistic competitor, with Sprint and MCI vying for buyers of long-distance phone service. Thus marketing is assuming a more important role for AT&T.

COMPONENTS OF COMPETITION

In developing a marketing program, companies must consider the components that drive competition: entry, bargaining, power of buyers and suppliers, existing rivalries, and substitution possibilities.[30] Scanning the environment requires a look at all of them. These relate to a firm's marketing mix decisions and may be used to develop a new entrant, create a barrier to entry, or intensify a fight for market share.

Entry In considering the competition, a firm must assess the likelihood of new entrants. Additional producers increase industry capacity and tend to lower prices. A company scanning its environment must consider the possible **barriers to entry** for other firms, which are business practices or conditions that make it difficult for new firms to enter the market. Barriers to entry can be in the form of capital requirements, advertising expenditures, product identity, distribution access, or switching costs. The higher the expense of the barrier, the more likely it will deter new entrants. For example, IBM has created a switching cost barrier for companies that may consider Apple Computer equipment because IBM has a different programming language for its machines.

Power of Buyers and Suppliers A competitive analysis must consider the power of buyers and suppliers. Powerful buyers exist when they are few in number, there are low switching costs, or the product represents a significant share of the buyer's total costs. This last factor leads the buyer to exert significant pressure for price competition. A supplier gains power when the product is critical to the buyer and when it has built up the switching costs.

Existing Competitors and Substitutes Competitive pressures among existing firms depend on the rate of industry growth. In slow-growth settings, competition is more heated for any possible gains in market share. High fixed costs also create competitive pressures for firms to fill production capacity. For example, hospitals are increasing their advertising in a battle to fill beds, which represent a high fixed cost.

INCREASING FOREIGN COMPETITION

Foreign competition has become a basic ingredient in the environmental scan for most U.S. industries today. The increasing impact of foreign competitors is clearly seen in the U.S. balance of trade—the difference between the monetary value of a nation's exports and imports. In 1971 the United States experienced its first trade deficit since 1888, and since 1984 the U.S. trade deficit has exceeded $100 billion annually. The United States is losing some of its market share to the rest of the world in industries such as automobiles[31] and shoes.[32] U.S. firms are turning increasing energies toward competing internationally as seen in Chapter 21 on international marketing.

THE NEW LOOK IN AMERICAN CORPORATIONS

Global competition has had two other important effects on corporate America, which are (1) the restructuring of giant corporations and (2) the birth and growth of many small businesses.

Restructuring Giant Corporations A process known by various names—*downsizing, streamlining,* or **restructuring**—the result is the same: striving for more efficient corporations that can compete globally by selling off unsatisfactory product lines and divisions, closing down unprofitable plants, and often laying off hundreds or thousands of employees.[33] The result is painful for those laid off. And employees still working for the company often find that their jobs are far different, sometimes with one person doing what two did before restructuring. One effect has been a huge reduction in the number of middle managers. Where a decade ago managers had only 2 or 3 people reporting to them, they now often have 8 or 10. The result: far fewer levels from the bottom to the top of corporations, far fewer managers, far different employment opportunities for those entering the work force, and far greater problems for restructured companies in gaining loyalty from their employees.[34]

Restructuring often happens fast. It often involves a *corporate takeover,* or the purchase of a firm by outsiders. For example, Reginald Lewis bought the McCall Pattern Company in 1984 and sold it on July 1, 1987, for $63 million—making $90 for each $1 of his original investment. A month after selling McCall

Pattern, Lewis' TLC Group paid $985 million for the foreign operations of Beatrice Foods, making TLC the largest black-owned business in the United States.[35]

Startup and Growth of Small Businesses One effect of restructuring on giant corporations is their increased reliance on **outsourcing**—contracting work that formerly was done in-house by employees in marketing research, advertising, public relations, data processing, and training departments to small, outside firms.[36] This has been one factor triggering the major growth in new business startups and in employment in small businesses. Many economists believe that entrepreneurs in these small businesses are the key to U.S. employment growth in the 1990's. Past statistics support this idea: from 1981 to 1985, firms having less than 20 employees added 1.8 million net new jobs to the U.S. economy, whereas firms with 500 or more employees lost a net of about 200,000 jobs.[37]

CONCEPT CHECK

1 **What is the difference between a consumer's disposable and discretionary income?**

2 **In pure competition there are ____________ number of sellers.**

3 **What does restructuring a firm mean?**

REGULATORY FORCES

For any organization, the marketing and broader business decisions are constrained, directed, and influenced by regulatory forces. **Regulation** consists of restrictions the state and federal laws place on business with regard to the conduct of its activities. Regulation exists to protect companies as well as consumers. Much of the regulation from the federal and state levels has been passed to ensure competition and fair business practices. For consumers, the focus of legislation is to protect them from unfair trade practices and to ensure their safety.

How Soho won its packaging battle: Zeltzer Seltzer *before* . . . and *after* the legal decision that their original packaging too closely resembled Soho's and was therefore an unfair trade practice

PROTECTING COMPETITION

Major federal legislation has been passed to encourage free competition, which is deemed desirable because it permits the consumer to determine which competitor will succeed and which will fail. The first such law was the *Sherman Antitrust Act* (1890). Lobbying by farmers in the Midwest against fixed railroad shipping prices led to the passage of this act, which forbids (1) contracts, combinations, or conspiracies in restraint of trade and (2) actual monopolies or attempts to monopolize any part of trade or commerce. Because of vague wording and government inactivity, however, there was only one successful case against a company in the 9 years after the act became law, and the Sherman Act was supplemented with the *Clayton Act* (1914). This Act forbids certain actions that are likely to lessen competition, although no actual harm has yet occurred.

In the 1930's the federal government had to act again to ensure fair competition. During that time, large chain stores appeared, such as the Great Atlantic & Pacific Tea Company (A&P). Small businesses were threatened, and they lobbied for the *Robinson-Patman Act* (1936). This act makes it unlawful to discriminate in prices charged to different purchasers of the same product, where the effect may substantially lessen competition or help to create a monopoly. Figure 3-7 summarizes some other laws that have been passed to protect competition, as well as for other purposes.

PRODUCT-RELATED LEGISLATION

Various federal laws in existence specifically address the product component of the marketing mix. Some are aimed at protecting the company, some at protecting the consumer, and at least one at protecting both.

Company Protection A company can protect its competitive position in new and novel products under the patent law, which gives inventors the right to exclude others from making, using, or selling products that infringe the patented invention. Polaroid, on the strength of its patents, has successfully driven Kodak out of the color instant photography market.

The federal copyright law is another way for a company to protect its competitive position in a product. The copyright law gives the author of a literary, dramatic, musical, or artistic work the exclusive right to print, perform, or otherwise copy that work. Copyright is secured automatically when the work is created. However, the published work should bear an appropriate copyright notice, including the copyright symbol, the first year of publication, and the name of the copyright owner and must be registered under the federal copyright law.

Consumer Protection There are many consumer-oriented federal laws regarding products. One of the oldest is the *Meat Inspection Act* (1906), which provides for meat products to be wholesome, unadulterated, and properly labeled. The *Food, Drug and Cosmetics Act* (1938) is one of the most important of the federal regulatory laws. This Act is aimed principally at preventing the adulteration or misbranding of the three categories of products. The various federal consumer protection laws include over 30 amendments and separate

FIGURE 3-7
Major federal laws related to marketing

LAWS TO ENCOURAGE COMPETITION

Celler-Kefauver Antimerger Act (1950) strengthened the Clayton Act to prevent corporate acquisitions that reduced competition.

Hart-Scott-Rodino Act (1976) required large companies to notify the government of their intent to merge.

PRODUCT-RELATED LAWS

National Traffic and Motor Vehicle Safety Act (1966) created compulsory safety standards for automobiles and tires.

Magnuson-Moss Warranty/FTC Improvement Act (1975) authorized rules for consumer warranties and class action suits.

PRICING-RELATED LAWS

Automobile Information Disclosure Act (1958) required manufacturers to post suggested retail prices on the cars.

Fair Credit Reporting Act (1970) required that a consumer's credit report contain only accurate, relevant, and recent information.

PROMOTION-RELATED LAWS

Truth in Lending Act (1968) makes lenders state the true cost of a loan.

Public Health Cigarette Smoking Act (1969) required cigarette ads and packages to warn of danger of cigarette smoking.

PLACE-RELATED (DISTRIBUTION) LAWS

Flammable Fabrics Act (1953) prohibited shipment in the United States of any clothing or material that could ignite easily.

laws relating to food, drugs, and cosmetics, such as the *Poison Prevention Packaging Act* (1970) and the *Infant Formula Act* (1980). Various other consumer protection laws have a broader scope, such as the *Fair Packaging and Labeling Act* (1966), the *Child Protection Act* (1966), and the *Consumer Product Safety Act* (1972), which established the Consumer Product Safety Commission to monitor product safety and establish uniform product safety standards.[38]

Both Company and Consumer Protection Trademarks are intended to protect both the firm selling a trademarked product and the consumer buying it. A Senate report states that:

> The purposes underlying any trademark statute is twofold. One is to protect the public so that it may be confident that, in purchasing a product bearing a particular trademark which it favorably knows, it will get the product which it asks for and wants to get. Secondly, where the owner of a trademark has spent energy, time and money in presenting to the public the product, he is protected in this investment from misappropriation by pirates and cheats.

This statement was made in connection with another product-related law, the *Lanham Act* (1946), which provides for registration of a company's trademarks. The first user of a trademark in commerce has the exclusive right to use that particular name or symbol in its business. Registration under the Lanham Act provides important advantages to a trademark owner that has used the trademark in interstate or foreign commerce, but it does not confer ownership. A company can lose its trademark if it becomes generic, which means that it has primarily come to be merely a common descriptive word for the product. Coca-Cola, Whopper, and Xerox are registered trademarks, and competitors cannot use these names. Aspirin and escalator are former trademarks that are now generic terms in the United States and can be used by anyone. As described in the Marketing Action Memo, an entrepreneur went to court to protect the trademark name of his Anti-Monopoly game. Branding and trademarks are covered again in Chapter 10.

REGULATORY CONTROLS ON PRICING

The pricing component of the marketing mix is the focus of regulation from two perspectives: price fixing and price discounting. Although the Sherman Act did not outlaw price fixing, the courts view this behavior as a *per se illegality* (*per se* means "through or of itself"), which means the courts see price fixing itself as illegal. This per se view has been held since an early court decision in 1897 against the railroads' price fixing agreements.[39]

Certain forms of price discounting are allowed. Quantity discounts are acceptable; that is, buyers can be charged different prices for a product provided there are differences in manufacturing or delivery costs. Promotional allowances or services may be given to buyers on an equal basis proportionate to volume purchased. And a firm can meet a competitor's price "in good faith." Legal aspects of pricing are covered in more detail in Chapter 12.

DISTRIBUTION AND THE LAW

The government has four concerns with regard to distribution—earlier referred to as "place" actions in the marketing mix—and the maintenance of competition.[40] The first, *exclusive dealing,* is an arrangement with a buyer to handle only the products of one manufacturer and not those of competitors. This practice is only illegal under the Clayton Act when it substantially lessens competition.

Requirement contracts require a buyer to purchase all or part of its needs for a product from one seller for a period of time. These contracts are not always illegal but depend on the court's interpretation of their impact on distribution.

Exclusive territorial distributorships are a third distribution issue often under regulatory scrutiny. In this situation a manufacturer grants a distributor the sole rights to sell a product in a specific geographical area. The courts have found few violations with these arrangements.

The fourth distribution strategy is a *tying arrangement,* whereby a seller requires the purchaser of one product to also buy another item in the line. These contracts may be illegal when the seller has such economic power in the tying product that the seller can restrain trade in the tied product. For example, IBM

MARKETING · ACTION · MEMO

"I'LL TRADE MARVIN GARDENS FOR BOARDWALK"

Boardwalk, Park Place, Electric Company, Go to Jail—Do Not Collect $200! Who hasn't sat for hours buying houses, putting up hotels, and trading for property? For Parker Brothers, all those hours spent with Monopoly have been rewarding, with 85 million sets sold. Since 1936 Monopoly has been a registered trademark of this company—that is, until the fight began.

In 1973 an economics professor, Ralph Anspach, created a game called Anti-Monopoly. Soon after he began to sell his version, Parker Brothers sued, complaining that Anti-Monopoly infringed on its trademark. In 1974 Anspach filed a counter suit in U.S. District Court in San Francisco. Three years later, after a decision upholding the trademark, Parker Brothers took 40,000 Anti-Monopoly games and crushed and buried them in a landfill. Yet in 1979 the Circuit Court reviewed the decision and ordered the District Court to review the case. The District Court then decided Anti-Monopoly was a name that could be used. Anspach tried to dig up the games as a symbol of victory.

After a review and appeal in 1983 it was again decided that Anti-Monopoly does not infringe on the trademark. This case produced an amendment to the Lanham Act in 1984 (public law 98-620) providing that a registered mark shall not be deemed to be the common descriptive name of goods or services solely because such mark is also used as a name of or to identify a unique product or service.

Source: Based on "Judge Rules for Monopoly Trademark," *Minneapolis Star and Tribune* (May 13, 1981); Susan Feyder, "Game Maker Loses Monopoly to Competitor . . .," *Minneapolis Star and Tribune* (February 23, 1983), pp. 5B, 10B.

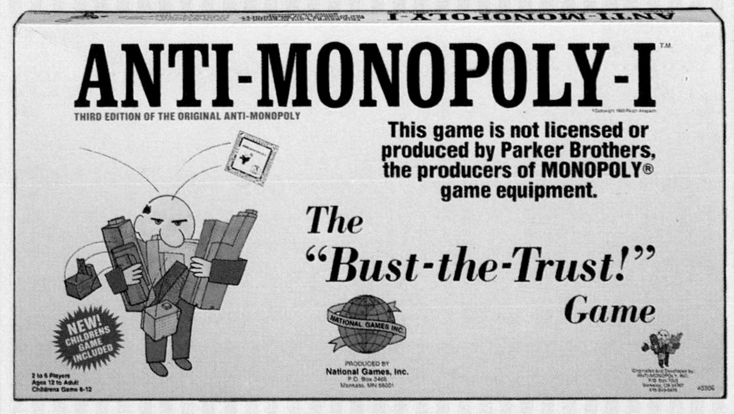

was not allowed to tie leasees of its automatic tabulating machines to the purchase of its tab cards.[41]

Legal aspects of distribution are reviewed in greater detail in Chapter 13.

PROMOTION CONTROLS

Promotion and advertising are aspects of marketing closely monitored by the FTC, which was established by the *FTC Act of 1914*. The FTC has been con-

A corrective ad—requested by the FTC

ADVERTISEMENT

FTC NOTICE

As a result of an investigation by the Federal Trade Commission into certain allegedly inaccurate past advertisements for STP's oil additive, STP Corporation has agreed to a $700,000 settlement. With regard to that settlement, STP is making the following statement:

It is the policy of STP to support its advertising with objective information and test data. In 1974 and 1975 an independent laboratory ran tests of the company's oil additive which led to claims of reduced oil consumption. However, these tests cannot be relied on to support the oil consumption reduction claim made by STP.

The FTC has taken the position that, in making that claim, the company violated the terms of a consent order. When STP learned that the test data did not support the claim, it stopped advertising containing that claim. New tests have been undertaken to determine the extent to which the oil additive affects oil consumption. Agreement to this settlement does not constitute an admission by STP that the law has been violated. Rather, STP has agreed to resolve the dispute with the FTC to avoid protracted and prohibitively expensive litigation.

February 13, 1978

cerned with deceptive or misleading advertising and unfair business practices and has the power to (1) issue cease and desist orders and (2) order corrective advertising. In issuing a *cease and desist order,* the FTC orders a company to stop practices it considers unfair. With *corrective advertising,* the FTC can require a company to spend money on advertising to correct previous misleading ads. For example, STP Corporation for years promoted an oil additive, but the FTC decided the claims were deceptive and made STP run a corrective advertisement.

CONTROL THROUGH SELF-REGULATION

The government has provided much legislation to create a competitive business climate and protect the consumer. An alternative to government control is **self-regulation,** where an industry attempts to police itself. The three major television networks have used self-regulation to set their own guidelines for TV ads for children's toys. These guidelines have generally worked well. The problem: cable TV and non-network TV have no such guidelines, and their commercials for a Barbie doll make her look almost lifelike, possibly increasing a child's desire for the doll. Critics complain that this double standard on TV commercials amounts to misleading advertising.[42] This example illustrates two problems with self-regulation: noncompliance by members and enforcement. If attempts at self-regulation are too strong, they may violate the Robinson-Patman Act. The best known self-regulatory group is the Better Business Bureau (BBB). This agency is a voluntary alliance of companies whose goal is to help maintain fair practices. Although the BBB has no legal power, it does try to use "moral suasion" to get members to comply with its ruling.

CONSUMERISM

Regulations by the government and industry are only two approaches to controlling business practices. As discussed in Chapter 1, **consumerism** is a movement to increase the influence, power, and rights of consumers in dealing with institutions. The consumer movement has grown over this century to have a powerful influence on corporate decisions.

The Consumer Bill of Rights Today's consumerism began in the 1960's. In a 1962 speech entitled "Consumer Bill of Rights," President John F. Kennedy listed four basic consumer rights: the right (1) to safety, (2) to be informed, (3) to choose, and (4) to be heard. Although not laws, these concerns have been strong guidelines for subsequent consumerism efforts. Also in the 1960's consumerism received a boost from an activist lawyer, Ralph Nader. First involved in questioning automobile safety, Nader continues his proconsumer lobbying today.

CONCEPT CHECK

1 **The ____________ Act was punitive toward monopolies, whereas the ____________ Act was preventive.**

2 **Explain the Lanham Act.**

3 **What is a per se illegality?**

SUMMARY

1 The population of the United States is aging, and the number of typical families as seen in the 1950's is diminishing. A blended family structure is becoming more common. Baby boomers are an important target market for companies because of their proportion in the population, as well as their high average disposable income. Mature households, those headed by people over age 50, are the fastest growing segment in America.
2 Recognition of geographical differences in product preferences has given rise to companies developing regional marketing plans.
3 Culture represents abstract values and material possessions. Values are changing toward work, quality of life, and the role of women and men.

4 Disposable income is the number of dollars left after taxes. Discretionary income is the money consumers have after purchasing their necessities. The median gross income (dollars before taxes) of the U.S. households has been stable since 1970 in real income terms.
5 There are various forms of competition ranging from pure competition to monopoly. The form of competition depends on the number of sellers and the substitutability of products. In analyzing competition, firms must consider the likelihood of new entrants, substitutes, the power of suppliers and buyers, and existing competitors.
6 The United States is experiencing a deficit balance of trade. Foreign competition is affecting a wide range of U.S. industries.
7 Global competition has had two major effects on U.S. corporations: (1) restructuring them to improve efficiency, and (2) stimulating the startup and growth of small businesses.
8 The Sherman Antitrust Act of 1890 made monopolies illegal, whereas the Clayton Act tried to outlaw actions believed to lead to monopolies.
9 A company's brand name or symbol can be protected under the Lanham Act, but if the name becomes generic, the company no longer has sole right to the trademark.
10 Price fixing has been viewed as illegal by the courts. However, price discounting is allowed to meet competition or to account for differences in the cost of manufacture or distribution.
11 There are four aspects of distribution reviewed by courts: exclusive dealing arrangements, requirements contracts, exclusive territorial distributorships, and tying arrangements.
12 The Federal Trade Commission, established in 1914, monitors unfair business practices and deceptive advertising. Two methods used in enforcement are (a) cease and desist orders and (b) corrective advertising.
13 Self-regulation attempts are common to some industries and organizations such as the Better Business Bureau.
14 Consumerism is the movement to increase the influence and power of consumers in dealing with institutions.

KEY TERMS AND CONCEPTS

environmental scanning p. 58
social forces p. 60
demographics p. 60
mature household p. 62
baby boomers p. 62
blended family p. 63
regional marketing p. 63
culture p. 65
economy p. 68
gross income p. 69
disposable income p. 70
discretionary income p. 70
technology p. 71
ecology p. 73
competition p. 74
barriers to entry p. 75
restructuring p. 76
outsourcing p. 77
regulation p. 77
self-regulation p. 82
consumerism p. 83

CHAPTER PROBLEMS AND APPLICATIONS

1 In recent years the Walt Disney Corporation expanded its amusement park by adding the World Showcase to the EPCOT Center, representing the sights, sounds, food, and culture of different countries. Based on the environmental trends discussed in this chapter, what factors do you think led to this addition?

2 Describe the target market for a luxury item such as the Mercedes Benz 190, the lowest-priced Mercedes. List four magazines in which you would advertise to appeal to this target market.

3 Regional marketing is becoming a strategy used by several companies. What difficulties might Con Agra have with their marketing of catfish as described in the Marketing Action Memo with business people in the United States who travel to different regions of America?

4 Battelle Corporation forecast the continued development of microprocessors. Some experts believe new advancements in this area would allow automobiles to be equipped with radar to detect oncoming crashes and then self-correct the steering to avoid impact. What industries would be affected by such technological change?

5 In recent years in the brewing industry, a couple of large firms that have historically had most of the beer sales (Anheuser-Busch and Miller) have faced competition from many small regional brands. In terms of the continuum of competition, how would you explain this change?

6 As the airline industry has become deregulated, how has the role of marketing changed? What elements of the marketing mix are more or less important since deregulation in 1978?

7 The Johnson Company manufactures buttons and pins with slogans and designs. These pins are inexpensive to produce and are sold in retail outlets such as discount stores, hobby shops, and bookstores. Little equipment is needed for a new competitor to enter the market. What strategies should they consider to create effective barriers to entry?

8 For many years Lennox Industries has defined its business as the "manufacturing of heating and air conditioning products." Based on the environmental scanning and analysis, how would you redefine Lennox's position? What would you add to the product line?

9 In 1978 the FTC required STP to run the corrective advertisement shown on p. 82. The ad was placed in *Business Week, The Wall Street Journal,* and *Forbes.* What is the profile of the buyer of STP? Where would you have ordered STP to place the ad? Why?

10 Why is Xerox concerned about having its name become generic?

SUGGESTED READINGS

"Can America Compete?" *Business Week* (April 20, 1987), pp. 45-66. *A special report that discusses several factors that are affecting the competitiveness of U.S. firms.*

Basia Hellwig, "How Working Women Have Changed America," *Working Woman* (November 1986), pp. 129-146. *A series of articles that reviews several changes brought about in the United States by the increasing numbers of women working full-time.*

Peter Petre, "Marketers Mine for Gold in the Old," *Fortune* (March 31, 1986), pp. 70-78. *This article discusses the past mistakes of companies as well as present strategies to market to mature households.*

Michael Porter, *Competitive Advantage* (New York: Freedom Press, 1985). *This book outlines strategies for dealing with different levels of competition.*

Mary Lou Roberts and Larry Wortzel, *Marketing to the Changing Household* (Cambridge, Mass.: Ballinger Publishing Co., 1984). *This book is a collection of articles that examines the impact of several sociodemographic changes in the United States on marketing.*

PART TWO

UNDERSTANDING BUYERS AND MARKETS

7 ELEVEN
7 ELEVEN
7-UP $1.97
Lottery Hotline
(213) (818) 976-4711
35¢ Local Phone Charge
Now...
Even Good
Prices
Come Easy!
7 ELEVEN

4

CONSUMER BEHAVIOR

After reading this chapter you should be able to:

Outline the stages in the consumer decision process.

•

Distinguish between three variations of the consumer decision process: routine, limited, and extended problem solving.

•

Explain how psychological influences affect consumer behavior and particularly purchase decision processes.

•

Identify major sociocultural influences on consumer behavior and their effects on purchase decisions.

•

Recognize how marketers can use knowledge of consumer behavior to better understand and influence individual and family purchases.

Know Thy Customer

Successful marketing begins with understanding why and how consumers behave as they do. Consider these examples of how consumer behavior is shaping marketing programs[1]:

- General Motors' Chevrolet Division launches an extensive dealer training program to woo women because they buy more than $40 billion worth of cars each year.
- Campbell's Soup, Metropolitan Life Insurance, and Procter & Gamble tailor their products, advertising, and sales efforts to fit the unique needs of various regional, ethnic, and racial subcultures in the United States.
- Southland's 7-Eleven stores, recognizing growing consumer interest in value and convenience, reduces its prices on many products, installs automatic teller machines, and advertises the theme "Now even good prices come easy" in some markets.

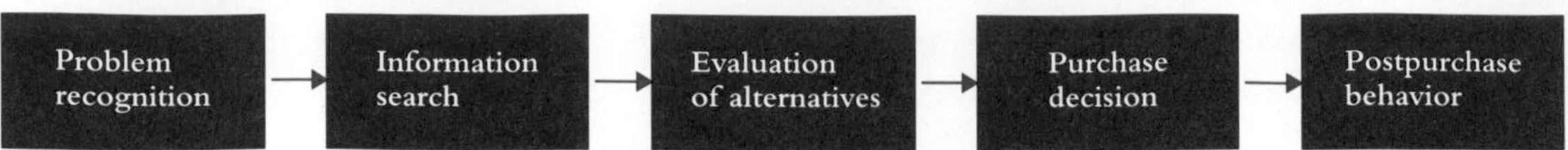

FIGURE 4-1
Purchase decision process

This chapter examines **consumer behavior**, the actions a person takes in purchasing and using products and services, including the mental and social processes that precede and follow these actions. This chapter shows how the behavioral sciences help answer questions such as why people choose one product or brand over another, how they make these choices, and how companies use this knowledge to market more effectively to consumers.

CONSUMER PURCHASE DECISION PROCESS

Behind the visible act of making a purchase lies an important decision process that must be investigated. The stages a buyer passes through in making choices about which products and services to buy is the **purchase decision process.** This process has the five stages shown in Figure 4-1: (1) problem recognition, (2) information search, (3) alternative evaluation, (4) purchase decision, and (5) postpurchase behavior.

PROBLEM RECOGNITION

Problem recognition, the initial step in the purchase decision, is perceiving a difference between a person's ideal and actual situations big enough to trigger a decision.[2] This can be as simple as finding an empty milk carton in the refrigerator or noting, as a college freshman, that your high school clothes are not in the style that others are wearing. Or a student's stereo system may not work properly.

In marketing, advertisements or salespeople can activate a consumer's decision process by showing the shortcomings of competing (or currently owned) products. For instance, an advertisement for a compact disc (CD) player could stimulate problem recognition because it emphasizes the sound quality of CD players over that of the conventional stereo system you may now own.[3]

INFORMATION SEARCH

After recognizing a problem, a consumer begins to search for information, the next stage in the purchase decision process. First, you may scan your memory for previous experiences with products or brands.[4] This action is called *internal search*. For frequently purchased products such as shampoo, this may be enough. Or a consumer may undertake an *external search* for information.[5] This is especially needed when past experience or knowledge is insufficient, the risk of making a wrong purchase decision is high, and the cost of gathering information is low.[6] The primary sources of external information are: (1) *personal sources,* such as relatives and friends whom the consumer trusts; (2) *public sources,* including various product-rating organizations such as *Consumer Reports,* government agencies, and TV "consumer programs"; and (3) *marketer-dominated sources,* such as information from sellers that include advertising, salespeople, and point-of-purchase displays in stores.

Suppose you consider buying an expensive or complex product such as a CD player. You will probably tap several of these information sources: friends and relatives, CD-player advertisements, and several stores carrying CD players for demonstrations. You might study the comparative evaluation of regular table model CD players that appeared in *Consumer Reports,* published by a product-testing organization, a portion of which appears in Figure 4-2.

ALTERNATIVE EVALUATION

The information search stage clarifies the problem for the consumer by suggesting criteria to use for the purchase and yielding brand names that might

FIGURE 4-2
Consumer Reports' evaluation of regular table model compact-disc players (abridged)

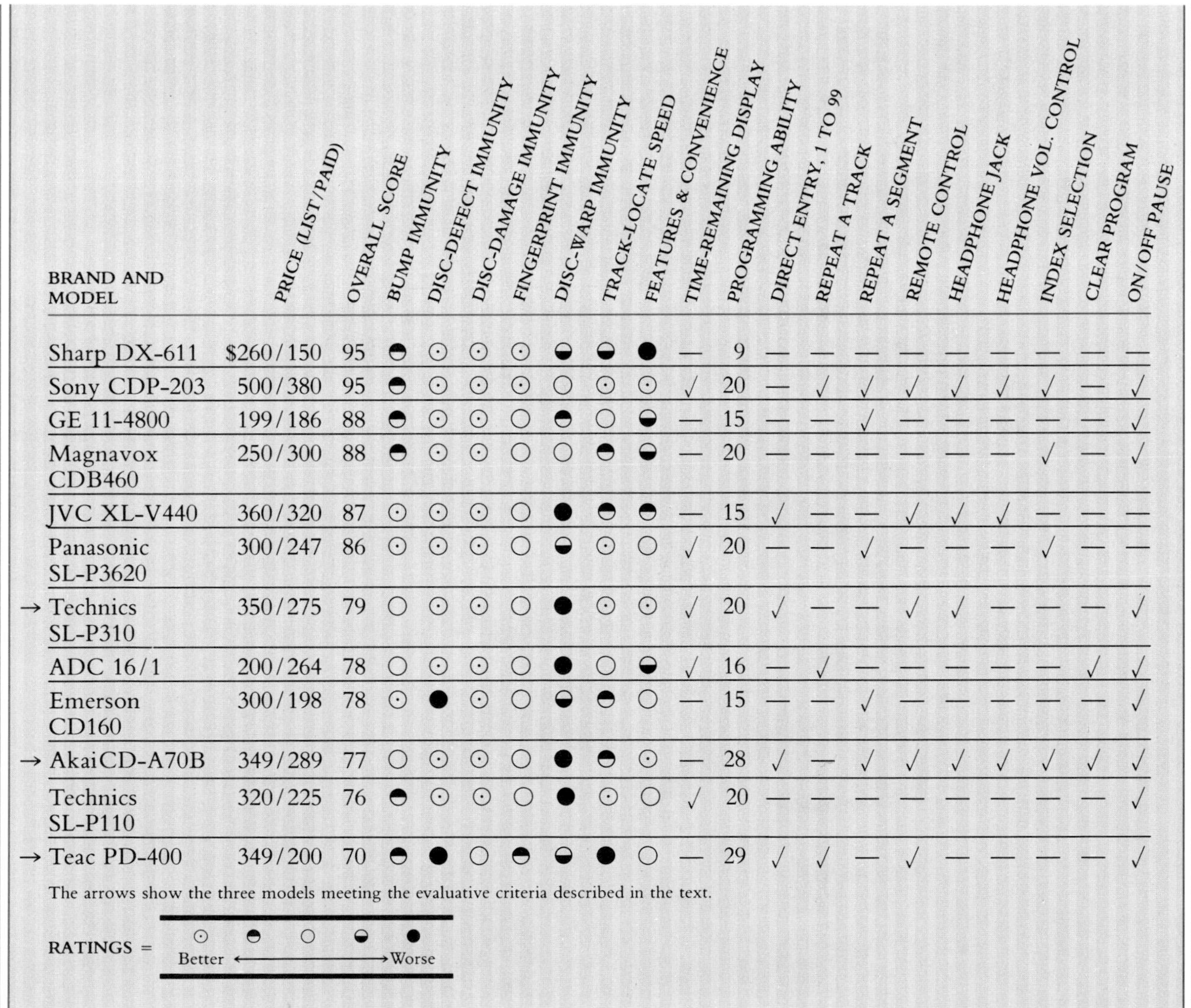

BRAND AND MODEL	PRICE (LIST/PAID)	OVERALL SCORE	BUMP IMMUNITY	DISC-DEFECT IMMUNITY	DISC-DAMAGE IMMUNITY	FINGERPRINT IMMUNITY	DISC-WARP IMMUNITY	TRACK-LOCATE SPEED	FEATURES & CONVENIENCE	TIME-REMAINING DISPLAY	PROGRAMMING ABILITY	DIRECT ENTRY, 1 TO 99	REPEAT A TRACK	REPEAT A SEGMENT	REMOTE CONTROL	HEADPHONE JACK	HEADPHONE VOL. CONTROL	INDEX SELECTION	CLEAR PROGRAM	ON/OFF PAUSE
Sharp DX-611	$260/150	95	◓	⊙	⊙	⊙	◒	◒	●	—	9	—	—	—	—	—	—	—	—	—
Sony CDP-203	500/380	95	◓	⊙	⊙	⊙	○	⊙	⊙	√	20	—	√	√	√	√	√	√	—	√
GE 11-4800	199/186	88	◓	⊙	⊙	○	◓	○	◒	—	15	—	—	√	—	—	—	—	—	√
Magnavox CDB460	250/300	88	◓	⊙	⊙	○	○	◓	◒	—	20	—	—	—	—	—	—	√	—	√
JVC XL-V440	360/320	87	⊙	⊙	⊙	○	●	◓	◓	—	15	√	—	—	√	√	√	—	—	—
Panasonic SL-P3620	300/247	86	⊙	⊙	⊙	○	◒	⊙	○	√	20	—	—	√	—	—	—	√	—	—
→ Technics SL-P310	350/275	79	○	⊙	⊙	○	●	⊙	⊙	√	20	√	—	—	√	√	—	—	—	√
ADC 16/1	200/264	78	○	⊙	⊙	○	●	○	◒	√	16	—	√	—	—	—	—	—	√	√
Emerson CD160	300/198	78	⊙	●	⊙	○	◒	◓	○	—	15	—	—	√	—	—	—	—	—	√
→ AkaiCD-A70B	349/289	77	○	⊙	⊙	○	●	◓	⊙	—	28	√	—	√	√	√	√	√	√	√
Technics SL-P110	320/225	76	◓	⊙	⊙	○	●	⊙	○	√	20	—	—	—	—	—	—	—	—	√
→ Teac PD-400	349/200	70	◓	●	○	◓	◒	●	○	—	29	√	√	—	√	—	—	—	—	√

The arrows show the three models meeting the evaluative criteria described in the text.

RATINGS = ⊙ ◓ ○ ◒ ●
Better ⟵ ⟶ Worse

Source: *Consumer Reports,* "Compact-disc Players" (May 1987), pp. 284-285.

meet the criteria. Based only on the information shown in Figure 4-2, what selection criteria would you use in buying a CD player?

For some of you, the information provided may be inadequate because it does not contain all the factors you might consider when evaluating CD players. These factors are a consumer's **evaluative criteria,** which represent both the objective attributes of a brand (such as programming capability) and the subjective ones (such as prestige) you may consider important.[7] Firms try to identify and capitalize on both types of criteria. So Sony emphasizes not only the performance characteristics of its products but also the prestige of owning one in its advertising message, "Sony, the one and only."

Consumers often have several criteria for evaluating brands. Didn't you in the exercise just finished? Knowing this, companies seek to identify the most important evaluative criteria consumers use when judging brands. For example, among the evaluative criteria shown in the columns of Figure 4-2, suppose that you use two in considering brands of a CD player to buy: (1) a price under $300 (the second price in column 2 of Figure 4-2) and (2) remote control (column 16 in Figure 4-2). These criteria establish the brands in your **evoked set,** the group of brands that a consumer would consider buying from among all the brands in the product class of which he or she is aware.[8] Your two evaluative criteria result in only three models in your evoked set, the ones shown by arrows in Figure 4-2. If these brands don't satisfy you, you can change your evaluative criteria to reach a different evoked set of models.

PURCHASE DECISION

Having examined the alternatives in the evoked set, the consumer makes a purchase decision. Not only is it not often observable by marketers—who aren't in the kitchen when a consumer makes the grocery list—but it is often impulsive, not following directly from alternative evaluation. The Marketing Research Report shows how often impulsive purchase decisions occur and their outcomes.

Consumers often read ads for products they have already bought to confirm that their decision was correct

Ad furnished compliments of Pioneer Electronics, Saatchi and Saatchi/DFS—Richard Noble, photographer

MARKETING·RESEARCH·REPORT

WHEN THE WHISPER BECOMES A SHOUT: BUY, BUY, BUY

Probably everyone has experienced a buying impulse—a sudden and powerful urge to buy something now, *now!* Only recently have researchers begun to uncover reasons for such behavior and its consequences. Dennis W. Rook at DDB Needham Worldwide, one of the world's largest advertising agencies, interviewed 133 men and women to study this phenomenon.

His findings suggest that feelings and emotions are decisive in buying impulses. One-third of those interviewed reported a spontaneous urge to buy that was triggered by seeing an item or an advertisement. Three in ten people felt a compulsion to buy, with an almost animal-like hunger or desire for the item. One in five described their buying impulse as a source of excitement or stimulation. According to one person, "It gives you goosebumps." Other descriptions of a buying impulse were fanciful or magical in tone: "The pants were shrieking 'buy me' . . ."

Impulsive buying can have dire consequences. Over 80 percent of people with a buying impulse said it led to some problems. These problems included financial difficulties, disappointment with the purchased item, guilt feelings, and friend and family disapproval.

No one knows how widespread impulsive buying is, but it does happen. It is clear that this behavior does not fit the standard purchase decision process, and it can create postpurchase anxiety.

Source: Dennis W. Rook, "The Buying Impulse," *Journal of Consumer Research* (September 1987), pp. 189–199.

POSTPURCHASE BEHAVIOR

After buying a product, the consumer compares it with his or her expectations and is either satisfied or dissatisfied. If the consumer is dissatisfied, marketers must decide whether the product was deficient or consumer expectations too high. Product deficiency may require a design change. If expectations are too high, perhaps the company's advertising or salesperson oversold the product's features.

Often a consumer is faced with two or more highly attractive alternatives, such as a Sony or a Pioneer CD player. If you choose the Sony, you may think, "Should I have purchased the Pioneer?" This feeling of postpurchase psychological tension or anxiety is called **cognitive dissonance.**[9] To alleviate it, consumers often attempt to applaud themselves for making the right choice. So after your purchase, you may seek information to confirm your choice by asking friends questions like, "Don't you like my CD player?" or by reading ads of the brand you chose. You might even look for negative information about the brand you didn't buy and decide that the track-locate speed of the Pioneer, which was rated "good" in Figure 4-2, was actually a serious deficiency.

Firms often use ads or follow-up calls by salespeople in this postpurchase stage to try to convince buyers they made the right decision. Dial soap, for example, conveys the message, "Aren't you glad you use Dial?"

INVOLVEMENT AND PROBLEM-SOLVING VARIATIONS

Sometimes consumers don't engage in the five-step purchase decision process just described. Instead, they skip one or more steps depending on the level of **involvement,** the personal and economic significance of the purchase to the consumer.[10] High-involvement products and purchases typically have at least one of three characteristics.[11] The item to be purchased (1) is expensive, (2) can have serious social consequences, or (3) could reflect on one's social image. Low-involvement products such as toothpaste and soap barely involve most of us at all, whereas college students typically say that stereo systems and automobiles are high-involvement products.[12] Researchers have identified three general variations in the consumer purchase process based on consumer involvement and product knowledge.[13]

Routine Problem Solving For products such as toothpaste and milk, consumers recognize a problem, make a decision, and spend little effort seeking external information and evaluating alternatives. The purchase decision is virtually a habit. Routine problem solving is typically the case for low-priced, frequently purchased products.

Limited Problem Solving In limited problem solving, consumers typically seek some information or rely on a friend to help them evaluate alternatives. In general, several brands might be evaluated using a moderate number of different attributes. You might use limited problem solving in choosing a toaster, a restaurant for dinner, and other purchase situations in which you have little time or effort to spend.

Extended Problem Solving In extended problem solving, each of the five stages of the consumer purchase decision process is used in the purchase, including considerable time and effort on external information search and in identifying and evaluating alternatives. Several brands usually are in the evoked set, and these are evaluated on many attributes. Extended problem solving exists in high-involvement purchase situations for items such as CD players, VCRs, and investments in stocks and bonds. Firms marketing these products put significant effort into informing and educating these consumers.

SITUATIONAL INFLUENCES

Often the purchase situation will affect the purchase decision process. Five **situational influences** have an impact on your purchase decision process: (1) the purchase task, (2) social surroundings, (3) physical surroundings, (4) temporal effects, and (5) antecedent states.[14] The purchase task is the reason for engaging in the decision in the first place. Information searching and evaluating alternatives may differ depending on whether the purchase is a gift, which often involves the social visibility, or for the buyer's own use. Social surroundings, including the other people present when a purchase decision is made, may also affect what is purchased. Physical surroundings such as decor and music in retail stores may alter how purchase decisions are made.[15] Temporal effects such as

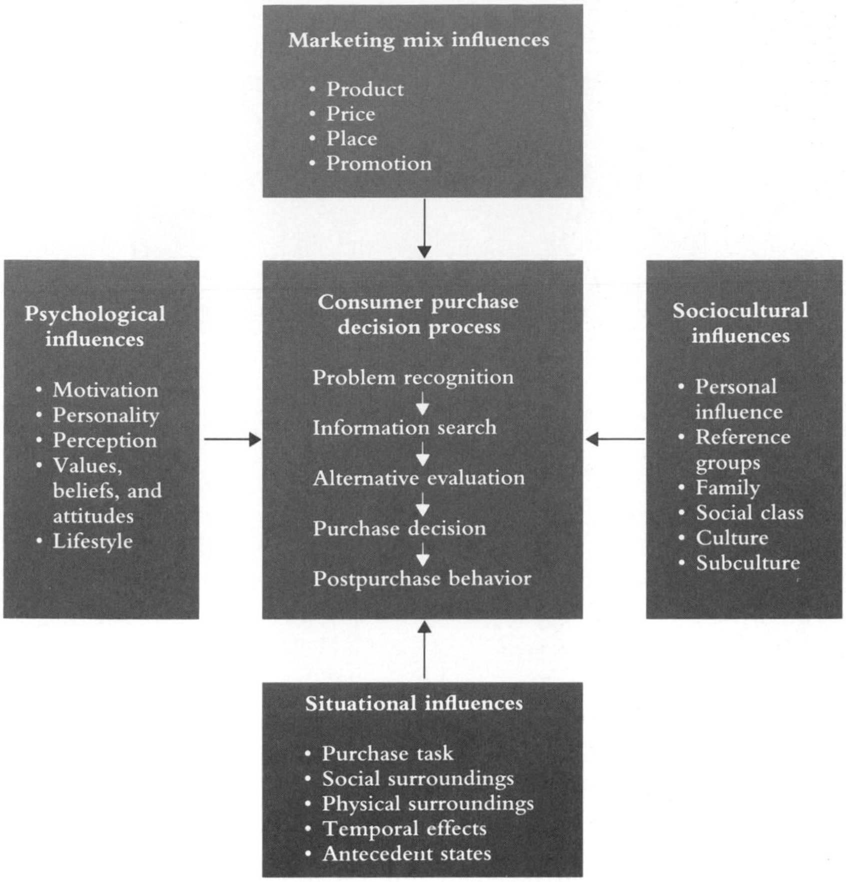

Marketing mix influences
- Product
- Price
- Place
- Promotion

Psychological influences
- Motivation
- Personality
- Perception
- Values, beliefs, and attitudes
- Lifestyle

Consumer purchase decision process

Problem recognition → Information search → Alternative evaluation → Purchase decision → Postpurchase behavior

Sociocultural influences
- Personal influence
- Reference groups
- Family
- Social class
- Culture
- Subculture

Situational influences
- Purchase task
- Social surroundings
- Physical surroundings
- Temporal effects
- Antecedent states

FIGURE 4-3
Influences on the consumer purchase decision process

time of day or the amount of time available will influence where consumers have breakfast and lunch and what is ordered. Finally, antecedent states, which include the consumer's mood or the amount of cash on hand, can influence purchase behavior and choice.

Figure 4-3 shows the many influences that affect the consumer purchase decision process. The decision to buy a product also involves important psychological and sociocultural influences, the two important topics discussed during the remainder of this chapter. Marketing mix influences are described in Chapters 9 through 20.

CONCEPT CHECK

1 **What is the first step in the consumer purchase decision process?**

2 **The brands a consumer considers buying out of the set of brands in a product class of which the consumer is aware is called the __________.**

3 **What is the term for postpurchase anxiety?**

FIGURE 4-4
Hierarchy of needs

PSYCHOLOGICAL INFLUENCES ON CONSUMER BEHAVIOR

Psychology helps marketers understand why and how consumers behave as they do. In particular, concepts such as motivation and personality; perception; learning; values, beliefs, and attitudes; and life-style are useful for interpreting buying processes and directing marketing effort.

MOTIVATION AND PERSONALITY

Motivation and personality are two familiar psychological concepts that have specific meanings and marketing implications.[16] They are both used frequently to describe why people do some things and not others.

Motivation **Motivation** is the energizing force that causes behavior that satisfies a need. Because consumer needs are the focus of the marketing concept, marketers try to arouse these needs.

An individual's needs are boundless. People possess physiological needs for basics such as water, sex, and food. They also have learned needs, including esteem, achievement, and affection. Psychologists point out that these needs are hierarchical; that is, once physiological needs are met, people seek to satisfy their learned needs. Figure 4-4 shows one need hierarchy and classification scheme that contains five need classes.[17] *Physiological needs* are basic to survival and must be satisfied first. A Burger King advertisement featuring a juicy hamburger attempts to activate the need for food. *Safety needs* involve self-preservation and physical well-being. Smoke detector and burglar alarm manufacturers focus on these needs. *Social needs* are concerned with love and friendship. Life insurance, dating services, and fragrance companies try to arouse these needs. *Personal needs* are represented by the need for achievement, status, prestige, and self-respect. The American Express Gold Card and Brooks Brothers Clothiers appeal to these needs. Sometimes firms try to arouse multiple needs to stimulate problem recognition. Michelin combined security with parental love to promote tire replacement as shown in the advertisement. *Self-actualization* needs involve personal fulfillment.

Personality **Personality** refers to a person's consistent behaviors or responses

Michelin appeals to security and parental love needs in its advertising

to recurring situations. Although numerous personality theories exist, most identify key traits—enduring characteristics within a person or in his or her relationship with others. Such traits include extroversion, compliance, dominance, and aggression, among others. For example, cigarette smokers have been identified as having traits such as aggression and dominance, but not compliance.[18]

Research suggests that compliant people prefer known brand names and use more mouthwash and toilet soaps. In contrast, aggressive types use razors, not electric shavers, and use more cologne and after-shave lotions.[19]

Mutual of America reminds people of their social needs with its ads

PERCEPTION

One person sees a Cadillac as a mark of achievement; another sees it as ostentatious. This is the result of **perception**—the process by which an individual selects, organizes, and interprets information to create a meaningful picture of the world.

Selective Perception Because the average consumer operates in a complex environment, the human brain attempts to organize and interpret information with a process called *selective perception,* a filtering of exposure, comprehension, and retention. *Selective exposure* occurs when people pay attention to messages that are consistent with their attitudes and beliefs and ignore messages that are inconsistent. Selective exposure often occurs in the postpurchase stage of the consumer decision process when consumers read advertisements for the brand they just bought. It also occurs when a need exists. You are more likely to "see" a McDonald's advertisement or the Golden Arches by the road when you are hungry rather than after you have eaten a pizza.

Selective comprehension involves interpreting information so that it is consistent with your attitudes and beliefs. A marketer's failure to understand this can have disastrous results. For example, Toro introduced a small, lightweight snow blower called the Snow Pup. Even though the product worked, sales failed to meet expectations. Why? Toro later found out that consumers perceived the name to mean that Snow Pup was a toy or too light to do any serious snow removal.[20] When the background color on Barrelhead Sugar-Free Root Beer containers changed to beige from blue, people said it tasted more like old-fashioned root beer even though the beverage was unchanged.[21]

Selective retention means that consumers do not remember all the information they see, read, or hear, even minutes after exposure to it. This affects the internal and external information search stage of the purchase decision process. This is why furniture and automobile retailers often give consumers product brochures to take home after they leave the showroom.

Perceived Risk Perception plays a major role in the perceived risk in purchasing a product or service. **Perceived risk** represents the anxieties felt because the consumer cannot anticipate the outcomes of a purchase but believes that there may be negative consequences. Examples of possible negative consequences are the size of the financial outlay required to buy the product (Can I afford $200 for those skis?), the risk of physical harm (Is the microwave oven safe?), and the performance of the product (Will the hair coloring work?). A more abstract form is psychosocial (What will my friends say if I wear that sweater?). Perceived risk affects information search because the greater the perceived risk, the more extensive the external search phase is likely to be.

Recognizing the importance of perceived risk, companies develop strategies to reduce the consumer's risk and encourage purchases. These strategies and examples of firms using them include[22]:

- Obtaining seals of approval: the Good Housekeeping seal or Underwriter's Laboratory seal
- Securing endorsements from influential people: Elizabeth Taylor's *Passion* line of perfume

Companies use a variety of strategies to reduce consumer-perceived risk

- Providing free trial of the product: sample packages of Duncan Hines Peanut Butter Cookies mailed by P&G
- Giving extensive usage instructions: Clairol haircoloring
- Providing warranties and guarantees: Chrysler's 70,000-mile, 7-year warranty for its cars

LEARNING

Much consumer behavior is learned. Consumers learn which information sources to use for information about products and services, which evaluative criteria to use when assessing alternatives, and, more generally, how to make purchase decisions. **Learning** refers to those behaviors that result from (1) repeated experience and (2) thinking.[23]

Behavioral Learning *Behavioral learning* is the process of developing automatic responses to a situation built up through repeated exposure to it. Four variables are central to how consumers learn from repeated experience: drive, cue, response, and reinforcement. A *drive* is a need that moves an individual to action. Drives, such as hunger, might be represented by motives. A *cue* is a stimulus or symbol perceived by consumers. A *response* is the action taken by a consumer to satisfy the drive, and a *reinforcement* is the reward. Being hungry (drive), a consumer sees a cue (a billboard), takes action (buys a hamburger), and receives a reward (it tastes great!).

Marketers use two concepts from behavioral learning theory. *Stimulus generalization* occurs when a response elicited by one stimulus (cue) is generalized to another stimulus. Using the same brand name for different products is an application of this concept. *Stimulus discrimination* refers to a person's ability to perceive differences in stimuli. Consumers' tendency to perceive all light beers

FIGURE 4-5
Brand loyalty of common consumer products

High-loyalty products	Medium-loyalty products	Low-loyalty products
• Cigarettes • Laxatives • Cold remedies • 35mm film • Toothpaste	• Cola drinks • Margarine • Shampoo • Hand lotion • Furniture polish	• Paper towels • Crackers • Scouring powder • Plastic trash bags • Facial tissues

as being alike led to *Budweiser Light* commercials that distinguished between many types of "lights" and *Bud Light.*

Cognitive Learning Consumers also learn through thinking, reasoning, and mental problem solving without direct experience. This type of learning, called *cognitive learning,* involves making connections between two or more ideas or simply observing the outcomes of others' behaviors and adjusting your own accordingly. Firms also influence this type of learning. Through repetition in advertising, messages such as "Medipren is a headache remedy" attempt to link a brand (Medipren) and an idea (headache remedy) by showing someone using the brand and finding relief.

Brand Loyalty Learning is also important because it relates to habit formation—the basis of routine problem solving. Furthermore, there is a close link between habits and **brand loyalty,** which is a favorable attitude toward and consistent purchase of a single brand over time. Brand loyalty results from the positive reinforcement of previous actions. So a consumer reduces risk and saves time by consistently purchasing the same brand of shampoo and has favorable results—healthy, shining hair. There is evidence of brand loyalty in many commonly purchased products (Figure 4-5). Note the strong brand loyalty for toothpaste and cold remedies compared with that for crackers and facial tissues.

VALUES, BELIEFS, AND ATTITUDES

Values, beliefs, and attitudes play a central role in consumer decision making and related marketing actions.

Attitude Formation An **attitude** is a "learned predisposition to respond to an object or class of objects in a consistently favorable or unfavorable way."[24] Attitudes are shaped by our values and beliefs, which are learned. Values vary by level of specificity. We speak of American core values, including material well-being and humanitarianism. We also have personal values such as thriftiness and ambition. Marketers are concerned with both, but focus mostly on personal values. **Values** represent personally or socially preferable modes of conduct or states of existence that are enduring.[25] Personal values affect attitudes by influencing the importance assigned to specific product attributes. Suppose thriftiness is one of your personal values. When you evaluate cars, fuel economy (a product attribute) becomes important. If you believe a specific car has this attribute, you are likely to have a favorable attitude toward it.

Many firms added calcium to their products to create a more favorable attitude

Beliefs also play a part in attitude formation. **Beliefs** are a consumer's subjective perception of *how well* a product or brand performs on different attributes.[26] Beliefs are based on personal experience, advertising, and discussions with other people. Beliefs about product attributes are important because, along with personal values, they create the favorable or unfavorable attitude the consumer has toward certain products and services.

Attitude Change Marketers use three approaches to try to change consumer attitudes toward products and brands, as shown in the examples below.[27]

1. Changing beliefs about the extent to which a brand has certain attributes. McDonald's ran an ad to allay consumer concerns about too much cholesterol in its french fries.
2. Changing the perceived importance of attributes. Seven-Up succeeded in building on its positively viewed "no-caffeine" attribute with its "Never had it, never will" slogan to build its market share.
3. Adding new attributes to the product. P&G added calcium to its Citrus Hill fruit juices hoping consumers would perceive this new product attribute favorably.

LIFE-STYLE

Life-style is a "mode of living that is identified by how people spend their time (activities); what they consider important in their environment (interests); and what they think of themselves and the world around them (opinions)."[28] Some activities, interests, and opinions that make up a person's life-style are shown in Figure 4-6. Moreover, life-style reflects consumers' **self-concept,** which is the way people see themselves and the way they believe others see them.[29] The men's clothier, Hart Schaffner & Marx, focused a recent promotional campaign on this theme: "The right suit might not help you achieve success. But the wrong suit could limit your chances."

The analysis of consumer life-styles (also called *psychographics*) has produced many insights into consumers' behavior. For example, life-style analysis has proven useful in segmenting and targeting consumers for new and existing

FIGURE 4-6
Life-style variable of activities, interests, and opinions influencing consumer purchase decision process

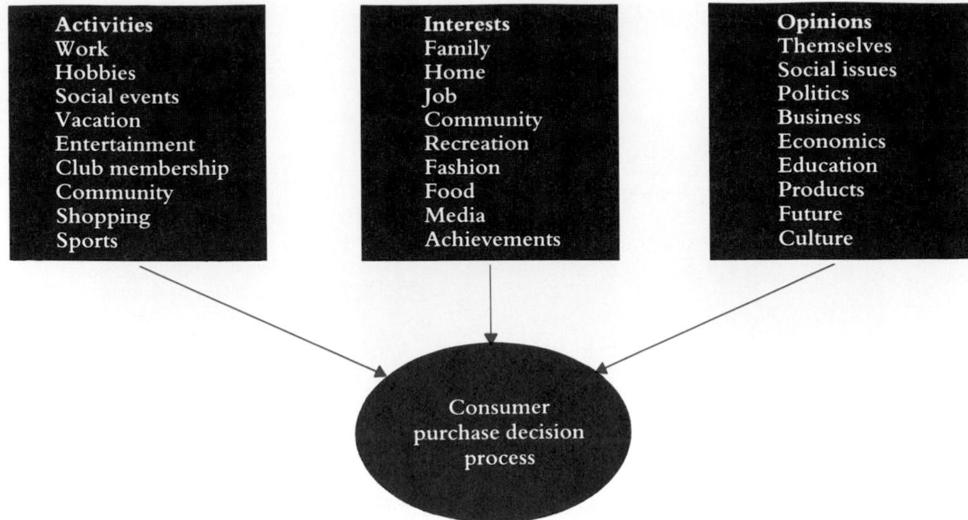

products (see Chapter 8). An example of using life-style research to identify five segments of perfume consumers is described in the Marketing Action Memo.

Life-style analysis has also focused on identifying general consumer profiles. The most prominent example of this type of analysis is the Stanford Research Institute (SRI) Value and Lifestyles (VALS) Program.[30] The VALS Program has identified categories of adult life-styles that relate to the behavior of segments of American consumers. *Need-driven* people are concerned with financial security and compose 11 percent of consumers. *Inner-directed* people seek self-expression and pursue individual needs; they account for 20 percent of consumers. *Outer-directed* people make up 67 percent of consumers and adhere to social norms and value appearances. *Integrated individuals* emphasize quality, uniqueness, and esthetics in their lives and account for 2 percent of consumers. Coca-Cola directs its advertising to two different VALS categories. Coca-Cola Classic "Red, White and You" ads appeal to outer-directed people; Max Headroom ads appeal to inner-directed people.

CONCEPT CHECK

1 **The problem with the Toro Snow Pup was an example of selective ___________.**

2 **What three attitude-change approaches are most common?**

3 **What does *life-style* mean?**

SOCIOCULTURAL INFLUENCES ON CONSUMER BEHAVIOR

Sociocultural influences, which evolve from a consumer's formal and informal relationships with other people, also exert a significant impact on consumer

MARKETING·ACTION·MEMO

There is More to Perfume than the Scent

Life-style research has opened new doors to the search for why people buy certain products. More often than not, life-style analysis reveals a rich portrait of present and potential product users. Research conducted on behalf of fragrance manufacturers, for example, illustrates some interesting findings.

Fragrance manufacturers have identified five types of women who use fragrances and represent five different market segments. One is the young, independent, carefree woman for whom Charlie was developed. Another is the incurable romantic; Jontue was made for her. Aviance was created for the housewife, and Enjoli was made for the working mother. A fifth type of woman wants the luxurious and adventurous life where the world is her toy; Scoundrel and Senchal were developed for her.

Each brand is directly linked and marketed to a particular type of woman as reflected in her self-concept and life-style. Lois Geraci Ernst, president and creative director of Advertising to Women, Inc., says "We're talking about a stupid little perfume, but we're dealing with the whole texture of life and relationships." Annette Green, director of the New York–based Fragrance Foundation, echoes this view: "We make a statement about ourselves—our personality, sexuality, and how we want to be remembered—by the way we smell."

Source: Julie Vargo-Turi, "Perfume: The Magical Fluid That Fantasies Are Made Of," *Dallas Times Herald* (February 12, 1986), p. 8; "Charles of the Ritz Discovers What It Is That Women Want," *Wall Street Journal* (August 20, 1981), p. 27.

behavior. These involve personal influence, reference groups, the family, social class, culture, and subculture.

Personal Influence

A consumer's purchases are often influenced by the views, opinions, or behaviors of others. Two aspects of personal influence are important to marketing: opinion leadership and word-of-mouth activity.

Opinion Leadership Individuals who exert direct or indirect social influence over others are called **opinion leaders.** Opinion leaders are more likely to be important for products that provide a form of self-expression. Automobiles, clothing, club membership, and PCs are products affected by opinion leaders, but appliances are not.[31]

Identifying, reaching, and influencing opinion leaders is a major challenge for companies. Some firms use sports figures or celebrities as spokespersons to represent their products, such as Dennis Conner for Wheaties or George C. Scott for Renault, in the hope that they are opinion leaders. Others promote their products in media believed to reach opinion leaders. Still others use more direct approaches. Ford Motor Company invited executives and professional

General Mills uses Dennis Conner in its advertising for Wheaties because he is an opinion leader

people to test drive its new Thunderbird.[32] Although only 10 percent said they would purchase the car, 84 percent said they would recommend it to a friend.

WHEATIES
"A DREAM COME TRUE" :30
GENERAL MILLS, INC.
GICO-0437
DDB NEEDHAM WORLDWIDE, INC.
A dream come true
(MUSIC UP AND UNDER)
DENNIS CONNER (VO): I guess all Americans grow up eating Wheaties
and dreaming about being a champion.
(OC): To actually bring the cup back home to America
(VO): was a dream
come true.
SONG: RIDE THE STARS,
RACE THE WIND,
THE BEST HAS JUST
BEGUN.
TO TASTE THE GLORY
THAT YOU FIND
WHEN YOU'RE THE CHAMPIONS.
ANNCR (VO): Wheaties salutes the Americas Cup champions.
SONG: WHEATIES, BREAKFAST OF CHAMPIONS.

Word-of-Mouth People influencing each other during their face-to-face conversations is called **word-of-mouth.** Word-of-mouth is perhaps the most powerful information source for consumers because it typically involves friends viewed as trustworthy. When consumers were asked what most influences their buying decisions in a recent survey, 37 percent mentioned a friend's recommendation and 20 percent said advertising.[33] Studies on automobile purchasing show that satisfied buyers tell 8 other people about their experience, whereas dissatisfied buyers complain to 22 people.[34]

The power of personal influence has prompted firms to promote positive, and retard negative, word-of-mouth.[35] For instance, "teaser" advertising campaigns are run in advance of new product introductions to stimulate conversations. Other techniques such as advertising slogans, music, and humor (California Raisins) also heighten positive word-of-mouth. On the other hand, rumors about K Mart (snake eggs in clothing), McDonald's (worms in hamburgers), and Corona Extra beer (contaminated beer) have resulted in negative word-of-mouth, none of which was based on fact. Overcoming or neutralizing negative word-of-mouth is difficult. However, firms have found that supplying factual information, providing toll-free numbers for consumers to call the company, and giving appropriate product demonstrations have been helpful.

REFERENCE GROUPS

Reference groups are people to whom an individual looks as a basis for self-appraisal or as a source of personal standards. Reference groups affect consumer purchases because they influence the information, attitudes, and aspiration levels that help set a consumer's standards. For example, one of the first questions asked of others when planning to attend a social occasion is "What are you going to wear?" Reference groups have an important influence in the purchase of luxury products but not of necessities; reference groups exert a strong influence on the brand chosen when its use and consumption is highly visible to others.[36]

Consumers have many reference groups, but three groups have clear marketing implications. A *membership group* is one to which a person actually belongs, including fraternities, social clubs, and the family. Such groups are easily identifiable and are targeted by firms selling insurance, insignia products, and charter vacations. An *aspiration group* is one that a person wishes to be a member of or wishes to be identified with, such as a professional society. Firms frequently rely on spokespeople or settings associated with their target market's aspiration group in their advertising. A *dissociative group* is one that a person wishes to maintain a distance from because of differences in values or behaviors.

California Raisins' commercials stimulated widespread word-of-mouth activity

FAMILY INFLUENCE

Family influences on consumer behavior result from three sources: consumer socialization, passage through the family life cycle, and decision making within the family.

Consumer Socialization The process by which people acquire the skills, knowledge, and attitudes necessary to function as consumers is **consumer socialization.** Children learn how to purchase by (1) interacting with adults in purchase situations and (2) their own purchasing and product usage experiences. As children mature into adults, brand preferences emerge that may last a lifetime. Knowledge of this has prompted Sony to introduce "My First Sony," a line of portable audio equipment for children.[37]

Family Life Cycle Consumers act and purchase differently as they go through life. The **family life cycle** concept describes the distinct phases that a family progresses through from formation to retirement, each phase bringing with it identifiable purchasing behaviors.[38] Figure 4-7 illustrates the traditional progression as well as contemporary variations of the family life cycle.

FIGURE 4-7
Modern family life cycle

Source: Redrawn from Patrick E. Murphy and William A. Staples, "A Modernized Family Life Cycle." Reprinted with permission from *The Journal of Consumer Research* (June 1979), p. 17.

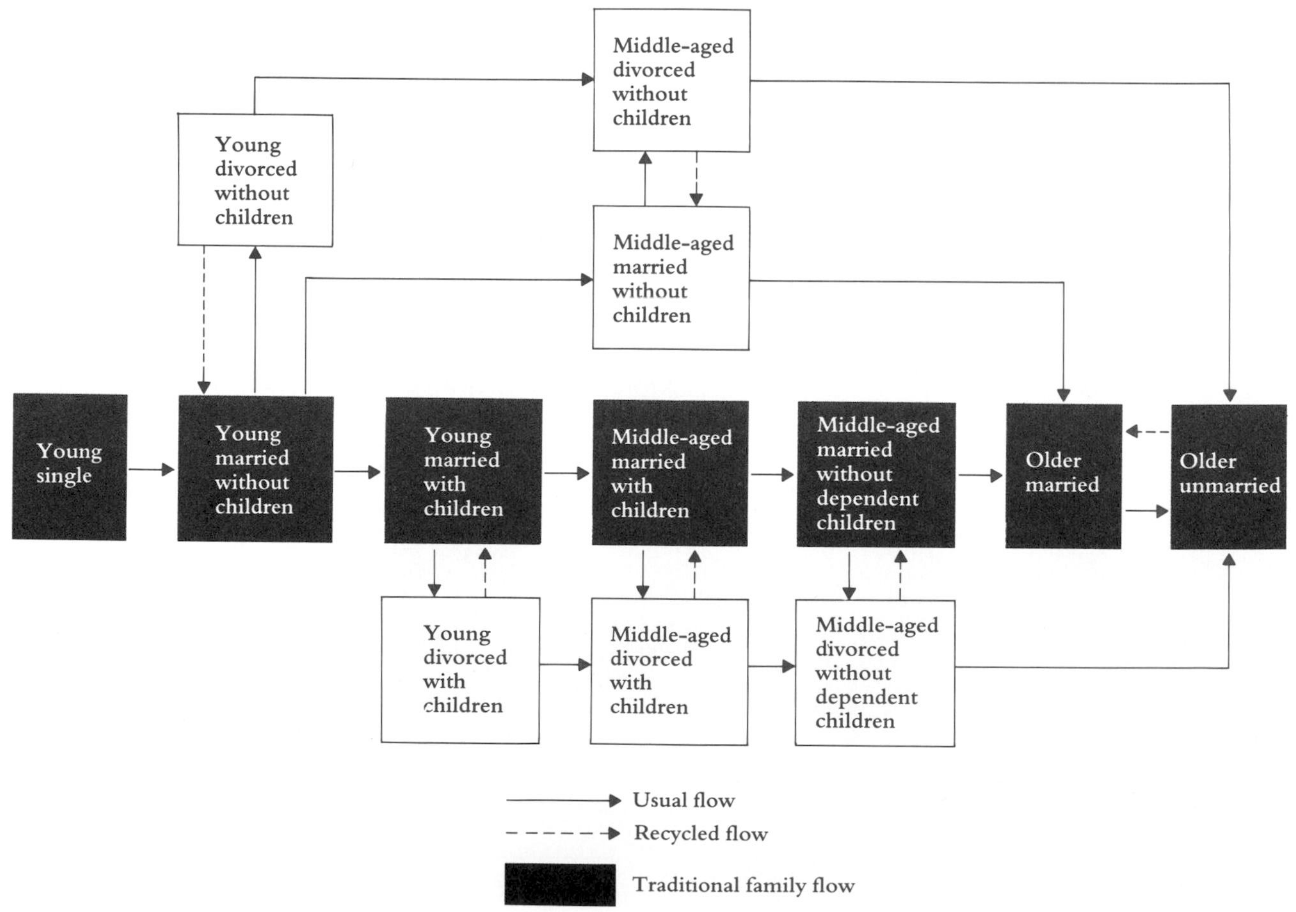

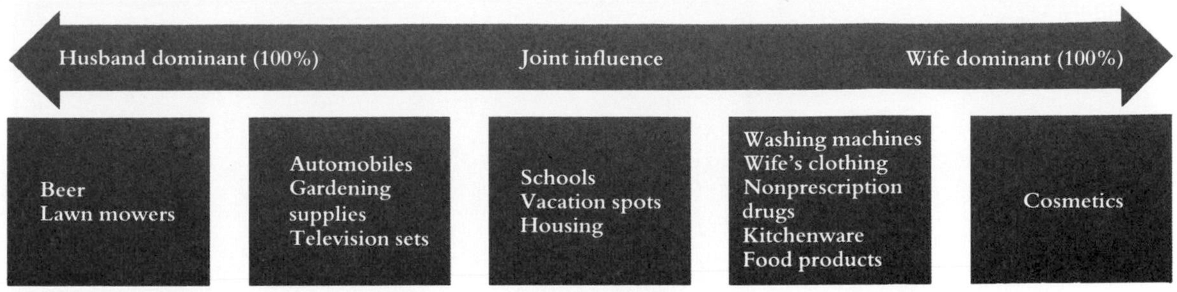

FIGURE 4-8
Influence continuum of spouse in family decision making

Young singles' buying preferences are for nondurable items, including food away from home, clothing, and entertainment. They represent a good market for recreational travel and automobiles. Young married couples without children are typically more affluent than young singles because both spouses are usually employed. They purchase home furnishings and automobiles. Young marrieds with a new baby may experience a decline in disposable income because spouses may cut back on working hours and must pay for necessities for the new arrival. Still, they represent a sizeable market for home furnishings, life insurance, and various infant products.

The middle-aged married couple with children is typically better off financially than their younger counterparts, because spouses often have better jobs. They are a significant market for leisure products and home improvement items. Middle-aged couples without children typically have a large amount of discretionary income. They buy better home furnishings, status automobiles, and financial services.

Persons in the last two phases—older married and older unmarried—represent a sizeable market for prescription drugs, medical services, vacation trips, and gifts for younger relatives.

Family Decision Making A third influence in the decision-making process occurs within the family. Two decision-making styles exist: spouse-dominant and joint decision making.[39] With a joint decision-making style, most decisions are made by both husband and wife. Spouse-dominant decisions are those for which either the husband or the wife is responsible. The types of products and services associated with the decision-making styles are shown in Figure 4-8. However, these tendencies are changing with the rise in dual-income families. Today, 42 percent of all food-shopping dollars are spent by male customers; and women influence 80 percent of all new car purchases.[40]

Roles of individual family members in the purchase process are another element of family decision making. Five roles exist: (1) information gatherer, (2) influencer, (3) decision maker, (4) purchaser, and (5) user. Family members assume different roles for different products and services. This knowledge is important to firms. Increasingly, teenagers are the information gatherers, decision makers, and purchasers of grocery items for the family, given the prevalence of working parents and single-parent households. Nabisco, Quaker Oats, Kellogg, P&G, and the American Sewing Association now advertise between the rock videos on MTV.[41]

McDonald's communicates directly to the Hispanic market

SOCIAL CLASS

A more subtle influence on consumer behavior than direct contact with others is the social class to which people belong. **Social class** may be defined as the relatively permanent, homogeneous divisions in a society in which people sharing similar values, interests, and behavior can be grouped. A person's occupation, source of income, and education determine his or her social class.

Companies use social class as a basis for identifying and reaching particularly good prospects for their products.[42] People in upper classes are targeted by companies for items such as financial investments, recreational apparel, and expensive cars. By comparison, working and lower classes are targeted for products such as plastic dinnerware and tablecloths. The middle class is a primary target for home improvement centers, automotive parts stores, and personal hygiene products. Firms also recognize differences in media preferences between classes. Lower and working classes prefer sports and romance magazines; upper classes tend to read literary, travel, and news magazines.

CULTURE AND SUBCULTURE

As described in Chapter 3, *culture* refers to the set of values, ideas, and attitudes that are accepted by a homogeneous group of people and transmitted to the next generation. Thus we often refer to the American culture, the Latin American culture, or the German culture.

Subgroups within the larger, or national, culture with unique values, ideas, and attitudes are referred to as **subcultures**. Various subcultures exist within the American culture based on race, nationality, and geography. Subculture affects media preferences, as evidenced by the existence of black and Spanish-language television and radio stations and Asian newspapers in several parts of the United States. In general, subcultural influences are most apparent for food products, clothing, beauty aids, and household items. Numerous firms have recognized the importance of subculture in marketing efforts. McDonald's frequently promotes its products in Spanish, Metropolitan Life Insurance has targeted Asians and Hispanics for its insurance policies, and Pro-Line Corporation markets a line of beauty products exclusively for blacks. Campbell's sells a mild cheese soup in the eastern, southern, and central regions of the United States.

However, in the West and Southwest, its cheese soup has more "bite." In the 1990's, increasing attention will be placed on modifying the products and promotion and distribution efforts of companies to better serve the preferences of subcultures, since one in five Americans is black, Hispanic, or Asian.[43]

CONCEPT CHECK

1 **What are the two primary forms of personal influence?**

2 **Marketers are concerned with which types of reference groups?**

3 **What are the five purchasing roles in family decision making?**

SUMMARY

1 When a consumer buys a product, it is not an act but a process. There are five steps in the purchase decision process: problem recognition, information search, alternative evaluation, purchase decision, and post-purchase behavior.

2 Consumers evaluate alternatives on the basis of attributes. Identifying which attributes are most important to consumers along with understanding consumer beliefs about how a brand performs on those attributes can make the difference between successful and unsuccessful products.

3 Consumer involvement with what is bought affects whether the purchase decision process involves routine, limited, or extended problem solving. Situational influences also affect the process.

4 Perception is important to marketers because of the selectivity of what a consumer sees or hears, comprehends, and retains.

5 Much of the behavior that consumers exhibit is learned. Consumers learn from repeated experience and reasoning. Brand loyalty is a result of learning.

6 Attitudes are learned predispositions to respond to an object or class of objects in a consistently favorable or unfavorable way. Attitudes are based on a person's values and beliefs concerning the attributes of objects.

7 Life-style is a mode of living reflected in a person's activities, interests, and opinions of himself or herself and the world. Life-style is a manifestation of a person's self-concept.

8 Personal influence takes two forms: opinion leadership and word-of-mouth activity. A specific type of personal influence exists in the form of reference groups.

9 Family influences on consumer behavior result from three sources: consumer socialization, family life cycle, and decision making within the household.

10 Within the United States there are social classes and subcultures that affect a consumer's values and behavior. Marketers must be sensitive to these sociocultural influences when developing a marketing mix.

KEY TERMS AND CONCEPTS

consumer behavior p. 90
purchase decision process p. 90
evaluative criteria p. 92
evoked set p. 92
cognitive dissonance p. 93
involvement p. 94
situational influences p. 94
motivation p. 96
personality p. 96
perception p. 98
perceived risk p. 98
learning p. 99
brand loyalty p. 100
attitude p. 100
values p. 100
beliefs p. 101
life-style p. 101
self-concept p. 101
opinion leaders p. 103
word-of-mouth p. 104
reference groups p. 105
consumer socialization p. 106
family life cycle p. 106
social class p. 108
subcultures p. 108

CHAPTER PROBLEMS AND APPLICATIONS

1 Think back over your decision of which college to attend and recreate what took place at each stage of the decision process.

2 Review Figure 4-2 in the text, which shows the CD-player attributes identified by *Consumer Reports*. Which attributes are important to you? What other attributes might you consider? Which brand would you prefer?

3 Suppose research at Apple Computer reveals that prospective buyers are anxious about buying PCs for home use. What strategies might you recommend to the company to reduce consumer anxiety?

4 A Porsche salesperson was taking orders on new cars because he was unable to satisfy the demand because of the limited number of cars in the showroom and lot. Several persons had backed out of the contract within 2 weeks of signing the order. What explanation can you give for this behavior, and what remedies would you recommend?

5 Think back about your most recent clothing purchase. How was your purchase affected by your motives, perceptions, learning, attitudes, and life-style? What role, if any, was played by your reference group?

6 Which social class would you associate with each of the following items or actions? (a) tennis club membership, (b) an arrangement of plastic flowers in the kitchen, (c) *True Romance* magazine, (d) *Smithsonian* magazine, (e) formally dressing for dinner frequently, and (f) being a member of a bowling team.

7 Assign one or more levels of the hierarchy of needs and the motives described in Figure 4-4 to the following products: (a) life insurance, (b) cosmetics, (c) *The Wall Street Journal*, and (d) hamburger.

8 With which stage in the family life cycle would the purchase of the following products and services be most closely identified? (a) bedroom furniture, (b) life insurance, (c) Caribbean cruise, (d) house mortgage, and (e) children's toys.

9 "The greater the perceived risk in a purchase situation, the more likely that cognitive dissonance will result." Does this statement have any basis given the discussion in the text? Why?

10 Which of the following products would be purchased with a routine problem-solving behavior and which with extended problem-solving behavior? (a) razor blades, (b) personal computer, (c) a gift for a close personal friend of the opposite sex, and (d) a soft drink.

SUGGESTED READINGS

Joseph W. Alba and J. Wesley Hutchinson, "Dimensions of Consumer Expertise," *Journal of Consumer Research* (March 1987), pp. 411-454. *Fundamental dimensions of consumer expertise are described with implications for consumer decision making.*

Sharon E. Beatty and Scott M. Smith, "External Search Effort: An Investigation Across Several Product Categories," *Journal of Consumer Research* (June 1987), pp. 83-95. *This article examines the role of involvement on consumers' external search effort.*

G.R. Dowling, "Perceived Risk: The Concept and Its Measurement," *Psychology and Marketing,* Vol. 3 (1986), pp. 193-210. *The nature of perceived risk and its relationship to risk-handling behavior are described in this article.*

Lawrence F. Feick and Linda Price, "The Market Maven: A Diffusion of Marketplace Information," *Journal of Marketing* (January 1987), pp. 83-97. *Personal influence is studied in this article.*

William O'Hare, "Blacks and Whites: One Market or Two?" *American Demographics* (March 1987), pp. 44-48. *This article explores subcultural aspects of purchasing behavior with specific reference to black consumers.*

GMF robotics

5

Industrial and Organizational Buyer Behavior

After reading this chapter you should be able to:

Distinguish between industrial, reseller, and government markets.

•

Recognize key characteristics of organizational buying that make it different from consumer buying.

•

Understand how types of buying situations influence organizational purchasing.

•

Describe actions organizations can take to improve their marketing to other organizations.

Robotics Designs Off the Kitchen Table

Joe Alvité got to know his kitchen table very well.

After accumulating more than 15 years of design experience working for robotics firms, Alvité decided to strike out on his own. With only his savings and money borrowed from relatives, he spent 18 months sitting at his kitchen table coming up with new, improved designs for robotic devices.

Alvité had originally considered designing the robots themselves—the programmable devices used to move material or parts or perform activities like welding (opposite page) or spray painting—to help American factories automate, improve quality, increase productivity, and lower costs. But he saw two problems with this strategy. First, by the mid-1980's, sales of all robotic equipment were only 33 percent of what forecasts had predicted 2 years earlier. In fact, only 25,000 robots were used in American firms by 1987, far short of expectations and far behind the 118,000 used by Japanese manufacturers. Second, he would be competing with several huge American firms that manufactured robots such as GM, GE, and Westinghouse, as well as with powerful, well-established European and Japanese robot producers.

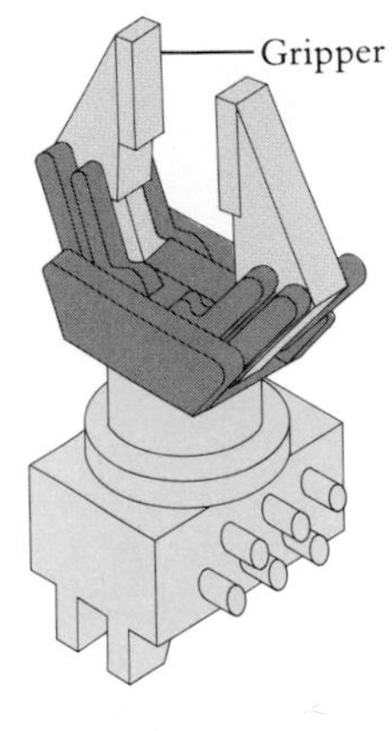

So Alvité decided to focus his effort on a niche in the robotics market—the "grippers" that go on the end of robot arms to provide the flexibility to perform the complex tasks required in a factory. Alvité designed numerous sizes of the devices on his kitchen table.

Alvité obtained additional funding and formed his own firm, Mecanotron Corporation. Now he faces the problem of trying to market his new grippers to the thousands of prospective organizational buyers—the industrial firms, resellers, and government agencies studied in this chapter. Further, he has to discover which individuals in these organizations influence and make the buying decision.[1]

The challenge facing Alvité is often encountered by both small, start-up corporations such as his and large, well-established companies. Important issues in marketing to organizations are examined in this chapter, which analyzes the types of organizational buyers, key characteristics of organizational buying, and some typical buying decisions. The chapter concludes with how organizations can market to other organizations more effectively.

THE NATURE AND SIZE OF ORGANIZATIONAL MARKETS

Organizational buyers are business firms and nonprofit establishments that buy goods and services and then resell them, with or without reprocessing, to other organizations or ultimate consumers. They include all the buyers in a nation except the ultimate consumers. These organizational buyers purchase and lease tremendous volumes of capital equipment, raw materials, manufactured parts,

FIGURE 5–1
Kind and number of organizational customers

KIND OF ORGANIZATION	NUMBER	KIND OF MARKET
Manufacturers	619,000	Industrial (business) markets, 13,534,000
Mining	250,000	
Construction	1,621,000	
Farms, forestry, and fisheries	2,479,000	
Services	5,800,000	
Finance, insurance and real estate	2,140,000	
Transportation and public utilities	625,000	
Wholesalers	511,000	Reseller markets, 3,341,000
Retailers	2,830,000	
Government units	82,000	Government markets, 82,000

Source: *Statistical Abstract of the United States*, 107th ed. (Washington, D.C.: U.S. Department of Commerce, 1987).

supplies, and business services. In fact, because they often buy raw materials and parts, process them, and sell the upgraded product several times before it is purchased by the final organizational buyer or ultimate consumer, the aggregate purchases of organizational buyers in a year are far greater than those by ultimate consumers. Because more than half of all U.S. business school graduates take jobs in firms that sell products or services to other organizations rather than to ultimate consumers,[2] it is important to understand the fundamental aspects of organizational buying behavior.

Organizational buyers are divided into three different markets: (1) industrial, (2) reseller, and (3) government markets.

INDUSTRIAL MARKETS

There are more than 13.5 million firms in the industrial, or business, market (Figure 5-1). These **industrial firms** in some way reprocess a product or service they buy before selling it again to the next buyer. This is certainly true of a steel mill that converts iron ore into steel. It is also true (if you stretch your imagination) of a firm selling services, such as a bank that takes money from its depositors, reprocesses it, and "sells" it as loans to its borrowers.

The importance of services in the United States today is emphasized by the composition of the industrial markets shown in Figure 5-1. The first four types of industrial firms (manufacturers; mining; construction; and farms, forestry, and fisheries) sell physical products and represent less than half of all the industrial firms, or about 5 million. The services market sells diverse services such as legal advice, auto repair, and dry cleaning. Along with finance, insurance and real estate businesses, and transportation and public utility firms, these service firms represent more than half of all industrial firms, or about 8.5 million. Because of the size and importance of service firms, service marketing is discussed in detail in Chapter 22.

Domtar Gypsum promotes its unique capabilities to industrial buyers

Courtesy of Domtar Gypsum

RESELLER MARKETS

Wholesalers and retailers who buy physical products and resell them again without any reprocessing are **resellers.** In the United States there are about 2.8 million retailers and 511,000 wholesalers. In Chapters 13 to 15 we shall see how manufacturers use wholesalers and retailers in their distribution ("place") strategies as channels through which their products reach ultimate consumers. In this chapter we look at these resellers mainly as organizational buyers in terms of (1) how they make their own buying decisions and (2) which products they choose to carry.

GOVERNMENT MARKETS

Government units are the federal, state, and local agencies that buy goods and services for the constituents they serve. There are about 82,000 of these government units in the United States. Their annual purchases vary in size from billions of dollars for federal agencies such as the Department of Defense and National Aeronautics and Space Administration (NASA) to millions or thousands of dollars for local school or sanitation districts.

MEASURING INDUSTRIAL, RESELLER, AND GOVERNMENT MARKETS

Measuring industrial, reseller, and government markets is an important first step for a firm interested in gauging the size of one, two, or all three markets. Fortunately, information is readily available from the federal government to do this. The federal government regularly collects, tabulates, and publishes data on these markets using its **Standard Industrial Classification (SIC) system.**[3] The SIC system groups organizations on the basis of major activity or the major product or service provided, which enables the federal government to publish the number of establishments, number of employees, and sales volumes for each group, designated by a numerical code. Geographic breakdowns are also provided where possible.

The SIC system begins with broad, two-digit categories such as food (SIC code 20), tobacco (SIC code 21), and apparel (SIC code 23). Often each of these two-digit categories is further divided into three-digit and four-digit categories, which represent subindustries within the broader two-digit category. Figure 5-2 presents a detailed breakdown within the food industry to illustrate the classification scheme.

The SIC system permits a firm to find the SIC codes of its present customers and then obtain SIC-coded lists for similar firms that may want the same types of products and services. Also, SIC categories can be monitored to determine the growth in the number of establishments, number of employees, and sales volumes to identify promising marketing opportunities.

However, SIC codes have important limitations. The federal government assigns one code to each organization based on its major activity or product, so large firms that engage in many different activities or provide different types

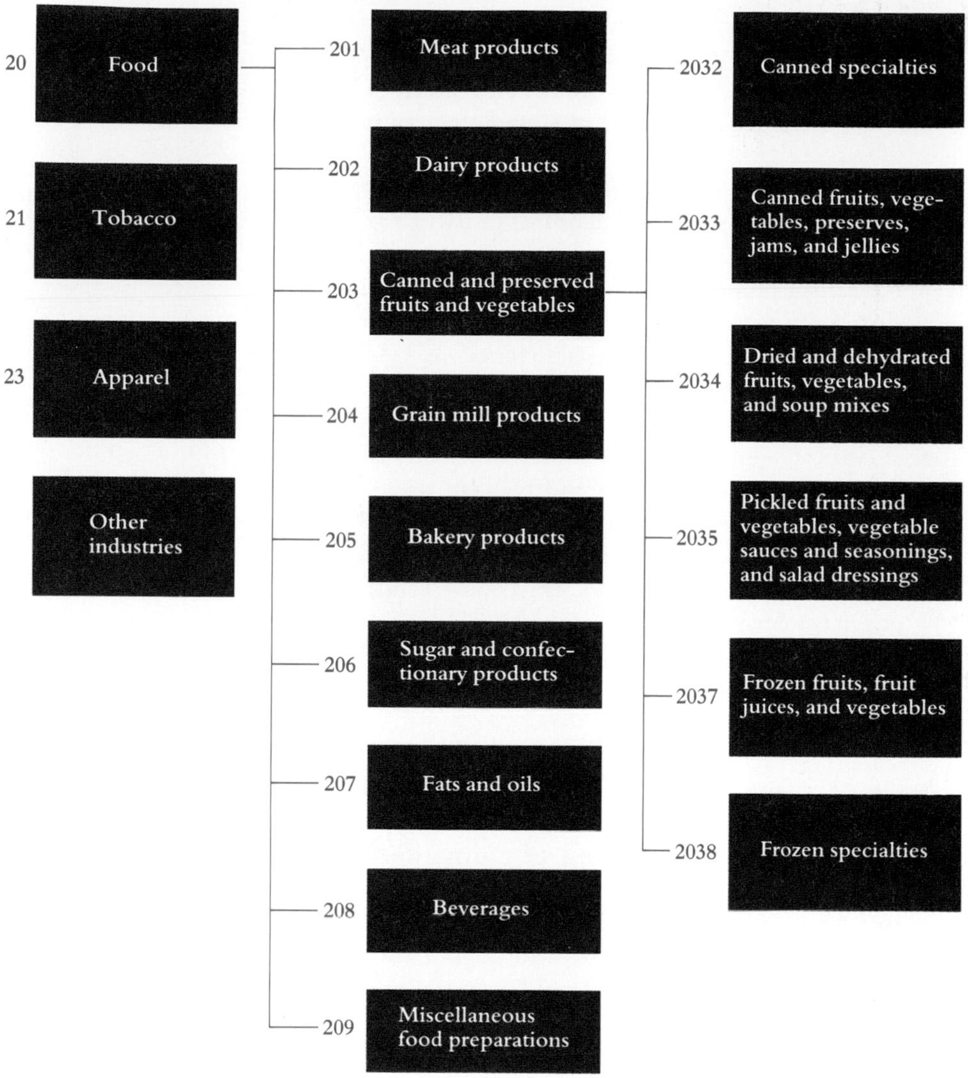

FIGURE 5–2
SIC breakdown for food industries

of products and services are still given only one SIC code. A second limitation is that four-digit codes are not available for all industries in every geographic area because the federal government will not reveal data when two or fewer organizations exist in an area.

Concept Check

1 **What are the three main types of organizational buyers?**

2 **What is the Standard Industrial Classification (SIC) system?**

FIGURE 5-3
Key characteristics of industrial and organizational buying behavior

Source: Adapted from Robert R. Reeder, Edward G. Brierty, and Betty H. Reeder, *Industrial Marketing: Analysis, Planning, and Control* (Englewood Cliffs, N.J.: Prentice-Hall, Inc., 1987), pp. 9-23; Robert W. Haas, *Industrial Marketing Management,* 2nd ed. (Boston: Kent Publishing Company, 1982), pp. 24-28; Michael D. Hutt and Thomas W. Speh, *Industrial Marketing Management,* 2nd ed. (Chicago: The Dryden Press, 1985), pp. 6-12; B. Charles Ames and James D. Hlavacek, *Managerial Marketing for Industrial Firms* (New York: Random House 1984), pp. 19-30.

Market characteristics

- Demand for industrial products and services is derived.
- Few customers typically exist, and their purchase orders are large.

Product or service characteristics

- Products or services are technical in nature and purchased on the basis of specifications.
- There is a predominance of raw and semifinished goods purchased.
- Heavy emphasis is placed on delivery time, technical assistance, post-sale service, and financing assistance.

Buying process characteristics

- Technically qualified and professional buyers exist and follow established purchasing policies and procedures.
- Buying objectives and criteria are typically spelled out, as are procedures for evaluating sellers and products (services).
- Multiple buying influences exist, and multiple parties participate in purchase decisions.
- Reciprocal arrangements exist, and negotiation between buyers and sellers is commonplace.

Other marketing mix characteristics

- Direct selling to organizational buyers is the rule, and physical distribution is very important.
- Advertising and other forms of promotion are technical in nature.
- Price is often negotiated, evaluated as part of broader seller and product (service) qualities, typically inelastic owing to derived demand, and frequently affected by trade and quantity discounts.

CHARACTERISTICS OF ORGANIZATIONAL BUYING

Organizations are different from individuals, so buying for an organization is different from buying for yourself or your family.[4] True, in both cases the objective in making the purchase is to solve the buyer's problem—to satisfy a need or want. But unique objectives and policies of an organization put special constraints on how it makes buying decisions. Understanding the characteristics of organizational buying is essential in designing effective marketing programs to reach these buyers.

Organizational buying behavior is the decision-making process that organizations use to establish the need for products and services and identify, evaluate, and choose among alternative brands and suppliers. Some key characteristics of organizational buying behavior are listed in Figure 5-3 and discussed in the following pages.

Consumer needs and wants provide a derived demand for Weyerhauser's pulp and paper products

Courtesy of Weyerhauser

DEMAND CHARACTERISTICS

Consumer demand for products and services is affected by their price and availability and by consumers' personal tastes and discretionary income. By comparison, industrial demand is derived.[5] **Derived demand** means that the demand for industrial products and services is driven by, or derived from, demand for consumer products and services. For example, the demand for Weyerhacuser's pulp and paper products is based on consumer demand for newspapers, Domino's "keep warm" pizza-to-go boxes, Federal Express packages, and disposable diapers. Derived demand is often based on expectations of future consumer demand. For instance, Whirlpool purchases parts for its washers and dryers in anticipation of consumer demand, which is affected by the replacement cycle for these products and by consumer income. Thus forecasting is very important in organizational buying, and it is discussed in Chapter 8.

NUMBER OF POTENTIAL BUYERS

Firms selling consumer products or services often try to reach thousands or millions of individuals or households. For example, your local supermarket or bank probably serves thousands of people, and Quaker Oats tries to reach 80 million American households with its breakfast cereals and probably succeeds in selling to a third or half of these in any given year. In contrast, firms selling to organizations are often restricted to far fewer buyers. Cray Research can sell its supercomputers to fewer than 1,000 organizations throughout the world, and B.F. Goodrich sells its original equipment tires to fewer than 10 car manufacturers.

Sylvania focuses on buyers' objective of reducing costs to improve profits

Courtesy of GTE Products Corporation

BUYING OBJECTIVES

Organizations buy products and services for one main reason: to help them achieve their objectives. For business firms the **buying objective** is usually to increase profits through reducing costs or increasing revenues. Southland Corporation buys automated inventory systems to increase the number of products that can be sold through its 7-Eleven outlets and to keep them fresh. Nissan Motor Company switched its advertising agency because it expects the new agency to devise a more effective ad campaign to help it sell more cars and increase revenues. To improve executive decision making, many firms buy advanced computer systems to process data. The objectives of nonprofit firms and government agencies are usually to meet the needs of the groups they serve. Thus a hospital buys a high-technology diagnostic device to serve its patients better, and the U.S. Department of Labor buys pencils and paper to help run its office so it can assist American workers. Understanding buying objectives is a necessary first step in marketing to organizations. Recognizing the high costs of energy, Sylvania promotes cost savings and increased profits made possible by its new fluorescent lights to prospective buyers.

BUYING CRITERIA

In making a purchase the buying organization must weigh key buying criteria that apply to the potential supplier and what it wants to sell. **Organizational buying criteria** are the objective attributes of the supplier's products and services and the capabilities of the supplier itself. These criteria serve the same purpose as the evaluative criteria used by consumers and described in Chapter 4. Seven

FIGURE 5-4
You be the industrial buyer and choose the buying criteria

Assume that you are the industrial buyer responsible for purchasing each of the items described below:

- Case A—paint. An industrial chemical producer must repaint the interior walls of its manufacturing plant. All the surfaces to be painted are cement and are exposed to severe chemical fumes, which cause paint to deteriorate. It's estimated that the project will require 10 barrels of paint.
- Case B—desks. A large university requires 200 new desks to be used by a large department in a soon-to-be completed university building. The university's policy is to furnish all new offices with metal desks.
- Case C—computers. A large aerospace firm has received a government contract to build two satellites for astronomical research. Each satellite is to have an on-board computer that must stabilize the orbit precisely. The two computers are to be subcontracted, since their electronics and manufacturing tolerances are so complex that only firms with prior experience could guarantee satisfactory performance. The satellites are scheduled to be launched in 2 years.

There are seven key buying criteria to consider in making each purchase, as outlined in the text below. For each of these cases, select the five criteria you consider most critical and rank them from most to least important. To discover which criteria a sample of actual purchasing managers thought were important, see the text.

of the most commonly used criteria are (1) price, (2) ability to meet the quality specifications required for the item, (3) ability to meet required delivery schedules, (4) technical capability, (5) warranties and claim policies in the event of poor performance, (6) past performance on previous contracts, and (7) production facilities and capacity.

Before reading further, study Figure 5-4 and play the role of an industrial buyer who must purchase a different product for three different firms. Try to select and rank five of the criteria just mentioned as most important in buying (1) paint, (2) desks, and (3) computers for the applications described.

A researcher[6] presented these 3 buying situations to 170 purchasing managers, who identified the 5 most important buying criteria for each case as follows:

RANK	CASE A—PAINT	CASE B—DESKS	CASE C—COMPUTERS
1	Quality	Price	Quality
2	Warranties	Quality	Technical capability
3	Delivery	Delivery	Delivery
4	Past performance	Warranties	Production facilities
5	Price	Past performance	Past performance

He observed that, despite the diverse nature of the purchases, three factors in each case were crucial in the choice of a supplier: (1) ability to meet quality standards, (2) ability to deliver the product on time, and (3) performance on previous contracts. He concluded that price is generally the key factor in buying standard items such as desks. Conversely, when buying more technically complex products such as computers, other criteria are likely to influence the decision and price becomes less important. With many U.S. manufacturers adopting a "just-in-time" inventory system that reduces the inventory of production parts to those used within hours or days, on-time delivery is becoming an even more critical buying criterion. Indeed, this buying criterion has assumed special significance in the U.S. automobile industry in recent years. Japanese automakers have long favored this inventory system, and U.S. automakers adopted it as a means to reduce inventory carrying costs and improve productivity. The "just-in-time" inventory system is discussed further in Chapter 14.

SIZE OF THE ORDER OR PURCHASE

The size of the purchase involved in organizational buying is typically much larger than that in consumer buying. The dollar value of a single purchase made by an organization often runs into the thousands or millions of dollars. For example, IBM's worldwide purchases of electronic components, subassemblies, and assembly services exceeds $13 billion annually.[7] With so much money at stake, most organizations place constraints on their buyers in the form of purchasing policies or procedures. Buyers must often get competitive bids from at least three prospective suppliers when the order is above a specific amount, such as $5,000. When the order is above an even higher amount, such as $50,000, it may require the review and approval of a vice president or even the president. Knowing how the size of the order affects buying practices is important in determining who participates in the purchase decision and makes the final decision and also the length of time required to arrive at a purchase agreement.

BUYER-SELLER INTERACTION

Another distinction between organizational and consumer buying behavior lies in the nature of the interaction between organization buyers and suppliers.[8] Specifically, organizational buying is more likely to involve complex and lengthy negotiations concerning delivery schedules, price, technical specifications, warranties, and claim policies. These negotiations can last as long as 5 years, as was the case in GE's recent purchase of a $9.5 million Cray Research supercomputer.[9]

Reciprocal arrangements also exist in organizational buying. **Reciprocity** is an industrial buying practice in which two organizations agree to purchase each other's products and services. For example, GM purchases Borg-Warner transmissions, and Borg-Warner buys trucks and cars from GM.[10] The U.S. Justice Department frowns on reciprocal buying because it restricts the normal operation of the free market. However, the practice exists and can limit the flexibility of organizational buyers in choosing alternative suppliers. Long-term relationships are also prevalent. As an example, Shanghai Aviation Industrial Corporation, owned by the government of China, has announced a $4.5 billion

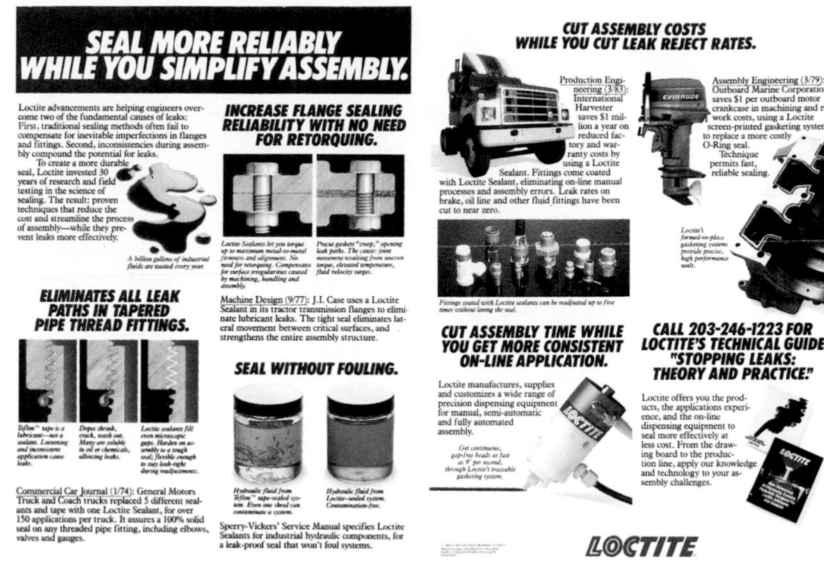

project to build 150 commercial airliners over 10 years. The contract will be awarded in 1991, and McDonnell Douglas, Boeing, and Europe's Airbus Industry are all vying for this lucrative, long-term project.[11]

Which ad should be targeted to maintenance engineers and which to design engineers? For the answers and the importance of "influencers" in the organizational buying process, see the Marketing Action Memo and text

THE BUYING CENTER

For routine purchases with a small dollar value, a single buyer or purchasing manager often makes the purchase decision alone. In many instances, however, several people in the organization participate in the buying process. The individuals in this group, called a **buying center**, share common goals, risks, and knowledge important to a purchase decision. For most large multistore chain resellers, such as Sears, 7-Eleven convenience stores, K Mart, Safeway, or Target, the buying center is highly formalized and is called a *buying committee*. However, most industrial firms or government units use informal groups of people or call meetings to arrive at buying decisions.

The importance of the buying center requires that a firm marketing to many industrial firms and government units understand the structure and behavior of these groups. One researcher has suggested four questions to provide guidance in understanding the buying center in these organizations[12]: Which individuals are in the buying center for the the product or service? What is the relative influence of each member of the group? What are the buying criteria of each member? How does each member of the group perceive our firm, our products and services, and our salespeople?

People in the Buying Center The composition of the buying center in a given organization depends on the specific item being bought. Although a buyer or purchasing manager is almost always a member of the buying center, individuals from other functional areas are included depending on what is to be purchased.

MARKETING·ACTION·MEMO

REACHING THE BUYING INFLUENCER WITH CUSTOMIZED ADVERTISEMENTS

What does a company do when it experiences 3 consecutive years of flat sales growth? Should its people work harder or smarter? Loctite Corporation, the producer of Super-Glue and an industry leader in industrial adhesives and sealants, chose to work smarter by conducting research on engineers who influence buying decisions.

The company recognized that engineers were uncomfortable with the idea of using adhesives and sealants in design, production, and maintenance applications. It seemed that the perception of Loctite's products, as opposed to their actual qualities, was the barrier to future sales growth. In-depth interviews with 450 design, production, and maintenance engineers found that *design engineers* are "risk avoiders." They want new technologies and products to be performance-proven and hence less risky. *Production engineers* are "today-oriented." They feel pressure to perform and are concerned about making costly mistakes. *Maintenance engineers* are "fixers" and are concerned with keeping things running smoothly. Moreover, each type of engineer had a preference for how they liked to have product information conveyed to them. For example, design engineers liked to see diagrams, charts, and graphs illustrating product performance characteristics. Maintenance engineers preferred visual illustrations of product benefits.

These insights led to a communication program targeting the detailed ad at left on p. 123 to design engineers and the "big picture" ad at right to maintenance engineers. This effort increased Loctite's influence on buying decisions among its potential customers and contributed to an average sales growth of slightly above 11 percent over the next 2 years.

Source: "Loctite: Home Is Where the Customers Are," *Business Week* (April 13, 1987), p. 63; Bob Donath, "What Loctite Learned with Psychographic Insights," *Business Marketing* (July 1984), pp. 100-101, 134.

In buying a million-dollar machine tool, the president (because of the size of the purchase) and the production vice-president or manager would probably be members. For key components to be incorporated in a final manufactured product, individuals from R&D, engineering, and quality control are likely to be added. For new word-processing equipment, experienced secretaries who will use the equipment would be members. Still, a major question in penetrating the buying center is finding and reaching the people who will initiate and influence the purchase process. The Marketing Action Memo shows how Loctite Corporation researched and pursued members of the buying centers in its customer organizations.

Roles in the Buying Center Researchers have identified five specific roles that an individual in a buying center can play.[13] In some purchases the same person may perform two or more of these functions.

- *Users* are the people in the organization who actually use the product or service, such as a secretary who will use the new word processor.
- *Influencers* affect the buying decision, usually by helping define the spec-

ifications for what is bought. The information systems manager would be a key influencer in the purchase of a new main-frame computer.

- *Buyers* have the formal authority and responsibility to select the supplier and negotiate the terms of the contract. The purchasing manager probably would perform this role in the purchase of a main-frame computer.
- *Deciders* have the formal or informal power to select or approve the supplier that receives the contract. Whereas in routine orders the decider is usually the buyer or purchasing manager, in important technical purchases it is more likely to be someone from R&D, engineering, or quality control. The decider for a key component being incorporated in a final manufactured product might be any of these three people.
- *Gatekeepers* control the flow of information in the buying center. Purchasing personnel, technical experts, and secretaries can all keep salespeople or information from reaching people performing the other four roles.

STAGES IN AN ORGANIZATIONAL BUYING DECISION

As shown in Figure 5-5 (and covered in Chapter 4), the five stages a student might use in buying a CD player also apply to industrial purchases

FIGURE 5-5
Comparing the stages in consumer and industrial purchases

STAGE IN THE BUYING DECISION PROCESS	CONSUMER PURCHASE: CD PLAYER FOR A STUDENT	INDUSTRIAL PURCHASE: HEADPHONES FOR A CD PLAYER
Problem recognition	Student doesn't like the sound of the stereo system now owned and desires a CD player.	Marketing research and sales departments observe competitors are including headphones on their models. Firm decides to include headphones on new models that will be purchased from an outside supplier.
Information search	Student uses past experience, that of friends, ads, and *Consumer Reports* to collect information and uncover alternatives.	Design and production engineers draft specifications for headphones. Purchasing department identifies suppliers of CD player headphones.
Alternative evaluation	Alternative CD players are evaluated on the basis of important attributes of what is desired in a CD player.	Purchasing and engineering personnel visit with suppliers and assess (1) facilities, (2) capacity, (3) quality control, and (4) financial status. They drop any suppliers not satisfactory on these factors.
Purchase decision	A specific brand of CD player is selected, the price is paid, and it is installed in the student's room.	They use (1) quality, (2) price, (3) delivery, and (4) technical capability as key buying criteria to select supplier. Then they negotiate terms and award a contract.
Postpurchase behavior	Student reevaluates the purchase decision, may return the CD player to the store if it is unsatisfactory, and looks for supportive information to justify the purchase.	They evaluate suppliers using a formal vendor rating system and notify supplier if phones do not meet its quality standard. If problem is not corrected, they drop firm as a future supplier.

However, comparing the two right-hand columns in Figure 5-5 reveals some key differences. For example, when a CD player manufacturer buys headphones for its units from a supplier, more individuals are involved, supplier capability becomes more important, and the postpurchase evaluation behavior is more formalized. The headphone-buying decision illustrated is typical of the steps in a purchase made by an organization.[14] Later in the chapter we analyze more complex purchases made by industrial, reseller, and government organizations.

TYPES OF BUYING SITUATIONS

The number of people in the buying center and the length and complexity of the steps in the buying process largely depend on the specific buying situation. Researchers who have studied organizational buying identify three types of buying situations, which they have termed **buy classes.**[15] These buy classes vary from the routine reorder, or **straight rebuy,** to the completely new purchase, termed **new buy.** In between these extremes is the **modified rebuy.** Some examples will clarify the differences:

- *Straight rebuy.* Here the buyer or purchasing manager reorders an existing product or service from the list of acceptable suppliers, probably without even checking with users or influencers from the engineering, production, or quality-control departments. Office supplies and maintenance services are usually obtained as straight rebuys.
- *Modified rebuy.* In this buying situation the users, influencers, or deciders in the buying center want to change the product specifications, price, delivery schedule, or supplier. Although the item purchased is largely the same as with the straight rebuy, the changes usually necessitate enlarging the buying center to include people outside the purchasing department.
- *New buy.* Here the organization is a first-time buyer of the product or service. This involves greater potential risks in the purchase, so the buying center is enlarged to include all those who have a stake in the new buy. The purchase of CD player headphones was a new buy.

The marketing strategies of sellers facing each of these three buying situations can vary greatly because the importance of personnel from functional areas such as purchasing, engineering, production, and R&D often varies with (1) the type of buying situation and (2) the stage of the purchasing process.[16]

Read the Marketing Research Report and suppose you are a sales representative selling a component part to a manufacturer for use in one of its products. How will your sales task differ depending on the purchase (buy-class) situation?

If it is a new buy for the manufacturer, you should be prepared to act as a consultant to the buyer, work with technical personnel, and expect a long time for a buying decision to be reached. However, if the manufacturer has bought the component part before from you so it is a straight or modified rebuy, your sales task should emphasize low price and a reliable supply in meetings with the purchasing agent.

MARKETING · RESEARCH · REPORT

How the Buying Situation Affects the Buying Center and Selling Actions

How does the buy class situation influence the size and behavior of the buying center? Professors Erin Anderson, Wujin Chu, and Barton Weitz looked into the question by asking sales managers about the behavior their salespeople encounter when dealing with their industrial customers. The research findings summarized below illustrate that the buy-class situation affects buying center tendencies in different ways. This research has important implications for industrial selling that are discussed in the text.

Source: Erin Anderson, Wujin Chu, and Barton Weitz, "Industrial Purchasing: An Empirical Exploration of the Buyclass Framework," *Journal of Marketing* (July, 1987), pp. 71-86.

BUYING CENTER DIMENSION	BUY-CLASS SITUATION: NEW BUY	BUY-CLASS SITUATION: STRAIGHT/MODIFIED REBUYS
People involved	Many	Few
Decision time	Long	Short
Problem definition	Uncertain	Well defined
Buying objective	Good solution	Low price supply
Suppliers considered	New/present	Present
Buying influencer	Technical personnel	Purchasing agent

Concept Check

1 What are some typical buying criteria that organizations use in making purchase decisions?

2 What one department is almost always represented by a person in the buying center?

3 What are the three types of buying situations, or buy classes?

Three Organizational New Buy Decisions

New buy purchase decisions are ones where the most purchasing expertise is needed and where both the benefits of good decisions and penalties of bad ones are likely to be greatest. This means that effective communication among people in the buying center is especially important.[17] Tracing the stages in the buying decisions made by an appliance manufacturer, a reseller, and a government agency highlights some of the similarities and differences of organizational buying. They also illustrate the challenges involved in marketing to organizations.

Standardized electric motors are used in many applications

AN INDUSTRIAL PURCHASE: AN ELECTRIC MOTOR

Suppose GE decides to design and build a new line of clothes dryers and needs an electric motor, a key component in the dryer. Let's track the five purchasing stages in this new buy situation.

Problem Recognition After top management in GE's appliance division decides to introduce a new line of clothes dryers, engineering and R&D personnel come up with a workable design that is tested and approved. They meet with the purchasing manager to reach a **make-buy decision**—an evaluation of whether a product or its parts will be purchased from outside suppliers or built by the firm itself. The group concludes that the electric motor in each dryer should be bought, not made.

Information Search The engineering and R&D personnel develop product specifications for the electric motor, which are detailed technical requirements the motor must meet such as its horsepower, life in hours, and ability to operate at a stated temperature and humidity. Members of the purchasing and production departments then perform a **value analysis** on the electric motor—a systematic appraisal of the design, quality, and performance requirements of the product to reduce purchasing costs. For example, suppose the GE engineers conclude that an at least ⅛-horsepower motor is needed to power the dryer. The purchasing department would recommend buying a ¼-horsepower motor, which is available as a standard item from many vendors, rather than a ⅛-horsepower motor, which must be made to order at a higher cost.

In its information search the purchasing department also relies on the technical expertise of vendors in developing appropriate design specifications. Specifications are generally stated in terms of material, dimensions, and performance characteristics rather than brand name to maximize the number of qualified vendors available and to ensure genuine competition among bidders.

Alternative Evaluation The buying center must develop the necessary buying criteria for the electric motor, which in this case are (1) quality requirements, (2) on-time delivery, and (3) price, in that order. The purchasing manager is given the responsibility to select the supplier and negotiate a contract for the motors.

The next step in purchasing is soliciting bids from potential suppliers. This involves selecting the names of vendors from a **bidders list**—a list of firms believed to be qualified to supply a given item—and sending each vendor a quotation request form describing the desired quantity, delivery date, and specifications of the product.

Most purchasing departments maintain a separate bidders list for each general class of items they order. These lists are updated continuously by adding the names of potential new vendors and deleting the names of unsatisfactory vendors. To further ensure competition, many firms require that at least three bids be solicited for purchases exceeding a specified dollar amount.

Purchase Decision Unlike the short purchase stage in a consumer purchase, such as buying a bag of potato chips, in organizations the purchase stage covers the period from vendor selection and placing the purchase order until the product is delivered, which often takes months or years. This period frequently involves performing vendor follow-up, expediting the order, and renegotiating the contract terms if specification changes are made after the initial contract is awarded.

Sometimes contracts are awarded directly to vendors based on the data they provide in the quotation request forms. At other times the purchasing manager may wish to negotiate with one or more bidders, particularly on high-dollar, high-volume items. Eventually the GE purchasing manager selects two vendors and awards each a contract in the form of a purchase order—an authorization for the vendor to provide the items under the agreed-on terms and to bill the purchasing firm.

If the purchased item is of minor value and if no design or delivery changes are made in the order after it has been issued, the purchasing manager rarely follows up on the order. However, vendor follow-up is essential if conditions change or if an item is of high value, in short supply, or crucial to the firm. In the case of the electric motors, they are so critical to producing the new clothes dryers that the purchasing manager periodically checks with the two vendors to see that no problems arise.

Postpurchase Behavior When the electric motors are finally delivered, the quality control department tests them to ensure they meet specifications. If they had been unsatisfactory, the purchasing manager would have negotiated with the supplier to rework the items according to specifications or arranged for an entirely new shipment.

Experienced buyers realize that evaluation of purchase decisions is essential. The vendor's performance is evaluated after final delivery of the purchased items. This information is often noted on a vendor-rating sheet and is used to update the bidders lists kept by the purchasing department. Performance on past contracts determines a vendor's chances of being asked to bid on future purchases, and poor performance results in a vendor's name being dropped from the list.

A RESELLER PURCHASE: A HOME FOOD DEHYDRATOR

Resellers—wholesalers and retailers—resell the products they purchase without physically changing the product. As a result, the stages in their buying decision process differ from those of manufacturers. As an example, let's look at Montgomery Ward's decision to stock a home food dehydrator.

Problem Recognition Members of Ward's buying committee for electric appliances continually look for appealing new items to stock in its stores and sell through its catalogs. Open to new ideas, the buying committee considered a home food dehydrator, an electric device that dries fresh fruit and vegetables and competes with canning and freezing in home food preservation.

Information Search Ward's committee assessed the market size to see if a genuine consumer demand exists for food dehydrators. It analyzed how the dehydrators work, their quality, and the chances that unhappy consumers would return these purchased appliances to the store for a refund.

Alternative Evaluation The buying committee found no home food dehydrators of satisfactory quality they wanted to sell. Then Ward was approached by a new, start-up firm—Alternative Pioneering Systems—who sells its home food dehydrator under the Harvest Maid brand name. Initial quality-control tests showed that it met Ward's high standards for electric appliances.

A senior buyer on Ward's buying committee checked on the firm itself. He found two young entrepreneurs who had manufactured 500 such dehydrators—a number Ward could sell in a day or two if the product "hit." These entrepreneurs were currently financed on a shoestring through bank loans obtained by using their cars as collateral. The two men had several patents on their device, and it had received the Underwriter's Laboratory approval. The Ward buyer persuaded the two men (1) to seek better financing and (2) to contract

Grumman's Lunar Module lands on the moon

out the production of their dehydrators to a larger manufacturer that could produce them in the quantities and with the quality Ward required.

Purchase Decision Ward's buyer signed a contract with Alternative Pioneering Systems for its Harvest Maid home food dehydrator. At that time no other major chain or catalog store (for example, Sears, Target, J.C. Penney, or K Mart) was selling such an appliance. But although Ward had no competition from its major rivals, there was no assurance the dehydrator would sell. On a big gamble, Ward advertised the Harvest Maid dehydrator on the inside front cover of its fall catalog—an extremely valuable advertising space.

Postpurchase Behavior Ward's buyer and buying committee hit paydirt. The company sold over 20,000 dehydrators in the two fall months—the peak period for using the appliance—at a retail price of $89. Ward concluded its decision was a good one and contracted for an expanded Harvest Maid line for the following fall. Today other chains such as Sears and J.C. Penney carry the line.

A GOVERNMENT PURCHASE: APOLLO LUNAR MODULE

Highly technical, first-of-a-kind purchases present special buying problems. This is especially true of the high-performance aircraft, missile, and space systems bought by the U.S. Department of Defense and NASA, but it also applies to technical purchases such as computers, buildings, and mass-transit systems bought by industrial firms and local governments. For example, the price of New Orlean's Super Dome stadium jumped from $35 million to $165 million between groundbreaking and completion. Frequently the period between the purchase—or signing the purchase contract—and delivery of the completed system is 3 to 8 years. The lunar module, the element of the Apollo spacecraft that landed on the moon, is an example of a successful government procurement.[18]

Problem Recognition For centuries people have dreamed about a visit to the moon, but the United States did not commit to landing an American on the moon until 1961. This commitment marked the problem recognition stage in a decision to procure a system to land a man on the moon and return him safely to earth.

Information Search President Kennedy gave the job of buying a system to NASA, which set to work assessing the technical problems and developing a feasible plan for the landing. Technically, NASA wasn't sure whether the moon landing should be made from an earth orbit or moon orbit. Also, no one was certain whether the moon's surface was solid enough to support the weight of a landing vehicle or even of a man walking on it. Still, NASA decided that the awarding of contracts could not wait until it had definite answers to these questions.

NASA divided the project into pieces, or subsystems, that could be purchased from separate vendors and also decided which parts of the system it should handle and which it should contract out—its own key make-buy decisions. It divided the Apollo system into several subsystems: the Saturn booster rocket and the command, service, and lunar modules of the Apollo spacecraft.

Alternative Evaluation NASA engineers and scientists wrote the basic performance specifications for each of these subsystems. They developed buying criteria in order of importance: (1) quality of the contractor's proposed technical design, (2) technical capability demonstrated on past aerospace projects, and (3) price. The first two criteria were critical because many of the specifications were unknown when the contract was awarded and men's lives were at stake. NASA decided to buy 16 lunar modules, counting several early prototypes that would be tested on land and never see space flight.

Purchase Decision NASA requested technical proposals and price quotations from aerospace firms that had produced successful aircraft or space systems in the past. It awarded the contract to build and test 16 lunar modules to Grumman for a price of $350 million, or about $22 million each.

Postpurchase Behavior In first-of-a-kind purchases the actual purchase stage is a minor part of the entire process. The years of work start *after* the purchase. Three months after the contract award for the lunar module, Grumman concluded that technical problems had been understated and raised its price to $650 million. Thousands of technical design changes were required, and the contract price grew to $1.6 billion, or $100 million per module—almost five times the initial price. In 1969, astronauts Neil Armstrong and Buzz Aldrin made a successful moon landing in Grumman's lunar module.

Although the success of the Apollo program has not been questioned, its cost overruns have been. The U.S. Congress wants more competition to occur in the production phase of these state-of-the-art systems procurements to both increase quality and lower costs. And since the Challenger space shuttle disaster in 1986, the government is trying to stimulate private business to share more of the risk in space exploration.[19]

CONCEPT CHECK

1 **What kind of buying situation is GE's purchase of an electric motor?**

2 **What problem did NASA encounter in buying the lunar module that resulted from the lack of precise specifications being available at the time of the contract award?**

MARKETING TO ORGANIZATIONS MORE EFFECTIVELY

The three preceding examples of organizational purchases suggest steps sellers can take to increase their chances of selling products and services to organizations. Firms selling to organizations must learn four key lessons to design and

MARKETING·RESEARCH·REPORT

HOW INDUSTRIAL BUYERS SELECT WINNING BIDDERS

Members of industrial buying centers develop rule-of-thumb guidelines to simplify the complex process of selecting a winning bidder. Researchers Niren Vyas and Arch Woodside interviewed and observed individuals in 18 industrial buying centers with an annual purchase volume of more than $100,000. Some sample decision-making rules people in these buying centers used in selecting the winning bidder are as follows:

- *Find candidate vendors for the bidders list.* For straight and modified rebuy products, use existing lists of potential suppliers kept by buyers. For new buys, talk to design engineers and other buyers, draw on past experience, and search trade journals.
- *Qualify" (verify) names of satisfactory vendors.* Use distributors when immediate local availability of large numbers of parts in small quantities is essential. Use manufacturers and avoid distributors' margin of profit when a predictable usage pattern exists for a large quantity needed; establish that manufacturers have the capacity, quality, and reasonable transportation costs to fill the order.
- *Invite bids from vendors.* Try to get bids from at least three bidders. Relax criteria, when necessary, to achieve this number. Increase the number of bids when the size and importance of the purchase warrant it. Tighten criteria when necessary to restrict the number of bidders to six.
- *Evaluate the bids.* Have the purchasing department conduct a commercial evaluation, covering price, transportation and tooling costs, delivery schedule, and past performance. Have engineering and production people conduct a technical evaluation to assess the bidder's ability to meet specifications. Drop bidders who are not within 3 percent to 6 percent of the lowest bid price or who do not satisfy technical requirements.
- *Select the winning bidder.* Select 2 suppliers if the volume and importance of the product warrant it, dividing the contract equally if their prices are within 1 percent of each other or giving a larger contract to the lower bidder. Otherwise select a single supplier. Select the lowest bidder unless past performance justifies choosing the second lowest.

These guidelines help firms that want to sell products to such buyers to develop effective marketing strategies.

Source: Based on Niren Vyas and Arch Woodside, "An Inductive Model of Industrial Supplier Choice Processes," *Journal of Marketing* (Winter 1984), pp. 30–45; by permission of the American Marketing Association.

implement successful marketing strategies: (1) understand the organization's needs, (2) get on the right bidders list, (3) find the right people in the buying center, and (4) do the job.

UNDERSTAND THE ORGANIZATION'S NEEDS

As important and obvious as understanding the organization's needs seems, this guideline is violated as often with industrial products as with consumer products. A small firm, I-Point, Inc., devised a temperature-sensitive strip for frozen food packages that would change color when the freezer's temperature got too warm.

A **NutraSweet ad directed at prospective users**

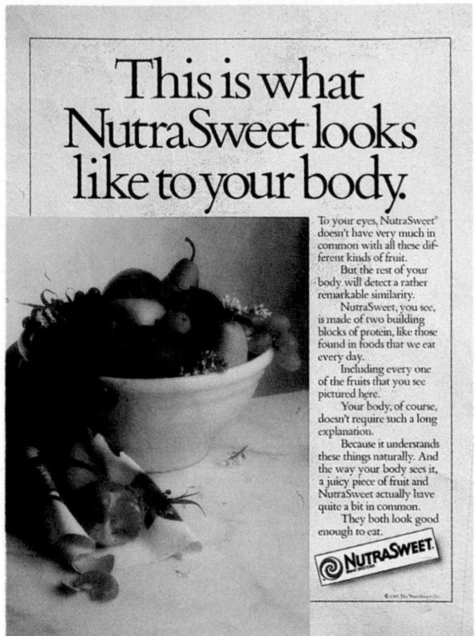

After spending $12 million developing the product, it found no food companies to buy it.[20] Airplane manufacturers such as Boeing and Lockheed conduct a "chicken test" on jet engines that potential suppliers want to sell them for their new commercial jets. To guarantee that the jet engines will be able to operate after ingesting flocks of birds, engineers buy 20 gross of chickens, stuff them into a cannon with a 4-foot diameter barrel, and fire them point-blank into a jet engine running at full throttle—as it would be running on takeoff. Rolls Royce spent several hundred million dollars on a new graphite jet engine. It had only one problem: it failed the chicken test.[21]

In contrast, the Timken Company has worked with its customers for years to design bearings to meet their requirements, rather than waiting for orders. Goodyear was able to provide the right tires for Chevrolet's newly redesigned Corvette by learning about the car's handling and performance characteristics.[22]

GET ON THE RIGHT BIDDERS LIST

As shown in the Marketing Research Report, it is critical for a firm to be considered a satisfactory or qualified supplier and to get its name on the bidders lists of organizations to which it hopes to sell. Ideally, it is desirable to know if the proposed purchase is a new buy or a straight or modified rebuy.[23] If it is a new buy, the organization must get wind of the buyer's need far enough in advance to understand it and offer a product or service to satisfy it. With a straight or modified rebuy the firm knows the need exists and understands what it is, but it can't compete unless its name is on the bidders list. This is accomplished through sending product samples to be tested and qualify its name for the list.

REACH THE RIGHT PEOPLE IN THE BUYING CENTER

One of the most difficult parts of an industrial salesperson's job is finding the "right" person in the buying center—the decider who really selects the product and supplier or the buyer who actually makes the purchase.[24] A major reason for the success of the Harvest Maid brand of home food dehydrator discussed earlier is that Alternative Pioneering Systems was able to convince the key senior buyer on the Montgomery Ward buying committee that the product was worth stocking and advertising in its catalog. Without that breakthrough, the Harvest Maid food dehydrator might not exist today.

DO THE JOB

Nothing succeeds like success; suppliers to organizations must provide what the customer wants, which leads to repeat orders and success. After G.D. Searle's chemists discovered a sweetener known as aspartame, it marketed the sweetener to Coca-Cola and 60 other manufacturers under the brand name NutraSweet, ringing up $600 million in industrial sales in the process. NutraSweet's low-calorie sweetening ability, coupled with its legitimate claim of "no unpleasant aftertaste," has generated millions of dollars of repeat business from industrial customers and the ultimate consumers who buy products, such as Diet Coke, containing NutraSweet.[25]

CONCEPT CHECK

1 **Why is getting on the right bidders list important to a prospective vendor?**

2 **When Alternative Pioneering Systems finally made its breakthrough in marketing its home food dehydrator, who was the key person in the buying center?**

SUMMARY

1 Organizational buyers are divided into three different markets: industrial, reseller, and government. There are about 13.5 million industrial firms, 3.3 million resellers, and 82,000 government units.

2 Measuring industrial, reseller, and government markets is an important first step for firms interested in gauging the size of one, two, or all three markets. The Standard Industrial Classification (SIC) system is a convenient starting point to begin this process.

3 Many aspects of organizational buying behavior are different from consumer buying behavior. Some key differences between the two include demand characteristics, number of potential buyers, dbuying objectives, buying criteria, size of the order or purchase, buyer-seller interaction, and multiple buying influences within companies.

4 The buying center concept is central to understanding organizational buying behavior. Knowing who composes the buying center and the roles they play in making purchase decisions is important in marketing to organizations. The buying center usually includes a person from the purchasing department and possibly representatives from R&D, engineering and production, depending on what is being purchased. These people can play one or more of five roles in a purchase decision: user, influencer, buyer, decider, or gatekeeper.

5 The three types of buying situations, or buy classes, are the straight rebuy, the modified rebuy, and the new buy. These form a scale ranging from a routine reorder to a totally new purchase.

6 The stages in an organizational buying decision are the same as those for consumer buying decisions: problem recognition, information search, alternative evaluation, purchase decision, and postpurchase behavior. Examples of organizational purchases described are the purchase of an electric motor by an appliance manufacturer (GE), a home food dehydrator by a reseller (Montgomery Ward), and a lunar module by a government unit (NASA).

7 To market more effectively to organizations, a firm must try to understand the organization's needs, get on the right bidders list, reach the right people in the buying center, and do the job properly.

KEY TERMS AND CONCEPTS

organizational buyers p. 114
industrial firms p. 115
resellers p. 116
government units p. 116
Standard Industrial Classification (SIC) system p. 116
organizational buying behavior p. 118
derived demand p. 119
buying objective p. 120
organizational buying criteria p. 120
reciprocity p. 122
buying center p. 123
buy classes p. 126
straight rebuy p. 126
new buy p. 126
modified rebuy p. 126
make-buy decision p. 128
value analysis p. 128
bidders' list p. 129

CHAPTER PROBLEMS AND APPLICATIONS

1 Describe the major differences between industrial firms, resellers, and government units in the United States.

2 Explain how the Standard Industrial Classification (SIC) system might be helpful in understanding industrial, reseller, and government markets and explain the limitations inherent in the SIC system.

3 Discuss the key characteristics of organizational buying that make it different from consumer buying.

4 The importance of buying criteria will often vary according to the type of product purchased. Describe the seven most commonly used buying criteria and how they might rate in importance in the purchase of paint and main-frame computers.

5 What is a buying center? Describe the roles assumed by people in a buying center and what useful questions should be raised to guide any analysis of the structure and behavior of a buying center.
6 Explain the relative influence of the purchasing function and the engineering function in the acquisition of an electronic component part during the first four stages of the organizational buying process in a new buy and in a straight rebuy situation.
7 Effective marketing is of increasing importance in today's competitive environment. How can firms more effectively market to organizations?
8 A foreign-based producer of apparel for men is interested in the sales volume for such products in the United States. The producer realizes that this is a difficult assignment but has given you a sizable fee to find these data. What information source would you examine first, and what kind of information would be found in this source?
9 A firm that is marketing multimillion-dollar wastewater treatment systems to cities has been unable to sell a new type of system. This setback has occurred even though the firm's systems are cheaper than competitive systems and meet U.S. Environmental Protection Agency (EPA) specifications. To date the firm's marketing efforts have been directed to city purchasing departments and the various state EPAs to get on approved bidders lists. Talks with city-employed personnel have indicated that the new system is very different from current systems. Therefore city sanitary and sewer department engineers, directors of these two departments, and city council members are unfamiliar with the workings of the system. Consulting engineers, hired by cities to work on the engineering and design features of these systems and paid on a percentage of system cost, are also reluctant to favor the new system. (a) What roles do the various individuals play in the purchase process for a wastewater treatment system? (b) How could the firm improve the marketing effort behind the new system?

SUGGESTED READINGS

Thomas V. Bonoma, "Major Sales: Who Really Does the Buying?" *Harvard Business Review* (May-June 1982), pp. 111–119. *This article describes the major roles played by individuals in organizational buying.*

Donald L. McCabe, "Buying Group Structure: Constriction at the Top," *Journal of Marketing* (October 1987), pp. 87–98. *This article examines how the structure of buying groups is affected by uncertainty in the buying situation.*

Ronald E. Michaels, Ralph L. Day, and Erich A. Joachimsthaler, "Role Stress Among Industrial Buyers: An Integrative Model," *Journal of Marketing* (April 1987), pp. 28–45. *This article describes the effects of role stress in the organizational buying process and implications for marketing to organizations.*

James R. Stock and Paul H. Zinszer, "The Industrial Purchase Decision for Professional Services," *Journal of Business Research* (February, 1987), pp. 1–16. *This article presents the results of one of the few studies on the buying of professional services by organizations.*

"Where Three Sales a Year Make You a Superstar," *Business Week* (February 17, 1986), pp. 76–77. *This short article details the lengthy and involved selling process for supercomputers to organizations.*

PART THREE

Targeting Marketing Opportunities

Coke
Trade-mark ®
Coca-Cola. 12 FL OZ 354 mL
PEPSI
Coca-Cola
Trade-mark®
CLASSIC

6

COLLECTING MARKETING INFORMATION

After reading this chapter you should be able to:

Identify the six steps a person can follow in reaching a decision and the significance of each step.

•

Explain the four key elements used to define a problem: the objectives, constraints, assumptions, and measures of success.

•

Structure a decision into two basic components: the controllable and uncontrollable factors.

•

Know three types of information collected to solve a problem: ideas, methods, and data.

•

Explain differences between primary and secondary data and the principal kinds of each.

•

Know how questionnaires, observations, experiments, and panels are used in marketing.

When 190,000 Taste Tests and $4 Million Were Wrong

Coca-Cola lovers who relish their Coke made with the century-old "secret formula 7X" still quake at the events that began the week of April 22, 1985.

That week the world was being prepared for a new, improved, and smoother-tasting Coke. Coca-Cola's major reason for changing the formula was that the company was getting a smaller share of the $22 billion U.S. soft-drink market. Archrival Pepsi-Cola was gaining market share, because of a sweeter taste than Coke's that had special appeal to many younger cola drinkers and also because of a series of very successful advertising campaigns featuring popular singers such as Michael Jackson and Lionel Ritchie. Because a loss of 1 percent in market share represents $220 million in lost sales, Coke executives were alarmed.

What finally triggered the Coke reformulation was a $4 million, three-year study involving over 190,000 taste tests around the United States. The study showed that in blind taste tests (the actual brand hidden from the taster) cola drinkers preferred the sweeter Pepsi to the crisper taste of the original Coke. So Coca-Cola marketing executives developed a new, sweeter formula for Coke—the formula that became "new" Coke. The result: in blind taste tests consumers preferred the new to old Coke formula 53 percent to 47 percent.

For the three months following the introduction of new Coke, Coca-Cola's Atlanta headquarters was bombarded by 1,500 phone calls daily from angry Coke drinkers asking the company to return to 7X—the original Coke formulation. On July 10, 1985, in front of TV cameras, the head of the company announced the return of 7X as "Coca-Cola Classic"—a name that won out over "Original Coke," "Coke 1886," "Old Coke," and "Coke 1"—and retained the new formulation as simply "Coke." The decision to bring 7X back seems wise: Coca-Cola Classic is now outselling new Coke 8 to 1.[1]

Why did the taste tests and marketing research lead to a wrong decision? Think about factors that can introduce bias into a taste test in a shopping mall in which people are asked to sip a sample of cola from two cups and tell which they prefer. What additional factors might influence a consumer's choice of a brand of cola?

The example of Coca-Cola shows both the potential benefits and dangers of marketing research, the topics of Chapters 6 and 7. At the end of this chapter we shall describe problems with the Coca-Cola taste tests and the lessons that were learned.

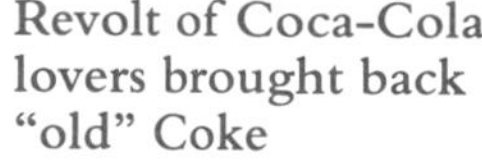

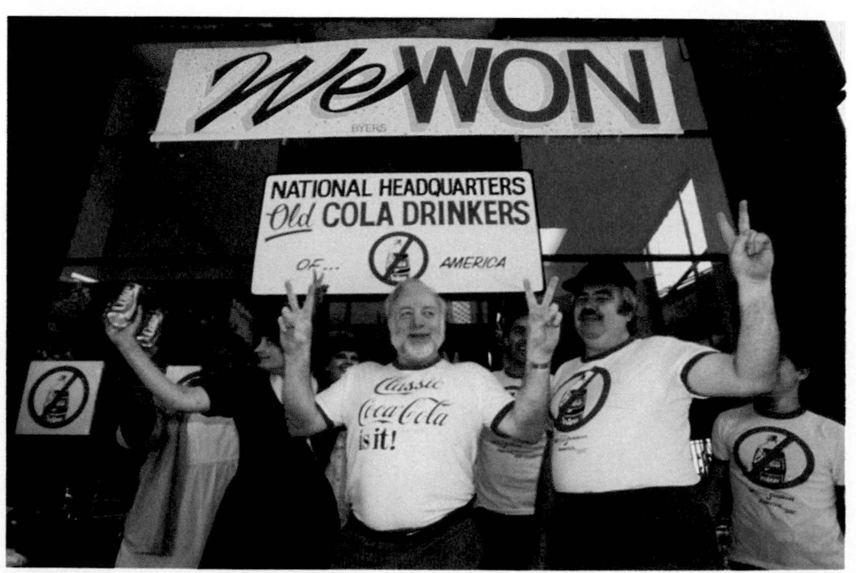

Revolt of Coca-Cola lovers brought back "old" Coke

Courtesy Philip Amdal/Time Magazine

THE ROLE OF MARKETING RESEARCH

To place marketing research in perspective, we can describe (1) what it is, (2) some of the difficulties in conducting marketing research, and (3) the process marketing executives can use to make effective decisions.

WHAT MARKETING RESEARCH IS AND DOES

Marketing research is the process of defining a marketing problem and opportunity, systematically collecting and analyzing information, and recommending actions to improve an organization's marketing activities.

A Means of Reducing Uncertainty Assessing the needs and wants of consumers and providing information to help design an organization's marketing program to satisfy them is the role that marketing research performs. This means marketing research attempts to identify and define both marketing problems and opportunities and to generate and evaluate marketing actions.[2] Although marketing research can provide few answers with complete assurance, it can reduce the uncertainty and increase the likelihood of the success of marketing decisions.[3] It is a great help to the marketing managers who make the final decisions.

Anyone for Juice in a Box? Suppose in the early 1980's you were asked by a marketing researcher whether you would drink unrefrigerated orange, apple, or cranberry juice that was packaged in a paper carton. This may have seemed farfetched then in most parts of the United States, but not in Europe, where it had become very common for packaging fruit juices and milk. The container is aseptic packaging, in which a sterilized product is put into a sterilized container.

Examples of aseptic packaging

Photo by Ray Marklin

The container is sealed airtight so the product requires neither refrigeration nor preservatives. The key question was whether the aseptic packaging technology could be moved successfully here from Europe, where refrigeration is less widespread than in the United States.

Would American consumers buy fresh juice in boxes stored on a retailer's shelf at room temperature? Do consumers need to be educated about the benefits of this product? Would they be suspicious of unrefrigerated, fresh juice in a box? The answers to these kinds of questions asked by Ocean Spray's marketing researchers resulted in advertisements to address such concerns when it introduced cranberry juice in a box in New England and New York. It led to Ocean Spray's very successful national introduction of aseptic packaging.

WHY GOOD MARKETING RESEARCH IS DIFFICULT

The dilemmas faced by marketing researchers at Ocean Spray when trying to assess consumers' willingness to buy juices sold in aseptic packages illustrate why good marketing research requires great care—especially because of the inherent difficulties in asking consumers questions.[4]

- Do consumers really know whether they are likely to buy a particular product that they probably have never thought about before? Can they really assess its advantages and disadvantages on the spur of the moment?
- Even if they know the answer, will they reveal it? When personal or status questions are involved, people may give wrong answers—knowingly or unknowingly.
- Will their actual purchase behavior be the same as their stated interest or intentions? Can they say with certainty when they are likely to buy their next car or suit? Will they buy the same brand they say they will? To appear progressive, consumers often overstate their likelihood of buying a new product.

When people know they are being measured, the very measurement process itself can significantly affect their answers and behaviors. A task of marketing research is to overcome these difficulties to provide useful information.

STEPS IN MAKING EFFECTIVE DECISIONS: DECIDE

A **decision** is a conscious choice from among two or more alternatives. All of us make many such decisions daily. At work we choose from alternative ways to accomplish an assigned task. At college we choose from alternative courses. As consumers we choose from alternative brands. No magic formula guarantees correct decisions all the time.

Managers and researchers have tried to improve the outcomes of decisions by using more formal, systematic approaches to *decision making,* the act of consciously choosing from alternatives. People who do not use some kind of system—and many do not—may make poor decisions. The systematic approach to making decisions (or problem solving) described in this chapter and the next is based on six steps, represented by the acronym DECIDE. It is one of several approaches that provide a mental checklist for making any decision—either business or personal. For example, suppose you are the product manager

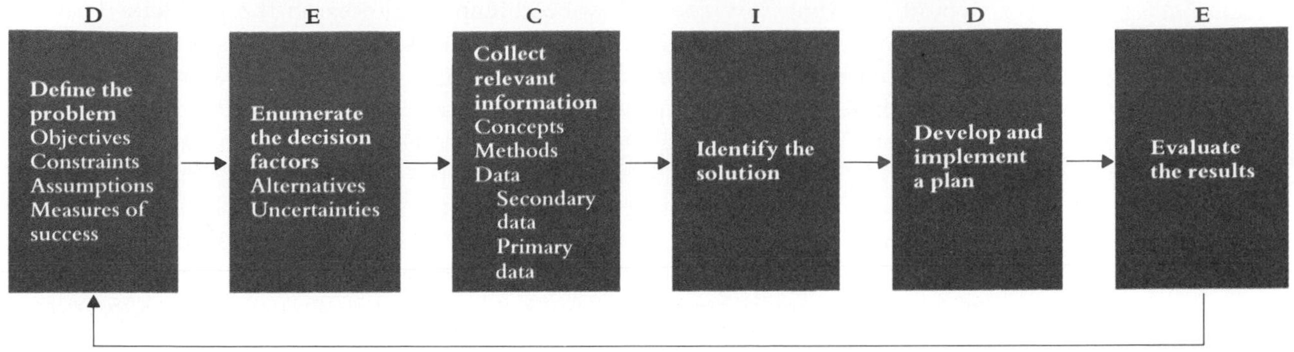

FIGURE 6-1
Details of the first three steps in the DECIDE process

for Ocean Spray cranberry juice. You might outline one of your typical decisions using the DECIDE process in this way:

- D—Define the problem: choose an advertising medium to introduce aseptically packaged cranberry juice nationally in the U.S. market.
- E—Enumerate the decision factors: consider (1) alternative media and (2) uncontrollable factors that might affect the decision.
- C—Collect relevant information: obtain the information pertinent to selecting a medium.
- I—Identify a solution: select the best advertising medium from among the alternatives enumerated.
- D—Develop and implement a plan: write a plan for using the advertising medium selected and put the plan into effect.
- E—Evaluate the results: assess whether the advertising medium chosen was successful and why.

Although Ocean Spray's marketing research and actions led the way, other U.S. firms soon adopted aseptic packages, and today Americans use more than 1.5 billion aseptic cartons annually.[5]

The first three steps in the DECIDE process (Figure 6-1) are analyzed in in this chapter and the last three steps in Chapter 7.

CONCEPT CHECK

1 **What is marketing research?**

2 **What are the problems in collecting marketing research data from consumers when they know they are being measured?**

STEP 1 IN DECIDE: DEFINE THE PROBLEM PRECISELY

Toy designers at Fisher-Price Toys, the nation's largest toy maker for children under 6, had a problem some years back: they developed toys they thought kids

would like, but how could they be certain? To research the problem, Fisher-Price got six children, aged 3 to 4, to make twice-a-week visits to play at its state-licensed nursery school in East Aurora, New York.[6] However, they soon lost their jobs: Fisher-Price changes its toy testers every 6 weeks to ensure that one group's way-out ideas don't lead to changes the nation's toy users don't want.

Fisher-Price's toy testing shows how to define the problem and its four key elements: objectives, constraints, assumptions, and measures of success. For example, the original model of a classic Fisher-Price toy, the chatter telephone, was simply a wooden phone with a dial that rang a bell. Observers noted, however, that the children kept grabbing the receiver like a handle to pull the phone along behind them, so a designer added wheels, a noisemaker, and eyes that bobbed up and down on an experimental version of the toy.

OBJECTIVES

Objectives are the goals the decision maker seeks to achieve in solving a problem. Typical marketing objectives are increasing revenues and profits, discovering what consumers are aware of and want, and finding out why a product isn't selling well. For Fisher-Price the immediate objective was to decide whether to market the old or new chatter telephone.

CONSTRAINTS

The **constraints** in a decision are the restrictions placed on potential solutions by the nature and importance of the problem. Common constraints in marketing problems are limitations on the time and money available to solve the problem. Thus Fisher-Price might set two constraints on its decision to select either the old or new version of the chatter telephone: the decision must be made in 10 weeks, and no research budget is available beyond that needed for collecting data in its nursery school.

In problem solving, there are human constraints as well: a person's mind can have "tunnel vision" that unnecessarily restricts the search for alternatives. Then the task is to uncover new alternatives that may lead to a solution. As an example of redefining a problem, solve these two puzzles, paying attention to what thoughts go through your mind[7]:

1. Connect the nine dots to the left using four straight lines without lifting your pen from the paper or retracing a line.
2. Arrange the six matches to the left in a pattern that gives four equilateral triangles of the same size. (If you've forgotten your geometry, an equilateral triangle is a triangle with three sides of equal length.)

The solutions appear in Figure 6-2, along with some suggestions for opening your mind and finding creative solutions to problems—techniques that marketing people looking for new products or original advertising copy often use.

ASSUMPTIONS

Constraints often require a person to make **assumptions,** or conjectures about factors or situations that simplify the problem enough to allow it to be solved within these constraints. If more money or time becomes available, sometimes the assumptions themselves are investigated. For example, the product manager for the Fisher-Price chatter telephone might make these assumptions: (1) the children in the Fisher-Price nursery school are typical of all American children and (2) an indication of their preference is the amount of time spent playing with each toy when other toys are also available.

MEASURES OF SUCCESS

Effective decision makers specify **measures of success,** which are criteria or standards used in evaluating proposed solutions to the problem. For the Fisher-Price problem, if a measure of success were the total time children spend playing with each of the two designs, the results of observing them would lead to clear-cut actions as follows:

OUTCOME OF DATA COLLECTION	MARKETING ACTION
Children spend more time playing with old design.	Continue with old design; don't introduce new design.
Children spend more time playing with new design.	Introduce new design; drop old design.

One test of whether marketing research should be undertaken is if different outcomes will lead to different marketing actions. If all the research outcomes lead to the same action—such as top management sticking with the older design regardless of what the observed children like—the research is useless and a waste of money.

In this case research results showed that kids liked the new design, so Fisher-Price introduced its noise-making pull-toy telephone, which has become a toy classic and sold millions.

Most marketing researchers would agree with philosopher John Dewey's observation that "a problem well-defined is half-solved," but they know that defining a problem is an incredibly difficult, although essential, task. For example, if the objectives are too broad, the problem may not be researchable. If they are too narrow, as was the situation in reformulating Coca-Cola, the value of the research results may be seriously lessened. This is why marketing researchers spend so much time in defining a marketing problem precisely and writing a formal proposal describing the research to be done.

STEP 2 IN DECIDE: ENUMERATE THE DECISION FACTORS

Decision factors are the different sets of variables—the alternatives and uncertainties—that combine to give the outcome of a decision. These two sets of variables differ by the degree of control that the decision maker can exert over them. **Alternatives** are the factors over which the decision maker has complete

FIGURE 6-2
Solutions to the dot and match problems

Source: Based on Martin Scheerer, "Problem Solving," *Scientific American* (April 1963), pp. 118-128.

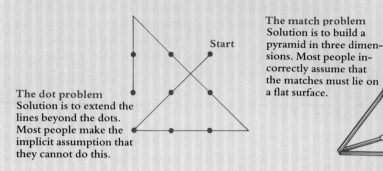

The solutions to the dot and match problems are shown below, along with the tricks a person's mind plays that may prevent solving the **problem**.

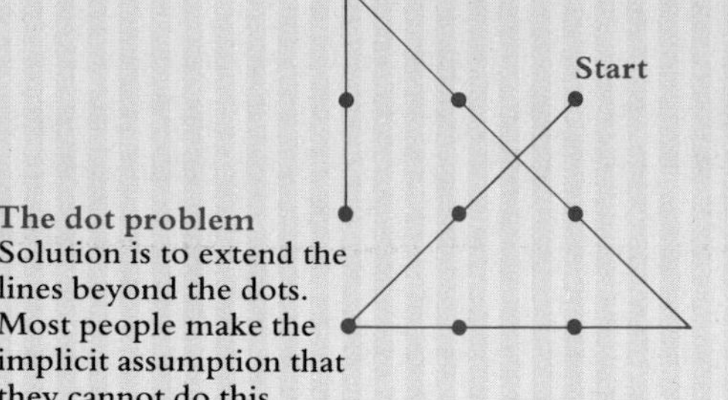

Start
The dot problem
Solution is to extend the lines beyond the dots. Most people make the implicit assumption that they cannot do this.

The match problem
Solution is to build a pyramid in three dimensions. Most people incorrectly assume that the matches must lie on a flat surface.

Experts say that people can do a number of things to open up their minds and overcome implicit constraints or assumptions that inhibit solutions:

1. Recast or restate the problem.
2. Make the problem more explicit by writing it down or stating it aloud to a friend or co-worker (including the objectives, constraints, assumptions, and measures of success).
3. Leave it for a while to "simmer on the back burner" before attacking it afresh.

command. **Uncertainties** are the uncontrollable factors that the decision maker cannot influence. In Step 2 of DECIDE the decision maker faces the problem of identifying in detail (1) the principal alternatives that can be considered reasonable approaches to solving the problem and (2) the major uncertainties that can affect a particular alternative and result in its being a good or a poor solution to the problem.

ALTERNATIVES: THE CONTROLLABLE DECISION FACTORS

Experienced marketing managers insist on searching for more than a single alternative solution to a problem because the new alternatives may lead to better solutions. One widely used method is to start the problem statement with, "In what ways can we . . .?" For example:

- In what ways can we put our Xerox copier to new uses?
- In what ways can we better demonstrate our Wang word processor to reach more customers?
- In what ways can we use our present technology at Texas Instruments to reach new markets?

With respect to the first question, the Xerox Corporation probably exists today because although its early plain-paper photocopier was a disaster for its intended use, it did make copies that could be used in offset printing. Discovering this

Duds 'N Suds

Photo by Ray Marklin

fact, the executives at Xerox used revenues from this application to perfect and sell the Xerox plain-paper copier. They had temporarily redefined their task to discover and produce a copier for a different application.[8]

To develop new alternatives, creative people often blend unusual elements into a winning combination that doesn't occur to the average person. An Iowa State University student observed that today's college students want a comfortable social atmosphere and also have to do their own laundry. The result: "Duds 'N Suds," a chain of laundromat-pubs located near more than 100 college campuses across the United States.

Talking to customers, trading ideas with co-workers, holding formal brainstorming sessions, and learning from competitors are efficient ways to search for alternative ideas for improving marketing mix actions. Using these techniques to uncover new products is discussed in Chapter 9.

UNCERTAINTIES: THE UNCONTROLLABLE DECISION FACTORS

Well-chosen alternatives can go haywire because of uncertainties, which can relate to factors within the firm or can involve consumers, competitors, national or international affairs, or even the weather.

Creative minds at Booz, Allen & Hamilton's research division slaved over what they were sure was a great new product idea: bubble gum a child could eat. But they could never lick two key uncertainties. First, tests with kids showed that until they got the knack of blowing bubbles, they would dribble the sticky stuff down their chins. This consumer uncertainty was also tied to a technical one: the research division found that foaming agents safe to eat made poor bubbles.

Even the weather can be a critical marketing uncertainty. Booz, Allen & Hamilton's research lab developed a temporary hair coloring the consumer applied by inserting a solid block of hair dye into a specially designed comb. It was a disaster. Researchers subsequently discovered that when people perspired on hot days, any extra dye applied to their hair simply ran down their foreheads and necks. One of the company's executives explained, "It just didn't occur to us to look at this under conditions where people perspire."[9]

CONCEPT CHECK

1 What are examples of constraints in solving a problem?

2 What does "measure of success" mean?

3 What is the difference between uncertainties and alternatives?

STEP 3 IN DECIDE: COLLECT RELEVANT INFORMATION

Collecting enough relevant information to make a rational, informed decision sometimes simply means using your knowledge to decide immediately. At other times it entails collecting an enormous amount of information at great expense.

Defined broadly, three kinds of information used to solve marketing problems are concepts, methods, and data. To understand the abstract topic of information, assume you are the marketing vice-president for Scripto and are struggling to find a new writing instrument to introduce into the market. The steps you have gone through are shown in the Marketing Action Memo and are illustrated in the following pages using the Scripto example.

CONCEPTS

One valuable type of concept, a **hypothesis,** is a conjecture about the relationship of two or more factors or what might happen in the future. Hypotheses that lead to marketing actions can come from many sources: theoretical reasoning, marketing studies, technical breakthroughs, informal conversations, and even educated guesses.

For example, as the marketing vice-president of Scripto, you can marshal the following facts:

- More than 1 billion ball-point disposable stick pens are sold in the United States annually.
- Stick pens are the most widely used writing instruments by students and teenagers. Eraser Mate has introduced an erasable ink pen with refills selling for $1.60 that is widely used by students.

From this information, you can develop a hypothesis: there is a substantial demand—especially among students and teenagers—for a disposable, erasable pen. A **new product concept** is a tentative description of a product or service a firm might offer for sale. A "disposable, erasable pen" is a new product concept that Scripto wanted to consider.

METHODS

Methods are the approaches a researcher can use to solve part or all of a problem. For example, as marketing vice-president of Scripto you face a number of methodological questions, including:

MARKETING·ACTION·MEMO

"ERASES THE INK, NOT THE PAPER": SCRIPTO'S ERASABLE PEN

When K. Douglas Martin took over as president of Scripto, the company had a problem: it was strong only in mechanical pencils, a small segment of the over $1 billion writing instrument market. Furthermore, the company was especially weak in sales to the teenage and young adult markets. What Martin felt was needed was "a mainstream writing instrument with appeal to a young audience."

About that time Gillette started marketing Eraser Mate, an erasable ink pen with refills that sold for $1.69 in retail stores. Scripto itself had been researching erasable ink for years and had filed for patents.

Scripto measured the movement of the Gillette pens out of warehouses serving 1,200 drug stores and discovered the pens were selling better than Flair markers or Paper Mate 98-cent ball-point pens. Scripto made a telephone survey of 2,000 randomly selected households and was astounded to discover 11 percent had the pens actually in their house and 86 percent of these would buy them again. In addition, 65 percent of the users were under 18 with a surprising 42 percent in the 11 to 14 age group.

Scripto concluded that erasable pens fill a real student need. Also, it knew teenagers used disposable, ball-point pens more than any other writing instrument. Trade association data showed that more than 1 billion such pens are sold a year. Scripto's conclusion: produce the world's first disposable, erasable pen.

Group interviews of students revealed they thought 98 cents was a reasonable price for a disposable, erasable pen and they'd buy this pen rather than a 25-cent disposable Bic. Test markets for the pen showed it sold well at 98 cents, so this became the introductory price.

Group interviews also came up with the sales slogan, "Erases the ink, not the paper." The resulting TV commercial was tested on a sample of potential consumers with fantastic results: 98 percent remembered the pen erased ink—the key product benefit—and 91 percent said they would probably or definitely buy the product when introduced at retail. The result of this marketing research is Scripto's very successful erasable pen.

Source: Based on "Success of Scripto Erasable Pen due to Marketing Research," *Marketing News* (January 23, 1981), p. 5; by permission of the American Marketing Association.

- How do you ask students about the price they might pay for the proposed pen?
- How do you phrase a question to determine whether they would buy the product if it were available?
- How do you forecast expected sales after the new product is introduced?

Millions of other people have asked exactly these same questions about millions of other products and services.

How can you find and use the methodologies that other marketing researchers have found successful? Information on useful methods is available in tradebooks, textbooks, and handbooks that relate to marketing and marketing

Journals that describe methods to help solve marketing problems

research.[10] Some periodicals and technical journals such as the *Journal of Marketing* and the *Journal of Marketing Research* summarize methods and techniques valuable in addressing marketing problems. Of course, as the Scripto marketing vice-president, you must apply the methods that have worked for others to your particular problems with your new pen. Special methods vital to marketing are (1) sampling and (2) statistical inference.

Sampling Marketing researchers often select a group of distributors, customers, or prospects, ask them questions, and treat their answers as typical of all those in whom they are interested. There are two ways of sampling, or selecting representative elements from a population: probability and nonprobability sampling. With **probability sampling** precise rules are used to select the sample such that each element of the population has a specific known chance of being selected. For example, if a college wants to know how last year's 1,000 graduates are doing, it can put their names in a bowl and randomly select 50 names of graduates to contact. The chance of being selected—50/1,000 or 0.05—is known in advance, and all graduates have an equal chance of being contacted. This procedure helps select a sample (the 50 graduates) that is representative of the entire population (the 1,000 graduates) and allows conclusions to be drawn about the entire population.

When time and budget are limited, researchers may use **nonprobability sampling** and use arbitrary judgments to select the sample so that the chance of selecting a particular element may be unknown or 0. If the college decides arbitrarily to select the 50 graduates from last year's class who live closest to the college, many members of the class have been arbitrarily eliminated. This has introduced a bias that makes it dangerous to draw conclusions about the population from this geographically restricted sample.

Statistical Inference The method of **statistical inference** is used to draw conclusions about a *population* (the "universe" of all people, stores, or salespeople about which they wish to generalize) from a *sample* (some elements of the universe) taken from that population.

To draw accurate inferences about the population, the sample elements should be representative of that universe. If the sample is not typical, bias can be introduced, resulting in bad marketing decisions. For example, had Scripto

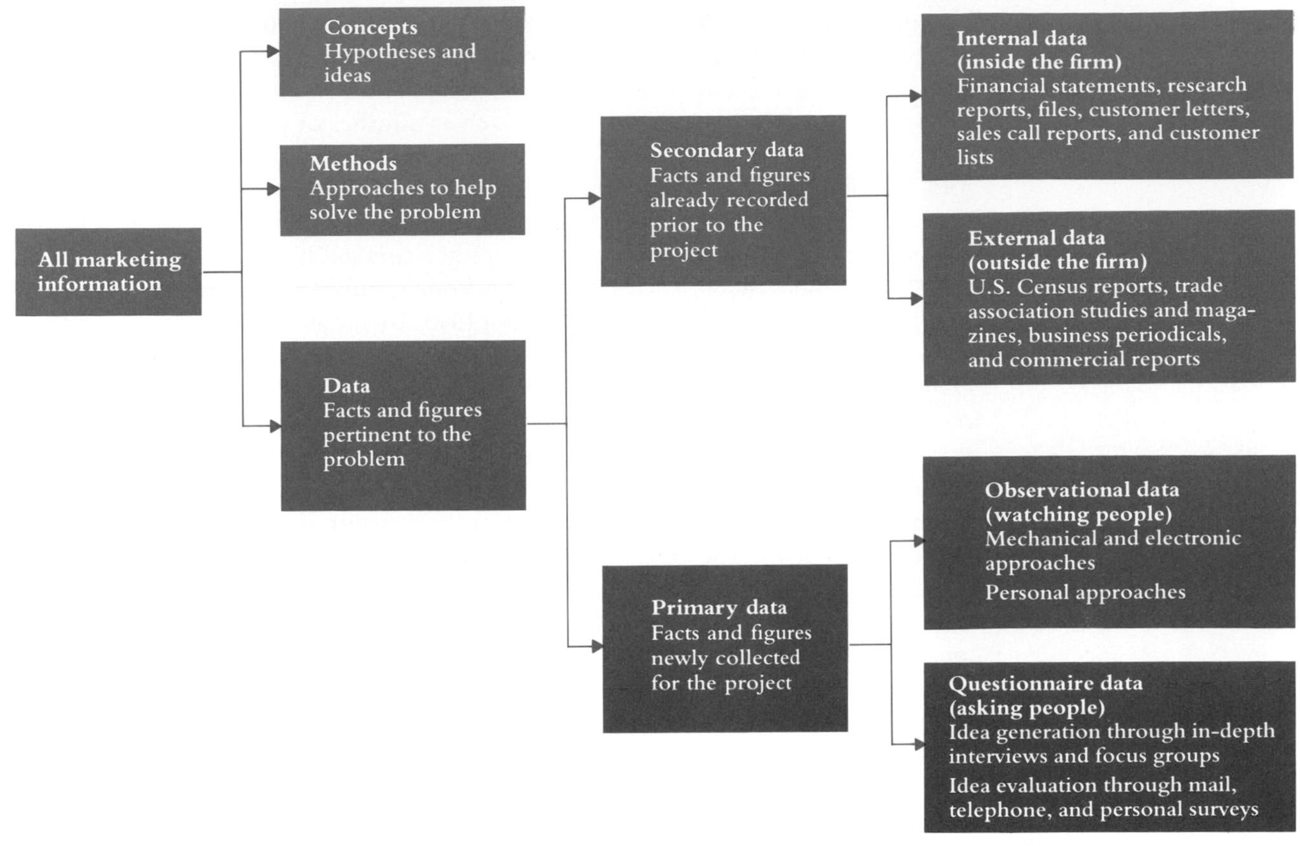

FIGURE 6-3
Types of marketing information

selected a nonrepresentative sample of people who said they didn't like Gillette's Eraser Mate pen, it probably would have dropped the idea of introducing its own competing pen.

SECONDARY DATA

Figure 6-3 shows how the different kinds of marketing information fit together. **Data,** the facts and figures pertinent to the problem, are divided into two main parts: secondary data and primary data. **Secondary data** are those which have already been recorded before the project at hand, whereas **primary data** are those facts and figures which are newly collected for the project.

Internal Secondary Data Data that have already been collected and exist inside the business firm or other organization are internal secondary data. These include financial statements (like the firm's balance sheet and income statement), research reports, customer letters, sales reports on customer calls, and customer lists. For example, Scripto's company records revealed that its strength lay in mechanical pencils, a relatively minor part of the billion dollar a year writing instrument market. The records also showed that Scripto's pen product line had not held its own against pens such as Flair and Bic.

External Secondary Data Published data from outside the firm are external secondary data. Probably the best known are U.S. Census Bureau reports. The *U.S. Census of Population* is published every 10 years and provides detailed information on American households, such as number of people per household, their ages, their sex, household income, and education of the head of the household. These are basic sources of information used by manufacturers and retailers to identify characteristics and trends of ultimate consumers.

Other census reports are vital to business firms selling products and services to organizations. The *U.S. Census of Manufactures,* published about every 5 years, lists the number and size of manufacturing firms by industry group (the Standard Industrial Classifications described in Chapter 5). The *U.S. Census of Retail Trade,* also published about every 5 years, provides comparable detailed information on retailers.

In addition, trade associations, universities, and business periodicals provide detailed data of value to marketing researchers. A number of commercial organizations also serve the research needs of consumer goods manufacturers. The best known is the A.C. Nielsen Company's Nielsen Television Ratings, discussed later in the chapter. *Sales and Marketing Management* magazine publishes four special issues each year that provide useful data for firms selling both consumer and industrial products; sample data from the magazine appear in Chapter 7. Selling Areas-Marketing, Inc. (SAMI), uses a large sample of warehouses nationwide to measure warehouse withdrawals of consumer products that in turn are sold to retail establishments such as grocery stores and discount stores. Also, hundreds of useful computerized data bases can be accessed by a telephone link from a personal computer on a marketer's desk.

As the Scripto vice-president, you could use the *U.S. Census of Population* data to identify the number of students and young adults according to age group. You also could use a commercial report produced by SAMI to measure warehouse withdrawals and determine that Gillette's Eraser Mate is selling better than Flair markers or Paper Mate ball-point pens.

Some new marketing data services sell *single-source data,* in which a single firm offers both general secondary data on consumer demographics and specific primary data such as consumer purchases in response to TV ads or free samples. An example of a single-source data service tailored to the needs of a marketing manager is BehaviorScan, which monitors both the TV viewing habits and supermarket purchases of more than 20,000 U.S. households—services that previously had to be bought from two or more separate suppliers. Some typical uses and results of single-source data services:

1. Campbell Soup's Swanson frozen dinners shifted a TV ad campaign from a serious to light theme and increased sales of Swanson dinners 14 percent.
2. After only eight weeks of market testing, Quaker Oats decided to launch its new "Oh!s" dry breakfast cereal nationally.
3. Richardson-Vicks dropped plans for stepped-up media advertising for its Olay Beauty Cleanser when tests showed the extra advertising wouldn't even pay for itself.[11]

To understand how single-source data services work, see the Marketing Action Memo.

Advantages and Disadvantages of Secondary Data A general rule among marketing people is to use secondary data first and then collect primary data. Two important advantages of secondary data are (1) the tremendous time savings if the data have already been collected and published and (2) the low cost (for example, most census reports are available for only a few dollars each). Furthermore, a greater level of detail is often available through secondary data. Because the U.S. Census Bureau can require business establishments to report information about themselves, industry data usually are more complete than if a private organization attempted to collect them.

However, these advantages must be weighed against some significant disadvantages. First, the secondary data may be out of date. If, working for Scripto, you use 1980 *U.S. Census of Population* data, by 1989—when you need it—the data would have been already 9 years old. Second, the definitions or categories might not be quite right for your purposes. For example, you are interested in the age group from 13 to 16, but many census data age statistics appear only from the 10 to 14 and 15 to 19 age groupings. Finally, because the data are collected for another purpose, they may not be specific enough for your needs as a marketing researcher. In such cases it may be necessary to collect primary data.

MARKETING·ACTION·MEMO

"SINGLE-SOURCE DATA"—A NEW SOURCE OF MARKETING INFORMATION

Since 1983 a new, state-of-the-art marketing research service has changed the way data are being collected to relate TV viewing and supermarket purchases.

This has turned up such unlikely—but useful—facts as "Search for Tomorrow" daytime TV serial watchers buy 27 percent more spaghetti sauce than average but 22 percent less V-8 vegetable juice. In contrast, "All My Children" viewers are about average buyers of spaghetti sauce but buy 46 percent more V-8 juice than average according to *Fortune* magazine. As a direct result, Campbell Soup has advertised its Prego spaghetti sauce on "Search" and V-8 on "Children."

The sources of such facts are "single-source data" services—data collection services that follow the behavior of specific households all the way from TV viewing to actual purchases at the grocery checkout counter. BehaviorScan, one example offered by Information Resources, Inc. (IRI), tracks about 2,500 households in each of eight small-town markets such as Visalia, California; Marion, Indiana; and Pittsfield, Massachusetts. Sampled households have their TV habits checked by telephone-linked microcomputers and their supermarket purchases monitored by checkout counter electronic scanners tied to a special identification card they show the clerk. To test the effect of different TV commercials on grocery purchases, IRI can change the commercials that part of its households see with a simple flick of a switch in the local TV station. The service also measures how consumers respond to price, coupons, free samples, newspaper ads, and point-of-purchase displays.

Source: Felix Kessler, "High-Tech Shocks in Ad Research," *Fortune*, July 7, 1986), pp. 58-62; *Nielsen Researcher*, Vol. 1, No. 2, (1987), pp. 16-19.

CONCEPT CHECK

1 What are methods?

2 What is the difference between secondary and primary data?

3 What kind of information did Scripto use from the *U.S. Census of Population* on the number of Americans in various age groups?

PRIMARY DATA

There are really only two ways to collect primary data, the original data for a marketing study: (1) by observing people and (2) by asking them questions.

Observational Data Watching, either mechanically or in person, how people actually behave is the way marketing researchers collect **observational data.** National TV ratings, such as those of the A.C. Nielsen Company shown in Figure 6-4, are an example of mechanical observational data collected by a "people meter," which is attached to TV sets in 4,000 homes across the country. The people meter is a small box wired to every TV set in the household. When a household member watches TV, he or she is supposed to push a button on the box and to push it again when he or she stops watching. All information is sent automatically through phone lines to Nielsen each night. So the people meter is supposed to measure who in the household is watching what program on every TV set owned. The Nielsen TV ratings in Figure 6-4 are the percentage of people-meter households whose TV sets are tuned to the program.

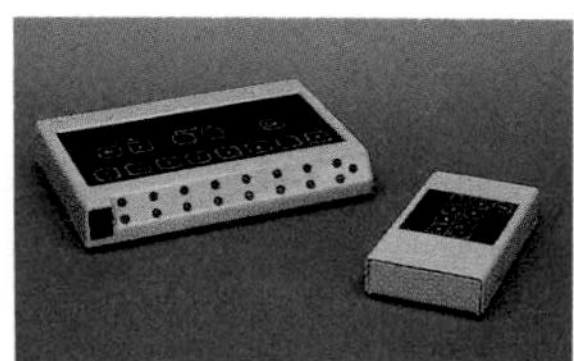

A Nielsen "people meter" collects information about a household's TV viewing

The people meter's limitations—as with all observational data collected mechanically—relate to how its measurements are taken. Critics of people meters aren't so sure the devices are measuring what they are supposed to. They are concerned that many household members, especially teenagers and the elderly, will find it annoying to hit the button every time they start or stop watching TV. If the intrusion of the device into a household's life-style is serious, it may refuse to let the Nielsen devices be attached. The potential result is a biased sample of households that may not be representative of U.S. TV viewing.[12] Supporters of people meters believe they are better than the two systems they replaced, which are described in Questions 2 and 3 at the end of the chapter.

Nielsen ratings report the percentage of the 88.6 million American households with TV that are watching a specific program. Precision in Nielsen ratings is critical because 1 percentage point change can mean gaining or losing up to $40 million during the main viewing season (the fall and winter months before spring reruns start). The Nielsen peoplemeter ratings show that for the main 1987-1988 viewing season the 3 major television networks (ABC, CBS, and NBC) lost 9 percent of their average prime time audience from the previous season—at least partly the result of cable television, independent stations, and VCRs. Because of the lower ratings, the 3 networks had to give advertisers $100 million in free advertising time to compensate for ratings that fell below guarantees.[13] The reason is that advertisers pay rates based on the guaranteed size of audience for a TV program. Programs that have consistently low rat-

RANK	PROGRAM	NIELSEN RATING
1	The Cosby Show	28.0
2	A Different World	25.1
3	Cheers	23.4
4	Golden Girls	22.0
5	Growing Pains	21.6
6	Who's The Boss	21.3
7	Night Court	21.2
8	60 Minutes	20.7
9	Murder, She Wrote	20.3
10	Alf	18.9

Source: CBS, A.C. Nielsen Company as reported in Dennis Kneale, "As TV Season Ends, Ratings Show Networks Lost Millions of Viewers," *The Wall Street Journal* (April 18, 1988), p. 34.

FIGURE 6-4
Nielsen ratings of the top 10 regularly scheduled national television shows (April 10, 1988)

ings—less than 15 percent or 16 percent—often can't get advertisers and are dropped from the air.

Personal observational data, which are collected by having a person watch a marketing activity, are also a type of primary data. For example, Procter & Gamble observes how consumers bake cakes in its Duncan Hines kitchens to see if the baking instructions on the cake mix box are understood and followed correctly. Chrysler watches how drivers sit behind the wheel of the car to see if they can turn or push the radio and air conditioner knobs conveniently. Marketing researchers for Breyers ice cream visited six families at home to see exactly when and how people ate their ice cream—the occasion and the toppings.[14]

Personal observation is both useful and flexible, but it can be costly and unreliable when different observers report different conclusions in watching the same event. Also, although observation can reveal *what* people do, it cannot easily determine *why* they do it, such as why they are buying or not buying a product. This is a principal reason for using questionnaires.

Questionnaire Data Marketing researchers obtain **questionnaire data** by asking people about their attitudes, awareness, intentions, and behaviors. So many questions might be asked in questionnaires, it is essential that the researcher concentrate on those directly related to the marketing problem at hand. Many marketing researchers divide questionnaire data used for hypothesis generation from those used for hypothesis evaluation.

Marketing studies for *hypothesis generation* seek to uncover hypotheses that can be evaluated in later research. Hamburger Helper didn't fare too well with consumers when General Mills introduced it. Initial instructions called for cooking a half pound of hamburger separately from the noodles or potatoes, which were later mixed with the hamburger. *Individual interviews* (a single researcher asking questions of one respondent) showed consumers (1) didn't think it contained enough meat and (2) didn't want the hassle of cooking in two different pots. So the Hamburger Helper product manager changed the recipe to call for

FIGURE 6-7
Typical problems in wording questions

PROBLEM	SAMPLE QUESTION	EXPLANATION
Leading question	Why do you like Wendy's fresh meat hamburgers better than those of competitors made with frozen meat?	Consumer is led to make statement favoring Wendy's hamburgers.
Ambiguous question	Do you eat at fast food restaurants regularly? ☐ Yes ☐ No	What is meant by word *regularly*—once a day, once a month, or what?
Unanswerable question	What was the occasion for your eating your first hamburger?	Who can remember the answer? Does it matter?
Two questions in one	Do you eat Wendy's hamburgers and chili? ☐ Yes ☐ No	How do you answer if you eat Wendy's hamburgers but not chili?
Nonexhaustive question	Where do you live? ☐ At home ☐ In dormitory	What do you check if you live in an apartment?
Nonmutually exclusive answers	What is your age? ☐ Under 20 ☐ 20 to 40 ☐ 40 and over	What answer does a 40-year-old check?

as "yes" to the researcher who tabulates them, but they suggest that dramatically different marketing actions be directed to each of these two prospective consumers. Therefore it is essential that marketing research questions be worded precisely so that all respondents interpret the same question similarly.

Interviews and surveys of distributors—retailers and wholesalers in the marketing channel—are also very important for manufacturers. A reason given for the success of many Japanese consumer products in the U.S. market, such as Sony Walkmans and Toyota automobiles, is the stress that Japanese marketers place on obtaining accurate information from their distributors.[18]

Ethical Aspects of Collecting Questionnaire Data Obtaining marketing research data through telephone and personal interviews is increasingly difficult. Not only do some consumers, retailers, and wholesalers feel they have been bombarded by too many questionnaires, but they are increasingly suspicious of interviewers who claim to be collecting marketing research data but instead are creating an opportunity to get a foot in the door—often both literally and figuratively—and start a sales presentation. This unethical practice has been condemned by legitimate marketing research organizations, which are working to stop such abuses.

Professional marketing researchers also have to make ethical decisions in collecting and using survey data. Examples of potential conflicts include covering up the problems caused by nonrespondents or poor samples, compromising the reliability of a study to complete it, or reporting only part of the data so the client will like the results. Using formal statements on ethical policies and instituting rewards and punishments can improve ethical behavior in marketing research.[19]

Experiments and Panels Two special ways that observations and questionnaires are sometimes used are experiments and panels.

In **experiments,** data are obtained by manipulating factors under tightly controlled conditions to test cause and effect. The interest is in whether changing one of the conditions (a cause) will change the behavior of what is studied (the effect). Both the causal conditions and the resulting behavior are variables. Two types of causal conditions can occur: (1) experimental and (2) extraneous independent variables. The causal condition called an **experimental independent variable** (or simply, the experimental variable) is manipulated or controlled by the experimenter. In contrast, the causal condition called an **extraneous independent variable** (or simply, the extraneous variable) is a result of outside factors that the experimenter cannot control but might change the behavior of what is studied.

The change in the behavior of what is studied is called the **dependent variable.** The experimenter tries to arrange a change in the independent variable and then measure the accompanying change, or absence of it, in the dependent variable.

In marketing experiments the experimental independent variables are often one or more of the marketing mix variables, such as the product features, price, or advertising used. The ideal dependent variable usually is a change in purchases of an individual, household, or entire organization. If actual purchases cannot be used as a dependent variable, factors that are believed to be highly related to purchases, such as preferences in a taste test or intentions to buy, are used.

A potential difficulty with experiments is that extraneous independent variables can distort the results of an experiment and affect the dependent variable. A researcher's task is to identify the effect of the experimental variable of interest on the dependent variable when the effects of extraneous variables in an experiment might hide it. The Coke taste test experiment described at the start of the chapter used various Coke formulas and Pepsi as the independent variables and people's preferences as the dependent variable.

Coca-Cola actually tested three different formulations of new Coke against "old" Coke and Pepsi. However, only 30,000 to 40,000 of these used the formulation that was actually introduced. These tests showed the new formula beat the old 53 percent to 47 percent in the blind taste tests.

By conventional standards the taste test was carefully controlled. For example, the tasting was "blind" (brands concealed to avoid brand bias), only one sample from each can or bottle was used (to avoid reduced carbonation in a stale sample), servings were at 32 degrees Fahrenheit (to avoid a temperature bias), and the taster was required to take a cup of water or unsalted cracker between sips (to neutralize the palate before the next taste). All of these controls reduced possible bias due to extraneous independent variables.

So what went wrong? The post mortems suggest that two key independent variables were omitted from the experiment: (1) the *actual* use of the Coke brand name in the experiment and (2) an explanation to taste-test participants that selecting the new formula would mean the old one would be taken off the market. While these factors were originally seen as minor extraneous independent variables, they now appear as very important factors that should have been made part of the taste-test experiments as experimental independent variables.

A PEOPLE-METER FAMILY OUT ENJOYING THE CALM NIGHT BREEZES WHILE CLAIMING TO BE INSIDE ENJOYING A RERUN OF "FALCON CREST"

This is because the strong personal association and brand loyalty that Coke drinkers have for the product cannot be captured in traditional blind taste tests.

Marketing researchers conclude that the design of future experiments that involve changing a well-established soft drink or grocery product should not only involve blind taste tests but should also reveal the brand to try to capture the effect of strong brand loyalty on the consumer's buying decision.[20] Question 7 at the end of the chapter addresses other issues in drawing conclusions from the Coke experiment.

Marketing researchers often want to know if consumers are changing their behavior through time and so they take successive measurements of the same people. A **panel** is a sample of consumers or stores from which researchers take a series of measurements. For example, in this way a consumer's switching from one brand of breakfast cereal to another can be measured. Nielsen's national TV ratings are developed from its people-meter households that make up a panel and are measured repeatedly through time.

Advantages and Disadvantages of Primary Data Compared with secondary data, primary data have the advantage of being more timely and specific to the problem being studied. The main disadvantages are that primary data are usually far more costly and time consuming to collect than secondary data.

CONCEPT CHECK

1 **A mail questionnaire asks you, "Do you eat pizza?" What kind of question is this?**

2 **Does a mail, telephone, or personal interview survey provide the greatest flexibility for asking probing questions?**

3 **What is the difference between an independent and dependent variable?**

SUMMARY

1 Marketing research is the process of defining the problem and then collecting and analyzing information to recommend actions to improve an organization's marketing activities.

2 Marketing research assists in decision making, the act of consciously choosing from alternatives. The DECIDE acronym is a six-step checklist that can lead to better decisions.

3 Defining the problem, Step 1 in DECIDE, involves identifying the objectives, constraints, assumptions, and measures of success related to the problem.

4 Enumerating two kinds of decision factors, Step 2 in DECIDE, requires specifying both the alternatives (the controllable variables) and the uncertainties (the uncontrollable variables) that interact to lead to the outcome—good or bad—of the decision.

5 Collecting relevant information, Step 3 in DECIDE, includes considering pertinent concepts, methods, and data.

6 Secondary data already have been recorded and include those internal and external to the organization. Examples of internal secondary data are financial statements, sales records, and customer records. Examples of external secondary data are U.S. Census Bureau data, Nielsen TV ratings, and *Sales and Marketing Management* magazine's information on consumer and industrial markets.

7 Primary data are collected specifically for the project and are obtained by either observing or questioning people. In the latter case ideas are often generated through individual interviews and focus groups. Ideas are often evaluated using large-scale mail, telephone, or personal interview surveys.

8 Experiments manipulate a situation to measure the effect of an independent variable (cause) on the dependent variable (result or effect).

9 With panels, repeated measurements are taken from the sample units—individuals, households, or stores.

KEY TERMS AND CONCEPTS

marketing research p. 143
decision p. 144
objectives p. 146
constraints p. 146
assumptions p. 147
measures of success p. 147
decision factors p. 147
alternatives p. 147
uncertainties p. 148
hypothesis p. 150
new product concept p. 150
methods p. 150
probability sampling p. 152
nonprobability sampling p. 152
statistical inference p. 152
data p. 153
secondary data p. 153
primary data p. 153
observational data p. 156
questionnaire data p. 157
experiments p. 163
experimental independent variable p. 163
extraneous independent variable p. 163
dependent variable p. 163
panel p. 164

CHAPTER PROBLEMS AND APPLICATIONS

1 Try to recast or restate the brainteasers below to "open your mind" and increase your chances of solving them. In the process try to recognize the underlying constraints that may reduce your likelihood of solving the problem.

a. Thomas A. Edison was approached by a young scientist with a perplexing problem: for several days, he had been trying to develop a mathematical equation to determine the volume of air inside an incandescent light bulb so that he would know how much air to pump out of it to form an adequate vacuum. Edison looked at the young man in shocked disbelief. In 30 seconds Edison had an answer. How did he solve the problem?

b. Eight soldiers have to cross a river. The only means of crossing the river is a small boat in which two small children are playing. At most the boat can carry two children or one soldier. How do the eight soldiers cross the river?

2 Before the people meter, Nielsen obtained national TV ratings by using "audimeters" attached to TV sets in 1,170 American households. These devices measured (1) if the TV set was turned on and (2) if so, to which channel. What are the limitations of this mechanical observation method?

3 Before the people meter, Nielsen obtained ratings of local TV stations by having households fill out diary questionnaires. These gave information on (1) who was watching TV and (2) what program. What are the limitations of this questionnaire method?

4 For the two questions in the legislator's questionnaire shown in the chapter, (a) what is the factual issue for which opinions are sought and (b) how has the legislator managed to bias the question to get the answer he wants?

5 Rework Question 1 in the legislator's questionnaire to make it an unbiased question in the form of (a) an open-end question and (b) a Likert scale question.

6 Suppose Fisher-Price wants to run an experimental and control group experiment to evaluate a proposed chatter telephone design. It has two different groups of children on which to run an experiment for 1 week each. The control group has the old toy telephone, whereas the experimental group is exposed to the newly designed pull toy with wheels, a noisemaker, and bobbing eyes. The dependent variable is the average number of minutes during the 2-hour play period that one of the children is playing with the toy, and the results are as follows:

ACTIVITY	EXPERIMENTAL GROUP	CONTROL GROUP
Experimental variable	New design	Old design
After measurement	62 minutes	13 minutes

Should Fisher-Price introduce the new design? Why?

7 In the Coca-Cola taste-test experiment described in the chapter, what might be the effect on the company's decision of (a) having the taster consume a 12-ounce can of the soft drink rather than just take sips, (b) labeling the products in the test "A" and "B" versus "386" and "473," and (c) weighting the respondents' taste preferences by the amount of cola they consume in a year?

8 A rich aunt has decided to set you up in a business of your own choosing. To her delight, you decide on a service business—giving flying lessons in ultralight planes to your fellow college students. Some questions from the first draft of a mail questionnaire you plan to use are shown below. In terms of Figure 6-7, (a) identify the problem with each question and (b) correct it. NOTE: Some questions may have more than one problem.

a. Have you ever flown in commercial airliners and in ultralight planes?
☐ Yes ☐ No

b. Why do you think ultralights are so much safer than hang gliders?
____
____

c. When did you first know you like to fly?
☐ Under 10 ☐ 10 to 20 ☐ 21 to 30 ☐ Over 30

d. How much did you spend on recreational activities last year?
☐ $100 or less ☐ $401 to $800 ☐ $1201 to $1600
☐ $101 to $400 ☐ $801 to $1201 ☐ $1600 or more

e. How much would you pay for ultralight flying lessons? ____________

f. Would you sign up for a class that met regularly? ☐ Yes ☐ No

SUGGESTED READINGS

Pamela L. Alreck and Robert B. Settle, *The Survey Research Handbook* (Homewood, Ill.: Richard D. Irwin, Inc., 1985). *Providing a wealth of detailed information, this handbook follows the chronology of survey research from project definition and planning through questionnaire design and analysis to writing the final report.*

Stanley L. Payne, *The Art of Asking Questions* (Princeton, N.J.: Princeton University Press, 1951). *This is a readable classic that systematizes the approach to questionnaire construction and identifies some practical do's and dont's.*

Robert A. Peterson, *Marketing Research* (Plano, Tex.: Business Publications, Inc., 1988). *Chapters 8 through 10 of this textbook describe basic techniques of questionnaire and scale construction.*

Betsy D. Gelb and Gabriel M. Gelb, "New Coke's Fizzle—Lessons for the Rest of Us," Sloan Management Review (Fall, 1986), pp. 71-76. *An insightful study of the new Coke introduction, the article also suggests ways to avoid similar problems in the future.*

Fatal
ATTRACTION

7

Analyzing Marketing Information and Making Forecasts

After reading this chapter you should be able to:

Apply a decision process to help structure and find a solution to marketing problems.

•

Understand how to make and execute plans to solve marketing problems.

•

Know how to evaluate both the decision and decision process to improve future decisions.

•

Recognize how the information used in a marketing decision support system helps marketing.

•

Recognize the top-down and buildup approaches to forecasting sales.

•

Use the lost-horse and linear trend extrapolation methods to make a simple forecast.

How Movies Use Marketing Research and Analysis

As far as plots go, the movies *Beverly Hills Cop II, Indiana Jones and the Temple of Doom, Star Wars,* and *Fatal Attraction* don't have much in common. But as production and marketing costs of motion pictures skyrocket, all these movies use increasingly sophisticated marketing research and analysis. Some examples of commonly used techniques include:

- Concept tests of plots. Concepts for new plots are described to members of the target audience to get their reactions. Used by Columbia Pictures, this concept-testing technique can result in a decision to not produce a film, to alter an element of the plot, or to change casting.[1]

- Sneak previews of completed films. These use a handful of screenings in "middle America"—cities away from both coasts such as Dallas, Minneapolis, and St. Louis—to gauge audience reaction.[2] In sneak previews of *Fatal Attraction,* audiences liked everything but the ending, which had Alex (Glenn Close) committing suicide and managing to frame Dan (Michael Douglas) as her murderer by leaving his fingerprints on the death knife. New scenes were then shot for the ending that regular audiences saw later.[3]
- Awareness tests before and after the movie release. For a movie to be a success, Columbia Pictures believes 60 percent of the target audience should be aware of it on the day it opens. Columbia and other film companies track audience awareness immediately before and after the opening and increase or decrease advertising expenditures depending on the results. Right before the opening of *Indiana Jones and the Temple of Doom,* 90 percent of people polled by Paramount were aware of it and 75 percent intended to see it, so Paramount reduced its advertising.[4]

These examples show how marketing research is done, from concept tests before production even starts to awareness tests after it is finished. This research reduces uncertainty and improves marketing decisions, but it doesn't eliminate all errors. For example, a Columbia Pictures marketing study caused the firm to turn down a chance to coproduce a film because concept tests suggested it "would appeal only to 8-year-olds."[5] That film was *E.T.*—the highest grossing film ever at $638 million. The concept tests probably failed to reveal the human emotions—built into the film later—that made *E.T.* a hit.

This chapter covers the last three steps of DECIDE, summarized in Figure 7-1, which describe how firms like Paramount and Columbia Pictures move from data collection to action. The chapter also describes how organizations use marketing decision support systems to systematize the collection and reporting

FIGURE 7-1
Details of the last three steps in the DECIDE process

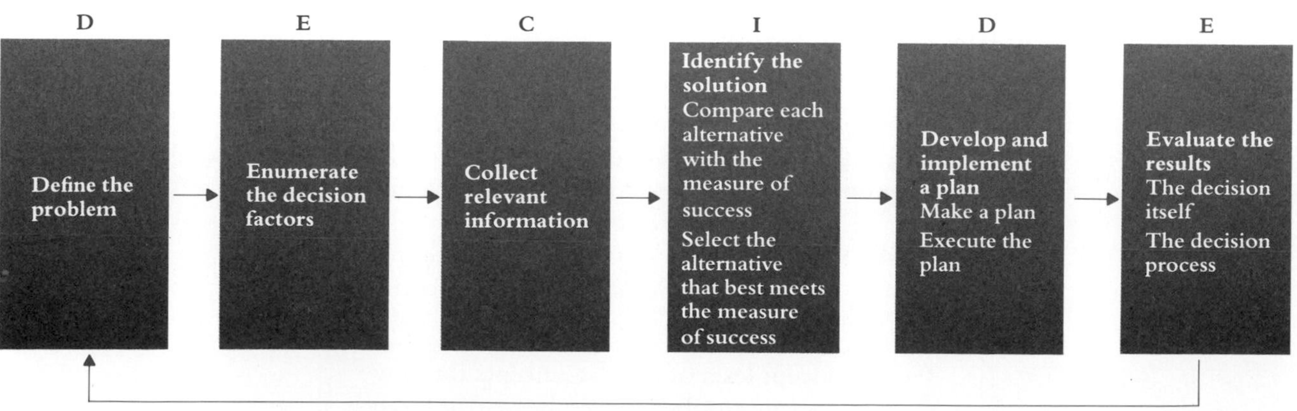

of data used for marketing decisions and how they make market and sales forecasts.

STEP 4 IN DECIDE: IDENTIFY THE BEST ALTERNATIVE

Mark Twain once observed, "Collecting data is like collecting garbage. You've got to know what you're going to do with the stuff before you collect it." The purpose of Step 4 in the DECIDE process is to analyze the collected data to find the alternative that best meets the measure of success the decision maker specified in defining the problem. While marketing managers use various approaches to find solutions to their problems, this section shows how experiments can be used to organize and analyze information for decision making.

BEST ALTERNATIVE: THE SOLUTION TO THE PROBLEM

The **solution** to the problem is simply the best alternative that has been identified. We recognize the best alternative by finding the one that best meets the measure of success established in defining the problem (Step 1 of DECIDE).

For example, suppose Pillsbury's marketing manager for prepared dough products is considering introducing Soft Breadsticks, sold in an 11-ounce refrigerated package of fresh dough with eight breadsticks each. After baking, the breadsticks are soft on the inside and crisp on the outside (Figure 7-2).

Pillsbury's decision makers tried to anticipate the possible results of later data collection and how this would relate to both the measure of success and future actions. So before undertaking a test market study, Pillsbury marketing personnel specified both (1) a quantifiable measure of success and (2) the actions that would be taken for each result of the data collection—points cited in Chapter 6.

Pillsbury decided to evaluate the consumer response to its new line of refrigerated Soft Breadsticks by putting them on trial for 12 months in a test market. Afterward marketing executives were shown results: projected annual sales for the entire United States.

Did the test market results justify introducing the product nationally? In the past this situation might have posed a problem at Pillsbury because those opposed to Soft Breadsticks from the start might use the results to justify dropping the product; those who had always favored Soft Breadsticks might see the same results as indicators of success and reason enough to distribute the product nationally.

Now Pillsbury's marketing and marketing research executives have devised a simple procedure to resolve this dilemma. How would you attack this problem? The text describes the procedure Pillsbury now uses.

FIGURE 7-2
How Pillsbury uses measures of success to guide its marketing decisions

In analyzing Soft Breadsticks, the measure of success was its projected annual U.S. sales volume in cases (containing 12 packages) based on the test market results. Accounting for considerations like production costs, marketing expenses, and return on investment for the new product, marketing executives developed the following "decision rules" to guide their future actions:

1. Projected annual U.S. sales volume of less than 1 million cases: drop product
2. Projected annual U.S. sales volume of 1 million to 1.5 million cases: reformulate the product in the laboratory
3. Projected annual U.S. sales volume of more than 1.5 million cases: introduce it nationally

The test market results showed that the Soft Breadsticks easily met the 1.5 million case measure of success for immediate national introduction.

Note that by clearly and objectively defining the measure of success and accompanying actions before the data are collected, Pillsbury reduced the chance of arguments after the results are in, when opposing points of view about success or failure are likely to be more emotional.

FINDING MARKETING SOLUTIONS THROUGH EXPERIMENTS

As mentioned in Chapter 6, experiments are potentially ideal for finding solutions to marketing problems because they are the only means of establishing a cause-and-effect relationship—that the "cause" (a reduction in price) causes a change in the "effect" or result (the number of units sold).

Laboratory Versus Field Experiments The **laboratory experiment** simulates some marketing-related activity in a highly controlled setting, such as consumers "going shopping" in a mock-up of a supermarket. The danger is that the artificiality of the situation may cause the subjects in the experiment to behave differently than they normally would. This may have been the reason for a bad forecast made for Beecham Products' new "Delicare"—a cold water detergent that was expected to topple Woolite, which had 90 percent of the $103 million annual market. Beecham's marketing research agency used a mock-store laboratory setting to estimate that Delicare could win 45 percent of the total market. When brought to market, Delicare's share was less than half of the projection, causing Beecham to sue the marketing research agency for faulty market forecasts.[6] This example also illustrates that marketing research contractors not only have an ethical responsibility to do a quality project for their clients but also may have a legal liability for their work.

Photo by Ray Marklin

In contrast, **field experiments** test some marketing variables in actual store or buying settings. Test markets, covered in more detail in Chapter 9, are a special kind of field experiment in which consumer purchases of a product or brand are measured under controlled conditions. The advantage of the reality of the buying situation—people actually spending their own money, not saying they would—is balanced against the high cost of such experiments. The cost of a test market, however, can easily pay for itself in money saved by not

Listerine's free-standing insert used in the field experiment

Reprinted with permission of Warner-Lambert Company

introducing bad products on a national scale, which can run into millions of dollars.

A Field Experiment Using Scanner Data Safeway Stores, Inc., a supermarket chain, uses electronic scanner data from its checkout counters to conduct in-store field experiments to benefit both itself and manufacturers whose products it sells. For example, Safeway measures the effects of in-store advertising—such as posterboards, aisle markers, and grocery-cart signs—on the sales of product classes and specific brands. This allows Safeway to use in-store advertising space more efficiently and also enables manufacturers to assess their budgets for these in-store ads.[7]

One of today's fastest growing promotional tools is the use of free-standing inserts (FSIs), which are multiple-page inserts in newspapers printed on heavy paper and containing coupons. Manufacturers of consumer products are the most frequent users of FSIs.

Warner Lambert Company undertook a "First thing in the morning" campaign to promote a wide range of its "morning" products. As one part of this campaign, it ran a national full-page FSI that contained a 25-cent coupon for a 32-ounce bottle of Listerine. Circulation for the FSI was 46 million.[8]

FIGURE 7-3
The effect of an FSI coupon and in-store advertising on sales of Listerine

Source: Redrawn from "Analyzing Promotions: The Free-Standing Insert Coupon," *Nielsen Researchers,* No. 4 (1982), pp. 16-20

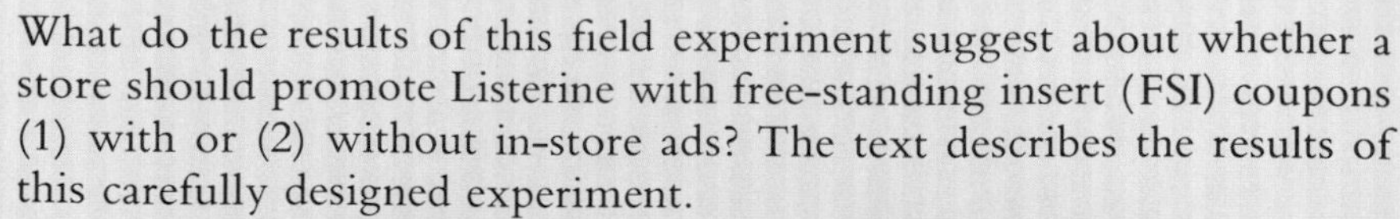

What do the results of this field experiment suggest about whether a store should promote Listerine with free-standing insert (FSI) coupons (1) with or (2) without in-store ads? The text describes the results of this carefully designed experiment.

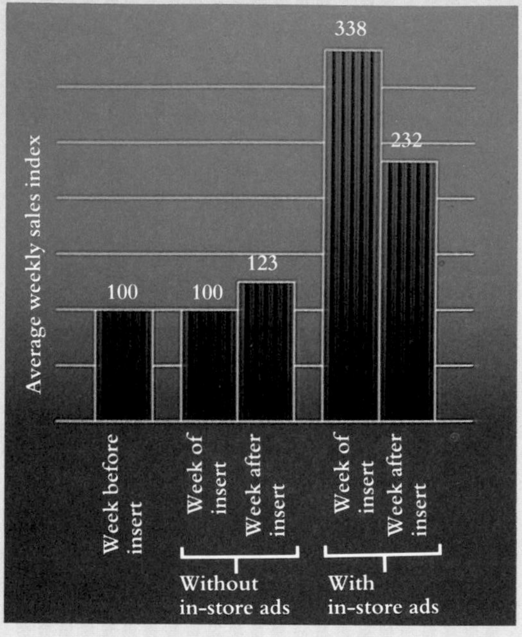

Warner Lambert and supermarkets like Safeway that distribute its products wanted to know if the FSI (1) by itself and (2) in combination with in-store ads increased Listerine sales the week of the insert and the following week. In this field experiment both the measure of success (retail sales) and the experimental variables (FSIs and in-store ads) were precisely identified. This precision enabled both Warner Lambert and the supermarkets to choose from among the alternatives (use or don't use FSIs; use or don't use in-store ads). Assume that Warner Lambert concluded that sales must at least double the 2 weeks after running the FSIs to justify repeating the promotion.

The results of the Listerine field experiment (Figure 7-3) used sales measured by scanner data from various supermarkets. Unit sales the week before the promotion were measured and indexed at 100. Without accompanying ads, the first week after the FSIs were introduced the sales index remained at 100, and the next week they increased slightly to 123 (or 1.23 times the "week before" sales). The stores supporting the FSI promotion with in-store ads showed a 338 index during the insert week and one of 232 a week later. The conclusion for Listerine was the FSIs alone have only a slight effect, but in conjunction with in-store ads they exceed the "doubling of sales" measure of success and justify being used again in the future.

Safeway also uses in-store experiments and scanner data to determine which in-store merchandising ideas advocated by manufacturers, such as end-of-aisle displays and temporary price reductions, actually increase sales. Safeway even tests alternative placement of products within its store. For example, it found that foil-packaged sauce mixes shouldn't be displayed together but should be spread around the store according to their contents—such as spaghetti sauce near bottled spaghetti sauce and gravy mix near canned gravy.

Value of Experiments in Finding a Solution With experiments—especially field experiments—the effect of key marketing variables on the measure of success can be evaluated directly in a realistic setting. For example, the Listerine experiment showed the effects of FSIs and in-store ads on sales of Listerine (the measure of success) in actual supermarkets without consumers being aware of an experiment. The drawbacks are the time and cost of these experiments.

CONCEPT CHECK

1. **How do you know how to select the best alternative from the group of alternatives in Step 4 of DECIDE?**
2. **What is the main advantage in using a field experiment to reach a marketing decision?**

STEP 5 IN DECIDE: DEVELOP AND IMPLEMENT A DETAILED PLAN

Identifying a problem's solution in Step 4 of DECIDE isn't enough. The potential problem: no one may get around to putting the solution into effect.

MAKING SOMETHING HAPPEN

The essence of Step 5 of DECIDE is making something happen; someone has to develop a detailed plan and see that it gets implemented. The goal is to use *both* effective planning and execution to achieve a successful marketing program.

Chapters 9 to 18 cover strategies dealing with each of the marketing mix elements, and Chapters 19 and 20 describe marketing planning, implementation, and control in depth, so these topics are not covered here in detail. But we can give a brief example from a small entrepreneurial startup company—Garid, Inc.—that illustrates how even small firms can develop, execute, and evaluate plans to solve a marketing problem.

MARKETING A PERSONAL COMMUNICATOR

Fernando Garcia decided to invent something for people whose deafness cut them off from the rest of the world; a device to help them communicate by telephone. He talked to dozens of hearing-impaired people and groups to try to understand their needs for a portable communications device. With the help of friends he started the business that today is Garid, Inc.

Garid's personal communicator

By 1983 Garcia had a laboratory model that worked, and two years later he and his technical staff had their "Personal Communicator" ready for market. It is a pocket-sized, portable terminal enabling people with speech and hearing impairments to communicate by telephone. It has a voice synthesizer that converts typed input to voice output, a liquid crystal display to print 40 letters that move across the screen at the user's reading rate, and an acoustic coupler to permit attachment to any telephone. Tests with users got the "bugs" out of the device and Garcia took the product to market. The marketing plan was straightforward:

- Product. Market a device that had word processing, videodisplay, message storage, voice synthesizer, and acoustic coupler features.
- Price. Set an initial price of $1,795 for the unit.
- Promotion. Advertise it in magazines, newspapers, and meetings directed at the hearing impaired. Sell it through salespeople who can add the product to their existing line.
- Place. Distribute it directly to customers and through the salespeople handling the device.

In terms of Step 5 of DECIDE, Garid and Fernando Garcia had developed the marketing plan very carefully and then worked hard to implement it. However, as is often the case with high-technology startup ventures, things didn't work out quite as expected. That is the reason for evaluation, the final step in the DECIDE process.

Step 6 in DECIDE: Evaluate the Results

Evaluating results is a continuing way of life for effective marketing managers. There are really two aspects of this evaluation process:

- Evaluate the decision itself. This usually involves comparing actual results with plans and taking corrective action if necessary—the evaluation activity described in Chapter 2.
- Evaluate the decision process used. This involves changing the activities

in one or more of the steps used in reaching a decision, such as altering the methods used to define the problem, collect the data, or implement the plan.

EVALUATION OF THE MARKETING OF THE PERSONAL COMMUNICATOR

After a year in the market, only 300 Personal Communicators had been sold—far less than forecast. This forced Garid to make a careful evaluation of both the decision to market the device and the decision process used. This revealed some vital information.

Evaluation of the Decision Itself While most buyers were pleased with the device, the bulk of prospective customers did not think the benefits were great enough to warrant spending $1,795 for it. Also, the device turned out to be too complex to be sold effectively by mail or by a sales force for whom it was too expensive to give detailed training. The company could not discover a way to market its device profitably, so it would either have to find a new product and additional outside funding or go bankrupt.

Evaluation of the Decision Process Fernando Garcia concluded that the decision process had introduced several pieces of incorrect information that led to some bad decisions. He concluded that his own enthusiasm had been contagious and doing his own marketing research interviews had caused prospective buyers to overstate their interest in the Personal Communicator. Also, his marketing research never actually asked prospects if they would buy the Personal Communicator. The company had also underestimated the difficulty of marketing a complex technical device to prospective buyers. Garcia concluded that if Garid ever had another chance, the process of reaching the decision could be improved.

IF AT FIRST YOU DON'T SUCCEED . . .

At about this time, Garcia got another brainstorm. He discovered that diabetics taking insulin often must run two or more blood sugar tests on themselves each day, which requires a drawer full of paraphernalia. He concluded there must be a better way, found none, and then invented his own. The invention: the Med-Pen System, a device the size of two felt-tip pens that takes a blood sample and then automatically gives a digital readout of the blood sugar level. The automatic process largely eliminates the problem found in competitive systems of the user making errors that result in incorrect blood sugar readings. The device even stores the last five readings in memory and has a built-in alarm to remind the user when it is time for the next blood sample.

Several evaluation lessons—Step 6 in the DECIDE process—learned from the Personal Communicator experience have especially helped with Garid's Med-Pen System. For example, the process of collecting marketing research information must be done by impartial outsiders who compare the Garid device with existing substitutes. Researchers also asked users of competitive products if they would actually buy the new system if it became available on the market.

Garid's Med-Pen System

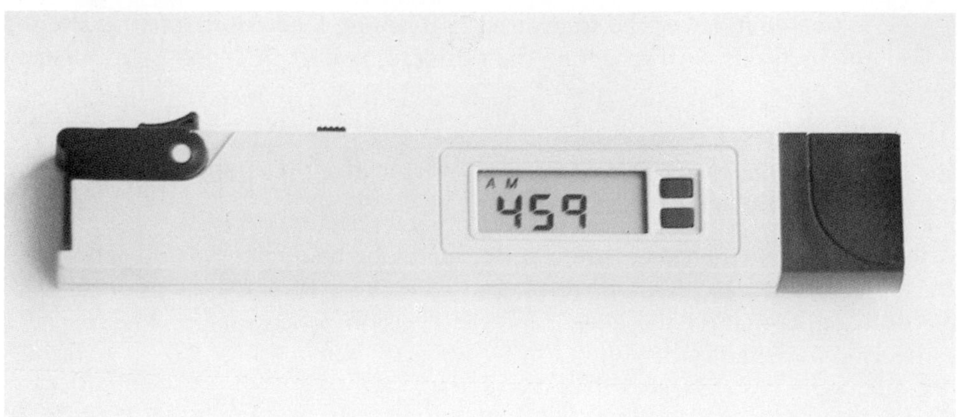

Vital to decision making is the need to conduct a systematic evaluation of past decisions and how they were made, and apply this information to future decisions.

Review of the DECIDE Process

The past two chapters have covered details of the six-step DECIDE process that can be used to make decisions. In studying these details, it is possible to lose sight of the larger picture: how the steps combine to contribute to better decisions. Let's briefly return to an example at the start of Chapter 6: as product manager for Ocean Spray, what advertising media should you use to gain consumer acceptance of aseptic packaging for your juice?

D: Define the Problem

Step 1 involves identifying four parts of the problem: (1) the objectives to be achieved, (2) the constraints placed on solving the problem (for example, its importance and the time and money available), (3) simplifying assumptions, and (4) the measures of success to be used initially in choosing the best alternative and later in judging whether it was a good one. In the case of Ocean Spray, assume your objective is to choose an advertising medium to introduce aseptically packaged cranberry juice nationally in the U.S. market. Constraints are 6 months and $400,000 allotted to reach a decision. A major assumption is that the quality of Ocean Spray juice in the new packaging is as good as or better than in the old. If this weren't true, you couldn't tell whether to attribute bad sales of the juice to the packaging or the quality. As a measure of success, you choose the number of cases of the juice sold in test markets.

E: Enumerate the Decision Factors

In any decision two kinds of factors determine its success or failure: (1) the alternatives (actions the decision maker can take to solve the problems) and (2) uncertainties (factors that can influence the outcome which are beyond the decision maker's control). The two alternative advertising media you choose to evaluate for your aseptic package are TV and newspapers. Factors beyond your control also must be considered. For example, important new product introductions by competitors that are advertised on national media can affect the success of your own choice of an advertising medium.

C: COLLECT RELEVANT INFORMATION

To help solve the problem, relevant information must be compiled. Sometimes this may be found quickly and easily, perhaps by recalling facts already stored in the decision maker's memory, by making a telephone call, or by examining existing reports. At other times obtaining the information may be expensive and time consuming, such as surveying hundreds of consumers about their reactions to a product. In this case you might collect information by introducing the Ocean Spray advertising campaign for the new aseptically packaged cranberry juice in four U.S. test market cities—two with TV advertising and two with newspaper advertising with equal dollar expenditures for each.

I: IDENTIFY THE SOLUTION

To select the best available alternative—the solution to the problem—summarize and analyze the collected information. Your test market shows that newspaper ads generated 50 percent more sales (your measure of success) than did TV ads.

D: DEVELOP AND IMPLEMENT A PLAN

Develop a plan, get approval for it, and execute it to put the chosen alternative into effect. At Ocean Spray you get national distribution for your new aseptically packaged cranberry juice, schedule the ads in newspapers across the country, and then run them. This requires organizing the activities of many people both inside and outside Ocean Spray.

E: EVALUATE THE RESULTS

The final step involves evaluating both the decision itself and the entire decision process after the plan has been implemented to determine if the results match the initial objectives set forth in the problem-definition step. Such an evaluation may reveal that modifications should be made in the solution that was developed, the decision process used to reach that solution, or both. At Ocean Spray you conclude that the national introduction is successful. But suppose subsequent research shows that the aseptically packaged juice is selling well with women but not with men. You discover that the reason is that the newspaper ad is better in reaching women but TV is better for men, so in future test markets you alter your measure of success to get more precise data on sales to both men and women. This might lead to a strategy combining TV and newspaper ads, which is what Ocean Spray actually did. The feedback arrow from Step 6 to Step 1 in Figure 7-1 stresses that lessons learned in the evaluation step are applied to future decisions.

CONCEPT CHECK

1 **Why can't a marketing manager's decision making stop with selecting the best alternative to solve a problem?**

2 **What two factors should be evaluated after reaching a decision?**

MARKETING DECISION SUPPORT SYSTEMS

Marketing data have become so important to today's marketing executives that many firms have designed their own information systems to process the data for use by the manager. A **marketing decision support system (MDSS)** is a computerized method of providing timely, accurate information to improve marketing decisions. Three points about this definition need elaboration. First, an MDSS is one of a number of management information systems—like those for finance, production control, and accounting—used by a firm, but it is employed mainly by marketing managers. Second, it is a computer-based system, *not* simply a term applied broadly to all the marketing managers who use it to formulate better decisions. Third, an MDSS doesn't make decisions itself but helps marketing managers who use it to formulate better decisions.

KEY ELEMENTS OF AN MDSS

The marketing information system of a decade ago stressed mainly the collection and organization of marketing data. Today's MDSS emphasizes the need for the system to be user friendly to encourage use by marketing managers requiring the information for the decisions. Four key elements of today's MDSS:

- *Data banks* are libraries of information. Often data bases from secondary sources mentioned in Chapter 6, these data banks usually include product sales by brand, package size, type of outlet, and geographical area. Also included are data on price, promotions, and customer characteristics.

Using an MDSS to make a better marketing decision

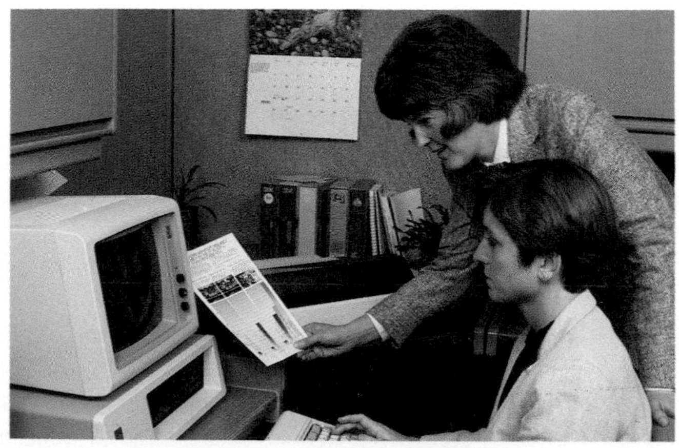

- *Models* are ideas or hypotheses about the relationship between the factors a marketing manager controls and the results sought, such as the sensitivity of sales to changes in price or levels of advertising.
- *Links* are means of tying the data bank to the models so that the available data can be fitted into the model.
- *System interrogation* is a means of communicating with the entire system so the manager can ask questions and get answers quickly. Today it is possible to have direct access to the system through a terminal or personal computer on the manager's desk.

The importance of the model element of the MDSS lies in establishing hypotheses that can be tested by the MDSS. An MDSS also facilitates the use of **sensitivity analysis** of marketing problems: analyzing how making slight changes in factors like price or advertising levels affect sales revenue or other results of marketing programs.

OCEAN SPRAY'S MDSS

Guava is not the first fruit juice that comes to mind when you are thinking about a quick pick-me-up! No kidding!

This lack of awareness about guava was exactly the problem faced by new products manager Terry Dinsmore of Ocean Spray Cranberries Company. Firmly entrenched in better-known fruit beverage markets with cranberry and grapefruit juices, Ocean Spray undertook a real break with tradition by developing Mauna La'i Hawaiian Guava Drink. "Guava is different in color, taste, and aroma from any other fruit drink on the market," observes Dinsmore.[12]

Photo by Ray Marklin

Based on results of a 1-year test market, Ocean Spray had to decide whether to introduce Mauna La'i nationally or not. Ocean Spray's MDSS included BehaviorScan data (see Chapter 6) that enabled Dinsmore to track Mauna La'i purchases by individual households. This is a big job because about 70 retail food brokers nationwide sell its more than 60 different sizes and flavors of sauces, juices, and drinks—from 8.5-ounce aseptic packages to 64-ounce bottles.

The planned target market was "older children through older adults with average income and education." But the BehaviorScan data found that these people weren't the heavy buyers of Mauna La'i and that the base of loyal consumers was smaller than expected. However, by using the data collected and asking key "what if . . ." questions of its MDSS, Ocean Spray had a successful national introduction of Mauna La'i.

Who did the target market turn out to be and how did the MDSS help find the reasons justifying the national introduction? The Marketing Action Memo provides the answers and illustrates the value of an effective MDSS.

WHEN AN MDSS IS NEEDED

Not every firm needs an MDSS. The need for it is largely determined by (1) the value versus the cost of marketing information and (2) the kinds of decisions a marketing manager makes and how they relate to the information included in an MDSS.

MARKETING · ACTION · MEMO

How an MDSS Helped Save a Guava Drink from the Scrap Heap

The decision: a go/no go choice on a new fruit drink.

For its new Mauna La'i Hawaiian Guava Drink, the Ocean Spray Cranberries Company had to decide whether to take the product nationally ("go") or not ("no go"). To help it decide, it ran a test market and turned to its marketing decision support system (MDSS) for help.

Its MDSS uses data bases to help Ocean Spray track case sales and promotions.

Using BehaviorScan (see Chapter 6) to track purchases of individual households, Mauna La'i went into a one-year test market in Eau Claire, Wisconsin and Midland, Texas. The target market was older children through older adults with average income and education. Ocean Spray established goals for "first trial" and "repeat" purchases needed for a profitable national introduction. Most of the ad budget went for TV commercials with Hawaiian scenes.

After six months of test market the product was headed for the scrap heap because first trial was good but repeat purchases were below those needed for national introduction. Detailed analysis of the BehaviorScan households buying Mauna La'i revealed two key surprises. First, the actual buyers were not the expected target market but were mainly upscale "yuppie" buyers for whom Mauna La'i was "a little bit cultish and special." Second, these upscale buyers consumed larger quantities than expected.

Asking the Ocean Spray MDSS a series of "what if . . ." questions about a series of hypotheses turned up an important conclusion: unusually large consumption rates of the smaller group of upscale consumers made it profitable to "go"—to take Mauna La'i national.

In the national introduction, sales even exceeded MDSS projections.

Sources: Leslie Brennan, "Test Marketing Put to the Test: Ocean Spray Mauna La'i Hawaiian Guava Drink," *Sales and Marketing Management* (March, 1987), p. 68; Thayer C. Taylor, "The Computer in Sales and Marketing: Software Juices Up Ocean Spray Promotions," *Sales and Marketing Management* (May, 1986), pp. 74–75.

Trade-Offs: Value Versus Cost of Marketing Data Information and data can be valuable commodities, but they can also be very expensive. The facts and figures that make up marketing information have no value by themselves. Their value comes from being organized and interpreted to help the decision maker reach better decisions.

In practice, a marketing manager (1) sets the priority of the data from most valuable to least valuable in solving a problem, (2) assesses the cost of collecting each kind of data, and (3) stops collecting more data on the list when the cost of collection outweighs their value in improving the decisions. Although these are very difficult guidelines to apply, they stress an important issue: the value of the data must be balanced against their cost of collection and use. Great care is needed to design an MDSS that is user-friendly and that marketing managers are comfortable using to help reach decisions.[13]

Kinds of Decisions a Marketing Manager Makes A marketing manager makes two distinctly different kinds of decisions. One type is *repetitive decisions,* the periodic decisions that are repeated at standard intervals during the work year. A product manager for a grocery products manufacturer such as Ocean Spray develops an annual plan at the same time every year, or a department store buyer develops two seasonal buying plans a year, one for the spring and the other for the fall. For example, at Ocean Spray one of the early MDSS applications involved planning the dozens of sales promotions (coupons and deals) used with its products that are repetitive decisions. Managers can access the MDSS to determine what the impact on case sales will be of moving the promotion up two weeks or changing a coupon's price allowance.[14]

In contrast, *nonrepetitive decisions* are those which are unique to a particular time and situation. For example, the manager of the department store buyer may ask for an assessment of the impact on sales of changing the department's location within the store.

One-time and special reports don't go into an MDSS. Only the cost-effective, repetitive information is typically included and becomes the data bank used with pertinent models to provide the standardized, periodic reports produced by the MDSS.

The importance of the MDSS to marketing managers is increasing daily. Current applications include retail buying, sales force planning and control, new product forecasting, and media selection decisions in advertising.

CONCEPT CHECK

1 **Of what value is a model in an MDSS?**

2 **What is the difference between repetitive and nonrepetitive decisions for a marketing manager?**

MARKET AND SALES FORECASTING

As we saw earlier in the chapter with Delicare, the cold water detergent that failed in the marketplace, forecasting or estimating the actual size of a market is critical. This is because overestimating the size of a market may mean wasting research and development, manufacturing, and marketing dollars on new products that fail. Underestimating it may mean missing the chance to introduce successful new products. We will discuss (1) some basic forecasting terms, (2) two major approaches to forecasting, and (3) specific forecasting techniques.

BASIC FORECASTING TERMS

Unfortunately there are no standard definitions for some forecasting concepts, so it's necessary to take care in defining the terms used.

Market or Industry Potential The term **market potential,** or **industry potential,** refers to the maximum total sales of a product by all firms to a segment under specified environmental conditions and marketing efforts of the firms. For example, the market potential for cake mix sales to U.S. consumers in 1995 might be 12 million cases—what Pillsbury, Betty Crocker, Duncan Hines, and other cake mix producers would sell to American consumers under the assumptions that (1) past patterns of dessert consumption continue and (2) the same level of promotional effort continues relative to other desserts. If one of these assumptions proves false, the estimate of market potential will be wrong. For example, if American consumers suddenly become more concerned about eating refined sugar and shift their dessert preferences from cakes to fresh fruits, the estimate of market potential will be too high.

Sales or Company Forecast What one firm expects to sell under the specified conditions for the uncontrollable and controllable factors that affect the forecast is the **sales forecast,** or **company forecast.** For example, Duncan Hines might develop its sales forecast of 4 million cases of cake mix for U.S. consumers in 1995, assuming past dessert preferences continue and the same relative level of advertising expenditures between it, Pillsbury, and Betty Crocker. If Betty Crocker suddenly cuts its advertising in half, Duncan Hines's old sales forecast will probably be too low.

With both market potential estimates and sales forecasts, it is necessary to specify some significant details: the product involved (all cake mixes, only white cake mixes, or only Bundt cake mixes); the time period involved (month, quarter, or year); the segment involved (United States, Southwest region, upper-income buyer, or single-person households); controllable marketing mix factors (price and level of advertising support); uncontrollable factors (consumer tastes and actions of competitors); and the units of measurement (number of cases sold or total sales revenues).

TWO BASIC APPROACHES TO FORECASTING

A marketing manager rarely wants a single number for an annual forecast, such as 5,000 units or $75 million in sales revenue. Rather, the manager wants this

A competitor's marketing actions can affect the sales forecast for a cake mix brand

Photo by Ray Marklin

total subdivided into elements the manager works with, such as sales by product line or sales to a market segment. The two basic approaches to sales forecasting are (1) subdividing the total sales forecast (top-down approach) or (2) building the total sales forecast by summing up the components (buildup approach).

Top-Down Approach The **top-down approach** to sales forecasting involves subdividing an aggregate estimate into its principal components. A shoe manufacturer can use the top-down approach to estimate the percentage of its total shoe sales in a state and develop state-by-state forecasts for shoe sales for the coming year. The "Survey of Buying Power" published annually by *Sales and Marketing Management* magazine is a widely used source of such top-down forecasting information.

For example, as shown in Figure 7-4, the state of New York has 7.39 percent of the U.S. population, 8.45 percent of the U.S. effective buying income, and 6.95 percent of the U.S. retail sales. If the shoe manufacturer wanted to use a single factor related to expected shoe sales, it would choose the factor that has been most closely related to shoe sales historically, in this case the percentage of U.S. retail sales. The top-down forecast would then be that 6.95 percent of the firm's sales would be made in the state of New York.

Sometimes multiple factors are considered, such as the *buying power index* (BPI) developed by *Sales and Marketing Management* magazine that gives weights of 0.2, 0.5, and 0.3, respectively, to the three previously mentioned factors, as follows:

$$\begin{aligned}\text{BPI} &= (0.2 \times \text{Percent of population}) + (0.5 \times \text{Percent of effective buying income}) + (0.3 \times \text{Percent of retail sales}) \\ &= (0.2 \times 7.3926) + (0.5 \times 8.4481) + (.03 \times 6.9465) \\ &= 1.4785 + 4.2240 + 2.0840 \\ &= 7.7425\% = 7.74\%\end{aligned}$$

Thus the BPI forecasts 7.74 percent of the firm's shoe sales will occur in New

FIGURE 7-4
U.S. population, effective buying income, and retail sales for selected states, 1986

Source: Adapted from "1986 Survey of Buying Power," Part I, *Sales and Marketing Management* (July 27, 1987), pp. B-3, B-5, B-7.

	1986 regional and state summaries of. . .					
	Population		Effective buying income		Retail sales	
Region State	2/31/86 Total population (thousands)	Percent of U.S.	1986 Total EBI ($1,000)	Percent of U.S.	1986 Total retail sales ($1,000)	Percent of U.S.
Middle Atlantic	**37,620.4**	**15.4681**	**509,853,234**	**17.0992**	**224,482,793**	**15.2071**
New Jersey	7,687.3	3.1607	116,085,968	3.8932	52,987,961	3.5896
New York	17,979.6	7.3926	251,898,226	8.4481	102,542,772	6.9465
Pennsylvania	11,953.5	4.9148	141,869,040	4.7579	68,952,060	4.6710

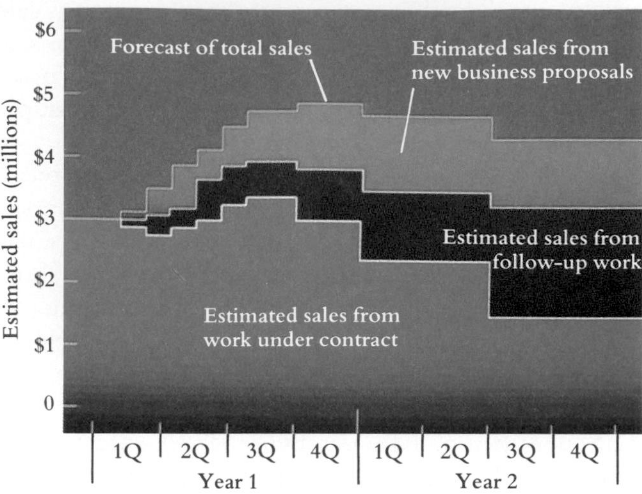

FIGURE 7-5
Buildup approach to a 2-year sales forecast for General Electric's Aerospace Vehicle Department

York—significantly higher than if retail sales alone were used for the forecast. The forecast can be converted into dollars by using *Sales and Marketing Management* magazine's "Survey of Buying Power," Part II (in an annual October issue), that gives retail sales of various lines of merchandise such as footwear.

Buildup Approach The **buildup approach** sums the sales forecasts of each of the components to arrive at the total forecast. It is a widely used method when there are identifiable components such as products, product lines, or market segments in the forecasting problem.

Figure 7-5 shows how GE's aerospace department uses the buildup approach to develop a sales forecast involving three broad categories of projects or products: (1) work currently under contract that can be forecast precisely, (2) follow-up work that is likely to result from current contracts, and (3) new business that results from GE's proposals for new business, which is difficult to forecast. Each of these three forecasts is the sum of a number of individual products or projects, which for simplicity are not shown. In turn, forecasts for each of the three kinds of business can be summed to give the total sales forecast for the entire department.

SPECIFIC SALES FORECASTING TECHNIQUES

Broadly speaking, three main sales forecasting techniques are available that can lead to the forecasts used in the top-down or buildup approaches. Ordered from least costly in terms of both time and money to most costly, these are (1) judgments of the decision maker, (2) surveys of knowledgeable groups, and (3) statistical methods.

Judgments of the Decision Maker Probably 99.9 percent of all sales forecasts are judgments of the person who must act on the results of the forecast—the individual decision maker. An example is the forecasts of likely sales, and hence the quantity to order, for the 8,500 items stocked in a typical supermarket that must be forecast by the stock clerk or manager. A **direct forecast** involves estimating the value to be forecast without any intervening steps. Examples appear in your daily life: How many quarts of milk should I buy? How much time should I allow to drive to the game? How much money should I get out of the instant cash machine? Your mind probably goes through some intervening steps but so quickly you're unaware of it.

Even in estimating the amount of money to get from the instant cash machine, you probably made some unconscious (or conscious) intervening estimates (such as counting the cash in your billfold or the special events you need cash for) to obtain your direct estimate. **Lost-horse forecasting** does this in a more structured way by asking you to start with the last known value of the item being forecast, list the factors that could affect the forecast, assess whether they have a positive or negative impact, and make the final forecast. The technique gets its name from how you'd find a lost horse: go to where it was last seen, put yourself in its shoes, consider those factors which could affect where you might go (to the pond if you're thirsty, the hayfield if you're hungry, and so on), and go there. For example, a product manager for Wilson's wooden tennis rackets in 1989 who needed to make a sales forecast through 1995 would start with the known value of 1989 sales and list the positive factors (more tennis courts, more TV publicity) and the negative ones (competition from metal, graphite, and ceramic rackets) to arrive at the final series of annual sales forecasts.

Surveys of Knowledgeable Groups If you wonder what your firm's sales will be next year, ask people who are likely to know something about future sales. Four common groups that are surveyed to develop sales forecasts are prospective buyers, the firm's sales force, its executives, and experts.

A **survey of buyers' intentions** asks prospective customers whether they are likely to buy the product or service during some future time period. For industrial products with few prospective buyers who are able and willing to predict their future buying behavior, this can be effective. For example, there are probably only a few hundred customers in the entire world for Cray Research's supercomputers, so Cray simply surveys these prospects to develop its sales forecasts.

A **sales force survey** asks the firm's salespeople to estimate sales during a coming period. Because these people are in contact with customers and are likely to know what customers like and dislike, there is logic to this approach. However, salespeople can be unreliable forecasters—painting too rosy a picture if they are enthusiastic about a new product and too grim a forecast if their sales quota is based on it.

A **jury of executive opinion** surveys knowledgeable executives inside the firm—such as vice-presidents of marketing, research and development, finance, and production—and combines their opinions to obtain the sales forecast. Although this approach is fast and includes judgments from diverse functional areas, it can be biased by a dominant executive whose judgments are deferred to by the others.

The **Delphi method** is an example of a **survey of experts** in which people knowledgeable about the forecast topic are polled. Now used regularly by more than 100 large corporations, the Delphi method gets its name from the ancient

CONCEPT CHECK

1 **What is the difference between the top-down and buildup approaches to forecasting sales?**

2 **How is the Delphi method used in making a sales forecast?**

3 **What is linear trend extrapolation?**

SUMMARY

1 Identifying the best available alternative, or solution, to a problem is Step 4 in DECIDE. It involves selecting the alternative that best meets the measures of success specified in Step 1. Experiments are a widely used method to help identify the best alternative from a set of options.

2 Experiments, especially those done in the field involving actual sales, help find a solution through establishing a causal link between marketing action and actual results such as sales or profits, which are often primary measures of success.

3 Developing and executing a plan to put the chosen alternative into effect (Step 5 in DECIDE) is the essence of marketing management. For success to occur, detailed plans must be made and implemented effectively.

4 Step 6 in DECIDE involves evaluating both the decision itself and the process used to reach it and helps the decision maker learn lessons that can be used in the future.

5 Marketing decision support systems (MDSSs) are computerized methods of providing timely, accurate information to improve marketing decisions. Because of the high cost of collecting and computerizing marketing data, an MDSS is most likely to be used only when standardized data can be collected and applied to repetitive marketing decisions.

6 Two basic approaches to forecasting sales are the top-down and buildup methods. Three forecasting techniques are judgments of individuals, surveys of groups, and statistical methods.

7 Individual judgments are the most widely used forecasting method. Two common examples are direct and lost-horse methods.

8 Asking questions of groups of people who are knowledgeable about likely future sales is another frequently used method of forecasting. Four such groups are prospective buyers, the sales force, executives, and experts.

FIGURE 7-6
Projected ye
scientific bre
according to
Delphi techn
forecast

KEY TERMS AND CONCEPTS

solution p. 171
laboratory experiment p. 172
field experiments p. 172
marketing decision support system (MDSS) p. 180
sensitivity analysis p. 181
market potential p. 184
industry potential p. 184
sales forecast p. 184
company forecast p. 184
top-down approach p. 185
buildup approach p. 186
direct forecast p. 187
lost-horse forecasting p. 187
survey of buyers' intentions p. 187
sales force survey p. 187
jury of executive opinion p. 187
Delphi method p. 187
survey of experts p. 187
technological forecasting p. 188
trend extrapolation p. 189

CHAPTER PROBLEMS AND APPLICATIONS

1 As owner of a chain of supermarkets, you get the idea that you could sell more fresh strawberries by leaving them individually out on a tray and letting customers then fill their own pint or quart box with strawberries. (a) Describe an experiment to test this idea. (b) What are some possible measures of success?

2 You walk up to the supermarket checkout counter with six cartons of yogurt you want to buy. (a) Describe circumstances under which the checkout procedure with electronic scanner (1) will measure all six items and (2) could miss the six items. (b) What problems do missing sales cause in field experiments?

3 Suppose on a rainy night you are driving on a two-lane highway at 50 miles per hour. As you come over the crest of the hill, you see that a car 100 yards ahead of you has plowed into a tank truck, obstructing your lane. You are afraid that too much braking will cause a bad skid, so your main choices are to steer into the left lane or into the right shoulder. Further, you can't tell if traffic is coming toward you. Apply the six steps of the DECIDE process to address this problem.

4 Aim toothpaste runs a field test evaluating a free-standing insert (FSI) coupon along with in-store advertising similar to that run for Listerine and shown in Figure 7-3. The results of the Aim experiment are as follows:

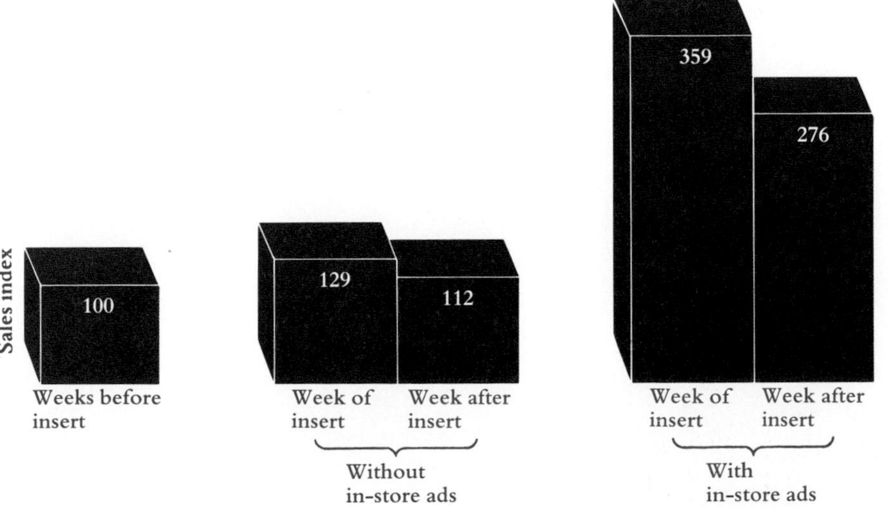

(a) What measures of success are appropriate? (b) What are your conclusions and recommendations?

5 Another field experiment with FSI coupons and in-store advertising for Wisk detergent is run. The index of sales is as follows:

	WEEKS BEFORE INSERT	WEEK OF INSERT	WEEK AFTER INSERT
Without in-store ads	100	144	108
With in-store ads	100	268	203

What are your conclusions and recommendations?

6 In designing an MDSS, the format in which information is presented to a harried marketing manager is often vital. (a) If you were a marketing manager and interrogated your MDSS, would you rather see the results shown in Question 4 or Question 5? (b) What are one or two strengths and weaknesses of each format?

7 Suppose you are associate dean of your college's business school responsible for scheduling courses for the school year. (a) What repetitive information would you include in your MDSS to help schedule classes? (b) What special, one-time information might affect your schedule? (c) What standardized output reports do you have to provide? When?

8 Suppose you are to make a sales forecast using a top-down approach to estimate the percentage of a manufacturer's total U.S. sales going to each of the 50 states. You plan to use only a single factor—percentage of U.S. population, percentage of effective buying income, or percentage of retail sales. Which of the three factors would you use if your sales forecast were for each of the following manufacturers, and why? (a) Morton salt, (b) Christian Dior dresses, and (c) Columbia records.

9 Which of the following variables would linear trend extrapolation be more accurate for? (a) Annual population of the United States or (b) annual sales of cars produced in the United States by General Motors. Why?

SUGGESTED READINGS

Alan R. Andreasen, "Cost-Conscious Marketing Research," *Harvard Business Review* (July-August 1983), pp. 74-79. *Addressing five common myths in marketing research, Andreasen shows how even smaller firms can use inexpensive marketing research to aid their decisions.*

Gilbert A. Churchill, Jr., *Marketing Research,* 4th ed. (Chicago: Dryden Press, 1987). *This marketing research textbook gives an in-depth discussion of designs of causal experiments and analysis of marketing data at the basic and advanced levels.*

"Decision Support Systems Cited by AMA," *Marketing News* (May 23, 1986), pp. 1, 16. *The article describes numerous applications of marketing decision support systems and why this area is seen as a "breakthrough for marketing management."*

"John Diebold on PCs in Marketing: The Best Is Yet to Come," *Sales and Marketing Management* (July 1987), pp. 42-45. *In an interview John Diebold, an expert in anticipating the advent of automation and computers, describes what he foresees for personal computers in marketing and sales.*

David M. Georgoff and Robert G. Murdick, "Manager's Guide to Forecasting," *Harvard Business Review* (January-February 1986), pp. 110-120. *The article gives a readable summary of major forecasting techniques—from judgment methods to statistical methods.*

AEROBICS
Reebok
Reebok
Reebok
Reebok
Reebok

8

Market Segmentation, Targeting, and Positioning

After reading this chapter you should be able to:

Explain what market segmentation is, when to use it, and the five steps used in segmentation.

•

Recognize the different factors used to segment consumer and industrial markets.

•

Understand the significance of heavy, medium, and light users and nonusers in targeting markets.

•

Develop a market-product grid to use in segmenting and targeting a market.

•

Interpret a cross tabulation to analyze market segments.

•

Understand how marketing managers position products in the marketplace.

Reebok: Turning Those Dirty Old Sneakers into a Gold Mine

Remember when you took all your exercise—running around the block, shooting baskets, and playing tennis—in the same pair of dirty old sneakers with the holes in them? Reebok changed all that.

In just 6 years, from 1981 to 1987, its annual sales grew from $1.5 million to $1 billion—an increase of 66,667 percent! It all started in 1979, when Paul Fireman, a camping equipment distributor, wandered through an international trade fair and saw Reebok's custom track shoes. He bought the U.S. license from the British manufacturer and started producing top-of-the-line running shoes. Sales hit $1.5 million in 1981, but Fireman saw that the running boom had peaked and that he needed other opportunities. That realization put him a giant step ahead of Nike, which kept churning out running shoes, which started piling up in warehouses.[1]

In a brilliant marketing decision, Fireman introduced the first soft-leather aerobic-dance shoe—the Reebok "Freestyle"—in 1982. The flamboyant colors of these Reebok designer sneakers captured the attention of aerobic-dance instructors and students alike. This color strategy still helps the sneakers get good display space in stores and attracts a lot of consumer attention.

Today known as Reebok International, Ltd., the firm successively introduced tennis shoes, children's shoes ("Weeboks"), and basketball shoes in 1984 and walking shoes in 1986. For those who don't want to buy 4 different pairs of shoes to run, play tennis, shoot baskets, and walk in, Reebok introduced—of course—"cross-trainers" in 1988; a pair of shoes made for the same activities you originally used your sneakers for, at a price of about $55 to $90 a pair.[2]

The Reebok strategy, making shoes designed to satisfy needs of different customers, illustrates successful market segmentation, the main topic of this chapter. After discussing why markets need to be segmented, this chapter covers the steps a firm uses in segmenting and targeting a market and then positioning its offering in the marketplace.

WHY SEGMENT MARKETS?

A business firm segments its markets so it can respond more effectively to the wants of groups of prospective buyers and thus increase its sales and profits. Nonprofit organizations also segment the clients they serve to satisfy client needs more effectively while achieving the organization's goals. Let's use the dilemma of sneaker buyers finding their ideal Reebok shoes to describe (1) what market segmentation is and (2) when it is necessary to segment markets.

WHAT MARKET SEGMENTATION MEANS

People have different needs and wants, even though it would be easier for marketers if they didn't. **Market segmentation** is aggregating prospective buyers into groups that (1) have common needs and (2) will respond similarly to a marketing action. The groups that result from this process are **market segments**, a relatively homogeneous collection of prospective buyers.

The existence of different market segments has caused firms to use a marketing strategy of **product differentiation,** a strategy that has come to have two different but related meanings. In its broadest sense, product differentiation involves a firm's using different marketing mix activities, such as product features and advertising, to help consumers perceive the product as being different and better than competing products. The perceived differences may involve physical features or nonphysical ones, such as image or price.[3]

In a narrower sense, product differentiation involves a firm's selling two or more products with different features targeted to different market segments. A firm can get into trouble when its different products blend together in consumers' minds and don't reach distinct market segments successfully—such as

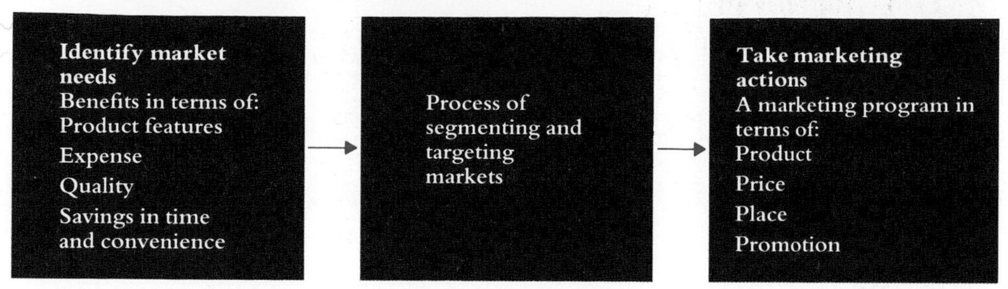

FIGURE 8-1
Market segmentation links market needs to an organization's marketing actions

GM's problem described in Chapter 2, in which customers couldn't separate the Chevrolet, Pontiac, Oldsmobile, Buick, and Cadillac cars in their minds. How GM is addressing this problem is described at the end of the chapter. However, the Reebok example discussed next shows how a manufacturer has succeeded in using a product differentiation strategy to offer different products targeted to separate market segments.

Segmentation: Linking Needs to Actions The definition of market segmentation first stresses the importance of aggregating—or grouping—people or organizations in a market according to the similarity of their needs and the benefits they are looking for in making a purchase. Second, such needs and benefits must be related to specific, tangible marketing actions the firm can take. These actions may involve separate products or other aspects of the marketing mix such as price, advertising or personal selling activities, or distribution strategies—the four *P*'s.

The process of segmenting a market and selecting specific segments as targets is the link between the various buyers' needs and the organization's marketing actions (Figure 8-1). Market segmentation is only a means to an end: in an economist's terms, it relates supply (the organization's actions) to demand (customer needs). A basic test of the usefulness of the segmentation process is whether it leads to tangible marketing actions.

Using Market-Product Grids A **market-product grid** is a framework to relate the segments of a market to products offered or potential marketing actions by the firm. The grid in Figure 8-2 shows different markets of sneaker users as rows in the grid, while the columns show the different shoe products (or marketing actions) chosen by Reebok.

The darker-shaded cells in Figure 8-2, labeled *P*, represent the primary market segment that Reebok targeted when it introduced each shoe. The lightly shaded cells labeled *S* represent the secondary market segments that also started buying the shoe. In some cases, Reebok discovered that large numbers of people in a segment not originally targeted for a style of shoe bought the shoe. In fact, as many as 75 to 80 percent of the running shoes and aerobic-dance shoes are bought by nonathletes represented by the (1) comfort and style conscious and (2) walker segments shown in Figure 8-2—although walkers may object to being labeled "nonathletes." When this trend became apparent to Reebok in 1986, it introduced its walking shoes targeted directly at the walker segment.[4]

MARKET		PRODUCT (STYLES OF SHOES)						
GENERAL	SPECIFIC	RUNNING (1981)	AEROBIC-DANCE (1982)	TENNIS (1984)	CHILDREN'S (1984)	BASKETBALL (1984)	WALKING (1986)	CROSS-TRAINERS (1988)
ATHLETES	Runners	P						P
	Aerobic-dance exercisers		P					P
	Tennis players			P				P
	Basketball players					P		P
NON ATHLETES	Comfort and style conscious	S	S	S			S	S
	Walkers	S	S	S			P	P
	Children				P			

Key: *P*, Primary market; *S*, secondary market.

FIGURE 8-2
Market-product grid showing how seven different styles of Reebok shoes reach segments of customers with different needs

WHEN TO SEGMENT MARKETS

A business firm goes to the trouble and expense of segmenting its markets when this increases its sales revenue, profit, and ROI. When its expenses more than offset the potentially increased revenues from segmentation, it should not attempt to segment its market. The specific situations that illustrate this point are the cases of (1) one product and multiple market segments and (2) multiple products and multiple market segments.

One Product and Multiple Market Segments When a firm produces only a single product or service and attempts to sell it to two or more market segments, it avoids the extra cost of developing and producing additional versions of the product, which often entail extremely high research, engineering, and manufacturing expenses. In this case the incremental costs of taking the product into new product segments are typically those of a separate promotional campaign or a new channel of distribution. Although these expenses can be high, they are rarely as large as those for developing an entirely new product.

Movies and magazines are single products frequently directed to two or more distinct market segments. Movie companies often run different TV commercials featuring different aspects of a newly released film (love, or drama, or spectacular scenery) that are targeted to different market segments.[5] As shown on p. 199 Street and Smith's official yearbook, *College Football*, uses different covers in different regions of the United States featuring a college football star from the region. Although multiple TV commercials for the movies or separate covers for magazines are expensive, this is minor compared with the costs of producing an entirely new movie or magazine for another market segment.

Multiple Products and Multiple Market Segments Reebok's seven different styles of shoes, each targeted at a different type of user, are an example of multiple products aimed at multiple markets. Manufacturing seven styles of shoes is clearly more expensive than producing one but seems worthwhile if it serves customers' needs better, doesn't reduce quality or increase the price they pay, and adds to the sales revenues and profits.

Product differentiation is generally an effective strategy, as in the Reebok example. But it can be carried too far. For example, in some cases American auto manufacturers have offered so many models and options to try to reach diverse market segments that sales revenue and profits have suffered in competition with imports.

The three basic elements that distinguish one model of car from another are (1) frames, (2) engines and drive trains, and (3) name plates. Adding other options in the form of various (4) body styles, (5) transmissions, (6) interiors, and (7) colors results in an incredible number of options. Perhaps the extreme case occurred in 1982 when Ford Thunderbird had exactly 69,120 options compared with 32 (including colors) on the 1982 Honda Accord (Figure 8-3). Some experts estimate the proliferation of these options has added an average of $1,000 to the sticker price of American cars—giving American consumers another reason to buy the lower-priced Japanese imports. Japanese manufacturers have

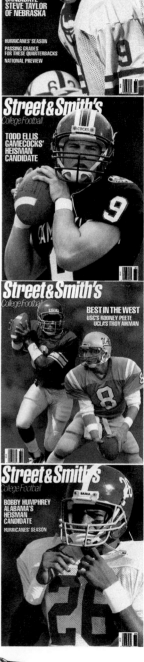

FIGURE 8-3
Product differentiation running wild; the number of options available on a 1982 Ford Thunderbird compared with those on a Honda Accord

Source: James Cook, "Where's the Niche?" *Forbes* (September 24, 1984), p. 54. © Forbes Inc., 1984.

Honda Accord: 32 option combinations

Ford Thunderbird: 69,120 option combinations

done extensive marketing research on American consumers and have selected a combination of options to meet the most typical needs.[6]

American car manufacturers are concluding that the costs of developing, producing, and servicing dozens of slightly different products probably outweigh the premium that consumers are willing to pay for the wider array of choices and are simplifying their product lines. For example, Ford's 1988 Thunderbird has fewer options, and its sales brochure stresses "preferred equipment packages" to simplify buying decisions for customers. GM, too, is trying to reduce the number of options and models it offers: by 1992 it hopes to eliminate 25 percent of the 175 models it offered in 1986.[7]

American appliance manufacturers are moving in the same direction: GE has reduced its number of dishwasher models and plans to do the same for refrigerators. Although there are fewer choices, this provides two benefits to consumers: (1) lower prices through higher volume production of fewer models and (2) higher quality because of the ability to debug fewer basic designs.

CONCEPT CHECK

1 **Market segmentation involves dividing a market into distinct groups that have two key characteristics. What are they?**

2 **What is product differentiation?**

3 **The process of segmenting and targeting markets is a bridge between what two marketing activities?**

STEPS IN SEGMENTING AND TARGETING A MARKET

The process of segmenting a market and then selecting and reaching the target segments is divided into the five steps discussed in this section. Segmenting a market is not a science. It requires large doses of common sense and managerial judgment.[8]

Market segmentation and target markets can be abstract topics, so put on your entrepreneur's hat to experience the process. Suppose you own a Wendy's fast food restaurant next to a large urban university that offers both day and evening classes. Your restaurant specializes in the Wendy's basics: hamburgers, french fries, Frosty milkshakes, and chili. Even though you are part of a chain and have some restrictions on menu and decor, you are free to set your hours of business and to undertake local advertising. How can market segmentation help?

FIND WAYS TO SEGMENT CUSTOMERS IN THE MARKET

Grouping customers into meaningful segments involves meeting some specific criteria for segmentation and finding specific variables to segment the consumer or industrial market being analyzed.[9]

Process of segmenting and targeting markets
Identify market needs
Benefits in terms of:
• Product features
• Expense
• Quality
• Savings in time and convenience
Form market segments
Develop segments based on:
• Potential for increased profit and ROI
• Similarity of needs of buyers within a segment
• Differences of needs of buyers between segments
• Feasibility of a marketing action to reach a segment
• Simplicity and cost of assigning potential buyers to segments
Select target segments
Focus on specific market segments based on:
• Size
• Expected growth
• Competitive position
• Cost of reaching the segment
• Compatibility with organization's objectives and resources
Take marketing actions
A marketing program in terms of:
• Product
• Price
• Place
• Promotion

FIGURE 8-4
Criteria used in segmenting a market and selecting target segments

Criteria to Use in Forming the Segments A marketing manager should develop segments for a market that meet five principal criteria (Figure 8-4):

- Potential for increased profit and ROI. The best segmentation approach is the one that maximizes the opportunity for future profit and ROI. If this potential is maximized through no segmentation, don't segment. For nonprofit organizations, the analogous criterion is the potential for serving client users more effectively.
- Similarity of needs of potential buyers within a segment. Potential buyers within a segment should be similar in terms of a marketing activity, such as product features sought or advertising media used.
- Difference of needs of buyers between segments. If the needs of the various segments aren't appreciably different, combine them into fewer segments. A different segment usually requires a different marketing action that in turn means greater costs. If increased revenues don't offset extra costs, combine segments and reduce the number of marketing actions.
- Feasibility of a marketing action to reach a segment. Reaching a segment requires a simple but effective marketing action. If no such action exists, don't segment.
- Simplicity and cost of assigning potential buyers to segments. A marketing manager must be able to put a market segmentation plan into effect. This means being able to recognize the characteristics of potential buyers and assign them to a segment.

Ways to Segment Consumer Markets Figure 8-5 shows a number of variables that can be used to segment consumer markets. They are divided into two general categories: customer characteristics and buying situation. Some examples of how certain characteristics can be used to segment specific markets include the following:

- Region, a geographical customer characteristic. Campbell's found that its

FIGURE 8-5
Segmentation variables and breakdowns for consumer markets

MAIN DIMENSION	SEGMENTATION VARIABLE	TYPICAL BREAKDOWNS
CUSTOMER CHARACTERISTICS		
Geographic	Region	Pacific; Mountain; West North Central; West South Central; East North Central; East South Central; South Atlantic; Middle Atlantic; New England
	City or metropolitan statistical area (MSA) size	Under 5,000; 5,000 to 19,999; 20,000 to 49,999; 50,000 to 99,999; 100,000 to 249,999; 250,000 to 499,999; 500,000 to 999,999; 1,000,000 to 3,999,999; 4,000,000 or over
	Density	Urban; suburban; rural
	Climate	Northern; Southern
Demographic	Age	Infant, under 6; 6 to 11; 12 to 17; 18 to 24; 25 to 34; 35 to 49; 50 to 64; 65 or over
	Sex	Male; female
	Family size	1 to 2; 3 to 4; 5 or over
	Stage of family life cycle	Young single; young married, no children; young married, youngest child under 6; young married, youngest child 6 or older; older married, with children; older married, no children under 18; older single; other older married, no children under 18
	Ages of children	No child under 18; youngest child 6 to 17; youngest child under 6
	Children under 18	0; 1; more than 1
	Income	Under $5,000; $5,000 to $14,999; $15,000 to $24,999; $25,000 to $34,999; $35,000 to $49,999; $50,000 or over
	Education	Grade school or less; some high school; high school graduate; some college; college graduate
	Race	White; black; Hispanic; Asian; other
	Home ownership	Own home; rent home
Psychographic	Personality	Gregarious; compulsive; extroverted; aggressive; ambitious
	Life-style	Use of one's time; values and importance; beliefs
BUYING SITUATIONS		
Benefits sought	Product features	Situation specific; general
	Needs	Quality; service; economy
Usage	Rate of use	Light user; medium user; heavy user
	User states	Nonuser; ex-user; potential user; first-time user; regular user
Awareness and intentions	Readiness to buy	Unaware; aware; informed; interested; desirous; intending to buy
	Brand familiarity	Insistence; preference; recognition; nonrecognition; rejection
Buying condition	Type of buying activity	Minimum effort buying; comparison buying; special effort buying
	Kind of store	Convenience; wide breadth; specialty

new canned nacho cheese sauce, which could be heated and poured directly onto nacho chips, was too hot for Americans in the East and not hot enough for those in the West and Southwest. The result: today Campbell's plants in Texas and California produce a hotter nacho cheese sauce to serve their regions than that produced in the other plants.[10]

- Family size, a demographic customer characteristic. More than half of all U.S. households have only one or two persons in them, so Campbell's packages meals with only one or two servings—from Great Starts breakfasts to L'Orient dinners. Because smaller households often have smaller kitchens, GE downsized its microwave oven, restyled it to hang under a kitchen cabinet, and moved into the number 2 position in microwaves. However, GE also offers extra large refrigerators for growing families at the beginning of their family life cycle.[11]
- Life-style, a psychographic customer characteristic. **Psychographic variables** are consumer activities, interests, and opinions. Knowing that a specific consumer segment is liberal politically, likes science fiction, and likes to take chances is of value in designing movies and TV commercials.
- Benefits offered, a situation characteristic. Important benefits offered different customers are a useful way to segment markets.[12] Because some consumers want or need a more healthy life-style, Del Monte now promotes a line of canned fruits with no artificial flavors or sweeteners.
- **Usage rate,** which refers to quantity consumed or patronage (store visits) during a specific period, varies significantly among different customer groups. This is often stated as the **80/20 rule,** which suggests that 80 percent of a firm's sales are obtained from 20 percent of its customers.

The percentages in the 80/20 rule are not really fixed at exactly 80 percent and 20 percent, but rather suggest that a small fraction of customers provides a large

GE's extra large refgrigerator caters to large families

USER OR NONUSER	SPECIFIC SEGMENT	ADULTS, 18 AND OVER NUMBER (1,000'S)	%	ACTUAL CONSUMPTION (%)	USAGE INDEX PER PERSON*	IMPORTANCE OF SEGMENT
Users	Heavy (14+ per month)	48,506	27.9	53.5	435	High
	Medium (6-13 per month)	51,471	29.6	36.5	280	
	Light (1-5 per month)	39,343	22.7	10.0	100	
TOTAL USERS		139,320	80.2	100.0	283	
Nonusers	Prospects	?	?	0	0	
	Nonprospects	?	?	0	0	Low
TOTAL NONUSERS		34,357	19.8	0	0	
TOTAL	Users and nonusers	173,677	100.0	100.0	—	—

*Where monthly consumption of a light user equals 100.

Source: *Simmons 1987 Study of Media and Markets: Restaurants, Stores, and Grocery Shopping—P-11* (Simmons Market Research Bureau, Inc., 1987), pp. 0001-0003.

FIGURE 8-6
Patronage (use) of fast food, drive-in, family, and steak house restaurants

fraction of a firm's sales. For example, Simmons Market Research Bureau, Inc., periodically surveys about 20,000 adults 18 years of age and older to discover how the products and services they buy and the media they watch relate to their demographic characteristics. Figure 8-6 shows the results of a question Simmons asks about the respondent's frequency of use (or patronage) of "fast-food, drive-in, family, and steak house restaurants."

As shown in the right column of Figure 8-6, the importance of the segment increases as we move up the table. Among nonusers of these restaurants, prospects (who *might become* users) are more important than nonprospects (who are *never likely* to become users). Moving up the rows to the users, it seems logical that **light users** of these restaurants (1 to 5 times per month) are important but less so than **medium users** (6 to 13 times per month), who in turn are a less important segment than the critical group—the **heavy users** (14 or more times per month). The "Actual Consumption" column in Figure 8-6 tells how much of the total monthly sales of these restaurants are accounted for by the heavy, medium, and light users. For example, the 48,506,000 American adults who go to these restaurants 14 or more times in a typical month represent about 53.5 percent of the sales revenues.

The "Usage Index per Person" column in Figure 8-6 emphasizes the importance of the heavy user group even more. Giving the light users (1 to 5 restaurant visits per month) an index of 100, the heavy users have an index of 435. In other words, for every $1.00 spent by a light user in one of these restaurants in a month, each heavy user spends $4.35. This is the reason for the emphasis in almost all marketing strategies on effective ways to reach these heavy users. Thus as a Wendy's restaurant owner you want to keep the heavy-user segment constantly in mind. Fortunately, many college students fall into the heavy-user segment for fast-food restaurants.

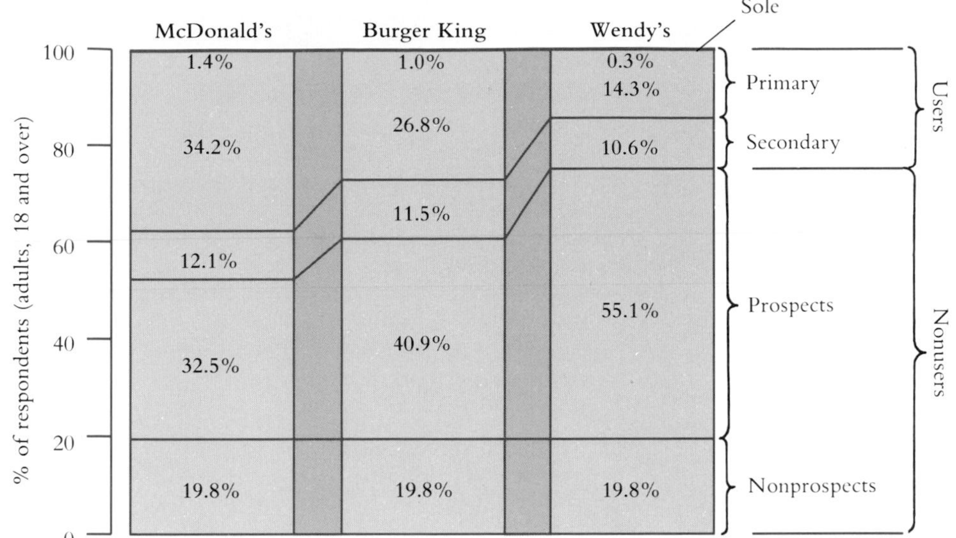

FIGURE 8-7 Comparison of various kinds of users and nonusers for McDonald's, Burger King, and Wendy's restaurants

As part of the Simmons survey, restaurant patrons were asked if each restaurant was (1) the sole restaurant they went to, (2) the primary one, or (3) one of several secondary ones. This national information, shown in Figure 8-7, might give you, as a Wendy's owner, some ideas in developing your local strategy. The Wendy's bar in Figure 8-7 shows that your sole (0.3 percent), primary (14.3 percent), and secondary (10.6 percent) user segments are somewhat behind Burger King and far behind McDonald's, so a natural strategy is to look at these two competitors and devise a marketing program to win customers from them.

The "nonusers" part of your own bar in Figure 8-7 also provides ideas. It shows that 19.8 percent of adult Americans don't go to these restaurants in a typical month (also shown in Figure 8-6) and are really **nonprospects**—unlikely to ever patronize your restaurant. But the 55.1 percent of the Wendy's bar shown as **prospects** may be worth detailed thought. These adults use the product category (fast-food, drive-in, family, and steak house restaurants) but *do not* go to Wendy's. New menu items or new promotional strategies might succeed in converting these "prospects" to "users." One key conclusion emerges about usage: in market segmentation studies, some measure of usage or revenues derived from various segments is central to the analysis.

In determining one or two variables to segment the market for your Wendy's restaurant, very broadly we find two main markets: students and nonstudents. To segment the students, we could try a variety of demographic variables, such as age, sex, year in school, or college major; or psychographic variables, such as personality characteristics, attitudes, or interests. But none of these variables really meets the five criteria listed previously—particularly the fourth criterion about leading to a feasible marketing action to reach the various segments. Four student segments that *do* meet these criteria include the following:

- Students living in dormitories (college residence halls, sororities, fraternities)

MAIN DIMENSION	SEGMENTATION VARIABLE	TYPICAL BREAKDOWNS
CUSTOMER CHARACTERISTICS		
Geographical	Region	Pacific; Mountain; West North Central; West South Central; East North Central; East South Central; South Atlantic; Middle Atlantic; New England
	Location	In MSA; not in MSA
Demographic	SIC code	2-digit; 3-digit; 4-digit categories
	Number of employees	1 to 19; 20 to 99; 100 to 249; 250 or over
	Number of production workers	1 to 19; 20 to 99; 100 to 249; 250 or over
	Annual sales volume	Less than \$1 million; \$1 million to \$10 million; \$10 million to \$100 million; over \$100 million
	Number of establishments	With 1 to 19 employees; with 20 or more employees
BUYING SITUATIONS		
Nature of good	Kind	Product or service
	Where used	Installation; component of final product; supplies
	Application	Office use; limited production use; heavy production use
Buying condition	Purchase location	Centralized; decentralized
	Who buys	Individual buyer; group
	Type of buy	New buy; modified rebuy; straight rebuy

FIGURE 8-8
Segmentation variables and breakdowns for industrial markets

- Students living near the college in apartments
- Day commuter students living outside the area
- Night commuter students living outside the area

These segmentation variables are really a combination of where the student lives and the time he or she is on campus (and near your restaurant). For nonstudents who might be customers, similar variables might be used:

- Faculty and staff members at the university
- People who live in the area but aren't connected with the university
- People who work in the area but aren't connected with the university

People in each of these segments aren't quite as similar as those in the students', which makes them harder to reach with a marketing program or action. Think about (1) whether the needs of all these segments are different and (2) how various advertising media can be used to reach these groups effectively.

Ways to Segment Industrial Markets Variables for segmenting industrial markets are shown in Figure 8-8. A product manager at Xerox responsible for a line of photocopiers might use a number of these segmentation variables, as follows:

Industrial products use different segmentation variables than do consumer products

- Location. Firms located in a metropolitan statistical area (MSA) might receive a personal sales call, whereas those outside the MSA might be contacted by telephone.
- SIC code. Firms categorized by the Standard Industrial Classification (SIC) code as manufacturers might have different photocopying needs than do retailers or lawyers.
- Number of employees. The size of the firm is related to the volume of photocopying done, for a given industry or SIC, so larger firms in terms of employment might require larger machines than do smaller firms.

FIND WAYS TO GROUP PRODUCTS TO BE SOLD

As important as grouping customers into segments is finding a means of grouping the products you're selling into meaningful categories. If the firm has only one product or service, this isn't a problem, but when it has dozens or hundreds, these must be grouped in some way so buyers can relate to them. This is why department stores and supermarkets are organized into product groups, with the departments or aisles containing related merchandise. Likewise manufacturers have product lines that are the groupings they use in the catalogs sent to customers.

What are the groupings for your restaurant? It could be the item purchased, such as a Frosty, chili, hamburgers, and french fries, but this is where judgment—the qualitative aspect of marketing—comes in. Students really buy an eating experience, or a meal that satisfies a need at a particular time of day, so the product grouping can be defined by meal or time of day as breakfast, lunch, between-meal snack, dinner, and after-dinner snack. These groupings are more closely related to the way purchases are actually made and permit you to market the entire meal, not just your french fries or Frosties.

DEVELOP A MARKET-PRODUCT GRID AND ESTIMATE MARKET SIZE

Developing a market-product grid means labeling the markets (or horizontal rows) and products (or vertical columns), as shown in Figure 8-9. In addition, the size of the market in each cell, or the market-product combination, must be estimated. For your restaurant this involves estimating the number of, or sales revenue obtained from, each kind of meal that can reasonably be expected to be sold to each market segment. This is a form of the usage rate analysis discussed earlier in the chapter.

The market sizes in Figure 8-9 may be simple "guesstimates" if you don't have time for formal marketing research and forecasting (as discussed in Chapters 6 and 7). But even such crude estimates of the size of specific markets using a market-product grid are far better than the usual estimates of the entire market.

SELECT TARGETS ON WHICH TO FOCUS EFFORTS

A firm must take care to choose its target market segments carefully. If it picks too narrow a group of segments, it may fail to reach the volume of sales and profits it needs. If it selects too broad a group of segments, it may spread its marketing efforts so thin that the extra expenses more than offset the increased sales and profits.

Criteria to Use in Picking the Target Segments There are two different kinds of criteria present in the market segmentation process: (1) those to use in dividing the market into segments (discussed earlier) and (2) those to use in actually picking the target segments (Figure 8-4). Even experienced marketing executives often confuse these two different sets of criteria. The five criteria to use in actually selecting the target segments apply to your Wendy's restaurant this way:

- Size. The estimated size of the market in the segment is an important

FIGURE 8-9
Selecting a target market for your fast food restaurant next to a metropolitan college. Target market is shaded

	PRODUCTS: MEALS				
MARKETS	BREAKFAST	LUNCH	BETWEEN-MEAL SNACK	DINNER	AFTER-DINNER SNACK
STUDENT					
Dormitory	0	S	L	0	L
Apartment	S	L	L	S	S
Day commuter	0	L	M	S	0
Night commuter	0	0	S	L	M
NONSTUDENT					
Faculty or staff	0	L	S	S	0
Live in area	0	S	M	M	S
Work in area	S	L	0	S	0

Key: *L*, Large market; *M*, medium market; *S*, small market; *0*, no market.

Packaged foods targeted at market segments with special tastes

factor in deciding whether it's worth going after. There is really no market for breakfasts among dormitory students (Figure 8-9), so why devote any marketing effort toward reaching a small or nonexistent market?

- Expected growth. Although the size of the market in the segment may be small now, perhaps it is growing significantly or is expected to grow in the future. Night commuters may not look important now, but with the decline in traditional day students in many colleges, the evening adult education programs are expected to expand in the future. Thus the future market among night commuters is probably more encouraging than the current picture shown in Figure 8-9.
- Competitive position. Is there a lot of competition in the segment now or is there likely to be in the future? The less the competition, the more attractive the segment is. For example, if the college dormitories announce a new policy of "no meals on weekends," this segment is suddenly more promising for your restaurant.
- Cost of reaching the segment. A segment that is inaccessible to a firm's marketing actions should not be pursued. For example, the few nonstudents who live in the area may not be economically reachable with ads in newspapers or other media. As a result, do not waste money trying to advertise to them.
- Compatibility with the organization's objectives and resources. If your restaurant doesn't have the cooking equipment to make breakfasts and has a policy against spending more money on restaurant equipment, then don't try to reach the breakfast segment.

As is often the case in marketing decisions, a particular segment may appear attractive according to some criteria and very unattractive according to others.

Choose the Segments Ultimately a marketing executive has to use these criteria to choose the segments for special marketing efforts. As shown in Figure 8-9, let's assume you've written off the breakfast market for two reasons: market size and compatibility with your objectives and resources. In terms of competitive position and cost of reaching the segment, you choose to focus on the four student segments and not the three nonstudent segments (although you're certainly not going to turn away business from the nonstudent segments). This combination of market-product segments—your target market—is shaded in Figure 8-9.

DEVELOP AND IMPLEMENT A MARKETING PROGRAM

The purpose of developing a market-product grid is to trigger marketing actions to increase revenues and profits. This means that someone must develop and execute an action plan.

Your Wendy's Segmentation Strategy With your Wendy's restaurant you've already reached one significant decision: there is a limited market for breakfast, so you won't open for business until 10:30 AM. In fact, a costly attempt at a Wendy's breakfast menu was a disaster and was discontinued in 1986.[13]

Another essential decision is where and what meals to advertise to reach specific market segments. An ad in the student newspaper could reach all the student segments, but you might consider this "shotgun approach" too expensive and want a more focused "rifle approach" to reach smaller segments. If you choose three segments for special actions (Figure 8-10), advertising actions to reach them might include:

- Day commuters, an entire market segment. Run ads inside commuter buses and put flyers under the windshield wipers of cars in parking lots used by day commuters. These ads and flyers promote all the meals at your restaurant to a single segment of students—a horizontal cut through the market-product grid.
- Between-meals snacks, directed to all four student markets. To promote eating during this downtime for your restaurant, offer "Ten percent off all purchases between 2:00 and 4:30 PM during winter quarter." This ad

FIGURE 8-10
Advertising actions to reach specific student segments

	PRODUCTS: MEALS			
MARKETS	LUNCH	BETWEEN-MEAL SNACK	DINNER	AFTER-DINNER SNACK
Dormitory students	S	L	0	L
Apartment students	L	L	S	S
Day commuter students	L	M	S	0
Night commuter students	0	S	L	M

Ads in buses; flyers under windshield wipers of cars in parking lots.

Ad campaign: "Ten percent off all purchases between 2:00 and 4:30 PM during winter quarter."

Ad on flyer under windshield wipers of cars in night parking lots: "Free Frosty with this coupon when you buy a hamburger and french fries."

Wendy's original menu

promotes a single meal to all four student segments—a vertical cut through the market-product grid.

- Dinners to night commuters. The most focused of all three campaigns, this ad promotes a single meal to a single student segment. The campaign might consist of a windshield flyer offering a free Frosty with the coupon when the person buys a hamburger and french fries.

Depending on how your advertising actions work, you can repeat, modify, or drop them and design new campaigns for other segments you feel warrant the effort. This example of advertising your Wendy's restaurant is just a small piece of a complete marketing program using all the elements of the marketing mix.

Apple's Segmentation Strategy Steven Jobs and Stephen Wozniak didn't realize they were developing today's multibillion-dollar PC industry when they invented the Apple II in a garage in 1976. Under Jobs' inspirational leadership through the early 1980's, Apple was run with a focus on products and little concern for markets. Apple's control of its brainy, creative young engineers was likened to "Boy Scouts without adult supervision."[14] When IBM entered the PC market in 1981, Apple lost significant market share, and many experts predicted it wouldn't survive.

Enter John Sculley, who in 1983 moved to Apple's presidency from Pepsi-Cola. Sculley, as shown in the Marketing Action Memo, formalized and gave cohesiveness to Apple's market segmentation strategy and targeted specific Apple machines to particular market segments. As in most segmentation situations, a single Apple product does not fit into an exclusive market niche. Rather, there is overlap among products in the product line and also among the markets to which they are directed. But a market segmentation strategy enables Apple to offer different products to meet the needs of the different market segments.

In talking to PC users, Sculley reached some key conclusions that redirected Apple's segmentation strategy. First, he concluded that the popularity of cheap, imported PCs meant that Apple could not count on significant revenues from individual households (the "home" market segment), so he reduced efforts to reach that segment. Next, he concluded that Apple must penetrate the business market, which meant designing Apple products that would network easily with

MARKETING · ACTION · MEMO

HOW APPLE SEGMENTS ITS MARKETS

When John Sculley moved from Pepsi-Cola to become president of Apple Computer in 1983, he took over the company that some computer industry wags called "Camp Runamok," because it had no coherent product line that was directed at identifiable market segments.

Sculley took immediate action to avoid potential disaster. The result is the market-product grid below that shows the target segments for each computer and Apple's LaserWriter printer. Because the market-product grid shifts as a firm's strategy changes, the one below is based on the product line that existed in early 1988. Apple's new market-product analysis has given it a coherent strategy to compete with IBM. Uses for these products range from word and data processing to sophisticated applications involving multicomputer networks, desktop publishing, and scientific work stations. Camp Runamok is back on track.

Sources: Brian O'Reilly, "Apple Finally Invades the Office," *Fortune* (November 9, 1987), pp. 52-64; "Apple Goes for a Bigger Bite of Corporate America," *Business Week* (August 24, 1987), pp. 74-75; "Corporate Antihero John Sculley," *Inc.* (October 1987), pp. 49-60; Brian O'Reilly, "Growing Apple Anew for the Business Market," *Fortune* (January 4, 1988), pp. 36-37.

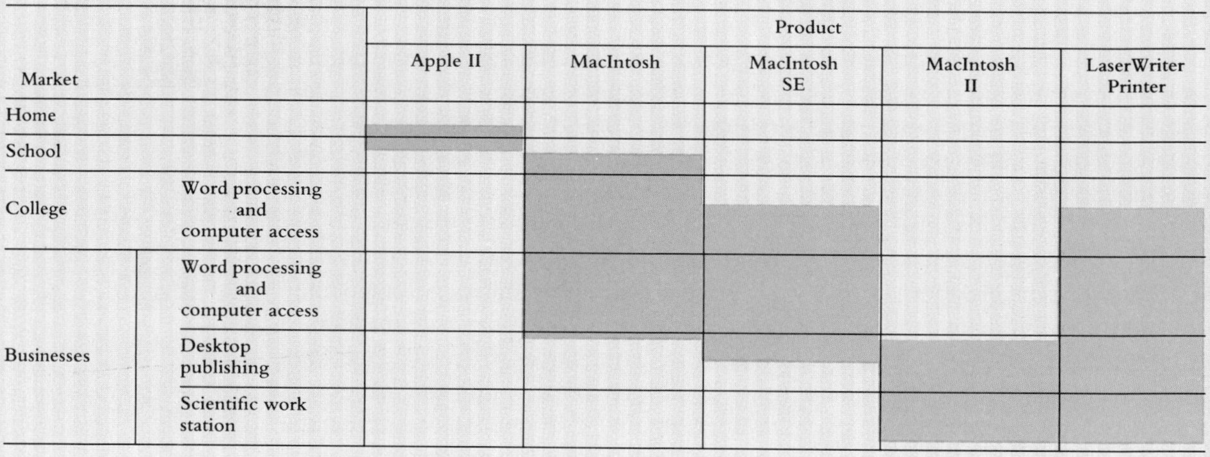

Market		Product				
		Apple II	MacIntosh	MacIntosh SE	MacIntosh II	LaserWriter Printer
Home						
School						
College	Word processing and computer access					
Businesses	Word processing and computer access					
	Desktop publishing					
	Scientific work station					

competitive machines and larger computers from IBM and Digital Equipment Corporation (DEC). So Sculley signed an agreement with DEC to make their machines swap data more easily. Finally, Sculley pushed the introductions of the Macintosh SE and Macintosh II lines to accommodate computer boards made by other companies, which significantly increased the appeal to businesses because they network better with other computers.[15]

Apple also had the vision to see a giant breakthrough triggered by tiny Aldus Corporation's software breakthrough for the Macintosh. This was desktop publishing, which enables a Macintosh user to produce brochures and graphics, such as those used in *USA Today,* in hours or days, a task that formerly took weeks.[16] Desktop publishing has enabled Apple to gain respectability among business users today and to compete with IBM for PC sales.

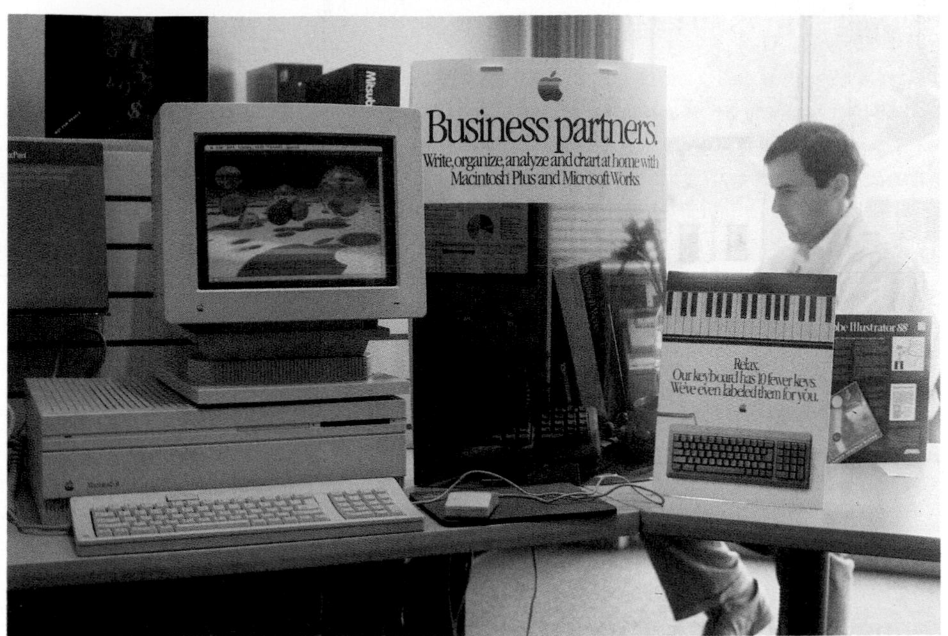

Examples of graphics created on the Macintosh computer

Segmentation Strategies of Small Firms Many startup firms attribute their success to finding a specialized market segment, or niche, in which their small size is not a major disadvantage relative to their giant competitors. Some have used this initial niche strategy to become large firms today. For example, An Wang built today's $2-billion-a-year Wang Laboratories by initially focusing on the networking of computer work stations years before it became fashionable. Similarly, Sirjang Lal Tandon successfully targeted Tandon Corporation's efforts toward specialized niches within the computer disk drive and PC markets.[17]

Other, less well-known firms operate successfully in smaller market segments. For example, rather than compete in the market for standard window glass, California's AFG Industries offers lines of specialty and tempered glass—enabling it to capture 70 percent of the market for glass for microwave oven doors and 75 percent of the market for glass for shower doors and patio tabletops. In its Akron, Ohio, factory, A. Shulman blends plastic resins and paint colors and sells these customized materials to manufacturers producing colorful products such as skateboard wheels and lobster pots. In this way, A. Shulman avoids being just another firm among hundreds of plastics compounders across the United States.[18]

Concept Check

1 **What are some of the variables used to segment consumer markets?**

2 **What are some criteria used to decide which segments to choose for targets?**

3 **Why is usage rate important in segmentation studies?**

ANALYZING MARKET SEGMENTS USING CROSS TABULATIONS

To do a more precise market segmentation analysis of your Wendy's restaurant, suppose you survey fast food patrons throughout the metropolitan area where your restaurant is located using the questionnaire shown in Figure 6-6. You want to use this information as best you can to study the market's segments and develop your strategy. Probably the most widely used approach today in marketing is to develop and interpret cross tabulations of data obtained by questionnaires.

DEVELOPING CROSS TABULATIONS

A **cross tabulation,** or "cross tab," is a method of presenting and relating data having two or more variables. It is used to analyze and discover relationships in the data. Two important aspects of cross tabulations are deciding which of two variables to pair together to help understand the situation and forming the resulting cross tabulations.

Pairing the Questions Marketers pair two questions to understand marketing relationships and to find effective marketing actions. The Wendy's questionnaire in Figure 6-6 gives many questions that might be paired to understand the fast food business better and help reach a decision about marketing actions to increase revenues. For example, if you want to study your hypothesis that as the age of the head of household increases, patronage of fast food restaurants declines, you can cross tabulate Questions 9d and 3.

FIGURE 8-11
Two forms of a cross tabulation relating age of head of household to fast food restaurant patronage

A, Absolute frequencies

AGE OF HEAD OF HOUSEHOLD (YEARS)	FREQUENCY: ONCE A WEEK OR MORE	FREQUENCY: 2 OR 3 TIMES A MONTH	FREQUENCY: ONCE A MONTH OR LESS	TOTAL
24 or less	144	52	19	215
25 to 39	46	58	29	133
40 or over	82	69	87	238
TOTAL	272	179	135	586

B, Row percentages: running percentages horizontally

AGE OF HEAD OF HOUSEHOLD (YEARS)	FREQUENCY: ONCE A WEEK OR MORE	FREQUENCY: 2 OR 3 TIMES A MONTH	FREQUENCY: ONCE A MONTH OR LESS	TOTAL
24 or less	67.0%	24.2%	8.8%	100.0%
25 to 39	34.6	43.6	21.8	100.0
40 or over	34.4	29.0	36.6	100.0
TOTAL	46.4%	30.6%	23.0%	100.0%

Forming Cross Tabulations Using the answers to Question 3 as the column headings and the answers to Question 9d as the row headings gives a cross tabulation, as shown in Figure 8-11, using the answers 586 respondents gave to both questions. The figure shows two forms of the cross tabulation:

- The raw data or answers to the specific questions are shown in Figure 8-11, *A*. For example, this cross tab shows that 144 households whose head was 24 years or younger ate at fast food restaurants once a week or more.
- Answers on a percentage basis, with the percentages running horizontally, are shown in Figure 8-11, *B*. Of the 215 households headed by someone 24 years or younger, 67.0 percent ate at a fast food restaurant at least once a week and only 8.8 percent ate there once a month or less.

Two other forms of cross tabulation using the raw data shown in Figure 8-11, *A*, are as described in Question 7 at the end of the chapter.

INTERPRETING CROSS TABULATIONS

A careful analysis of Figure 8-11 shows that patronage of fast food restaurants is related to the age of the head of the household. Note that as the age of the head of the household increases, fast food restaurant patronage declines, as shown by highlighted numbers on diagonal lines in Figure 8-11. This means that if you want to reach the heavy user segment, you should direct your marketing efforts to the segment that is 24 years old or younger.

As discussed earlier in the chapter, there are various ways to segment a consumer market besides according to age. For example, you could make subsequent cross tabulations to analyze patronage related to where students live and the meals they eat to obtain more precise information for the market-product grid in Figure 8-11.

VALUE OF CROSS TABULATIONS

Probably the most widely used technique for organizing and presenting marketing data, cross tabulations have some important advantages.[19] The simple format permits direct interpretation and an easy means of communicating data to management. They have great flexibility and can be used to summarize experimental, observational, and questionnaire data. Also, cross tabulations may be easily generated by today's personal computers.

Cross tabulations also have some disadvantages. For example, they can be misleading if the percentages are based on too small a number of observations. Also, cross tabulations can hide some relations because each typically only shows two or three variables. Balancing both advantages and disadvantages, more marketing decisions are probably made using cross tabulations than any other method of analyzing data.

The ultimate value of cross tabulations to a marketing manager lies in obtaining a better understanding of the wants and needs of buyers and targeting key segments. This enables a marketing manager to "position" the offering in the minds of buyers, the topic discussed next.

Head-to-head positioning: Volvo versus Porsche

Positioning the Product

When a company offers a product commercially, a decision critical to its long-term success is how to position it in the market on introduction. **Product positioning** refers to the place an offering occupies in consumers' minds on important attributes relative to competing offerings.

Two Approaches to Product Positioning

There are several approaches to positioning a new product in the market. Head-to-head positioning involves competing directly with competitors on similar product attributes in the same target market. Using this strategy, Gillette positioned Earth Borne shampoo head-to-head against Clairol's Herbal Essence; Dollar competes directly with Avis and Hertz; and Volvo pits its turbo-charged cars against Porsche (see advertisement above).

Differentiation positioning involves seeking a smaller market niche that is less competitive in which to locate a brand. Curtis Mathes has promoted its television sets for the quality market with the slogan, "The most expensive television sets money can buy." Sylvania, on the other hand, competes head-to-head with Sony in direct product comparison advertising. Intel successfully competed head-to-head with Motorola in the computer chip business by positioning itself as a firm with a broad and deep product line having a plan for the future.[20]

Companies also follow a differentiation strategy among brands within their own product line to minimize cannibalization of a brand's sales or shares (which occurs when a company's new brand steals sales from other products in its line). For example, it has been estimated that 20 percent to 25 percent of the share of Michelob Light has come from Michelob. When Hanes introduced its less expensive pantyhose, L'eggs, in supermarkets, sales of its more expensive hosiery in department stores dropped by 20 percent.[21] For many companies, however, although cannibalization is not desired, it's a risk they're willing to take.

PRODUCT POSITIONING USING PERCEPTUAL MAPS

A key to positioning a product effectively is the perceptions of consumers.[22] In determining a brand's position and the preferences of consumers, companies obtain three types of data from consumers:

1. Evaluations of the important attributes for a product class
2. Judgments of existing brands with the important attributes
3. Ratings of an "ideal" brand's attributes

From these data, it is possible to develop a **perceptual map,** a means of displaying or graphing in two dimensions the location of products or brands in the minds of consumers.

As mentioned earlier, by the 1980's GM was concerned that the image of its five main models of U.S. cars—Chevrolet, Pontiac, Oldsmobile, Buick, and Cadillac—had so blurred in the minds of American consumers that they could not distinguish one brand from another. In 1982 GM interviewed consumers and developed the perceptual map shown in Figure 8-12, *A*. Note that the two dimensions on the perceptual map are (1) low price versus high price and (2) family/conservative versus personal/expressive appeal. Figure 8-12, *A*, shows that GM indeed had a problem. Although there was some variation in the vertical

FIGURE 8-12
The General Motors strategy to reposition its major car brands

Source: Jesse Synder, "4 GM Car Divisions Are Repositioned in an Effort to Help Sales," *Automotive News* (September 15, 1986), pp. 1, 49.

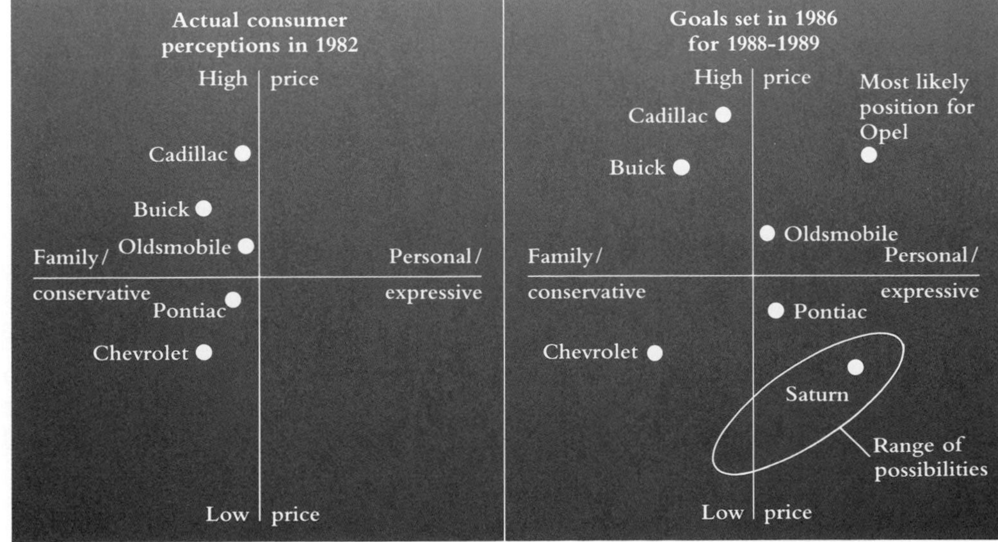

dimension (consumers' perception of price), there was little difference in the horizontal dimension (family/conservative appeal versus personal/expressive appeal). So in 1986 GM set new goals for where it wanted its models (including a possible Opel import) to be in 1988 to 1989. This involves **repositioning** the models, or changing their images in consumers' minds. Note the repositioning changes intended for two of its models by 1988 to 1989[23].

1. Oldsmobile is to be reduced slightly in price and repositioned as a more personal/expressive car.
2. Pontiac is to be made a more personal/expressive car to move it further away from Chevrolet than it has been in the past.

To fill in glaring gaps in its brands, GM is trying to position its new Saturn and an Opel import as shown in Figure 8-12, *B*. To convert these perceptual maps to actions, GM is changing both its basic designs and the advertising used to describe its models to prospective buyers.[24] Some of the intervening steps in GM's positioning strategy are explained in a case in the back of this text.

The example illustrates how a manager can use perceptual maps to see how consumers perceive competing products or brands and then take actions to try to change the product offering and the image it projects to consumers.

Concept Check

1 **What is cross tabulation?**

2 **What are some advantages of cross tabulations?**

3 **Why do marketers use perceptual maps in product positioning decisions?**

Summary

1 Market segmentation is aggregating prospective buyers into groups that have common needs and will respond similarly to a marketing action.

2 A straightforward approach to segmenting, targeting, and reaching a market involves five steps: (a) group customers into segments according to characteristics such as their needs, (b) group the products offered or marketing actions into meaningful categories, (c) develop a market-product grid that relates potential sales of product lines to the segments, (d) select the target segments for emphasis, and (e) take marketing actions to reach those target segments.

3 Marketing variables often are used to represent customer needs in the market segmentation process. For consumer markets, typical customer variables are region, metropolitan statistical area, age, income, and benefits sought, and usage rate. For industrial markets, comparable variables are geographical location, size of firm, and Standard Industrial Classification (SIC) code.

4 Usage rate is an important factor in a market segmentation study. Users are often divided into heavy, medium, and light users.
5 Nonusers are often divided into prospects and nonprospects. Nonusers of a firm's brand may be important because they are prospects—users of some other brand in the product class that may be convinced to change brands.
6 Criteria used (a) to segment markets and (b) to choose target segments are related but different. The former includes potential to increase profits, similarity of needs of buyers within a segment, difference of needs between segments, and feasibility of a resulting marketing action. The latter includes market size, expected growth, the competitive position of the firm's offering in the segment, and the cost of reaching the segment.
7 A market-product grid is a useful way to display what products can be directed at which market segments, but the grid must lead to marketing actions for the segmentation process to be worthwhile.
8 Cross tabulations are widely used today in market segmentation studies to identify needs of various customer segments and the actions to reach them.
9 A company can position a product head-to-head against the competition or seek a differentiated position. A concern with positioning is often to avoid cannibalization of the existing product line. In positioning, a firm often uses consumer judgments in the form of perceptual maps to locate its product relative to competing ones.

KEY TERMS AND CONCEPTS

market segmentation p. 196
market segments p. 196
product differentiation p. 196
market-product grid p. 197
psychographic variables p. 203
usage rate p. 203
80/20 rule p. 203
light users p. 204
medium users p. 204
heavy users p. 204
nonprospects p. 205
prospects p. 205
cross tabulation p. 214
product positioning p. 216
perceptual map p. 217
repositioning p. 218

CHAPTER PROBLEMS AND APPLICATIONS

1 What variables might be used to segment these consumer markets? (a) lawn mowers, (b) frozen dinners, (c) dry breakfast cereals, and (d) soft drinks.
2 What variables might be used to segment these industrial markets? (a) industrial sweepers, (b) photocopiers, (c) computerized production control systems, and (d) car rental agencies.
3 In Figure 8-10 the dormitory market segment includes students living in college-owned residence halls, sororities, and fraternities. What market needs are common to these students that justify combining them into a single segment in studying the market for your Wendy's restaurant?

4 You may disagree with the estimates of market size given for the rows in the market-product grid in Figure 8-10. Estimate the market size and give a brief justification for these market segments: (a) dormitory students, (b) day commuters, and (c) people who work in the area.
5 Suppose you want to increase revenues from your fast food restaurant shown in Figure 8-10 even further. What advertising actions might you take to increase revenues from (a) dormitory students, (b) dinners, and (c) after-dinner snacks from night commuters?
6 Look back at Figure 6-6. Which questions would you pair to form a cross tabulation to uncover the following relationships? (a) frequency of fast food restaurant patronage and restaurant characteristics important to the customer, (b) age of the head of household and source of information used about fast food restaurants, (c) frequency of patronage of Wendy's and source of information used about fast food restaurants, and (d) how much children have to say about where the family eats and number of children in the household.
7 Look back at Figure 8-11, *A*. (a) Run the percentages vertically and tell what they mean. (b) Express all numbers in the table as a percentage of the total number of people sampled (586) and tell what the percentages mean.
8 In Figure 8-11, (a) what might be other names for the three patronage levels shown in the columns? (b) Which is likely to be of special interest to Wendy's and why?
9 Using GM's 1988 to 1989 positioning goals that it set in 1986 (Figure 8-12, *B*) as a reference, what product design changes would it have to make to reposition the Oldsmobile and Pontiac lines on the family/conservative versus personal/expressive dimension and (b) where should it position Saturn and why?

SUGGESTED READINGS

Peter Dickson and James L. Ginter, "Market Segmentation, Product Differentiation, and Marketing Strategy," *Journal of Marketing* (April 1987), pp. 1-10. *In this article the authors try to clarify the often-misused phrases "market segmentation" and "product differentiation."*

Brian O'Reilly, "Apple Finally Invades the Office," *Fortune* (November 9, 1987), pp. 52-64. *After a frontal assault in 1984 with MacIntoshes to try to get Apple's computers into large corporations, John Sculley developed a "back-door" strategy targeted at these same firms by stressing desk-top publishing.*

"The Fast Food Industry Is Slowing Down," *Business Week* (May 18, 1987), pp. 50-51. *With one restaurant for every 685 Americans, Wendy's and Burger King are developing new strategies to regain customers.*

Stuart Gannes, "The Riches in Market Niches," *Fortune* (April 27, 1987), pp. 227-230. *This article describes the success of small-sized and medium-sized companies in reaching specialized market segments in which they avoid competing directly with the giants.*

PART FOUR

SATISFYING MARKETING OPPORTUNITIES

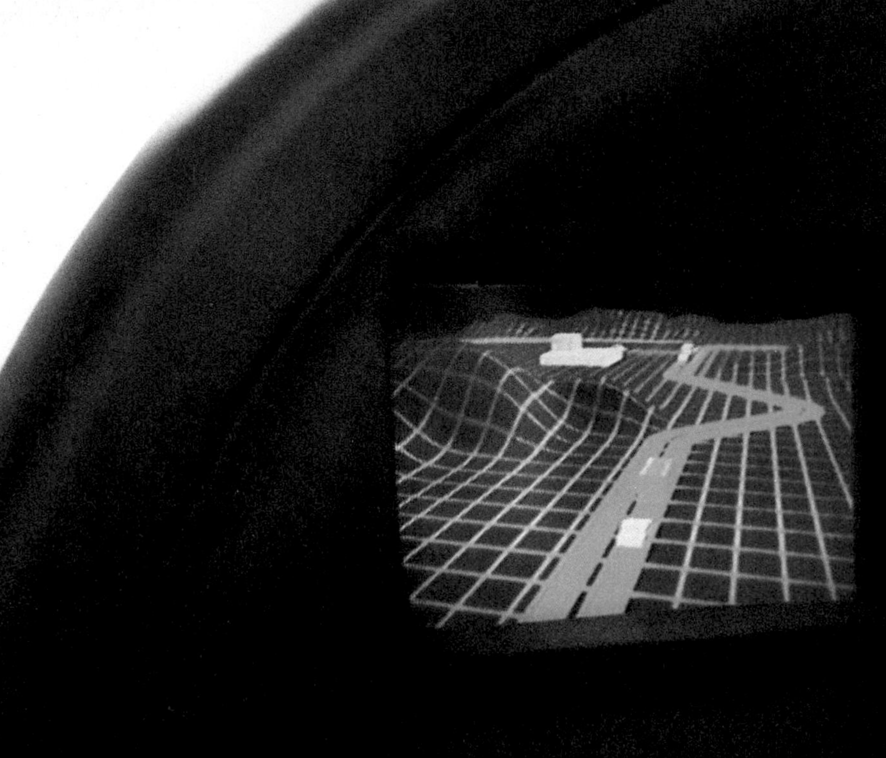

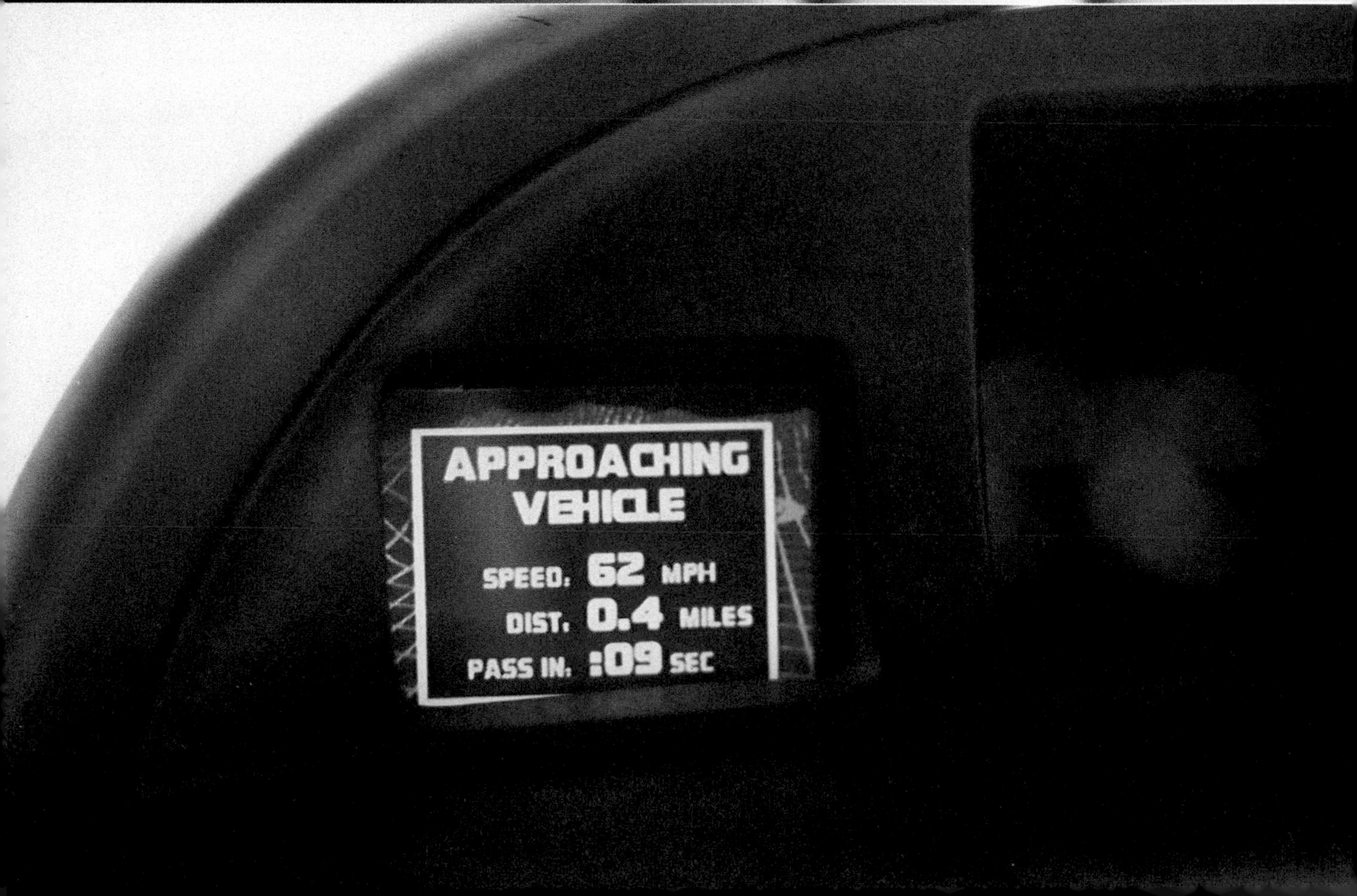

APPROACHING
VEHICLE
SPEED: 62 MPH
DIST. 0.4 MILES
PASS IN: :09 SEC

9

DEVELOPING NEW PRODUCTS

After reading this chapter you should be able to:

Understand the ways in which consumer and industrial products can be classified.

•

Recommend strategies for marketing the different types of consumer products.

•

Explain the implications of alternative ways of viewing "newness" in new products.

•

Understand the purposes of each step of the new product process.

•

Analyze the factors contributing to a product's success or failure.

Smart Cars for 1995: More Computer Power than an IBM PC

Cars built in 1995 are likely to have so many new gadgets and controls that even James Bond would be shocked. On board these cars may be two or three master computers, each with the power of IBM's latest PC.

These computers will revolutionize the design and driving of these new "smart" cars. And when you sit behind the wheel, you will experience major differences in four areas[1]:

- *Outside the car.* Already on Pontiac's Banshee concept car (opposite page), a dashboard video screen will show you road conditions and the surrounding terrain. Using radar, sonar, or laser technology, an anticollision system will signal you when it's unsafe to pass or change lanes.
- *Inside the car.* Heads-up-displays (HUD), originally developed for airplane pilots, will make the dashboard displays seem

to hover in the air so you don't have to look down, and image-enhancement techniques will improve your view in fog and at night.

- *Under the hood.* Electronic signals will replace cumbersome mechanical and hydraulic linkages to control gas fed to the engine and braking messages sent to the wheels.
- *Beneath the floor.* Advanced traction-control systems will help stop skidding on ice and brake locking during quick stops. Special pressure sensors will tell you when your tires need more air.

Do we really need these devices on our 1995 cars? Many consumers remember gadgetry such as talking cars and fancy digital dashboards that are now largely gone because consumers found they didn't really want or need the devices. And with the high costs of research, development, and production of these new products, many car manufacturers are understandably nervous about consumer reactions.

Some car experts are even concerned that the new high-technology cars may make driving less safe by making their drivers overconfident. Perhaps some designs are even going too far already: BMW is designing a system to make the steering wheel more difficult to turn when the system senses it is dangerous to pass another car.

The essence of marketing is in developing products such as new features on cars to meet consumers' needs. A **product** is a good, service, or idea consisting of a bundle of tangible and intangible attributes that satisfies consumers and is received in exchange for money or another unit of value. Tangible benefits include physical items such as cars or soap, and intangible benefits include becoming healthier or wealthier. This comprehensive definition of a product includes the breakfast cereal you eat, the accountant who fills out your tax return, or the American Red Cross, which provides you self-satisfaction when you donate your blood. In many instances we exchange money to obtain the product, whereas in other instances we exchange our time and other valuables, such as our blood.

The life of a company often depends on how it conceives, produces, and markets new products. In this chapter we discuss the decisions involved in developing and marketing a new product. Chapter 10 covers the process of managing existing products.

THE VARIATIONS OF PRODUCTS

A product varies in terms of whether it is a consumer or industrial good. For most organizations the product decision is not made in isolation because companies often offer a range of products. To better appreciate the product decision, let's first define some terms pertaining to products.

PRODUCT LINE AND PRODUCT MIX

A **product line** is a group of products that are closely related because they satisfy a class of needs, are used together, are sold to the same customer group, are

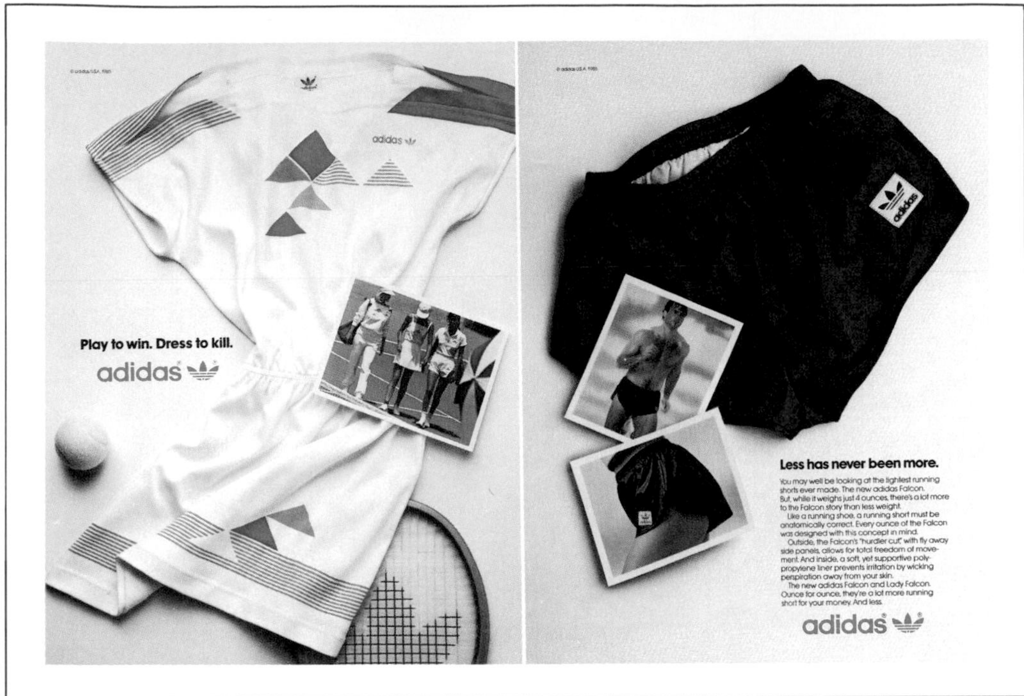

Some items in Adidas' broadening product line

distributed through the same type of outlets, or fall within a given price range.[2] Polaroid has two major product lines consisting of cameras and film; Adidas' product lines are shoes and clothing. Each product line has its own marketing strategy.

Within each product line is the *product item,* a specific product as noted by a unique brand, size, or price. For example, Downy softener for clothes comes in 12-ounce and 22-ounce sizes; each size is considered a separate item and assigned a distinct ordering code, or *stock keeping unit (SKU).*

The third way a company looks at its products is by the **product mix**, or the number of lines it carries. Cray Research has a single product line consisting of supercomputers, which are sold mostly to governments and military agencies. American Brands, Inc., however, has many product lines consisting of cigarettes (Pall Mall), sporting equipment (Titleist golf balls), distilled beverages (Jim Beam liquors), and even services (Pinkerton security) among others.

CLASSIFYING PRODUCTS

Both the federal government and companies classify products but for different purposes. The government's classification method helps it collect information on industrial activity. Companies classify products to help develop similar marketing strategies for the wide range of products offered. Two major ways to classify products are by degree of product tangibility and by type of user.

Shoes are an example of consumer goods

Degree of Tangibility Classification by degree of tangibility divides products into one of three categories.[3] First is a *nondurable good,* an item consumed in one or a few uses, such as food products and fuel. A *durable good* is one that usually lasts over an extended number of uses, such as appliances, automobiles, and stereo equipment. *Services* are defined as activities, benefits, or satisfactions offered for sale, such as marketing research, health care, and education. As noted in Chapter 1, services are intangible. According to this classification, government data indicate that the United States is becoming a service economy.

This classification method also provides direction for marketing actions. Nondurable products such as Wrigley's gum are purchased frequently and at relatively low cost. Advertising is important to remind consumers of the item's existence, and wide distribution in retail outlets is essential. A consumer wanting Wrigley's Spearmint Gum would most likely purchase another brand of spearmint gum if Wrigley's were not available. Durable products, however, generally cost more than nondurable goods and last longer, so consumers usually deliberate longer before purchasing them. Therefore personal selling is an important component in durable-product marketing because it assists in answering consumer questions and concerns.

Marketing is increasingly being used with services. Services are intangibles, so a major goal in marketing is to make the benefits of purchasing the product real to consumers. Thus Northwest Airlines shows the fun of a Florida vacation or the joy of seeing grandparents. People who provide the service are often the key to its success in the market because consumers often evaluate the product by the service provider they meet—the Hertz reservation clerk, the receptionist at the university admission office, or the nurse in the doctor's office.

Type of User The second major type of product classification is according to the user. **Consumer goods** are products purchased by the ultimate consumer, whereas **industrial goods** are used in the production of other products for ultimate consumers. In many instances the differences are distinct: Charles of the Ritz face moisturizer and Bass shoes are clearly consumer products, whereas Wang word processors and high-tension steel springs are industrial goods used in producing other products or services.

There are difficulties, however, with this classification because some products can be considered both consumer and industrial items. A Macintosh computer can be sold to consumers as a final product or to industrial firms for office use. Each classification results in different marketing actions. Viewed as a consumer product, the Macintosh would be sold through computer stores like ComputerLand. As an industrial product, the Macintosh might be sold by a salesperson offering discounts for multiple purchases. Classifying by the type of user focuses on the market and the user's purchase behavior, which determine the marketing mix strategy.

CLASSIFYING CONSUMER AND INDUSTRIAL GOODS

Because the buyer is the key to marketing, consumer and industrial product classifications are discussed in greater detail.

CLASSIFICATION OF CONSUMER GOODS

Convenience, shopping, specialty, and unsought products are the four types of consumer goods. They differ in terms of (1) the effort the consumer spends on the decision, (2) the attributes used in purchase, and (3) the frequency of purchase.

Convenience goods are items that the consumer purchases frequently, conveniently, and with a minimum of shopping effort. **Shopping goods** are the type for which the consumer compares several alternatives on criteria such as price, quality, or style. **Specialty goods** are those items, such as a Rolex watch, that a consumer makes a special effort to search out and buy. **Unsought goods** are those products which the consumer either does not know about or knows about but does not initially want. Figure 9-1 shows how the classification of a consumer product into one of these four types results in different aspects of the marketing mix being stressed. Different degrees of brand loyalty and amounts of shopping effort are displayed by the consumer for a product in each of the four classes.

The manner in which a consumer good is classified depends on the individual. One person may view a camera as a shopping good and visit several stores before deciding on a brand, whereas a friend may view cameras as a specialty good and will only buy a Nikon.

The product classification of a consumer good can change the longer a product is on the market. When first introduced, the Litton microwave oven was unique, a specialty good. Now there are several competing brands on the market, and microwaves are a shopping good for many consumers.

Some watches are specialty goods

ENDURING CLASSICS
There are rare instances when performance is an artform in itself. Such is the case with the legendary 1928 Hispano Suiza and the Rolex® Day-Date® chronometer and companion Lady Datejust®. Each handcrafted timepiece in 18kt. gold with matching President® bracelet features a silver dial and bezel punctuated with diamonds. And each is self-winding and pressure-proof down to 330 feet in its renowned Oyster® case.
Only at your Official Rolex Jeweler.
ROLEX
MONDAY
28

FIGURE 9-1
Classification of consumer goods

BASIS OF COMPARISON	TYPE OF CONSUMER GOOD			
	CONVENIENCE	SHOPPING	SPECIALTY	UNSOUGHT
Product	Toothpaste, cake mix, hand soap, laundry detergent	Cameras, TVs, briefcases, appliances, and clothing	Ralph Lauren Polo shirts, Rolls Royce cars, Rolex watches	Burial insurance, thesaurus
Price	Relatively inexpensive	Fairly expensive	Usually very expensive	Varies
Place (distribution)	Widespread; many outlets	Large number of selective outlets	Very limited	Often limited
Promotion	Price, availability, and awareness stressed	Differentiation from competitors stressed	Uniqueness of brand and status stressed	Awareness is essential
Brand loyalty of consumers	Aware of brand, but will accept substitutes	Prefer specific brands, but will accept substitutes	Very brand loyal; will not accept substitutes	Will accept substitutes
Purchase behavior of consumers	Frequent purchases; little time and effort spent shopping; routine decision	Infrequent purchases; comparison shopping; uses decision time	Infrequent purchases; extensive time spent to make the decision and get the item	Very infrequent purchases, some comparison shopping

CLASSIFICATION OF INDUSTRIAL GOODS

A major characteristic of industrial goods is that sales of items are often the result of *derived demand;* that is, sales of industrial products frequently result (or are derived) from the sale of consumer goods. For example, if consumer demand for Fords (a consumer product) increases, the firm may increase its demand for paint spraying equipment (an industrial product). Industrial goods are classified not only on the attributes the consumer uses, but also on how the item is to be used. Thus industrial products may be classified as production or support goods.

Production Goods Raw materials such as grain or lumber are **production goods**, which enter the manufacturing of the final product. Also included in this category are component parts. For example, a company that manufactures door hinges used by GM in its car doors is producing a component part. As noted in Chapter 5, the marketing of production goods is based on factors such as price, quality, delivery, and service. Marketers of these products tend to sell directly to industrial users.

Support Goods The second class of industrial goods, **support goods**, includes installations, accessory equipment, supplies, and services, which are purchased to assist in the production of the finished product.

- *Installations* consist of buildings and fixed equipment. Because a significant amount of capital is required to purchase installations, the industrial buyer deals directly with the manufacturer through a sales representative. The pricing of installations is often by competitive bidding.
- *Accessory equipment* includes tools and office equipment and is usually purchased in small-order sizes by buyers. As a result, instead of dealing directly with buyers, sellers of industrial accessories use distributors to contact a large number of buyers.
- *Supplies* are similar to consumer convenience goods and consist of products such as stationery, paper clips, and brooms. These are purchased with little effort, using the straight rebuy decision sequence discussed in Chapter 5. Price and delivery are major attributes considered by the buyers of supplies.
- *Services* are benefits provided to assist the ongoing activities of the industrial buyer. This category can include maintenance and repair services and advisory services such as tax or legal counsel. The reputation of the seller of services is a major factor in marketing these industrial goods.

CONCEPT CHECK

1 **Explain the difference between product mix and product line.**

2 **To which type of good (industrial or consumer) does the term *derived demand* generally apply?**

3 **A limited problem-solving approach is common to which type of consumer good?**

NEW PRODUCTS AND WHY THEY FAIL

New products are the lifeblood of a company and keep it growing. The importance placed on the sale of new products is increasing in most companies. This fact is demonstrated by the growing number of new-product introductions. In 1987, 7,866 new food products were introduced, up 29 percent from 1986.[4] A separate study of only industrial firms found that 15 percent of current sales were from products introduced within the last 5 years.[5] Before discussing how new products reach the stage of commercialization when they are available to the consumer, we'll begin by looking at *what* a new product is.

WHAT IS A NEW PRODUCT?

The term *new* is difficult to define. Does changing the color of a laundry detergent mean it is a new product, as a lap-top computer would be considered new? There are several ways to view the newness of a product.

Newness Compared with Existing Products If a product is functionally different from existing offerings, it can be defined as new. The microwave oven and automobile were once functionally new, but for most products the innovation is more a modification of an old product than a dramatic functional change.

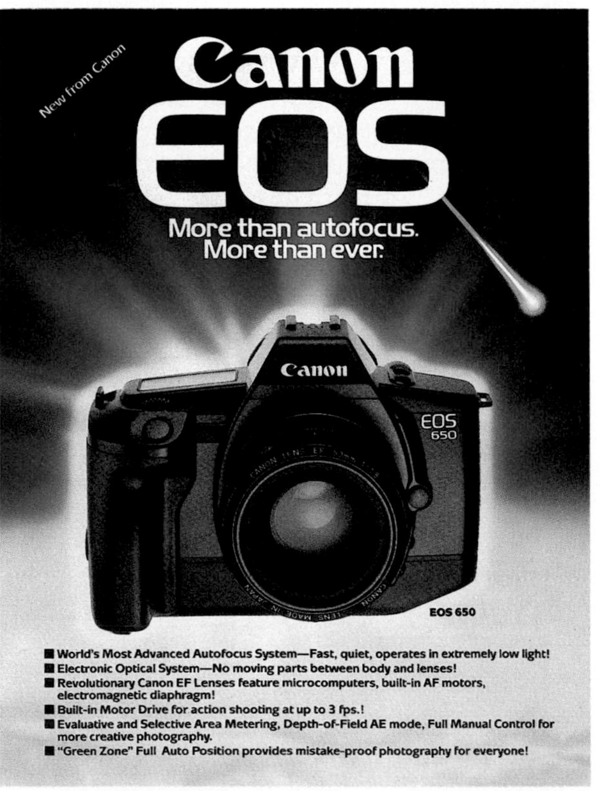

The autofocus feature makes this 35mm camera a new product

Newness in Legal Terms The Federal Trade Commission advised that the term *new* be limited to use with a product up to 6 months after it enters regular distribution.[6] The difficulty with this suggestion is in the interpretation of the term *regular distribution*.

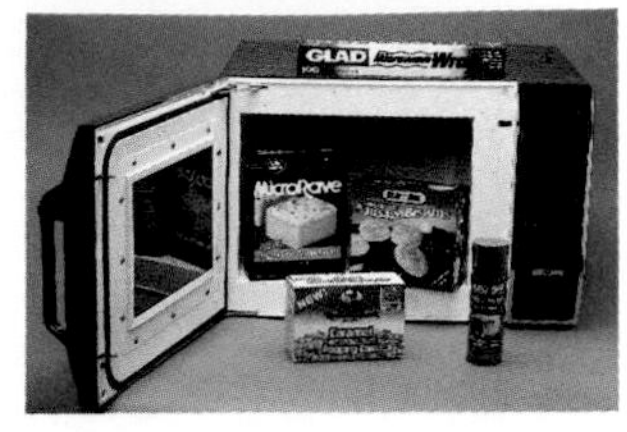

Microwave cooking: a discontinuous innovation that has revolutionized some consumption patterns

Newness from the Company's Perspective Companies generally view a new product as either a revised item or a completely new innovation. With a revised product the modifications can be either major or minor. Major revisions in 35 mm cameras are the automatic focus capability of Canon's EOS (for electrical optical system) and the talking ability of Minolta's camera. A minor revision is the self-contained lens protector of Pentax's 35 mm camera. A completely new product might be a technological breakthrough (such as the cellular car telephone) or a product new to the company but offered by competing firms.

Rather than viewing a product as new for a specified period (such as 6 months), companies often use an objective measure such as sales, market share, or percentage of sales potential. When a product is introduced to the market, a large advertising expenditure is often required to inform potential buyers. If a company considers a product new for only 6 months, advertising expenditures may be reduced prematurely.

Newness from the Consumer's Perspective A fourth way to define new products is in terms of their effects on consumption.[7] This approach classifies new products according to the degree of learning required by the consumer, as shown in Figure 9-2.

With a *continuous new product,* no new behaviors must be learned. The all-wheel-drive vehicles offered by Honda and Mazda improve the handling of a car, but require no new driver education. When little consumer education is required, marketing depends on generating awareness and having strong distribution in appropriate outlets.

The *dynamically continuous innovation* is represented by the electric tooth-

FIGURE 9-2
Consumption effects define newness

Low — Degree of change behavior and learning needed by consumer — High

BASIS OF COMPARISON	CONTINUOUS INNOVATION	DYNAMICALLY CONTINUOUS INNOVATION	DISCONTINUOUS INNOVATION
Definition	Requires no new learning by consumers	Disrupts consumer's normal routine but does not require totally new learning	Establishes new consumption patterns among consumers
Examples	Trac II Blade and New Improved Tide	Electric toothbrush, automatic transmission, and automatic flash units for cameras	Automobile, microwave oven, and home computer
Marketing emphasis	Generate awareness among consumers and obtain widespread distribution	Advertise benefits to consumers, stressing point of differentiation and consumer advantage	Educate consumers through product trial and personal selling

Recently introduced new consumer products

brush. Although this new product was somewhat disruptive, totally new behavior by the consumer was not required for its use. People knew how to brush their teeth, and an automatic toothbrush merely changed the brushing action.

A *discontinuous innovation* involves making the consumer establish entirely new consumption patterns. In marketing these new products, a significant amount of time must often be spent initially educating the consumer on how to use the product, such as cooking with a microwave oven or operating a personal computer.

WHY PRODUCTS FAIL

Thousands of product failures occurring every year cost American businesses billions of dollars. Some estimates place 35 percent of all products launched as resulting in commercial failures.[8] To learn marketing lessons from these failures, we can analyze why new products fail and then study several failures in detail. As we go through the new product process later in the chapter, we can identify ways such failures might have been avoided—admitting that hindsight is clearer than foresight.

Reasons for New Product Failures Many factors contribute to new product failures or are symptoms of them: incompatibility with the firm's objectives and capabilities, competition that is too tough, lack of top management support, and lack of money. However, six factors, often present in combination, are far more fundamental:

1. Too small a target market. The market for the product is too small to warrant the R&D, production, and marketing expenses to reach it. Among other problems, Polaroid's instant home movie, Polavision, had too small a market. Polavision was introduced in 1978, a year in which 560,000 8 mm home movie cameras were sold—half the volume

sold 6 years earlier. So the growth of Polavision's target market, small to begin with, was slowing significantly.

2. Insignificant point of difference. The expected benefit or point of difference compared with competitive offerings is not that important in consumers' eyes. Menley & James introduced Duractin, an aspirin that gave 8 hours of pain relief to headache sufferers. The longer time period wasn't important because people with headaches want immediate pain relief. If the headache comes back in 4 hours, they take two more aspirin tablets.
3. Poor product quality. The quality of the product sold is either poor in an absolute sense or worse than first buyers had expected, leaving them disappointed. General Foods introduced its Post Cereals with freeze-dried fruit, which turned out to be a disaster. By the time the milk or cream on the cereal reconstituted its freeze-dried fruit to look and taste like bananas or strawberries, the cereal itself was soggy.
4. No access to consumers. Manufacturers of potentially better products can't communicate this to prospective buyers or gain retail shelf space. Dozens of useful computer software programs can't get the attention of prospective buyers or the space in computer stores.
5. Bad timing. The product is introduced too soon, too late, or at a time when consumer tastes are shifting dramatically. Dozens of creative video games appeared for Christmas 1983, when consumers were getting bored with most video games.
6. Poor execution of the marketing mix. One or more elements in the marketing mix—besides the product element mentioned separately in number 3 above—aren't right. Revlon's Supernatural Hair Spray failed because purchasers were unclear on what the product was supposed to do. Some expected it to provide more holding power for their hair, and others expected less holding power.

FIGURE 9-3
Why did these new products fail?

As explained in detail in the text, new products often fail because of one or a combination of six reasons: (1) too small a target market, (2) insignificant point of difference, (3) poor product quality, (4) no access to market, (5) poor timing, and (6) poor execution of the marketing mix.

Look at the three products described below, and try to give the reason they failed in the marketplace:

- Nestea's Ice Teasers was a fruit-flavored instant tea with caffeine aimed at baby boomers.
- Del Monte's Barbecue Ketchup contained finely chopped onions and was aimed at the heavy catsup-eating segment.
- Holly Farms' fully roasted chicken in supermarkets was targeted at households who didn't want to spend time cooking.

Compare your insights with those given in the text.

but may be augmented with sketches, mock-ups, or promotional literature.[20] Several key questions are asked during concept testing: How does the customer perceive the product? Who would use it? For what purposes would the product be used?

Concept testing is a basic step used by Airwick Industries, Inc., in its screening and evaluation stage. Early concept tests for Carpet Fresh, a rug deodorizer, suggested that the product could not be granular because consumers were afraid the granules would lodge under their furniture. As a result, the later success was in powder form.[21]

CONCEPT CHECK

1. **What step in the new product process has been added in recent years?**
2. **What are four sources of new product ideas?**
3. **What is a weighted point system, as used internally by a firm in the new product process?**

BUSINESS ANALYSIS

Business analysis involves specifying the features of the product and the marketing strategy needed to commercialize it and making necessary financial projections. This is the last checkpoint before significant capital is invested in creating a prototype of the product. Economic analysis, marketing strategy review, and legal examination of the proposed product are conducted at this stage.

The marketing strategy analysis reviews the new product idea in relation to the marketing program to support it. The proposed product is assessed to determine whether it will help or hurt sales of existing products. Likewise, the product is examined to assess whether it can be sold through existing channels or if new outlets will be needed.

After the product's important features are defined, economic considerations focus on several issues, starting with costs of R&D, production, and marketing. For financial projections, the firm must also forecast the possible revenues from future product sales and forecast market shares. American Hospital Supply considers factors such as total market dollars, market growth rate, market share, relative growth share, gross profitability, net earnings after tax, return on net working assets, and cash flow.[22] At the business analysis stage the firm does a break-even analysis and estimates return on investment to determine the profitability of the product.

As an important aspect of the business analysis, the proposed new product is studied to determine whether it can be protected with a patent. An attractive new product proposal is one in which the technology can be patented or not easily copied.[23]

DEVELOPMENT

Product ideas that survive the business analysis proceed to actual **development,** turning the idea on paper into a prototype—a demonstrable, producible product

MARKETING · ACTION · MEMO

That's Not a Radio, It's a Visual Metaphor!

What do the following terms have in common: visual metaphor, product semantics, and visual imagery?

They all pertain to today's attitude toward the design of new products, or *strategic design.* The idea behind *product semantics* is that a consumer good ought to communicate its purpose visually in very explicit ways. The dramatic success of Ford's Taurus-Sable automobiles reveals the importance of design in a new product's success. Peter Wooding, President of the Industrial Designers Society of America, termed "the aero look a major design statement by Ford."

A new product developed in the past was designed to meet the needs and constraints of the manufacturing process. Production costs led to products that were boxy and less descriptive, such as the shape of a microwave oven. Today design is seen as a potential competitive advantage. Polaroid wanted their Spectra camera to appeal to an upscale audience. After seeing the subdued colors of European automobiles such as Mercedes and BMW, the company chose a dark metallic gray for the camera body to give it a sophisticated look. Also to heighten the design appeal, the camera's body is thin and molded for the hand.

The goal of designers is to make the products attractive and more expressive of what they are, a *visual metaphor.* In 1986, Phillips introduced a radio with huge circular speakers—to convey the sense of sound. And in 1988 the company planned to introduce a hair dryer with a wavy shape that would evoke images of heat and long, flowing curls. New products, new designs are the watchwords of the next decade.

Source: "Smart Design Quality Is the New Style," *Business Week* (April 11, 1988), pp. 102-117; Stephen MacDonald, "Looking Good: More Firms Place Higher Priority on Product Design," *The Wall Street Journal* (January 22, 1987); Alex M. Freedman, "Forsaking the Black Box: Designers Wrap Products in Visual Metaphors," *The Wall Street Journal* (March 26, 1987), p. 41.

in hand. Outsiders seldom understand the technical complexities of the development stage, which involves not only manufacturing the product but also performing laboratory and consumer tests to ensure it meets the standards set. Design of the product becomes an important element. Many marketers believe design will be a key to success in the 1990's, as discussed in the Marketing Action Memo.

Liquid Tide, introduced by P&G, looks like a simple modification of its original Tide detergent. However, P&G sees this product as a technological breakthrough: the first detergent without phosphates that cleans as well as existing phosphate detergents.

To achieve this breakthrough, P&G spent 400,000 hours and combined technologies from its laboratories in three countries. The new ingredient in Liquid Tide that helps suspend the dirt in wash water came out of the P&G research lab in Cincinnati. The cleaning agents in the product came from P&G scientists in Japan. Cleaning agent technology is especially advanced in Japan because consumers there wash clothes in colder water (about 70° F) than consumers in the United States (95° F) and Europe (160° F). P&G scientists thought

A technological breakthrough

Liquid Tide also needed water-softening ingredients to make the cleaning agents work better. For this technology it turned to P&G's lab in Belgium, whose experience was based on European water, which has more than twice the mineral content of U.S. wash water.[24]

The prototype product is tested in the laboratory to see if it achieves the physical standards set for it. Prototypes of disposable consumer goods are also subjected to consumer tests, often in-home placements of the product to see if consumers actually perceive it as a better product after they use it. In a blind test consumers preferred Liquid Tide nine to one over the detergent of their own choice tested in their own washers. Most grocery products are actually used and tested by consumers in their own homes.

MARKET TESTING

The **market testing** stage of the new product process involves exposing actual products to prospective consumers under realistic purchase conditions to see if they will buy. Often a product is developed, tested, refined, and then tested again to get consumer reactions through either test marketing or purchase laboratories.

Test Marketing Test marketing involves offering a product for sale on a limited basis to see if consumers will actually buy the product and to try different ways of marketing it.[25] Only about a third of the products test marketed reach

Metro area	New products tested*
1 Minneapolis-St Paul	92
2 Portland, Ore.	91
3 Columbus, Ohio	69
4 Syracuse, N.Y.	62
5 Kansas City, Mo.	60
6 Buffalo, N.Y.	53
7 Denver	51
8 Atlanta	50
9 Seattle-Tacoma	49
10 Milwaukee	48
11 Albany-Schenectady-Troy, N.Y.	42
12 Rochester, N.Y.	39
13 Grand Rapids-Kalamazoo-Battle Creek, Mich.	38
14 St. Louis	36
15 Orlando-Daytona Beach-Melbourne, Fla.	29
16 Fort Wayne, Ind.	28
17 Portland-Poland Spring, Maine	25
18 Spokane, Wash.	24
19 Des Moines, Iowa	23
20 Cincinnati	22
20 Green Bay-Appleton, Wis.	22
20 Sacramento-Stockton, Calif.	22

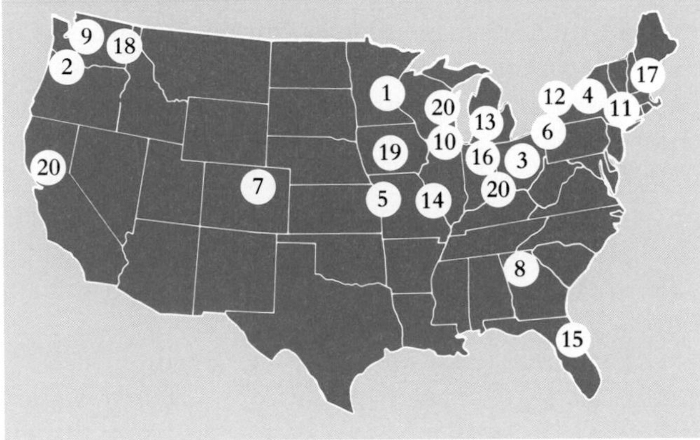

*Includes only food and drug products

FIGURE 9-8
The most popular test markets. Ranked by number of new products* tested from January, 1985, to April, 1987

Source: "Market Watch/Proving Grounds," *The Wall Street Journal* (January 26, 1988), p. 34.

the next phase.[26] These test markets are usually conducted in cities that are viewed as being representative of U.S. consumers and of small enough size so tests of different advertising media and appeals can be run. If you live in one of the 20 cities shown in Figure 9-8, you are more likely to see new consumer products than are people living elsewhere.

In examining the commercial viability of the new product, companies measure sales in the test area, often with *store audits*. These audits, conducted by groups such as the A.C. Nielsen Company, measure the sales in grocery stores and the number of cases ordered by a store from the wholesaler. This gives the company an indication of potential sales volume and market share in the test area. Although test markets have not been able to predict exact future sales or share, they do help a company with an idea of relative product performance and the likelihood of having a loser or a winner.[27]

Test markets are also used to check other elements of the new product marketing mix besides the product itself, such as price and level of advertising support. Campbell's withdrew their line of Fresh Chef refrigerated soups, salads, and snacks in 1987 after consumers sent back large numbers of spoiled packages. The company found it difficult to move its product, with its short shelf life, through the distribution channel quickly enough. In 1988 the company began experimenting with door-to-door delivery, placing the product in consumers' homes only 48 hours after manufacture.[28] In industrial marketing, test markets are often used to gain a record of product performance. This experience can then be used as part of the sales presentation when the product is offered elsewhere.

There is no required time period for an appropriate test market. In the brewing industry Coors tested its Herman Joseph's brew for about 3 years.[29] Manufacturers prefer to shorten the test period to minimize competitive reaction, but for consumer products time is required to build retail store distribution, develop consumer interest, and provide opportunities for repeat purchase.

There are difficulties with test marketing, a primary one being how well the results can be projected. Representativeness of the test market to the target market for the product is very important. Test markets also are expensive because production lines must be set up, as well as promotion and sales programs. Costs can run from $250,000 to $1 million, depending on the size of the city and the cost of buying media time or space to advertise the product.[30] Also, test markets reveal plans to competitors, sometimes enabling them to get a product into national distribution first. Although Hunt-Wesson got its Prima Salsa Tomato Sauce into the test market first, Chesebrough-Pond's Ragu Extra Thick & Zesty beat it into national introduction. Publications such as *Advertising Age* regularly list products being tested and the location of the test market. Companies also instruct their salespeople to look for new competing products in test markets and report their existence to headquarters.

The disadvantages of test markets have led some consumer goods firms to shorten them, simplify them, or drop them entirely. *Controlled distribution minimarkets* are test markets run in smaller test areas that electronically monitor product purchases at checkout counters more carefully, and they can reduce test

A beer tested for 3 years

market costs by 60 percent to 80 percent. Some companies have recently chosen to skip test marketing entirely in new product introductions: Sara Lee Corporation with its meat-filled frozen croissants, General Foods with its sugar-free International Coffee, and Quaker Oats with its Cherry Granola bars and Granola Dipps.

Purchase Laboratories Because of the limitations of test markets, one of the best assessment techniques for a new product launch is the purchase laboratory, in which competing test brands are displayed.[31] These purchase labs are usually run in shopping malls, where consumers are questioned to identify those who use the product class being tested. Willing participants are questioned on usage, reasons for purchase, and important product attributes. Consumers are also shown advertising for the new brand along with competitors' advertising and are given money to buy or not buy a package of the product (or the competitors') from a mock grocery shelf. Consumers who purchase the test brand are interviewed later for their reactions.[32] Based on these reactions, the company may decide to proceed to the last stage of the new product process.

Market testing is a valuable step in the new product process, but not all products can be judged in this way. Testing a service beyond the concept level is very difficult because the service is intangible and consumers can't see what they are buying. Similarly, market testing of expensive consumer products such as cars or VCRs or costly industrial products like jet engines or computers is impractical.

COMMERCIALIZATION

Finally, the product idea is brought to the point of **commercialization**—launching the product in full-scale production and sales. Because new product introductions are so expensive, they often involve huge risks that may result in long

FIGURE 9-9
The time from the original idea for various new products to their commercialization

NEW PRODUCT	YEAR OF FIRST CONCEPTION	YEAR OF FIRST REALIZATION	DURATION (YEARS)
Heart pacemaker	1928	1960	32
Oral contraceptives	1951	1960	9
Bird's Eye frozen foods	1908	1923	15
Ban Roll-On	1948	1954	6
Crest toothpaste	1945	1955	10
Videocassette recorders	1950	1956	6
Minute rice	1931	1949	18
Scripto felt-tip pen	1959	1961	2
Talon zippers	1884	1939	55
Marlboro filter cigarettes	1953	1955	2
Decaffeinated instant coffee	1947	1953	6

Source: Based on Glen L. Urban and John R. Hauser, *Design and Marketing of New Products* (Englewood Cliffs, N.J.: Prentice-Hall, Inc., 1980); Robert D. Hirsch and Michael P. Peters, *Marketing a New Product* (Menlo Park, Calif.: Benjamin/Cummings Publishing Company, 1978).

delays between the development of the original idea and the appearance of the idea as a new product in the market.

Lag from Idea to New Product Figure 9-9 shows the time from the original idea for various new products until the product appeared on the market. Thirty-two years for the heart pacemaker, 55 years for the zipper, 18 years for minute rice—the process from idea generation to commercialization can be lengthy. Companies generally proceed carefully because, at this last stage, commercialization, production, and marketing expenses are greatest. To minimize the financial risk of a market failure of a new product introduction, many grocery product manufacturers use *regional rollouts,* introducing the product sequentially into geographical areas of the United States to allow production levels and marketing activities to build up gradually.

In recent years, some companies—such as NEC, Honda, Fuji, and Xerox—have moved away from the development approach that uses the sequence of stages described in this chapter. A new trend, termed *parallel development,* is being tried. With this approach, multidisciplinary *venture teams* of marketing, manufacturing, and R&D personnel stay with the product from conception to production. The results appear impressive in speeding up new product development: using this approach, Xerox has reduced its time to develop a new copier

FIGURE 9-10
Marketing information and methods used in the new product process

STAGE OF PROCESS	PURPOSE OF STAGE	MARKETING INFORMATION AND METHODS USED
New product strategy development	Identify new product niches to reach in light of company objectives	Company objectives; assessment of firm's current strengths and weaknesses in terms of market and product
Idea generation	Develop concepts for possible products	Ideas from employees and co-workers, consumers, R&D, and competitors; methods of brainstorming and focus groups
Screening and evaluation	Separate good product ideas from bad ones inexpensively	Screening criteria, concept tests, and weighted point systems
Business analysis	Identify the product's features and its marketing strategy, and make financial projections	Product's key features, anticipated marketing mix strategy; economic, marketing, production, legal, and profitability analyses
Development	Create the prototype product, and test it in the laboratory and on consumers	Laboratory and consumer tests on product prototypes
Market testing	Test product and marketing strategy in the marketplace on a limited scale	Test markets, controlled distribution minimarkets, purchase laboratories
Commercialization	Position and offer product in the marketplace	Perceptual maps, product positioning, regional rollouts

from 5 years to 2, and Honeywell has reduced the time to design and build a new thermostat from 4 years to 1.[33]

Ingredients for a Successful New Product In 1968 it took companies 58 ideas to generate 1 commercial product, but since the addition of the new product strategy development stage in the new product process, only 7 ideas have been required to generate 1 successful new product. However, the success rate of new products is as low as 65 percent.[34] What contributes to the success of a new product?

Look back to the Marketing Research Report on p. 236 to see how careful execution of the activities in the seven new product development steps just described relates to the factors separating winners from losers and increases the chances of success.

How the New Product Process Reduces Failures Figure 9-10 identifies the purpose of each stage of the new product process and the kinds of marketing information and methods used. Firms that follow the seven stages in the new product process reduce risks and have a better chance of averting new-product failures. A look at Figure 9-10 suggests stages where some of the product failures mentioned at the start of the chapter might have been avoided or been identified early enough to be dropped before undergoing the more expensive, later stages of the new product process. For example, running the idea of Del Monte's Barbecue Ketchup with finely chopped onions in a concept test on children and teenagers—the heavy using segment—should have shown most didn't like onions. Although using the new product process does not guarantee successful products, it does increase a firm's success rate.

CONCEPT CHECK

1 **How does the development stage of the new product process involve testing the product inside and outside the firm?**

2 **What is a test market?**

3 **What is product positioning?**

SUMMARY

1 A product is a good, service, or idea consisting of a bundle of tangible and intangible attributes that satisfies consumers and is received in exchange for money or another unit of value. A company's product decision involves the product item, product line, and range of its product mix.

2 Products can be classified by tangibility and by user. By user, the major distinctions are consumer or industrial goods. Consumer goods consist of convenience, shopping, and specialty products. Industrial goods are for either production or support.

3 There are several ways to define a new product, such as the degree of distinction from existing products, a time base specified by the FTC, a company perspective, or consumption effects.
4 In terms of its effect on a consumer's use of a product, a discontinuous innovation represents the greatest change and a continuous innovation the least. A dynamically continuous innovation is disruptive but not totally new.
5 The failure of a new product is usually attributable to one of six reasons: too small a target market, insignificant point of difference, poor product quality, no access to market, poor timing, and poor execution of the marketing mix.
6 The new product process consists of seven stages. Objectives for new products are determined in the first stage, new product strategy development; this is followed by idea generation, screening and evaluation, business analysis, development, market testing, and commercialization.
7 Ideas for new products come from several sources, including consumers, employees, R&D, laboratories, and competitors.
8 In market testing new products, companies often rely on test markets to see that consumers will actually buy the product when it's offered for sale and that other marketing mix factors are working.
9 Screening and evaluation are often done internally using a weighted point system or externally using concept tests.
10 Business analysis involves defining the features of the new product, a marketing strategy to introduce it, and a financial forecast.
11 Development involves not only producing a prototype product but also testing it in the lab and on consumers to see that it meets the standards set for it.

KEY TERMS AND CONCEPTS

product p. 226
product line p. 226
product mix p. 227
consumer goods p. 229
industrial goods p. 229
convenience goods p. 229
shopping goods p. 229
specialty goods p. 229
unsought goods p. 229
production goods p. 231
support goods p. 231
new product process p. 238
new product strategy development p. 238
proactive strategies p. 239
reactive strategies p. 239
idea generation p. 240
screening and evaluation p. 242
business analysis p. 244
development p. 244
market testing p. 246
commercialization p. 249

CHAPTER PROBLEMS AND APPLICATIONS

1 Products can be classified as either consumer or industrial goods. How would you classify the following products? (a) Johnson's baby shampoo, (b) a Black & Decker two-speed drill, and (c) an arc gas welder.

2 Are products like Nature Valley Granola bars and Eddie Bauer hiking boots convenience, shopping, specialty, or unsought goods?

3 Based on your answer to Question 2, how would the marketing actions differ for each product and the classification to which you assigned it?

4 In terms of the behavioral effect on consumers, how would the PC, such as a Macintosh or IBM PS/2, be classified? In light of this classification, what actions would you suggest to the manufacturers of these products to increase their sales in the market?

5 Several alternative definitions were presented for a new product. How would a company's marketing strategy be affected if it used (a) the legal definition or (b) a behavioral definition?

6 In terms of the weighted point system used to screen new product ideas at Medtronic (Figure 9-7), what is the significance of the following factors: incidence of malady, treatment evaluation, restore natural physiology, and physician users know Medtronic name? What are the advantages and disadvantages of such a system?

7 Test marketing and purchase laboratories are two approaches for assessing the potential commercial success of a new product. Based on the strengths and weaknesses of each approach, what methods would you suggest for the following items? (a) A new, improved catsup, (b) a three-dimensional television system that took the company 10 years to develop, and (c) a new children's toy on which the company holds a patent.

8 Look back at Figure 9-6 outlining the roles for new products. If a company followed the role of defending market share position, what type of positioning strategy might be followed?

9 Concept testing is an important step in the new product process. Outline the concept tests for (a) an electrically powered car and (b) a new loan payment system for automobiles that is based on a variable rate interest. What are the differences in developing concept tests for products as opposed to services?

SUGGESTED READINGS

Marvin Berkowitz, "Product Shape as a Design Innovation Strategy," *Journal of Product Innovation Management* (December 1987), pp. 274-283. *This article highlights the value of design as an innovative strategy for a successful product.*

Christopher Knowlton, "What America Makes Best," *Fortune* (March 28, 1988), pp. 40-54. *The article lists 100 products for which U.S. firms are the world leader and gives in-depth looks at several of them.*

William Moore, "New Product Development Practices of Industrial Marketers," *Journal of Product Innovation Management* (March 1987), pp. 6-20. *This study presents results from interviews with 25 industrial marketers on their approach to the new product process.*

Bro Uttal, "Speeding New Ideas to Market," *Fortune* (March 2, 1987), pp. 62-66. *This article describes the strategies several companies are taking to get their ideas to commercialization as fast as possible.*

VHS
AT HOME
WITH
MINOLTA VIDEO
Panasonic
eumig
KODAK
BOLEX 160 MACROZOOM

10

MANAGING THE PRODUCT

After reading this chapter you should be able to:

Explain the product life cycle concept and relate a marketing strategy to each stage.

•

Recognize the differences in product life cycles for various products and their implications for marketing decisions.

•

Understand alternative approaches to managing a product's life cycle.

•

Identify the attributes of a successful brand name.

•

Explain the rationale for alternative brand name strategies employed by companies.

•

Understand the benefits of packaging and warranties in the marketing of a product.

The Demise of 8 mm Home Movies

Through the 1950's, 1960's, and 1970's, 8 mm film cameras were the rage. In 1972 over 1 million 8 mm movie cameras were sold, but by 1981 sales had dropped to only 180,000 units. Seeing what lay ahead, Kodak stopped producing 8 mm cameras in 1980. What happened?

Jay Seth of Minifilm Photo Corporation in New York City says that sales of movie cameras "hit the skids" in 1981, probably never to return. The reason was new product development in the form of VCRs. As a new product enters, it often kills demand for an existing product in the market. Look at the sales curve in Figure 10-1—1982 was the year of demise for movie cameras

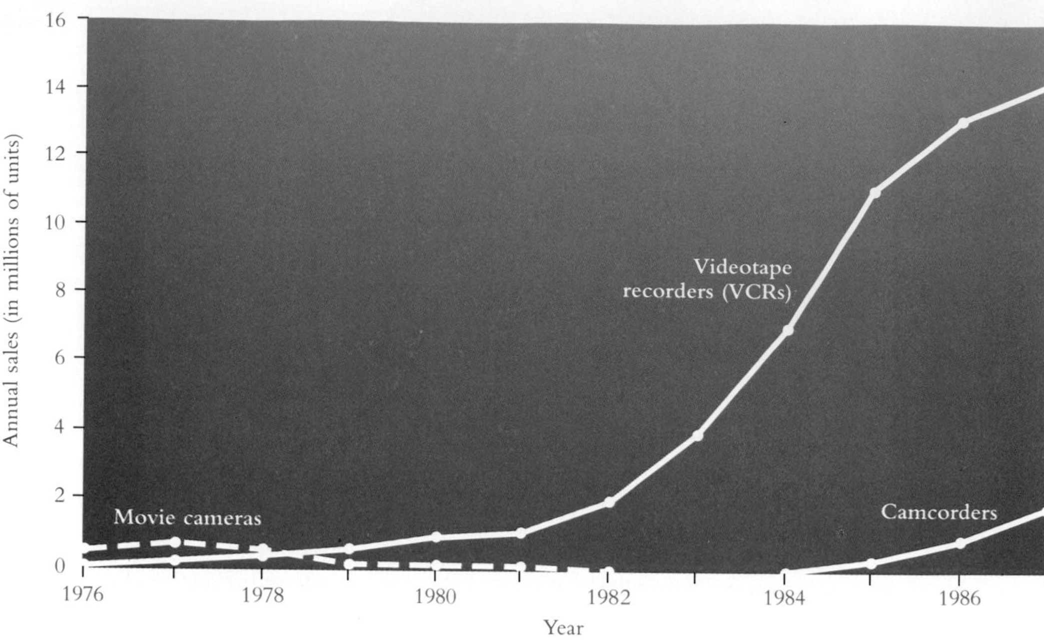

FIGURE 10-1
The birth and death of three products

and the beginning of a dramatic rise in the sales of VCRs. In 1987 sales of VCRs were slightly over 14 million units.

The home movie buff who once bought an 8 mm movie camera and projector is now more likely to buy video equipment. The ease of instant playback and lack of need for 8 mm movie film development make video equipment a very attractive replacement. Movies require a projector and screen, whereas VCRs work through the TV set. However, a new question is whether 8 mm camcorders—combination of video cameras and tape recorders—will in turn replace the ½-inch VCR cameras.[1] Just as VCRs replaced 8 mm movie cameras, camcorders are beginning to climb in sales (see Figure 10-1).

The development process of new products, discussed in Chapter 9, is expensive and often time consuming, but the results can lead to commercialization—a product for the marketplace. This chapter covers the marketing of a product when it enters the market, the life of a product, the brand name, and package design. Consumers first see new products at the commercialization stage but these products don't always live forever.

PRODUCT LIFE CYCLE

Products, like people, have been viewed as having a life cycle. The **product life cycle** concept describes the stages a new product goes through in the marketplace: introduction, growth, maturity, and decline (Figure 10-2).[2] There are two curves shown in this figure: total industry sales revenue and total industry profit, which represent the sum of sales revenue and profit of all firms producing the product. The reasons for the changes in each curve and the marketing decisions involved are discussed in the following pages.

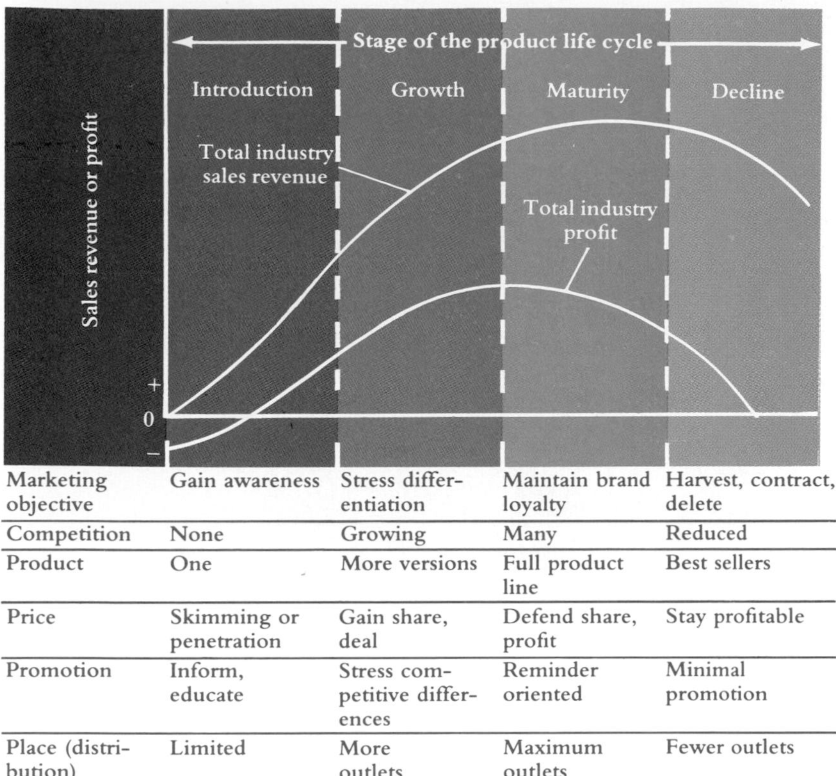

Marketing objective	Gain awareness	Stress differentiation	Maintain brand loyalty	Harvest, contract, delete
Competition	None	Growing	Many	Reduced
Product	One	More versions	Full product line	Best sellers
Price	Skimming or penetration	Gain share, deal	Defend share, profit	Stay profitable
Promotion	Inform, educate	Stress competitive differences	Reminder oriented	Minimal promotion
Place (distribution)	Limited	More outlets	Maximum outlets	Fewer outlets

FIGURE 10-2
How stages of the product life cycle relate to a firm's marketing objectives and marketing mix actions

INTRODUCTION STAGE

The introduction stage of the product life cycle occurs when the product first enters the market, sales grow slowly, and profit is little. Look at Figure 10-3, which shows the product life cycle for windsurfers, after they were introduced into the United Kingdom. Sales grew slowly until 1978. The lack of profit is

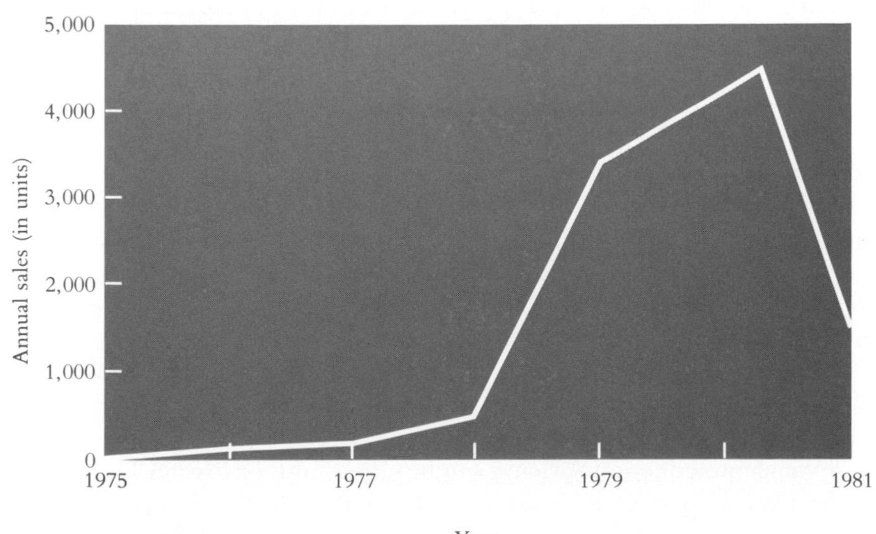

FIGURE 10-3
Product life cycle for windsurfers (a.k.a. boardsailers) in the United Kingdom

An ad building primary demand

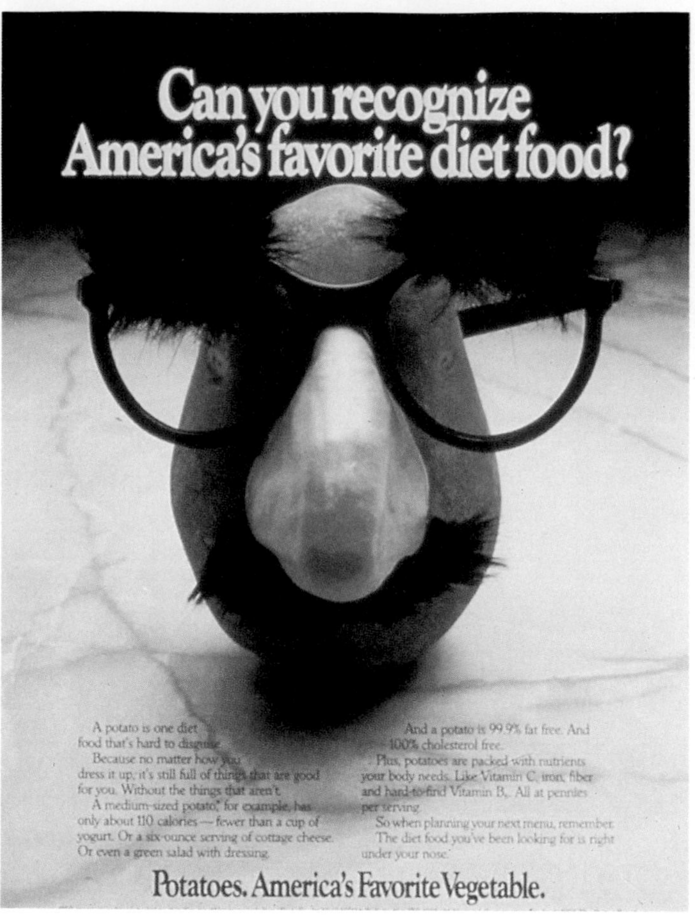

often a result of the large investment costs of product development and a shift of industry profit from negative to positive during the introductory stage. The marketing objective for a company at this stage is to promote consumer awareness and gain trial—the initial purchase of a product by a consumer. In the introduction stage there are no competitors with the same product, and heavy promotional expenditures are often made to build *primary demand,* or a desire for the product class (such as food processors or potatoes) rather than for a specific brand. To induce primary demand, early sailboard companies such as Mistral offered free lessons with every board purchase. Demand for a specific brand is referred to as *selective demand* and occurs later in the life cycle.

Other marketing mix variables also are important at this stage. Gaining distribution outlets for the product is often difficult because retailers may be hesitant to carry a new product. Moreover, in this stage a company often restricts the number of variations of the product to ensure control of product quality. For example, the first windsurfers were designed to be stable and easy to use. Variations on board design occurred later.

During introduction, pricing can be either high or low. A high initial price may be used as part of a *skimming* strategy to help the company recover the costs of development, as well as capitalize on the price insensitivity of early buyers. However, high prices also tend to make competitors more eager to enter the market because they see the opportunity for profit. To discourage competitive entry, a company can price low, referred to as *penetration pricing*. This pricing strategy also helps build market share, but a company must closely monitor costs. These and other pricing techniques are covered in depth in Chapter 12.

GROWTH STAGE

The second stage of the product life cycle, growth, is characterized by rapid increases in sales, and it is in this stage that competitors appear. For example, Figure 10-3 shows the dramatic increase in sales of windsurfers from 1978 to 1979. The number of companies selling windsurfers was also increasing: from one in 1975 to eight in 1979. In 1984 Dole Food introduced a frozen fruit juice bar, "Fruit and Juice." Quickly followed by the Dove Bar, Nestle's, and Häagen-Dazs versions, there were 120 different competitors by 1987.[3]

The result is that industry profit usually peaks during the growth stage. The emphasis of advertising shifts to selective demand in which product benefits are compared with those of competitors' offerings.

Products in the growth stage have an increase in sales because of new people trying the product and a growing proportion of *repeat purchasers*—people who tried the product, were satisfied, and buy again. As a product moves through the life cycle, the ratio of repeat to trial purchases grows. Failure to achieve substantial repeat purchasers usually means an early death for a product. Alberto-Culver introduced Mr. Culver's Sparklers, which were solid air fresheners that looked like stained glass. The problem was there were almost no repeat purchasers because buyers treated the product like cheap window decorations, left them there, and didn't buy new ones.

At the growth stage changes start to appear in the product. To help differentiate the brand from those of competitors, an improved version or new features may be added to the original design. Variations on the early, stable windsurfer appeared in 1977. Racing sailboards were introduced, which had different sail sizes and board lengths. Also, in 1980, "fun" boards, a third version, were offered for wave jumping.

In the growth stage it is important to gain as much distribution for the product as required. In the retail store, for example, this often means that competing companies fight for shelf space.

MATURITY STAGE

The third stage, maturity, is characterized by a leveling off of total industry sales revenue. Most consumers who would buy the product are either repeat purchasers of the item or have tried and abandoned it. As you can see in Figure 10-2, there is a slight sales increase in the maturity stage, as the last buyers enter the market. Profit declines because there is fierce price competition among many sellers and the cost of gaining each new buyer at this stage is greater than the resulting revenue.

Figure 10-3 shows the flattening of sales of windsurfers from 1979 to 1980 when the product is in its maturity stage in the United Kingdom. Retail prices fell by 40 percent the 5 years up to 1980 as the number of competitors grew. The marketing objective for a company is to maintain its existing buyers because few new customers are available to replace any who are lost.

Promotional expenses in the maturity stage often are directed towards contests or games to keep people using the product, and price competition continues through cents-off coupons. Companies are often hurt when distribution outlets drop the mature product in favor of other new products in the

Where are these products in their life cycles?

Look at each of the three products and (1) estimate where the products are in their life cycles and (2) decide which products they displaced or are being displaced by. The text gives the answers, along with explanations of factors affecting product life cycles.

A few words for those who haven't experienced Sony's new Compact Disc Player.

CD players provide high-fidelity sound

Swiss Swatches, stylish water-resistant watches for $35

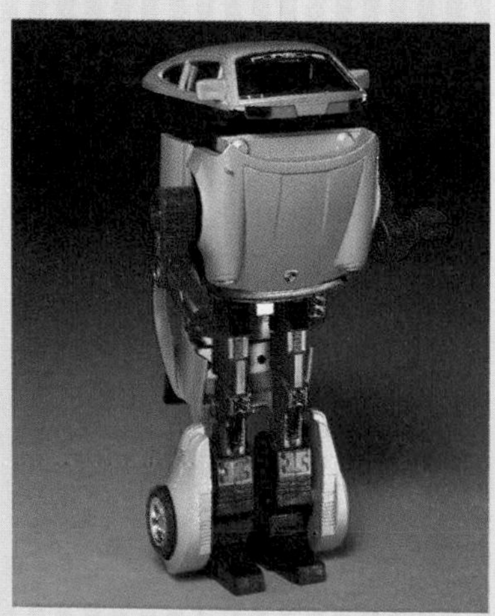

Tonka's GoBot, which converts from robot to car

introductory or growth stage. A major factor in a company's strategy is to reduce overall marketing costs by improving its promotional and distribution efficiency.[4]

DECLINE STAGE

The decline stage is the beginning of the end and occurs when sales and profits are steadily dropping. Frequently a product enters this stage not because of any wrong strategy of the company but because of environmental changes. New technology led to video cameras, which pushed 8 mm movie cameras into decline. The Salk vaccine for polio reduced the need for iron lung machines and moved their manufacturers into decline. Advertising support for a product in this stage diminishes. The decline stage is often the most difficult for a company to address. Dropping a product is an emotional decision in that many individuals have committed time and effort to its early successes in the product life cycle. Products on decline, however, tend to consume a disproportionate share of management time and financial resources relative to their worth. To handle a declining product, a company follows one of three strategies.

Deletion The most drastic action, deletion, is dropping the product from the line. Studies have shown that few companies which delete a product have specified policies to meet customer obligations, but customer objections to a product deletion are common.[5]

Harvesting A second strategy, harvesting, is when a company retains the product but reduces support costs. The product continues to be offered, but salespeople do not allocate time in selling, nor are advertising dollars spent. The purpose of harvesting is to maintain the ability to meet customer requests.

Contracting Some companies operate on a scale that makes it financially unwise for them to carry a product after sales decline below a certain level. However, this same sales level might be profitable for a smaller company, and the larger firm may contract with a smaller company to manufacture the product. In this way its production budget is freed for more profitable items, but the item is still available to customers. An alternative to contracting manufacturing is to contract the marketing. Some companies find that their manufacturing efficiencies allow them to continue producing the product but require others to sell it.

SOME DIMENSIONS OF THE PRODUCT LIFE CYCLE

Some important aspects of product life cycles are (1) their length, (2) the shape of their curves, and (3) how they vary with different levels of the products. Look at the photos on the opposite page and think about where the three products are in their life cycles and why.

Length of the Product Life Cycle There is no exact time that a product takes to move through its life cycle. If a company introduces products that are similar to others in its line, rough estimates can be made, but several factors can affect the length of a product's life. Credit alters a product's life cycle by making it available to more consumers sooner than if purchases were only by cash, and mass communication informs the market of a new product introduction at a quicker rate. Technological advances and company experience can also move products quickly through their life cycles. In the United Kingdom, it took 5 years after stable sailboards were introduced until new technology and design led to racing boards. And in only 3 years, technology led to the introduction of fun boards.

The Shape of the Product Life Cycle The product life cycle curve shown in Figure 10-2 might be referred to as a generalized life cycle, but not all products have the same shape to their curve.[6] In fact, there are several different life cycle curves, each type suggesting different marketing strategies.[7] Figure 10-4 shows the shape of life cycle curves for four different types of products: high learning, low learning, fashion, and fad products.

A *high learning product* is one for which significant education of the customer is required and there is an extended introductory period (Figure 10-4, *A*). Products such as home computers have this type of life cycle curve because consumers have to understand the benefits of purchasing the product or be educated in a new way of performing a familiar task. Microwave ovens, for example, necessitate that the consumer learn a new way of cooking and alter familiar recipes.

Sony faced an education problem for the CD player, a high learning product. When it was first introduced in the United States in 1983, there was little understanding of the benefits of this new technology. The company ran ads explaining the advantages of the CD player in *Audio, Stereo Review,* and *High Fidelity,* three publications often read by audiophiles. Moreover, to better show the benefits of sound reproduction, Sony gave 200 rock music stations a free CD player.[8] The use of educational advertisements such as that shown on p.

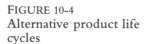

FIGURE 10-4
Alternative product life cycles

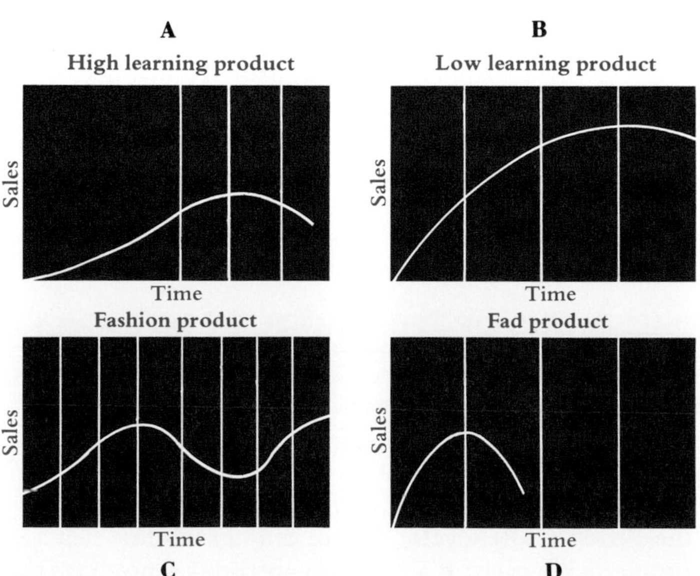

MARKETING·ACTION·MEMO

TIRED? RUN DOWN? HAVE A JOLT!!!

Is Jolt for real or simply a fad?

Americans are on a health-consciousness kick. Jogging, exercise bicycles, and natural foods all testify to the growing concern of Americans for health and nutrition.

So how about this slogan for a new soft drink: "All the sugar and twice the caffeine"? It may seem strange, but in 1987 and 1988, consumers in Chicago, Denver, Vancouver, and Rochester began to buy the soft drink that claims to "give you a boost every time you drink it." "Wow," said David Letterman, after he tried his first sip of Jolt Cola on national TV. Jolt is not a joke. It was developed by Joseph F. Rapp, a former Canada Dry bottling plant operator, along with his 27-year-old son C.J. They believe their new product will stand out among what they call "the parade of wimpy tasting colas."

Jolt is made with natural cane sugar and is loaded with 5.9 mg of caffeine per ounce (just under the Federal limit of 6 mg per ounce). The caffeine level is twice that of Coke or Pepsi. Jolt is getting a reaction. One public-interest health group has nominated Mr. Rapp for the "nutrition hall of shame." But Mr. Rapp says Jolt has one-fifth the caffeine of coffee.

Consumers are also starting to notice this new product. Jolt obtained a 4.5 percent market share in a test in Chicago. And Gary Mullins of Seattle, the premier cola drinker who took credit for forcing Coca-Cola to return to its original formula, tried Jolt—and says he's switching. So the next time you're up late studying for a marketing exam and need a little pick-me-up, look for the new cola on your grocer's shelf—have a Jolt.

Source: "New Markets Give Share to Jolt," *Beverage Industry* (January 1987), p. 12; Richard W. Stevenson, "Jolt Cola's Contrary Strategy," *The New York Times* (August 20, 1986), p. 11; "C.J. Rapp Has Formulated A Jolting Drink That's Creating Plenty of Fizz in The Cola Biz," *People* (September 15, 1986), p. 67.

260 for Sony's Compact Disc Player resulted in sales slowly picking up in the early 1980's. Today CD players are an accepted technology and are in the growth stage in Figure 10-4, *A*.

In contrast, for a *low learning product* sales begin immediately because little learning is required by the consumer and the benefits of purchase are readily understood (Figure 10-4, *B*).[9] This product often can be easily imitated by competitors, so the marketing strategy is to gain strong distributor outlets at the beginning. In this way, as competitors rapidly enter, the best retail outlets already have the innovator's product. It is also important to have the manufacturing capacity to meet demand. Swatch watches from Switzerland are an example of a low learning new product that are in the growth stage of their life cycle. Water-resistant tested to 100 feet, with high fashion styling and costing

FIGURE 10-5
Life cycles of product form and product class

Source: Redrawn from Richard N. Cardozo, *Product Policy* (Reading, Mass.: Addison-Wesley Publishing Company, Inc., 1979), p. 6.

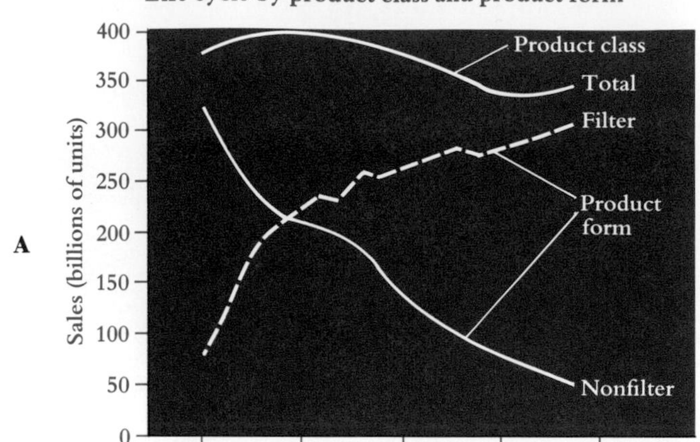

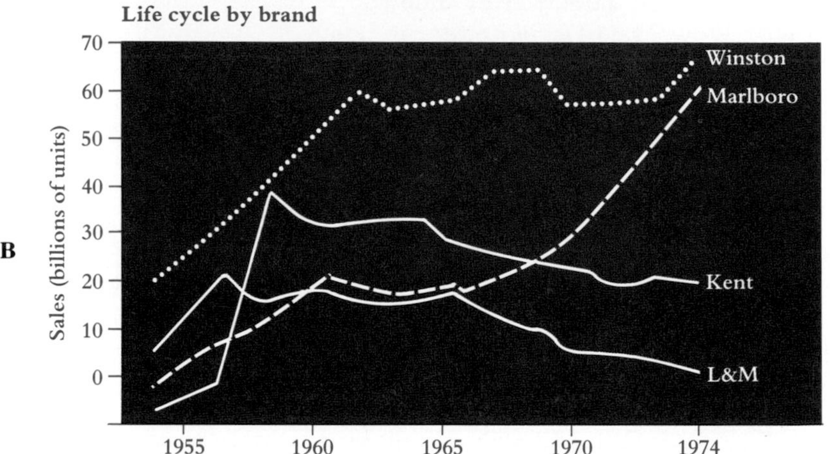

about $35, they can't be repaired, are thrown away if they break down, and have replaced more expensive, repairable watches.

A *fashion product* (Figure 10-4, *C*), for example, such as hemline lengths on skirts or lapel widths on sport jackets, is introduced, declines, and then seems to return. Life cycles for fashion products most often appear in women's and men's clothing styles. The length of the cycles may be years or decades.

A *fad,* such as wall walkers or toe socks, experiences rapid sales on introduction and then an equally rapid decline (Figure 10-4, *D*). Tonka's GoBots and Hasbro's Transformers, toys that convert from robots to cars or airplanes and back again, may be a fad or may become a more permanent toy. Some companies make fads their primary business. Creative Programming, Inc., produces novelty videotapes. In 1988 they introduced "Video Baby" for $19.95, which they promote as letting you have the full, rich experience of parenthood, without the mess and inconvenience of the real thing. The company also sells "Video Dog" and "Video Cat" and says more are on the way.[10]

Following Coca-Cola's 1985 New Coke experience, two entrepreneurs introduced their Jolt Cola, with "all the sugar and twice the caffeine" of competing colas (see the Marketing Action Memo). Their marketing task is to move

Jolt from being simply a fad in the minds of consumers to being a permanent entry in the very competitive cola market.

The Product Level: Class, Form, and Brand The product life cycle can vary depending on whether it applies to a class, form, or brand of product. **Product class** refers to the entire product category or industry, such as the total cigarette industry shown in Figure 10-5, *A*. **Product form** pertains to variations within the class. For example, in the cigarette industry there are filter or nonfilter product forms (Figure 10-5, *A*). A final type of life cycle curve can represent the brand, such as the four brands of cigarettes in Figure 10-5, *B*. During the period shown, sales of the Marlboro brand were growing and the Kent and L&M brands were in the decline stage of the product life cycle as cigarette smokers shifted from nonfiltered to filtered cigarettes or quit smoking entirely. Today many companies offer nonfiltered and filtered cigarettes.

The Life Cycle and Consumers The life cycle of a product depends on sales to consumers. Not all consumers rush to buy a product in the introductory stage, and the shapes of the life cycle curves indicate that most sales occur after the product has been on the market for some time. In essence, a product diffuses, or spreads, through the population, a concept called the *diffusion of innovation*.

Some people are attracted to a product early, others buy it only after they see their friends with the item. Figure 10-6 shows the consumer population divided into five categories of product adopters based on when they adopt a new product. Brief profiles accompany each category. For any product to be successful, it must be purchased by innovators and early adopters. This is why manufacturers of new pharmaceuticals try to gain adoption by leading hospitals, clinics, and physicians that are widely respected in the medical field. Once accepted by innovators and early adopters, the adoption of new products moves on to the early majority, late majority, and laggard categories.

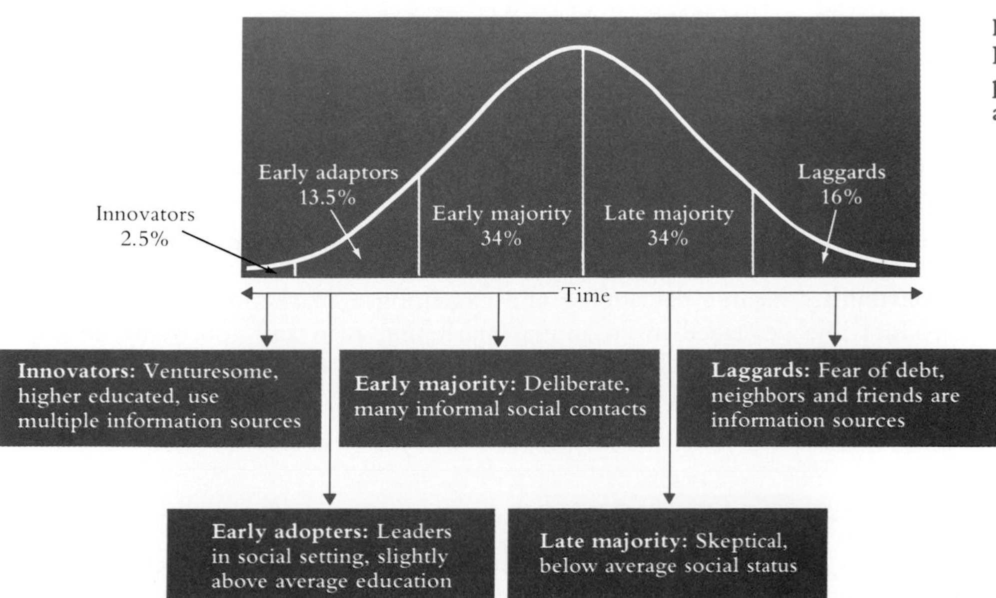

FIGURE 10-6
Five categories and profiles of product adopters

Recognizing the concept of the product life cycle helps a marketing manager to remember that a product may need continual adjustments to prevent sales declines and to formulate a marketing strategy to stimulate sales. Failure to recognize the life cycle concept often has dramatic consequences. In the 1960's, airline passenger miles increased by 15 percent a year, and airline companies ordered dozens of new wide-body jets such as the Boeing 747 and McDonnell Douglas DC-10. By the mid-1970's these same planes were standing empty on the runways because airline officials had just extrapolated past trends on passenger usage and failed to see that smaller, more fuel-efficient planes would replace the 747 and DC-10 jets on shorter domestic flights.[11] Today, even though some new models are being produced, these wide-body jets are in the mature or declining stage of their product life cycle.

CONCEPT CHECK

1 **Advertising plays a major role in the __________ stage of the product life cycle, and __________ plays a major role in maturity.**

2 **How do high learning and low learning products differ?**

3 **What does the life cycle for a fashion product look like?**

MANAGING THE PRODUCT'S LIFE CYCLE

An important task for a firm is to manage its products through the successive stages of their life cycles. This section discusses the role of the product manager who is usually responsible for this and analyzes three ways to manage a product through its life cycle: modifying the product, modifying the market, and repositioning the product.

ROLE OF A PRODUCT MANAGER

The product manager (sometimes called brand manager) manages the marketing efforts for a close-knit family of products or brands. Introduced by P&G in 1927, the product manager style of marketing organization is used by consumer goods firms such as General Foods and Revlon and by industrial firms such as Intel and Hewlett-Packard. All product managers are responsible for managing existing products through the stages of the life cycle, and some are also responsible for developing new products. The product manager's marketing responsibilities include developing and executing a marketing program for the product line described in an annual marketing plan and approving ad copy, media selection, and package design. The role of product managers in planning, implementing, and controlling marketing strategy is covered in depth in Chapters 19 and 20.

MODIFYING THE PRODUCT

Strategies of **product modification** involve altering a product's characteristic, such as its quality, performance, or appearance, to try to increase and extend a

A longer hotdog was Oscar Mayer's product modification

product's sales and life cycle. Wilson Sporting Goods, for example, has changed the quality of tennis rackets with the addition of graphite and ceramics and revived sales as tennis players replace their wooden, aluminum, and steel rackets. Mazda has introduced a dramatic feature change in its RX-7 rotary engine–powered sport car.

New features, packages, or scents can be used to change a product's characteristics and give the sense of a revised product line. For example, Dial Corporation introduced lemon-scented Brillo cleaning pads in 1987. Oscar Mayer introduced its bun-length weiner that "fits the bun, bite for bite" so that hot dog gourmets aren't left with their last bite being only the bun.

MODIFYING THE MARKET

With **marketing modification** strategies, a company tries to increase a product's use among existing customers, to create new use situations, or to find new customers.

Increasing Use Promoting more frequent use has been a strategy of Heineken brewery, which has used the slogan, "Come to think of it, I'll have a Heineken." For several years, the manufacturer of Dentyne gum has advised people to chew Dentyne if they can't brush after every meal.

Creating New Use Situation Finding new uses for an existing product has been the major strategy in extending the life of Arm & Hammer Baking Soda. This product, originally intended as a baking ingredient, is now being promoted as toothpaste; a deodorizer for cat litter, carpeting, and refrigerators; and a fire extinguisher.

Finding New Users To prevent sales declines in wall-to-wall carpeting, carpet manufacturers found new user groups such as schools and hospitals. To expand company sales, Nautilus, a manufacturer of fitness equipment for gyms, entered the home market in 1988. Commercial accounts represented 95 percent of the company's sales in 1987, but the home market has a $1 to $5 billion sales potential. U.S. sales of video games plummeted from $3 billion in 1982 to $100 million in 1985. But they are making a comeback by having improved games targeted at two new segments: (1) 8- to 14-year-olds, most of whom can't remember the old games, and (2) adults who want more sophisticated games.[12]

REPOSITIONING THE PRODUCT

Often a company decides to reposition its product or product line in an attempt to prevent sales decline. As mentioned in Chapter 8, *product repositioning* is changing the place a product occupies in a consumer's mind relative to competitive products. A firm can reposition a product by changing one or more of the four marketing mix elements. Four factors that trigger a repositioning action are discussed below.

Reacting to a Competitor's Position One reason to reposition a product is because a competitor's entrenched position is adversely affecting sales and market share. As noted earlier in the book, RCA's SelectaVision Videodisc player failed to compete successfully with VCRs and was withdrawn from the market. However, the success of the CD player in the audio market today may give new life to laser videodiscs. Now priced as low as $400, the new units have been repositioned to stress not only the higher quality audio and video available on the laser videodiscs as compared with that on VCRs, but also the ability to accommodate the entire width (and thus view) of a 70 mm movie theater film, a view that a VCR can't show. "Combi" laser players play both laser and compact discs.[13] The question of the 1990's is whether the repositioning strategy will succeed in relaunching laser videodiscs. To cloud the markets for audio and videodisc players even more, in 1988 Tandy announced that within 2 years it would sell an inexpensive CD player that can both record and erase music.[14]

Reaching a New Market Dannon Yogurt introduced Yop, a liquid yogurt, in France in 1974. The product flopped because the French were not interested in another dairy product. Dannon repositioned Yop as a soft drink for the health-conscious consumer, and in 1988 sales were booming.[15]

Repositioning can involve more than changing advertising copy. The New Balance Company changed its product's position as a running shoe for the serious runner to the shoe for the mass market. The distribution strategy was altered from selling only through specialty running stores to selling through discount and department stores as well.

Catching a Rising Trend Analysis of changing consumer trends can lead to repositioning. For many years, tanning was an important summer ritual that led to $400 million in sales of tanning lotions in 1986. Yet growing concern over skin cancer has led to a repositioning of tanning lotions to that of being skin protectors. American Home Products repositioned its Youthe Garde facial moisturizer as an item to help protect against skin cancer.[16]

Changing the Value Offered In repositioning the product line, a company can decide to change the value it offers buyers and trade up or down. **Trading up** involves adding value to the product (or line) through additional features or higher quality materials. BMW built its reputation in the United States with small, sporty sedans that sell for $20,000 to $35,000. In 1988, BMW traded up with a new model, 750sci, which costs $67,000. The car is targeted at the Mercedes Benz buyer, who is 45 to 55 years old and has an income above $150,000.[17] A department store can trade up by adding a designer clothes section to the store.

Trading down involves reducing the number of features, quality, or price. Mercedes traded down its line with the introduction of the Mercedes 190 sedan. During the energy crisis of the early 1970's, companies downgraded their lines to improve profitability or help overcome product supply shortages. For example, Scovill Manufacturing Company shortened appliance cords and reduced the number of models of electric fans in its line.[18]

CONCEPT CHECK

1 **How does a product manager help manage a product's life cycle?**

2 **What does "creating new use situations" mean in managing a product's life cycle?**

3 **Explain the difference between trading up and trading down in repositioning.**

BRANDING

A basic decision in marketing products is **branding,** in which an organization uses a name, phrase, design, symbols, or combination of these to identify its

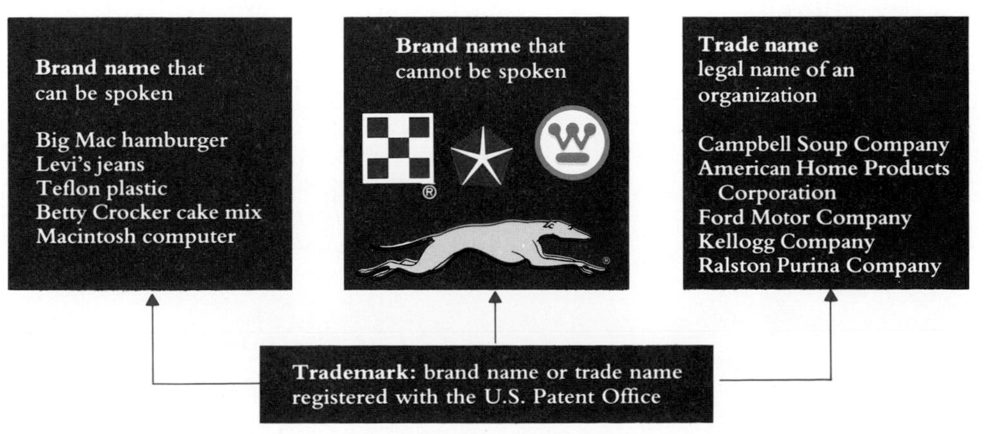

FIGURE 10-7
Examples of well-known trademarks

products and distinguish them from those of competitors. A **brand name** is any word, "device" (design, sound, shape, or color), or combination of these used to distinguish a seller's goods or services. Some brand names can be spoken, such as a Big Mac hamburger. Other brand names cannot be spoken, such as the rainbow-colored apple (the *logotype* or *logo*) that Apple Computer puts on its machines and in its ads. A **trade name** is a commercial, legal name under which a company does business. The Campbell Soup Company is the trade name of that firm.

A **trademark** identifies that a firm has legally registered its brand name or trade name so the firm has its exclusive use, thereby preventing others from using it. In the United States, trademarks are registered with the U.S. Patent Office. As discussed in Chapter 3, trademarks are protected under the Lanham Act. A well-known trademark can help a company advertise its offerings to customers and develop their brand loyalty. Figure 10-7 shows examples of well-known trademarks.

MARKETING·ACTION·MEMO

Is There Life After Death? Ask Black Jack or Grandma

The product life cycle is pretty clear. Much as with people, it implies some distinct stages from birth to death. However, some people, including famous actress Shirley MacLaine, claim to have lived several lives. So, too, are some brands being reborn to the marketplace.

Warner Lambert has introduced a new gum, Black Jack. Ask your parents or grandparents if they remember this "new" brand. It was first introduced in 1870 as the first mass-produced chewing gum. Now it has been brought back because tests have shown that its distinct taste has renewed appeal. Coca-Cola has revitalized Fresca, a grapefruit-flavored drink, first offered in 1966. The new Fresca now contains NutraSweet and 10 percent real grapefruit juice.

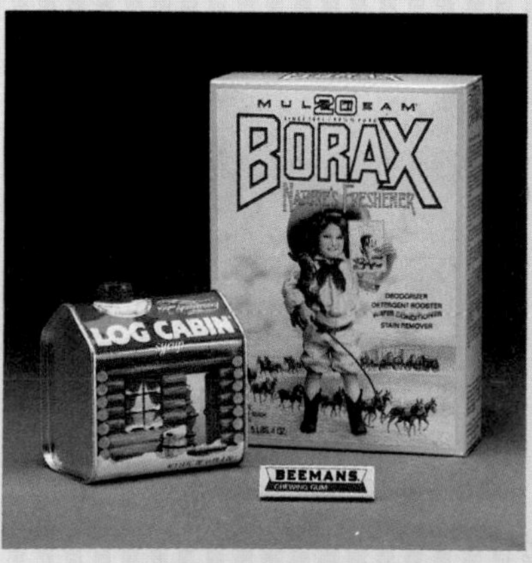

Why this rebirth of old brands? As noted in the last chapter, the launch of a new product is expensive. Estimates for national distribution of a consumer food product are as high as $40 million. Taking an old brand and resurrecting it may cost less because the market may still be aware of the name. Or, as in the case of the Goobers and Raisinets candies, Nestle's changed their distribution strategy. For 50 years, these 2 candies were sold only in movie theaters. Now you can drop by your local supermarket and pick up some Goobers.

So the next time you try that new brand, such as Clove gum, Log Cabin syrup, Brylcreem, Maypo, or Ipana toothpaste—ask your grandparents. Chances are, they've already tried it.

Source: Bill Saporito, "Has-Been Brands Go Back To Work," *Fortune* (April 28, 1986), pp. 123-124; Arthur Bragg, "Back to the Future," *Sales and Marketing Management* (November 1986), pp. 61-62.

THE VALUE OF BRANDING

Branding policy is important not only for manufacturers but also for retailers and consumers. Retailers value branding because consumers shop at stores that carry their desired brands. Some retailers have created their own store brands to further enhance loyalty from their customers. Sears exclusively offers the Kenmore brand for its appliance line and Craftsman as the brand for tools.

Consumers, however, may benefit most from branding. Recognizing competing products by distinct trademarks allows them to be more efficient shoppers. Consumers can recognize and avoid products with which they are dissatisfied, while becoming loyal to other, more satisfying brands. As discussed in Chapter 4, brand loyalty often eases the consumers' decision making by eliminating the need for an external search. Also, the expense of establishing a brand on the marketplace means that some brands are reintroduced years after they apparently died (see the Marketing Action Memo).

LICENSING

The value of brand names is seen more in marketing through a strategy of licensing. **Licensing** is a contractual agreement whereby a company allows someone else to use its brand name and usually requires the product be made to its specifications. Winnebago, a manufacturer of campers, has licensed its name to a line of tents and camping accessories.[19] Coca-Cola has licensed clothing, and Old Spice, a manufacturer of men's after-shave lotion, has licensed a line of safety razors. This approach allows a company to enter new markets without engaging in the new product development process.

PICKING A GOOD BRAND NAME

We take brand names such as Dial, Sanyo, Porsche, and Danskin for granted, but it is often a difficult and expensive process to pick a good name. Four criteria are mentioned most often in selecting a good brand name.[20]

The name should suggest the product benefits. For example, Accutron (watches), Easy Off (oven cleaner), Glass Plus (glass cleaner), Cling-Free (anti-static cloth for clothes drying), and Tidy Bowl (toilet bowl cleaner) all clearly describe the value of purchasing the product.

The name should be memorable, distinctive, and positive. In the car industry, when a competitor has a memorable name, others quickly imitate. In the 1960's Ford named a car the Mustang. Soon there were Pintos, Colts, Mavericks, and Broncos. The Thunderbird stimulated a Phoenix, Eagle, Sunbird, and Firebird.

The name should fit the company or product image. Sharp is a name that can apply to audio and video equipment. NCR (the National Cash Register Company) has had difficulty extending its name to its line of computers. Excedrin is a scientific-sounding name, good for an analgesic. Anacin, however, is perceived negatively because of its prefix meaning "not." The name *Apple* is considered a stroke of genius. When Apple Computer was created, there wasn't any PC market. The name was friendly, safe, and trustworthy. Name experts believe the name *TI99/4* helped kill Texas Instruments' entry into the PC market because it sounds so complex.[21]

Distinctive names suggest product benefits

The name should have no legal restrictions. Recently the largest provider of legal services—Hyatt Legal Services—was ordered by a federal court to indicate in advertising that it's named after the founder, Joel Hyatt. Hyatt Hotels argued *Hyatt Legal Services* was a name that infringed on its trademark.[22] Similarly, Baskin-Robbins, which has a registered trademark on Pralines 'N Cream ice cream, sued Häagen-Dazs for trademark infringement when it introduced its Pralines & Cream flavor.

BRANDING STRATEGIES

In deciding to brand a product, companies have several possible strategies, including manufacturer branding, reseller branding, or mixed branding approaches.

Manufacturer Branding With **manufacturer branding,** the producer dictates the brand name using either a multiproduct or multibrand approach. **Multiproduct branding** is when a company uses one name for all its products. This approach is often referred to as a *blanket* or *family* branding strategy (Figure 10-8). There are several advantages to this approach. Consumers who have had a good experience with a Honda lawn mower may carry a favorable attitude toward the purchase of a Honda snow blower or Honda generator. This is an example of *line extension* because the new product is seen as extending an existing line rather than starting a completely new one. This approach also can result in lower advertising costs because the same name is used on all products within the line, raising the level of brand awareness.

In recent years there has been an increasing trend toward *brand extensions,* applying the same brand name to related products within the same product category. North American Systems, Inc., manufacturers of Mr. Coffee machines, is introducing a line of coffee called Mr. Coffee. Coca-Cola is taking its Minute Maid name from orange juice and using it on orange soda.[23] A blanket branding approach can also facilitate acceptance of the product by retail stores. A retailer that knows customers are satisfied with Gerber's baby food will be more open to carrying the new line of Gerber's diapers.

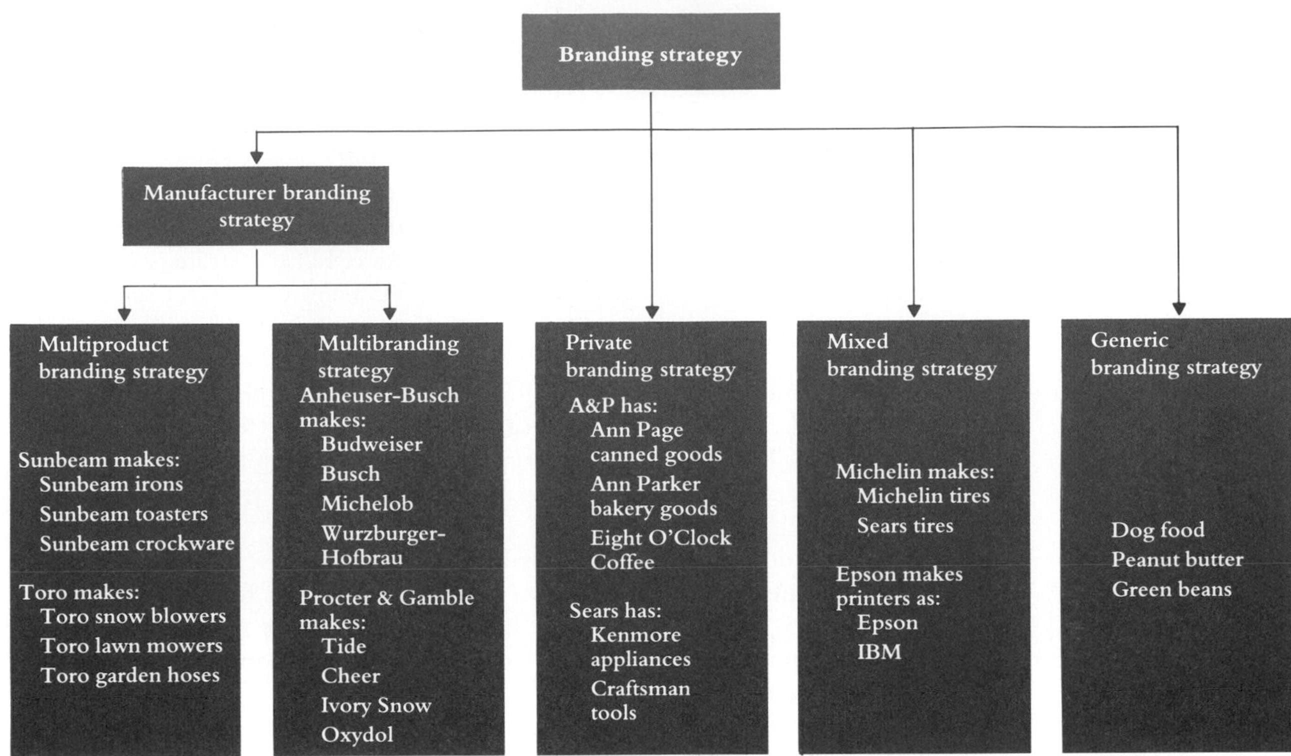

FIGURE 10-8
Alternative branding strategies

However, there are some risks to the multiproduct branding approach. Poor performance of one item may have a negative impact on similarly named items in the line. Also, too many uses for one brand name can dilute the image of a product line.

An alternative manufacturer's branding strategy, **multibranding,** involves giving each product a distinct name. Multibranding is a useful strategy when each brand is intended for a different marketing segment. P&G makes Camay soap for those concerned with soft skin, Safeguard for those who want deodorant protection, and Lava for those who desire a strong cleaner.

Compared with the multiproduct approach, promotional costs tend to be higher with multibranding. The company must generate awareness among consumers and retailers for each new brand name without the benefit of any previous impressions. The advantages of this approach are that each brand is unique to each market segment and there is no risk that a product failure will affect other products in the line.

Private Branding A company uses **private branding,** often called private labeling or reseller branding, when it manufactures products but sells them under the brand name of a wholesaler or retailer. Radio Shack, Sears, and K Mart are large retailers that have their own brand names. 3M, for example, manufactures photographic film for K Mart branded under K Mart's name, *Focal*. Manufacturers follow this approach when the retailer has a large number of outlets and a strong reputation. The advantage to the manufacturer of using reseller branding is that promotional costs are shifted to the retailer.[24] There is a risk, though, because the manufacturer's sales depend heavily on the efforts of the retailer.

Mixed Branding A compromise between the two previously described approaches is a **mixed branding** strategy. Some manufacturers (Figure 10-8) market products under their own name and that of a reseller because the segment attracted to the manufacturer's brand name is different from the type of customer who shops at the reseller. Thus by following a mixed brand strategy and selling tires under the names of Michelin and Sears, Michelin can attract sales from a broader market.

Generic Branding Introduced in 1977, an alternative branding approach is the **generic brand,** which is a no-brand product such as dog food, peanut butter, or green beans. There is no identification other than a description of the contents. The major appeal is that the price is up to one-third less than that of branded items.

The sale of generic brands peaked in 1982, at the height of a recession in the United States. In late 1987, generic brands accounted for only 1.5 percent of total grocery sales. The decline in generics has been attributed to lower inflation, the importance of brand name, and greater promotional efforts for brand-name items.[25]

Consumers who use generics see these products as being as good as brand-name items, and in light of what they expect, users of these products are relatively pleased with their purchases.[26] The Marketing Research Report shows a consumer evaluation of generic brands compared with national (manufacturer) brands and private (reseller) brands; it shows that national brands are clearly judged the best, except in the categories for "high shopping convenience" (tied with private brands) and "value for money" (private brands are rated best).

PACKAGING

The **packaging** component of a product refers to any container in which it is offered for sale and on which information is communicated. To a great extent,

New packaging for traditional products

the customer's first exposure to the product is the package, and it is an expensive and important part of the marketing strategy. A grocery product package is especially important because packaging designers using eye cameras have discovered that a typical consumer's eye sweep of a grocery shelf is a mere 2.3 seconds.[27] Today's packaging costs exceed $50 billion and are also substantial for the consumer: an estimated 10 cents of every dollar spent by a consumer goes to packaging.[28]

BENEFITS OF PACKAGING

Despite the cost, packaging is essential because packages provide important benefits for the manufacturer, retailer, and ultimate consumer.

MARKETING · RESEARCH · REPORT

DO BRAND NAMES MAKE A DIFFERENCE?

Three branding strategies described in the text are: manufacturer's brands (often national brands such as Fritos, Renault, and Smuckers); private brands (those of the reseller such as Kenmore for Sears); and generic (no-name) brands. The competition between these brands is related to how consumers evaluate them. Do consumers believe a quality difference exists between the three brands? If not, the consumer may buy the cheapest: the generic brand. To answer the question, four researchers conducted a study.

The 125 grocery shoppers interviewed were asked to evaluate a list of statements on a five-point scale from (1) strongly agree to (5) strongly disagree for a variety of food and nonfood items. Results are shown in the next column.

Did people perceive a difference? A close look at the table reveals important differences in perceptions on many of these statements. In general, national brands were perceived as superior in terms of reliability, prestige, and quality. Private and generic brands were seen to offer more value for the money. The private brands were generally perceived to be between generic and national brands. Which won on dimensions of freshness, confidence, and packaging?

FACTOR EVALUATED	NATIONAL BRANDS*	PRIVATE BRANDS	GENERIC BRANDS
Eye-catching package	1.79	2.52	3.37
High reliability	1.90	2.32	3.14
Highly appealing	1.99	2.42	3.19
High quality	2.02	2.64	3.34
Confidence in use	2.05	2.38	3.15
Inviting package	2.10	2.72	3.53
High freshness	2.25	2.47	2.74
Informative package	2.26	2.30	2.71
High prestige	2.28	3.32	3.77
High shopping convenience	2.42	2.42	2.73
Gives a sense of brand loyalty	2.70	2.88	3.24
Value for money	2.97	2.33	2.41

*The lower the mean (average) score, the higher is the level of agreement from (1) strongly agree to (5) strongly disagree.

Source: Based on Joseph A. Bellizzi, Harry F. Krueckeberg, John R. Hamilton, and Warren S. Martin, "Consumer Perceptions of National, Private, and Generic Brands," *Journal of Retailing* (Winter 1981), pp. 56-70.

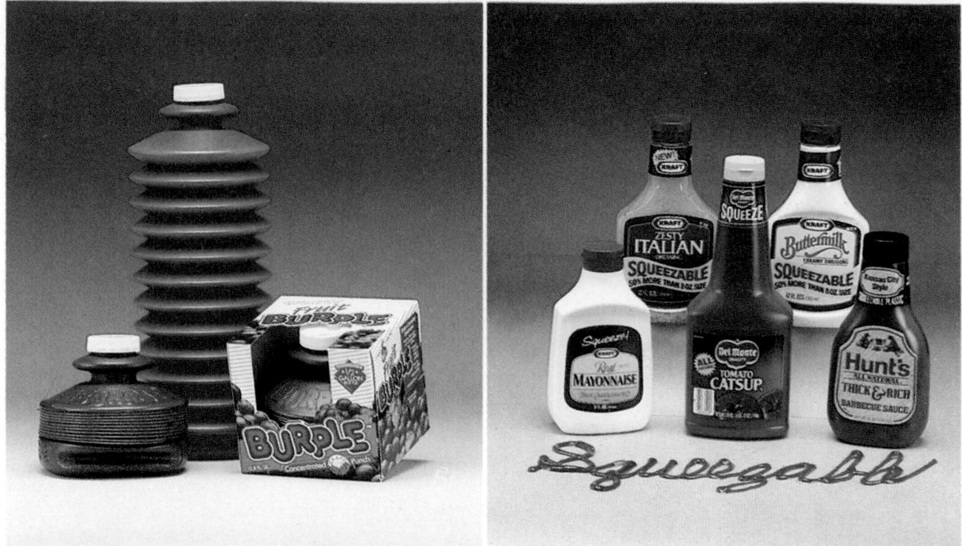

More packaging today stresses functional benefits

Communication Benefits A major benefit of packaging is the information on it conveyed to the consumer, such as directions on how to use the product and the composition of the product, which is needed to satisfy legal requirements of product disclosure.[29] Other information consists of seals and symbols, either government-required or commercial seals of approval (such as the Good Housekeeping seal).[30]

Functional Benefits Packaging often plays an important functional role, such as convenience, protection, or storage. Quaker State has changed its oil containers to eliminate the need for a separate spout, and Borden has changed the shape of its Elmer's Wonder Bond adhesive to prevent clogging of the spout. To increase convenience, Colgate and Check-Up brands of toothpaste are now sold in pump dispensers. Introduced in 1984, pumps captured 12 percent of all toothpaste sales within 1 year. Both General Foods (with Post's Natural Raisin Bran) and Oscar Mayer (with weiners) recently introduced easy-to-open-and-reseal plastic bags for their products.[31]

Consumer protection is becoming a growing role of packaging. In 1982 a mentally ill person put cyanide into several bottles of Tylenol, which resulted in several deaths. Since that time, the development of tamper-resistant packaging has become important. Companies such as that producing Skippy Peanut Butter have turned to safety seals or pop tops, which reveal previous opening. The concern among many is that no package is truly tamper resistant. The Federal government now has a law that carries maximum penalties of life imprisonment and $250,000 fines for tampering.[32]

Another functional value of packaging is in extending storage and *shelf life* (the time a product can be stored before it spoils). New technology allows products requiring refrigeration to be packaged in paper-sealed containers, which dramatically increases their shelf life.

Perceptual Benefits A third component of packaging is the perception created in the consumer's mind. To achieve a modern look that could cover both its Coke sold in the United States and Coca-Cola (sold abroad), the Coca-Cola Company undertook a 2½-year redesign effort of its logo and package design. Involving at least 25 designers and 800 variations on the word *Coke,* the company sought to retain the perceptual benefits of the world's best-known brand of cola when it introduced its new package design in 1988.[33]

A package can connote status, economy, or even product quality. Equally fresh potato chips were wrapped in two different types of bags: wax paper and polyvinyl. Consumers rated the chips in the polyvinyl as crisper and even tastier, even though the chips were identical.[34]

In the past, the color of packages was selected subjectively. For example, the famous Campbell's soup can was the inspiration of a company executive who liked Cornell University's red and white football uniforms. Today, there is greater recognition that color affects consumers' perceptions. When the color of the can of Barrelhead Sugar-Free Root Beer changed to beige from blue, consumers said it tasted more like old-fashioned root beer.[35] And Owens-Corning judged the pink color of its fiber insulation to be so important that the color was given trademark status by the courts.[36]

TRENDS IN PACKAGING

Packaging is becoming an increasingly important aspect of marketing strategy. Companies are seeing packaging as a way to attract customers to new and existing brands. For existing brands, there is a growing tendency to repackage; that is, to redesign the existing package or container. Breyers Ice Cream was a respected premium brand name for many years until the superpremium ice creams such as Häagen-Dazs appeared. Breyers redesigned its package to give it a sleek black look with an appetizing product shot. Jergen's soap redesigned its package and saw sales increase 15 percent in 6 months. Redesigns cost as little as $100,000 to $150,000 and are seen as a potentially cost-effective way to boost sales.[37]

There are two differing trends in packaging. One involves downsizing, or reducing, the package size. One company is marketing "Breakfast in Bed," a 2-ounce package of their Breakfast Blend coffee and a bag of their doughnut mix. Best Kosher Sausage Company now offers three-packs of six different sausages. The opposite trend is increasing the size. Lever Bros., for example, is offering 80-ounce plastic bottles of Liquid Sunlight automatic dishwasher detergent. Citrus Hill Select orange juice is being tested in 96-ounce plastic containers.

A significant packaging issue facing marketers is the environmental impact of packages. Concern is growing about the effects of plastic packaging on animals and humans. Sea animals and birds mistake discarded plastic packaging foam, beads, and bags for food, which results in blockages of their digestive tracts. And some plastic-based foam packaging has been found to be harmful to the earth's ozone layer. As a result, in 1987, McDonald's discontinued use of hamburger containers made of chlorofluorcarbons. Because today's plastic packaging can remain intact for up to 4 centuries, packaging producers are putting millions of dollars into research to find biodegradable plastic packaging.[38]

PRODUCT WARRANTY

A final component for product consideration is the **warranty,** which is a statement indicating the liability of the manufacturer for product deficiencies. There are various degrees of a product warranty with different implications for manufacturers and customers.

THE VARIATIONS OF A WARRANTY

Some companies offer *express warranties,* which are written statements of liabilities. In recent years the government has required greater disclosure on express warranties to indicate whether the warranty is a limited-coverage or full-coverage alternative. A *limited-coverage warranty* specifically states the bounds of coverage and, more important, areas of noncoverage, whereas a *full warranty* has no limits of noncoverage. Peugeot boldly touts its warranty coverage. The Magnuson-Moss Warranty / FTC Improvement Act (1975) regulates the content of consumer warranties and so has strengthened consumer rights with regard to warranties.

With greater frequency, manufacturers are being held to *implied warranties,* which assign responsibility for product deficiencies to the manufacturer. Studies show warranties are important and affect a consumer's product evaluation. Brands that have limited warranties tend to receive less positive evaluations compared with full-warranty items.[39]

THE GROWING IMPORTANCE OF WARRANTIES

Warranties are important in light of increasing product liability claims. In the early part of this century the courts protected companies, but the trend now is toward "strict liability" rulings, where a manufacturer is liable for any product defect, whether it followed reasonable research standards or not. This issue is hotly contested by companies and consumer advocates.

Warranties represent much more to the buyer than just protection from negative consequences. Warranties can hold a significant marketing advantage for the producer. Sears has built a strong reputation for its Craftsman tool line with a simple warranty: if you break a tool, it's replaced with no questions asked. Zippo has an equally simple guarantee: "If it ever fails, we'll fix it free."

CONCEPT CHECK

1 **How does a generic brand differ from a private brand?**

2 **Explain the role of packaging in terms of perception.**

3 **What is the difference between an expressed and an implied warranty?**

SUMMARY

1 Products have a finite life cycle consisting of four stages: introduction, growth, maturity, and decline. The marketing objectives for each stage differ.

2 In the introductory stage the need is to establish primary demand, whereas the growth stage requires selective demand strategies. In the maturity stage the need is to maintain market share; the decline stage necessitates a deleting, harvesting, or contracting strategy.

3 There are various shapes to the product life cycle. High learning products have a long introductory period, and low learning products rapidly enter the growth stage. There are also different curves for fashions and fads. Different product life cycle curves can exist for the product class, product form, and brand.

4 In managing a product's life cycle, changes can be made in the product itself or in the target market. Product modification approaches include changes in the quality, performance, or appearance. Market modification approaches entail increasing a product's use among existing customers, creating new use situations, or finding new users.

5 Product repositioning can be done by modifying the product, as well as through changes in advertising, pricing, or distribution.

6 Branding enables a firm to distinguish its products in the marketplacc from those of its competitors. A good name brand should suggest the product benefits, be memorable, fit the company or product image, and be free of legal restrictions.

7 Licensing of a brand name is being used by more companies. The company allows the name to be used without having to manufacture the product.

8 Manufacturers can follow one of three branding strategies: a manufacturer's brand, a reseller brand, or a mixed brand approach. With a manufacturer's branding approach, the company can use the same brand name for all products in the line (multiproduct, or family, branding) or can give products different brands (multibranding).

9 A reseller, or private, brand is used when a firm manufactures a product but sells it under the brand name of a wholesaler or retailer. A generic brand is a product with no identification of manufacturer or reseller that is offered on the basis of price appeal.

10 Packaging provides communication, functional, and perceptual benefits.

11 The warranty, a statement of a manufacturer's liability for product deficiencies, is an important aspect of a manufacturer's product strategy.

KEY TERMS AND CONCEPTS

product life cycle p. 256
product class p. 265
product form p. 265
product modification p. 266
marketing modification p. 267
trading up p. 269
trading down p. 269
branding p. 269
brand name p. 270
trade name p. 270
trademark p. 270
licensing p. 271
manufacturer branding p. 272
multiproduct branding p. 272
multibranding p. 273
private branding p. 273
mixed branding p. 274
generic brand p. 274
packaging p. 274
warranty p. 278

CHAPTER PROBLEMS AND APPLICATIONS

1 Several years ago, Apple Computer was one of the first to mass market PCs. IBM, the giant, had no competing product, but within a short time it announced its PC model. Steven Jobs, the founder of Apple, is said to have exclaimed, "We're glad to see IBM is entering the market." According to the product life cycle, is there any rationale for this statement?

2 Several manufacturers of aseptic packaging (paper containers) have formed a trade association to advertise its merits. What is the rationale for competitors collectively advertising in the early stages of a product's life?

3 Listed below are three different products in various stages of the product life cycle. What marketing strategies would you suggest to these companies? (a) Sony's laser disc stereo—introductory stage, (b) manual typewriters—decline stage, and (c) solar panels for home heating—growth stage.

4 In many communities the birth rate has dropped substantially, adversely affecting hospitals' pediatric medicine departments. Although pediatrics as a specialty is declining, hospitals still need a complete service mix. As the chief executive of a hospital, what decline strategies would you suggest?

5 It has often been suggested that products are intentionally made to break down or wear out. Is this strategy a planned product modification approach?

6 The product manager of GE is reviewing the penetration of trash compactors in American homes. After more than a decade in existence, this product is in relatively few homes. What problems account for this poor penetration? What is the shape of the trash compactor life cycle?

7 Several alternative product life cycles were reviewed in this chapter. Why is it important for a company to realize what type of life cycle curve may represent its product?

8 For years, the Linx Company has had a reputation for producing high-quality crystal stemware. Because of economic pressures on consumers, the company plans to market a lower priced glass for the mass market. What branding strategy would you recommend? What are the trade-offs with your recommended strategy?

9 The nature of product warranties has changed as the federal court system reassesses the meaning of warranties. How does the regulatory trend toward warranties affect product development?

10 Generic brands are a new entry into the marketplace. Assume you are the manufacturer of Green Giant canned vegetables. Would you introduce a generic line of canned vegetables? Explain your rationale.

SUGGESTED READINGS

Michael Brody, "When Products Turn," *Fortune* (March 3, 1986), pp. 20-24. *The exploding litigation problem for companies regarding product performance is highlighted in this article.*

Michael Gershman, "Packaging's Role in Remarketing," *Management Review* (May 1987), p. 41. *This article explores the value of packaging in bringing a product's sales back to life.*

Theodore Levitt, "Exploit the PLC," *Harvard Business Review* (November-December 1965), pp. 81-94. *This is a classic article on the product life cycle.*

Marisa Manley, "Product Liability: You're More Exposed than You Think," *Harvard Business Review* (September-October 1987), p. 28-34. *This article describes several approaches companies should consider to avoid product liability problems.*

Bill Saporito, "The Fly in Campbell's Soup," *Fortune* (May 9, 1988), pp. 67-70. *This article describes the potential problems of line and brand extensions—cannibalizing sales of the original brands.*

Mark Traylor, "Cannibalism In MultiBrand Firms," *The Journal of Consumer Marketing* (Spring 1986), pp. 69-75. *This article shows when cannibalism may not be bad for the multiproduct firm.*

Ladies' Home Journal
$1.50 October 1988
The war against BREAST CANCER
EXCLUSIVE Jessica McClure The little girl in the well: One year later
Woman's Day
PLAY TO WIN 52 MAZDA CARS
Woman's Day
CRASH COURSE COOKING THE HEALTHY WAY
GREAT CHRISTMAS GIFTS TO MAKE
INSTANT WINNER 2 CAR GIVEAWAY
HOW TO PROTECT YOUR CHILD FROM CRIME
LITTLE SIGNS OF BIG HEALTH PROBLEMS
VANITY FAIR
OCTOBER 1988/$2.00
MARY TYLER MO
SEPTEMBER 20, 1988
GIANT FALL ISSUE
familycircle
HOT GOSSIP FROM JOAN COLLINS
WHAT MAKES YOU
Lose 20, 30, 40 Pounds
10 WAYS TO A HAPPY
SPECIAL BONUS
FAMILY HEALTH GUIDE
Stress Test
Checkup Calendar
Nutrition Makeover
Fitness Plan
DAYCARE NIGHTMARE: One Mother's Story
Newsweek
RECORDS AND RUMBLES
THE DEBATE
HARDBALL
Dukakis and Bush Go on the Attack
A Newsweek Poll Assesses the Results

11

PRICING: RELATING OBJECTIVES TO REVENUES AND COSTS

After reading this chapter you should be able to:

Identify the elements that make up a price.

•

Recognize the constraints on a firm's pricing latitude and the objectives a firm has in setting prices.

•

Explain what a demand curve is and how it affects a firm's total and marginal revenue.

•

Recognize what price elasticity of demand means to a manager facing a pricing decision.

•

Explain the role of costs in pricing decisions.

•

Calculate a break-even point for various combinations of price, fixed cost, and variable cost.

Magazine Economics 101 at the Newsstand

Even though the magazines on the opposite page appeal to diverse tastes, they all have something in common. Each magazine has recently conducted a price experiment. Why? According to a *Newsweek* executive, "We want to figure out what the demand curve for our magazine at the newsstand is." And you thought that demand curves only existed to confuse you on a test in basic economics!

In July, August, and September of 1986, *Newsweek* conducted a pricing experiment at newsstands in 12 cities throughout the United States. Houston newsstand buyers paid \$2.25. In Fort Worth, New York, Los Angeles, San

Francisco, and Atlanta, newsstand buyers paid the regular $2 price. In San Diego and Dallas, the price was $1.50. The price in Minneapolis-St. Paul, New Orleans, and Detroit was only $1. By comparison, the regular newsstand price for *Time* and *U.S. News and World Report, Newsweek's* competitors, was $1.95.

The economics of newsstand cover pricing considers the manufacturing cost of the magazine, the relationship between price and volume sold, the effect of newsstand price on consumer subscription price, competitors' prices, and the likelihood of converting one-shot newsstand magazine buyers to permanent subscribers. *Newsweek's* weekly circulation had leveled off at 3 million copies, and company executives had reason to believe *Newsweek* could attract new subscribers at the newsstand. For example, *Ladies Home Journal* executives estimate that 5 percent of the *Journal's* newsstand readers become subscribers each month.

Price experiments in the magazine industry are common. *Woman's Day, Family Circle, Vanity Fair,* and *Ladies Home Journal* recently conducted experiments like *Newsweek*. *Vanity Fair's* price experiment indicated that a price reduction from $3 per single copy to $2 increased newsstand sales 60 percent. On the other hand, *Woman's Day* and *Family Circle* raised their prices after conducting price experiments.[1] The result of *Newsweek's* pricing experiment: keep the newsstand price at $2.

This chapter and Chapter 12 cover important factors organizations use in developing prices. The role of price in marketing strategy and a step-by-step procedure organizations use to set prices for products and services are discussed. Relevant concepts from economics and accounting show how each assists the marketing executive in developing the price component in the marketing mix.

NATURE AND IMPORTANCE OF PRICE

The price paid for goods and services goes by many names. You pay *tuition* for your education, *rent* for an apartment, *interest* on a bank credit card, and a *premium* for car insurance. Your dentist or physician charges you a *fee,* a professional or social organization charges *dues,* and transportation companies charge a *fare*. In business a consultant may require a *retainer* for services rendered, an executive is given a *salary,* a salesperson receives a *commission,* and a worker is paid a *wage*. Of course, what you pay for clothes or a haircut is termed a *price*.

WHAT IS A PRICE?

These examples highlight the many varied ways that price plays a part in our daily lives. From a marketing viewpoint, **price** is the money or other considerations (including other goods and services) exchanged for the ownership or use of a good or service. For example, Shell Oil recently exchanged 1 million pest control devices for sugar from a Caribbean country and consumers exchange trading stamps such as S&H Green Stamps for a variety of products.[2]

For most products and services, money is exchanged, although the amount is not always the same as the list or quoted price. Suppose you decide to buy five identical Rolls Royce Corniche models in peacock blue at a list price of

ITEM PURCHASED	PRICE	=	LIST PRICE	−	DISCOUNTS AND ALLOWANCES	+	EXTRA FEES
	PRICE EQUATION						
New car bought by an individual	Final price	=	List price	−	Quantity discount Cash discount Trade-ins	+	Financing charges Special accessories
Term in college bought by a student	Tuition	=	Published tuition	−	Scholarship Other financial aid Discounts for number of credits taken	+	Special activity fees
Bank loan obtained by a small business	Principal and interest	=	Amount of loan sought	−	Allowance for collateral	+	Premium for uncertain credit worthiness
Merchandise bought from a wholesaler by a retailer	Invoice price	=	List price	−	Quantity discount Cash discount Season discount Functional or trade discount	+	Penalty for late payment

FIGURE 11-1
The price of four different purchases

$150,000 each. As a quantity discount for buying five Corniches, you get $7,000 off the list price for each. You agree to pay half down and the other half in 3 months when the cars are delivered, which results in a financing fee of $2,000 per car. You are allowed $500 for your only trade—your 1978 Honda—amounting to $100 off the price of each car.

Applying the "price equation" (Figure 11-1) to your purchase, your price per car is:

Price = List price − Discounts and allowances + Extra fees
= $150,000 − ($7,000 + $100) + $2,000
= $144,900

Are you still interested? Figure 11-1 also illustrates how the price equation applies to a variety of different products and services.

PRICE AS AN INDICATOR OF VALUE

From a consumer's standpoint, price is often used to indicate value when it is paired with the perceived quality of a product or service. Specifically, **value** can be defined as the ratio of perceived quality to price (Value = Perceived quality/Price).[3] This relationship shows that for a given price, as perceived quality increases, value increases. Also, for a given price, value decreases when perceived quality decreases. The U.S. automobile industry struggled to overcome this latter relationship throughout the 1980's in its battle with foreign cars.[4]

BMW uses price to convey an image of value

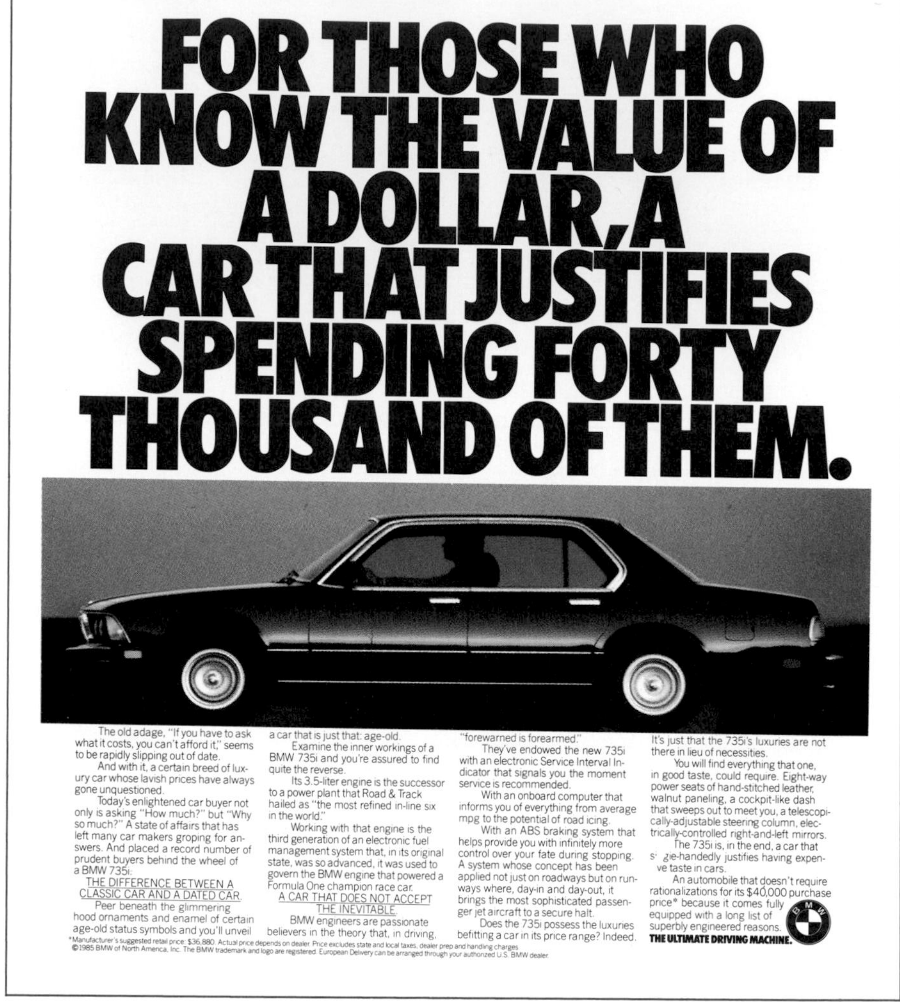

For some products, price itself influences the perception of quality, and ultimately value, to consumers.[5] For example, in a survey of home furnishing buyers, 84 percent agreed with the statement: "The higher the price, the higher the quality." For computer software it has been shown that consumers believe a low price implies poor quality.[6]

Consumer value assessments are often comparative. Here value involves the judgment by a consumer of the worth and desirability of a product or service relative to substitutes which satisfy the same need.[7] In this instance, a "reference value" emerges which involves comparing the costs and benefits of substitute items. For example, although Equal, a sugar substitute with NutraSweet, might be more expensive than sugar, some consumers "value" it more highly than sugar because Equal contains no calories.

How consumers make value assessments is not fully understood.[8] Nevertheless, companies consider this factor when making price decisions, as will be shown in Chapter 12.

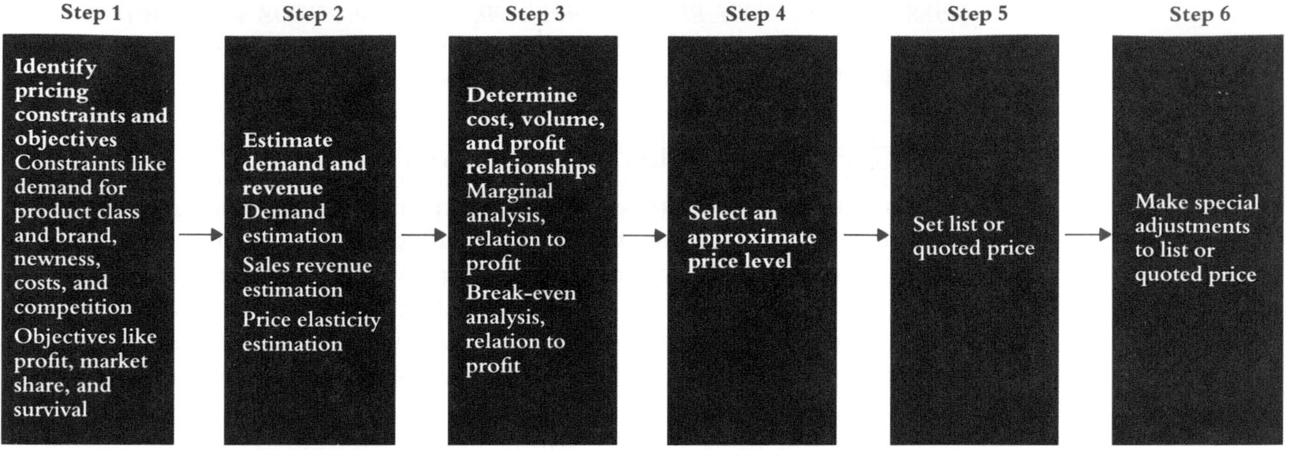

FIGURE 11-2
Steps in setting price

PRICE IN THE MARKETING MIX

Pricing is also a critical decision made by a marketing executive because price has a direct effect on a firm's profits. This is apparent from a firm's **profit equation:**

Profit = Total revenue − Total cost

or

Profit = (Unit price × Quantity sold) − Total cost

What makes this relationship even more important is that price affects the quantity sold, as illustrated with demand curves later in this chapter. Furthermore, since the quantity sold sometimes affects a firm's costs because of efficiency of production, price also indirectly affects costs. So pricing decisions influence both total revenue and total cost, which makes pricing one of the most important decisions marketing executives face.[9]

The importance of price in the marketing mix necessitates an understanding of six major steps involved in the process organizations go through in setting prices (Figure 11-2):

- Identify pricing constraints and objectives.
- Estimate demand and revenue.
- Determine cost, volume, and profit relationships.
- Select an approximate price level.
- Set list or quoted price.
- Make special adjustments to list or quoted price.

The first three steps are covered in this chapter and the last three in Chapter 12.

STEP 1: IDENTIFYING PRICING CONSTRAINTS AND OBJECTIVES

To define a problem, Chapter 6 showed that it is important to consider both the objectives and constraints that narrow the range of alternatives available to

erogeneous (main-frame computers), and informative advertising is used that avoids head-to-head price competition.

- *Monopolistic competition.* Dozens of regional, private brands of peanut butter compete with national brands like Skippy and Jif. Both price competition (regional, private brands being lower than national brands) and non-price competition (product features and advertising) exist.
- *Pure competition.* Hundreds of local grain elevators sell corn whose price per bushel is set by the marketplace. Within strains, the corn is identical, so advertising only informs buyers that the seller's corn is available.

The purpose of the government's breakup of AT&T was to stimulate competition in pricing telephone services by encouraging other firms to enter the market, thereby replacing the pure monopoly with an oligopoly.

Competitors' Prices A firm must know what specific price its competitors are charging. Price changes by competitors affect a firm's latitude for pricing to an important degree, as evidenced by the pricing experience of Texas Instruments (TI) with its 99/4A home computer. TI introduced its product at a list price of $1,100, only to see its competitors introduce similar models at much lower prices. A price war resulted, with TI ultimately selling the 99/4A for $49.95, having 1 million unsold units in inventory and recording losses of millions of dollars.[11]

IDENTIFYING PRICING OBJECTIVES

Goals that specify the role of price in an organization's marketing and strategic plans are **pricing objectives.** To the extent possible, these organizational pricing objectives are also carried to lower levels in the organization, such as in setting objectives for marketing managers responsible for an individual brand. Chapter 2 discussed six broad objectives that an organization may pursue, which tie in directly to the organization's pricing policies.

Profit Three different objectives relate to a firm's profit, usually measured in terms of return on investment (ROI) or return on assets. One objective is *managing for long-run profits,* which is followed by many Japanese firms that are willing to forgo immediate profit in cars, TV sets, or computers to develop quality products that can penetrate competitive markets in the future. A *maximizing current profit* objective, such as during this quarter or year, is common in many firms because the targets can be set and performance measured quickly. American firms are sometimes criticized for this short-run orientation. A *target return* objective involves a firm like Du Pont or Exxon setting a goal (such as 20 percent) for pretax ROI. These three profit objectives have different implications for a firm's pricing objectives.

Sales Given that a firm's profit is high enough for it to remain in business, its objectives may be to increase sales revenue. The hope is that the increase in sales revenue will in turn lead to increases in market share and profit. Cutting price on one product in a firm's line may increase its sales revenue but reduce

MARKETING·ACTION·MEMO

Hardball Contact Lens Pricing to Regain Market Share

Bausch & Lomb (B&L) introduced the world's first soft contact lens, so for several years, until competitors came up with their own soft contacts, B&L had a 100 percent market share.

However, extended-wear contacts (a soft lens that users could wear an entire month without removal) were a different matter. B&L had no share of this market for 2 years after competitors introduced this new product. A month after the U.S. Food and Drug Administration approved B&L's own extended-wear lens, it was in the hands of more than 90 percent of the 12,000 professional eye-care outlets in the United States that sell contact lenses. Within 4 months B&L had the highest market share—37 percent—for the extended-wear contact.

One key to B&L's success in obtaining this market share was what *Business Week* magazine called "hardball pricing." B&L priced its new extended-wear contacts at $20 to wholesalers—50 percent or more below the prices of its main competitors, CooperVision and Revlon's Barnes-Hind division.

Then the pricing game got even rougher:

- CooperVision introduced a new contact lens to wholesalers for $15.
- B&L responded by cutting prices on its own lens to $10 to $15, depending on volume purchased, and cut prices on the rest of its contact lens line as well.

The result was that B&L's sales tripled the following month and its market share jumped.

Source: Based on "Bausch & Lomb is Correcting Its Vision of Research," *Business Week* (March 30, 1987), p. 91; "Bausch & Lomb: Hardball Pricing Helps It Regain Its Grip on Contact Lenses," *Business Week* (July 16, 1984), pp. 78-80.

those of related products. Objectives related to sales revenue or unit sales have the advantage of being translated easily into meaningful targets for marketing managers responsible for a product line or brand—far more easily than with an ROI target, for example.

Market Share Market share is the ratio of the firm's sales revenue or unit sales to those of the industry (competitors plus the firm itself). Bausch & Lomb watched its market share decline below 50 percent as competitors introduced extended-wear contact lenses. When its president announced its own extended-wear contact lens, he declared, "Losing market share now is just not an alternative."[12] As described in the Marketing Action Memo, he embarked on an aggressive price-cutting strategy to regain lost market share. Although increased market share is a pricing goal of some firms, others see it as a means to other ends: increasing sales and profits.

Unit Volume Many firms use unit volume, the quantity produced or sold, as a pricing objective. These firms often sell multiple products at very different-prices and are sensitive to matching production capacity with unit volume. Using unit volume as an objective, however, can sometimes be misleading from a

General Motors uses low-interest financing and rebates to increase unit sales

profit standpoint. Volume can be increased by employing sales incentives (such as lowering prices, giving rebates, or offering lower interest rates). By doing this the company chooses to lower profits in the short run to quickly sell their product. This was the case in 1987 when General Motors, in an attempt to clear out older models, offered low-interest car loans and rebates. Although profits declined temporarily, they satisfied their objective of increasing volume to make room for the new model year cars.[13]

Survival In some instances, profits, sales, and market share are less important objectives of the firm than mere survival. Braniff Airlines has struggled to attract passengers with low fares, no penalty advance-booking policies, and aggressive promotions to improve the firm's cash flow. This pricing objective has helped Braniff to stay alive in the competitive airline industry.

Social Responsibility A firm may forgo higher profit on sales and follow a pricing objective that recognizes its obligations to customers and society in general. Medtronics followed this pricing policy when it introduced the world's first heart pacemaker. Government agencies, which set many prices for services they offer, use social responsibility as a primary pricing objective. As a result, in the arid South and Southwest the federal government sells water to users at a price that is only about 19 percent of the total cost of providing it.[14]

CONCEPT CHECK

1 **What do you have to do to the list price to determine the final price?**

2 **How does the type of competitive market a firm is in affect its latitude in setting price?**

STEP 2: ESTIMATING DEMAND AND REVENUE

Basic to setting a product's price is the extent of customer demand for it. Understanding demand requires a look at how both economists and business people view it.

FUNDAMENTALS IN ESTIMATING DEMAND AND REVENUE

Reflecting on the example that opened this chapter, would you buy a weekly issue of *Newsweek* if its price were $20? Probably not. If its price were 50 cents? You and many others might get trampled in the stampede to the local newsstand.

The Demand Curve The demand curve in Figure 11-4 illustrates these answers about *Newsweek*. A **demand curve** shows a maximum number of products consumers will buy at a given price. Demand curve D_1 shows the newsstand demand for *Newsweek* under present conditions. Note that as price falls, people buy more. But price is not the complete story in estimating demand. Economists stress three other key factors:

1. Consumer tastes. As we saw in Chapter 3, these depend on many factors such as demographics, culture, and technology. Because consumer tastes can change quickly, up-to-date marketing research is essential.
2. Price and availability of other products. As the price of close substitute products falls (*Time* for *Newsweek*) and their availability increases, the demand for a product declines.
3. Consumer income. In general, as real consumer income (allowing for inflation) increases, demand for a product also increases.

The first of these two factors influences what consumers *want* to buy, and the third affects what they *can* buy. Along with price, these are often called **demand**

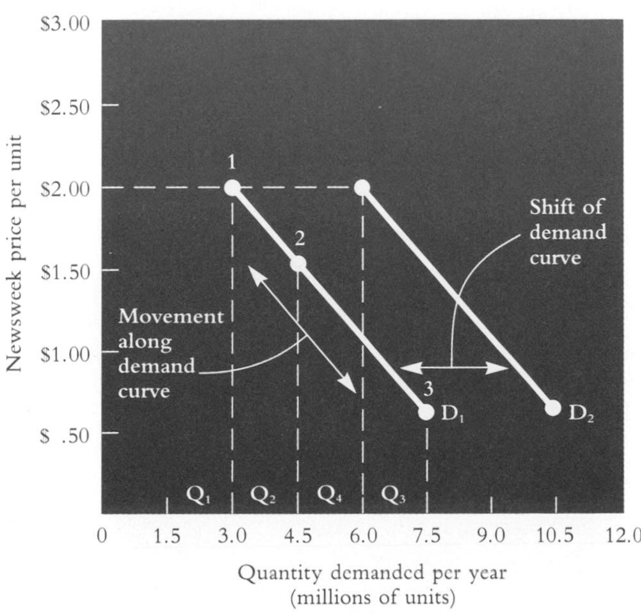

FIGURE 11-4 Illustrative demand curves for *Newsweek* magazine

factors, or factors that determine consumers' willingness and ability to pay for goods and services.

Movement Along Versus Shift of a Demand Curve Demand curve D_1 in Figure 11-4 shows that as the price is lowered from $2 to $1.50, the quantity demanded increases from 3 million to 4.5 million units per year. This is an example of a movement along a demand curve and assumes that other factors (consumer tastes, price and availability of substitutes, and consumer income) remain unchanged.

What if some of these factors change? For example, if advertising causes more people to want *Newsweek,* newsstand distribution is increased, and consumer incomes double, then the demand increases. This is shown in Figure 11-4 as a shift of the demand curve to the right, from D_1 to D_2. This means that more *Newsweek* magazines are wanted for a given price: at a price of $2, the demand is 6 million units per year (Q_4) on D_2 rather than 3 million units per year (Q_1) on D_1.

FUNDAMENTALS IN ESTIMATING REVENUE

While economists may talk about "demand curves," marketing executives are more likely to speak in terms of "revenues generated." Demand curves lead directly to three related revenue concepts critical to pricing decisions: **total revenue, average revenue,** and **marginal revenue** (Figure 11-5).

Demand Curves and Revenue Figure 11-6, *A,* again shows the demand curve for *Newsweek,* but it is now extended to intersect both the price and quantity

FIGURE 11-5
Fundamental revenue concepts

Total revenue (TR) is the total money received from the sale of a product. If:

TR = Total revenue

P = Unit price of the product

Q = Quantity of the product sold

then:

$$TR = P \times Q$$

Average revenue (AR) is the average amount of money received for selling one unit of the product, or simply the price of that unit. Average revenue is the total revenue divided by the quantity sold:

$$AR = \frac{TR}{Q} = P$$

Marginal revenue (MR) is the change in total revenue obtained by selling one additional unit:

$$MR = \frac{\text{change in TR}}{\text{1 unit increase in Q}} = \frac{\Delta TR}{\Delta Q}$$

axes. The demand curve shows that as price is reduced, the quantity of *Newsweek* magazines sold throughout the United States increases. This relationship holds whether the price is reduced from $3 to $2.50 on the demand curve or is reduced from $1 to $0 on the curve. In the former case the market demands no *Newsweek* magazines, whereas in the latter case 9 million could be given away at $0 per unit.

It is likely that if *Newsweek* was given away, more than 9 million would be demanded. This fact illustrates two important points. First, it can be dangerous to extend a demand curve beyond the range of prices for which it really applies. Second, most demand curves are rounded (or convex) to the origin, thereby avoiding an unrealistic picture of what demand looks like when a straight-line curve intersects either the price axis or the quantity axis.

Figure 11-6, *B*, shows the total revenue curve for *Newsweek* calculated from the demand curve shown in Figure 11-6, *A*. The total revenue curve is developed by simply multiplying the unit price times the quantity for each of the points on the demand curve. Total revenue starts at $0 (point A), reaches a

FIGURE 11-6
How a downward-sloping demand curve affects total, average, and marginal revenue

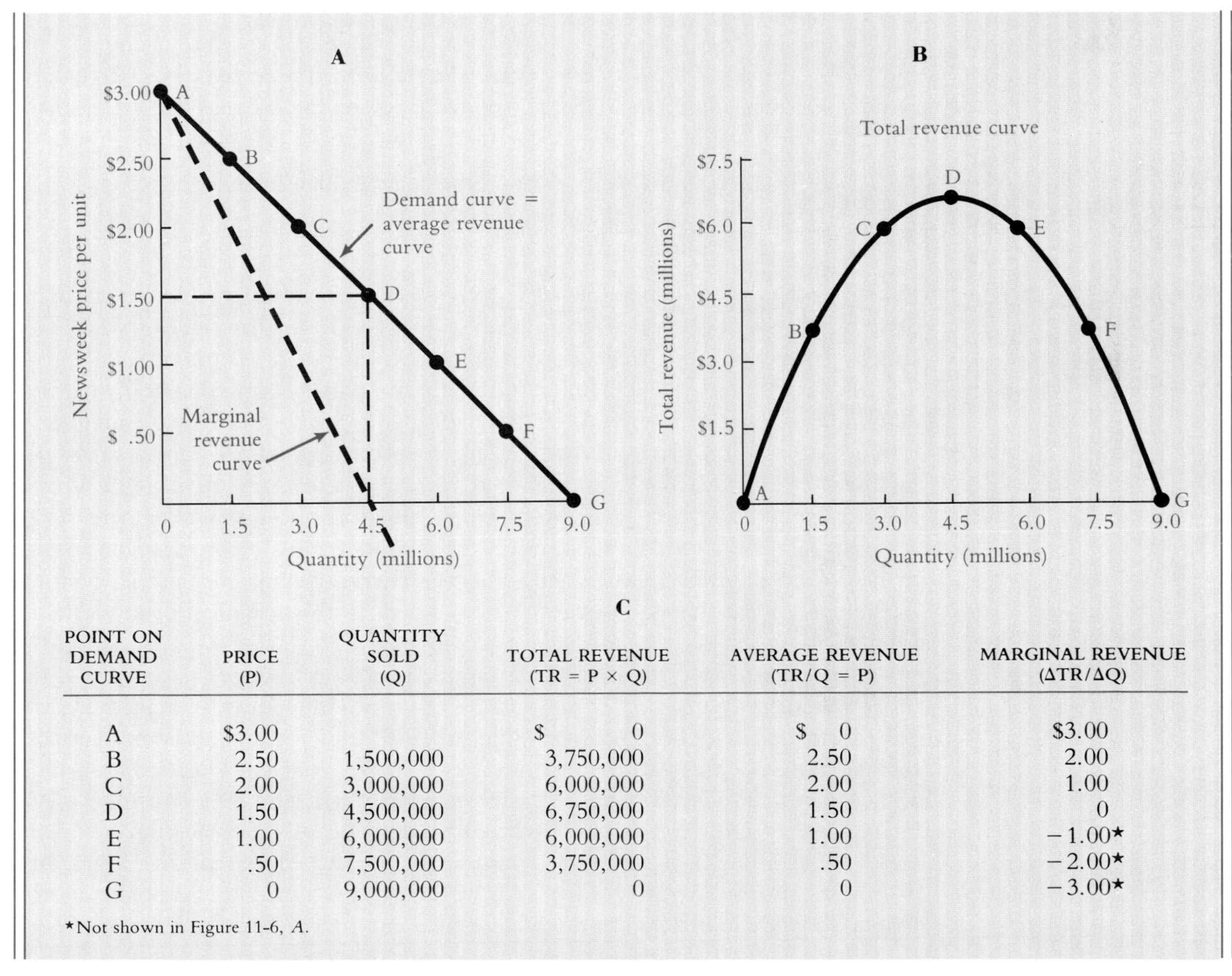

POINT ON DEMAND CURVE	PRICE (P)	QUANTITY SOLD (Q)	TOTAL REVENUE (TR = P × Q)	AVERAGE REVENUE (TR/Q = P)	MARGINAL REVENUE (ΔTR/ΔQ)
A	$3.00		$ 0	$ 0	$3.00
B	2.50	1,500,000	3,750,000	2.50	2.00
C	2.00	3,000,000	6,000,000	2.00	1.00
D	1.50	4,500,000	6,750,000	1.50	0
E	1.00	6,000,000	6,000,000	1.00	−1.00★
F	.50	7,500,000	3,750,000	.50	−2.00★
G	0	9,000,000	0	0	−3.00★

★Not shown in Figure 11-6, *A*.

maximum of $6,750,000 at point D, and returns to $0 at point G. This shows that as price is reduced in the A-to-D segment of the curve, total revenues are increased. However, cutting price in the D-to-G segment results in a decline in total revenue.

Marginal revenue, which is the slope of the total revenue curve, is positive but decreasing when the price lies in the range from $3 to above $1.50 per unit. But below $1.50 per unit, marginal revenue is actually negative, so the extra quantity of magazines sold is more than offset by the decrease in the price per unit.

For any downward-sloping, straight-line demand curve, the marginal revenue curve always falls at a rate twice as fast as the demand curve. As shown in Figure 11-6, *A,* the marginal revenue becomes $0 per unit at a quantity sold of 4.5 million units—the very point at which total revenue is maximum (see Figure 11-6, *B*). Because a rational marketing manager would never operate in the region of the demand curve in which marginal revenue is negative, only the positive portion is shown in typical graphs of demand curves.

Price Elasticity of Demand With a downward-sloping demand curve, we have been concerned with the responsiveness of demand to price changes. This can be conveniently measured by **price elasticity of demand,** or the percentage change in quantity demanded relative to a percentage change in price. Price elasticity of demand (E) is expressed as follows:

$$E = \frac{\text{(Initial quantity demanded} - \text{New quantity demanded)/Initial quantity demanded}}{\text{(Initial price} - \text{New price)/Initial price}}$$

Because quantity demanded usually decreases as price increases, price elasticity of demand is usually a negative number. However, for the sake of simplicity and by convention, elasticity figures are shown as positive numbers.

Price elasticity of demand assumes three forms: elastic demand, inelastic demand, and unitary demand elasticity. *Elastic demand* exists when a small percentage decrease in price produces a larger percentage increase in quantity demanded. Price elasticity is greater than 1 with elastic demand. *Inelastic demand* exists when a small percentage decrease in price produces a smaller percentage increase in quantity demanded. With inelastic demand, price elasticity is less than 1. *Unitary demand* exists when the percentage change in price is identical to the percentage change in quantity demanded. In this instance, price elasticity is equal to 1.

Price elasticity of demand is determined by a number of factors. First, the more substitutes a product or service has, the more likely it is to be price elastic. For example, butter has many possible substitutes in a meal and is price elastic, but gasoline has almost no substitutes and is price inelastic. Second, products and services considered to be necessities are price inelastic. For example, open-heart surgery is price inelastic, whereas airline tickets for vacation are price elastic. Third, items that require a large cash outlay compared with a person's disposable income are price elastic. Accordingly, cars and yachts are price elastic; books and movie tickets are price inelastic.

Price elasticity is important to marketing managers because of its relation-

A Vision of Sterling Elegance.
The Trojan International.
Whittaker
TROJAN YACHT

An elastic demand exists for products such as Trojan yachts

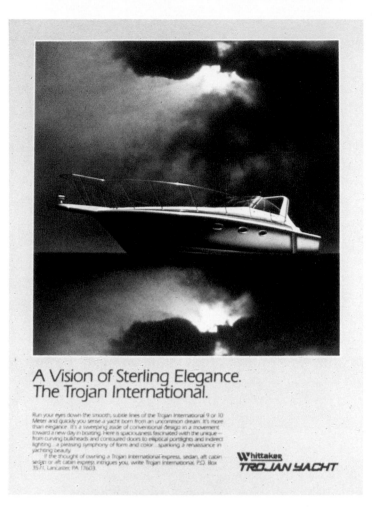

ship to total revenue. For example, with elastic demand, total revenue increases when price decreases, but decreases when price increases. With inelastic demand, total revenue increases when price increases and decreases when price decreases. Finally, with unitary demand total revenue is unaffected by a slight price change.

Because of this relationship between price elasticity and a firm's total revenue, it is important that marketing managers recognize that price elasticity of demand is not the same over all possible prices of a product. Figure 11-6, *B,* illustrates this point using the *Newsweek* demand curve shown in Figure 11-6, *A*. As the price decreases from $2.50 to $2, total revenue increases, indicating an elastic demand. However, when the price decreases from $1 to 50 cents, total revenue declines, indicating an inelastic demand. Unitary demand elasticity exists at a price of $1.50.

Price Elasticities for Brands and Product Classes Marketing executives also recognize that the price elasticity of demand is not always the same for product classes (such as stereo receivers) and brands within a product class (such as Sony and Marantz). For example, marketing experiments on brands of cola, coffee,

Snack foods evidence elastic demand, whereas fruits and vegetables evidence inelastic demand

and snack and specialty foods generally show elasticities of 1.5 to 2.5,[15] indicating they are price elastic. By comparison, entire product classes of fruits and vegetables have elasticities of about 0.8—they are price inelastic.[16]

The importance of understanding this difference in price elasticities for brands and product classes is shown in the Marketing Research Report. Before going further, assume you are a product manager for breakfast cereals for General Foods or Kellogg and try to answer the questions at the end of the Marketing Research Report.

Neslin and Shoemaker[17] found that in general, presweetened cereals are price elastic (E = 1.97), whereas the entire ready-to-eat cereal market is price inelastic (E = 0.36). Hence they concluded that when prices of presweetened cereals are raised, consumers substitute low-sugar and granola cereals rather than skip dry cereals entirely. They recommended that manufacturers of presweetened cereals such as General Foods, Kellogg, and Quaker Oats have a balanced product line that includes low-sugar and granola brands as well.

Concept Check

1 **What is the difference between a movement along and a shift of a demand curve?**

2 **What does it mean if a product has a price elasticity of demand that is greater than 1?**

MARKETING · RESEARCH · REPORT

CAP'N CRUNCH, FROSTED FLAKES, AND PRICE ELASTICITY

Remember back in 1974 when you were 5 years old(?) and the price of your Cap'n Crunch cereal went up so much your folks made you eat Shredded Wheat? There was a reason.

A world sugar shortage caused its price in world commodity markets to jump from 9 cents a pound in 1973 to more than six times that price—58 cents a pound—in November 1974. Related to this price increase in sugar, the average retail price of presweetened cereals (in real dollars) rose by 24 percent from March to December 1974, as shown in the chart.

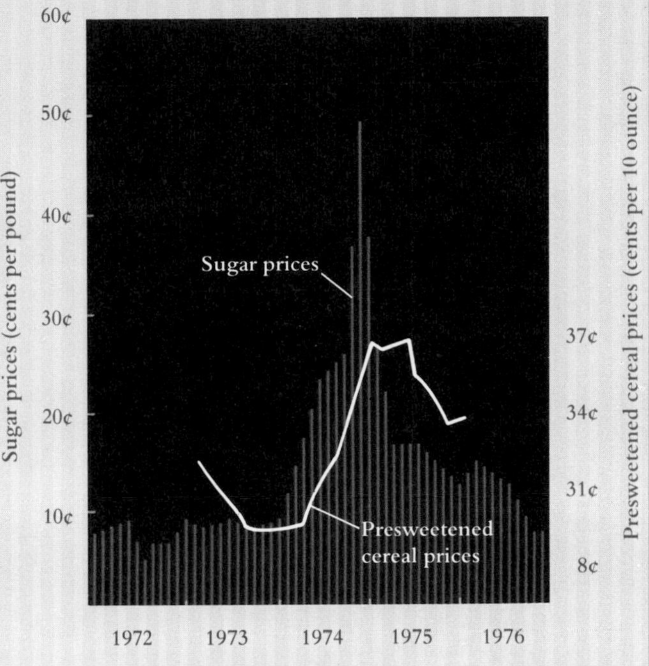

Researchers Neslin and Shoemaker used monthly data from January 1973 to December 1975 as a "natural experiment" to analyze the price elasticity of presweetened cereals. In contrast to a typical field experiment conducted by a firm under carefully controlled conditions, a natural experiment is an after-the-fact analysis of some dramatic event such as this jump in the price of sugar.

The researchers studied prices and sales for 61 brands of presweetened cereals (such as Cap'n Crunch and Frosted Flakes) and 50 nonpresweetened cereals (such as Cheerios and Kellogg's Corn Flakes). They also considered some other factors:

- Advertising for competing products by various cereal manufacturers
- Prices of competing products
- New products introduced, such as granola cereals
- Adverse publicity, such as the question of the nutritive value of presweetened cereals
- Industry growth trends

After allowing for these other factors, Neslin and Shoemaker estimated the price elasticity for presweetened cereals to be 1.97 and for the entire ready-to-eat cereal market to be 0.36.

What do these results mean (1) by themselves, (2) in comparison to each other, and (3) in terms of strategy for a ready-to-eat cereal manufacturer? The researchers' interpretations are discussed in the text.

Source: Based on Scott A. Neslin and Robert W. Shoemaker, "Using a Natural Experiment to Estimate Price Elasticity: The 1974 Sugar Shortage and the Ready-to-Eat Cereal Market," *Journal of Marketing* (Winter 1983), pp. 44-57; by permission of the American Marketing Association.

STEP 3: DETERMINING COST, VOLUME, AND PROFIT RELATIONSHIPS

The profit equation described at the beginning of the chapter showed that Profit = Total revenue − Total cost. Therefore understanding the role and behavior of costs is critical for all marketing decisions, particularly pricing decisions. Four cost concepts are important in pricing decisions: **total cost, fixed cost, variable cost,** and **marginal cost** (Figure 11-7).

MARGINAL ANALYSIS AND PROFIT MAXIMIZATION

A basic idea in business, economics, and indeed everyday life is marginal analysis. In personal terms, marginal analysis means that people will continue to do something as long as the incremental return exceeds the incremental cost. This same idea holds true in marketing and pricing decisions. In this setting, **marginal analysis** means that as long as revenue received from the sale of an additional product (marginal revenue) is greater than the additional cost of producing and selling it (marginal cost), a firm will expand its output of that product.[18]

Marginal analysis is central to the concept of maximizing profits. In Figure 11-8, *A,* marginal revenue and marginal cost are graphed. Marginal cost starts out high at lower quantity levels, decreases to a minimum through production and marketing efficiencies, and then rises again due to the inefficiencies of overworked labor and equipment. Marginal revenue follows a downward slope. In Figure 11-8, *B,* total cost and total revenue curves corresponding to the marginal cost and marginal revenue curves are graphed. Total cost initially rises as quantity increases but increases at the slowest rate at the quantity where marginal cost is lowest. The total revenue curve increases to a maximum and then starts to decline, as shown in Figure 11-6, *B.*

FIGURE 11-7
Fundamental cost concepts

Total cost (TC) is the total expense incurred by a firm in producing and marketing the product. Total cost is the sum of fixed cost and variable cost.

Fixed cost (FC) is the sum of the expenses of the firm that are stable and do not change with the quantity of product that is produced and sold. Examples of fixed costs are rent on the building, executive salaries, and insurance.

Variable cost (VC) is the sum of the expenses of the firm that vary directly with the quantity of product that is produced and sold. For example, as the quantity sold doubles, the variable cost doubles. Examples are the direct labor and direct materials used in producing the product and the sales commissions that are tied directly to the quantity sold. As mentioned above:

$$TC = FC + VC$$

Variable cost expressed on a per unit basis is called *unit variable cost (UVC).*

Marginal cost (MC) is the change in total cost that results from producing and marketing one additional unit:

$$MC = \frac{\text{Change in TC}}{\text{1 unit increase in Q}} = \frac{\Delta TC}{\Delta Q}$$

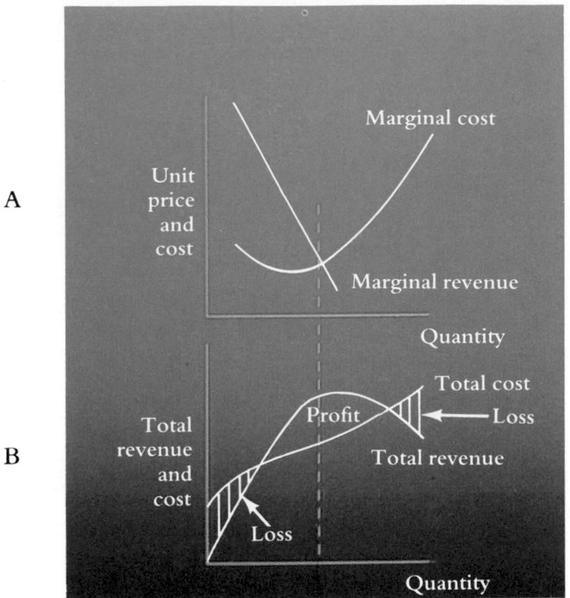

FIGURE 11-8
Profit maximization pricing

The message of marginal analysis, then, is to operate up to the quantity and price level where marginal revenue equals marginal cost (MR = MC). Up to the output quantity at which MR = MC, each increase in total revenue resulting from selling one additional unit exceeds the increase in the total cost of producing and marketing that unit. Beyond the point at which MR = MC, however, the increase in total revenue from selling one more unit is less than the cost of producing and marketing that unit. At the quantity at which MR = MC, the total revenue curve lies farthest above the total cost curve and they are parallel. The Marketing Action Memo illustrates this by showing how General Motors has adopted both a price strategy to increase revenue and a cost strategy to control expenses on its new Saturn generation of small cars.

BREAK-EVEN ANALYSIS

Marketing managers often employ a simpler approach for looking at cost, volume, and profit relationships, which is also based on the profit equation. **Break-even analysis** is a technique that analyzes the relationship between total revenue and total cost to determine profitability at various levels of output. The **break-even point** (BEP) is the quantity at which total revenue and total cost are equal and beyond which profit occurs. In terms of the definitions in Figure 11-7:

$$\text{BEP}_{\text{Quantity}} = \frac{\text{Fixed cost}}{\text{Unit price} - \text{Unit variable cost}}$$

Calculating a Break-Even Point Consider, for example, a corn farmer who wishes to identify how many bushels of corn he must sell to cover his fixed cost at a given price. Suppose the farmer had a fixed cost (FC) of $2,000 (for real estate taxes, interest on a bank loan, and other fixed expenses) and a unit

MARKETING·ACTION·MEMO

GENERAL MOTORS CHOOSES A PRICE AND COST STRATEGY FOR 1991

In 1980 the Big Three U.S. auto manufacturers—General Motors (GM), Ford, and Chrysler—lost $4 billion dollars, and in 1985 they made $8 billion. What happened in the meantime?

There are three main answers. First, the American economy moved out of a recession, causing more consumers to buy new cars, especially larger ones, which have better profit margins than do small cars. Second, import quotas were placed on Japanese cars shipped to the United States, thereby increasing sales of Big Three cars. Third, and perhaps most important, the Big Three embarked on massive programs to both cut costs and increase productivity through scrapping old plants and building new automated plants.

The strategy of GM is an example of what the Big Three are planning for the 1990's. In the early 1980's GM succeeded in making a profit on its bigger, more luxurious cars such as Cadillacs and Oldsmobile Cutlass Supremes. However, the combination of high labor costs per hour and many labor hours per car made the total labor costs per car for GM and its suppliers about three times those of Japanese auto manufacturers for a typical subcompact car.

Because of this, GM must find a strategy to compete in the small car market (see GM repositioning analysis in Chapter 8). It has initiated "Project Saturn" to design a new generation of small cars (which will be on the market by 1991) having two primary strategies:

- Price strategy. The Saturns will be priced as low as possible to try to lure into new car showrooms the 1 to 2 million Americans each year who buy used cars.
- Cost strategy. Intelligent robots will be paired with teams of workers responsible for whole subassemblies or modules, which will then be combined on the final assembly line to produce the wedge-shaped Saturn.

Will GM's strategy work? Visit a Saturn showroom in 1991 and find out.

Source: Based on "Downsizing Detroit: The Big Three's Strategy for Survival," *Business Week* (April 14, 1986), pp. 86-87; Anne B. Fisher, "Can Detroit Live Without Quotas?" *Fortune* (June 25, 1984), pp. 20-25,

variable cost (UVC) of $1 per bushel (for labor, corn seed, herbicides, and pesticides). If the price (P) is $2 per bushel, his break-even quantity is 2,000 bushels:

$$BEP_{\text{Quantity}} = \frac{FC}{P - UVC} = \frac{\$2{,}000}{\$2 - \$1} = 2{,}000 \text{ bushels}$$

Figure 11-9 shows that the break-even quantity at a price of $2 per bushel is 2,000 bushels, since at this quantity total revenue equals total cost. At less than 2,000 bushels the farmer incurs a loss, and at more than 2,000 bushels he makes a profit. Figure 11-10 shows a graphic presentation of the break-even analysis, called a **break-even chart.**

QUANTITY SOLD (Q)	PRICE PER BUSHEL (P)	TOTAL REVENUE (TR) (P × Q)	UNIT VARIABLE COST (UVC)	TOTAL VARIABLE COSTS (TVC) (UVC × Q)	FIXED COST (FC)	TOTAL COST (TC) (TVC + FC)	PROFIT (TR − TC)
0	$2	$ 0	$1	$ 0	$2,000	$2,000	−$2,000
1,000	2	2,000	1	1,000	2,000	3,000	−1,000
2,000	2	4,000	1	2,000	2,000	4,000	0
3,000	2	6,000	1	3,000	2,000	5,000	1,000
4,000	2	8,000	1	4,000	2,000	6,000	2,000
5,000	2	10,000	1	5,000	2,000	7,000	3,000
6,000	2	12,000	1	6,000	2,000	8,000	4,000

FIGURE 11-9
Calculating a break-even point

Applications of Break-Even Analysis Because of its simplicity, break-even analysis is used extensively in marketing, most frequently to study the impact on profit of changes in price, fixed cost, and variable cost. The mechanics of break-even analysis are the basis of the widely used electronic spread sheets offered by computer programs such as Lotus 1-2-3 that permit managers to answer hypothetical "what if . . ." questions about the effect of changes in price and cost on their profit.

Although use of electronic spread sheets in pricing is covered in Chapter 12, an example here will show the power of break-even analysis. As described in Figure 11-11, if an electronic calculator manufacturer automates its production, thereby increasing fixed cost and reducing variable cost by substituting machines for workers, this increases the break-even point from 333,333 to 500,000 units per year.

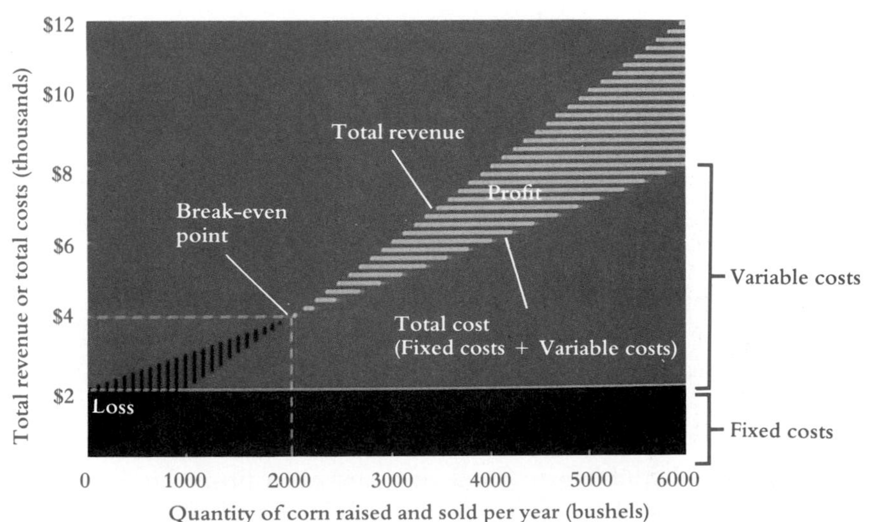

FIGURE 11-10
Break-even analysis chart

GM weighs the marginal cost and marginal revenue of each expenditure—including new windshields

Reproduced courtesy of General Motors Corporation

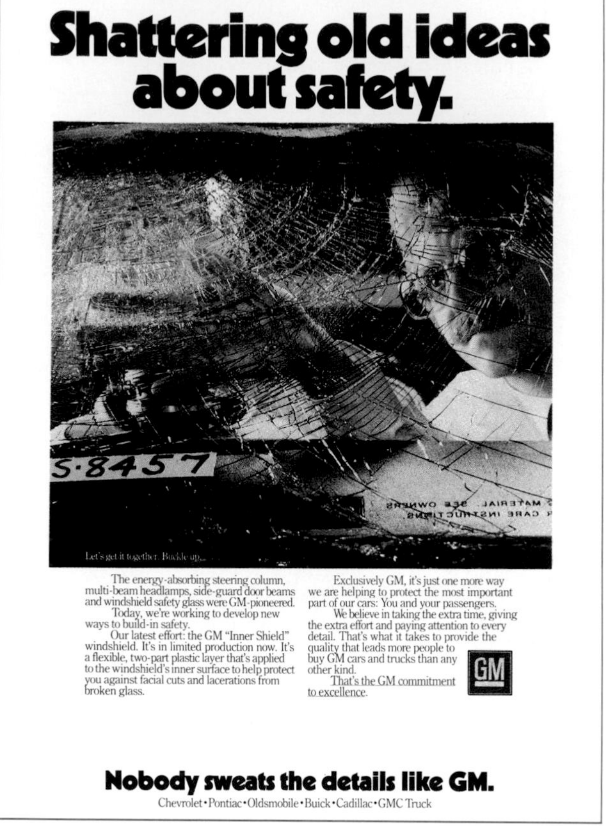

But what about the impact of the higher level of fixed cost on profit? Remember, profit at any output quantity is given by:

$$\begin{aligned} \text{Profit} &= \text{Total revenue} - \text{Total cost} \\ &= (P \times Q) - [FC + (UVC \times Q)] \end{aligned}$$

So profit at 1 million units of sales before automation is:

$$\begin{aligned} \text{Profit} &= (P \times Q) - [FC + (UVC \times Q)] \\ &= (\$10 \times 1{,}000{,}000) - [\$1{,}000{,}000 + (\$7 \times 1{,}000{,}000)] \\ &= \$10{,}000{,}000 - \$8{,}000{,}000 \\ &= \$2{,}000{,}000 \end{aligned}$$

After automation, profit is:

$$\begin{aligned} \text{Profit} &= (P \times Q) - [FC + (UVC \times Q)] \\ &= (\$10 \times 1{,}000{,}000) - [\$4{,}000{,}000 + (\$2 \times 1{,}000{,}000)] \\ &= \$10{,}000{,}000 - \$6{,}000{,}000 \\ &= \$4{,}000{,}000 \end{aligned}$$

Automation, by adding to fixed cost, increases profit by $2 million at 1 million units of sales. Thus as the quantity sold increases for the automated plant, the potential increase or leverage on profit is tremendous. This is why

Executives in virtually every mass-production industry—from locomotives and cars to electronic calculators and breakfast cereals—are searching for ways to increase quality and reduce production costs to remain competitive in world markets. Increasingly they are substituting robots, automation, and computer-controlled manufacturing systems for blue- and white-collar workers.

To understand the implications of this on the break-even point and profit, consider this example of an electronic calculator manufacturer:

BEFORE AUTOMATION	AFTER AUTOMATION
$P = \$10$ per unit	$P = \$10$ per unit
$FC = \$1{,}000{,}000$	$FC = \$4{,}000{,}000$
$UVC = \$7$ per unit	$UVC = \$2$ per unit
$BEP_{Quantity} = \dfrac{FC}{P - UVC}$	$BEP_{Quantity} = \dfrac{FC}{P - UVC}$
$= \dfrac{\$1{,}000{,}000}{\$10 - \$7}$	$= \dfrac{\$4{,}000{,}000}{\$10 - \$2}$
$= 333{,}333$ units	$= 500{,}000$ units

The automation increases the fixed cost and increases the break-even quantity from 333,333 to 500,000 units per year. So if annual sales fall within this range, the calculator manufacturer will incur a loss with the automated plant, whereas it would have made a profit if it had not automated.

But what about its potential profit if it sells 1 million units a year? Look carefully at the two break-even charts below and see the text to check your conclusions.

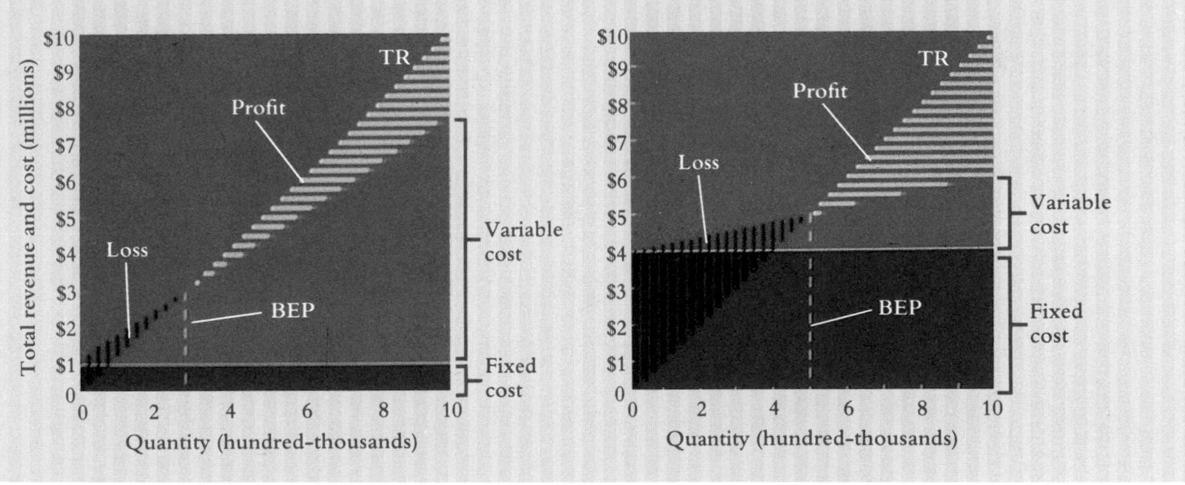

FIGURE 11-11
The cost trade-off: fixed versus variable costs

with large production and sales volumes, automated plants for GM cars or Texas Instruments calculators produce large profits. Also, firms in other industries, such as airline, railroad, and hotel and motel industries, that require a high fixed cost can reap large profits when they go even slightly beyond the break-even point.

CONCEPT CHECK

1 What is the difference between fixed cost and variable cost?

2 What is a break-even point?

SUMMARY

1 Price is the money or other considerations exchanged for the ownership or use of a product or service. Although price typically includes money, the amount exchanged is often different from the list or quoted price because of allowances and extra fees.

2 Consumers use price as an indicator of value when it is paired with the perceived quality of a good or service. Sometimes price influences consumer perceptions of quality itself and at other times consumers make value assessments by comparing the costs and benefits of substitute items.

3 Pricing constraints such as demand, product newness, costs, competitors, other products sold by the firm, and the type of competitive market restrict a firm's pricing latitude.

4 Pricing objectives, which specify the role of price in a firm's marketing strategy, may include pricing for profit, sales revenue, market share, unit sales, survival, or some socially responsible price level.

5 A demand curve shows the maximum number of products consumers will buy at a given price and for a given set of (a) consumer tastes, (b) price and availability of other products, and (c) consumer income. When any of these change, there is a shift of the demand curve.

6 Price elasticity of demand measures the sensitivity of units sold to a change in price. When demand is elastic, a reduction in price is more than offset by an increase in units sold, so that total revenue increases.

7 It is necessary to consider cost behavior when making pricing decisions. Important cost concepts include total cost, variable cost, fixed cost, and marginal cost.

8 Break-even analysis shows the relationship between total revenue and total cost at various quantities of output for given conditions of price, fixed cost, and variable cost. The break-even point is where total revenue and total cost are equal.

KEY TERMS AND CONCEPTS

price p. 284
value p. 285
profit equation p. 287
pricing constraints p. 288
pricing objectives p. 290
demand curve p. 293
demand factors p. 293
total revenue p. 294
average revenue p. 294
marginal revenue p. 294
price elasticity of demand p. 296
total cost p. 300
fixed cost p. 300
variable cost p. 300
marginal cost p. 300
marginal analysis p. 300
break-even analysis p. 301
break-even point p. 301
break-even chart p. 302

CHAPTER PROBLEMS AND APPLICATIONS

1 How would the price equation apply to the purchase price of (a) gasoline, (b) an airline ticket, and (c) a checking account?

2 When the telephone industry was deregulated and AT&T (the Bell System) lost its virtual monopolistic position, the company experienced an immediate change in its pricing practices for telephones and long-distance phone rates because of a barrage of new competitors entering the market. How might this new competitive environment bring about new or different pricing constraints for AT&T?

3 What would be your response to the statement, "Profit maximization is the only legitimate pricing objective for the firm"?

4 How is a downward-sloping demand curve related to total revenue and marginal revenue?

5 A marketing executive once said, "If the price elasticity of demand for your product is inelastic, then your price is probably too low." What is this executive saying in terms of the economic principles discussed in this chapter?

6 A marketing manager reduced the price on a brand of cereal by 10 percent and observed a 25 percent increase in quantity sold. The manager then thought that if the price were reduced by another 20 percent, a 50 percent increase in quantity sold would occur. What would be your response to the marketing manager's reasoning?

7 A student theater group at a university has developed a demand schedule that shows the relationship between ticket prices and demand based on a student survey, as follows:

TICKET PRICE	NUMBER OF STUDENTS WHO WOULD BUY
$1	300
2	250
3	200
4	150
5	100

a. Graph the demand curve and the total revenue curve based on these data. What ticket price might be set based on this analysis?
b. What other factors should be considered before the final price is set?

8 Touché Toiletries, Inc., has developed an addition to its Lizardman Cologne line tentatively branded Ode d'Toade Cologne. Unit variable costs are 45 cents for a 3-ounce bottle, and heavy advertising expenditures in the first year would result in total fixed costs of $900,000. Ode d'Toade Cologne was priced at $7.50 for a 3-ounce bottle. How many bottles of Ode d'Toade must be sold to break even?

9 Suppose that marketing executives for Touché Toiletries reduced the price to $6.50 for a 3-ounce bottle of Ode d'Toade and the fixed costs were $1,100,000. Suppose further that the unit variable cost remained at 45 cents for a 3-ounce bottle. (a) How many bottles must be sold to break even? (b) What dollar profit level would Ode d'Toade achieve if 200,000 bottles were sold?

10 Executives of Random Recordings, Inc., produced an album entitled *Sunshine/ Moonshine* by the Starshine Sisters Band. The cost and price information was as follows:

Album cover		$1.00 per album
Songwriter's royalties		0.30 per album
Recording artists' royalties		0.70 per album
Direct material and labor costs to produce the album		1.00 per album
Fixed cost of producing an album (advertising, studio fee, etc.)	100,000.00	
Selling price		7.00 per album

a. Prepare a chart like Figure 11-10 showing total cost, fixed cost, and total revenue for album quantity sold levels starting at 10,000 albums through 100,000 albums at 10,000 album intervals, that is, 10,000, 20,000, 30,000, and so on.

b. What is the break-even point for the album?

SUGGESTED READINGS

"Break-Even Analysis," *Small Business Report* (August 1986), pp. 22-24. *This article provides a tutorial on the basics of break-even analysis.*

John Morton, "Pricing for Profits," *Marketing Communications* (February 1988), pp. 33-35. *This short article illustrates how price elasticity of demand can be used in a variety of practical applications.*

Thomas T. Nagle, *The Strategy & Tactics of Pricing* (Englewood Cliffs, N.J.: Prentice-Hall, Inc., 1987). *This short book provides a thorough review of pricing fundamentals. Chapters 2, 3, and 4 cover economics of pricing, price sensitivity, and the role of competition.*

Saeed Samiee, "Pricing in Marketing Strategies of U.S.- and Foreign-Based Companies," *Journal of Business Research* (February 1987), pp. 17-31. *This article describes the pricing objectives, strategies, and tactics of domestic and foreign companies.*

Valerie A. Ziethaml, "Consumer Perceptions of Price, Quality, and Value," *Journal of Marketing* (July 1988), pp. 2-22. *This article provides a comprehensive review of the literature on price-quality-value relationships.*

Choosing a long distance company is a lot like choosing a roommate.

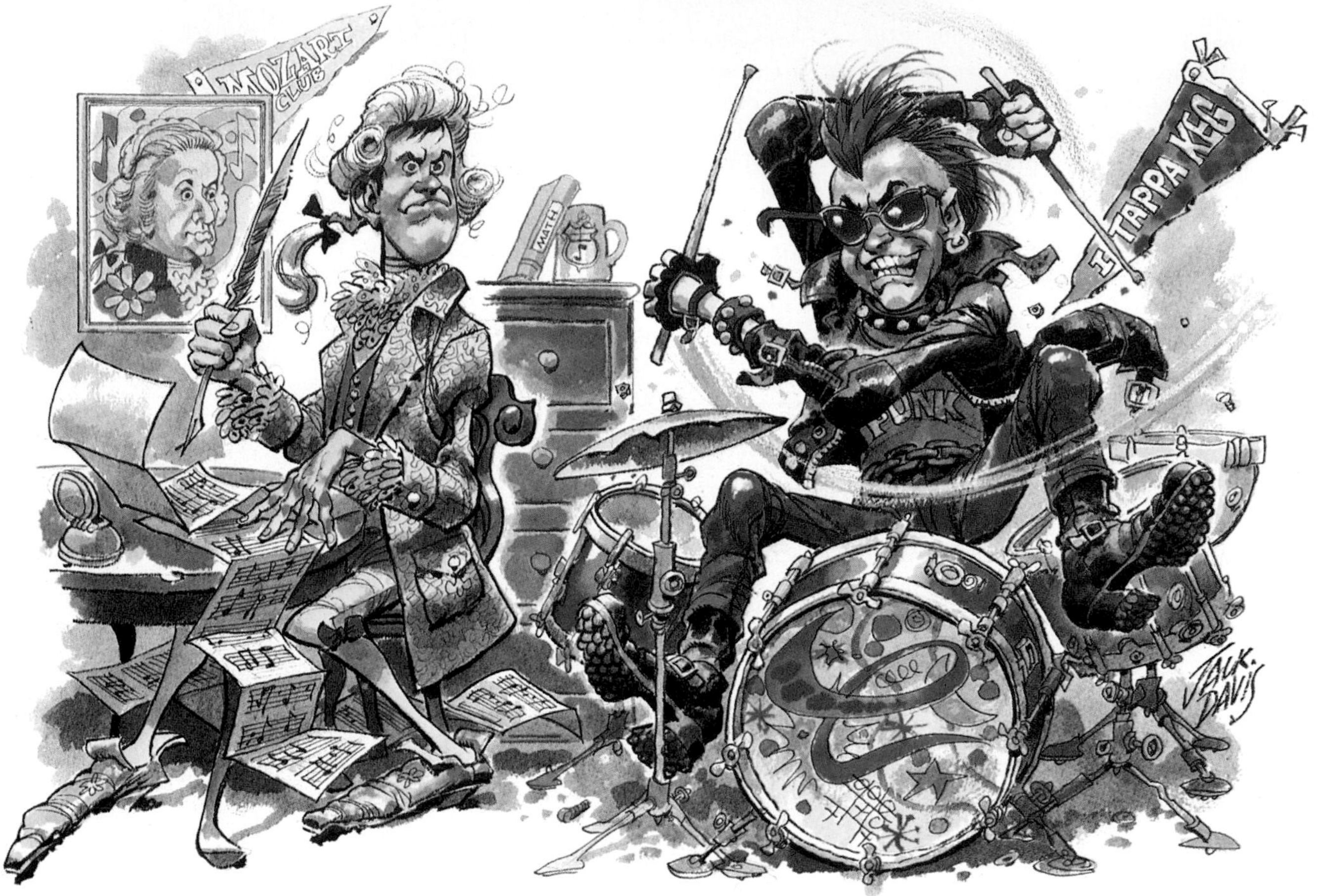

It's better to know what they're like before you move in.

Some long distance companies are easier to live with than others.

Because not everyone provides you with all the services you've come to expect from AT&T.

But when you pick AT&T, there won't be any surprises when you move in. You'll get the same high-quality, trouble-free service you've always had.

So when you're asked to choose a long distance company, choose AT&T. Because whether you're into Mozart or metal, quality is the one thing everyone can agree on.

Reach out and touch someone.®

12

PRICING: ARRIVING AT THE FINAL PRICE

After reading this chapter you should be able to:

Understand how to establish the initial "approximate price level" using demand-based, cost-based, profit-based, and competition-based methods

•

Identify the major factors considered in deriving a final list or quoted price from the approximate price level

•

Describe adjustments made to the approximate price level based on geography, discounts, and allowances

•

Prepare basic financial analyses useful in evaluating alternative prices and arriving at the final sales price

•

Describe the principal laws and regulations affecting pricing practices

Reach Out and Touch Everybody!

A 36 percent price reduction ain't hay! Less than 4 years after deregulation of the telephone industry, AT&T had systematically reduced its basic long-distance rates by a whopping 36 percent! Deregulation spurred fierce price competition and aggressive promotions to attract customers to the long-distance service provided by firms like AT&T, MCI, GTE Sprint, and ITT. At the same time, billions of dollars were being spent to increase the quality of domestic and global telecommunications. Comments one expert on the telecommunications industry, "These guys are going to kill each other."

Pricing decisions became critical for the competitors, including AT&T. Not only were prices changing constantly, but allowances in the form of free calls and discounts for evening and weekend calls and call frequency became commonplace. Through all of this, AT&T operated at a disadvantage. Its costs were higher than competitors' and its interstate long-distance rates were set by the Federal Communications Commission's limits on the company's return on its $9.1 billion investment in interstate equipment. Still, AT&T pricing decisions and creative promotion allowed it to capture about 80 percent of the long-distance telephone service market.[1]

The AT&T experience documents how factors related to cost, the company, and competition affect prices for a single firm and an entire industry.

This chapter describes how companies select an appropriate price level, highlights important considerations in setting a list or quoted price, and identifies various price adjustments that can be made to prices set by the firm—the last three steps an organization uses in setting price (Figure 12-1). In addition, an overview of legal and regulatory aspects of pricing is provided.

STEP 4: SELECT AN APPROXIMATE PRICE LEVEL

A key to a marketing manager's setting a final price for a product is to find an "approximate price level" to use as a reasonable starting point. Four common approaches to helping find this approximate price level are (1) demand-based, (2) cost-based, (3) profit-based, and (4) competition-based methods (Figure 12-2). Although these methods are discussed separately below, some of them overlap, and an effective marketing manager will consider several in searching for an approximate price level.[2]

DEMAND-BASED METHODS

Demand-based methods of finding a price level weigh factors underlying expected customer tastes more heavily than such factors as cost, profit, and competition.

Skimming Pricing A firm introducing a new or innovative product can use **skimming pricing,** setting the highest initial price that customers really desiring

FIGURE 12-1
Steps in setting price

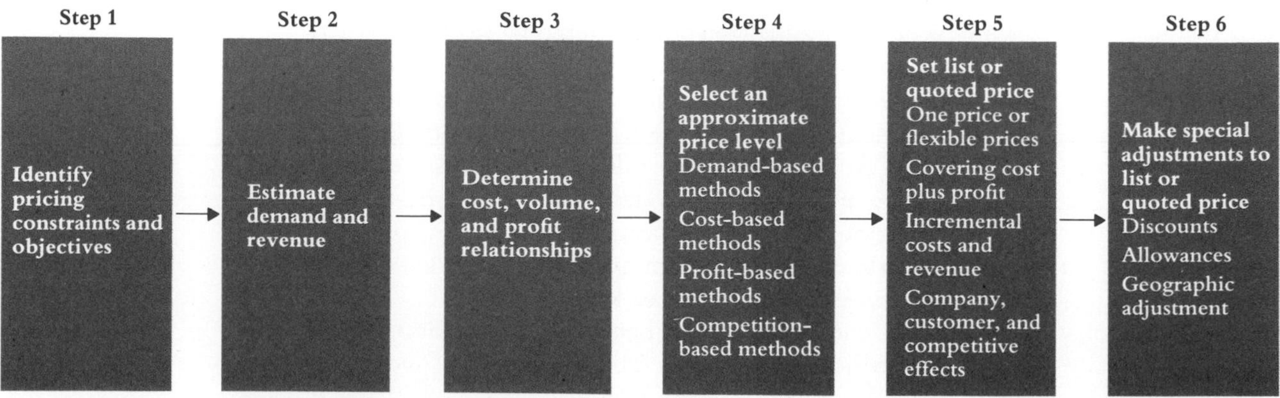

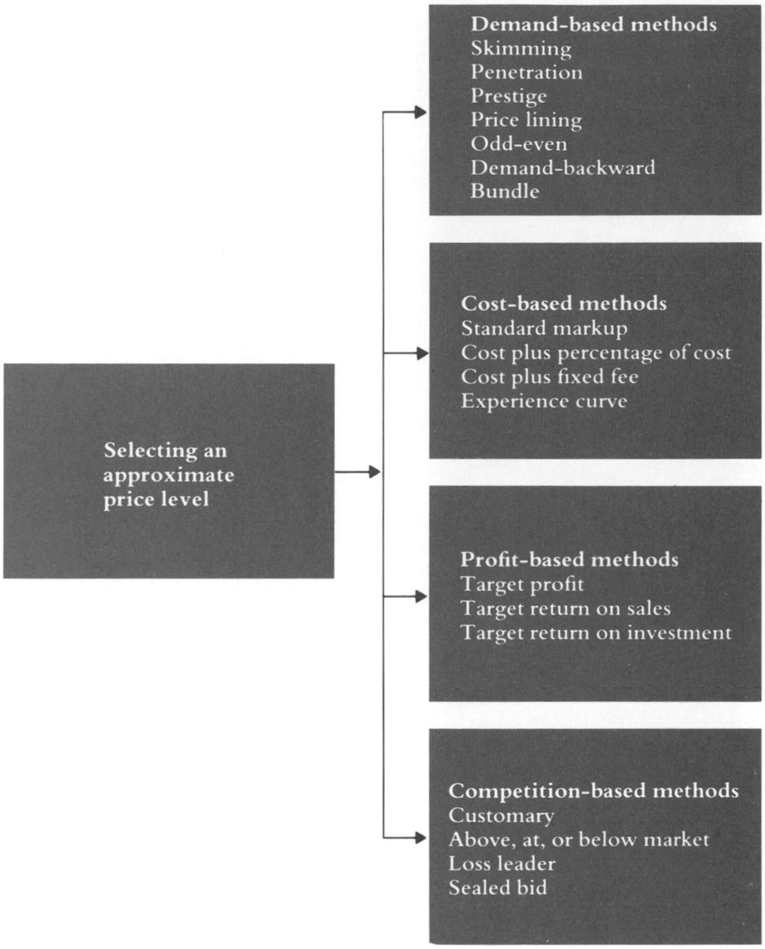

FIGURE 12-2
Four methods of selecting an approximate price level

the product are willing to pay. These customers are not very price sensitive because they weigh the new product's price, quality, and ability to satisfy their needs against the same characteristics of substitutes. As the demand of these customers is satisfied, the firm lowers the price to attract another, more price-sensitive segment. Thus skimming pricing gets its name from skimming successive layers of "cream," or customer segments, as prices are lowered in a series of steps.

The initial pricing of VCRs at more than $1,500 and the Trivial Pursuit game at $39.95 are examples of skimming pricing. Within 3 years after their introductions, both products were often priced at less than half their initial prices. Sometimes minor modifications are made in the product when it is offered at a lower price to a new segment; publishing hardback bestselling novels in paperback is an example. Skimming pricing is an effective strategy when (1) enough prospective customers are willing to buy the product immediately at the high initial price to make these sales profitable, (2) the high initial price will not attract competitors, (3) lowering price has only a minor effect on increasing

Trivial Pursuit was priced high on introduction and subsequently priced lower to reach a broader audience

the sales volume and reducing the unit costs, and (4) customers interpret the high price as signifying high quality. These four conditions are most likely to exist when the new product is protected by patents or copyrights or its uniqueness is understood and appreciated by customers. The Marketing Research Report shows the results of an experiment to help set the retail price of pure maple syrup when national brands are priced at 75 cents each. Read the report and decide what price you would set for pure maple syrup and whether you would use an informative point-of-purchase display if you were the marketing manager responsible.

The demand curves in the Marketing Research Report show that the demand for 100 percent maple syrup is inelastic when buyers are informed about the percentage of maple syrup and other additives of branded maple-flavored syrups. Consumers who are not given such information are far more price sensitive, so point-of-purchase information seems to be a good device to increase sales of pure maple syrup at higher prices for some consumers. The researchers suggest that if maximizing revenue is the only consideration, a price of $2.25 would be best if no information were provided; you can see the horizontal spike in the no-information demand curve at $2.25.[3]

Penetration Pricing Setting a low initial price on a new product to appeal immediately to the mass market is **penetration pricing,** the exact opposite of skimming pricing. Texas Instruments (TI) consciously chose a penetration strategy when it introduced its hand-held calculators and digital watches. As demand

MARKETING·RESEARCH·REPORT

PRICING PURE MAPLE SYRUP: A LABORATORY EXPERIMENT

If 12-ounce bottles of Aunt Jemima, Log Cabin, and Vermont Maid maple-flavored syrup are priced at 75 cents each, what price will consumers pay for a bottle of pure, 100 percent maple syrup?

To answer this question, women in the greater Boston area were given \$2.75 and were shown the three brand-name flavored syrups priced at 75 cents each and a bottle of pure maple syrup. They were told to buy the bottle they wanted and to keep whatever money was left after their purchases. A fifth of the women saw each of the following prices for the maple syrup and only that price: \$1.50, \$1.75, \$2.00, \$2.25, and \$2.50.

In addition, half these women saw an information card and half did not. The card showed the composition (percentage of maple, sugar, and corn syrup), presence of additives and preservatives, and calories per ounce for the three syrup brands and the pure maple syrup.

TREATMENT	PRICE LEVEL	PERCENT BUYING PURE MAPLE SYRUP
Price	\$1.50	48.3%
	1.75	36.7
	2.00	26.7
	2.25	33.3
	2.50	28.3
Information card	Present	41.3%
	Not present	28.0

The results were the percentages of women buying the 100 percent maple syrup for the price and information treatments shown in *A*. Two different demand curves appear in *B*: D_1 for consumers not seeing the information card and D_2 for consumers seeing it.

What price would appear to maximize revenue? Should information be given in a point-of-purchase display? The answers to these and other questions, as seen by the researchers, are discussed in the text.

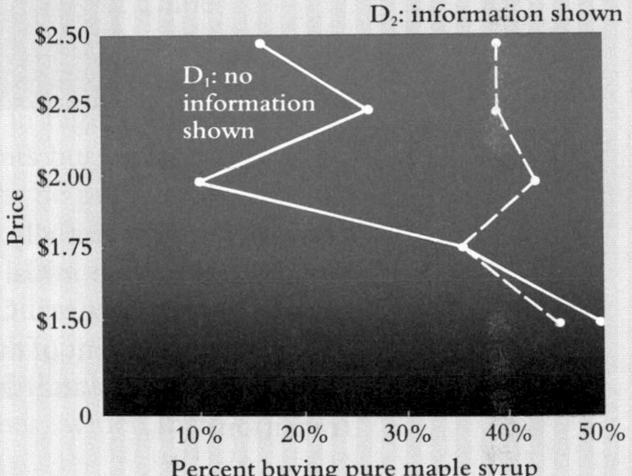

Source: Based on Alan G. Sawyer, Parker M. Worthing, and Paul E. Sendak, "The Role of Laboratory Experiments to Test Marketing Strategies," *Journal of Marketing* (Summer 1979), pp. 60–67; by permission of the American Marketing Association.

for these products increased, unit production costs fell, which permitted TI to lower its prices further.

The conditions favoring penetration pricing are the reverse of those supporting skimming pricing: (1) many segments of the market are price sensitive, (2) a low initial price discourages competitors from entering the market, and (3) unit production and marketing costs fall dramatically as production volumes increase. Thus the firm using penetration pricing may (1) maintain the initial price for a time to gain profit loss from its low introductory level or (2) lower the price further, counting on the new volume to generate the necessary profit.

In some situations penetration pricing may follow skimming pricing. A

FIGURE 12-4
Markups of the manufacturer, wholesaler, and retailer on a home appliance sold to the consumer for $100

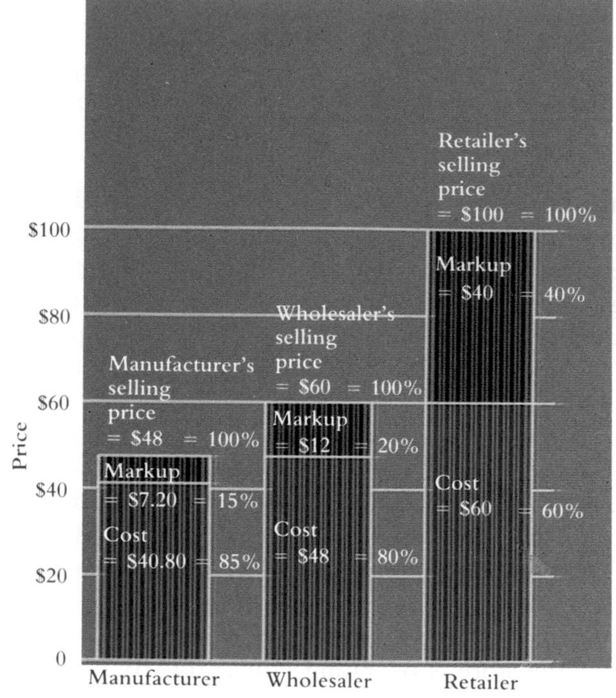

the markups on snacks and beverages purchased at your local movie theater. As shown in the Marketing Action Memo, markups for these products can be as large as 87 percent! An explanation of how to compute a markup, along with operating statement data and other ratios, is given in Appendix A to this chapter.

Figure 12-4 shows the way standard markups combine to establish the selling price of the manufacturer to the wholesaler, the wholesaler to the retailer, and the retailer to the ultimate consumer. For example, the markups on a home appliance (for simplicity, sold to consumers for exactly $100) can increase as the product gets closer to the ultimate consumers; that is, the manufacturer has a 15 percent markup on its selling price, the wholesaler 20 percent, and the retailer 40 percent.

These larger markups later in the channel reflect the fact that as the product gets closer to the ultimate consumer, the seller has a smaller volume of the product and must provide a greater number of services or amount of individual attention to the buyer. The manufacturer gets $48 for selling the appliance to the wholesaler, who gets $60 from the retailer, who gets $100 from the ultimate consumer. As noted in the discussion of demand-backward pricing, if the manufacturer targets the price to the ultimate consumer at $100, it must verify that this includes adequate markups for the retailer, wholesaler, and itself.

Cost Plus Percentage-of-Cost Pricing Some manufacturing, architectural, and construction firms use a variation of standard markup pricing. In **cost plus percentage-of-cost pricing,** they add a fixed percentage to the production or construction cost. This is often used to price one- or few-of-a-kind items, as when an architectural firm charges a fee of 13 percent of the construction costs

measure the cost quite easily, but the incremental revenue gene
is difficult to measure. She could partly solve this problem by
the purchase price with use of a coupon printed in the ad to
resulted from the ad.

COMPANY, CUSTOMER, AND COMPETITIVE EFF

As the final list or quoted price is set, the effects on the comp
and competitors must be assessed.

Company Effects For a firm with several products, a decisio
a single product must also consider the impact on the demand fo
in the line. IBM has an enviable record of assessing the impact
in a main-frame computer on the substitutes (its other main-fr
and complements (its peripheral equipment) in its product line
had to stop development of its 99/2 home computer when pr
products in the line made the price of the 99/2 unrealistic in t
provided and potential consumer acceptance.[13]

Customer Effects In setting price, retailers weigh factors he
the perceptions or expectations of ultimate consumers, such a
prices of vending machine items or the odd prices on sofas or
ufacturers and wholesalers must choose prices that result in p
in the channel to gain their cooperation and support. Toro fai
its lines of lawn mowers and snow throwers. Toro decided
traditional hardware outlet distribution by also selling through
such as K Mart and Target. To do so, it set prices for the discoun
below those for its traditional hardware outlets. When after
winters Toro fell on hard times, many of the unhappy hardw
doned Toro products in favor of mowers and snow throwers
ufacturers.

Competitive Effects Regardless of whether a firm is a price le
it wants to avoid cutthroat price wars in which no firm in the in
a profit. With the deregulation of the airline industry, Braniff
to expand its route structure and cut airline fares to gain m
result was disastrous, and Braniff incurred huge losses. A n
decision is immediately apparent to most competitors, who m
price changes of their own, so a manager who sets a final lis
must anticipate potential price responses from competitors.
American Airlines makes between 50,000 and 60,000 fare ch
sponse to competitor fare adjustments.[14]

STEP 6: MAKE SPECIAL ADJUSTMENTS TO THE LIST OR QUOTED PRICE

When you pay 50 cents for a bag of M&M's in a vending ma
quoted price of $5,000 from a contractor to build a new kit

Prices p
policies, alth
as well. Whe
Wilson Sting
at a single p
under the sel
uses a flexibl
lies within a
setting the fi
Deregu
banking indu
shows four
Dallas-Fort

PRICING

Unless you
in the long
or you'll go
even apply to
as loss leader
buy other h
Barbie dolls
Barbie's clot
exist because
adequate pro

Experience curve pricing is often used to set prices for electronic products

of a house. Thus for a house whose construction cost was $100,000 and the architect's fee was 13 percent of construction cost, or $13,000, the final price would be $113,000.

Cost Plus Fixed-Fee Pricing In buying highly technical, few-of-a-kind products such as aircraft or space satellites, the government has found its contractors are reluctant to specify a formal, fixed price for the procurement. Therefore it uses **cost plus fixed-fee pricing,** which means that a supplier is reimbursed for all costs, regardless of what they turn out to be, but is allowed only a fixed fee as profit that is independent of the final cost of the project. For example, suppose that NASA agreed to pay McDonnell Douglas $1.2 billion as the cost of the first space shuttle and agreed to a $100 million fee for providing that space shuttle. Even if McDonnell Douglas's cost increased to $2 billion for the space shuttle, its fee would remain $100 million.

In the late 1980's some GM car dealers across the country used this cost plus fixed-fee pricing method. Whether it was a Chevette or a Cadillac, a flat $49 fee was added by the dealer to the factory invoice to establish the final selling price to the buyer. Dealers made money by eliminating their inventory and much of their sales force. However, although consumers got a no-nonsense auto purchase without price bargaining, they had to wait from 6 weeks to 3 months for delivery of their car.[8]

Experience Curve Pricing The method of **experience curve pricing** is based on the learning effect, which holds that the unit cost of many products and services declines by 10 percent to 30 percent each time a firm's experience at producing and selling them doubles.[9] This reduction is regular or predictable enough that the average cost per unit can be mathematically estimated. For example, if the firm estimates that costs will fall by 15 percent each time volume doubles, then the cost of the 100th unit produced and sold will be about 85

FIGURE 12-7
The power of marginal analysis in real-world decisions

Suppose the owner of a pictur
a series of magazine ads to reach
of the ads is $1,000, the average
the unit variable cost (materials p
This is a direct application of m
uses to estimate the incremental r
that must be obtained to at leas
example the number of extra pictu
as follows:

Incremental number of frames =

=

=

So unless there are some other l
good will, she should only buy t
picture frame sales by at least 50

BALANCING INCREMENTAL

CONCEPT

When a price is changed or new adv
their effect on the quantity sold mu
marginal analysis (Chapter 11), invo
cremental costs against incremental r
Do marketing and business ma
they do, but they often don't use phr
elasticity of demand.
Think about these managerial c

- How many extra units do we tisement?
- How much savings on unit v break-even point the same if w
- Should we hire three more sa

All these questions are a form of man
these exact words are not used.
Figure 12-7 shows the power—
applied to a marketing decision. No
conclude that a simple advertising
additional sales or not undertake the c
made to increase the average price c
campaign, but the principle still ap
pricing and other marketing actions
The example in Figure 12-7 sho
of marginal analysis. The advantag
difficulty is obtaining the necessary

FIGURE 12-8
Three special adjustments to list or quoted price

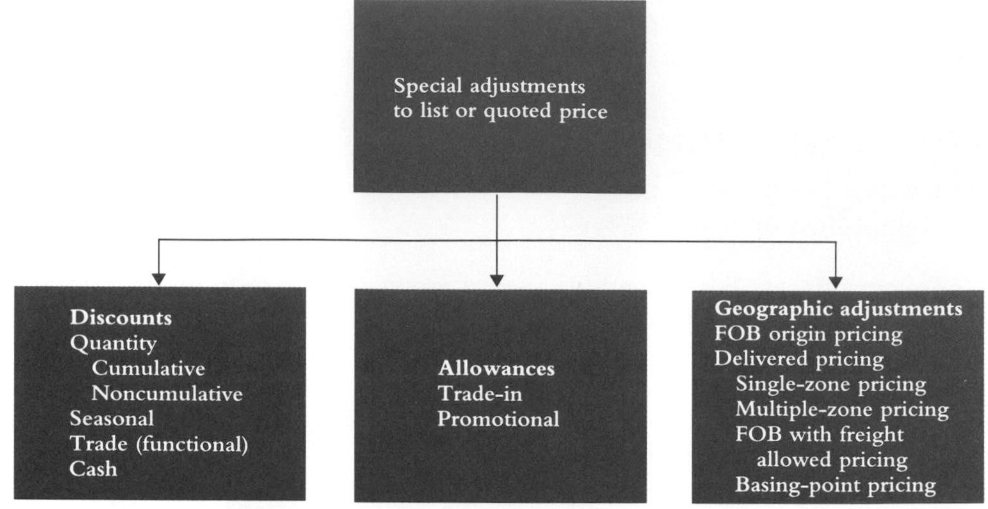

sequence ends with the last step just described: setting the list or quoted price. But when you are a manufacturer of M&M candies or gas grills and sell your product to dozens or hundreds of wholesalers and retailers in your channel of distribution, you may need to make a variety of special adjustments to the list or quoted price. Wholesalers also must adjust list or quoted prices they set for retailers. Three special adjustments to the list or quoted price are (1) discounts, (2) allowances, and (3) geographical adjustments (Figure 12-8).

DISCOUNTS

Discounts are reductions from list price that a seller gives a buyer as a reward for some activity of the buyer that is favorable to the seller. Four kinds of discounts are especially important in marketing strategy: (1) quantity, (2) seasonal, (3) trade (functional), and (4) cash discounts.

Quantity Discounts To encourage customers to buy larger quantities of a product, firms at all levels in the channel of distribution offer **quantity discounts,** which are reductions in unit costs for a larger order.[15] For example, an instant photocopying service might set a price of 10 cents a copy for copies 1 to 25, 9 cents a copy for 26 to 100, and 8 cents a copy for 101 or more. Because the photocopying service gets more of the buyer's business and has longer production runs that reduce its order-handling costs, it is willing to pass on some of the cost savings in the form of quantity discounts to the buyer.

Quantity discounts are of two general kinds: noncumulative and cumulative. *Noncumulative quantity discounts* are based on the size of an individual purchase order. They encourage large individual purchase orders, not a series of orders. *Cumulative quantity discounts* apply to the accumulation of purchases of a product over a given time period, typically a year. Cumulative quantity discounts encourage repeat buying by a single customer to a far greater degree than do noncumulative quantity discounts.

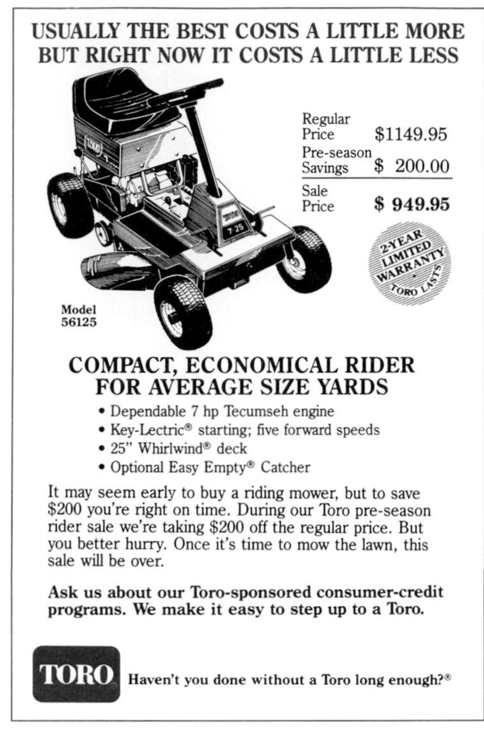

Toro uses seasonal discounts to stimulate consumer demand

Seasonal Discounts To encourage buyers to stock inventory earlier than their normal demand would require, manufacturers often use seasonal discounts. A firm like Toro that manufactures lawn mowers and snow throwers offers seasonal discounts to encourage wholesalers and retailers to stock up on lawn mowers in January and February and on snow throwers in July and August—5 or 6 months before the seasonal demand by ultimate consumers. This enables Toro to smooth out seasonal manufacturing peaks and troughs, thereby contributing to more efficient production. It also rewards wholesalers and retailers for the risk they accept in assuming increased inventory carrying costs and having supplies in stock at the time they are wanted by customers.

Trade (Functional) Discounts To reward wholesalers and retailers for marketing functions they will perform in the future, a manufacturer often gives trade, or functional, discounts. These reductions off the list or base price are offered to resellers in the channel of distribution on the basis of (1) where they are in the channel and (2) the marketing activities they are expected to perform in the future.

Suppose a manufacturer quotes price in the following form: list price—$100 less 30/10/5. The first number in the percentage sequence always refers to the retail end of the channel, and the last number always refers to the wholesaler or jobber closest to the manufacturer in the channel. The trade discounts are simply subtracted one at a time. This price quote shows $100 in the manufacturer's suggested retail price; 30 percent of the suggested retail price is available to the retailer to cover costs and provide a profit of $30

FIGURE 12-9
The structure of trade discounts

Terms	List price less 30/10/5 Manufacturer's suggested retail price	\$100.00
Subtract	Retail discount, 30 percent of manufacturer's suggested retail price	30.00
Yields	Retail cost or wholesaler sales price	\$ 70.00
Subtract	Wholesaler discount, 10 percent of wholesaler sales price	7.00
Yields	Wholesaler cost or jobber sales price	\$ 63.00
Subtract	Jobber discount, 5 percent of jobber sales price	3.15
Yields	Jobber cost, or manufacturer's sales price	\$ 59.85

(\$100 × 0.3 = \$30); wholesalers closest to the retailer in the channel get 10 percent of their selling price (\$70 × 0.1 = \$7); and the final group of wholesalers in the channel (probably jobbers) that are closest to the manufacturer get 5 percent of their selling price (\$63 × 0.05 = \$3.15). Thus starting with the manufacturer's retail price and subtracting the three trade discounts shows that the manufacturer's selling price to the wholesaler or jobber closest to it is \$59.85 (Figure 12-9).

Traditional trade discounts have been established in various product lines such as hardware, food, and pharmaceutical items. Although the manufacturer may suggest the trade discounts shown in the example just cited, the sellers are free to alter the discount schedule depending on their competitive situation.

Cash Discounts To encourage retailers to pay their bills quickly, manufacturers offer them cash discounts. Suppose a retailer receives a bill quoted as \$1,000, 2/10 net 30. This means that the bill for the product is \$1,000, but the retailer can take a 2 percent discount (\$1,000 × 0.02 = \$20) if payment is made within 10 days and send a check for \$980. If the payment cannot be made within 10 days, the total amount of \$1000 is due within 30 days. It is usually understood by the buyer that an interest charge will be added after the first 30 days of free credit.

Naive buyers may think that the 2 percent discount offered is not substantial. What this means is that the buyer pays 2 percent on the total amount to be able to use that amount an extra 20 days—from day 11 to day 30. In a 360-day business year, this is an effective annual interest rate of 36 percent (2% × 360/20 = 36%). Because the effective interest rate is so high, firms that cannot take advantage of a 2/10 net 30 cash discount often try to borrow money from their local banks at rates far lower than the 36 percent they must pay by not taking advantage of the cash discount.

Retailers provide cash discounts to consumers as well to eliminate the cost of credit granted to consumers.[16] These discounts take the form of discount-for-cash policies. For example, Breuners, a furniture dealer in California, offers a 5 percent discount for cash, 4 Day Tire Stores advertise a 2 percent discount, and gasoline stations offer a "cents-off" discount for cash, as opposed to credit card, purchases.

Discounts for cash as opposed to credit have become popular

ALLOWANCES

Allowances—like discounts—are reductions from list or quoted prices to buyers for performing some activity.

Trade-In Allowances A new car dealer can offer a substantial reduction in the list price of that new Mazda RX-7 by offering you a trade-in allowance of $500 for your 1976 Chevrolet. A trade-in allowance is a price reduction given when a used product is part of the payment on a new product. Trade-ins are an effective way to lower the price a buyer has to pay without formally reducing the list price.

Promotional Allowances Sellers in the channel of distribution can qualify for **promotional allowances** for undertaking certain advertising or selling activities to promote a product. Various types of allowances include an actual cash payment or an extra amount of "free goods" (as with a free case of pizzas to a retailer for every dozen cases purchased).[17] Frequently a portion of these savings is passed on to the consumer, as shown in the Marketing Action Memo.

GEOGRAPHICAL ADJUSTMENTS

Geographical adjustments are made by manufacturers or even wholesalers to list or quoted price to reflect the cost of transportation of the products from seller to buyer. The two general methods for quoting prices related to transportation costs are (1) FOB origin pricing and (2) uniform delivered pricing.

MARKETING · ACTION · MEMO

SECRETS BEHIND THE PRICE SPECIALS

Do you ever wonder what goes on behind the scene when your local supermarket features specials on its products? In a New York City supermarket, whose advertisement is shown here, the price specials reflect the allowances that the manufacturer gave the supermarket to push the product. The retailer usually pays $1.15 for a can of Bumble Bee white tuna ($55.43 ÷ 48 = $1.15), but the allowance reduced the cost per can to 96 cents. In this instance the retailer had a 3-cent retail markup on the product (99-cent retail price in ad − 96-cent cost). Similar calculations apply to the other examples.

The use of discounts and allowances is very common. It is estimated that $8 billion a year is spent on price adjustments, and the figure is growing. A decade ago, 20 percent to 30 percent of sales carried allowances and discounts, which averaged 6 percent to 8 percent of manufacturers' list price. Today about 60 percent of manufacturers' sales carry price adjustments, which average about 12 percent of their list price.

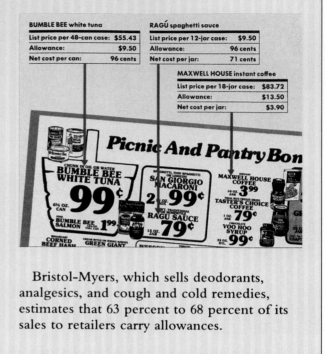

Bristol-Myers, which sells deodorants, analgesics, and cough and cold remedies, estimates that 63 percent to 68 percent of its sales to retailers carry allowances.

Source: Based on Joanne Lipman, "Firms Bid to Cut Sales Coupons, Other Incentives," *Wall Street Journal* (February 3, 1987), p. 37; Monci Jo Williams, "The No-Win Game of Price Promotions," *Fortune* (July 11, 1983), pp. 92-102;

FOB Origin Pricing FOB means "free on board" some vehicle at some location, which means the seller pays the cost of loading the product onto the vehicle that is used (such as a barge, railroad car, or truck). **FOB origin pricing** usually involves the seller's naming the location of this loading as the seller's factory or warehouse (such as "FOB Detroit" or "FOB factory"). The title to the goods passes to the buyer at the point of loading, so the buyer becomes responsible for picking the specific mode of transportation, for all the transportation costs, and for subsequent handling of the product. Buyers farthest from the seller face the big disadvantage of paying the higher transportation costs.

Uniform Delivered Pricing When a **uniform delivered pricing** method is used, the price the seller quotes includes all transportation costs. It is quoted in a contract as "FOB buyer's location," and the seller selects the mode of transportation, pays the freight charges, and is responsible for any damage that may occur, since the seller retains title to the goods until delivered to the buyer. Although they go by various names, four kinds of delivered pricing methods are (1) single-zone pricing, (2) multiple-zone pricing, (3) FOB with freight allowed pricing, and (4) basing-point pricing.

In *single-zone pricing* all buyers pay the same delivered price for the products, regardless of their distance from the seller. This method is also called *postage stamp pricing* because it is the way that U.S. postal rates are set for first-class mail. So although a store offering free delivery in a metropolitan area has lower transportation costs for goods shipped to customers nearer the store than for those shipped to distant ones, customers pay the same delivered price.

In *multiple-zone pricing* a firm divides its selling territory into geographic areas, or zones. The delivered price to all buyers within any one zone is the same, but prices across zones vary depending on the transportation cost to the zone and the level of competition and demand within the zone. The U.S. postal system uses multiple-zone pricing for mailing packages. This system is also used in setting prices on long distance phone calls.

With *FOB with freight allowed pricing,* also called *freight absorption pricing,* the price is quoted by the seller as "FOB plant—freight allowed." The buyer is allowed to deduct freight expenses from the list price of the goods, so the seller agrees to pay, or "absorbs," the transportation costs.

Basing-point pricing involves selecting one or more geographical locations (basing-point) from which the list price for products plus freight expenses are charged to the buyer. For example, a company might designate St. Louis as the basing-point and charge all buyers a list price of $100 plus freight from St. Louis to their location. Basing-point pricing methods have been used in the steel, cement, and lumber industries where freight expenses are a significant part of the total cost to the buyer and products are largely undifferentiated.

LEGAL AND REGULATORY ASPECTS OF PRICING

Arriving at a final price is clearly a complex process. The task is further complicated by legal and regulatory restrictions. Chapter 3 described the regulatory environment of companies. Here we elaborate on the specific laws and regulations affecting pricing decisions. Five pricing practices have received the most scrutiny: (1) price-fixing, (2) price discrimination, (3) deceptive pricing, (4) geographical pricing, and (5) predatory pricing.

Price-Fixing A conspiracy among firms to set prices for a product is termed **price-fixing.**[18] Price-fixing is illegal per se under the Sherman Act (*per se* means in and of itself). When two or more competitors explicitly or implicitly set prices, this practice is called *horizontal price-fixing*. For example, a federal grand jury once indicted Saks Fifth Avenue and I. Magnin, two retailers, on charges of conspiring to fix prices on women's clothing.[19]

Vertical price-fixing involves controlling agreements between independent buyers and sellers (a manufacturer and a retailer) whereby sellers are required to not sell products below a minimum retail price. This practice, called resale price maintenance, was declared illegal per se in 1975 under provisions of the Consumer Goods Pricing Act.

It is important to recognize that a manufacturer's "suggested retail price" is not illegal per se. The issue of legality only arises when manufacturers enforce such a practice by coercion. Furthermore, there appears to be a movement toward a "rule of reason" in pricing cases. This rule holds that circumstances surrounding a practice must be considered before making a judgment about its legality. The "rule of reason" perspective is the direct opposite of the per se rule, which holds that a practice is illegal in and of itself.

Price Discrimination The Clayton Act as amended by the Robinson-Patman Act prohibits **price discrimination**—the practice of charging different prices to different buyers for goods of like grade and quality.[20] However, not all price differences are illegal. Only those which substantially lessen competition or create a monopoly are deemed unlawful. Moreover, "goods" is narrowly defined and does not include discrimination in services.

A unique feature of the Robinson-Patman Act is that it allows for price differentials to different customers under the following conditions:

1. When price differences charged to different customers do not exceed the differences in the cost of manufacture, sale, or delivery resulting from differing methods or quantities in which such goods are sold or delivered to buyers. This condition is called the "cost justification" defense.
2. Price differences resulting from meeting changing market conditions, avoiding obsolescence of seasonal merchandise including perishables or closing out sales.
3. When price differences are quoted to selected buyers in good faith to meet competitors' prices and are not intended to injure competition. This condition is called the "meet the competition" defense.

The Robinson-Patman Act also covers promotional allowances. To legally offer promotional allowances to buyers, the seller must do so on a proportionally equal basis to all buyers distributing the seller's products. In general, the rule of reason applies frequently in price discrimination cases and is often applied to cases involving flexible pricing practices of firms.

Deceptive Pricing Price deals that mislead consumers fall into the category of deceptive pricing. Deceptive pricing is outlawed by the Federal Trade Commission Act. The FTC monitors such practices and has published a regulation titled "Guides Against Deceptive Pricing" designed to help business people avoid a charge of deception. The five most common deceptive pricing practices are described in Figure 12-10. As you read about these practices, it should be clear that laws cannot be passed and enforced to protect consumers and competitors against all of these practices. So it is essential to rely on the ethical standards of those making and publicizing pricing decisions.

Geographical Pricing FOB origin pricing is legal, as are FOB freight-allowed pricing practices, providing no conspiracy to set prices exists. Basing-point pricing can be viewed as illegal under the Robinson-Patman Act and the Federal Trade Commission Act if there is clear-cut evidence of a conspiracy to set prices.

FIGURE 12-10
Five most common deceptive pricing practices

- *Bait and Switch* A deceptive practice exists when a firm offers a very low price on a product (the bait) to attract customers to a store. Once in the store, the customer is persuaded to purchase a higher priced item (the switch) using a variety of tricks, including (1) downgrading the promoted item and (2) not having the item in stock or refusing to take orders for the item.
- *Bargains Conditional on Other Purchases* This practice may exist when a buyer is offered "1-Cent Sales," "Buy 1, Get 1 Free," and "Get 2 for the Price of 1." Such pricing is legal only if the first items are sold at the regular price, not a price inflated for the offer. Substituting lower quality items on either the first or second purchase is also considered deceptive.
- *Comparable Value Comparisons* Advertising such as "Retail Value $100.00, Our Price $85.00," is deceptive if a verified and substantial number of stores in the market area did not price the item at $100.
- *Comparisons with Suggested Prices* A claim that a price is below a manufacturer's suggested or list price may be deceptive if few or no sales occur at that price in a retailer's market area.
- *Former Price Comparisons* When a seller represents a price as reduced, the item must have been offered "in good faith" at a higher price for a substantial previous period. Setting a high price for the purpose of establishing a reference for a price reduction is deceptive.

In general, geographical pricing practices have been immune from legal and regulatory restrictions, except in those instances in which a conspiracy to lessen competition exists under the Sherman Act or price discrimination exists under the Robinson-Patman Act.

Predatory Pricing **Predatory pricing** is the practice of charging a very low price for a product with the intent of driving competitors out of business. Once competitors have been driven out, the firm raises its prices. This practice is illegal under the Sherman Act and the Federal Trade Commission Act. Proving the presence of this practice has been difficult and expensive because it must be shown that the predator explicitly attempted to destroy a competitor and the predatory price was below the defendant's average cost. Nevertheless, suits are common when foreign competitors enter markets in the United States.[21]

CONCEPT CHECK

1 **Why would a seller choose a flexible-price policy over a one-price policy?**

2 **If a firm wished to encourage repeat purchases by a buyer throughout a year, would a cumulative or noncumulative quantity discount be a better strategy?**

3 **Which pricing practices are covered by the Sherman Act?**

SUMMARY

1 Four general methods of finding an approximate price level for a product or service are demand-based, cost-based, profit-based, and competition-based pricing methods.
2 Demand-based pricing methods stress consumer demand and revenue implications of pricing and include seven types: skimming, penetration, prestige, price lining, odd-even, demand-backward pricing, and bundle pricing.
3 Cost-based pricing methods emphasize the cost aspects of pricing and include four types: standard markup, cost plus percentage-of-cost, cost plus fixed-fee, and experience curve pricing.
4 Profit-based pricing methods focus on a balance between revenues and costs to set a price and include three types: target profit, target return-on-sales, and target return-on-investment pricing.
5 Competition-based pricing methods stress what competitors or the marketplace is doing and include four types: customary; above-, at-, or below-market; loss-leader; and sealed-bid pricing.
6 Given an approximate price level for a product, a manager must set a list or quoted price by considering factors such as one-price versus a flexible-price policy; pricing to cover cost plus profit in the long run; balancing incremental costs and revenues; and the effects of the proposed price on the company, customer, and competitors.
7 List or quoted price is often modified through discounts, allowances, and geographical adjustments.
8 Legal and regulatory issues in pricing focus on price-fixing, price discrimination, deceptive pricing, geographical pricing, and predatory pricing.

KEY TERMS AND CONCEPTS

skimming pricing p. 312
penetration pricing p. 314
prestige pricing p. 316
price lining p. 317
odd-even pricing p. 317
demand-backward pricing p. 317
bundle pricing p. 318
standard markup pricing p. 319
cost plus percentage-of-cost pricing p. 320
cost plus fixed-fee pricing p. 321
experience curve pricing p. 321
target profit pricing p. 322
target return-on-sales pricing p. 322
target return-on-investment pricing p. 323
customary pricing p. 324
above-, at-, or below-market pricing p. 324
loss-leader pricing p. 326
sealed-bid pricing p. 326
one-price policy p. 326
flexible-price policy p. 326
quantity discounts p. 330
promotional allowances p. 333
FOB origin pricing p. 334
uniform delivered pricing p. 334
basing-point pricing p. 335
price-fixing p. 335
price discrimination p. 336
predatory pricing p. 337

CHAPTER PROBLEMS AND APPLICATIONS

1 Under what conditions would a camera manufacturer adopt a skimming price approach for a new product? A penetration approach?

2 What are some similarities and differences between skimming pricing, prestige pricing, and above-market pricing?

3 A producer of microwave ovens has adopted an experience curve pricing approach for its new model. The firm believes it can reduce the cost of producing the model by 20 percent each time volume doubles. The cost to produce the first unit was $1,000. What would be the approximate cost of the 4,096th unit?

4 The Hesper Corporation is a leading manufacturer of high-quality upholstered sofas. Current plans call for an increase of $600,000 in the advertising budget. If the firm sells its sofas for an average price of $850 and the unit variable costs are $550, then what dollar sales increase will be necessary to cover the additional advertising?

5 Suppose executives estimate that the unit variable cost for their VCR is $100, the fixed cost related to the product is $10 million annually, and the target volume for next year is 100,000 recorders. What sales price will be necessary to achieve a target profit of $1 million?

6 A manufacturer of motor oil has a trade discount policy whereby the manufacturer's suggested retail price is $30 per case with the terms of 40/20/10. The manufacturer sells its products through jobbers, who sell to wholesalers, who sell to gasoline stations. What will the manufacturer's sale price be?

7 What are the effective annual interest rates for the following cash discount terms? (a) 1/10 net 30, (b) 2/10 net 30, and (c) 2/10 net 60.

8 Suppose a manufacturer of exercise equipment sets a suggested price to the consumer of $395 for a particular piece of equipment to be competitive with similar equipment. The manufacturer sells its equipment to a sporting goods wholesaler who receives a 25 percent markup and a retailer who receives a 50 percent markup. What demand-based pricing method is being used, and at what price will the manufacturer sell the equipment to the wholesaler?

9 A furniture manufacturer located in North Carolina operates at a freight cost disadvantage relative to competitors in the Midwest and West. What methods of quoting prices could this firm adopt to make it more competitive in these states?

10 Is there any truth in the statement, "Geographical pricing schemes will always be unfair to some buyers"? Why or why not?

SUGGESTED READINGS

George S. Day and Adrian B. Ryans, "Using Price Discounts for a Competitive Advantage," *Industrial Marketing Management* (February 1988), pp. 1-14. *This article reviews types of discount programs and how they can be used.*

Joseph P. Guiltinan, "The Price Bundling of Services: A Normative Framework," *Journal of Marketing* (April 1987), pp. 74-85. *This article describes the theory behind bundle pricing, including demand and cost perspectives.*

Thomas T. Nagle, *The Strategy & Tactics of Pricing* (Englewood Cliffs, N.J.: Prentice-Hall, Inc., 1987). *This short book provides a thorough review of pricing practices related to arriving at a final price (Chapters 5 to 9).*

Gerard J. Tellis, "Beyond the Many Faces of Price: An Integration of Pricing Strategies," *Journal of Marketing* (October 1986), pp. 146-160. *Pricing strategies are reviewed and integrated with practical examples.*

APPENDIX A

FINANCIAL ASPECTS OF MARKETING

Basic concepts from accounting and finance provide valuable tools for marketing executives. This appendix describes an actual company's use of accounting and financial concepts and illustrates how they assist the owner in making marketing decisions.

The Caplow Company

An accomplished artist and calligrapher, Jane Westerlund, decided to apply some of her experience to the picture framing business in Minneapolis. She bought an existing retail frame store, The Caplow Company, from a friend who owned the business and wanted to retire. She avoided the do-it-yourself end of the framing business and chose two kinds of business activities: (1) cutting the frame, mats, and glass for customers who brought in their own pictures or prints to be framed and (2) selling prints and posters that she had purchased from wholesalers.

To understand how accounting, finance, and marketing relate to each other, let's analyze (1) the operating statement for her frame shop, (2) some general ratios of interest that are derived from the operating statement, and (3) some ratios that pertain specifically to her pricing decisions.

THE OPERATING STATEMENT

The operating statement (also called an *income statement* or *profit-and-loss statement*) summarizes the profitability of a business firm for a specific time period, usually a month, quarter, or year. The title of the operating statement for The Caplow Company shows it is for a 1-year period (Figure A-1). The purpose of an operating statement is to show the profit of the firm and the revenues and expenses that led to that profit. This information tells the owner or manager what has happened in the past and suggests actions to improve future profitability.

The left side of Figure A-1 shows that there are three key elements to all operating statements: (1) sales of the firm's goods and services, (2) costs incurred in making and selling the goods and services, and (3) profit or loss, which is the difference between sales and costs.

Sales Elements The sales element of Figure A-1 has four terms that need explanation:

FIGURE A-1
Example of an operating statement

THE CAPLOW COMPANY
OPERATING STATEMENT
FOR THE YEAR ENDING DECEMBER 31, 1989

Sales	Gross sales			$80,500
	Less: Returns and allowances			500
	Net sales			80,000
Costs	Cost of goods sold:			
	Beginning inventory at cost		$ 6,000	
	Purchases at billed cost	$21,000		
	Less: Purchase discounts	300		
	Purchases at net cost	20,700		
	Plus freight-in	100		
	Net cost of delivered purchases		20,800	
	Direct labor (framing)		14,200	
	Cost of goods available for sale		41,000	
	Less: Ending inventory at cost		5,000	
	Cost of goods sold			36,000
	Gross margin (gross profit)			44,000
	Expenses:			
	Selling expenses:			
	Sales salaries	2,000		
	Advertising expense	3,000		
	Total selling expense		5,000	
	Administrative expenses:			
	Owner's salary	18,000		
	Bookkeeper's salary	1,200		
	Office supplies	300		
	Total administrative expense		19,500	
	General expenses:			
	Depreciation expense	1,000		
	Interest expense	500		
	Rent expense	2,100		
	Utility expenses (heat, electricity)	3,000		
	Repairs and maintenance	2,300		
	Insurance	2,000		
	Social security taxes	2,200		
	Total general expense		13,100	
	Total expenses			37,600
Profit or loss	Profit before taxes			6,400

- *Gross sales* are the total amount billed to customers. Dissatisfied customers or errors may reduce the gross sales through returns or allowances.
- *Returns* occur when a customer gives the item purchased back to the seller, who either refunds the purchase price or allows the customer a credit on subsequent purchases. In any event the seller now owns the item again.
- *Allowances* are given when a customer is dissatisfied with the item purchased and the seller reduces the original purchase price. Unlike returns, in the case of allowances the buyer owns the item.
- *Net sales* are simply gross sales minus returns and allowances.

The operating statement for The Caplow Company shows that:

Gross sales	$80,500
Less: Returns and allowances	500
Net sales	$80,000

The low level of returns and allowances shows the shop generally has done a good job in satisfying customers, which is essential in building the repeat business necessary for success.

Cost Elements The *cost of goods sold* is the total cost of the products sold during the period. This item varies according to the kind of business. A retail store purchases finished goods and resells them to customers without reworking them in any way. In contrast, a manufacturing firm combines raw and semifinished materials and parts, uses labor and overhead to rework these into finished goods, and then sells them to customers. All these activities are reflected in the cost of goods sold item on a manufacturer's operating statement. Note that the frame shop has some features of a pure retailer (prints and posters it buys that are resold without alteration) and a pure manufacturer (assembling the raw materials of molding, matting, and glass to form a completed frame).

Some terms that relate to cost of goods sold need clarification:

- *Inventory* is the physical material that is purchased from suppliers, may or may not be reworked, and is available for sale to customers. In the frame shop inventory includes molding, matting, glass, prints, and posters.
- *Purchase discounts* are reductions in the original billed price for reasons like prompt payment of the bill or the quantity bought.
- *Direct labor* is the cost of the labor used in producing the finished product. For the frame shop this is the cost of producing the completed frames from the molding, matting, and glass.
- *Gross margin (gross profit)* is the money remaining to manage the business, sell the products or services, and give some profit. Gross margin is net sales minus cost of goods sold.

The two right-hand columns in Figure A-1 between "Net sales" and "Gross margin" calculate the cost of goods sold:

Net sales		$80,000
Cost of goods sold		
Beginning inventory at cost	$ 6,000	
Net cost of delivered purchases	20,800	
Direct labor (framing)	14,200	
Cost of goods available for sale	41,000	
Less: ending inventory at cost	5,000	
Cost of goods sold		36,000
Gross margin (gross profit)		$44,000

This section considers the beginning and ending inventories, the net cost of purchases delivered during the year, and the cost of the direct labor going into making the frames. Subtracting the $36,000 cost of goods sold from the $80,000 net sales gives the $44,000 gross margin.

Three major categories of expenses are shown in Figure A-1 below the gross margin:

- *Selling expenses* are the costs of selling the product or service produced by the firm. For The Caplow Company there are two such selling expenses: sales salaries of part-time employees waiting on customers and the advertising expense of simple newspaper ads and direct-mail ads sent to customers.
- *Administrative expenses* are the costs of managing the business and for The Caplow Company include three expenses: the owner's salary, a part-time bookkeeper's salary, and office supplies expense.
- *General expenses* are miscellaneous costs not covered elsewhere; for the frame shop these include seven items: depreciation expense (on her equipment), interest expense, rent expense, utility expenses, repairs and maintenance expense, insurance expense, and social security taxes.

As shown in Figure A-1, selling, administrative, and general expenses total $37,600 for The Caplow Company.

Profit Element What the company has earned, the *profit before taxes,* is found by subtracting cost of goods sold and expenses from net sales. For The Caplow Company, Figure A-1 shows that profit before taxes is $6,400.

GENERAL OPERATING RATIOS TO ANALYZE OPERATIONS

Looking only at the elements of Caplow's operating statement that extend to the right-hand column highlights the firm's performance on some important dimensions. Using operating ratios such as *expense-to-sales ratios* for expressing basic expense or profit elements as a percentage of net sales gives further insights:

ELEMENT IN OPERATING STATEMENT	DOLLAR VALUE	PERCENTAGE OF NET SALES
Gross sales	$80,500	
Less: Returns and allowances	500	
Net sales	80,000	100%
Less: Cost of goods sold	36,000	45
Gross margin	44,000	55
Less: Total expenses	37,600	47
Profit (or loss) before taxes	6,400	8%

Westerlund can use this information to compare her firm's performance from one time period to the next. To do so, it is especially important that she keep the same definitions for each element of her operating statement, also a significant factor in using the electronic spread sheets discussed in Chapter 12. Performance comparisons between periods are more difficult if she changes definitions for the accounting elements in the operating statement.

She can use either the dollar values or the operating ratios (the value of the element of the operating statement divided by net sales) to analyze the firm's performance. However, the operating ratios are more valuable than the dollar values for two reasons: (1) the simplicity of working with percentages rather than dollars and (2) the availability of operating ratios of typical firms in the same industry, which are published by Dun & Bradstreet and trade associations. Thus Westerlund can compare her firm's performance not only with that of *other* frame shops but also with that of *small* frame shops that have annual net sales, for example, of under $100,000. In this way she can identify where her operations are better or worse than other similar firms. For example, if trade association data showed a typical frame shop of her size had a ratio of cost of goods sold to net sales of 37 percent, compared with her 45 percent, she might consider steps to reduce this cost through purchase discounts, reducing inbound freight charges, finding lower cost suppliers, and so on.

RATIOS TO USE IN SETTING AND EVALUATING PRICE

Using The Caplow Company as an example, we can study four ratios that relate closely to setting a price: (1) markup, (2) markdown, (3) stockturns, and (4) return on investment. These terms are defined in Figure A-2 and explained below.

Markup Both markup and gross margin refer to the amount added to the cost of goods sold to arrive at the selling price, and they may be expressed either in dollar or percentage terms. However, the term markup is more commonly used in setting retail prices. Suppose the average price Westerlund charges for a framed picture is $80. Then in terms of the first two definitions in Figure A-2 and the earlier information from the operating statement:

ELEMENT OF PRICE	DOLLAR VALUE
Cost of goods sold	36
Markup (or gross margin)	44
Selling price	80

The third definition in Figure A-2 gives the percentage markup on selling price:

$$\text{Markup on selling price (\%)} = \frac{\text{Markup}}{\text{Selling price}} \times 100$$

$$= \frac{44}{80} \times 100$$

$$= 55\%$$

And the percentage markup on cost is obtained as follows:

$$\text{Markup on cost (\%)} = \frac{\text{Markup}}{\text{Cost of goods sold}} \times 100$$

$$= \frac{44}{36} \times 100$$

$$= 122.2\%$$

Inexperienced retail clerks sometimes fail to distinguish between the two definitions of markup, which (as the above calculations show) can represent a tremendous difference, so it is essential to know whether the base is cost or selling price. Marketers generally use selling price as the base for talking about "markups" unless they specifically state they are using cost as a base.

NAME OF FINANCIAL ELEMENT OR RATIO	WHAT IT MEASURES	EQUATION
Selling price ($)	Price customer sees	Cost of goods sold (COGS) + Markup
Markup ($)	Dollars added to COGS to arrive at selling price	Selling price − COGS
Markup on selling price (%)	Relates markup to selling price	$\frac{\text{Markup}}{\text{Selling price}} \times 100 = \frac{\text{Selling price} - \text{COGS}}{\text{Selling price}} \times 100$
Markup on cost (%)	Relates markup to cost	$\frac{\text{Markup}}{\text{COGS}} \times 100 = \frac{\text{Selling price} - \text{COGS}}{\text{COGS}}$
Markdown (%)	Ability of firm to sell its products at initial selling price	$\frac{\text{Markdowns} + \text{Allowances}}{\text{Net sales}} \times 100$
Stockturn rate	Ability of firm to move its inventory quickly	$\frac{\text{COGS}}{\text{Average inventory at cost}}$ or $\frac{\text{Net sales}}{\text{Average inventory at selling price}}$
Return on investment (%)	Profit performance of firm compared with money invested in it	$\frac{\text{Net profit after taxes}}{\text{Investment}} \times 100$

FIGURE A-2
How to calculate selling price, markup, markdown, stockturn, and return on investment

Retailers and wholesalers that rely heavily on markup pricing (discussed in Chapter 12) often use standardized tables that convert markup on selling price to markup on cost, and vice versa. The two equations on the next page show how to convert one to the other:

$$\text{Markup on selling price (\%)} = \frac{\text{Markup on cost (\%)}}{100\% + \text{Markup on cost (\%)}} \times 100$$

$$\text{Markup on cost (\%)} = \frac{\text{Markup on selling price (\%)}}{100\% - \text{Markup on selling price (\%)}} \times 100$$

Using the data from The Caplow Company gives:

$$\begin{aligned}\text{Markup on selling price (\%)} &= \frac{\text{Markup on cost (\%)}}{100\% + \text{Markup on cost (\%)}} \times 100 \\ &= \frac{122.2}{100 + 122.2} \times 100 \\ &= 55\%\end{aligned}$$

$$\begin{aligned}\text{Markup on cost (\%)} &= \frac{\text{Markup on selling price (\%)}}{100\% - \text{Markup on selling price (\%)}} \times 100 \\ &= \frac{55}{100 - 55} \times 100 \\ &= 122.2\%\end{aligned}$$

The use of an incorrect markup base is shown in Westerlund's business. A markup of 122.2 percent on her cost of goods sold for a typical frame she sells gives 122.2% × $36 = $44 of markup. Added to the $36 cost of goods sold, this gives her selling price of $80 for the framed picture. However, a new clerk working for her who erroneously priced the framed picture at 55 percent of cost of goods sold set the final price at $55.80 ($36 of cost of goods sold plus 55% × $36 = $19.80). The error, if repeated, can be disastrous: frames would be accidentally sold at $55.80, or $24.20 below the intended selling price of $80.

Markdown A markdown is a reduction in a retail price that is necessary if the item will not sell at the full selling price to which it has been marked up. The item might not sell for a variety of reasons: the selling price was set too high or the item is out of style or has become soiled or damaged. The seller "takes a markdown" by lowering the price to sell it, thereby converting it to cash to buy future inventory that will sell faster.

The markdown ratio cannot be calculated directly from the operating statement. As shown in the fifth item of Figure A-2, the numerator of the markdown ratio is the total dollar amounts of both markdowns and allowances. Both markdowns and allowances are reductions in the prices of goods that are purchased by customers. Returns are often available for resale and are not included in calculating the markdown ratio.

Suppose The Caplow Company had $300 in customer allowances and $700 in markdowns on the prints and posters that are stocked and available for sale. Since the frames are custom made for individual customers, there is little reason for a markdown there. Caplow's markdown ratio is then:

$$\text{Markdown} = \frac{\text{Markdowns} + \text{Allowances}}{\text{Net sales}} \times 100$$

$$= \frac{\$700 + \$300}{\$80{,}000} \times 100$$

$$= 1.25\%$$

Other kinds of retailers often have markdown ratios several times this amount. For example, women's dress stores have markdowns of about 25 percent, and menswear stores have markdowns of about 1 percent.

Stockturn Rate A business firm is anxious to have its inventory move quickly, or "turn over." Stockturn rate, or simply stockturns, measures this inventory movement. For a retailer a slow stockturn rate may show it is buying merchandise customers don't want, so this is a critical measure of performance. When a firm sells only a single product, one convenient way to measure stockturn rate is simply to divide its cost of goods sold by average inventory at cost. The sixth item in Figure A-2 shows how to calculate stockturn rate using information in the operating statement:

$$\text{Stockturn rate} = \frac{\text{Cost of goods sold}}{\text{Average inventory at cost}}$$

The dollar amount of average inventory at cost is calculated by adding the beginning and ending inventories for the year and dividing by 2 to get the average. From Caplow's operating statement, we have:

$$\text{Stockturn rate} = \frac{\text{Cost of goods sold}}{\text{Average inventory at cost}}$$

$$= \frac{\text{Cost of goods sold}}{\dfrac{\text{Beginning inventory + Ending inventory}}{2}}$$

$$= \frac{\$36{,}000}{\dfrac{\$6{,}000 + \$5{,}000}{2}}$$

$$= \frac{\$36{,}000}{\$5{,}500}$$

$$= 6.5 \text{ stockturns per year}$$

What is considered a "good stockturn" varies by the kind of industry. For example, supermarkets have limited shelf space for thousands of new products from manufacturers each year, so they watch stockturn carefully by product line. The stockturn rate in supermarkets for breakfast foods is about 17 times per year, for pet food is about 22 times, and for paper products is about 25 times per year.

Return on Investment A better measure of the performance of a firm than the amount of profit it makes in a year is its ROI, which is the ratio of net income to the investment used to earn that net income. To calculate ROI, it is necessary to subtract income taxes from profit before taxes to obtain net income, then divide this figure by the investment that can be found on a firm's balance sheet (another accounting statement that shows the firm's assets, liabilities, and net worth). While financial and accounting experts have many definitions for "investment," an often-used definition is "total assets."

For our purposes, let's assume that Westerlund has total assets (investment) of $20,000 in The Caplow Company, which covers inventory, store fixtures, and framing equipment. If she pays $1,000 in income taxes, her store's net income is $5,400, so her ROI is given by the seventh item in Figure A-2:

$$\text{Return on investment} = \text{Net income/investment} \times 100$$

$$= \$5{,}400/\$20{,}000 \times 100$$

$$= 27\%$$

If Westerlund wants to improve her ROI next year, the strategies she might take are found in this alternative equation for ROI:

$$\text{ROI} = \text{Net sales/investment} \times \text{Net income/net sales}$$

$$= \text{Investment turnover} \times \text{Profit margin}$$

This equation suggests that The Caplow Company's ROI can be improved by raising turnover or increasing profit margin. Increasing stockturns will accomplish the former, whereas lowering cost of goods sold to net sales will cause the latter.

EXIT
THIS DOOR TO REMAIN UNLOCKED DURING BUSINESS HOURS
TRACER
SCORPIO
SCORPIO PERFORMS
TO EUROPEAN

13

MARKETING CHANNELS AND WHOLESALING

After reading this chapter you should be able to:

Explain what is meant by a marketing channel of distribution and why intermediaries are needed.

•

Recognize differences between marketing channels for consumer and industrial products and services.

•

Describe the types and functions of firms that perform wholesaling activities.

•

Distinguish between traditional marketing channels and different types of vertical marketing systems.

•

Describe factors considered by marketing executives when selecting and managing a marketing channel.

Why You Can't Buy an Acura from Your Honda Dealer

Why are Ford, GM, Honda, and Nissan spending millions of dollars developing entirely new distribution and dealer networks when each already has hundreds of dealers? The answer: because these manufacturers can't entice young, upscale American buyers of expensive European cars such as Mercedes Benz, Porsche, BMW, and Audi into the showrooms of their existing dealers!

Licensing new dealers and not selling through existing ones is occurring because target market buyers for upscale American cars are not shopping at existing dealers. Ford and Honda led the way when they used separate dealerships for the Merkur and Acura, respectively. Ford's Merkur was designed for "trendsetters," specifically, young professionals who earn about

$40,000 per year. These buyers respond to such terms and phrases as "lower lumbar support," "user friendly," and "braking systems designed to cope with Autobahn cruising speeds." One Ford executive observed, "The customer we're after with Merkur isn't coming into our store." Commented a Honda executive, "People looking for those (expensive European) cars don't come to a Honda dealer for that sort of merchandise, and I don't expect they ever will."

In 1989, Nissan started using a new dealer distribution network, dubbed Infiniti, which sells its new line of high-priced sports and luxury cars. GM's subsidiary Saturn Corporation will establish a separate dealer system for its Saturn car, which is due out in 1991. Toyota is expected to do the same for its new line of luxury cars, called Lexus.

The new dealer distribution efforts reflect automaker strategies to reach different target markets and better satisfy buyer wants. For example, R.G. LeFauve, Saturn's president, said that each Saturn dealer will tailor its sales and service facilities to handle the ways buyers select and purchase their cars and then have their cars serviced.[1]

Distribution is critical not only for cars but also for the marketing success of such diverse products as magazines, PCs, snack foods, beverages, record albums, health care services, and cosmetics. Similarly, distribution is so important in marketing private and business airplanes that Cessna Aircraft considers its dealers to be the firm's greatest asset.

This chapter focuses on marketing channels of distribution and why they are an important component in the marketing mix. It then shows how such channels benefit consumers and the sequence of firms that make up a marketing channel. Finally, it describes factors that influence the choice and management of marketing channels, including channel conflict and legal restrictions.

NATURE AND IMPORTANCE OF MARKETING CHANNELS

Reaching prospective buyers, either directly or indirectly, is a prerequisite for successful marketing. At the same time buyers benefit from distribution systems used by firms.

DEFINING MARKETING CHANNELS OF DISTRIBUTION

You see the results of distribution every day. You may have purchased Lay's Potato Chips at the 7-Eleven store, your lunch at McDonald's, and Levi jeans at K Mart. Each of these items was brought to you by a marketing channel of distribution, or simply a **marketing channel,** which consists of individuals and firms involved in the process of making a product or service available for use or consumption by consumers or industrial users.

Marketing channels can be compared to a pipeline through which water flows from a source to terminus. Marketing channels make possible the flow of goods from a producer, through intermediaries, to a buyer. Intermediaries go by various names (Figure 13-1) and perform various functions. Some intermediaries actually purchase items from the seller, store them, and resell them

FIGURE 13-1
Terms used for marketing intermediaries

INTERMEDIARY	MEANING
Middleman	Any intermediary between manufacturer and end-user markets
Agent or broker	Any middleman with legal authority to act on behalf of the manufacturer
Wholesaler	A middleman who sells to other middlemen, usually to retailers; usually applies to consumer markets
Retailer	A middleman who sells to consumers
Distributor	An imprecise term, usually used to describe a middleman who performs a variety of distribution functions, including selling, maintaining inventories, extending credit, and so on; a more common term in industrial markets but may also be used to refer to wholesalers
Dealer	An even more imprecise term that can mean the same as distributor, retailer, wholesaler, and so forth; virtually synonymous with *middleman*

Source: Adapted from Frederick E. Webster, Jr., *Marketing for Managers* (New York: Harper & Row, Publishers, Inc., 1974), p. 191.

to buyers. For example, Sunshine Biscuits produces cookies and sells them to food wholesalers. The wholesalers then sell the cookies to supermarkets and grocery stores, which in turn sell them to consumers. Other intermediaries such as brokers and agents represent sellers but do not actually take title to products. Their role is to bring a seller and buyer together. Century 21 real estate agents are examples of this type of intermediary. The importance of intermediaries is made even clearer when we consider the functions they perform and the benefits they create for buyers.

RATIONALE FOR INTERMEDIARIES

Few consumers appreciate the value of intermediaries; however, producers recognize that intermediaries make selling goods and services more efficient because they minimize the number of sales contacts necessary to reach a target market. Figure 13-2 shows a simple example of how this comes about in the PC industry. Without a retail intermediary (such as ComputerLand), IBM, Apple, Compaq, and AT&T would each have to make four contacts to reach the four buyers shown who are in the target market. However, each producer has to make only one contact when ComputerLand acts as an intermediary. Equally important from a macromarketing perspective, the total number of industry transactions is reduced from 16 to 8, which reduces producer cost and hence benefits the consumer. This simple example also illustrates why computer manufacturers constantly compete with each other to gain display space in computer stores such as ComputerLand and MicroAge.[2]

Functions Performed by Intermediaries Intermediaries make possible the flow of products from producers to buyers by performing three basic functions

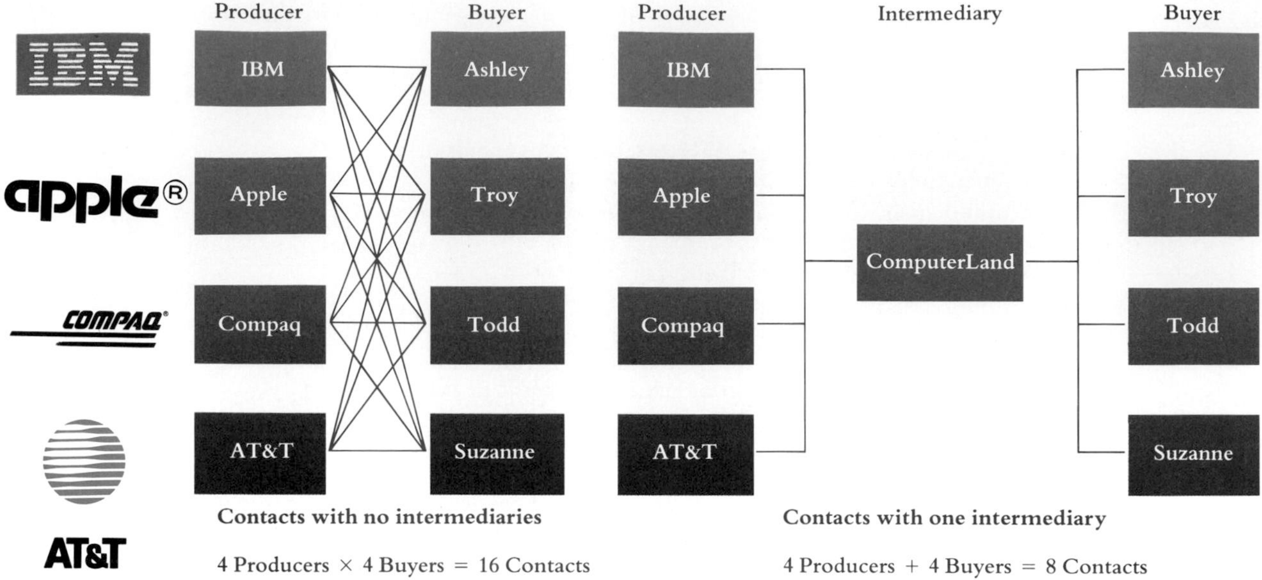

FIGURE 13-2
How intermediaries minimize transactions

(Figure 13-3). Most prominently, intermediaries perform a transactional function that involves buying, selling, and risk taking because they stock merchandise in anticipation of sales. Intermediaries perform a logistical function evident in

FIGURE 13-3
Marketing channel functions performed by intermediaries

TYPE OF FUNCTION	DESCRIPTION
Transactional functions	Buying: purchasing products for resale or as an agent for supply of a product
	Selling: contacting potential customers, promoting products, and soliciting orders
	Risk taking: assuming business risks in the ownership of inventory that can become obsolete or deteriorate
Logistical functions	Assorting: creating product assortments from several sources to serve customers
	Storing: assembling and protecting products at a convenient location to offer better customer service
	Sorting: purchasing in large quantities and breaking into smaller amounts desired by customers
	Transporting: physically moving a product to customers
Facilitating functions	Financing: extending credit to customers
	Grading: inspecting, testing, or judging products and assigning them quality grades
	Marketing information and research: providing information to customers and suppliers, including competitive conditions and trends

Source: Based on Frederick E. Webster, Jr., *Industrial Marketing Strategy* (New York: John Wiley & Sons, Inc., 1979), pp. 162-163.

Marketing intermediaries create utilities for customers

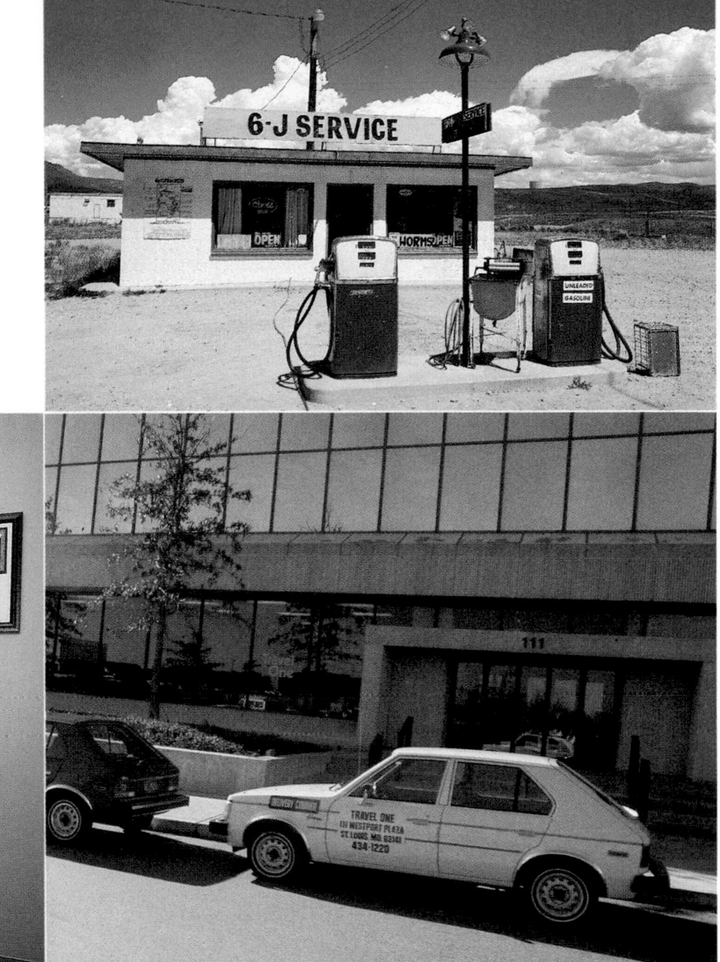

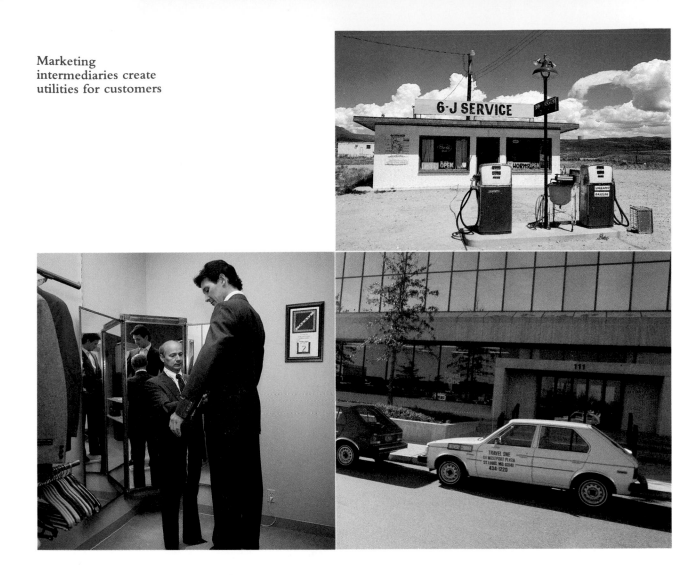

the gathering, storing, and dispersing of products (see Chapter 14, "Physical Distribution"). Finally, intermediaries perform facilitating functions, which assist producers in making goods and services more attractive to buyers.

All three groups of functions must be performed in a marketing channel even though each channel member may not participate in all three. Channel members often negotiate about which specific functions they will perform. Sometimes conflict results, and a breakdown in relationships between channel members occurs. Nevertheless, because all functions must be performed, a producer can eliminate an intermediary but not the functions it performs. So when Porsche AG management considered eliminating its dealers in the United States in the mid-1980's, it developed a plan to identify the transactional, logistical, and facilitating functions that the dealers performed.[3]

Utilities Created by Intermediaries Consumers also benefit from intermediaries. Having the goods and services you want, when you want them, where you want them, and in the form you want them is the ideal result of marketing channels. In more specific terms, marketing channels help create the four utilities described in Chapter 1: time, place, form, and possession. Time utility refers to having a product or service when you want it. For example, Federal Express provides next morning delivery. Place utility means having a product or service available where consumers want it, such as having a Gulf gas station located on a long stretch of lonely highway. Form utility involves enhancing a product or service to make it more appealing to buyers, for example, tailoring services provided by the men's shop in Foley's Department Store in Houston. Possession utility entails efforts by intermediaries to help buyers take possession of a product or service, such as having airline tickets delivered by a travel agency.

CONCEPT CHECK

1 **What is meant by a marketing channel?**

2 **What are the three basic functions performed by intermediaries?**

3 **What utilities are created by intermediaries?**

CHANNEL STRUCTURE AND ORGANIZATION

A product can take many routes on its journey from a producer to buyers, and marketers search for the most efficient route from the many alternatives available.

MARKETING CHANNELS FOR CONSUMER GOODS AND SERVICES

Figure 13-4 shows the four most common marketing channels for consumer goods and services. It also shows the number of levels in each marketing channel, as evidenced by the number of intermediaries between a producer and ultimate buyers. As the number of intermediaries between a producer and buyer increases, the channel is viewed as increasing in length. Thus the producer → wholesaler → retailer → consumer channel is longer than the producer → consumer channel.

Channel *A* represents a **direct channel,** because a producer and ultimate consumers deal directly with each other. Many products and services are distributed this way. Merrill Lynch sells its financial services using a direct channel and branch sales offices. Krastner Chemical, a manufacturer of household cleaning agents in the Southwestern United States, sells its products directly to consumers using door-to-door salespeople. Because there are no intermediaries with a direct channel, the producer must perform all channel functions.

The remaining three channel forms are **indirect channels** because intermediaries are inserted between the producer and consumers and perform numerous channel functions.

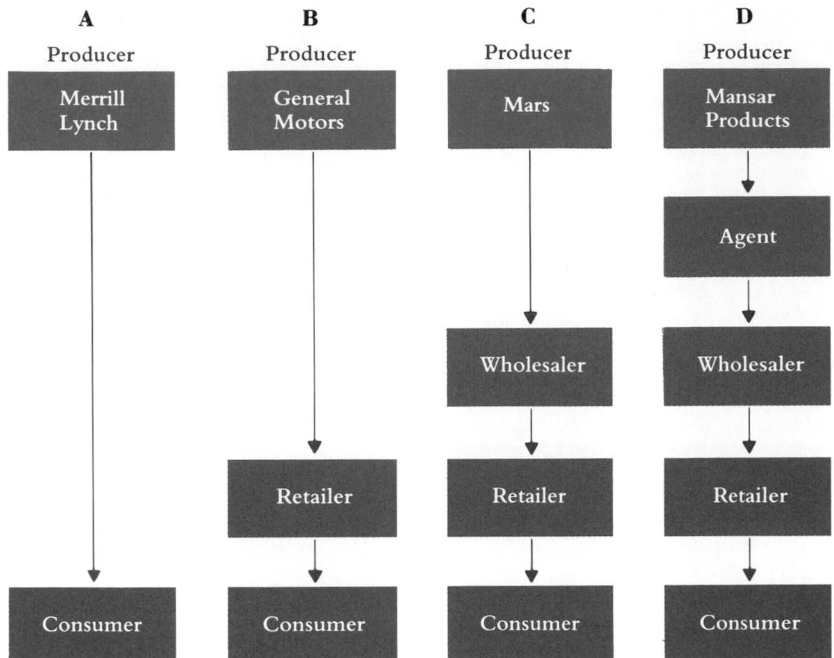

FIGURE 13-4
Common marketing channels for consumer goods and services

Channel *B,* with a retailer added, is most common when a retailer is large and can buy in large quantities from a producer or when the cost of inventory makes it too expensive to use a wholesaler. Manufacturers such as GM, Ford, and Chrysler use this channel, and a local car dealer acts as a retailer. Why is there no wholesaler? So many variations exist in the product that it would be impossible for a wholesaler to stock all the models required to satisfy buyers; in addition, the cost of maintaining an inventory would be too high. However, large retailers such as Sears, 7-Eleven, Safeway, and J.C. Penney buy in sufficient quantities to make it cost effective for a producer to deal with only a retail intermediary.

Adding a wholesaler in Channel *C* is most common for low-cost, low–unit value items that are frequently purchased by consumers such as candy, confectionary items, and magazines. For example, Mars sells its line of candies to wholesalers in case quantities; then they can break down (sort) the cases so that individual retailers can order in boxes or much smaller quantities.

Channel *D,* the most indirect channel, is used when there are many small manufacturers and many small retailers and an agent is used to help coordinate a large supply of the product. Mansar Products, Ltd., is a Belgian producer of specialty jewelry that uses agents to sell to wholesalers in the United States, which sell to many small retailers.

MARKETING CHANNELS FOR INDUSTRIAL GOODS AND SERVICES

The four most common channels for industrial goods and services are shown in Figure 13-5. In contrast with channels for consumer products, industrial

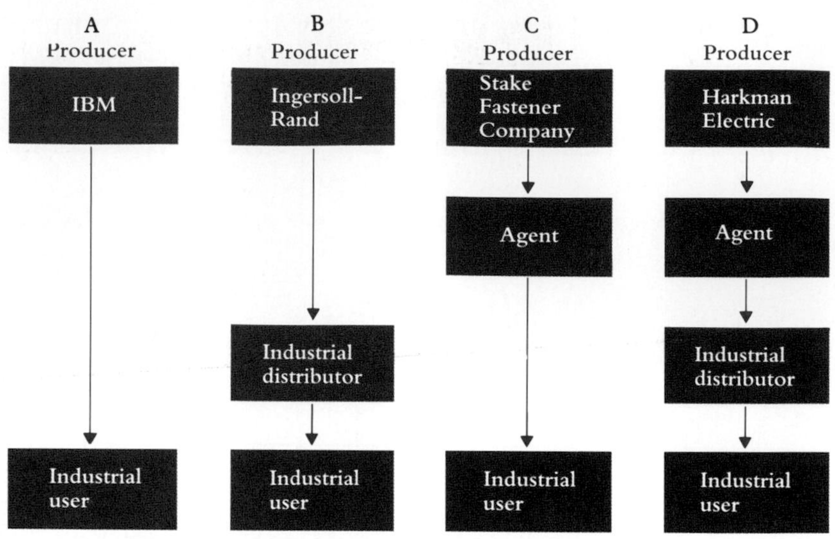

FIGURE 13-5
Common marketing channels for industrial goods and services

channels typically are shorter and rely on one intermediary or none at all because industrial users are fewer in number, tend to be more concentrated geographically, and buy in larger quantities (see Chapter 5).

Channel *A*, represented by IBM's large, main-frame computer business, is a direct channel. Firms using this channel maintain their own sales force and are responsible for all channel functions. This channel arrangement is employed when buyers are large and well defined, the sales effort requires extensive negotiations, and the products are of high unit value and require hands-on expertise in terms of installation or use.[4]

Channels *B, C,* and *D* are indirect channels with one or more intermediaries to reach industrial users. In Channel *B* an **industrial distributor** performs a variety of marketing channel functions, including selling, stocking, and delivering a full product assortment and financing.[5] In many ways industrial distributors are like wholesalers in consumer channels. Ingersoll-Rand, for example, uses industrial distributors to sell its line of pneumatic tools.

Channel *C* introduces a second intermediary, an *agent,* who serves primarily as the independent selling arm of producers and represents a producer to industrial users. For example, Stake Fastener Company, a California-based producer of industrial fasteners, has an agent call on industrial users rather than employing its own sales force.

Channel *D* is the longest channel and includes both agents and distributors. For instance, Harkman Electric, a small Texas-based producer of electric products, uses agents to call on distributors who sell to industrial users.

MULTIPLE CHANNELS

In some situations producers use **dual distribution,** an arrangement whereby a firm reaches different buyers by employing two or more different types of channels for the same basic product.[6] For example, GE sells its large appliances directly to home and apartment builders but uses retail stores to sell to consumers. In some instances, firms use multiple channels when a multibrand strategy is employed (see Chapter 10). Hallmark sells its Hallmark greeting cards through Hallmark stores and select department stores. Its Ambassador brand of cards is sold through discount and drugstore chains. In other instances, a firm will distribute modified products through different channels. Zoecon Corporation sells its insect control chemicals to professional pest control operators such as Orkin and Terminex. A modified compound is sold to the Boyle-Midway Division of American Home Products for use in its Black-Flag Roach Ender brand.

Dual distribution is frequently used to gain broad market coverage quickly—an essential requirement for firms selling fad products. Crowd Caps, which marketed stylish painter caps for students and special promotions, achieved distribution not only through college bookstores, sporting goods stores, and clothing stores, but also by selling to firms such as Pepsi-Cola and Wendy's that used the hats in sales promotions.

These examples illustrate the creative routes to the marketplace available through multiple channels. They also show how firms can reach more buyers (both consumer and industrial) and increase sales volume. However, dual distribution can cause conflict in a marketing channel and may raise legal questions as well, concerns considered later in this chapter.

DIRECT MARKETING CHANNELS

Increasingly, many firms are using direct marketing to reach buyers. **Direct marketing** allows consumers to buy products by interacting with various advertising media without a face-to-face meeting with a salesperson.[7] Direct marketing includes mail-order selling, direct-mail sales, catalog sales, telemarketing, video-text, and televised home shopping (for example, the Home Shopping Network).

Some firms sell products almost entirely through direct marketing. These firms include L.L. Bean (apparel) and Sharper Image (expensive gifts and novelties). Manufacturers such as Nestle and Sunkist, in addition to using traditional channels composed of wholesalers and retailers, employ direct marketing through catalogs and telemarketing to reach more buyers.[8] At the same time, retailers such as Sears and J.C. Penney use direct marketing techniques to augment conventional store merchandising activities. Some experts believe that direct marketing will account for as much as 20 percent of all retail transactions in the United States in the 1990's.[9] Direct marketing is covered in greater depth in Chapter 15.

A CLOSER LOOK AT WHOLESALING INTERMEDIARIES

Channel structures for consumer and industrial products assume various forms based on the number and type of intermediaries. Knowledge of the roles played by these intermediaries is important for understanding how channels operate in practice.

The terms *wholesaler, agent,* and *retailer* have been used in a general fashion consistent with the meanings given in Figure 13-1. However, on closer inspection a variety of specific types of intermediaries emerges. Figure 13-6 shows a common classification of intermediaries that engage in wholesaling activities—those activities involved in selling products and services to those who are buying for the purposes of resale or business use. Intermediaries engaged in retailing activities are discussed in detail in Chapter 15. Figure 13-7 describes the functions performed by major types of independent wholesalers.

Merchant Wholesalers Merchant wholesalers are independently owned firms that take title to the merchandise they handle. They go by various names, including industrial distributor (described earlier). About 80 percent of the firms engaged in wholesaling activities are merchant wholesalers.

Merchant wholesalers are classified as either full-service or limited-service wholesalers, depending on the number of functions performed. Two major types of full-service wholesalers exist. **General merchandise** (or *full-line*) **wholesalers** carry a broad assortment of merchandise and perform all channel functions. This type of wholesaler is most prevalent in the hardware, drug, and clothing industries. However, these wholesalers do not maintain much depth of assortment within specific product lines. **Specialty merchandise** (or *limited-line*) **wholesalers** offer a relatively narrow range of products but have an extensive

FIGURE 13-6
Types of wholesaling intermediaries

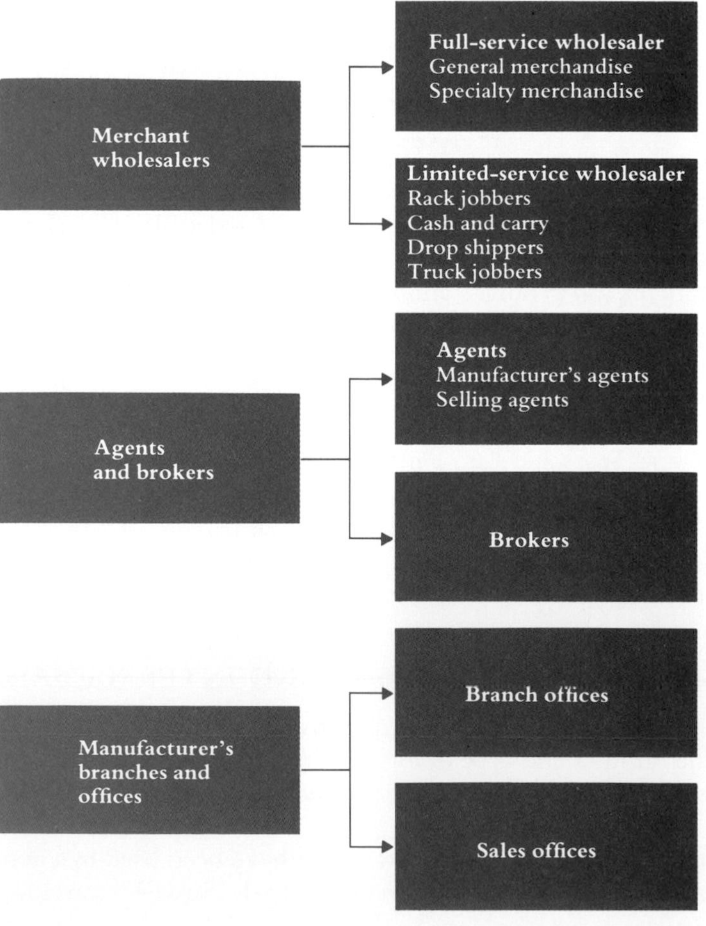

assortment within the product lines carried. They perform all channel functions and are found in the health foods, automotive parts, and seafood industries.

Four major types of limited-service wholesalers exist. **Rack jobbers** furnish the racks or shelves that display merchandise in retail stores, perform all channel functions, and sell on consignment to retailers, which means they retain the title to the products displayed and bill retailers only for the merchandise sold. Familiar products such as hosiery, toys, housewares, and health and beauty aids are sold by rack jobbers. **Cash and carry wholesalers** take title to merchandise but sell only to buyers who call on them, pay cash for merchandise, and furnish their own transportation for merchandise. They carry a limited product assortment and do not make deliveries, extend credit, or supply market information. This wholesaler is common in electric supplies, office supplies, hardware products,

FIGURE 13-7
Functions performed by independent wholesaler types

FUNCTIONS PERFORMED	MERCHANT WHOLESALERS						AGENTS AND BROKERS		
	FULL SERVICE		LIMITED SERVICE						
	GENERAL MERCHANDISE	SPECIALTY MERCHANDISE	RACK JOBBERS	CASH AND CARRY	DROP SHIPPERS	TRUCK JOBBERS	MANUFACTURER'S AGENTS	SELLING AGENTS	BROKERS
TRANSACTIONAL FUNCTIONS									
Buying	●*	●	●	●	●	●	○	○	○
Sales calls on customers	●	●	●	○	●	●	●	●	●
Risk-taking (taking title to products)	●	●	●	●	●	●	○	○	○
LOGISTICAL FUNCTIONS									
Creates product assortments	●	●	●	●	○	●	◒	○	●
Stores products (maintains inventory)	●	●	●	●	○	●	○	○	◒
Sorts products	●	●	●	●	●	●	○	○	○
Transports products	●	●	●	○	○	●	◒	◒	◒
FACILITATING FUNCTIONS									
Provides financing (credit)	●	●	●	○	●	○	○	◒	○
Provides market information and research	●	●	◒	○	◒	○	◒	◒	●
Grading	●	●	◒	○	◒	○	○	◒	●

*Key: ●, Yes; ◒, sometimes; ○, no.

Source: Adapted from Joel R. Evans and Barry Berman, *Marketing,* 2nd ed. (New York: Macmillan Publishing Company, 1987), p. 361; Louis W. Stern and Adel I. El-Ansary, *Marketing Channels,* 2nd ed. (Englewood Cliffs, N.J.: Prentice-Hall, Inc., 1988), pp. 139-143; Bert Rosenblum, *Marketing Channels,* 3rd ed. (Chicago: The Dryden Press, 1987), pp. 44-47.

and groceries. **Drop shippers,** or *desk jobbers,* are wholesalers who own the merchandise they sell but do not physically handle, stock, or deliver it. They simply solicit orders from retailers and other wholesalers and have the merchandise shipped directly from a producer to a buyer. Drop shippers are used for bulky products such as coal, lumber, and chemicals, which are sold in extremely large quantities. **Truck jobbers** are small wholesalers who have a small warehouse from which they stock their trucks for distribution to retailers. They usually handle limited assortments of fast-moving or perishable items that are sold for cash directly from trucks in their original packages. Truck jobbers handle products like bakery items, dairy products, meat, and tobacco.

Agents and Brokers Unlike merchant wholesalers, agents and brokers do not take title to merchandise and typically provide fewer channel functions. They make their profit from commissions or fees paid for their services, whereas merchant wholesalers make their profit from the sale of the merchandise they own.

Manufacturer's agents and selling agents are the two major types of agents used by producers. **Manufacturer's agents,** or *manufacturer's representatives,* work for several producers and carry noncompetitive, complementary merchandise in an exclusive territory.[10] Manufacturer's agents act as a producer's sales arm in a territory and are principally responsible for the transactional channel functions, primarily selling. They are used extensively in the automotive supply, footwear, and fabricated steel industries. However, Swank Jewelry, Japanese computer firms, and Apple have used manufacturer's agents as well. By comparison, **selling agents** represent a single producer and are responsible for the entire marketing function of that producer. They design promotional plans, set prices, determine distribution policies, and make recommendations on product strategy. Selling agents are used by small producers in the textile, apparel, food, and home furnishing industries.

Brokers are independent firms or individuals whose principal function is to bring buyers and sellers together to make sales. Brokers, unlike agents, usually have no continuous relationship with the buyer or seller but negotiate a contract between two parties and then move on to another task. Brokers are used extensively by producers of seasonal products (such as fruits and vegetables) and in the real estate industry.

A unique broker that acts in many ways like a manufacturer's agent is a food broker, representing buyers and sellers in the grocery industry. Food brokers differ from conventional brokers because they act on behalf of producers on a permanent basis and receive a commission for their services. For example, Nabisco uses food brokers to sell its candies, margarine, and Planters peanuts, but it sells its line of cookies and crackers directly to retail stores.[11] Do agents and brokers make a difference in a product's success? The Marketing Action Memo describes how Mr. Coffee used both manufacturer's agents and brokers to become the leader in the electric-drip coffee maker market.

Manufacturer's Branches and Offices Unlike merchant wholesalers, agents and brokers, manufacturer's branches and offices are wholly owned extensions of the producer that perform wholesaling activities. Producers will assume whole-

MARKETING·ACTION·MEMO

MR. COFFEE + AGENTS + BROKERS = SUCCESS

Vincent Marotta hated the way coffee tasted, but he was convinced that its poor taste was not caused by bad coffee but by the machines that brewed it. In 1972 he developed the prototype for what is now known as Mr. Coffee, the first electric-drip coffee maker. By 1988, over 40 million Mr. Coffees had been sold, as well as billions of coffee filters. Was Mr. Coffee's success only a result of a high-quality product that satisfied a need and of effective advertising using Joe DiMaggio as its spokesman? Not quite. Distribution played an integral role.

Mr. Coffee and its filters were sold by manufacturer's agents who called on appliance and department stores. In time, however, it became apparent that Mr. Coffee users found it inconvenient to visit appliance and department stores to buy replacement filters. These customers would benefit by having filters in the stores where they bought their coffee, namely, in the 168,000 retail food outlets throughout the United States. Therefore a national network of food brokers was hired to sell Mr. Coffee filters to supermarkets and grocery stores. The result? It is estimated that about 67 percent of Mr. Coffee's filter sales come from retail food outlets.

Source: Based on an interview with Mr. Tim McGinnity, Vice President, Mr. Coffee, Inc., April 15, 1988; "Can Mr. Coffee's Own Brew Jolt the Java Giants?" *Business Week* (March 4, 1985), pp. 76–77; Nancy Giges, "Grocers 'Middlemen' Step to the Forefront," *Advertising Age* (October 11, 1982), pp. M18, M19ff.

saling functions when there are no intermediaries to perform these activities, customers are few in number and geographically concentrated, or orders are large or require significant attention.[12] Wholesaling activities performed by producers are conducted by means of a branch office or sales office. A *manufacturer's branch office* carries a producer's inventory, performs the functions of a full-service wholesaler, and is an alternative to a merchant wholesaler. A *manufacturer's sales office* does not carry inventory, typically performs only a sales function, and serves as an alternative to agents and brokers.

VERTICAL MARKETING SYSTEMS

The traditional marketing channels described so far represent a loosely knit network of independent producers and intermediaries brought together to distribute goods and services. However, new channel arrangements are emerging

FIGURE 13-8
Types of vertical marketing systems

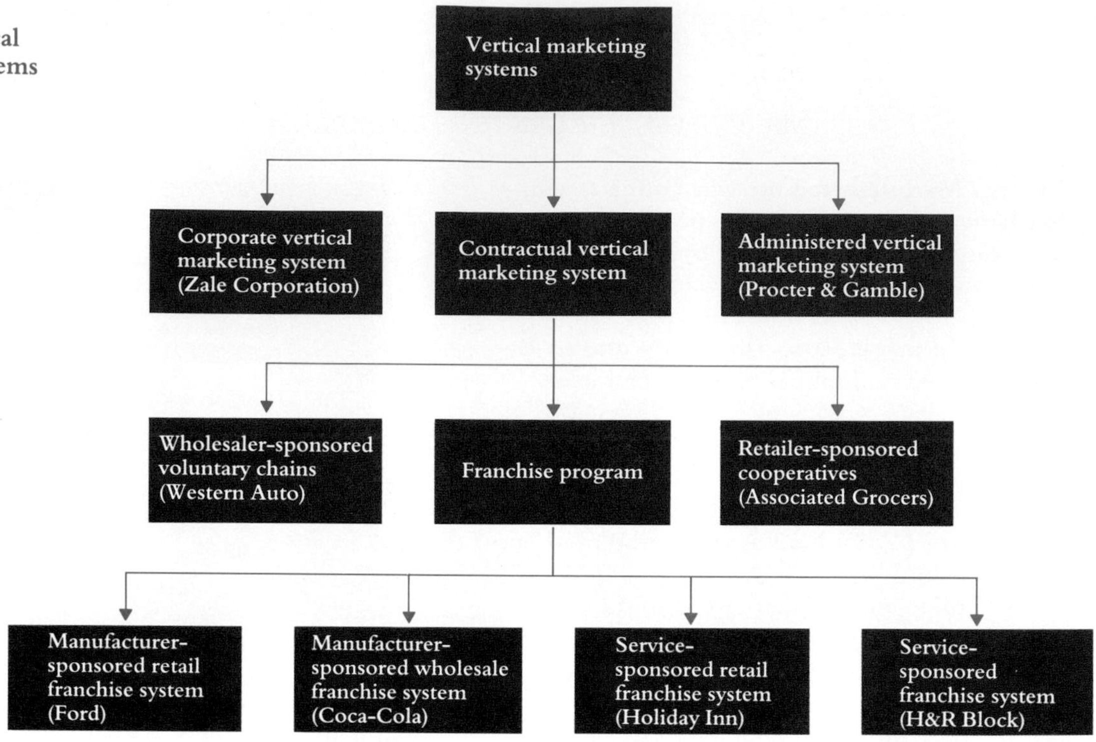

to improve efficiency in performing channel functions and achieving greater marketing impact. For example, **vertical marketing systems** are professionally managed and centrally coordinated marketing channels designed to achieve channel economies and maximum marketing impact.[13] Figure 13-8 depicts the major types of vertical marketing systems: corporate, contractual, and administered.

Corporate Systems The combination of successive stages of production and distribution under a single ownership is a *corporate vertical marketing system*. For example, a producer might own the intermediary at the next level down in the channel. This practice, called *forward integration,* is exemplified by Hart Schaffner & Marx, which manufactures men's clothing and also owns men's retail clothing stores. Other examples of forward integration include Goodyear, Singer, Sherwin Williams, and the building materials division of Boise Cascade. Alternatively, a retailer might own a manufacturing operation, a practice called *backward integration*. For example, Southland Corporation (7-Eleven), the nation's largest convenience store chain, operates its own gasoline refineries (Citgo).

Contractual Systems Under a *contractual vertical marketing system,* independent production and distribution firms integrate their efforts on a contractual basis to obtain greater functional economies and marketing impact than they could achieve alone. Contractual systems are the most popular among the three types of vertical marketing systems and are estimated to account for about 40 percent of all retail sales.

Western Auto is an example of a wholesaler-sponsored voluntary chain

Three variations of contractual systems exist. *Wholesaler-sponsored voluntary chains* involve a wholesaler that develops a contractual relationship with small, independent retailers to standardize and coordinate buying practices, merchandising programs, and inventory management efforts. With the organization of a large number of independent retailers, economies of scale and volume discounts can be achieved to compete with chain stores. Western Auto, IGA, and Ben Franklin stores represent wholesaler-sponsored voluntary chains. *Retailer-sponsored cooperatives* exist when small, independent retailers form an organization that operates a wholesale facility cooperatively. Member retailers then concentrate their buying power through the wholesaler and plan collaborative promotional and pricing activities. Examples of retailer-sponsored cooperatives include Associated Grocers and Certified Grocers.

The most visible variation of contractual systems is **franchising,** a contractual arrangement between a parent company (a franchisor) and an individual or firm (a franchisee) that allows the franchise to operate a certain type of business under an established name and according to specific rules. Franchises generate almost $500 billion in sales through about 576,000 establishments annually in the United States.[14] Four types of franchise arrangements are most popular.[15] Manufacturer-sponsored retail franchise systems are most prominent in the automobile industry, where a manufacturer such as Ford licenses dealers to sell its cars subject to various sales and service conditions. Manufacturer-sponsored wholesale systems are evident in the soft drink industry, where Pepsi-Cola licenses wholesalers (bottlers) who purchase concentrate from Pepsi-Cola and then carbonate, bottle, promote, and distribute its products to supermarkets and restaurants. Service-sponsored retail franchise systems are provided by firms that have designed a unique approach for performing a service and wish to profit by selling the franchise to others. Holiday Inn, Avis, and McDonald's represent

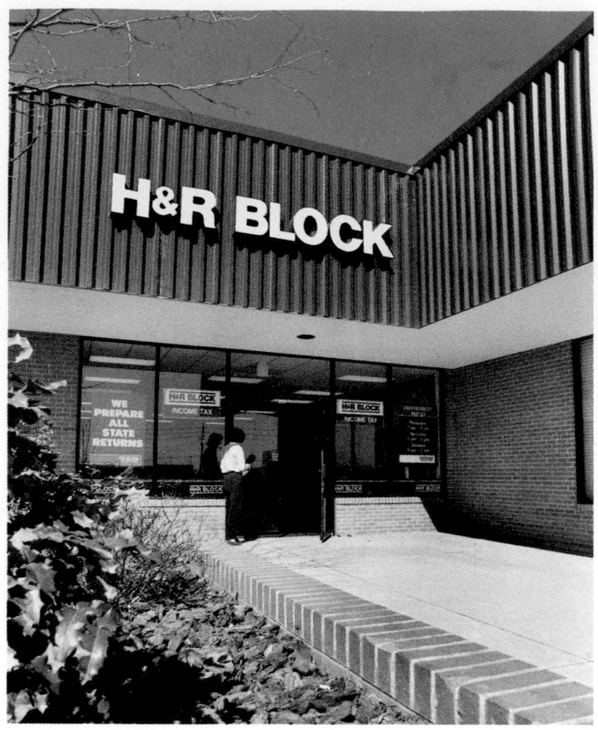

H&R Block represents a successful service franchise system

this franchising approach. Service-sponsored franchise systems exist when franchisors license individuals or firms to dispense a service under a trade name and specific guidelines. Examples include Snelling and Snelling, Inc., employment services, and H&R Block tax services. Franchising is discussed further in Chapter 15.

Administered Systems In comparison, *administered vertical marketing systems* achieve coordination at successive stages of production and distribution by the size and influence of one channel member rather than through ownership. P&G, given its broad product assortment ranging from disposable diapers to detergents, is able to obtain excellent cooperation from supermarkets in displaying, promoting, and pricing its products. Sears gains numerous concessions from manufacturers in terms of product specifications, price levels, and promotional support.

CONCEPT CHECK

1 **What is the difference between a direct and an indirect channel?**

2 **Why are channels for industrial products typically shorter than channels for consumer products?**

3 **What is the principal distinction between a corporate vertical marketing system and an administered vertical marketing system?**

CHANNEL CHOICE AND MANAGEMENT

Marketing channels not only link a producer to its buyers, but also provide the means through which a firm implements various elements of its marketing strategy. For example, when the U.S. division of Perrier decided to broaden the target market for Perrier water, it changed its marketing channel from one that focused solely on gourmet shops to one that also gave it access to supermarkets. Coca-Cola bottlers institute retail advertising and sales plans, which make the Coca-Cola national advertising program more effective.[16] So choosing a marketing channel is a critical decision.

FACTORS AFFECTING CHANNEL CHOICE AND MANAGEMENT

The final choice of a marketing channel by a producer depends on a number of factors that often interact with each other. The Marketing Action Memo illus-

MARKETING·ACTION·MEMO

MARKETING CHANNELS FOR MICROCOMPUTERS INTO THE 21ST CENTURY

The 1990's will witness major changes in marketing channels for microcomputers. Some will be carryover effects from the 1980's.

Apple Computer has pruned its dealer network, and IBM and Sears have closed most of their computer retail stores. Atari has announced plans to distribute some of its products through mass merchandise stores. ComputerLand and BusinessLand, two large chain retailers, are stocking Asian-manufactured computers. New retailing forms have emerged, called *value-added resellers (VARs)*. VARs, which provide already assembled (turnkey) or customized computer systems for special applications in business, have captured market share from computer stores that sell only computers.

Intense competition, a refocus away from consumer to business users, and increased user sophistication and knowledge about microcomputers have revolutionized the choice and management of marketing channels. The dominant channel at each stage of the product life cycle for microcomputers into the 21st century is shown at right. For Atari, the 21st century may be here already: it's experimenting now with selling its microcomputers through some mass merchandisers.

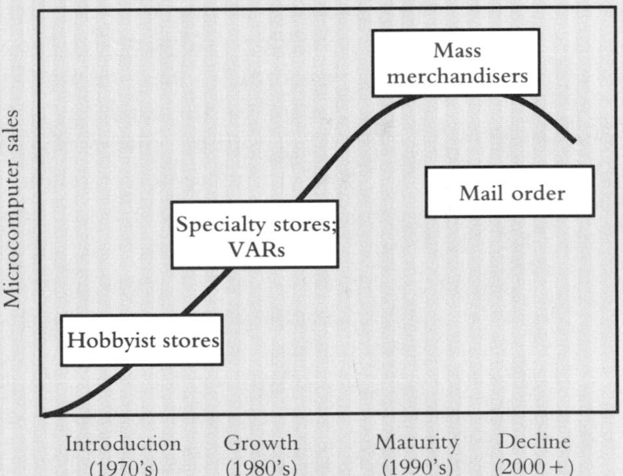

Source: "Computer Retailers: Things Have Gone from Worse to Bad," *Business Week* (June 8, 1987), pp. 104–105; Milind Lele, "Matching Your Channels to Your Product's Life Cycle," *Business Marketing* (December 1986), pp. 61ff; "Atari to Start Selling 520 ST Computer in Mass-Market Stores in Risky Strategy," *Wall Street Journal* (January 3, 1986), p. 2; "Apple Drops Contracts," *Dallas Times Herald* (April 8, 1986), p. 1D.

Technology helped Kroger become the nation's largest flower retailer

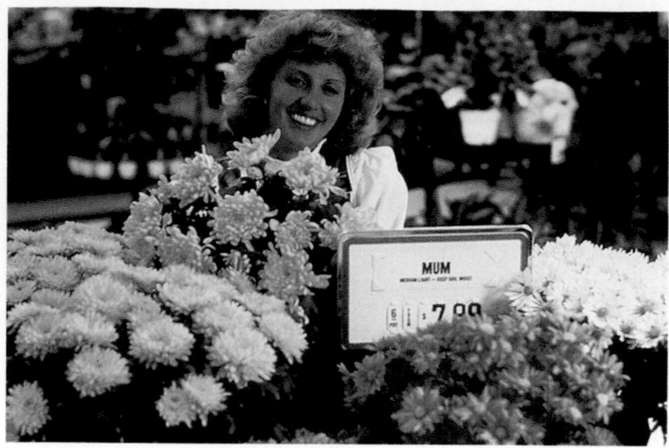

trates how numerous factors combine to alter marketing channels for microcomputers.

Environmental Factors The changing environment described in Chapter 3 has an important effect on the choice and management of a marketing channel. For example, the Fuller Brush Company, which is a name synonymous with door-to-door selling, began using catalogs in 1986 and opened retail stores in some cities in 1987.[17] Rising employment among women resulting in fewer being at home during working hours prompted this action. Deregulation of the financial services industry led Merrill Lynch to reconsider its direct selling effort and examine indirect channels and intermediaries (for example, retail stores such as Sears) for the many investment services it provides.[18] Advances in the technology of growing, transporting, and storing perishable cut flowers has allowed Kroger to eliminate flower wholesalers and buy direct from flower growers around the world. Today, Kroger's annual cut-flower sales exceed $100 million, making it the largest flower retailer in the United States.[19] Technological advances have also made it possible to market microcomputers that require less training for users. This advance has enabled the broadened distribution of these products.

Consumer Factors Consumer characteristics have a direct bearing on the choice and management of a marketing channel. Determining which channel is most appropriate is based on answers to fundamental questions such as: Who are potential customers? Where do they buy? When do they buy? How do they buy? What do they buy? These answers also indicate the type of intermediary best suited to reaching target buyers. For example, Ricoh Company, Ltd., studied the serious (as opposed to recreational) camera user and concluded a change in marketing channels was necessary. The company terminated its contract with a wholesaler who sold to mass merchandise stores and began using manufacturer's agents who sold to photo specialty stores. These stores agreed to stock and display Ricoh's full line and promote it prominently, and sales volume tripled within 18 months.[20] Similarly, increased user sophistication and unique needs have spurred the growth of VARs in the microcomputer marketing channel.

Product Factors In general, highly sophisticated products such as large, scientific computers, unstandardized products such as custom-built machinery, and products of high unit value are distributed directly to buyers. Unsophisticated, standardized products with low unit value such as table salt are typically distributed through indirect channels. A product's stage in the life cycle also affects marketing channels, as shown earlier in the Marketing Action Memo on microcomputers.

Company Factors A firm's financial, human, or technological capabilities affect channel choice. For example, firms that are unable to employ a sales force might use manufacturer's agents or selling agents to reach wholesalers or buyers. If a firm has multiple products for a particular target market, it might use a direct channel, whereas firms with a limited product line might use intermediaries of various types to reach buyers. The role of company factors is evident in the distribution of correctable typewriter ribbons.[21] IBM distributes its ribbons directly through its own sales force, which sells and services IBM office products. However, Burroughs, Frankel, Eaton Allen Corporation, Liquid Paper Corporation, and General Ribbon use indirect channels partially because of more limited resources and a narrower product line. They reach buyers through wholesalers, office supply dealers, and typewriter machine dealers.

Company factors also apply to intermediaries. For example, microcomputer hardware and software producers wishing to reach business users might look to VARs such as Micro Age, which has its own sales force that calls on businesses.

CHANNEL DESIGN CONSIDERATIONS

Recognizing that numerous routes to buyers exist and also recognizing the factors just described, marketing executives typically consider three questions when choosing a marketing channel and intermediaries:

1. Which channel and intermediaries will provide the best coverage of the target market?
2. Which channel and intermediaries will best satisfy the buying requirements of the target market?
3. Which channel and intermediaries will be the most profitable?

Target Market Coverage Achieving the best coverage of the target market requires attention to the density and type of intermediaries to be used at the retail level of distribution. Three degrees of distribution density exist: intensive, exclusive, and selective. **Intensive distribution** means that a firm tries to place its products or services in as many outlets as possible. Intensive distribution is usually chosen for convenience products or services; for example, chewing gum, automatic teller machines, and cigarettes. Increasingly, medical services are distributed in this fashion.

Exclusive distribution is the extreme opposite of intensive distribution because only one retail outlet in a specified geographical area carries the firm's product. Exclusive distribution is typically chosen for specialty products or

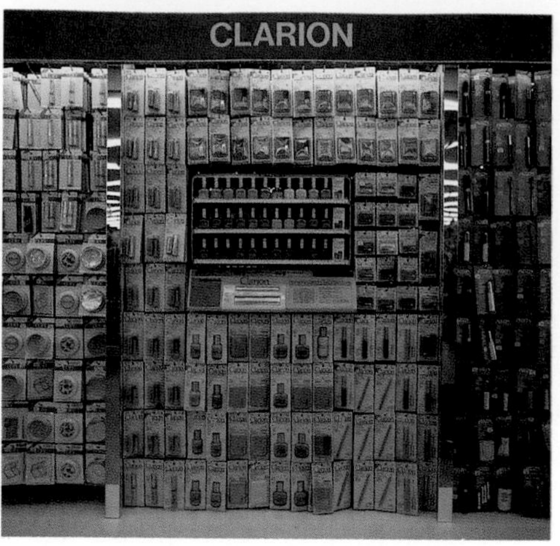

Clarion cosmetics display gives color information at the point of sale

services; for example, automobiles, some women's fragrances, men's suits, and yachts.

Selective distribution lies between these two extremes and means that a firm selects a few retail outlets in a specific area to carry its products. This is the most common form of distribution intensity and is usually associated with shopping goods or services such as Rolex watches, Ben Hogan golf clubs, and Henredon furniture.

The type or availability of a retail outlet will also influence whether a target market is reached. For example, Ford, GM, Toyota, Nissan, and Honda have recently established new dealers for their new European line of expensive cars to reach the young professional market, as described in the beginning of the chapter. The L'eggs division of the Hanes Corporation now distributes fashionable white pantyhose to nurses through catalogs because supermarkets and department stores do not typically carry these items.[22]

Satisfying Buyer Requirements A second consideration in channel design is gaining access to channels and intermediaries that satisfy at least some of the interests buyers might want fulfilled when they purchase a firm's products or services. These interests fall into four categories: (1) information, (2) convenience, (3) variety, and (4) attendant services.[23]

Information is an important requirement when buyers have limited knowledge or desire specific data about a product or service. Properly chosen intermediaries communicate with buyers through in-store displays, demonstrations, and personal selling. Computer stores have grown in popularity as a source for small computers because they provide such information. The decision by Ford to develop new dealerships for its Merkur model car was also based on this requirement. For example, new Ford dealers have been given "the most comprehensive training possible in terms of the mindset of the European [car] buyer and can talk knowledgeably in the jargon of the genre."[24]

Convenience has multiple meanings for buyers, such as proximity or driving time to a retail outlet. For example, 7-Eleven stores with 7,500 outlets nationwide satisfy this interest for buyers, and candy, tobacco, and snack food firms benefit by gaining display space in these stores. For other consumers, convenience means a minimum of time and hassle associated with shopping. Buying through catalogs is a way to reduce shopping time, and firms such as Sears, 3M, Hanes, and J.C. Penney have expanded their catalog operations accordingly.

Variety reflects buyers' interest in having numerous competing and complementary items from which to choose. Variety is evident in both the breadth and depth of products and brands carried by intermediaries, which enhances their attraction to buyers. Thus a manufacturer of men's ties would seek distribution through stores that offer a full line of men's clothing.

Attendant services provided by intermediaries are an important buying requirement for products such as appliances that require delivery, installation, and credit. Therefore Whirlpool seeks dealers that provide such services.

Profitability The third consideration in designing a channel is profitability, which is determined by the margins earned (revenues minus cost) for each channel member and for the channel as a whole. Channel cost is the critical dimension of profitability. These costs include distribution, advertising, and selling expenses associated with different types of marketing channels. The extent to which channel members share these costs determines the margins received by each member and by the channel as a whole.

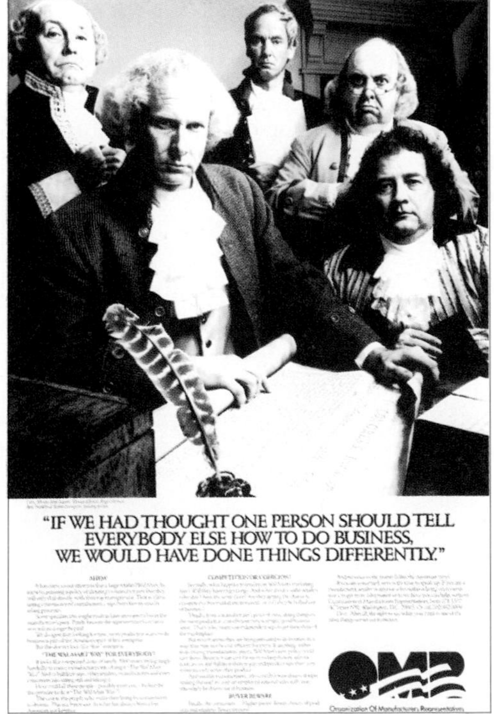

For the relation between these "Founding Fathers" of the United States and independent manufacturers' representatives, see the text

CHANNEL RELATIONSHIPS: CONFLICT, COOPERATION, AND LAW

Unfortunately, because channels consist of independent individuals and firms, there is always potential for disagreements concerning who performs which channel functions, how profits are allocated, which products and services will be provided by whom, and who makes critical channel-related decisions. These channel conflicts necessitate measures for dealing with them. Sometimes they result in legal action.

Conflict in Marketing Channels Channel conflict arises when one channel member believes another channel member is engaged in behavior that prevents it from achieving its goals.[25] Two types of conflict occur in marketing channels: vertical conflict and horizontal conflict.

Vertical conflict occurs between different levels in a marketing channel; for example, between a manufacturer and a wholesaler or retailer or between a wholesaler and a retailer. Three sources of vertical conflict are most common.[26] First, conflict arises when a channel member bypasses another member and sells or buys products direct. This conflict emerged when Wal-Mart elected to purchase products direct from manufacturers rather than through manufacturers' agents as described in the Marketing Action Memo. Second, disagreements over how profit margins are distributed among channel members produce conflict.

MARKETING·ACTION·MEMO

WAL-MART STORES' "DITCH THE REP" POLICY MEANS WAR!

What do Thomas Jefferson and Benjamin Franklin have to do with marketing channels? Just ask the Organization of Manufacturers Representatives (OMR). According to OMR, these founding fathers symbolize free enterprise. People dressed like them picketed Wal-Mart Stores on July 3, 1987, to protest the company's practice of dealing with manufacturers directly instead of buying products through independent manufacturers' representatives, or "reps." This action followed a full-page ad in the *Wall Street Journal* describing OMR's complaint (see previous page).

OMR is concerned that if Wal-Mart stops dealing with reps, then other large retailers like Target, Sears, and J.C. Penney and then mid-size retailers will do likewise. An OMR spokesperson noted, "The functions a rep performs would have to be performed by somebody. A lot of those functions would have to be performed by the retailers themselves. Those that aren't would have to be performed by manufacturers." The final result, according to OMR, is that expenses to retailers and consumers would increase. Moreover, manufacturers' reps would lose business, and according to Joseph B. Mittelman, chairman of OMR, "We're standing up and fighting."

Source: "Sales Representatives' Group to Stage Protest at Wal-Mart," *Dallas Times Herald* (July 2, 1987), p. C2; "Independent Sales Reps Launch Wal-Mart Fight," *Dallas Morning News* (January 4, 1987), p. 5Hff; "Wal-Mart Faces a Fight Over Purchasing Policy," *Wall Street Journal* (December 11, 1986); Telephone interview with George W. Brown, OMR Executive Director, July 10, 1987.

A third conflict situation arises when manufacturers believe wholesalers or retailers are not giving their products adequate attention. For example, H.J. Heinz Company found itself in a conflict situation with its supermarkets in Great Britain when supermarkets promoted and displayed private brands at the expense of Heinz brands.[27]

Horizontal conflict occurs between intermediaries at the same level in a marketing channel, such as between two or more retailers (Target and K Mart) or two or more wholesalers that handle the same manufacturer's brands. Two sources of horizontal conflict are most common. First, horizontal conflict arises when a manufacturer increases its distribution coverage in a geographical area. For example, a franchised Cadillac dealer in Chicago might complain to GM that another franchised Cadillac dealer has located too close to its dealership. Second, dual distribution causes conflict when different types of retailers carry the same brands. For instance, Revlon's Charlie perfume can be found in drugstores, department stores, and discount stores, which may lead to complaints by any one of the retailers.

Securing Cooperation in Marketing Channels Conflict can have destructive effects on the workings of a marketing channel, so it is necessary to secure cooperation among channel members. One means is through a **channel captain**, a channel member that coordinates, directs, and supports other channel members.[28] Channel captains can be producers, wholesalers, or retailers. P&G assumes this role because it has a strong consumer following in brands such as Crest, Tide, and Pampers. Therefore it can set policies or terms that supermarkets will follow. McKesson-Robbins, a drug wholesaler, is a channel captain because it coordinates and supports the product flow from numerous small drug manufacturers to more than 20,000 drugstores and nearly 6,000 hospitals nationwide. Sears and K Mart are retail channel captains because of their strong consumer image, number of outlets, and purchasing volume.

A firm becomes a channel captain because it is typically the channel member with the greatest power to influence the behavior of other members.[29] Power can take four forms. First, economic power arises from the ability of a firm to reward or influence other members given its strong financial position or customer franchise. IBM and Sears have such economic power. Expertise is a second source of power over other channel members. For example, American Hospital Supply helps its customers (hospitals) manage inventory and streamline order processing for hundreds of medical supplies. Third, identification with a particular channel member may also create power for that channel member. For instance, retailers may compete to carry the Ralph Lauren line, or clothing manufacturers may compete to be carried by Neiman-Marcus or Bloomingdale's. In both instances the desire to be associated with a channel member gives that firm power over others. Finally, power can arise from the legitimate right of one channel member to dictate the behavior of other members. This situation would occur under contractual vertical marketing systems where a franchisor could legitimately direct how a franchisee behaves. Other means for securing cooperation in marketing channels rest in the different variations of vertical marketing systems.

Legal Considerations Conflict in marketing channels is typically resolved through negotiation or the exercise of power by channel members. Sometimes conflict produces legal action. Therefore knowledge of legal restrictions affecting channel strategies and practices is important. Some restrictions were described in Chapter 12, namely vertical price-fixing and price discrimination. However, other legal considerations unique to marketing channels warrant attention.[30]

In general, suppliers can select whomever they want as channel intermediaries and may refuse to deal with whomever they choose. This right was established in the case of the *United States vs. Colgate and Company* in 1919. However, the Federal Trade Commission and the Justice Department monitor channel practices that restrain competition, create monopolies, or otherwise represent unfair methods of competition under the Sherman Act (1890) and Clayton Act (1914). Six practices have received the most attention (Figure 13-9).

Dual distribution, although not illegal, can be viewed as anticompetitive in some situations. The most common situation arises when a manufacturer distributes through its own vertically integrated channel in competition with independent wholesalers and retailers that also sell its products. If the manufacturer's behavior is viewed as an attempt to lessen competition by eliminating wholesalers or retailers, then such action would violate both the Sherman and Clayton Acts.

Vertical integration is viewed in a similar light. Although not illegal, this practice is sometimes subject to legal action under the Clayton Act if it has the potential to lessen competition or foster monopoly.

The Clayton Act specifically prohibits exclusive dealing and tying arrangements when they lessen competition or create monopolies. *Exclusive dealing* exists when a supplier requires channel members to sell only its products or restricts distributors from selling directly competitive products. *Tying arrangements* occur when a supplier requires a distributor purchasing some products to buy others from the supplier. These arrangements often arise in franchising. They are illegal if the tied products could be purchased at fair market values from other suppliers at desired quality standards of the franchiser. Full-line forcing is a special kind of tying arrangement. This practice involves a supplier requiring that a channel

FIGURE 13-9
Channel strategies and practices affected by legal restrictions

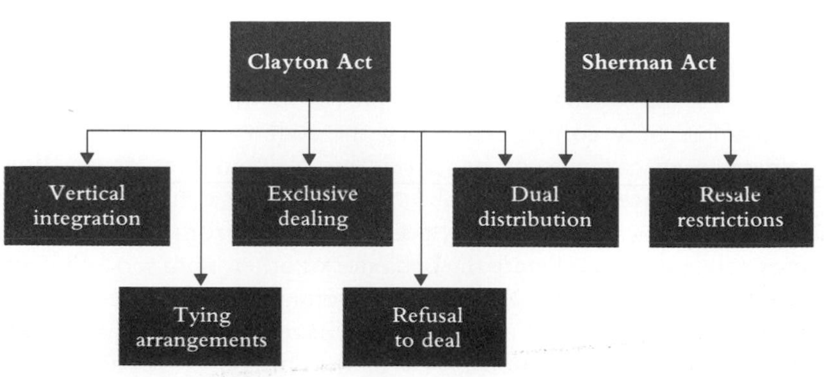

member carry its full line of products to sell a specific item in the supplier's line.

Even though a supplier has a legal right to choose intermediaries to carry and represent its products, a *refusal to deal* with existing channel members may be illegal under the Clayton Act. For example, an attempt to coerce an intermediary to perform in a certain way by refusing to deal with that firm would be illegal.

Resale restrictions refer to a supplier's attempt to stipulate to whom distributors may resell the supplier's products and in what specific geographical areas or territories they may be sold. These practices have been prosecuted under the Sherman Act. Today, however, the courts apply the "rule of reason" in such cases and consider whether such restrictions have a "demonstrable economic effect."

CONCEPT CHECK

1 **What are the three degrees of distribution density?**

2 **What are the three questions marketing executives consider when choosing a marketing channel and intermediaries?**

3 **What is meant by "exclusive dealing?"**

SUMMARY

1 A marketing channel consists of individuals and firms involved in the process of making a product or service available for use by consumers or industrial users.
2 Intermediaries make possible the flow of products and services from producers to buyers by performing transactional, logistical, and facilitating functions. At the same time, intermediaries create time, place, form, and possession utility for consumers.
3 Channel structure describes the route taken by products and services from producers to buyers. Direct channels represent the shortest route because producers interact directly with buyers. Indirect channels include intermediaries between producers and buyers.
4 In general, marketing channels for consumer products and services contain more intermediaries than do channels for industrial products and services. In some situations, producers use multiple channels for reaching buyers, a practice called *dual distribution*.
5 Numerous types of wholesalers can exist within a marketing channel. The principal distinction between the various types of wholesalers lies in whether they take title to the items they sell and the channel functions they perform.

6 Vertical marketing systems are professionally managed and centrally coordinated marketing channels designed to achieve channel function economies and marketing impact. A vertical marketing system may be one of three types: corporate, administered, or contractual.
7 Marketing managers consider environmental, consumer, product, and company factors when choosing and managing marketing channels.
8 Channel design considerations are based on the target market coverage sought by producers, the buyer requirements to be satisfied, and the profitability of the channel. Target market coverage comes about through one of three levels of distribution density: intensive, exclusive, and selective distribution. Buyer requirements are evident in the amount of information, convenience, variety, and service sought by consumers. Profitability relates to the margins obtained by each channel member and the channel as a whole.
9 Conflicts in marketing channels are inevitable. Vertical conflict occurs between different levels in a channel. Horizontal conflict occurs between intermediaries at the same level in the channel.
10 Legal issues in the management of marketing channels typically arise from six practices: dual distribution, vertical integration, exclusive dealing, tying arrangements, refusal to deal, and resale restrictions.

KEY TERMS AND CONCEPTS

marketing channel p. 350
direct channel p. 354
indirect channels p. 354
industrial distributor p. 356
dual distribution p. 356
direct marketing p. 357
general merchandise wholesalers p. 358
specialty merchandise wholesalers p. 358
rack jobbers p. 359
cash and carry wholesalers p. 359
drop shippers p. 360
truck jobbers p. 360
manufacturer's agents p. 360
selling agents p. 360
brokers p. 360
vertical marketing sytems p. 362
franchising p. 363
intensive distribution p. 367
exclusive distribution p. 367
selective distribution p. 368
channel captain p. 371

CHAPTER PROBLEMS AND APPLICATIONS

1 In what ways do marketing channels play an instrumental role in implementing a producer's marketing strategy?
2 A distributor for Celanese Chemical Company stores large quantities of chemicals, blends these chemicals to satisfy requests of customers, and delivers the blends to a customer's warehouse within 24 hours of receiving an order. What utilities does this distributor provide?

3 Suppose the president of a carpet manufacturing firm has asked you to look into the possibility of bypassing the firm's wholesalers (who sell to carpet, department, and furniture stores) and selling directly to these stores. What caution would you voice on this matter, and what type of information would you gather before making this decision?
4 What type of channel conflict is likely to be caused by dual distribution, and what type of conflict can be reduced by direct distribution? Why?
5 Suppose a Swedish-based manufacturer of home entertainment equipment such as stereos and VCRs is interested in designing a marketing channel in the United States to sell these products. What advice would you give the company? Be specific.
6 How does the channel captain idea differ between corporate, administered, and contractual vertical marketing systems with particular reference to the use of the different forms of power available to firms?
7 Suppose 10 firms in an industry wished to reach 10,000 potential customers by selling directly to them. How many sales contacts would be required in this industry if each firm called on each customer? How many sales contacts would be required if an intermediary were placed between the firms and potential customers?
8 Comment on this statement: "The only distinction between merchant wholesalers and agents and brokers is that merchant wholesalers take title to the products they sell."
9 How do specialty, shopping, and convenience goods generally relate to intensive, selective, and exclusive distribution? Give a brand name that is an example of each goods-distribution matchup.
10 Look at the chapter opening example on pp. 349-350. Do you think the new dealer networks developed by Ford, GM, Nissan, and Honda will be successful? Why or why not?

SUGGESTED READINGS

Kate Bertrand, "Changing Channels in the Microcomputer Market," *Business Marketing* (September 1986), pp. 89-94. *This article describes past, present, and future changes in microcomputer marketing channels.*

James A. Narus and James C. Anderson, "Turn Your Industrial Distributors Into Partners," *Harvard Business Review* (March-April 1986), pp. 66-71. *This article describes how firms can better understand distributor needs and build and manage working relationships.*

John A. Quelch, "Why Not Exploit Dual Marketing?" *Business Horizons* (January-February 1987), pp. 52-60. *This article describes the benefits, challenges, and approaches for dual distribution.*

Louis W. Stern and Adel I. El-Ansary, *Marketing Channels,* 3rd ed. (Englewood Cliffs, N.J.: Prentice-Hall, Inc., 1988). *This book provides an encyclopedic treatment of theory and practice in marketing channels.*

Louis W. Stern and Frederick D. Sturdivant, "Customer-driven Distribution Systems," *Harvard Business Review* (July-August 1987), pp. 34-35ff. *This article describes an eight-step process for selecting and structuring marketing channels.*

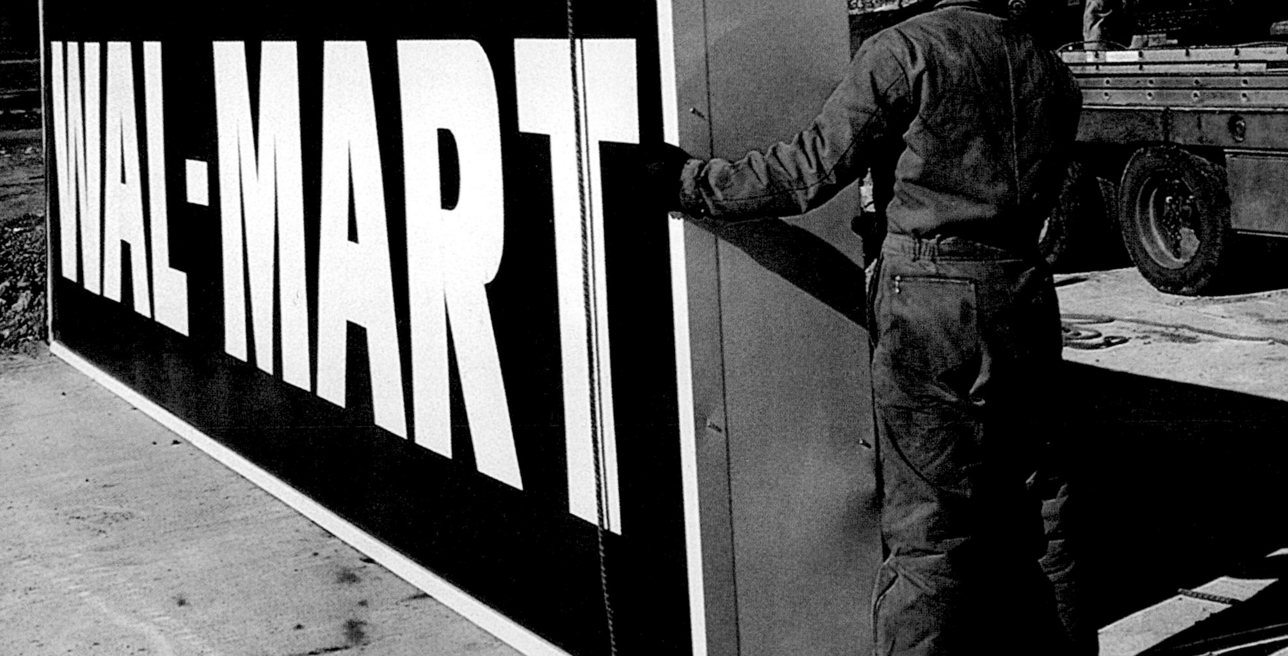
DISCOUNT CITY
WE SELL FOR LESS
Guaranteed Quality at Discount Prices
WAL-MART

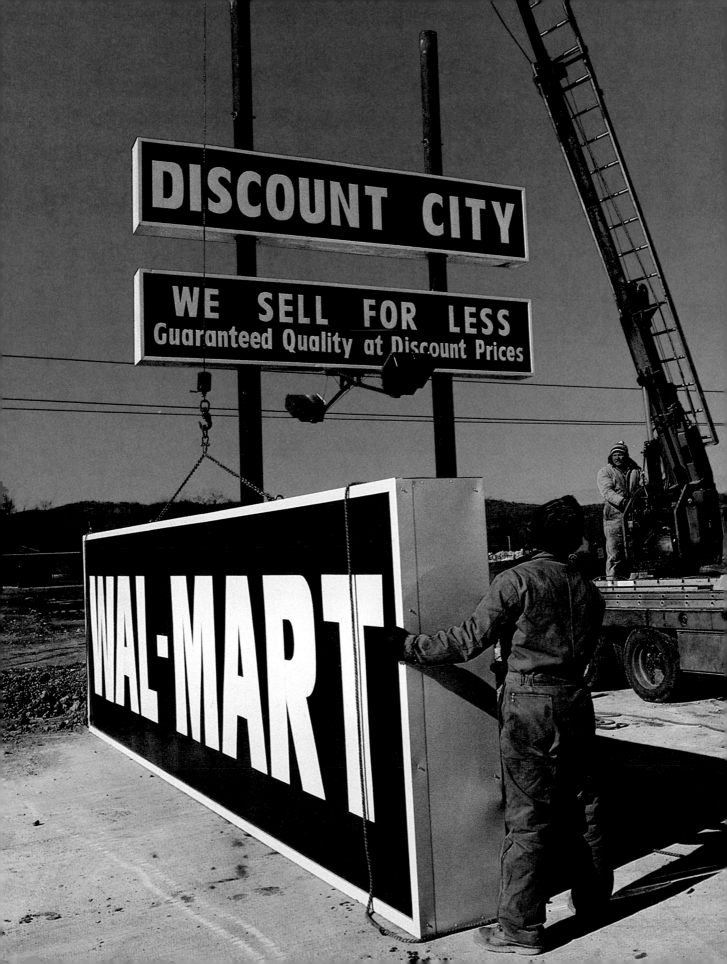

14

Physical Distribution and Logistics

After reading this chapter you should be able to:

Explain what physical distribution and business logistics are and how they relate to the marketing mix.

•

Recognize the growing importance of customer service in successful marketing.

•

Explain how costs are balanced with customer service factors to reach a logistics decision.

•

Describe the various transportation and warehousing options available to logistics managers.

•

Understand the various reasons for holding inventory and newer philosophies that are intended to reduce inventory costs.

Distribution: Often the Key to a Satisfied Customer

After procrastinating through a long winter, you've finally decided to strip and refinish your dining room table. In the spring you see a television ad demonstrating Black & Decker's Heat and Strip paint stripper and you read a newspaper ad telling you it's on sale at your local Wal-Mart store. You set off for the store.

At the Wal-Mart store you find the Heat and Strip paint stripper in stock, pay for it at the checkout counter, and happily go home, ready to tackle your dining room table. This is the way the distribution system is supposed to work, and it results in a happy customer. In fact, as discussed later in the chapter, Wal-Mart's efficient warehouse distribution contributes mightily to its success and is the envy of many competing discounters.

But what happens if you go to a competing store instead of Wal-Mart and discover that the Heat and Strip isn't in stock? Although you're offered a "rain check" for a later purchase when more stock arrives, this doesn't solve your immediate need for an efficient paint stripper.

Was this a deliberately misleading promotion by the chain? Probably not. More likely the problem was poor planning by the chain in stocking enough inventory to satisfy consumer demand. Or maybe a truck broke down or the inventory got misplaced in a warehouse so the paint stripper didn't arrive on the retail shelves in time for the sale. Regardless of the cause, very expensive advertising efforts by both the manufacturer and retailer were largely wasted.

The paint stripper that isn't in the right place at the right time for sale to consumers who have already decided to buy it illustrates the critical nature of the movement and storage of products in a firm's marketing program. The best-laid product and promotional strategies of a firm may be hurt or destroyed by poor physical distribution of the products it wishes to sell. This chapter examines the physical distribution process that moves products from the producer to buyer and how a firm tries to balance distribution costs against the need for effective customer service. It also presents an overview of the tools that are used in the movement and storage system.

MEANING AND SCOPE OF PHYSICAL DISTRIBUTION AND LOGISTICS

Physical distribution is the part of marketing that addresses how products are moved and stored. A physical distribution channel includes intermediaries often not considered to be part of the marketing channel described in Chapter 13, such as transportation companies, public warehouses, and insurance companies that participate in the movement and storage of products. These agents, who do not take title to (actually own) the goods they handle, are referred to as *facilitators* because their main function is to facilitate the movement of goods.

INCREASING IMPORTANCE OF PHYSICAL DISTRIBUTION

Today American business firms are placing more importance on their physical distribution systems. Several factors account for this trend. Soaring fuel prices into the 1980's meant it cost far more to move products than previously. Also, cost experts turned their attention to physical distribution because many of the quick savings had been obtained from production efficiencies. Because retail inventory philosophy changed so that retailers stocked less and wholesalers and manufacturers stocked more, and manufacturers' product lines proliferated to reach new segments, the demands for an efficient physical distribution system increased. Finally, improved computer technology permitted more sophisticated tracking of the thousands of items manufacturers produce and send through their distribution channels.[1]

A logistical component—moving products

TWO VIEWS OF PHYSICAL DISTRIBUTION

Marketing managers have different views on what physical distribution really is. Some see physical distribution only as the flow of finished goods to the consumer, whereas others see it as including activities that occur earlier in the process, such as procuring and moving raw materials.

A traditional marketing view of physical distribution looks at only the outbound considerations and ignores the physical supply and processing or manufacturing activities. This view, typically referred to as **physical distribution management,** or simply distribution management, fails to consider activities such as inventory policies and forecasting that often have a great impact on the success of the marketing program. Marketers justify this narrow view of physical movements by concentrating on activities that they might control while leaving the earlier movement and storage activities involving materials supply to the manufacturing, traffic, or purchasing departments that often control them. However, because marketers are often responsible for forecasting future demand, they may be able to influence inventory policy to help avoid out-of-stock problems. So it is important to consider the broader view of this concept.

A more comprehensive term for all these physical movement and storage activities is **business logistics,** which involves the coordination of movements of raw materials, parts, and finished goods to achieve a given service level while minimizing total costs.[2] This concept contains four elements and includes *both* physical supply and physical distribution, that is, both inbound and outbound activities. On a practical level, there is no consistent use of physical distribution terms generally, and many people use them loosely. The term *business logistics,*

FIGURE 14-1
Relation of physical distribution and logistics to a firm's operations

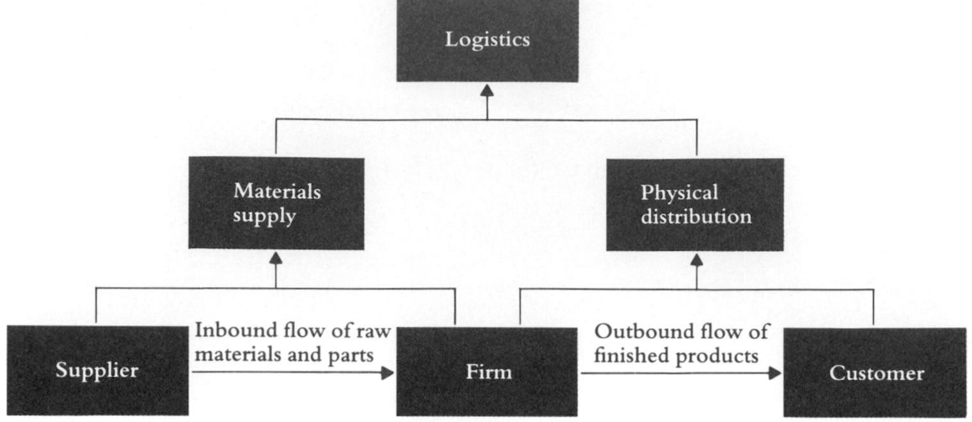

or logistics, is used in this chapter. Figure 14-1 shows the relation of physical distribution and logistics to the operations of a firm.

Another issue is the scope of the activities that fall within a logistics system. Most basic systems would include transportation, warehousing, and materials handling. The most advanced system would also include order processing, inventory management, and packaging. The range of logistics activities within a particular business firm lies somewhere on a scale between the basic and advanced systems.

HOW MOVEMENT AND STORAGE ACTIVITIES VARY AMONG FIRMS

The importance of these movement and storage activities varies greatly among firms, but the U.S. average for these costs is in excess of 20 percent of sales.[3] For firms that don't physically move or store many items, the costs will be negligible. For example, insurance companies and banks deal mainly with distributing paperwork, and most of their inbound materials are supplies.

At the other end of the spectrum are firms that produce many products from diverse raw materials and distribute them to wide geographic markets. Large consumer food companies like Lever Brothers or Quaker Oats have many manufacturing or processing plants dedicated exclusively to particular products. Each plant must receive raw materials, produce the product, and ship it to a warehouse before sale in decentralized markets. These geographic consumption points for consumer food items are spatially separated—essentially anywhere the firm wishes to compete. In considering the logistical problems for Procter & Gamble competing in the national market, the problems become apparent. It may produce more than 80 brands, all needing different raw materials, that are nationally distributed; the system has to move all the raw materials to the manufacturing plants and then all the finished products (brands) to the marketplace.

Most firms lie between these extreme examples. The importance of logistics to a firm can be placed on a scale from very low to very high, generally based

Product perishability makes logistics very important to the food industry

on these key factors that reflect the amount of movement and storage needed for the system to function:

- Number of final products and the raw materials needed to produce them
- Number of material supply points
- Number of material processing points
- Number of product consumption points
- Inbound/outbound relationships

A firm that doesn't manufacture anything has fewer logistical concerns, and producers of tangible goods usually have more complex systems than those of service providers. Some service firms may have extensive logistics systems, but they are usually dominated by inbound (or supply) considerations. Retailing is a type of business focusing on the inbound side, whereas mining and timber production concentrate on the outbound side. Figure 14-2 shows the percentage of sales accounted for by logistical costs for several U.S. industries. The figure shows that the average logistical costs for companies in all industries is 8 cents on each dollar of sales. Figure 14-3 shows that transportation is the largest component and takes 3.3 cents of each dollar of sales.

RELATION TO MARKETING STRATEGY

Bernard LaLonde, a prominent distribution expert, has remarked, "American management's philosophy has been: 'If you're smart enough to make it, aggressive enough to sell it—then any dummy can get it there!' Now we're paying for [that philosophy]."[4]

FIGURE 14-2
Variations in logistical (distribution) costs by industry, 1987

INDUSTRY	AS A PERCENT OF SALES
All consumer nondurable	7.0%
• Soap	8.4
• Dry and packaged food	6.3
• Canned and processed food	9.6
• Nonfood groceries	6.8
All consumer durable	8.7
All industrial nondurable	9.9
• Plastics	10.4
• Chemicals	7.9
• Hospital supplies	13.1
All industrial durable	8.3
All retailing	7.4
All companies	8.0

Source: Herbert W. Davis, "Physical Distribution Costs: Performance in Selected Industries, 1987," in *Proceedings of the Council of Logistics Management* (1987), pp. 371-379.

What this means is that the best-laid marketing strategies can fail if the logistics system doesn't support them; a product cannot be purchased if it is not on the shelf when the consumer attempts to buy it. Suppose Procter & Gamble attempts to boost trial for its Crest toothpaste with tartar control using a massive coupon campaign. If consumers attempting to redeem the coupons found the product was out of stock because of a lack of field inventory, it is doubtful that they would save the coupons and try to redeem them later. If they did, trial would still have been delayed, along with the real key to the new product success: repeat buys. So a good product, attractively priced and effectively promoted, could be destroyed through poor logistics.

Product Factors Some of the logistical factors affecting product decisions are physical product characteristics, packaging, and product differentiation. Physical product characteristics with implications for the movement and storage of the product include the weight/bulk relationship, the weight/value relationship,

FIGURE 14-3
Breakdown of the 8 cents of each sales dollar used for logistical (distribution) activities

Source: Herbert W. Davies, "Physical Distribution Costs: Performance in Selected Industries, 1987," in *Proceedings of the Council of Logistics Management,* 1987, pp. 371-379.

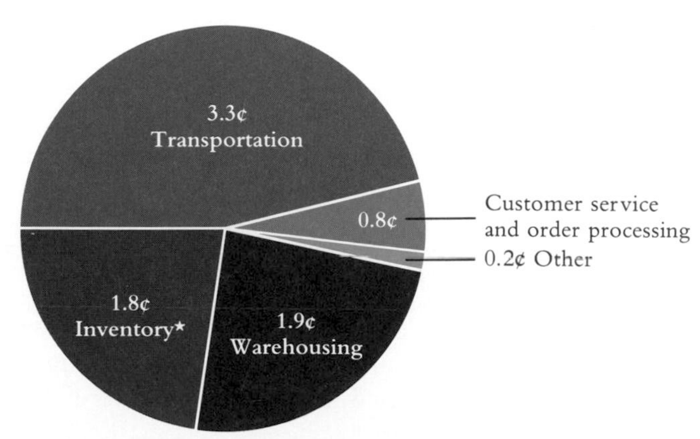

*Cost of carrying inventory valued at 18 percent per year

and the risk associated with buying the product. For example, since a product such as coal is of low value compared with its weight, transportation costs are high and could erode any profits from sales. To prevent this, a drop shipper is employed who takes title but not the physical possession of the goods and arranges for the coal to move directly from the mine to the customer. The important point is that physical product characteristics often dictate logistical actions.

Packaging is an area where both product and promotional factors interact with logistics. The marketer may view the interior package as a point-of-purchase device at retail but not consider its logistical implications. For instance, does the package provide adequate protection? Does the product's package allow it to be easily placed in an exterior package (such as a carton)? Do any factors such as unique shapes make handling, stacking, or filling of the package difficult? How many cartons can be placed in a vehicle? Various departments within a firm must coordinate efforts to ensure that a package desirable from a marketing standpoint is logistically acceptable.

A product can be differentiated through customer service and on-time delivery, especially if it is a mature product with many nearly identical competitors and low brand loyalty. In manufacturing firms, customer service and delivery have been found to rank behind product development and pricing in importance but ahead of personal selling and advertising.[5]

Pricing Factors Pricing interacts with logistics in several ways. Terms of transfer of the product's title and responsibility for transfer are determined by the specific geographic pricing system used. Some of these methods build transportation costs into the quoted price of the product.

Pricing discounts also may have logistical implications. A quantity discount is used to encourage buyers to purchase large quantities and to reward them for holding inventory. When these pricing discounts are combined with volume transportation discounts, buyers gain even larger savings.

Promotional Factors Promotion interacts with logistics in the areas of advertising, sales promotion, and personal selling. Advertising and promotional campaigns must be planned and coordinated with the logistics system to ensure product availability at the appropriate time. Distribution must be synchronized with sales to ensure timely and efficient handling of orders. Trade promotions and contests or incentives for the sales force also may create irregular demand that logistics will have to deal with efficiently.

Place Factors Many middlemen in marketing channels got their start because of logistical problems that existing intermediaries couldn't solve to the consumers' satisfaction. For example, careful attention to movement and storage of food products helped to make Cub Foods (a Midwestern chain) superwarehouses a retailing innovation copied across the country. While a conventional supermarket has sales of $150,000 a week, a Cub Foods store has sales of about $1 million a week. Its high-volume, low-price strategy is possible because of basic logistical decisions: taking some shipments directly from the manufacturer and storing and displaying merchandise in the original cartons stacked to the store's 24-foot ceilings.[6]

CONCEPT CHECK

1 **What is the broader business logistics view of physical distribution?**

2 **Why is logistics more important to a consumer good manufacturer than to a bank?**

3 **How does logistics interact with the product element of the marketing mix?**

OBJECTIVES OF THE LOGISTICS SYSTEM

The definition of business logistics presented previously contains four integral terms: coordination, movement, total cost, and service level. As just discussed, there is a need to *coordinate* activities among functional departments, including marketing. *Movement* refers to the continuous flow of physical goods into and out of the firm, much like a pipeline. Parts, supplies, and raw materials flow into the firm so it can produce the product and have finished goods flow out of the firm to be distributed through the marketing channel. The total cost and service aspects of the definition will be explored in more detail.

TOTAL COST CONCEPT

Logistics attempts to minimize the **total cost** of moving and storing the goods a firm uses and produces. There are many individual cost elements present in a logistics system, including transportation, warehousing and materials handling, various inventory costs, stockouts (being out of inventory), and order processing. Often as one of these costs decreases, another increases. For example, as inventory levels (and costs) rise, stockouts probably drop, so the net impact of both must be assessed. By considering all relevant costs as part of a logistics system, this effect can be determined, as shown in Figure 14-4. As the number of warehouses increases, inventory costs rise and transportation costs fall because more overall inventory is warehoused, but it is closer to customers. The net

FIGURE 14-4
How costs vary with number of warehouses used

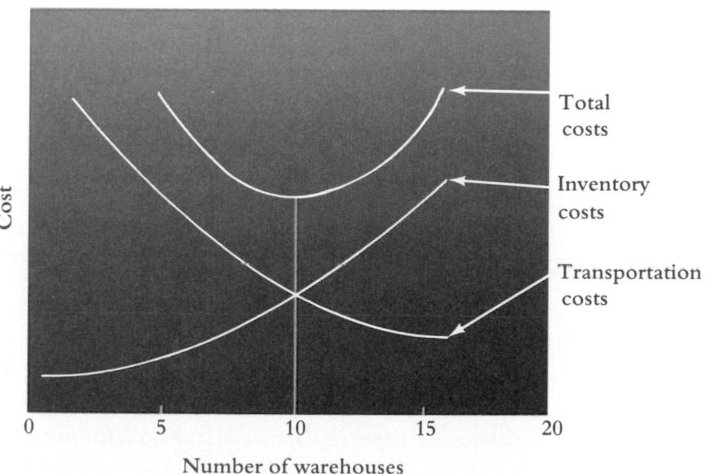

effect is to minimize the total costs of the logistics system by having 10 warehouses. This means the total cost curve is minimized at a point where neither of the two individual cost elements is at a minimum but the overall system is.

CUSTOMER SERVICE CONCEPT

Customer service representatives used to be only down in the trenches handling customer complaints. They straightened out various mixups like lost or incorrect orders and tried to satisfy irate customers. Now customer service managers are moving up in the organization. This new status comes from a push for better **customer service** and its use as a key element in marketing strategy.

If logistics is a pipeline, the end of it—or output—is the service delivered to customers. Unfortunately customer service is one of the most misunderstood areas in business, perhaps because no general definition exists. Certainly a definition must reflect both the quality of the system in delivering products to users and a customer orientation.[7] For our purposes, customer service is the ability of a logistics system to satisfy users in terms of time, dependability, communications, and convenience.[8]

Recent trends toward vendor evaluation, single sourcing, increased competition, and a renewed customer focus have propelled the changes in the role of customer service jobs. Companies now see customer service as a strategic tool for increasing customer satisfaction and sales, not merely as an expense.[9]

It would be simple to cut the total costs of a logistics system if customer service could be ignored, but competition prevents this. A firm's goal is to provide adequate customer service while controlling the associated costs. Unrealistically high customer service could lead to runaway costs, whereas minimum customer service could antagonize customers and destroy the firm's competitive position. Thus a balance or trade-off between costs and customer service is required, as suggested in Figure 14-5.

Time Time in a logistics setting refers to **lead time** for an item, which means the lag from ordering an item until it's received in stock. This is sometimes also referred to as **order cycle time** or **replenishment time.** The various elements that make up the typical order cycle for businesses include recognition of the need to order, order transmittal, processing, preparation, and shipment.

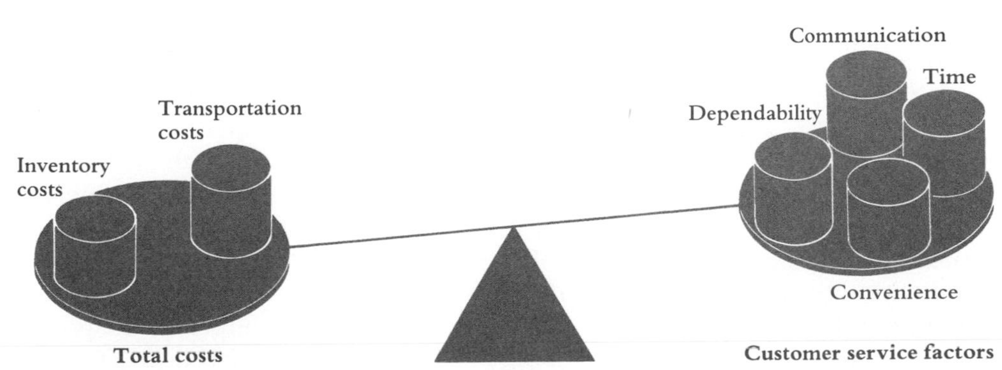

FIGURE 14-5
Logistics balances total costs against customer service factors

These issues may not seem important to consumers unless desired items are out-of-stock due to long lead times. However, in buying products such as cars and some furniture brands, where specific orders are placed with manufacturers, the consumer may directly face lead-time issues. Although effective customer service seeks to reduce lead times, achieving this goal often increases associated costs.

Dependability Dependability is the consistency, or reliability, or replenishment. It can be broken into three elements: consistent lead time (the period from order placement to delivery), safe delivery, and correct delivery. Studies indicate that dependability is the most important element in customer service.[10] Consistent service allows planning (such as appropriate inventory levels), whereas inconsistencies thwart this planning. Customers may be willing to accept longer lead times if they know about it in advance and can adjust their operations. Surprise delays may shut down a production line, and early deliveries may cause problems for the inventory system.

Communication Communication is a two-way link between buyer and seller that helps in monitoring service. Each party can try to resolve problems if it is aware of them at an early stage. Status reports on orders are a typical area where communication is important. Clear, timely communication is essential to achieve effective customer service.

Convenience Since different customers have different service needs, a customer service system should be flexible to accommodate these needs. For example, if an important customer requires deliveries before 7 AM, this must be done. Convenience levels may be established for separate groups of customers based on their potential profitability to the seller. A growing customer that already accounts for 30 percent of a firm's sales volume requires good service, whereas another customer that provides only 1 percent of sales may not warrant the higher, more costly levels of service.

Service Context Customer service is highly situational. A manufacturer like Wang or Westinghouse will probably include all the service elements that have been discussed. However, a retailer like Sears or K Mart usually focuses on communication and convenience (specifically, location, hours open, and credit policy) because order cycle time and dependability have little significance in dealing with a retailer's customers but are important when the retailer deals with suppliers.

COST-SERVICE TRADE-OFFS

Costs set an upper limit on the amount of customer service a firm can provide. The same service levels may be obtained with different combinations of resources (such as low-cost transportation with warehouses versus high-cost transportation without them). For example, IBM has begun closing 120 parts warehouses because Federal Express (the overnight air service) now inventories high-priced parts for IBM's computer workstations. The inventories kept at Federal's sorting hubs in Memphis, Oakland, and Newark mean that its high-cost overnight

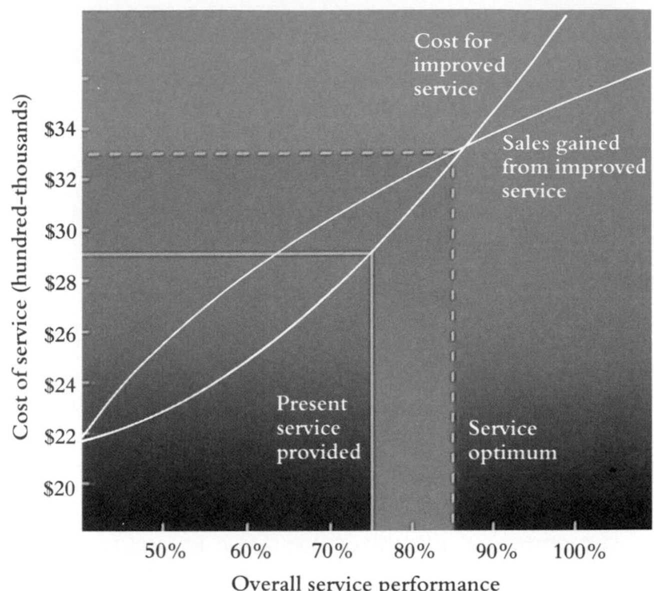

FIGURE 14-6
How much a firm should spend improving customer service to increase sales

Source: "Does Your Customer Service Program Stack Up?" *Traffic Management* (September 1982), p. 55.

transportation is being substituted for IBM's higher-cost parts warehouses scattered across the United States. The result: better service for IBM customers at a lower cost.[11]

Factors that affect the customer service level required are degree of product differentiation and alternate product sources, competitive service levels, product and customer profitability, importance of certain customers, and the possibility of cultivating new customers. In addition, there must be some company-wide standards for service, or operational chaos will result, further impeding cost minimization.

Studies indicate that service costs grow at an increasing rate. One firm found that to increase on-time delivery from a 95 percent rate to a 100 percent rate tripled costs.[12] Another study concluded that a switch from an 85 percent level to a 96 percent level (substituting telephone for mail, truck for water transportation, and higher inventories) more than tripled the costs.[13] This general relationship is shown in Figure 14-6. Higher levels of service require tactics such as more inventory to cut stockouts, more expensive transportation to improve speed and lessen damage, possibly more warehouses, and double or triple checking of orders to ensure correctness. These actions all add to costs, so judgments have to be made about the proper levels of customer service. Figure 14-6 suggests that the extra sales gained from a firm increasing its customer service from 74 percent to 85 percent more than offset the increased costs. Beyond 85 percent, however, the extra costs exceed the extra sales.

CUSTOMER SERVICE STANDARDS

Firms operating effective logistics systems develop a set of written customer service standards. These serve as objectives and provide a benchmark against which results can be measured for control purposes. In developing these standards, the place to start is with the customers. What are their service needs?

FIGURE 14-7
Examples of customer service standards

TYPE OF FIRM	STANDARD
Wholesaler	At least 98% of orders filled accurately
Manufacturer	Order cycle time of no more than 5 days
Retailer	Returns accepted within 30 days
Airline	At least 90% of arrivals on time
Trucker	A maximum of 5% loss and damage per year
Restaurant	Lunch served within 5 minutes of order

What do competitors offer them? Are the customers willing to pay a bit more for better service? After these questions are answered, realistic standards can be set and an ongoing measurement program established to monitor results. Typical standards relate to time, reliability, and loss and damage. They must be quantifiable and measurable, as shown in Figure 14-7.

During the control process, deviations from standards must be noted and investigated. For example, a high loss and demand record may indicate a need for a more expensive mode of transport, a different carrier, or better protective packaging. These will result in some added costs but improve service and decrease costs of loss and damage.

CONCEPT CHECK

1 **What is the trade-off between total costs and customer service in a logistics system?**

2 **In what ways do key customer service factors differ between a manufacturer and a retailer?**

MAJOR LOGISTICS FUNCTIONS

As mentioned earlier, a business firm can adopt a logistics strategy varying between basic and advanced, depending on the extent to which it adopts the concept. Four key elements in a logistics system described in the following sections include: (1) transportation, (2) warehousing and materials handling, (3) order processing, and (4) inventory management.

TRANSPORTATION

Transportation provides the movement of goods necessary in a logistics system. There are five basic modes of transportation: railroads, motor carriers, air carriers, pipelines, and water carriers. In addition, there are modal combinations involving two or more of the five basic modes. All can be evaluated on six basic service criteria:

MODE	RELATIVE ADVANTAGES	RELATIVE DISADVANTAGES
Rail	Full capability Extensive routes Low cost	Some reliability, damage problems Not always complete pickup and delivery Sometimes slow
Truck	Complete pickup and delivery Extensive routes Fairly fast	Size and weight restrictions Higher cost More weather sensitive
Air	Fast Low damage Frequent departures	High cost Limited capabilities
Pipeline	Low cost Very reliable	Limited capabilities and routes Slow
Water	Low cost Huge capacities	Slow Limited routes and schedules More weather sensitive

FIGURE 14-8
Advantages and disadvantages of five modes of transportation

- Cost: charges for transportation services only—usually on a ton-mile basis
- Time: speed of transit
- Capability: what can be realistically carried with this mode
- Dependability: reliability of service regarding time, loss, and damage
- Accessibility: convenience of the mode's routes (such as pipeline availability)
- Frequency: scheduling

Figure 14-8 summarizes service advantages and disadvantages of the modes of transportation available.

The process of picking a mode of transportation involves making tradeoffs among these often conflicting service criteria. In a decision about moving a specific product from the point of origin to a specific destination, the modes can then be evaluated on each criterion. However, one criterion or factor, such as cost or time, may assume such great importance in a particular situation that several alternative modes of transportation are ruled out. Typically, in the final decision, the user will likely strike a balance between cost and the level of customer service required.

Railroads Railroads today usually carry heavy, bulky items over fairly long distances. Their predominant cargos are coal, ores, and grain. They can carry items that won't fit on trucks or that exceed highway weight limits, and their routes are more extensive than those of either water carriers or pipelines.

Railroads still dominate the five modes of transportation in terms of ton-miles carried. A ton-mile is a standard transport measure that reflects both weight carried and distance moved, or one ton of cargo moved one mile. So 5 tons moved 100 miles is 500 ton-miles. But railroads have lost higher valued traffic to other modes and now account for only about 12 percent of freight dollars.

Railroads dominate shipping

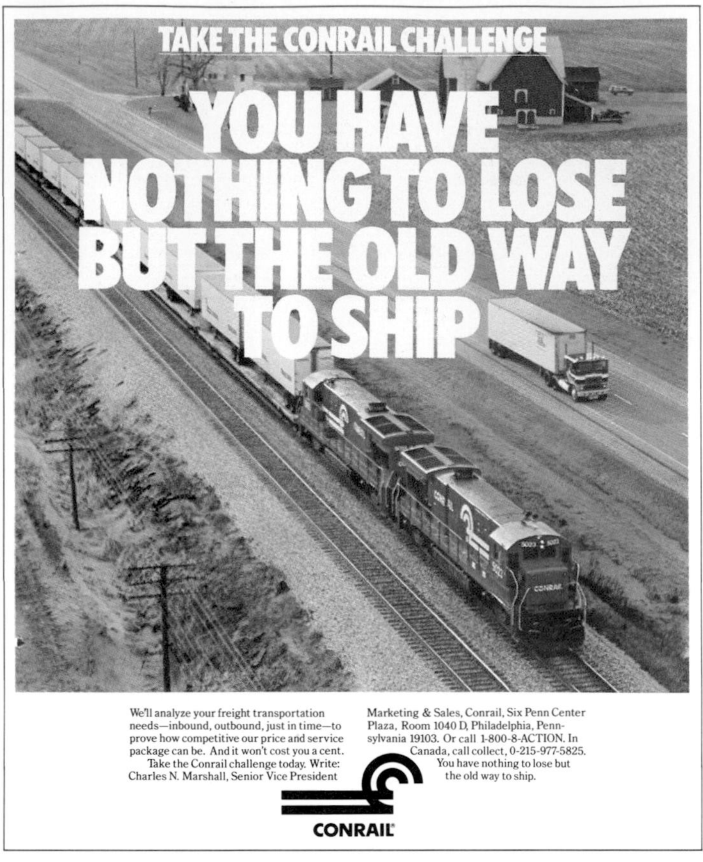

Railroads dominate other modes in bulky, lower-value products. The 1970's was a decade of turbulence for many railroads, with many bankruptcies and reorganizations. The Conrail (Consolidated Rail Corporation) system is a result of the bankruptcy of several railroads in the Northeastern United States. It was formerly owned by the federal government, but was sold to investors in 1987 through a common stock offering. Several mergers have also occurred, creating a national system dominated by a half dozen regional railroads. Railroads have generally been profitable in the 1980's aided greatly by the Staggers Rail Act of 1980, which enacted deregulation provisions allowing the railroads more operating freedom. Among the important freedoms to rail shippers are more flexible rates and the availability of contracts to provide service to individual customers.

Today's railroads have improved their service and are using more sophisticated equipment than a decade ago. Service innovations include unit trains, run-through trains, and minitrains. A *unit train* is a train dedicated to one commodity (often coal) that is loaded with sophisticated handling equipment, runs from origin to destination at high speed, and is unloaded mechanically. A *run-through train* carries more than one commodity but makes no stops. *Minitrains* are shorter trains that run on more frequent schedules and often help implement a new, just-in-time inventory system described later in the chapter.

Motor Carriers The motor carrier, or trucking, industry is composed of many small firms, as opposed to railroading. There are about 35,000 regulated truckers in the United States, in addition to many more independent truckers and private carriage operations owned by firms that transport their own products in their own trucks. The congressional deregulation of trucking in 1980 has led to severe financial problems for many truckers but has afforded shippers more service options and latitude in negotiating rates.

The biggest advantage of motor carriage is the complete door-to-door service. Trucks can go almost anywhere there is a road; however, they cannot carry all items because of size and weight restrictions. They typically carry higher valued items than do railroads, often items that are packaged. Trucks carry only about a quarter of all ton-mile traffic but about three-quarters of the total dollar value of traffic.

Trucks are often faster than rail, especially for shorter distances, but are more sensitive to interruptions by bad weather. Rates are generally higher than rail, although extreme price cutting has appeared in some segments of the industry as a result of the increased competition from trucking deregulation. This has enabled Procter & Gamble to reduce the unit cost of getting its products to its customers and has been an important factor in its decision to reduce the number of production sites from 12 to 9 for laundry granules and from 7 to 3 for shortening and oil.[14]

Air Carriers Most of the general public's interest in air carriers, or airlines, centers around passenger traffic, but shippers look at their freight operations. Air freight is costly, but its speed may create savings in lower inventory levels to offset the cost. The items that can be carried are limited by space constraints and are usually valuable and lightweight, such as perishable flowers, clothing, and electronic parts. The items have to be delivered to an airport and picked up at the destination, although this service is available from specialized firms. Products moved in containers are especially amenable to this mode of shipment.

Pipelines Usual cargos for pipelines are oil-related and chemical-related liquids such as natural gas. Pipelines are an inexpensive, automated mode and are very reliable. Routes are fixed and tend to be concentrated regionally. The speed is slow, but operation is continuous. Currently pipelines are second to railroads in ton-miles carried domestically.

Water Carriers Several forms (or "trades") exist within the water transportation mode. Domestically, the major options are the river systems (barges) and the St. Lawrence Seaway. The ships and barges are large and tend to haul bulky items of low value (such as coal and iron ore). Rates are low, and so is transit speed. Technological innovations have enabled some of the Great Lakes ships to carry huge cargos. Water transportation is available only to firms shipping certain commodities that have access to the river systems, the Great Lakes, or ocean ports. Most overseas traffic moves on ships.

Intermodal Transportation Sometimes it is possible to use **intermodal transportation,** which involves coordinating or combining modes to get the best features of each, while minimizing the shortcomings. The most popular coordination approach is truck-rail, also referred to as *piggyback* or *trailer on flatcar* (TOFC). Other intermodal arrangements involve some form of water transport.

The basic idea in TOFC is to achieve the door-to-door capabilities of truck, along with the long-haul economies of rail. Trucks pick up shipments and proceed to rail yards, where the trailers are disconnected, are loaded onto flatcars, and travel by rail to a destination point. The trailers then are unloaded, hooked up to a power unit (tractor), and driven away. TOFC rates are now largely deregulated, spurring a growth in this traffic. Packaged goods and some agricultural shipments are good candidates for TOFC movement.

All the intermodal approaches share one theme: use of some form of container moved by truck for part of the distance. TOFC uses a truck trailer as a container, whereas the water plans generally employ conventional containers. They can be easily stacked and sorted and provide added product protection. Expensive handling equipment is required for these containers and is available only at certain locations.

Freight Consolidators Firms that accumulate small shipments into larger lots and then hire a carrier to move them are **freight forwarders,** or consolidators.

Different modes offer different advantages: trucks give door-to-door service; pipelines and barges are inexpensive; and ships carry bulk

Since per-pound rates for heavy shipments are lower than light ones, the forwarder's profit comes from the rate differential between large and small lots. Some of these firms specialize in air freight and others in surface freight. Shippers can form their own cooperative forwarders, termed **shippers' associations.**

The main advantage of using a forwarder is service. Pickup and delivery are provided, and the forwarders generally give more attention to small shipments (which they consolidate) than do carriers.

Package and Express Companies Several alternatives exist for moving small packages and letters. In addition to the government post offices, package services such as United Parcel Service (UPS) specialize in parcels under 70 pounds and provide pickup and delivery. Express companies such as Federal Express (see the Marketing Action Memo) and Purolator Courier offer fast movement of small packages. Pickup and delivery are provided, and next morning delivery is guaranteed. Since these services are generally high cost, they are usually reserved for vital and lightweight shipments. Emery Air Freight, which merged with Purolator in 1987, concentrates in air-expressing the over 70-pound packages and is trying to take advantage of the popularity of just-in-time inventory systems (discussed later in the chapter) to serve customers in this large-package segment.

CONCEPT CHECK

1 **What are some new kinds of train service offered by railroads to compete more effectively with other modes of transportation?**

2 **What is intermodal transportation?**

WAREHOUSING AND MATERIALS HANDLING

Warehouses not only allow firms to hold their stock in decentralized locations but also they are used for sorting, consolidation, product-recall programs, product "aging" (for example, wine and tobacco), "mixing" (or blending) of items, and for tax reasons, such as state inventory taxes. Warehouses are second to transportation in cost significance for logistics systems.

Warehouses may be an integral part of customer service policy, as when a firm has warehouses within 500 miles of all customers to provide rapid resupply. They also have important implications for inventory policy. Availability of warehouse space permits taking quantity discounts or transportation volume discounts and stockpiling materials in anticipation of shortages or price increases. Unfortunately, overall levels will likely rise as well, resulting in higher costs, so a trade-off between costs and customer service must be made.

Warehousing presents several managerial issues: (1) the number, type, and location of warehouses needed and (2) ownership arrangements. The first of these decisions is based on the location of a company's markets, sources of inbound raw materials or parts, and transportation routes and rates. Volumes moving in each direction must be considered, and a balance struck between the total costs incurred and the benefits received from having a warehouse in a particular place.

MARKETING · ACTION · MEMO

FLY-BY-NIGHT IDEA + CUSTOMER SERVICE + KISS = FEDERAL EXPRESS

Armed with his college term paper, which got a C− grade, Frederick W. Smith didn't build a better mousetrap and wait for the world to beat a path to his door. Instead, he set out to show the world that with his simple new innovation *he* could beat a path to everybody else's door.

He gave the name *Federal Express* to his door-to-door flying parcel service that uses garish orange, white, and purple jets. And he advertised "absolutely, positively overnight" delivery for his small-parcel service—limited to 70 pounds, the weight one person can carry. "I figured we had to be enormously reliable," says Smith, "since our service is frequently used for expensive spare parts, live organs, or other emergency shipments."

But Federal Express isn't your typical fly-by-night outfit. After all, Smith *did* write his term paper at Yale, and he *did* use a family trust of $4 million to get started—and Federal Express *did* lose $29 million in its first 26 months of operation.

What Smith had was a good idea, a good understanding of customer service, and the tenacity and resources to stick with it. First, Smith reasoned, he had to own his own jet aircraft so *all* parcels had to be picked up early in the evening, flown to a single sorting center (Memphis), and rerouted to their final destination before dawn. That's part of Fred Smith's KISS ("Keep it simple, stupid") principle. Finally, in spite of heavy early losses, some loans and a lot of hustle turned the business around. Always looking for a better idea, Federal Express started ZapMail, an electronic mail service, in 1984. The idea sounded great: use satellite transmission and facsimile machines to transport documents quickly. Unfortunately some technical glitches developed that hurt reliability. The price tag ($35 for ten pages, later cut to $25) also proved too steep for many customers. So ZapMail had huge customer service and pricing problems. Result? After losing more than $300 million in ZapMail, Federal Express killed the service.

Sources: Based on "Why Federal Express has Overnight Anxiety," *Business Week* (November 9, 1987), pp. 62-66; "Why ZapMail Finally Got Zapped," *Business Week* (October 13, 1986), pp. 48-49; Roy Rowan, "Business Triumphs of the Seventies," *Fortune* (December 1979), pp. 34.

Once the number, type, and location of warehouses is determined, then ownership issues can be addressed. Public and private warehouses are the major options and will be discussed next, along with several types of warehouses that provide specific benefits.

Public Warehouses Space and miscellaneous services are provided by **public warehouses** on a rental basis. All the costs are variable, so for limited warehouse usage this option is cheaper. They also are flexible because they can be used only when the space is required (for example, seasonally) or to fulfill some task

Warehouse space is a key to customer service

such as a product recall. Public warehouses entail no fixed costs, long-term commitment, or ownership risks and are managed by people who know the warehouse business.

Additional services include filing monthly inventory status reports, preparing transportation documents, weighing, monitoring loss and damage from transportation, and assisting in claim filing for such errors. These services can be purchased as required and eliminate the need for this expertise on the part of the user.

Many situations lend themselves to the use of public warehouses, as when new geographical markets (or test markets) are entered and product demand is uncertain. Vehicle load transportation rates (for larger shipments) can also be used if added space is available. They're also beneficial for firms that don't have the money or expertise to run their own warehouse.

Over 10,000 public warehouses are available in the United States. Some of these concentrate on specific types of goods (such as farm products or frozen food), whereas others serve general storage needs. Public warehouses also offer specialized services. **Bonded warehouses** allow deferment of taxes on items such as liquor and tobacco until the stocks are released. The warehouse is bonded to the tax collection agency to ensure tax payment on release of the goods.

Private Warehouses An alternative to renting warehouse space is owning it. Private warehouses are owned and operated by a firm in the channel of distribution, such as the manufacturer or retailer. The owner of a warehouse is

A one-story distribution center

responsible for its management and operation, including hiring, labor and union negotiations, investment in handling equipment, insurance, and utility bills. A concern with private warehouses is their adaptability. Specialized warehouses may not be attractive for resale, which could be important if market conditions necessitate relocating the inventory to be warehoused.

Distribution centers use a computerized approach to order processing and private warehousing and focus on rapid movement of goods (or "throughput") through the warehouse. They are designed accordingly, usually are one story (although it may be high) to avoid elevators, and are strategically located for transportation access, often near interstate highways. Distribution centers may serve as consolidation points for other warehouses within the system. The tremendous success of rural retailing chains such as Wal-Mart stores, Ames Department Stores, and Duckwell-Alco stores is due to sophisticated distribution centers that serve their retail outlets.[15] In fact, as noted in the Marketing Action Memo, Wal-Mart's low retail prices are in large part a result of an efficient network of warehouse distribution centers that serves its retail stores within a 400-mile radius.[16]

The major benefit of distribution centers is improved customer service. They receive orders from customers and fill them quickly from local stocks. They are also entwined with production by receiving and consolidating shipments of materials and perhaps providing some production capabilities such as blending or final assembly to meet customer needs as close to the consumption point as possible.

In private warehousing both fixed and variable costs are present. In comparing the costs with those of public warehousing, a break-even analysis can be used. To cover the fixed costs, a high level of use is necessary. Private warehousing is cheaper in the long run if it is used extensively, although the adaptability and real estate risks remain. An operational benefit of private warehousing is control over operations. Products not amenable to public warehousing include hazardous materials, sterile materials, or products such as fine wine that require long aging.

MARKETING·ACTION·MEMO

WAL-MART: WHERE WAREHOUSE LOCATION MATTERS

Chairman Sam Walton's Wal-Mart chain has grown from a small cluster of stores in Arkansas to a 22-state chain of more than 1,100 stores, selling more than $15 billion annually in discounted merchandise. In late 1987 Wal-Mart opened its first "Hypermarket USA" outside Dallas—a giant combined discount-supermarket with more than 70,000 products for sale (see Chapter 15).

Sam Walton gives much of the credit for growth in sales and profitability to the Wal-Mart version of hub-and-spoke distribution marketing. Like most retailers, Wal-Mart endorses the first three guidelines to retail success—location, location, and location—but then comes the surprise: Wal-Mart is primarily concerned with *warehouse* location. As reported in *Forbes* magazine: "Other retailers built warehouses to serve existing outlets, but Walton went at it the other way around. He started with a giant warehouse, then spotted stores all around it. One large Walton warehouse served a radius of 400 miles."

Today, some 80 percent of store needs are fulfilled from eight distribution centers in six hub cities. A typical 650,000 square-foot center serves 150 stores in a 6-hour drive radius. All centers are highly automated, with online receipt of orders from store registers, automatic inventory control, and re-ordering on-line from 200 vendors. It is rare that store orders take more than 36 to 48 hours for fulfillment.

The distribution system is being fine-tuned constantly, although distribution costs now stand at a remarkably low 2 cents on the dollar—believed to be less than half the standard for the industry. Supplying its existing stores plus the new hypermarkets—each of which needs $100 million annual sales to be profitable—will be a tough test for Wal-Mart's distribution system.

Sources: Adapted from *Marketing News* (June 20, 1986), p. 18; Thomas C. Hayes, "Hypermarkets Catching On in U.S.," *International Herald Tribune* (February 6-7, 1988), pp. 9, 11; "Here Come the 'Malls Without Walls'," *Time* (February 8, 1988), p. 50.

Conditions that generally favor private warehousing include a large, stable volume of stock moving through the warehouse, adequate financial resources to make the purchase, available managerial expertise, and a need for control of warehousing operations or some specific capabilities.

Materials Handling Warehouse operations are supported through **materials handling,** which involves moving small amounts of goods over shorter distances. The two major problems with this activity are high labor costs and high rates of loss and damage. Every time an item is handled, there is a chance for loss or damage. Common materials handling equipment includes forklifts, cranes, and conveyors. Many versions of each exist.

A more recent approach to materials handling is the **automated warehouse,** which uses computer-controlled technologies to replace people with machines in warehouses, cut labor costs, reduce loss and damage, improve safety, and provide better inventory record keeping.

The automated warehouse replaces trucks and operators with robot equip-

Material handling through automation

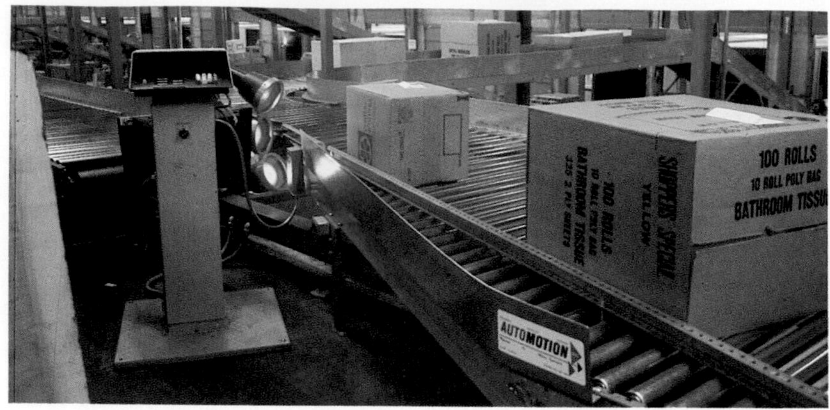

ment that places goods into storage and retrieves them under direction of a computer control system. Fewer than 10 people can operate the warehouse from a control center. Records are immediately updated to yield precise inventory data, and productivity is greatly enhanced. The warehouse can have a higher ceiling, since the equipment can safely reach greater heights. The best applications for this technology are warehouses that handle high-turnover items of similar shape, such as packaged foods and cosmetics. This is why firms such as General Mills, Revlon, and Frito-Lay use automated warehouses.

ORDER PROCESSING

There are several stages in the processing of an order. An order request starts the process, which is followed by entering the order, notifying production or a warehouse to prepare an order, checking inventory, possibly creating a back-order (an order for an out-of-stock item), checking credit, preparing all paperwork that follows the order, and possibly sending a confirmation of the order to the customer. This information transfer within the firm is facilitated by an accurate computerized information system. Data from this system can be used for other purposes later, such as product planning, market planning, customer analysis, and various other marketing research activities. Many firms have invested heavily in these systems and differentiate themselves in the marketplace in this manner.

INVENTORY MANAGEMENT

The major problem in managing inventory is maintaining the delicate balance between too little and too much of it. Too little may result in poor service, stockouts, brand switching, and loss of market share. Too much leads to higher costs because of the money tied up in the inventory and the chance that it may become obsolete.

Different departments within the firm may have directly opposing views on inventory. Marketing and production managers may favor higher levels to improve customer service and aid in long production runs, whereas financial managers may be worried about the increased cost.

Inventory management has received renewed attention in the 1980's because of an increased emphasis on increasing profit through effective cost reduction. Estimates of average U.S. inventory costs usually range from 12 percent to 35 percent of the inventory's value. However, several recent studies indicate the costs may be at the high end of this range. One detailed study found that true inventory costs were 38 percent, although the firm believed they were 19 percent.[17]

Reasons for Inventory Traditionally, carrying inventory has been justified on several grounds: (1) to offer a buffer against variations in supply and demand, often caused by poor forecasting, (2) to provide better customer service, (3) to promote production efficiencies, (4) to provide a hedge against price increases by suppliers, (5) to promote purchasing and transportation discounts, and (6) to protect the firm from contingencies such as strikes and shortages.

Inventory Costs Specific inventory costs are often hard to detect because they are spread throughout the firm and in diverse locations such as production warehouses and decentralized warehouses. A typical general set of inventory costs includes:

- Capital costs: the opportunity costs resulting from tying up funds in inventory instead of using them in other, more profitable investments; these are related to investment rates
- Inventory service costs: items such as insurance and taxes that are present in most states
- Storage costs: warehousing space and materials handling
- Risk costs: possible loss, damage, pilferage, perishability, and obsolescence

Just-in-time inventory management is gaining importance in U.S. manufacturing

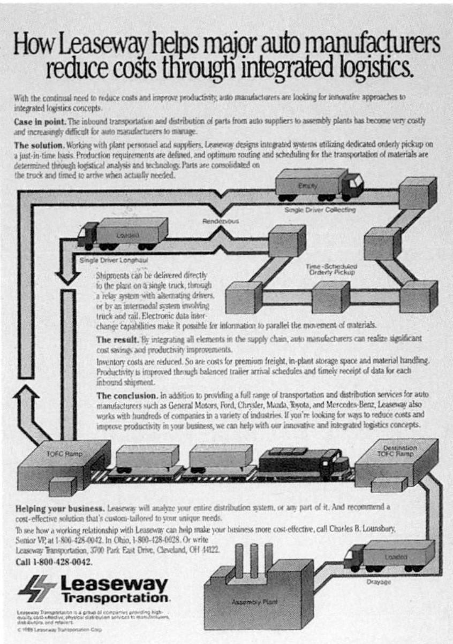

MARKETING · ACTION · MEMO

HOW GENERAL MOTORS TAILORS RAIL AND TRUCK SERVICE FOR JUST-IN-TIME SYSTEMS

Just-in-time (JIT) inventory systems require reliable replenishment of supplies to prevent a production shutdown, since these systems run with very low inventories of raw materials and parts. Ideally, suppliers should be located near the production plant to improve the reliability of delivery.

General Motors (GM) requires overnight delivery to implement a JIT system at its Lansing, Michigan, Oldsmobile assembly plant. Various parts are consolidated in a shipment that comes from Kalamazoo, 118 miles away, and are delivered during the night for the next day's production. Thus Oldsmobile production can operate with only a day's inventory of those parts. What GM needs is reliable, overnight deliveries of these items at a reasonable cost. It found this in the form of Conrail's Minitrain, a shorter-than-normal train that makes no stops between Kalamazoo and Lansing. The Minitrain leaves Kalamazoo at 6 PM. When the production workers arrive at the Lansing plant at 6 AM the next morning, the parts are in the factory and available for use that day.

JIT systems can cause difficulties when labor relations problems or bad weather disrupts tightly scheduled deliveries. GM manufactures its Pontiac Fiero in Pontiac, Michigan. It buys plastic body panels for the Fiero from an Ohio firm, the Budd Company, located 131 miles away. These panels are delivered by truck five times a day. When a February snowstorm hit Michigan, the panel deliveries were delayed, which slowed the Fiero assembly plant from a 20-hour per day operation to 8 hours per day.

JIT savings can be tremendous: GM estimates that it saved $1 billion over a 2-year period by reducing its average inventory by $30 billion.

Sources: Based on "Freight Transportation: A Revitalized Industry Emerges," *Forbes* (August, 1, 1983), pp. Ad1-12; Jeremy Main, "The Trouble with Managing Japanese Style," *Fortune* (April 2, 1984), pp. 50-56; Mike Meyers, "Low Inventory Manufacturing Arrives Just in Time," *Minneapolis Star and Tribune* (March 11, 1984), p. ID.

Storage costs, risk costs, and some service costs vary according to the characteristics of the item inventoried. Capital costs are always present and are proportional to the *value* of the item and prevailing interest rates. Controlling inventory costs requires accurate forecasts of future demand.

Inventory Strategies Several methods exist for improving inventory management. Increasingly important is the **just-in-time** (JIT) **concept** advocated by Japanese industry. JIT systems operate with very lean inventories to hold down costs. When items are needed for production, they arrive "just in time."[18]

Proponents cite several advantages to JIT. First, there are the financial advantages that come from lower inventory levels and/or faster inventory turnover. Second, the Japanese experience suggests that JIT yields better reliability in production scheduling and product quality. Smaller, more frequent shipments to manufacturers seem to lead to better quality levels.

For JIT to work properly, suppliers must be able to provide fast, reliable deliveries, or there will be a production disruption for the buyer. Ideally, to reduce these risks, the suppliers are near the user. This is often the case in Japan, where many suppliers are purposely located near the manufacturers. Although the United States doesn't lend itself as readily to such location strategies, certain industries, such as the automotive industry, have located many facilities quite close together in the Midwest. It's not surprising that many of the U.S. JIT users are located there.

Firms in the United States have had problems adapting to JIT systems. Besides the spatial dispersion of U.S. industry, to implement a JIT strategy effectively, suppliers probably need to maintain a warehouse near their customers. Reliable transportation is also crucial. Different transportation modes have different degrees of reliability, so the choice of mode is very important. The Marketing Action Memo on JIT describes how General Motors uses both railroads and trucks in its JIT systems.

Several philosophical issues have also created barriers to the effective use of JIT systems in this country. One is the lack of an orientation toward quality (although this is changing), since quality is a prerequisite to effective use of JIT (there is no backup inventory if parts with unsatisfactory quality are received). Another factor is that American managers don't view inventory as inherently wasteful as do Japanese managers. Finally, the Japanese practice of building long-term partnerships between manufacturers and suppliers is not as prevalent in the United States. The U.S. posture is more likely an adversarial one that focuses on buyers negotiating with suppliers.

The realities of U.S. JIT systems are probably different than what its advocates suggest. In many cases, manufacturers merely push inventory back in the channel, forcing their suppliers to hold it. Containers for consumer products (such as shampoo and beer) may be held by the vendor until they are needed in production. So inventory hasn't been eliminated from the system, it has just moved around. JIT systems also often lead to a reduction in the number of suppliers used by a manufacturer, so some suppliers lose business. For those that can adapt, however, it may mean a large amount of stable business and a competitive advantage in the marketplace.

In summary, a well-managed logistics system that delivers high levels of customer service is a valuable marketing tool. Instead of being just another expense, it can serve to generate sales and possibly to allow premium prices to be obtained because of the value provided to customers. With increased global competition in many industries, improved logistics performance—especially customer service—is a means for a firm to gain a competitive advantage.

CONCEPT CHECK

1 **What are the basic trade-offs between the modes of transportation?**

2 **What are the advantages of using public warehouses? Private warehouses?**

3 **What are the strengths and weaknesses of a just-in-time system?**

SUMMARY

1 A comprehensive definition of physical distribution activities, called *business logistics,* includes both inbound and outbound activities.

2 The importance of logistical activities varies among firms. Production activities generally create a more complex system, as do the width of the product line and number of geographic markets served.

3 Although some marketers may pay little attention to logistics, they do so at their own peril. Logistics directly affects the success of the marketing program and all areas of the marketing mix.

4 The total cost concept suggests that a system of costs is present. The individual elements can be balanced against one another to minimize total costs.

5 Cost minimization is irrelevant without specifying an acceptable service level that must be maintained. The importance of customer service varies among industries, but many of them are becoming more aware of its importance.

6 Although key customer service factors depend on the service situation, important elements of the customer service program are likely to be time-related dependability, communications, and convenience.

7 The five modes of transportation (railroads, motor carriers, air carriers, pipelines, and water carriers) offer shippers different service benefits. Better service often costs more, although it may result in savings in other areas of the logistics system.

8 A variety of warehousing arrangements exists to serve various needs. Public warehouses are rented as needed, so they provide flexibility. Two important developments in private (owned) warehousing are the distribution center concept and automated warehousing.

9 Inventory management is critical, since too much inventory greatly increases costs and too little may result in stockouts. Various methods are available to manage inventory. A popular approach currently is the just-in-time concept, which attempts to minimize inventory in the system.

KEY TERMS AND CONCEPTS

physical distribution management p. 379
business logistics p. 379
total cost p. 384
customer service p. 385
lead time p. 385
order cycle time p. 385
replenishment time p. 385
intermodal transportation p. 391
freight forwarders p. 392
shippers' associations p. 393
public warehouses p. 394
bonded warehouses p. 395
distribution centers p. 396
materials handling p. 397
automated warehouse p. 397
just-in-time concept p. 400

CHAPTER PROBLEMS AND APPLICATIONS

1 List several companies whose logistical activities are unimportant. Also list several whose focus is only on the inbound or outbound side.

2 Give an example of how logistical activities might affect trade promotion strategies.

3 What are some types of business in which order processing may be among the paramount success factors?

4 What behavioral problems might arise to negate the logistics concept within the firm?

5 What customer service factors would be vital to buyers in the following types of companies? (a) manufacturing, (b) retailing, (c) hospitals, and (d) construction.

6 Name some cases when extremely high service levels (for example, 99 percent) would be warranted.

7 What mode of transportation would be the best for the following products? (a) farm machinery, (b) liquid ammonia, (c) wheat, and (d) coal.

8 Assume you work for a Chicago firm expanding to California. You are uncertain whether to rent or buy needed warehouse space. You have a forecast that you feel is reliable which indicates you will have enough sales volume to justify owning a warehouse. Make a list of *specific fixed* and *variable* costs that you will have to cover if you choose this option.

9 How would *location decisions* vary for these types of warehouses? (a) distribution center and (b) automated warehouse.

10 The auto industry is a heavy user of the just-in-time concept. Why? What other industries would be good candidates for its application? What do they have in common?

SUGGESTED READINGS

James C. Johnson and Kenneth C. Schneider, "Marketing Managers Discuss the Strengths and Weaknesses of Logistics Personnel," *The Logistics and Transportation Review* (August 1987), pp. 325-333. *This article describes the perceptions of 156 marketing managers about the strengths and weaknesses of the logistics people with whom they work and notes the special importance of customer service.*

James C. Johnson and Donald F. Wood, *Contemporary Physical Distribution and Logistics*, 3rd ed. (New York: MacMillan Publishing Company, 1986). *This book provides a good overview of logistics. It is written in lay terms and features an abundance of explanatory diagrams and photos.*

Roy D. Shapiro, "Get Leverage from Logistics," *Harvard Business Review* (May-June 1984), pp. 119-126. *This article relates the ideas of customer service and cost minimization to corporate strategy.*

"Why Federal Express has Overnight Anxiety," *Business Week* (November 9, 1987), pp. 62-66. *This article describes how changes in competition, facsimiles, market growth, and technology are affecting Federal Express and other air express companies.*

PIGALLE
Le FAUBOURG

15

Retailing

After reading this chapter you should be able to:

Identify retailers in terms of the utilities they provide.

•

Explain the alternative ways to classify retail outlets.

•

Classify retailers in terms of the retail positioning matrix.

•

Develop retailing mix strategies over the life cycle of a retail store.

•

Explain the impact of computers on retail methods and store operations.

Need a Vacation? Skip Florida. Try the Mall—In Canada!

Want to go ice skating, ride a Spanish galleon, visit 20,000 leagues under the sea, or play golf (opposite page)? Skip Disneyworld. Just take a trip to Edmonton, Alberta—home of the world's largest shopping mall. This Canadian mall is so large that it's listed in the *Guinness Book of World Records*.

How large is large? Is 800 stores enough for you to browse in? Choose, if you like, from 11 major department stores, 110 eating places, 200 women's clothing stores, 50 shoe stores, and 35 shops for menswear. This mall is so large that shoppers can rent motorized scooters with baskets attached for their purchases.

Retailing is a visible and exciting part of marketing. In Canada, the Ghermezians have taken the mall shopping concept to new heights, even to the surprise of super-heroes in Marvel Comics. Nedar Ghermezian says, "Here you will be able to visit an attraction superior to Disneyland, Malibu Beach, Epcot Center,

Houston Space Center, or the Champs d' Elysees." This super-mall is the center of community activity. Regardless of the temperature, Edmonton shoppers can slide down 1 of 22 waterslides, or jump the waves in the machine-made wave pool. But don't worry, eventually you won't need to fly to Edmonton for this kind of vacation. The Ghermezians are planning a second such mall in some balmy location in the United States. Bring your bathing suit and charge cards. Let's go shopping.[1]

Where do your customers shop? If you're selling books, cosmetics, or auto accessories, what retail outlet should you use? If you're thinking of opening a store, what type should it be? How much will you charge for the record albums you plan to sell? These are difficult and important questions that are an integral part of retailing. In the channel of distribution, retailing is where the customer meets the product. It is through retailing that exchange (a central aspect of marketing) occurs. **Retailing** includes all activities involved in selling, renting, and providing services to ultimate customers for personal, nonbusiness use.

The Value of Retailing

Retailing is an important marketing activity. Not only do producers and consumers meet in a retailing outlet, but retailing also provides multiple values to the consumer and the economy as a whole. To consumers, these values are in the form of services provided, or utilities. Retailing's economic value is represented by the people employed in retailing, as well as by the total amount of money exchanged in retail sales.

CONSUMER UTILITIES OFFERED BY RETAILING

The utilities provided by intermediaries is a major value of retailers. Time, place, possession, and form utilities are offered by most retailers in varying degrees, but one utility is often stressed more than others. Look at Figure 15-1 to see how well you can match the retailer with the utility being stressed in the description.

Having 750,000 representatives, as Amway does, puts the company's products close to the customer—place utility. And for those of us who face the holiday crunch, stores such as Dayton-Hudson help possession utility with

FIGURE 15-1
Which company best represents which utilities?

Amway	Since 1959 Amway has grown to 750,000 representatives who sell soap and related products. Although relatively new, Amway alone accounts for about one sixth of all direct sales in the United States. Amway products are not sold in stores.
Dayton-Hudson	A large Midwest department store chain, Dayton-Hudson has always been viewed as an aggressive merchandiser. While other stores opened furniture departments, it opened Home Stores, large free-standing furniture stores. Furniture is expensive, but here you may pay cash if you like or use the store charge. If it's December and you'd like to buy an Oriental rug for Christmas, use Holiday Dollars, a charge plan where you aren't billed until February of the next year.
Legal Sea Foods	Opened in the 1970's with one restaurant, Legal Sea Foods now has four locations. Known for high-quality, fresh fish, Legal's has become a popular Boston eating establishment. It will also sell you fresh, uncooked fish. The staff will cut, fillet, or trim anything from octopus to shark to meet your needs.
Toys 'Я Us:	A distinctive toy store with a backwards *R*, this company is what every kid dreams about. Walking into a Toys 'Я Us store is like living under the Christmas tree. Unlike most stores, which reduce their space allotted to toys after the Christmas season, everything is always available at Toys 'Я Us.

MATCH THEM UP

Time	Place	Possession	Form
________	________	________	________

A typical hotel room—and bed—is not to be found in the Edmonton shopping mall

deferred payment plans and Holiday Dollars. Form utility is offered by Legal Sea Foods as it cuts and fillets a shark to the customer's specifications. Finding toy shelves stocked in May is the time utility dreamed about by every child who enters Toys 'Я Us.

Shopping malls sponsor antique shows, and department stores often offer guest speakers or fashion shows, both of which provide entertainment to prospective customers. Many consumers find shopping a wonderful form of recreation and entertainment that is composed of several of the four basic utilities. The Marketing Research Report describes two segments: those that browse and those that don't, and how they differ.

Dolphins perform at the Edmonton shopping mall

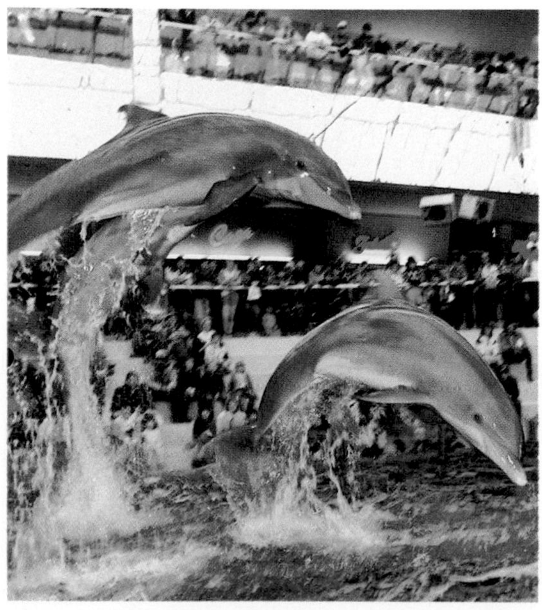

MARKETING · RESEARCH · REPORT

ARE YOU BUYING? OR JUST LOOKING? WHAT'S THE DIFFERENCE?

You see them all the time as you dash into the mall to make a quick purchase: two people leisurely strolling past the store windows, stopping to gaze. "Just who are those people?," you might ask. They're the browsers. But do they ever buy anything? Are they important to a retailing and marketing strategy? To answer this, Glen R. Jarboe and Carl D. McDaniel asked 190 randomly chosen people at two regional malls about their shopping habits. They were first asked whether they were browsers, and 72 percent of the people said "yes." And do the browsers differ from the shoppers? Look at the table below. If you're a retailer, browsers are an important segment to attract. As you'll see in the text, the differences between these groups are dramatic.

Source: Glen R. Jarboe and Carl D. McDaniel, "A Profile of Browsers in Regional Shopping Malls," *Journal of the Academy of Marketing Science* (Spring 1987), pp. 46-53.

QUESTION	ANSWER	BROWSER	NONBROWSER
Do you like to look around in stores?	Yes	94%	46%
	No	6	54
How often do you make unplanned purchases?	Always	32	14
	Sometimes	33	37
	Never	35	49
How often do you window shop?	Always	77	53
	Sometimes	23	45
	Never	0	2
How long is your normal visit to a mall?	Under 60 min.	17	41
	60 to 119 min.	46	35
	120 min. or more	37	21

As we discuss retailing, consider the importance of these browsers and how you might attract them to your store. Browsers like to look around stores (94 percent to 46 percent), they make unplanned purchases more often, and they tend to stay in a mall for more than 2 hours (37 percent to 21 percent) compared with nonbrowsers. At the Edmonton super-mall, browsers might never go home.

THE ECONOMIC IMPACT OF RETAILING

Retailing provides values to the individual consumer and is important to the economy as a whole. The 50 largest retailers in the United States account for $319 billion of sales and employ over 3.88 million people.[2] Food stores, automobile dealers, and general merchandise outlets such as department stores are significant contributors to the U.S. economy (Figure 15-2). As the figure shows, mail order sales are small compared with those through other outlets, but this is a growing phase of retailing and is discussed in greater depth later.

FIGURE 15-2
1985 retail sales by type of business

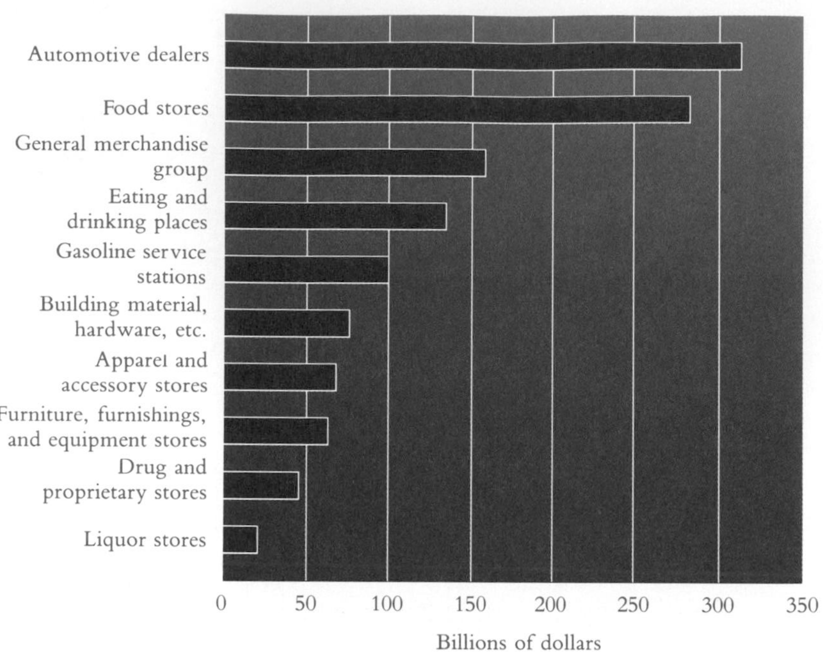

The magnitude of retailing sales is hard to imagine; the sales of the five largest retailing chains in the U.S. are more than many countries' gross national product (GNP). Sears' $44 billion of sales in 1986 far surpassed the GNP of Egypt for that same year, and Safeway, K Mart, and J.C. Penney have sales in excess of the GNPs of both the Sudan and Burma (Figure 15-3).

CONCEPT CHECK

1 **When an Amway sales representative brings products into a potential buyer's home, what utility is provided?**

2 **Two measures of the importance of retailing in the American economy are ________________ and ________________.**

CLASSIFYING RETAIL OUTLETS

For manufacturers, consumers, and the economy, retailing is an important component of marketing that has several variations. To understand retailing, it is helpful to recognize that outlets can be classified in several ways:

- **Form of ownership:** who owns the outlet
- **Level of service:** the degree of service provided the customer
- **Merchandise line:** how many different types of products a store carries and in what assortment
- **Method of operation:** the manner in which services are provided—how and where the customer purchases products

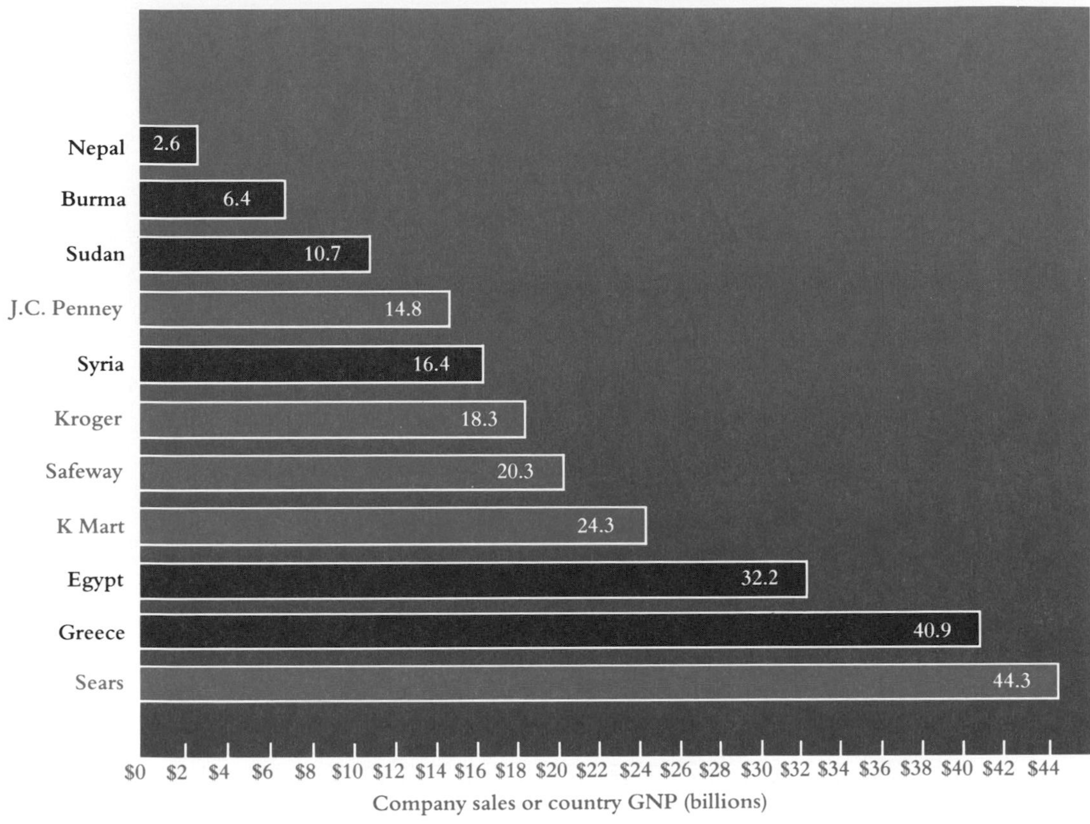

FIGURE 15-3
Republic of K Mart?

Within each method of classification there are several alternative types of outlets, as shown in Figure 15-4 and explained in the following pages.

FORM OF OWNERSHIP

Independent One of the most common forms of retail ownership is the independent business, owned by an individual. The neighborhood dry cleaner or florist is often an independent retailer. The advantage of this form of ownership for the owner is that she can be her own boss. For customers the independent store often provides a high level of personal service.

Corporate Chain A second ownership form, the corporate chain, involves multiple outlets under common ownership. If you've ever shopped at Jordan Marsh, The Bon, Maas Brothers, Stern's, Bonwit Teller, Blochs, Cain Sloan, Garfinkel, Brooks Brothers, or Miller Rhoads, you've shopped at a chain outlet owned by Allied Stores.

In a chain operation, centralization in decision making and purchasing is common. Chain stores have advantages in dealing with manufacturers, particularly as the size of the chain grows. A large chain can bargain with a manufacturer to obtain good service or volume discounts on orders. Sears' large volume makes it a strong negotiator with manufacturers of most products. The

FIGURE 15-4
Classifying retail outlets

METHOD OF CLASSIFICATION	DESCRIPTION OF RETAIL OUTLET

Form of ownership	Independent
	Corporate chain
	Consumer cooperative
	Contractual system
	  Retailer-sponsored cooperative
	  Wholesaler-sponsored voluntary chain
	  Franchise

Level of service	Self-service Limited service Full service

Merchandise line	Depth
	  Single line
	  Limited line
	Breadth
	  General merchandise
	  Scrambled merchandising

Method of operation	Store retailing
	Nonstore
	  Direct marketing
	  In-home retailing

power of chains is seen in the retailing of computers: small independents buy at 75 percent of list price, but large chains such as ComputerLand pay only 60 to 65 percent of list price.[3] Consumers also benefit in dealing with chains because there are consistent merchandise and policies, as well as multiple outlets.

Consumer Coöperative A consumer cooperative is an outlet owned by a group of consumers who also manage, operate, and shop at the store. This form of retailing is most common in food marketing. Although estimates show that food cooperatives account for less than 1 percent of all U.S. grocery sales,[4] not all co-ops are small. The Berkeley co-op in California, for example, has 12 stores. In Scandinavian countries food cooperatives have significant market shares: Finland, 37 percent; Norway, 25 percent; Sweden, 21 percent; and Denmark, 19 percent.[5]

For consumers the attractiveness of a cooperative is often in terms of price. Co-op food prices have been estimated to be 18 percent to 25 percent lower than at a regular grocery store.[6] However, to gain these savings, a consumer usually must devote a certain number of hours per month to activities in the cooperative. Although co-ops have been strong in some Scandinavian countries, this form of retailing has not grown significantly in the United States.

Contractual System Contractual systems involve independently owned stores that band together to act like a chain. The three kinds described in Chapter 13 are retailer-sponsored cooperatives, wholesaler-sponsored voluntary chains, and franchises. A retailer-sponsored cooperative is the Associated Grocers, which consists of neighborhood grocers that agree with several other independent grocers to all buy their meat from the same wholesaler. In this way, members

CarX is a franchise system

can take advantage of volume discounts commonly available to chains and also give the impression of being a large chain, which may be viewed more favorably by some consumers. Wholesaler-sponsored voluntary chains such as Western Auto and Independent Grocers' Alliance (IGA) try to achieve similar benefits.

As noted in Chapter 13, in a franchise system an individual or firm (the franchisee) contracts with a parent company (the franchisor) to set up a business or retail outlet. McDonald's, CarX, and Holiday Inn all involve some level of franchising. The franchisor usually assists in setting up the store, selecting the store location, advertising, and training personnel. The franchisee pays a yearly fee usually tied to the store's sales. Although this might be seen as a relatively new phenomenon, this ownership approach has been used with gas stations since the early 1900's. Franchising is attractive because of the opportunity for people to enter a well-known, established business where managerial advice is provided. Also, the franchise fee may be less than the cost of setting up an independent business. License fees paid to the franchisor can range from as little as $9,750 for a business card operation, to as much as $350,000 to open a McDonald's.[7]

For the organization deciding to franchise, the trade-off is the advantage of reduced expenses to expand but the loss of some control. A good franchisor has strong control of the outlets in terms of delivery and presentation of merchandise.

The hottest trend in franchising is **piggyback franchising,** in which stores operated by one chain sell the products of another franchised firm. For example, Dairy Queens are beginning to sell the products of Mr. Donut.

LEVEL OF SERVICE

Even though most customers perceive little variation in retail outlets by form of ownership, differences between retailers are more obvious in terms of level of service. In some department stores, such as Loehman's, individual dressing room stalls are not provided. Rather, all the women try on clothes in a large, enclosed area. Some grocery stores, such as the Cub chain, have customers individually mark the price on their purchases and bag the food in sacks brought from home. Other outlets, such as Ayers in Cincinnati, provide a wide range of customer services from gift wrapping to wardrobe consultation.

Self-Service Self-service is at the extreme end of the level of service continuum because the customer performs many functions, and little is provided by the outlet. Home building supply outlets, discount stores, and catalog showrooms are often self-service. Warehouse stores, usually in buildings several times larger than a conventional store, are self-service with all nonessential customer services eliminated. Levitz furniture stores, Big E food stores in Indiana, and Hinky Dinky in Nebraska, Missouri, and Texas are examples of the no frills, self-service approach.

Limited Service Limited service outlets provide some services, such as credit, merchandise return, and telephone ordering, but not others, such as custom making clothes. Department stores typically are considered limited-service outlets.

Full Service The full-service retailer provides a complete list of services to cater to its customer. Specialty stores are among the few stores in this category. Nordstrom's, a Seattle-based retail chain, sets the standard for full service. Clerks keep notebooks on customers' dress sizes and fashion preferences. And in some stores a tuxedoed bootblack will shine your shoes while another clerk serenades you on a baby grand piano.[8]

MERCHANDISE LINE

Retail outlets also vary by their merchandise lines, the key distinction being the breadth and depth of the items offered to customers (Figure 15-5). **Breadth of product line** means the store carries a wide variety of different items. **Depth of product line** means the store carries a large assortment of each item, such as a shoe store that offers running shoes, dress shoes, and children's shoes.

Depth of Line Stores that carry a considerable assortment (depth) of a related line of items are limited line stores. Herman's sporting goods stores carry considerable depth in sports equipment ranging from weight lifting accessories to running shoes. Stores that carry tremendous depth in one primary line of merchandise are single line stores. Victoria's Secret, a nationwide chain, carries great depth in women's lingerie. Both limited and single line stores are often referred to as specialty outlets.

FIGURE 15-5
Breadth versus depth of merchandise lines

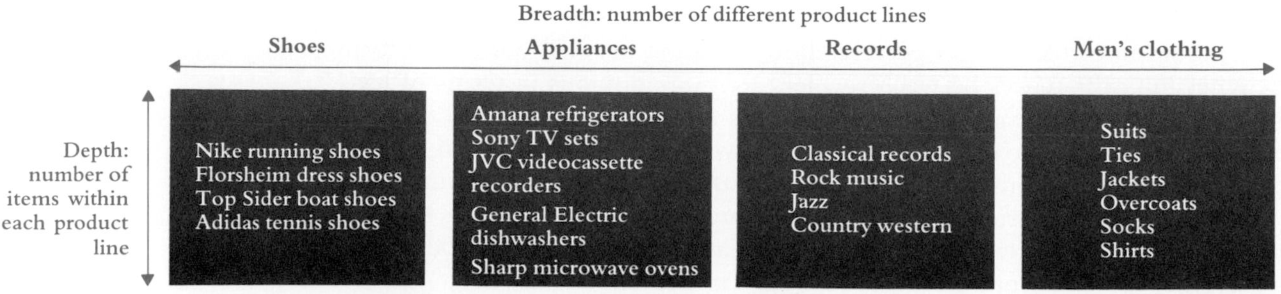

Breadth of Line Stores that carry a broad product line, with limited depth, are referred to as general merchandise stores. For example, a large department store carries a wide range of different types of products but not unusual sizes. The breadth and depth of merchandise lines are important decisions for a retailer. Traditionally, outlets carried related lines of goods. Today, however, **scrambled merchandising,** offering several unrelated product lines in a single store, is common. The modern drugstore carries food, camera equipment, magazines, paper products, toys, small hardware items, and pharmaceuticals. Department stores repair automobiles, provide travel planning services, and sell insurance.

A major new form of scrambled merchandising in the United States opened in Dallas, Texas, on December 28, 1987, when the Wal-Mart chain opened its first Hypermarket, U.S.A. Showing strong sales, the company quickly followed with a second in January, 1988, in Topeka, Kansas, and a third in Washington, Missouri, not far from St. Louis. A French firm called Carrefour, the largest hypermarket company in Europe, opened a store during 1988 in Philadelphia.[9]

FIGURE 15-6
Layout of Hypermarket U.S.A.

Source: Redrawn from "Wal-Mart Launches Hypermarket U.S.A.," *Discount Store News* (January 18, 1988), p. 11.

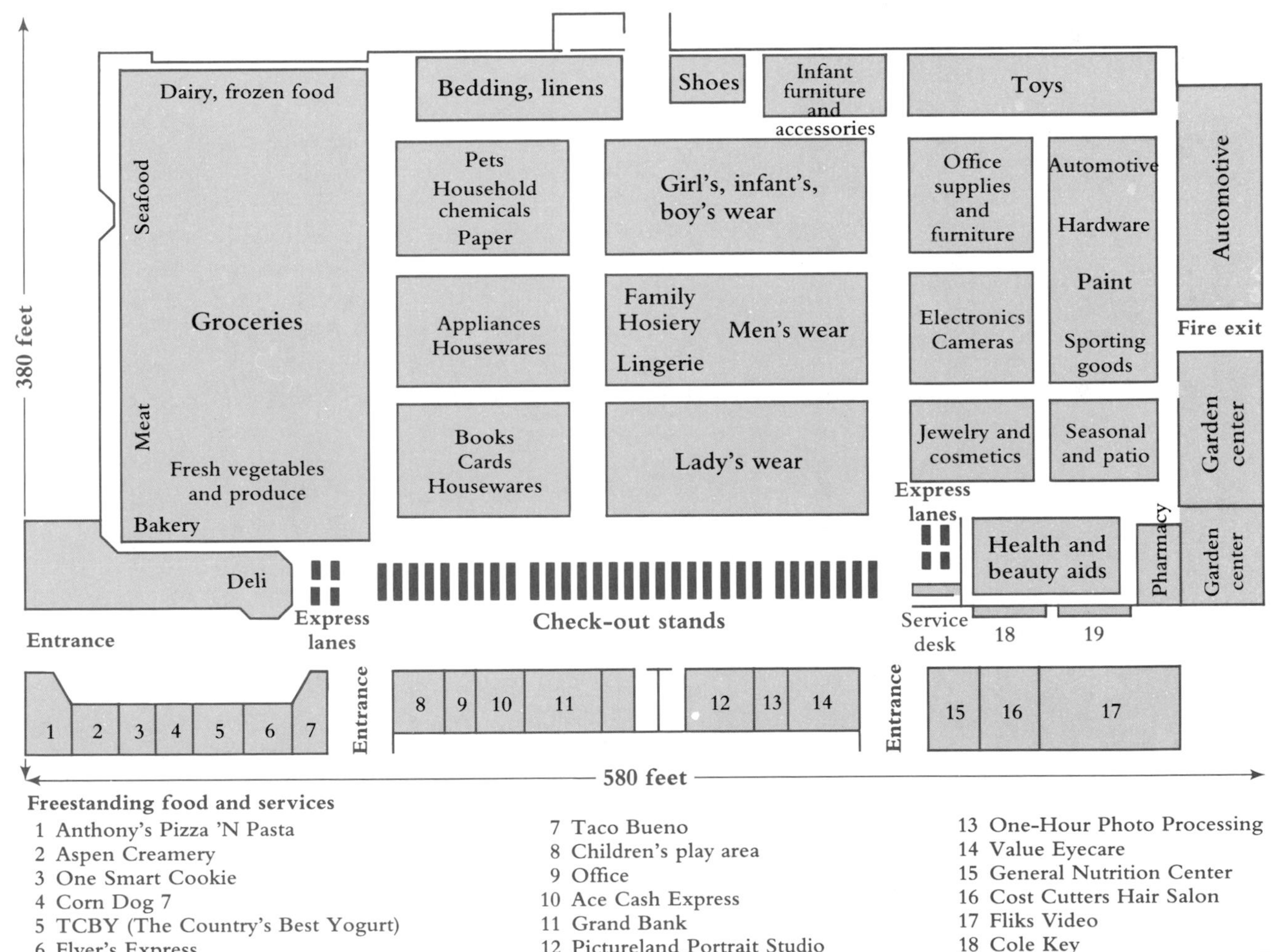

Freestanding food and services

1 Anthony's Pizza 'N Pasta
2 Aspen Creamery
3 One Smart Cookie
4 Corn Dog 7
5 TCBY (The Country's Best Yogurt)
6 Flyer's Express
7 Taco Bueno
8 Children's play area
9 Office
10 Ace Cash Express
11 Grand Bank
12 Pictureland Portrait Studio
13 One-Hour Photo Processing
14 Value Eyecare
15 General Nutrition Center
16 Cost Cutters Hair Salon
17 Fliks Video
18 Cole Key
19 Heel Quik

Hypermarkets are defined as large stores (over 100,000 square feet), offering a mix of 40 percent food products, and 60 percent general merchandise items.[10] Figure 15-6 shows the layout of the new Hypermarket U.S.A. store with its 50 checkout lines within the 220,000 square feet of selling space—about the area of five football fields.

Scrambled merchandising is convenient for consumers because it eliminates the number of stops required in a shopping trip. However, for the retailer this merchandising policy means there is competition between very dissimilar types of retail outlets, or **intertype competition.** A local bakery may compete with a department store, discount outlet, or even a local gas station. Scrambled merchandising and intertype competition make it more difficult to be a retailer.

METHOD OF OPERATION

Retail outlets have begun to vary widely in the way their services are provided, or the method of operation. Throughout this discussion, we have talked in terms of retail outlets, rather than stores. Classifying retail outlets by method of operation means dividing these outlets into store and nonstore retailing.

Store Retailing Traditionally retailing meant the consumer went to the store and purchased a product—which is store retailing. Most of the retailing examples discussed earlier in the chapter, such as corporate chains, department stores, and limited and single line specialty stores, involve store retailing.

Nonstore Retailing Viewing retailing as an activity limited to sales in a store is too narrow an approach. Nonstore retailing occurs outside a retail outlet, such as through direct marketing, described in Chapter 13 (mail order, vending machines, computer, and teleshopping), and in-home retailing.

Few areas of retailing have grown as rapidly during the decade as mail order. During the early 1980's yearly sales increases averaged 15 percent, but during the latter half of the decade these increases have slowed to a still strong 10 percent. The flood of catalogs continues, with the average household receiving about 50 per year.[11] The computer has stimulated the big spurt in direct mail efforts, because orders can be received, processed, and billed in very little time.

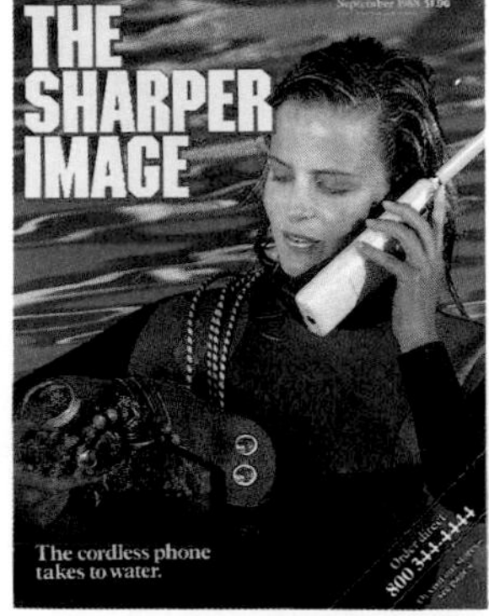

THE
SHARPER
IMAGE
The cordless phone
takes to water.

Mail order retailing is attractive because it eliminates the costs of a store, clerks, and merchandising. American Express Company, active in direct mail selling, sends out 4 million Christmas catalogs and has no retail stores. Inventory is often stored in low-cost warehouse space in areas less accessible to consumers.

As sales growth in the direct mail industry begins to moderate, direct mail companies are changing their strategies. One approach being tried involves selling catalogs in bookstores, libraries, and supermarkets. Another major strategy is to have direct-mail companies open their own retail stores.[12] Look at the Marketing Action Memo for one of the more unusual operations that may sell the necessities (?) you can't find in your local department store.

Direct marketing also encompasses vending machines, which make it possible to serve customers when and where stores cannot. Maintenance and operating costs are high, so product prices tend to be higher in vending machines. Typically, small convenience products are available in vending machines, but

MARKETING · ACTION · MEMO

FROM A BUMPER STICKER: "WHOEVER DIES WITH THE MOST TOYS WINS!"

A strange motto, fit for a bumper sticker!

You might be right, except it is the theme which drives Richard Thalheimer, a 38-year-old graduate of Yale and president of a unique company—The Sharper Image. Need a $69 GoBall, a round, green-striped high-tech object that scurries around the house at the beck and call of whoever is running the remote control device? Or, would you rather have the $69 Petster, a synthetic, furry electronic beast that resembles a household pet and responds to voice commands? It's the perfect thing for those who live where pets are not allowed.

These items may sound strange to you, but they meet the goal of Mr. Thalheimer, who describes his mission as "coming up with the new and unique product." The Sharper Image is one of the companies that began as a direct-mail marketer in the early 1980's. Since its first store opened in San Francisco in 1983, the company has seen tremendous growth. In 1988 there were 50 stores with plans for an eventual 100. In 1984 catalog sales accounted for three-quarters of the company's sales, but in 1988 sales split about evenly between catalog and store sales.

The Sharper Image's main idea is to be on the cutting edge of the new, technologically advanced product like the $29 CheckGo. This gizmo spins your golf ball at 10,000 rpm to determine the "sweet spot." The company employs five people whose only job is to search for the new and different.

And who is the target for this stuff? Mr. Thalheimer says it is people like him, the 30- to 55-year-old with a high disposable income. So the next time you're bored with the everyday gift, check out the Sharper Image for that new whizmo, hot geegaw, or latest whatchamacallit.

Source: Jim Sullivan, "He Plays Santa to the Yuppies," *The Boston Globe* (December 15, 1986) pp. 8, 9.

with improved technology, more expensive, larger items are being sold in machines. In Paris, businesses sell Levi's jeans in vending machines for $47 apiece.[13]

Computer-assisted retailing is a new approach by which customers view products on their TV screen or computer monitor and then order the desired item on the terminal. One company, Comp-U-Card, provides computer shopping to subscribers who pay $25 a year for access to the computerized data bank. These subscribers get price quotes and comparison shopping information and then order products. Comp-U-Card has over 1 million members who talk to sales consultants on a toll-free 800 line.[14] The Arthur Andersen Co., an accounting and consulting firm, did a study of 200 telecommunication experts and predicted that 25 percent of the United States will do some form of interactive shopping by 1990.[15]

The success of computerized retailing depends on the growth of home computers and cable systems that will support it. Initial results of computer-interactive home shopping services have been disappointing. In 1986, three companies that had invested heavily in this form of retailing—Times-Mirror, Knight-Ridder Newspapers, and CBS, Inc.—gave up.[16] Several reasons have been cited for the problems of interactive shopping such as the size and cultural diversity of the United States, the large number of existing on-line services, such as Comp-U-Card, and the growth of new competition such as television shopping.

A fourth form of direct marketing that has grown quickly since the mid-1980's is television home shopping (teleshopping). Unlike interactive computer shopping, the consumer sits at home and tunes into a television show on which products are displayed. The consumer can then call an 800 number and purchase whatever item he or she sees displayed. This form of nonstore shopping experienced rapid growth from mid-1985 to 1987. But during 1988, it entered a more mature phase. Several home shopping networks, such as the Consumer Discount Network, Shoppers University, the Home Shopping Game Show, and Value television, all went off the air. The limited growth is attributed to the set number of cable television channels. Industry leaders still predict a bright future. And although the dramatic sales increases of the early 1980's are slowing, home shopping sales are forecast to be $6 billion by 1990, a significant rise from the 1986 level of $1.1 billion.[17] Future growth is expected to come from television shopping channels that appeal to specific market segments, such as a separate show for the fashion-oriented consumer.

With in-home retailing, customers buy products in their own home from retailers such as Amway (soap), Shaklee (vitamins), and Tupperware (plastic dishes). The advantage of this approach is that often the customer and salesperson are friends or acquaintances, which may increase the chance of a sale.

CONCEPT CHECK

1. **Centralized decision making and purchasing are an advantage of ________ ownership.**
2. **Would a shop for big men's clothes carrying size 40 to 60 pants have a broad or deep product line?**
3. **What are some examples of direct marketing?**

RETAILING STRATEGY

This section identifies how a retail store positions itself and three areas where it can take actions to establish or alter that position: (1) retail pricing, (2) store location, or (3) image and atmosphere.

POSITIONING A RETAIL STORE

The four classification alternatives presented in the previous section help determine one store's position relative to its competitors.

Retail Positioning Matrix A framework for viewing the **retail positioning matrix** has been developed by the MAC Group, Inc., a management consulting firm.[18] The matrix positions retail outlets on two dimensions: breadth of product

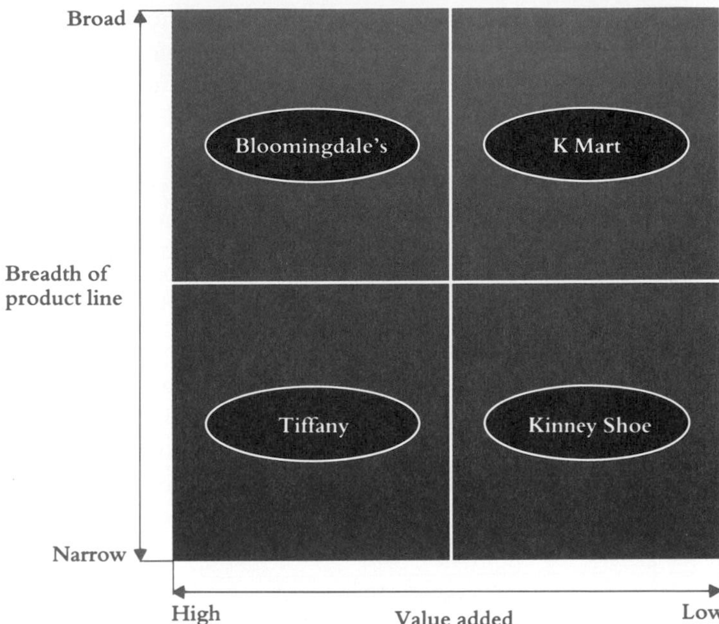

FIGURE 15-7
Retail positioning map

line and value added. As defined previously, breadth of product line is the range of products sold through each outlet. The second dimension, *value added,* involves the service level and method of operation, which includes elements such as location (as with 7-Eleven stores), consistent product (as with Holiday Inn or McDonald's), or a prestigious image (as with Saks Fifth Avenue or Brooks Brothers).

The retail positioning map in Figure 15-7 shows four possible positions. An organization can be successful in any box, but unique strategies are required within each quadrant. Consider the four stores shown in the map:

1. Bloomingdale's has high value added and a broad product line. Retailers in this quadrant pay great attention to store design and product lines. Merchandise often has a high margin of profit and is of high quality. The stores in this position typically provide high levels of service.
2. K Mart has low value added and a broad line. K Mart and similar firms typically trade a higher price for increased volume in sales. Retailers in this position focus on price with low service levels and an image of being a place for good buys.
3. Tiffany has high value added and a narrow line. Retailers of this type typically sell a very restricted range of products that are of high status quality. Customers are also provided with high levels of service.
4. Kinney has a low value added and narrow line. Such retailers are specialty mass merchandisers. Kinney, for example, carries attractively priced shoes for the entire family. These outlets appeal to value-conscious consumers. Economies of scale are achieved through centralized advertising, merchandising, buying, and distribution. Stores are usually the same in design, layout, and merchandise; hence they are often referred to as "cookie-cutter" stores.

Keys to Positioning To successfully position a store, it must have an identity that has some advantages over the competitors yet is recognized by consumers. A company can have outlets in several positions on the matrix, but this approach is usually done with different store names. Dayton-Hudson, for example, owns Dayton's, Diamonds, and Hudson's department stores (with a high value added and broad line) and Target and Lechemere discount stores (low value added and broad line). Shifting from one box in the retail positioning map to another is also possible, but all elements of retailing strategy must be reexamined.

RETAILING MIX

In developing retailing strategy, managers work with the **retailing mix,** which includes the (1) goods and services, (2) physical distribution, and (3) communications tactics chosen by a store[19] (Figure 15-8). Decisions relating to the mix focus on the consumer. Each of the areas shown is important, but we will cover only three basic areas: (1) pricing, (2) store location, and (3) image and atmo-

FIGURE 15-8
The retailing mix

Source: Redrawn from William Lazer and Eugene J. Kelley, "The Retailing Mix: Planning and Management," *Journal of Retailing*, Vol. 37 (Spring 1961), pp. 34-41.

sphere. The communications and promotion component is discussed in Chapter 17 on advertising and Chapter 18 on personal selling.

Retail Pricing In setting prices for merchandise, retailers must decide on the markup, markdown, and timing for markdowns. Off-price retailers are one type of outlet stressing low-price policies.

As mentioned in the appendix to Chapter 12, the *markup* refers to how much should be added to the cost the retailer paid for a product to reach the final selling price. Retailers decide on the *original markup*, but by the time the product is sold, they end up with a *maintained markup*. The original markup is the difference between retailer cost and initial selling price. When products do not sell as quickly as anticipated, their price is reduced. The difference between the final selling price and retailer cost is the maintained markup, which is also called the gross margin.

Discounting a product, or taking a *markdown*, occurs when the product does not sell at the original price and an adjustment is necessary. Often new models or styles force the price of existing models to be marked down. Remember the original Sony Walkman? It first sold in stores for $150. However, to meet competition, Sony developed new Walkman models. As demand for the original version dropped, retailers began to take markdowns. The original Walkman was being sold for less than $70 within 8 months of its introduction.

Although most retailers plan markdowns, many retailers use price discounts as part of their regular merchandising policy. In the Northeast, Filene's is a well-established department store that operates a basement store for out-of-season and slow-selling merchandise. Filene's has an automatic discount policy:

- Merchandise not sold after 12 selling days is reduced 25 percent.
- Merchandise not sold after 18 selling days is reduced 50 percent.
- Merchandise not sold after 24 selling days is reduced 75 percent.
- After 30 selling days merchandise is given to charity.

All items in Filene's basement store are tagged with the initial date on which they were displayed. The automatic discount policy adjusts price as a function of demand. If you want that suit now discounted at 25 percent, will you risk waiting 6 more days to get it for 50 percent off?

A final issue, *timing*, involves deciding when to discount the merchandise. Many retailers take a markdown as soon as sales fall off to free up valuable selling space and cash. However, other stores delay markdowns to discourage bargain hunters and maintain an image of quality. There is no clear answer, but retailers must consider how the timing might affect future sales.

Off-Price Retailing Off-price retailing is a new trend having a dramatic impact on retail pricing, most commonly in clothing sales. **Off-price retailing** is defined as selling brand-name merchandise at lower than regular prices. In 1983 off-price sales accounted for 4 to 6 percent of all clothing sales. Yet by 1987 off-price retailing began to take a major portion of apparel sales in the United States. Look at Figure 15-9 for the growing percent of purchases bought at off-price retailers.

FIGURE 15-9
The growing impact of off-price retailing

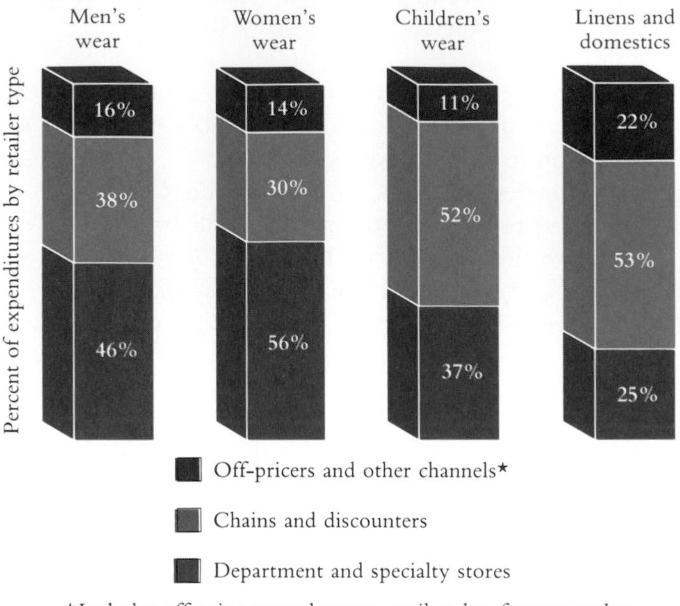

Figure 15-9 shows that off-price sales are increasing dramatically in factory outlet stores. Filene's has turned its original basement into off-price, free-standing basement stores. Other off-price outlets familiar to women are Hit n' Miss (Zayre Corporation) and Loehman's (Associated Dry Goods Corporation); men know Kuppenheimer Manufacturing Company (Hartmarx); and for the general population there are T.J. Maxx (Zayre Corporation) and Marshall's (Melville Corporation) stores.

There is a difference between the off-price retailer and a discount store. Off-price merchandise is bought by the retailer at prices below wholesale prices, while the discounter buys at full wholesale price but takes less of a markup (compared with traditional department stores). Merchandise in off-price retailers turns over eight to ten times a year rather than the four times for the department store. Savings to the consumer at off-price retailers are reported as high as 70 percent off the price at a traditional department store.

There are two growing variations of off-price retailing. One is the warehouse club. These large stores (over 100,000 square feet) are rather stark with no elaborate displays, customer service, or home delivery. They require a yearly membership fee (usually $25) for the privilege of shopping.[20] There has been rapid growth in this new type of off-price retailer. In 1984 there were only 66 outlets in the United States, with predictions for 350 with $20 billion in sales by 1990.[21] Their deep discount of 40 percent off regular discount store prices is again the appeal.

A second trend is the "one-price" apparel chain. These outlets, such as Dre$$ to the Nine$ in Ft. Lauderdale or $5 Clothing Store in California and Nevada, sell everything in their store (usually women's apparel and accessories) for one price. These outlets have begun as many of the early off-price retailers have started to appeal to the more affluent shopper. The one-price outlet targets the lower- and middle-income, value-oriented consumer.[22]

Store Location A second aspect of the retailing mix involves deciding where to locate the store and how many stores to have. Department stores, which started downtown in most cities, have followed customers to the suburbs, and in recent years more stores have been opened in large regional malls. Most stores today are near several others in one of four settings: the central business district, the regional center, the community shopping center, or the strip.

The **central business district** is the oldest retail setting, the community's downtown area. Until the regional outflow to suburbs, it was the major shopping area, but the suburban population has grown at the expense of the downtown shopping area. Detroit, experiencing a decade of population decline, lost its last major department store in 1982 when Hudson's left the central city.

Regional centers are the suburban malls of today, containing up to 100 stores. The typical drawing distance of a regional center is over 5 to 10 miles from the mall. These large shopping areas often contain one or two *anchor stores*, which are well-known national or regional stores such as Sears, Saks Fifth Avenue, and Bloomingdale's. In some communities such as Fargo, North Dakota, or Missoula, Montana, the large regional shopping center has replaced the downtown as the major shopping area. In North Dakota a weekend shopping trip of 300 miles to the mall in Fargo is common for many families.

A more limited approach to retail location is the **community shopping center,** which typically has one primary store (usually a department store branch) and often about 20 to 40 smaller outlets. Generally, these centers serve a population base of about 100,000.

Not every suburban store is located in a shopping mall. Many neighborhoods have clusters of stores, referred to as a **strip location,** to serve people who are within a 5- to 10-minute drive and live in a population base of under 30,000. Gas station, hardware, laundry, and grocery outlets are commonly found in a strip location. Unlike the larger shopping centers, the composition of these stores is usually unplanned.

Retail Image and Atmosphere Deciding on the image of a retail outlet is an important retailing mix factor that has been widely recognized and studied since the late 1950's. Pierre Martineau described image as "the way in which the store is defined in the shopper's mind, partly by its functional qualities and partly by an aura of psychological attributes.[23] In this definition, *functional* refers to mix elements such as price ranges, store layouts, and breadth and depth of merchandise lines. The psychological attributes are the intangibles, such as a sense of belonging, excitement, style, or warmth. Image has been found to include a store's personnel, return policies, and cleanliness.[24]

In designing a store's image, retailers must consider the area in which they're located and the type of customers they attract. On Rodeo Drive in Beverly Hills, status is the image promoted by "bijan's," an exclusive men's clothing store. Entry to the store is by appointment only. The store only averages six customers a day, but the typical shopper spends several thousand dollars per visit. It's not difficult when silk ties are $100, cotton shirts $200, shoes $400,

bijan's *(left)* offers an exclusive image, whereas Quincy Market is exciting

and suits start at $1000. Price, appointments, and personal attention by Mr. Bijan give this store a distinct image.

Closely related to the concept of image is the store's atmosphere, or ambiance. Many retailers believe that sales are affected by layout, color, lighting, and music in the store, as well as by how crowded it is.

Hardware stores, for example, are attempting to shift from their earlier all-male image and meet the demands of a growing segment of female buyers. ServiStar in Virginia has redesigned their stores with bright lighting, chrome display gridwork, and wall murals.[26] In creating the right image and atmosphere, a retail store tries to identify its target audience and what the target audience seeks from the buying experience so its atmosphere will fortify the beliefs and the emotional reactions buyers are seeking.[27]

Concept Check

1 **What are the two dimensions of the retail positioning map?**

2 **How does original markup differ from maintained markup?**

3 **An area with two anchor stores and up to 100 other stores is a __________ center.**

The Changing Nature of Retailing

Retailing is the most dynamic aspect of the channel of distribution. Stores like bijan's or pricing approaches such as off-price retailing show that new retailers are always entering the market, searching for a new position that will attract customers The reason for this continual change is explained by two concepts: the wheel of retailing and the retail life cycle.

THE WHEEL OF RETAILING

The **wheel of retailing** describes how new forms of retail outlets enter the market.[28] Usually they enter as low-status, low-margin stores such as a drive-in hamburger stand with no indoor seating and a limited menu (Figure 15-10, Box 1). Gradually these outlets add fixtures and more embellishments to their stores (in-store seating, plants, and chicken sandwiches as well as hamburgers) to increase the attractiveness for customers. With these additions, prices and status rise (Box 2). As time passes, these outlets add still more services and their prices and status increase even further (Box 3). These retail outlets now face some new form of retail outlet that again appears as a low-status, low-margin operator (Box 4), and the wheel of retailing turns as the cycle starts to repeat itself.

In the 1950's McDonald's and Burger King had very limited menus of hamburgers and french fries. Most stores had no inside seating for customers. Over time, the wheel of retailing for fast-food restaurants has turned. These chains have changed by expanding their menu and altering their stores. Today the wheel has come full circle. Hooker's Hamburgers in the South and Burger Street in Texas are very small, fast-food hamburger chains with a very limited menu. The stores can run with six employees, and only offer take-out service. The prices are about 80 cents lower than McDonald's for a burger, fries, and cola.[29]

Discount stores were a major new retailing form in the 1950's and priced their products below those of department stores. As prices in discount stores

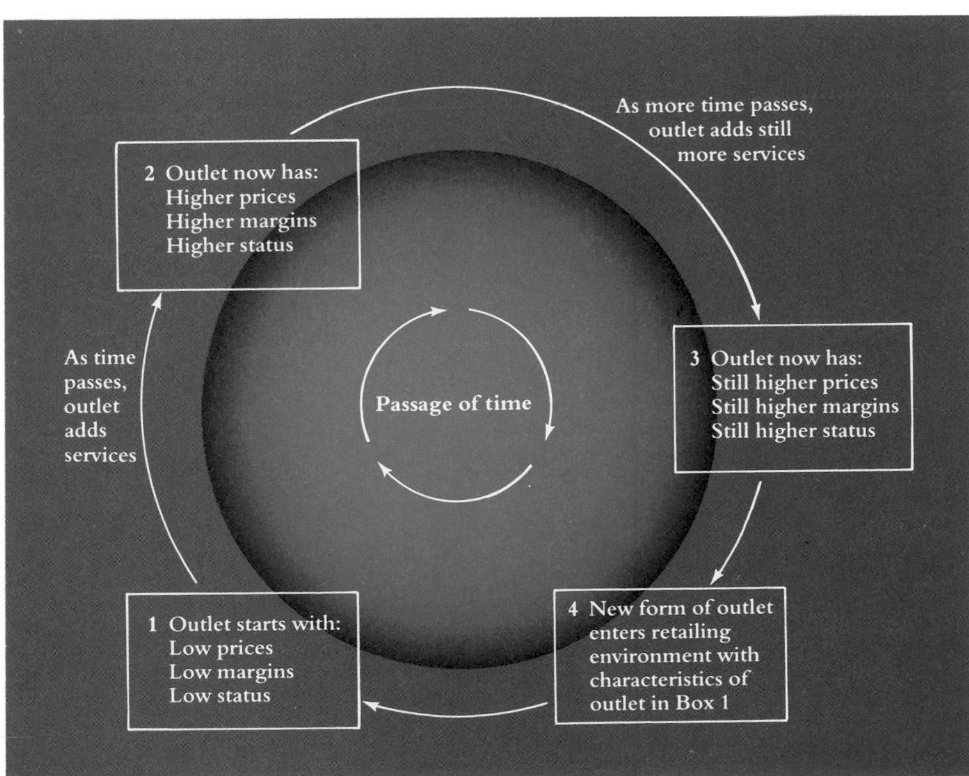

FIGURE 15-10
The wheel of retailing

rose, they found themselves overpriced in the 1970's compared with a new form of retail outlet—the warehouse retailer.

THE RETAIL LIFE CYCLE

The process of growth and decline that retail outlets, like products, experience is described by the **retail life cycle**.[30] Figure 15-11 shows the retail life cycle and the position of various current forms of retail outlets on it. Early growth is the stage of emergence of a retail outlet, with a sharp departure from existing competition. Market share rises gradually, although profits may be low because of start-up costs. In the next stage, accelerated development, both market share and profit achieve their greatest growth rates. Usually multiple outlets are established as companies focus on the distribution element of the retailing mix. In this stage some later competitors may enter. Wendy's, for example, appeared on the hamburger chain scene almost 20 years after McDonald's had begun operation. The key goal for the retailer in this stage is to establish a dominant position in the fight for market share.

The battle for market share is usually fought before the maturity phase, and some competitors drop out of the market. In the wars among hamburger chains, Jack In The Box, Gino Marchetti's, and Burger Chef used to be more dominant outlets. New retail forms enter in the maturity phase, stores try to maintain their market share, and price discounting occurs. The battle among retailers is to delay entering the decline stage in which market share and profit fall rapidly.

Figure 15-12 shows how many of today's retail institutions evolved. It shows the difficult challenge facing today's retailers: the time to move from early growth to maturity is decreasing so there is less time for a retail outlet to achieve profitability. Department stores took 100 years to reach maturity,

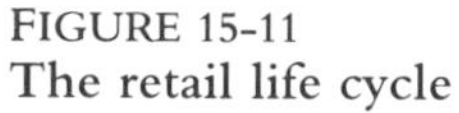
FIGURE 15-11
The retail life cycle

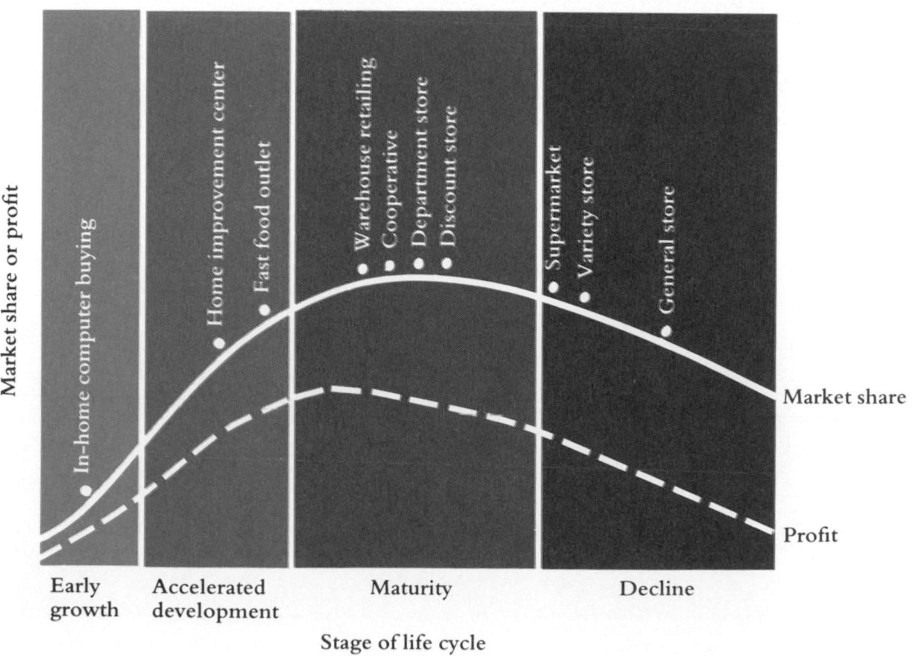

INSTITUTIONAL TYPE	PERIOD OF FASTEST GROWTH	PERIOD FROM INCEPTION TO MATURITY (YEARS)	STAGE OF LIFE CYCLE	REPRESENTATIVE FIRMS*
General store	1800–1840	100	Declining	A local store
Single-line store	1820–1840	100	Mature	Hickory Farms
Department store	1860–1940	80	Mature	Marshall Field's
Variety store	1870–1930	50	Declining	Morgan-Lindsay
Mail-order house	1915–1950	50	Mature	Spiegel
Corporate chain	1920–1930	50	Mature	Sears
Discount store	1955–1975	20	Mature	K Mart
Supermarket	1935–1965	35	Mature/declining	A&P
Shopping center	1950–1965	40	Mature	Paramus
Cooperative	1930–1950	40	Mature	Ace Hardware
Gasoline station	1930–1950	45	Mature	Texaco
Convenience store	1965–1975	20	Mature	7-Eleven
Fast-food outlet	1960–1975	15	Late growth	Shoney's
Home improvement center	1965–1980	15	Late growth	Lowes
Warehouse retailing	1970–1980	10	Maturity	Levitz
Super specialists	1975–1985	10	Late growth	The Limited

*These firms are representative of institutional types and are not necessarily in the stage of life cycle specified for the institutional group as a whole.

Source: Adapted from: J. Barry Mason & Morris L. Mayer, *Modern Retailing: Theory and Practice* (Plano, Texas: Business Publications, Inc., 1981), p. 93.

FIGURE 15-12
The evolution of today's retail institutions

whereas warehouse retailing took only 10 years. As a result, retailers must continually modify their mix to avoid early decline.

FUTURE CHALLENGES IN RETAILING

The challenges facing retailers come from many directions, including (1) the advent of computerization, (2) the cost of shrinkage, and (3) the retailing of services. Because services marketing has become a dominant trend in recent years, Chapter 22 covers this topic. The following sections address the former two issues.

COMPUTERIZATION OF THE RETAIL STORE

Computers are in use today in most medium to large stores in the form of computerized checkouts (or scanning systems) that read the item being purchased. They are rapidly replacing traditional cash registers. In 1986 over 50 percent of the nation's supermarkets were equipped with scanners.[31] Although slow to catch hold, scanning systems are being rapidly adopted.

Scanning systems use the **universal product code** (UPC) as the basis to record the item being purchased. The code is a number assigned to identify each product and is represented by a series of bars with varying widths. The scanner converts this UPC symbol, identifies the product, and accesses the price stored in the firm's computer. Scanners provide retailers with savings through faster checkouts, fewer misrings, and better control of inventory.

Dillard's department stores built a centralized computer system that links 115 stores in 11 Midwestern and Southern states to track inventory. Consumers also benefit: speed, accuracy, and more courteous checkout clerks have been reported as advantages.[33] Studies have shown that the common uses for scanner data have been in five areas: monitoring current products, new product research, monitoring prices, studying the impact of coupons, and assessing advertising effectiveness.[34] Also, some supermarkets benefit by selling the scanner data on unit sales to firms manufacturing consumer products.

THE SHRINKAGE PROBLEM

A long-standing, growing problem threatening retailing is **shrinkage,** or theft of merchandise by customers and employees. According to the National Coalition of Retailers to Prevent Shoplifting, the cost of shrinkage represents

MARKETING · RESEARCH · REPORT

WANT TO CATCH A THIEF? GO SHOPPING!

Retail losses are assuming epidemic proportions. But how big are the losses and who is doing the stealing?

To answer these questions, Warren French, Melvin Crask, and Fred Mader analyzed surveys from 670 retailers in 21 states. These researchers also tried to assess whether this problem differs by the type of retail outlet. The table below shows the estimates of retailers about the seriousness of shoplifting problems.

Employee theft appears to be a major problem for department stores (59 percent). Yet shoplifting appears to be a major concern for most types of stores. And, more than half of the discount stores (54 percent) estimate that their losses from shoplifting are 5 percent or more of the sales. Controlling this significant expense is a major challenge for retailers.

Source: Warren A. French, Melvin R. Crask, and Fred H. Mader, "Retailer's Assessment of the Shoplifting Problem," *Journal of Retailing* (Winter 1984), pp. 108-115.

		TYPE OF RETAILER					
PROBLEM	TOTAL (n = 670)	FOOD (n = 115)	SPECIALTY (n = 146)	DEPARTMENT (n = 98)	DISCOUNT (n = 49)	APPAREL (n = 129)	DRUG (n = 65)
Retailers saying they have a problem with employee theft	27%	44%	7%	59%	41%	11%	19%
Retailers saying they have a problem with shoplifting	73	71	48	91	83	67	86
Retailers estimating that their shoplifting losses as a percentage of sales are:							
0 to 4.9%	63	63	74	62	46	62	70
5% or more	37	37	26	38	54	38	30

7 percent of retail sales.[35] And, as the Marketing Research Report indicates, retailers are not optimistic about the future trend in this area. Unfortunately, the cost of shrinkage must be passed on to the consumer in the form of higher prices.

Retailers have started to use a wide range of approaches such as locked display cases, observation towers, two-way mirrors, and magnetic detectors to combat this problem. As the Marketing Research Report shows, the problem is not just with the customer, but for some outlets the problem is the employees. In one study, half of all the employees surveyed said they had taken merchandise from their place of employment without paying for it. Some companies (such as the Lerner stores) have begun posting the amount lost per day in the employee lounge. Athlete's Foot, a specialty footwear retailer, uses pencil-and-paper "honesty tests" to reduce employee theft by screening dishonest job applicants and rewarding reliable and productive workers. This is an example of how many firms are now taking steps to anticipate and control shrinkage.[36]

CONCEPT CHECK

1 According to the wheel of retailing, when a new retail form appears, how would you characterize its image?

2 Market share is usually fought out before the ____________ stage of the retail life cycle.

3 What is shrinkage?

SUMMARY

1 Retailing provides a number of values to the consumer in the form of various utilities: time, place, possession, and form. Economically, retailing is important in terms of the people employed and sales represented.

2 Retailing outlets can be classified along several dimensions: the form of ownership, level of service, merchandise line, or method of operation.

3 There are several forms of ownership: the independent, chain, consumer cooperative, trade cooperative, or franchise.

4 Stores vary in the level of service, being self-service, limited service, or full service.

5 In terms of method of operation, retailing includes store and direct marketing operations. Direct-mail retailers are now setting up store operations. Interactive computer buying services have had disappointing growth, whereas teleshopping has rapidly matured in the past few years.

6 Retail outlets vary in terms of the breadth and depth of their merchandise lines. Breadth refers to the number of different items carried, and depth refers to the assortment of each item offered. In assessing their com-

petitive position, retail outlets should consider their position in terms of breadth of merchandise line and the amount of value added, which is the service level and method of operation.

7 Retailing strategy is based on the retailing mix, consisting of goods and services, physical distribution, and communications.

8 In retail pricing, retailers must decide on the markup, markdown, and timing for the markdown. A growing trend is off-price retailing in which the retailer offers nonbrand merchandise at lower than regular prices. This retailing form is most common in the clothing industry.

9 Retail site location is an important retailing mix decision. The common alternatives are the central business district, a regional shopping center, a community shopping center, or a strip location. These alternatives differ in terms of the distance from which they draw customers and the number and type of stores.

10 New retailing forms are explained by the wheel of retailing. Stores enter as low-status, low-margin outlets. Over time, they add services and raise margins, which allows a new form of low-status, low-margin retailing outlet to enter.

11 Like products, retail outlets have a life cycle consisting of four stages: early growth, accelerated development, maturity, and decline. Over the past 100 years the time it takes for each new retailing form to reach maturity has declined.

12 Computerized scanning systems are playing a major role in retail store operations. These scanners read the UPC symbol for each item and provide timely sales and inventory data.

KEY TERMS AND CONCEPTS

retailing p. 407
form of ownership p. 411
level of service p. 411
merchandise line p. 411
method of operation p. 411
piggyback franchising p. 413
breadth of product line p. 414
depth of product line p. 414
scrambled merchandising p. 415
hypermarkets p. 416
intertype competition p. 416
retail positioning matrix p. 418
retailing mix p. 420
off-price retailing p. 421
central business district p. 423
regional centers p. 423
community shopping center p. 423
strip location p. 423
wheel of retailing p. 425
retail life cycle p. 426
universal product code p. 427
shrinkage p. 428

CHAPTER PROBLEMS AND APPLICATIONS

1 In the Marketing Research Report on p. 409, two types of shoppers were profiled. What aspects of the retailing mix might you use to attract the browser segment into your store?
2 In recent years in the United States, more households have both the husband and wife employed outside the home. Assuming this trend were to continue, discuss the impact on (a) consumer cooperatives, (b) nonstore retailing alternatives, and (c) scrambled merchandising practices.
3 How does value added affect a store's competitive position?
4 In retail pricing, retailers often have a maintained markup. Explain how this maintained markup differs from original markup and why it is so important.
5 What are the similarities and differences between the product and retail life cycles?
6 How would you classify K Mart in terms of its position on the wheel of retailing versus that of the off-price retailer?
7 Develop a chart to highlight the role of each of the three main elements of the retailing mix across the four stages of the retail life cycle.
8 In Figure 15-7, Kinney Shoe was placed on the retail positioning matrix. What strategies should Kinney follow to move itself into the same position as Tiffany?
9 Compare and contrast the four types of store location alternatives in terms of drawing power of customers, number of stores, and type of stores.
10 According to the wheel of retailing and the retail life cycle, what will happen to off-price retailers?
11 The text discusses the development of teleshopping in the United States. How does the development of this form of direct marketing agree with the implications of the retail life cycle?

SUGGESTED READINGS

Jean C. Darian, "In Home Shopping: Are There Consumer Segments," *Journal of Retailing* (Summer 1987), pp. 163-186. *This study profiles who is most likely to be the in-home shopper of today.*

Richard J. George, "In Home Electronic Shopping: Disappointing Past, Uncertain Future," *The Journal of Consumer Marketing* (Fall 1987), pp. 47-56. *This article critically evaluates the growth in computer-assisted buying and teleshopping.*

Jack KaiKati, "The Boom in Warehouse Clubs," *Business Horizons* (March-April 1987), pp. 68-73. *This article reviews a growing trend in member-only retail outlets.*

Marthe Riche and Peter Francese, "Vital Trends in Consumer Demographics (I) & (II)," *Retail Control* (March 1987), pp. 28-51. *This two-part discussion highlights retailers' possible responses to the changing sociodemographics in the United States.*

"The Future of Hypermarkets," *Supermarket News* (February 15, 1988), pp. 1, 8, 38. *This article discusses the likely success of this retailing trend along with interviews from prominent retailers.*

BUD
LIGHT
BUD
LIGHT
BUD
LIGHT
BUD
LIGHT

16

PROMOTIONAL PROCESS, SALES PROMOTION, AND PUBLICITY

After reading this chapter you should be able to:

Explain the communication process and its elements.

•

Understand the promotional mix and the uniqueness of each component.

•

Select the promotional approach appropriate to a product's life cycle stage and characteristics.

•

Differentiate between the advantages of push and pull strategies.

•

Understand the alternative strengths and weaknesses of consumer-oriented and trade-oriented sales promotions.

•

Appreciate the value of an integrated publicity approach.

How Spuds MacKenzie Helped Anheuser-Busch Win in a Dog Market

Beer has been described as a "dog of a market."

Yet for any firm that wants to sell more but thinks it can't because the market has stagnated, Anheuser-Busch should be an inspiration. Although beer consumption per capita in the United States has been declining for years, Anheuser-Busch sells twice as much beer as it sold a decade ago, more beer than its two largest competitors combined, and more beer than anyone else in the world.[1]

The key to this brewer's success is marketing excellence, especially in its promotion, in which it dominates all other firms in the industry. Although many claim that Miller brought modern marketing to the brewing industry in the 1970's with the success of Miller Lite, Anheuser-Busch is the best student of marketing and is doing it better than anyone else.

Today, Anheuser-Busch combines state-of-the-art promotion with careful target marketing to produce such advertising classics as "I'll have a light . . . *Bud Light*" and wonderdog "Spuds MacKenzie," which together increased *Bud Light*'s sales by 20 percent in 1987.[2] Another illustration of Anheuser-Busch's promotional muscle is its dominance in professional sports. The company puts about 70 percent of its $450 million advertising budget into sports advertising and has exclusive advertising deals with 21 of 24 major league baseball teams, 21 of 28 National Football League franchises, 300 college sports teams, and most professional basketball, hockey, and soccer teams.

Although promotion to the beer-drinking consumer is critical to Anheuser-Busch, it doesn't come at the expense of promotion to its world-class distribution network. Every 3 years, it holds a Las Vegas–style extravaganza of monumental scale. Celebrities such as Paul Newman, Bernadette Peters, and Gene Kelly, plus company spokesmen such as Ed McMahon, Lou Rawls, and John Forsythe, appear on stage before an audience of about 5,000 local beer distributors.

At the same time, the company strongly encourages their distributors to promote Anheuser-Busch locally. Each year every wholesaler is asked to suggest a special local promotion for each brand. Anheuser-Busch often covers half the cost, and it almost always outdoes its rivals.

Promotion represents the fourth element in the marketing mix. The promotional element comprises a mix of tools available for the marketer called the *promotional mix,* which consists of advertising, personal selling, sales promotion, and publicity. All of these elements can be used to (1) inform prospective buyers about the benefits of the product, (2) persuade them to try it, and (3) remind them later about the benefits they enjoyed by using the product. This chapter first gives an overview of the communications process and the promotional elements used in marketing and then discusses sales promotion and publicity. Chapter 17 covers advertising, and Chapter 18 discusses personal selling.

FIGURE 16-1
The communication process

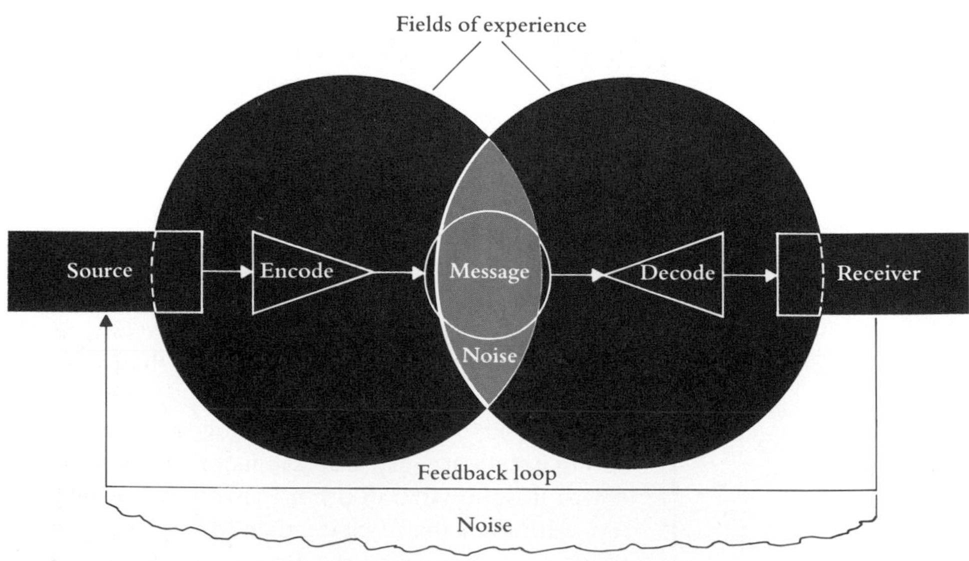

THE COMMUNICATION PROCESS

Communication is the sharing of meaning and requires five central elements: a source, a message, a receiver, and the processes of encoding and decoding[3] (Figure 16-1). The **source** may be a company or salesperson who has information to convey. This information, such as the particulars on a new weight reduction drink, forms the **message.** Consumers who read, hear, or see the message are the **receivers.** The message is communicated by means of a channel—the television, radio, or a salesperson standing outside your door.

ENCODING AND DECODING

Encoding and decoding are essential to communication. **Encoding** is the process of having the sender transform an abstract idea into a set of symbols. **Decoding** is the reverse process of having the receiver take a set of symbols, the message, and transform them back to an abstract idea. Look at the Jaguar advertisement: who is the source, and what is the message?

Decoding is performed by the receivers according to their own frame of reference: their attitudes, values, and beliefs.[4] In the ad, Jaguar is the source and the message is this advertisement, which appeared in *Fortune* magazine (the channel). How would you interpret (decode) this advertisement? The picture and text in the advertisement show that the source's intention is to position the Jaguar XJ-S as a product with quality V-12 engine performance and "impeccable road manners"—an ad targeted to the upper income market segment.

A source and message

The process of communication is not always a successful one. Errors in communication can happen in several ways. The source may not adequately transform the abstract idea into an effective set of symbols. Or a properly encoded message may be sent through the wrong channel and never make it to the receiver. Or the receiver may not properly transform the set of symbols into the correct abstract idea. Finally, feedback may be so delayed or distorted that it is of no use to the sender. Although communication appears easy to perform, truly effective communication can be very difficult.

COMMUNICATING THE MESSAGE EFFECTIVELY

For the message to be communicated effectively, the sender and receiver must have a mutually shared **field of experience**—similar understanding and knowledge. Figure 16-1 shows two circles representing the fields of experience of the sender and receiver, which overlap in the message. Some of the better-known communication problems have occurred when U.S. companies have taken their messages to cultures with different fields of experience. Many misinterpretations are merely the result of bad translations. For example, General Motors made a mistake when its "Body by Fisher" claim was translated into Flemish as "Corpse by Fisher."[5]

FEEDBACK

Figure 16-1 shows a line labeled *feedback loop*. **Feedback** closes the communication flow from receiver back to sender and indicates whether the message was decoded and understood as intended. Chapter 17 reviews approaches called *pretesting* to ensure that advertisements are decoded properly.

NOISE

Noise includes extraneous factors that can work against effective communication, such as distorting a message or the feedback received (Figure 16-1). Noise can be a simple error, such as a printing mistake that affects the meaning of a newspaper advertisement, or using words or pictures that fail to communicate the message clearly. Or noise occurs when a salesperson's message is misunderstood by a buyer who concentrates on not liking the salesperson's smoking rather than hearing the sales message.

CONCEPT CHECK

1 What are the five elements required for communication to occur?

2 A difficulty for U.S. companies advertising overseas is that the audience does not share the same ____________.

3 A misprint in a newspaper ad is an example of ____________.

THE PROMOTIONAL MIX

To communicate to consumers, a company can use one or more of four promotional alternatives: advertising, personal selling, sales promotion, and publicity. A firm's **promotional mix** is the combination of one or more of the elements it chooses to use. Figure 16-2 summarizes the distinctions between these four elements. Three of these elements—advertising, sales promotion, and publicity—are often said to use *mass selling* because they are used with groups of prospective buyers. In contrast, personal selling uses *interpersonal selling* because the seller usually talks person-to-person with an individual who is a prospective buyer.

FIGURE 16-2
The promotional mix

PROMOTIONAL ELEMENT	MASS VERSUS INTERPERSONAL	PAYMENT	STRENGTHS	WEAKNESSES
Advertising	Mass	Fees paid for space or time	• Efficient means for reaching large numbers of people	• High absolute costs • Difficult to receive good feedback
Personal selling	Interpersonal	Fees paid to salespeople as either salaries or commissions	• Immediate feedback • Very persuasive • Can select audience • Can give complex information	• Extremely expensive per exposure
Publicity	Mass	No direct payment to media	• Often most credible source in the consumer's mind	• Difficult to get media cooperation
Sales promotion	Mass	Wide range of fees paid depending on promotion selected	• Effective at changing behavior in short run • Very flexible	• Easily abused • Can lead to promotion wars • Easily duplicated

ADVERTISING

Advertising is a paid form of nonpersonal communication about an organization, good, service, or idea by an identified sponsor. The *paid* aspect of this definition is important because the space for the advertising message normally must be bought. An occasional exception is the public service announcement, where the advertising time or space is donated. A full-page, four-color ad in *Time* magazine, for example, costs $120,130. The *nonpersonal* component of advertising is also important. Advertising involves mass media (such as TV, radio, and magazines), which are nonpersonal and do not have an immediate feedback loop as does personal selling. So before the message is sent, marketing research plays a valuable role; for example, it determines that the message is understood by the target market and that the target market will actually see the medium chosen.

There are several advantages to a firm using advertising in its promotional mix. It can be attention-getting—as with the Oreo cookie ad shown—and also communicate specific product benefits to prospective buyers. By paying for the

An attention-getting advertisement

advertising space, a company can control *what* it wants to say and, to some extent, to *whom* the message is sent. If a stereo company wants college students to receive its message on CD players, advertising space is purchased in a college campus newspaper. Advertising also allows the company to decide *when* to send its message (which includes how often). The nonpersonal aspect of advertising also has its advantages. Once the message is created, the same message is sent to all receivers in a market segment. If the message is properly pretested, the company can trust that the same message will be decoded by all receivers in the market segment.

Advertising has some disadvantages. As shown in Figure 16-2 and discussed in depth in Chapter 17, the costs to produce and place a message are significant, and the lack of direct feedback makes it difficult to know how well the message was received.

PERSONAL SELLING

The second major element of the promotional mix is **personal selling,** defined as any paid form of *interpersonal* presentation of goods and services. Unlike advertising, personal selling is usually face-to-face communication between the sender and receiver (although, as discussed in Chapter 18, use of telephone sales is growing). Why do companies use personal selling?

There are important advantages to personal selling, as summarized in Figure 16-2. A salesperson can control to *whom* the presentation is made. Although some control is available in advertising by choosing the medium, some people may read the college newspaper, for example, who are not in the target audience for CD players. For the CD-player manufacturer, those readers outside the target audience are *wasted coverage*. Wasted coverage can be reduced with personal selling. The personal component of selling has another advantage over advertising in that the seller can see or hear the potential buyer's reaction to the message. If the feedback is unfavorable, the salesperson can modify the message.

Face-to-face sales presentation

The flexibility of personal selling can also be a disadvantage. Different salespeople can change the message so that no consistent communication is given to all customers. The high cost of personal selling is probably its major disadvantage. On a cost-per-contact basis, it is generally the most expensive of the four elements in the promotional mix.

PUBLICITY

A nonpersonal, indirectly paid presentation of an organization, service, or product is termed **publicity.** It can take the form of a news story, editorial, or product announcement. A difference between publicity and both advertising and personal selling is the "indirectly paid" dimension. With publicity a company does not pay for space in a mass medium (such as television or radio) but attempts to get the medium to run a favorable story on the company. In this sense there is an indirect payment for publicity in that a company must support a public relations staff.

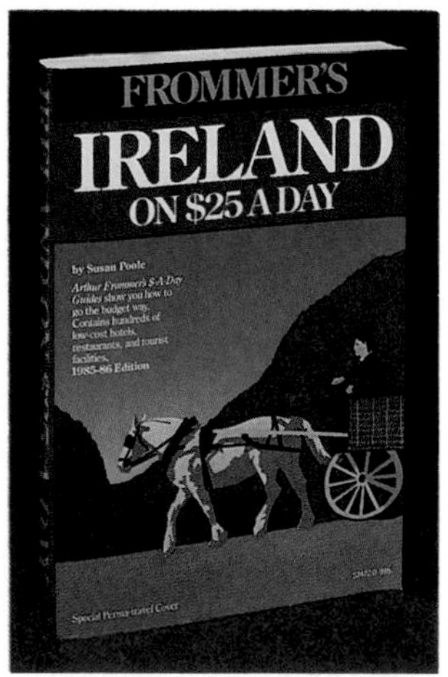

An advantage of publicity is credibility. When you read a favorable story about a company's product (such as a glowing restaurant review), there is a tendency to believe it. Travelers throughout the world have relied on Arthur Frommer's guides such as *Ireland on $25 a Day*. These books outline out-of-the-way, inexpensive restaurants, hotels, inns, and bed-and-breakfast rooms, giving invaluable publicity to these establishments. They do not (nor can they) buy a mention in the guide, which in recent years has sold millions of copies.

The disadvantages of publicity relate to the lack of the user's control over it. A company can invite a news team to preview its innovative exercise equipment and hope for a favorable mention on the 6 PM newscasts. But without buying advertising time, there is no guarantee of any mention of the new equipment or that it will be aired when the target audience is watching. The company representative who calls the station and asks for a replay of the story may be told, "Sorry, it's only news once." With publicity there is little control over what is said, to whom, or when. As a result, publicity is rarely the main component of a promotional mix.

SALES PROMOTION

A fourth, and also supplemental, promotional element is **sales promotion,** a short-term inducement of value offered to arouse interest in buying a good or service. Used in conjunction with advertising or personal selling, sales promotions are offered to intermediaries as well as to ultimate consumers. Coupons, rebates, samples, and sweepstakes like that of Bali Blinds shown below are just a few examples of sales promotions discussed later in this chapter.

The advantage of sales promotions is that the short-term nature of these programs (such as the expiration date of a coupon or sweepstakes) often stimulates sales for their duration. Offering value to the consumer in terms of a cents-off coupon or rebate provides an incentive to buy.

Sales promotions cannot be the sole basis for a campaign because gains are often temporary and sales drop off when the deal ends.[6] Advertising support is needed to convert the customer who tried the product because of a sales promotion into a long-term buyer.[7] If sales promotions are conducted continuously, they lose their effectiveness. Customers begin to delay purchase until a coupon is offered, or they question the product's value. Some aspects of sales promotions also are regulated by the federal government. These issues are reviewed in detail later in this chapter.

Sales promotions arouse interest

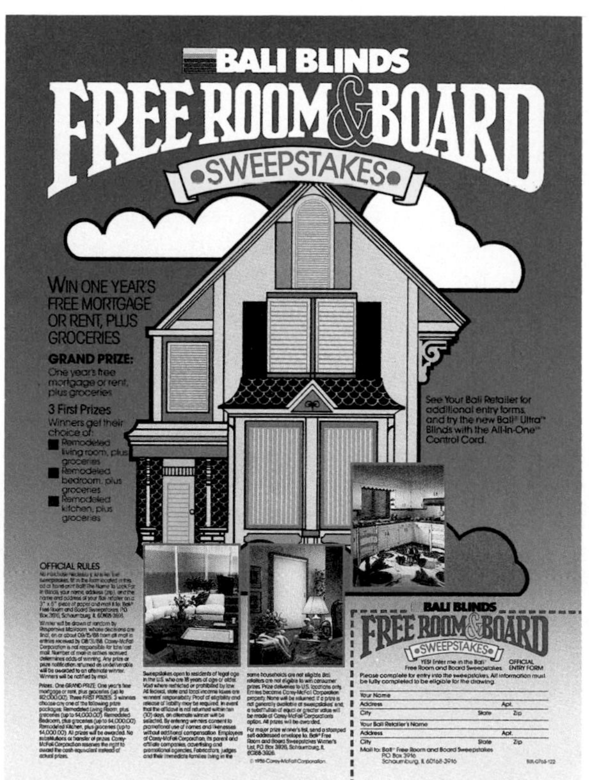

CONCEPT CHECK

1 **Explain the difference between advertising and publicity when both use television.**

2 **Which promotional element should be offered only on a short-term basis?**

3 **Cost per contact is high with the __________ element of the promotional mix.**

SELECTING PROMOTIONAL TOOLS

In putting together the promotional mix, a marketer must consider the balance of elements to use. Should advertising be emphasized more than personal selling? When should a promotional rebate be offered? Several factors affect such decisions: the target audience for the promotion, the stage of the product's life cycle, characteristics of the product, decision stage of the buyer, and even the channel of distribution.

THE TARGET AUDIENCE

Promotional programs are directed to the ultimate consumer, intermediary (retailer, wholesaler, or industrial distributor), or both. Promotional programs of consumer products to ultimate consumers use mass media. Geographical dispersion and the number of potential buyers are the primary reasons for a mass approach. Personal selling is used at the place of purchase, generally the retail store.

To industrial buyers, advertising is used more selectively, as in trade publications such as *Fence* magazine for buyers of fencing material. Because industrial buyers often have specialized needs or technical questions, personal selling is particularly important. The salesperson can provide information and the necessary support after sales.

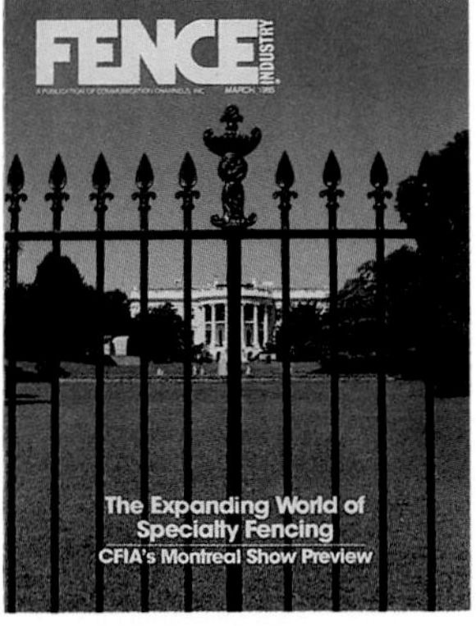

Intermediaries are often the focus of promotional efforts. As with industrial buyers, personal selling is the major promotional ingredient. The salespeople inform retailers on future advertising efforts to ultimate users, for example, and they assist retailers in making a profit. Intermediaries' questions often pertain to the allowed markup, merchandising support, and return policies, which are best handled by a salesperson.

Related to the issue of the target audience is the composition of the *decision-making unit* (DMU), or the people in a household or in a buying center in an organization involved in making the decision to buy the product. The more people in the DMU, the greater the emphasis on personal selling. A salesperson can provide a specific message for each member of the DMU to try to address her or his concerns and objections. For example, in office equipment sales, a salesperson can address more efficiently the technical concerns of the office worker, the cost concerns of the financial officer, and the service questions of the purchasing agent. Three separate messages in very different magazines would be required if advertising were used.

FIGURE 16-3
Promotional tools used over the product life cycle of Purina Puppy Chow

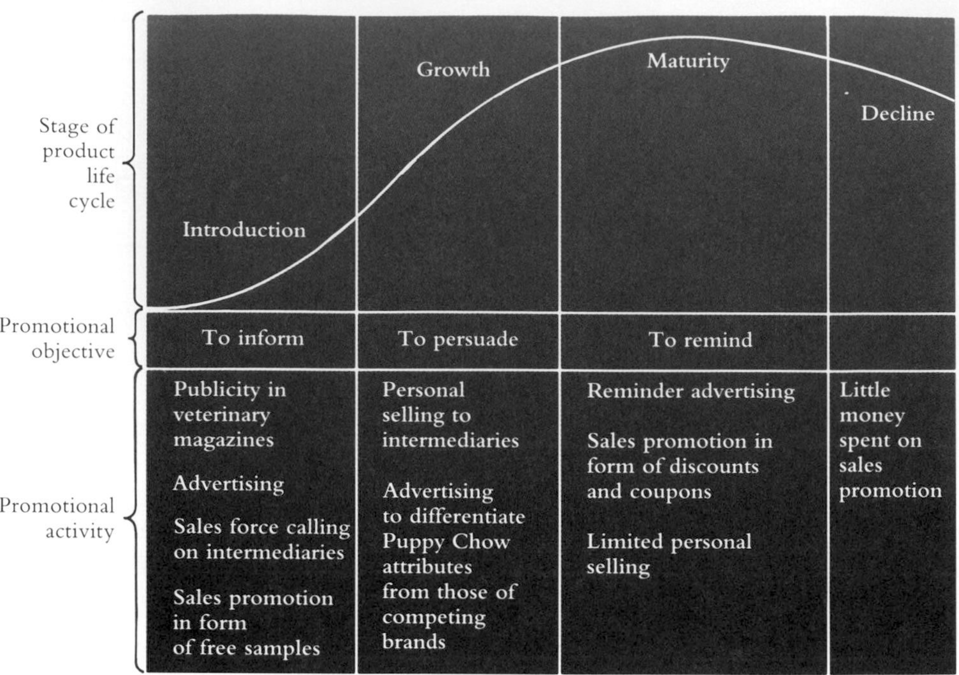

THE PRODUCT LIFE CYCLE

All products have a product life cycle (see Chapter 10), and the composition of the promotional mix changes over the four life-cycle stages, as shown for Purina Puppy Chow in Figure 16-3.

Introduction Stage Informing consumers in an effort to increase their level of awareness is the primary promotional objective in the introduction stage of the product life cycle. In general, all the promotional mix elements are used at this time, although the use of specific mix elements during any stage depends on the product and situation. Stories on Purina's new nutritional food are placed in *Dog World* magazine, trial samples are sent to registered dog owners in 10 major cities, advertisements are placed during reruns of the TV show *Lassie,* and the sales force begins to approach supermarkets to get orders. Advertising is particularly important as a means of reaching as many people as possible to build up interest. Publicity may even begin slightly before the product is commercially available.

Growth Stage The main promotional objective of the growth stage is to persuade the consumer to buy the product—Purina Puppy Chow—rather than substitutes. So the marketing manager seeks to gain brand preference and solidify distribution. Sales promotion assumes less importance in this stage, and publicity is not a factor because it depends on novelty of the product. The main promotional element is advertising, which stresses brand differences. Personal selling is used to solidify the channel of distribution. For consumer products such as dog food the sales force calls on the wholesalers and retailers in hopes of increasing inventory levels and gaining shelf space. For industrial products the

Purina Puppy Chow: a product in the maturity stage of its life cycle

sales force often tries to get contractual arrangements to be the sole source of supply for the buyer.

Maturity Stage In the maturity stage the need is to maintain existing buyers, and advertising's role is to remind buyers of the product's existence. Sales promotion, in the form of discounts and coupons offered to both ultimate consumers and intermediaries, is important in maintaining loyal buyers. In a test of one mature consumer product, it was found that 80 percent of the product's sales at this stage resulted from sales promotions.[8] Price cuts and discounts can also significantly increase a mature brand's sales. The sales force at this stage seeks to satisfy intermediaries. An unsatisfied customer who switches brands is hard to replace.

Decline Stage The decline stage of the product life cycle is usually a period of phase out for the product, and little money is spent in the promotional mix—especially in sales promotions.

PRODUCT CHARACTERISTICS

The proper blend of elements in the promotional mix also depends on the type of product. Three specific characteristics should be considered: complexity, risk, and ancillary services. *Complexity* refers to the technical sophistication of the product and hence the amount of understanding required to use the product. It's hard to provide much information in a one-page magazine ad or 30-second television ad, so the more complex the product, the greater is the emphasis on personal selling.

A second element is the degree of *risk* represented by the product's purchase. Risk for the buyer is a cost in financial terms, such as $6,000 spent for the IBM PS/2 personal computer, or risk can be social or physical. A hair transplant procedure might represent all three risks. Expensive, yes. But will it work? Does it hurt? Although advertising helps, the greater the risk, the more the need for personal selling.

FIGURE 16-4
How the importance of three promotional elements varies during the consumer's purchase decision

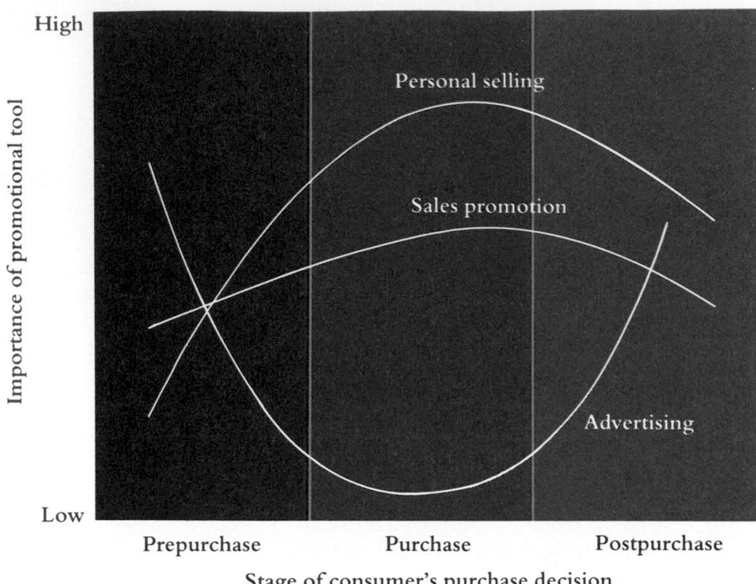

The level of *ancillary services* required by a product also affects the promotional strategy. Ancillary services pertain to the degree of service or support required after the sale. This characteristic is common to many industrial products and consumer purchases. Who will repair your automobile or microwave oven? Advertising's role is to establish the seller's reputation. However, personal selling is essential to build buyer confidence and provide evidence of follow-up.

STAGES OF THE BUYING DECISION

Knowing the customer's stage of decision making can also affect the promotional mix. Figure 16-4 shows how the importance of the three directly paid promotional elements varies with the three stages in a consumer's purchase decision.

Prepurchase Stage In the prepurchase stage advertising is more helpful than personal selling because advertising informs the potential customer of the existence of the product and the seller. Sales promotion in the form of free samples also can play an important role to gain low-risk trial. When the salesperson calls on the customer after heavy advertising, there is some recognition of what the salesperson represents. This is particularly important in industrial settings in which sampling of the product is usually not possible.

Purchase Stage At the purchase stage the importance of personal selling is highest to close the sale, whereas the impact of advertising is lowest. Sales promotion in the form of coupons, deals, point-of-purchase displays, and rebates can be very helpful in encouraging demand. Figure 16-4 oversimplifies the importance of advertising. Although by itself it is not an active influence during the purchase stage, it is the means of delivering the coupons, deals, and rebates that are often important.

Postpurchase Stage In the postpurchase stage the salesperson is still important. In fact, the more personal contact after the sale, the more the buyer is satisfied. Advertising is also important to assure the buyer that the right purchase was made. Advertising and personal selling help reduce the buyer's postpurchase anxiety.[9] Sales promotion in the form of coupons can help encourage repeat purchases from satisfied first-time triers.

CHANNEL STRATEGIES

Chapter 13 discussed the channel flow from producer to intermediaries to consumer. Achieving control of the channel is often difficult for the manufacturer, and promotional strategies can assist in moving a product through the channel of distribution. This is where a manufacturer has to make an important decision about whether to use a push strategy, pull strategy, or both in its channel of distribution.

Push Strategy Figure 16-5, *A*, shows how a manufacturer uses a **push strategy,** directing the promotional mix to channel members to gain their cooperation in ordering and stocking the product. In this approach, personal selling and sales promotions play major roles. Salespeople call on wholesalers to encourage orders and provide sales assistance. Sales promotions, such as case discount allowances (20 percent off the regular case price), are offered to stimulate demand. By pushing the product through the channel, the goal is to get channel members to push it to their customers.

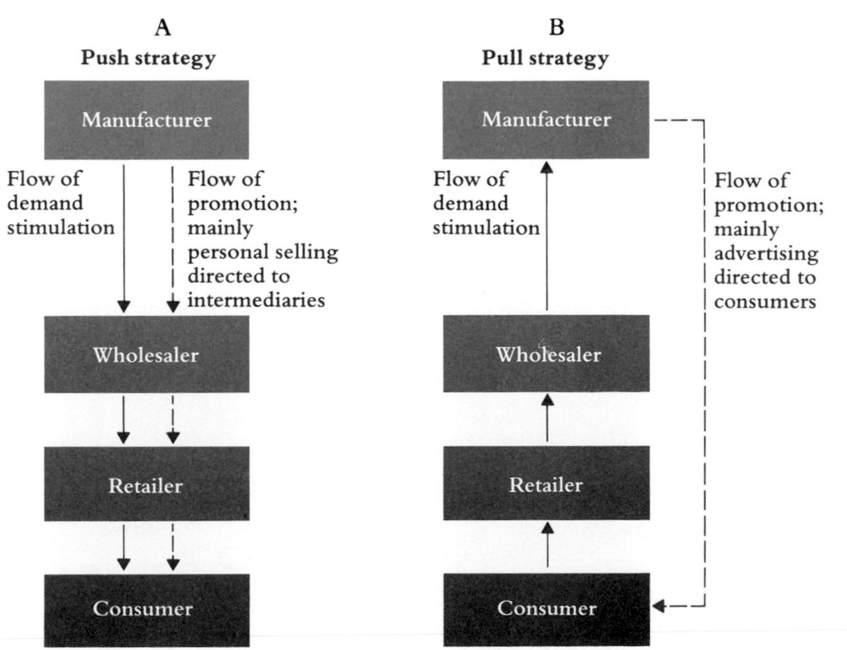

FIGURE 16-5
A comparison of push and pull promotional strategies

Anheuser-Busch, for example, spends a significant amount of its marketing resources on maintaining its relationship with its distributors, and through them, with retailers. Anheuser-Busch provides a series of incentives and assistance to its distribution system to maintain its channel dominance. The company arranges group discounts on purchase of trucks, insurance, and even the IBM computers that wholesalers use to order beer. Even specialized computer software is provided to help retailers maximize the shelf space of Anheuser-Busch products.[10]

Pull Strategy In some instances manufacturers face resistance from channel members who do not want to order a new product or increase inventory levels of an existing brand. As shown in Figure 16-5, *B,* a **pull strategy** is then warranted, in which a manufacturer directs its efforts in the form of advertising and sales promotions to ultimate consumers to encourage them to ask the retailer for the product. Seeing demand from ultimate consumers, retailers order the product from wholesalers and thus the item is pulled through the intermediaries. In the beer industry, efforts to pull the brand through the channel are also important. As mentioned earlier, Anheuser-Busch spends about $450 million on media advertising to stimulate consumer demand for its brands. Successful advertising campaigns, such as the Spuds MacKenzie *Bud Light* campaign, can have dramatic effects on the sales of a brand. The distinguishing elements in a push or pull strategy are (1) the target audience for promotional efforts and (2) the emphasis on personal selling or advertising. As the Anheuser-Busch example points out, most companies rely on elements of both push and pull strategies because both intermediaries and consumers are crucial to the brand's success.

WHEN TO STRESS ADVERTISING AND PERSONAL SELLING

In the promotional mix, publicity and sales promotions are supportive and rarely the key elements in a firm's strategy. Often a firm must make a trade-off between emphasizing advertising or personal selling. Figure 16-6 summarizes the major factors that lead to an emphasis on either approach.

FIGURE 16-6
When to emphasize advertising or personal selling

	HEAVIER RELIANCE ON . . .	
BASIS OF COMPARISON	ADVERTISING	PERSONAL SELLING
Target audience	Ultimate consumers	Resellers and industrial buyers
Risk in purchase	Low	High
Size of decision-making unit	Small	Large
Complexity of product	Simple	Complex
Level of ancillary services	Low	High
Stage of purchase decision	Prepurchase	Purchase
Channel strategy	Pull	Push
Geographical dispersion of customers	Great	Little

CONCEPT CHECK

1 For consumer products, why is advertising emphasized more in promotion than is personal selling?

2 When is publicity a key element in the product life cycle?

3 Explain a push versus a pull strategy.

SALES PROMOTION

THE IMPORTANCE OF SALES PROMOTION

Sales promotion is a supplemental ingredient of the promotional mix and is not as visible as advertising, but more than $100 billion is spent annually on sales promotion. As shown in Figure 16-7, during the first half of the 1980's, there was a major shift of dollars from media advertising to trade and consumer promotion. By 1987 about 65 percent of these expenditures were for trade and consumer promotion.[11]

CONSUMER-ORIENTED SALES PROMOTIONS

Directed to ultimate consumers, **consumer-oriented sales promotions,** or simply **consumer promotions,** are used to support advertising and personal selling. A variety of these sales promotion tools exist to achieve the objectives outlined previously. The alternative consumer-oriented sales promotion tools are shown in Figure 16-8.

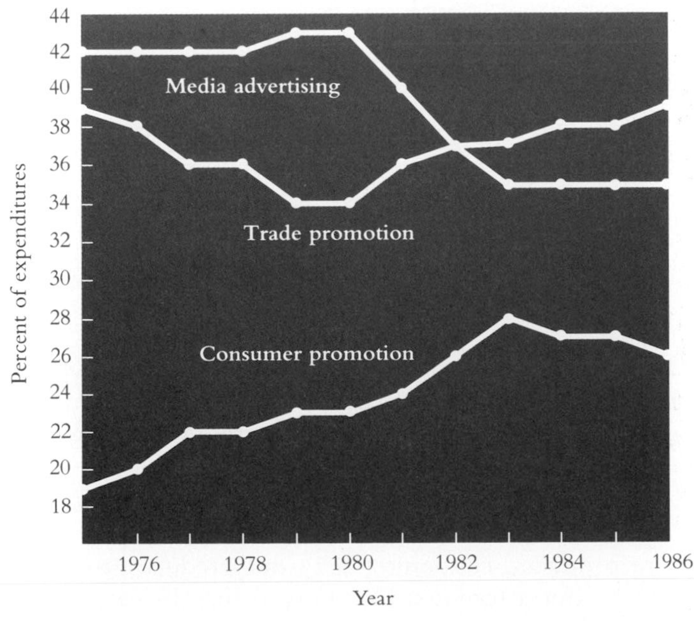

FIGURE 16-7
Trends in expenditures for media advertising, trade promotion, and consumer promotion

Source: "Promotional Practices Survey," *Adweek's Marketing Week* (March 14, 1988), pp. 10-11.

KIND OF SALES PROMOTION	OBJECTIVES	ADVANTAGES	DISADVANTAGES
Coupons	Stimulate demand	Encourage retailer support	Consumers delay purchases
Deals	Increase trial; retaliate against competitor's actions	Reduce consumer risk	Consumers delay purchases; reduce perceived product value
Premiums	Build goodwill	Consumers like free or reduced-price merchandise	Consumers buy for premium, not product
Contests	Increase consumer purchases; build business inventory	Encourage consumer involvement with product	Require creative or analytical thinking
Sweepstakes	Encourage present customers to buy more; minimize brand-switching behavior	Get customer to use product and store more often	Sales drop after sweepstakes
Samples	Encourage new product trial	Low risk for consumer to try product	High cost for company
Trading stamps	Encourage repeat purchases	Help create loyalty	High cost for company
Point-of-purchase displays	Increase product trial; provide in-store support for other promotions	Provide good product visibility	Hard to get retailer to allocate high-traffic space
Rebates	Encourage customers to purchase; stop sales decline	Effective stimulate demand	Easily copied; steal sales from future; reduce perceived product value

FIGURE 16-8
Sales promotion alternatives

A study of consumer-oriented sales promotions showed the following types are most frequently used[12]:

TYPE OF PROMOTION	FREQUENCY OF USE
Coupons	66%
Price/quantity promotions	11
Refunds	10
Premiums	8
Prize promotions	4
Samples	1
TOTAL	100%

Coupons Coupons such as those offered by Gillette in an effort to reach black consumers are sales promotions that usually offer a discounted price to the consumer, which encourages trial. As noted in the Marketing Action Memo, coupons are experiencing explosive growth. In 1985, Americans redeemed about 6.5 billion (almost 4 percent) of the 180 billion coupons used by packaged goods producers.[13]

For mature products, couponing may only reduce gross revenues from already loyal users. But a recent study showed that 14 percent of coupon redeemers were first-time buyers of the brand, 34 percent rarely or occasionally used the brand, and 52 percent almost always bought the brand.[14] Manufacturers are offering coupons with greater values, such as $5 coupons for pots and pans sold by Wear-Ever Cookware. Coupon use is also expanding beyond food products to drugs, toys, and appliances.[15]

Coupons are often far more expensive than the face value showing the price discount; a 20-cent coupon can cost 3 times that after paying for the advertisement to deliver it, handling, redemption, and so on.

Deals Deals are short-term price reductions, commonly used to increase trial among potential customers or to retaliate against a competitor's actions. For example, if a rival manufacturer introduces a new cake mix, the company responds with a "two packages for the price of one" deal. This short-term price reduction builds up the stock on the kitchen shelves of cake mix buyers and makes the competitor's introduction more difficult.

Premiums A promotional tool often used with consumers is the premium, which consists of merchandise offered free or at a significant savings over retail. This latter type of premium is called self-liquidating because the cost charged

MARKETING·ACTION·MEMO

SALES PROMOTION: OFTEN TWICE THE EXPENDITURES OF MEDIA ADVERTISING

Although consumer-product companies such as Kraft and Nabisco Brands still spend billions of dollars on media advertising to build long-term consumer loyalty for their brands, *Fortune* magazine reports the big dollar increase lies in sales promotions. Sales promotions are of two main types: (1) consumer promotions such as coupons, trading stamps, sweepstakes, and premiums ("mail in two box tops for . . .") and (2) trade promotions such as merchandise, finance, and case ("one case free for every ten purchased") allowances directed at intermediaries in the marketing channel.

Fortune reports that consumer-product firms such as Kraft and Nabisco Brands' Del Monte division spend $2 in sales promotions (both consumer and trade) for every $1 spent on media advertising. *Fortune* also reports an increasing shift of promotional expenditures from media advertising to sales promotion. The reasons for the shift to sales promotion expenditures include:

1. Greater difficulty of consumer-product firms in differentiating their brand from competitive brands.
2. Gaining precious shelf space for products using sales promotions.
3. Short-term performance measurement for brand managers, who have an incentive to "drop a coupon" to give a quick sales jolt to a brand rather than use media advertising, which builds long-run brand image.

The net effect is often a form of fierce price competition among weaker brands that can least afford it.

Coupons have experienced the most explosive growth. In 1985, packaged-goods producers issued 180 billion coupons with a face value of $50 billion. The A.C. Nielsen Company, a division of Dun and Bradstreet, estimates consumers saved $2 billion dollars by redeeming 6.5 billion of them.

Source: Felix Kessler, "The Costly Coupon Craze," *Fortune* (July 9, 1986), pp. 83-84.

Gillette coupons heavily

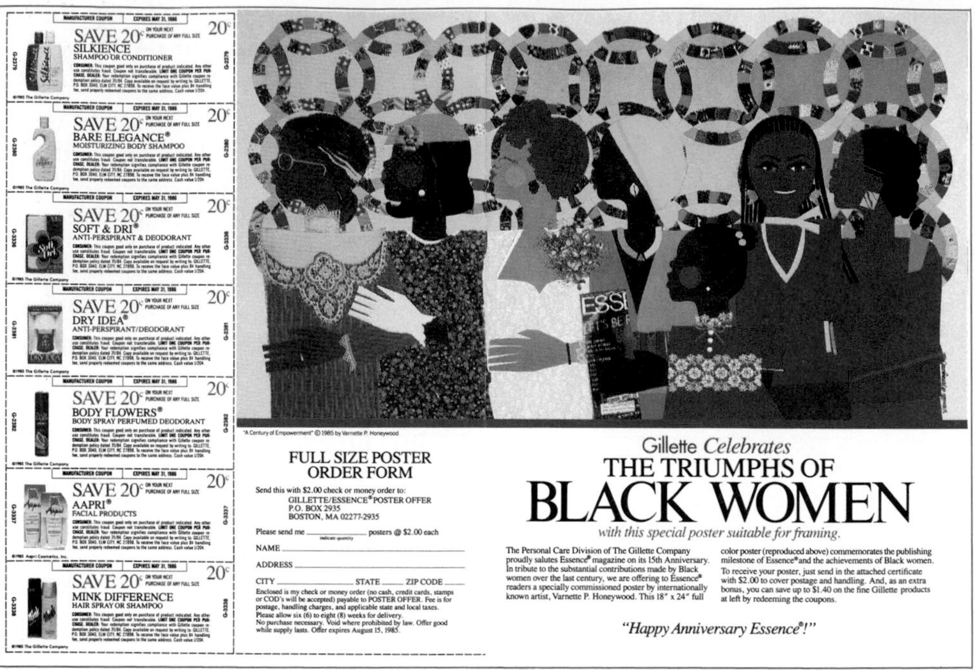

the consumer covers the cost of the item. When *Return of the Jedi* opened in U.S. theaters, 2,500 Burger King restaurants offered *Star Wars* glasses as a premium 2 days later. A different glass with the likeness of Luke Skywalker, Darth Vader, or R2-D2 was offered each week for 49 cents and the purchase of a medium soft drink. McDonald's countered with Snoopy and the gang from *Peanuts*.[16] Weekly visits were required to collect the full set.

Perhaps the most unusual premiums: 10 scale-model red Corvettes among the 11 million tiny car models in 6 of Ralston-Purina's children's cereal boxes. What is so unusual is that each of the 10 red Corvette premiums could be turned in for the real thing—a $29,000 1988 Chevrolet Corvette.[17]

Successful premiums must have consumer appeal, and when they are offered on a self-liquidating basis, the cost must represent a real value. The more effective premiums have a functional or logical relationship to the product being promoted. Gatorade offered a squeeze bottle for its drink that was similar to that used by athletic teams.[18] A baby food manufacturer offers a sterling silver baby spoon for $1.

Contests A fourth sales promotion in Figure 16-8, the contest, is where consumers apply their analytical or creative thinking to try to win a prize. For example, White Horse scotch whiskey ran a contest based on information on the back of the bottle. Although not requiring purchase, it resulted in the customer going to the store, reading the label, and buying the product. More than 250,000 entries were received, and sales rose consistently during the contest.[19]

Sweepstakes *Reader's Digest* and Publisher's Clearing House are two of the better-promoted sweepstakes. These sales promotions require participants to submit some kind of entry form but are purely games of chance requiring no analytical or creative effort by the consumer. In October 1969 the Federal Trade Commission issued trade rules covering sweepstakes, contests, and games to regulate their fairness, ensure that the chance for winning is represented honestly, and ensure that the prizes are actually awarded.[20]

MARKETING · RESEARCH · REPORT

DOES THAT DISPLAY AT THE CHECKOUT COUNTER REALLY WORK?

When you approach the checkout counter at your local supermarket, do the point-of-purchase displays really result in sales? Woodside and Waddle studied the effects of both point-of-purchase displays and a price reduction on the retail sales of a product. Over the course of 4 weeks these researchers ran an experiment in 4 supermarkets. Consumers who entered the stores were exposed to one of four experimental treatments for a brand of instant coffee:

- Treatment 1: No price reduction and no promotion display
- Treatment 2: Price reduction (20 percent off) and no promotion display
- Treatment 3: No price reduction and a promotion display
- Treatment 4: Price reduction (20 percent off) and a promotion display

The promotion display consisted of a 5 × 7 inch hand-lettered card showing the brand name, size, price, the words "No limit," and a 1 × 2 inch sticker of the package. Each alternative treatment was in each store for 1 day and then changed. At the end of each day the coffee brand sales were counted, with results as shown to the right.

The price reduction had indeed led to greater sales compared with sales of the coffee at a regular price. Furthermore a price reduction and point-of-purchase display led to increased sales, but even without a price reduction, a display helped sales. Sales with the display with no price reduction (T_3) were higher than when the regular-priced coffee did not have a display (T_1).

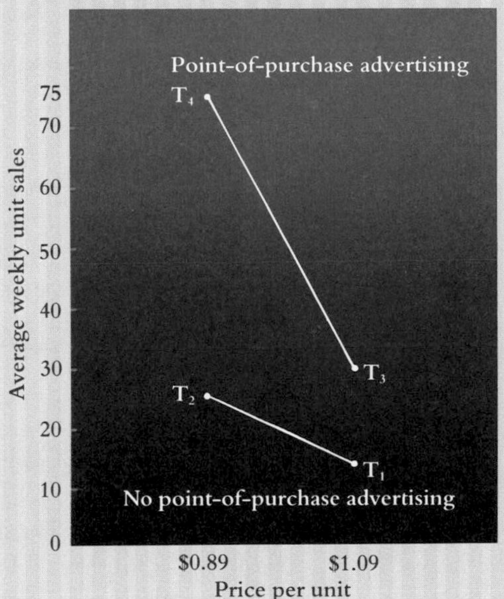

So a point-of-purchase promotion helps draw the customer's attention to the brand and increases sales. Even when the price was not reduced to 89 cents, a display helped sales. A surprising finding is that a point-of-purchase display with no reduced price (T_3) is better than a reduced price with no display (T_2).

Source: Based on Arch G. Woodside and Gerald L. Waddle, "Sales Effects of In-Store Advertising," *Journal of Advertising Research*, Vol. 15 (June 1975), pp. 29-34; by permission of the American Marketing Association.

The VideOcart: gentle video reminders on your shopping trip through your supermarket

A gravity-feed bin that doubles as a point-of-purchase display

Samples Another common consumer sales promotion is sampling, which is offering the product free or at a greatly reduced price. Used for new products, sampling puts the product in the consumer's hands. A trial size is generally offered that is smaller than the regular package size. If consumers like the sample, it is hoped they will remember and buy the product. Sampling is appropriate for products that are frequently purchased, have a low unit cost, and are new. Sampling is often done in test marketing a new product. For example, P&G test marketed Tide with Bleach powder detergent in Denver in 1988 using samples, print ads, and TV ads.[21]

Trading Stamps Trading stamps are a sales promotion tool in which customers are given stamps in relation to the dollar size of their purchase. These stamps can be redeemed for merchandise or cash. This sales promotion was widely used by supermarkets and gas stations in the 1960's and 1970's to encourage store loyalty but has declined recently because of the cost involved.

Point-of-Purchase Displays In a store aisle, you often encounter a sales promotion called a *point-of-purchase display*. These product displays take the form of advertising signs, which sometimes actually hold or display the product, and are often located in high-traffic areas near the cash register or the end of an aisle. The picture above shows gravity-feed bins that Nabisco uses for its animal crackers; it helps ensure product freshness, provides storage, and captures the consumer's attention as an end-aisle, point-of-purchase display.[22] Because of the space needed, some retailers avoid such displays. As the Marketing Research Report shows, point-of-purchase displays can increase sales significantly even with no price discounts.

Some studies estimate that two-thirds of a consumer's buying decisions are made in the store. This means that grocery product manufacturers want to get their message to you at the instant you are next to their brand in your supermarket aisle—perhaps through a point-of-purchase display. In the next few years this may be done through the VideOcart. Sitting on the handlebar of your supermarket shopping cart, the VideOcart's liquid-crystal screen will remind you twice per aisle about products next to your cart that you might consider buying. The displays on your screen are triggered by transmitters on the store shelves. Although the technology exists today to make it talk to you, your VideOcart will remain silent. The reason: try to imagine 100 VideOcarts in a large supermarket all talking at the same time![23]

Rebates A final consumer sales promotion in Figure 16-7, the cash rebate, offers a return of money based on proof of purchase. This tool has been used heavily by car manufacturers facing increased competition. Computer companies like Apple have also used it effectively in selling PCs to ultimate consumers. When the rebate is offered on lower-priced items such as detergent or dog food, the time and trouble of mailing in a proof-of-purchase to get the rebate check means that many buyers—attracted by the rebate offer—never take advantage of it. However, this "slippage" is less likely to occur with those frequent users of rebate promotions.[24]

TRADE-ORIENTED SALES PROMOTIONS

Trade-oriented sales promotions, or simply **trade promotions**, also supplement advertising and personal selling but are directed to wholesalers, retailers, or distributors. Some of the sales promotions just reviewed are used for this purpose, but there are three other common approaches targeted uniquely to these intermediaries: (1) allowances and discounts; (2) cooperative advertising; and (3) training of distributors' sales force.

Allowances and Discounts Trade promotions often focus on maintaining or increasing inventory levels in the channel of distribution. An effective method for encouraging such increased purchases by intermediaries is the use of allowances and discounts. However, overuse of these "price reductions" can lead to retailers changing their ordering patterns in the expectation of such offerings. Although there are many variations that manufacturers can use with discounts and allowances, three common approaches include the merchandise allowance, the case allowance, and the finance allowance.[25]

Reimbursing a retailer for extra in-store support or special featuring of the brand is a *merchandise allowance*. Performance contracts between the manufacturer and trade member usually specify the activity to be performed, such as a picture of the product in a newspaper with a coupon good at only one store. The merchandise allowance then consists of a percentage deduction from the list case price ordered during the promotional period. Allowances are not paid by the manufacturer until it sees proof of performance (such as a copy of the ad placed by the retailer in the local newspaper).

A second common trade promotion, a *case allowance,* is a discount on each

Chrysler-Plymouth and Dodge rebate offer

case ordered during a specific time period. These allowances are usually deducted from the invoice. A variation of the case allowance is the "free goods" approach, whereby retailers receive some amount of the product free based on the amount ordered, such as 1 case free for every 10 cases ordered.[26]

A final trade promotion, the *finance allowance,* involves paying retailers for financing costs or financial losses associated with consumer sales promotions. This trade promotion is regularly used and has several variations. One type is the floor stock protection program. Manufacturers give retailers a case allowance price for products in their warehouse, which prevents shelf stock from running down during the promotional period. Also common are freight allowances, which compensate retailers that transport orders from the manufacturer's warehouse.

Cooperative Advertising Resellers often perform the important function of promoting the manufacturer's products at the local level. One common sales promotional activity is to encourage both better quality and greater quantity in the local advertising efforts of resellers through **cooperative advertising**. These are programs by which a manufacturer pays a percentage of the retailer's local advertising expense for advertising the manufacturer's products.

Usually the manufacturer pays a percentage, often 50 percent, of the cost of advertising up to a certain dollar limit, which is based on the amount of the purchases the retailer makes of the manufacturer's products. In addition to paying for the advertising, the manufacturer often furnishes the retailer with a selection of different ad executions, sometimes suited for several different media. A manufacturer may provide, for example, several different print layouts as well as a few broadcast ads for the retailer to adapt and use.

Cooperative advertising represents a substantial investment for the manufacturer. However, it is very effective because both the manufacturer and the retailer receive benefits. The retailer receives partial payment of the local advertising expenses along with better quality ads. The manufacturer, on the other hand, involves the retailer in local advertising and generally receives stronger support in other areas such as maintaining sufficient inventory and receiving prominent display space for their products in the retailer's store.

Training of Distributors' Sales Forces One of the many functions the intermediaries perform is customer contact and selling for the producers they represent. Both retailers and wholesalers employ and manage their own sales personnel. A manufacturer's success often rests on the ability of the reseller's sales force to represent its products.

So it is in the best interest of the manufacturer to help train the reseller's salesforce. Because the reseller's sales force is often less sophisticated and knowledgeable about the products than the manufacturer might like, training can increase their sales performance. Training activities include producing manuals and brochures to educate the reseller's salesforce. The salesforce then uses these aids in selling situations. Other activities include national sales meetings sponsored by the manufacturer and field visits to the reseller's location to inform and motivate the salesperson to sell the products. Manufacturers also develop incentive and recognition programs to motivate reseller's salespeople to sell their products.

CONCEPT CHECK

1 **Which sales promotional tool is most common for new products?**

2 **What's the difference between a coupon and a deal?**

3 **Which trade promotion is used on an ongoing basis?**

PUBLICITY

As noted previously, publicity is a form of promotion that is not paid for directly. The responsibility for publicity usually rests with a public relations director, who maintains or creates a favorable image of the organization and its products. The nonpaid aspect of publicity pertains only to the placement of the message. Money is required for staff and for creating opportunities to obtain media coverage of a product. Media representatives may have to be entertained in the hopes of getting a favorable story. News releases have to be prepared and sent. All these efforts result in some internal, indirect cost of publicity. In days of increasing consumerism and skepticism, many companies have begun to hire public relations directors and public relations firms to help their credibility.[27]

THE TOOLS OF PUBLICITY

In developing a campaign, several **publicity tools** are available to the public relations director. Many companies frequently use the *news release,* consisting of an announcement regarding changes in the company or the product line. The objective of a news release is to inform a newspaper, radio station, or other medium of an idea for a story.

A second common publicity tool is the *news conference*. Representatives of the media are all invited to an informational meeting, and advance materials regarding the content are sent.

Nonprofit organizations rely heavily on *PSAs (public service announcements),* which are free space or time donated by the media. For example, the charter of the American Red Cross prohibits any local chapter from advertising, so to solicit blood donations, local chapters often depend on PSAs on radio or television to announce their needs.

A PLANNED CAMPAIGN

For publicity to be effective, a planned campaign integrated into the total promotional plan is necessary. In this way the advantages of advertising, personal selling, publicity, and sales promotion can complement each other. This planned approach often has not been used, but the success of the Cabbage Patch Kids dolls—perhaps the most successful publicity campaign for a consumer product in the 1980's—highlights its advantages.

To start the sales snowball rolling, the Coleco public relations department sent Jane Pauley, co-host of the morning *Today* show, a Cabbage Patch Kids doll with its own birth certificate. This gift led to 5 minutes of valuable air time on *Today*. Major women's magazines were also sent some dolls, resulting in several publications featuring a Cabbage Patch Kids doll in their Christmas gift layouts. Two Coleco representatives also went on a media tour to 12 major cities, appearing on talk shows to discuss the dolls' development and success.

During December the effort went all out. The dolls were featured several times on the *Tonight* show. Then, with Brooke Shields as a life-size Cabbage Patch Kids doll, the dolls appeared on Bob Hope's Christmas special. The dolls, which became scarce in the final days before Christmas, were flown to children's hospitals for distribution to sick patients.[28] The shortage of these dolls allowed Coleco to raise prices an additional $10 as sales reached 2.5 million units in December 1983. An integrated publicity campaign was the stimulus for the sales success.

CAUSE-RELATED MARKETING

A recent development that lies on the borderline between sales promotion and publicity is **cause-related marketing** (CRM), which is when the charitable contributions of a firm are tied directly to the customer revenues produced through the promotion of one of its products. This definition distinguishes CRM from a firm's standard charitable contributions, which are outright donations. At the same time, CRM is clearly a sales promotion effort that often wins much free publicity for the sponsoring firm.

Statue of Liberty restoration: an example of cause-related marketing

In 1983, American Express' Travel Related Services Company was searching for a "cause"—something that Americans could identify with easily that would also help promote its services. It considered supporting a national arts program, historical preservation, and higher education, but all these ideas seemed to lack real punch. Then American Express found *the* cause: the Statue of Liberty.

This decision triggered a tremendously successful CRM campaign in which American Express contributed a penny to the restoration of the Statue of Liberty every time one of its credit cards was used during a 3-month period. This project provided $1.7 million to the Statue of Liberty restoration and helped increase the usage of American Express cards during the 3-month promotion by 30 percent. American Express has copyrighted the "*cause-related marketing*" phrase.[29]

ETHICAL DIMENSIONS OF PROMOTION IN TODAY'S SOCIETY

Promotional activities often reflect the values of society. Perhaps this explains why in recent years greater concern has arisen about (1) misleading sales promotions and advertisements, (2) advertising and TV programs directed toward children, and (3) more realistic portrayals of women and minorities. Although laws and court decisions have set some standards, sound ethical judgments of key marketing executives are needed in most of the areas described below.

MISLEADING SALES PROMOTIONS AND ADVERTISEMENTS

Unfortunately, over the years many consumers have been misled—or even deceived—by some sales promotions and advertisements. Examples include sweepstakes in which the gifts were not awarded, rebate offers that were a terrible hassle, and advertisements whose promises were great, until the buyer read the small print.

As noted earlier, the Federal Trade Commission stepped in to set precise guidelines on sweepstakes to protect consumers, an example of formal government regulation by an agency of the federal government. Concerning rebates, the buyer usually needs to send proof-of-purchase evidence to the manufacturer to receive a check for the offered price reduction. Suppose that the hassle of finding the proof-of-purchase rebate offer at the bottom of the giant-size package of detergent you bought—because of the rebate—discourages you from sending it in. This slippage raises ethical questions about the manufacturer perhaps deliberately making it difficult for you to take advantage of the rebate. To address some advertising abuses in airline ads, 21 states got together in 1987 to try to set standards for (1) the fine print in airline ads that said special tickets were nonrefundable and (2) sudden changes in frequent flyer programs that penalized past users.[30]

It is clearly too expensive to rely on formal regulation by federal, state, and local governments of all sales promotions and advertisements. As a result, there are increasing efforts by private organizations at *self-regulation,* ethical guidelines set by advertisers, industries, advertising agencies, and advertising associations.[31] This requires solid, continuing ethical judgments by individuals in these organizations.

ADVERTISING AND TV PROGRAMS FOR CHILDREN

Advertising to children is a subject of great debate. Some critics have suggested prohibiting advertising on all TV programs watched by a significant proportion of children under 8 years of age. Because it has been estimated that the average 2- to 11-year-old American child watches about 26 hours of TV a week and sees between 22,000 and 25,000 TV commercials a year,[32] the concern is real. Children who watch a great amount of TV want more advertised products and ask for them more often than do children who watch less TV.

Clear policies by the government and companies remain to be developed to ensure advertising to children is responsible and ethical. Advertisers and consumers have clear differences of opinion on what TV ads and programs are appropriate for children.[33] This concern has escalated as companies develop TV programs that feature a toy character in a cartoon program after the toy is marketed. The *Care Bears* Saturday morning TV cartoon is a recent example that has raised some questions. The issue came to a head when a Los Angeles TV station ran a children's program partly produced by Mattel—*He-Man and the Masters of the Universe*—without identifying the toy manufacturer as the sponsor. A federal appeals court directed the Federal Communications Commission to study this problem and the related barter arrangement in which toy manufacturers exchange a TV program they offer for free advertising time from the station.[34]

REALISTIC PORTRAYALS OF MINORITIES AND WOMEN

Just 2 decades ago, fewer than 5 percent of all advertisements portrayed blacks, but today blacks appear far more often in TV and print advertisements. Further, they are now shown in more favorable jobs and environments than they were in the past. The same is true of other minority groups: Hispanics, American Indians, and Asian Americans.

Advertisers are also presenting a more realistic view of women's roles in society. Women are now shown in advertisements as having a multifaceted role extending beyond housekeeping chores, which was still the way they were portrayed in many ads in the 1970's. In fact, showing a realistic role of today's women—more than half of whom work outside the home—not only is ethically sound but also makes good marketing sense: one study showed that realistic role portrayals of women strongly influence advertising effectiveness, such as the recall of major selling points in an ad and a willingness to consider buying a product.[35]

Advertisers and advertising agencies are increasingly staffed by minorities and women, both to improve the effectiveness of their communications to targeted audiences and to avoid offending these audiences.

Concept Check

1 **What is a news release?**

2 **What is cause-related marketing?**

3 **What is the difference between government regulation and self-regulation?**

Summary

1 Communication is the sharing of meaning and requires a source, message, receiver, and the processes of encoding and decoding.
2 For communication to occur, the sender and receiver must have a shared field of experience. Feedback from receiver to sender helps determine whether decoding has occurred or noise has distracted the message.
3 The promotional mix consists of advertising, personal selling, sales promotion, and publicity. These tools vary according to whether they are personal, can be identified with a sponsor, and can be controlled with regard to whom, when, where, and how often the message is sent.
4 The target for promotional programs is both the ultimate consumer and an intermediary. Ultimate consumer programs rely more on advertising, whereas personal selling is more important in reaching industrial buyers and intermediaries.
5 The emphasis on the promotional tools varies with a product's life cycle. In introduction, awareness is important. During growth, creating brand preference is essential. Advertising is more important in the former stage and personal selling in the latter. Sales promotion helps maintain buyers in the maturity stage.

6 In selecting the appropriate promotional mix, marketers must consider the characteristics of the product and the stage of the consumer purchase decision.
7 When a push strategy is used, personal selling and sales promotions directed to intermediaries play major roles. In a pull strategy, advertising and sales promotions directed to ultimate consumers are important.
8 More money is spent in sales promotion than in advertising. There are several objectives for sales promotion: encouraging new product trial, increasing business inventory, increasing repeat purchases by customers, and reducing price cutting.
9 There is a wide range of consumer-oriented sales promotions: coupons, deals, premiums, contests, sweepstakes, samples, point-of-purchase displays, and rebates.
10 Trade-oriented promotions consist of allowances and discounts, cooperative advertising, and training of distributors' sales forces. These are used in all levels of the channel.
11 Publicity is an indirectly paid form of promotion conducted through news releases, news conferences, or public service announcements.
12 Special ethical concerns in today's promotional activities include misleading sales promotions and ads, ads and TV programs directed toward children, and realistic portrayals of minorities and women.

KEY TERMS AND CONCEPTS

communication p. 435
source p. 435
message p. 435
receivers p. 435
encoding p. 435
decoding p. 435
field of experience p. 436
feedback p. 436
promotional mix p. 437
advertising p. 437
personal selling p. 438
publicity p. 439
sales promotion p. 440
push strategy p. 445
pull strategy p. 446
consumer-oriented sales promotions p. 447
consumer promotions p. 447
trade-oriented sales promotions p. 453
trade promotions p. 453
cooperative advertising p. 454
publicity tools p. 456
cause-related marketing p. 456

CHAPTER PROBLEMS AND APPLICATIONS

1 After listening to a recent sales presentation, Mary Smith signed up for membership at the local health club. On arriving at the facility, she learned there was an additional fee for racquetball court rentals. "I don't remember that in the sales talk; I thought they said all facilities were included with the membership fee," complained Mary. Describe the problem in terms of the communication process.

2 Product managers who are responsible for most of the promotional decisions for a brand are usually well-paid, well-educated marketing professionals. Consider for a minute the average consumer for Kraft Macaroni and Cheese. Are there any potential problems in terms of the fields of experience of these two groups with respect to promotional campaigns? How might any potential differences be overcome?

3 Develop a matrix to compare the four elements of the promotional mix on the three *W*'s criteria—to *w*hom you deliver the message, *w*hat you say, *w*hen you say it.

4 Explain how the promotional tools used by an airline would differ if the target audience were (a) consumers who travel for pleasure and (b) corporate travel departments that select the airlines to be used by company employees.

5 Suppose you introduced a new consumer food product and invested heavily both in national advertising (pull strategy) and in training and motivating your field sales force to sell the product to food stores (push strategy). What kinds of feedback would you receive from both the advertising and your sales force? How could you increase both the quality and quantity of each?

6 Fisher-Price Company, long known as a manufacturer of children's toys, has introduced a line of clothing for children. Outline a promotional plan to get this product introduced in the marketplace.

7 Cray Research makes supercomputers to handle the information and computing needs of government agencies, such as the weather service, and entire countries, such as France. Unlike Apple Computer, Cray does no advertising on television. Explain why two computer companies have such different promotional strategies.

8 Many insurance companies sell health insurance plans to companies. In these companies the employees pick the plan, but the set of offered plans is determined by the company. Recently Blue Cross–Blue Shield, a health insurance company, ran a television ad stating, "If your employer doesn't offer you Blue Cross–Blue Shield coverage, ask why." Explain the promotional strategy behind the advertisement.

9 Identify the sales promotion tools that might be useful for (a) Tastee Yogurt—a new brand introduction, (b) 3M self-sticking Post-it notes, and (c) Wrigley's Spearmint Gum.

10 A few years ago the Gannett Corporation introduced a new daily newspaper intended to be a nationwide periodical. To introduce *USA Today,* free copies were distributed at airports and check-in counters of car rental companies such as Hertz and Avis. (a) What was the rationale behind this promotional strategy? (b) Who was the original target audience?

SUGGESTED READINGS

Felix Kessler, "The Costly Coupon Craze," *Fortune* (July 9, 1986), pp. 83-84. *The article gives insights into the magnitude of coupon use in the United States today.*

Marvin A. Jolson, Joshua L. Weiner, and Richard Rosecky, "Correlates of Rebate Proneness," *Journal of Advertising Research* (February-March 1987), pp. 33-43. *The article analyzes who uses "rebates"—defined as a money-refund offer available to consumers who mail in a proof-of-purchase and receive a check from the manufacturer in return.*

Scott A. Neslin and Darral G. Clarke, "Relating the Brand Use Profile of Coupon Redeemers to Brand and Coupon Characteristics," *Journal of Advertising Research* (February-March 1987), pp. 23-32. *As the title states, the article relates who uses coupons to factors such as the face value of the coupon and the market share enjoyed by the brand.*

P. Rajan Varadarajan and Anil Menon, "Cause-Related Marketing: A Coalignment of Marketing Strategy and Corporate Philanthropy," *Journal of Marketing* (July 1988), pp. 58-74. *This article describes cause-related marketing from the viewpoints of promotion, philanthropy, social responsibility, fund-raising, and public relations.*

17

ADVERTISING

After reading this chapter you should be able to:

Explain the differences between product and institutional advertising and the variations within each type.

•

Understand the steps used to develop, execute, and evaluate an advertising program.

•

Understand alternative ways to set an advertising budget.

•

Explain the advantages and disadvantages to alternative advertising media.

A Zapper's Profile: A 3-Minute, 42-Second Attention Span

"I'm a zapper," states Bruce Hoenig of Brooklyn, New York. Remote control held tightly in hand, he pingpongs among the 68 channels in his cable system for 3 hours a night—zapping himself away from a stream of TV ads.

Although his nighttime zapping behavior is typically American, his daytime job is not. He is a media-services director responsible for spending $70 million annually to make and air TV ads for Lipton's tea bags and its other products. He's concerned that if everyone else zaps like he does, Lipton's ads aren't reaching the amount of TV viewers it is paying for.

Hoenig's concerns are real. The average U.S. household zaps its TV set every 3 minutes and 42 seconds.[1] So companies are frantically searching for "zap-proof advertising" that will capture viewers' attention enough to discourage their switching channels.

To combat zapping, several approaches such as celebrities and docudramas are being used. To gain young consumers' attention, Honda motor scooters used several famous, offbeat celebrities. In a very avant-garde television commercial, actress Grace Jones was shown biting rock singer Adam Ant's ear.

In another, Chicago Bears' quarterback Jim McMahon, sunglasses and all, says, "Outrageousness!" He continues, "It's nothin' more than a way to wake people up, especially yourself." Although such a statement is certainly not typical

Advertisements serve varying purposes

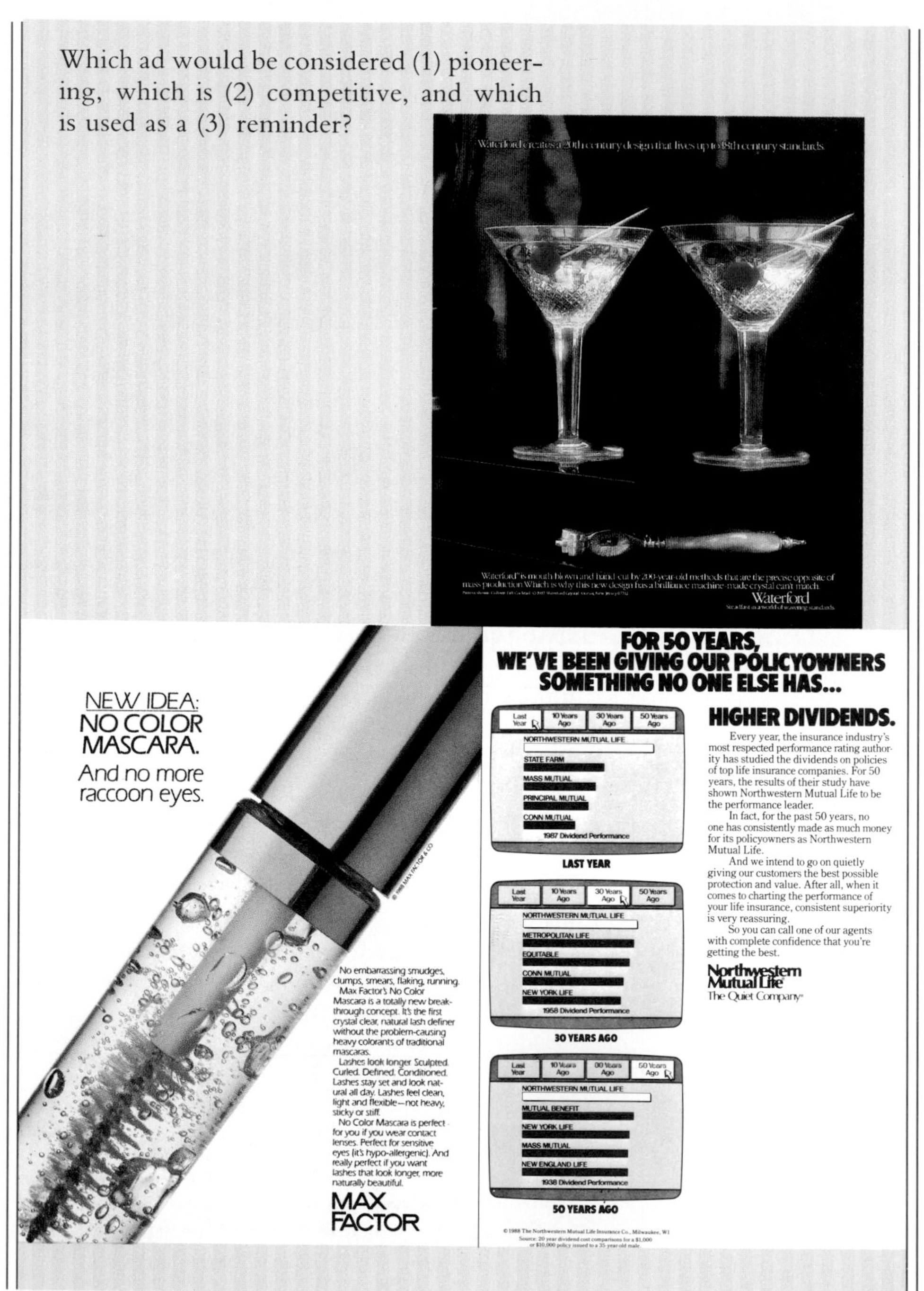

Which ad would be considered (1) pioneering, which is (2) competitive, and which is used as a (3) reminder?

of most television commercials, the real surprise comes halfway through the 30-second spot. Suddenly, the commercial runs in reverse, and viewers see the entire McMahon routine performed backwards.[2]

These creative approaches can succeed in neutralizing zapping. For example, measurements of TV viewing revealed that most TV ads shown during the 1988 Grammy music awards program lost 10 percent of the audience by zapping. But Pepsi-Cola's TV ads, which featured Michael Jackson, lost only 1 to 2 percent.[3]

Successful advertising is a challenge. The first few seconds are the key, or all that is discussed in this chapter is zapped. Movies, soap, hospitals, politicians, various causes, and even AIDS prevention are all promoted by advertising. Advertising is the most visible and highly criticized element of the marketing mix and an important aspect of promotion.

Advertising is defined as any *paid* form of *nonpersonal* presentation of goods, services, or ideas by an identified sponsor. Two terms are highlighted: *paid* distinguishes advertising from publicity, and *nonpersonal* separates it from personal selling.

TYPES OF ADVERTISEMENTS

As you look through any magazine, the number of advertisements and the varying themes are overwhelming. Advertisements are prepared for different purposes, but they basically consist of two types: product or institutional.

PRODUCT ADVERTISEMENTS

Focused on selling a good or service, **product advertisements** take three forms: (1) pioneering (or informational), (2) competitive (or persuasive), and (3) reminder. Look at the ads for Waterford Crystal, Northwestern Mutual Life Insurance, and Max Factor clear mascara and guess the type and objective of each ad.

Used in the introductory stage of the life cycle, *pioneering* advertisements tell people what a product is, what it can do, and where it can be found. The key objective of a pioneering ad (such as that for Max Factor clear mascara) is to inform the target market. Informative ads have been found to be interesting, convincing, and effective according to consumer judgment.[4]

Advertising that promotes a specific brand's features and benefits is *competitive*. The objective of these messages is to persuade the target market to select the firm's brand rather than that of a competitor. An increasingly common form of competitive advertising is *comparative* advertising, which shows one brand's strengths relative to competitors'.[5] The Northwestern Mutual Life ad, for example, highlights its competitive advantage in life insurance policies. Before the late 1970's, two of the three national TV networks would not allow comparative ads in which a competitor's brand name was used. However, the Federal Trade Commission (FTC) endorsed comparative advertising in 1979, and now over one-fifth of network radio and television commercials are comparative ads.[6] Firms that use comparative advertising (such as Northwestern Mutual Life) need market research and test results to provide legal support for their claims.[7]

Dial soap uses reinforcement ads to encourage consumers to keep using the product

Reminder advertising is used to reinforce previous knowledge of a product. The Waterford Crystal ad shown reminds consumers about the quality and history associated with its product. Reminder advertising is good for products that have achieved a well-recognized position and are in the mature phase of their product life cycle. Maxwell House used a creative form of reminder advertising during the 1988 Winter Olympics in Calgary when it used two hot air balloons in the shape of its coffee cans.[8] One type of reminder ad, reinforcement, is used to assure current users they made the right choice. One example: "Aren't you glad you use Dial? Don't you wish everybody did?"

INSTITUTIONAL ADVERTISEMENTS

The objective of **institutional advertisements** is to build goodwill or an image for an organization, rather than promote a specific product or service. Institutional advertising has been used by companies such as GTE, Beatrice, and TRW to build confidence in the company name.[9] Often this form of advertising is used to support the public relations plan or counter adverse publicity. Four alternative forms of institutional advertisements are often used:

1. *Advocacy* advertisements state the position of a company on an issue. Anheuser-Busch places ads discussing its views on the responsible use of alcohol, as shown on the opposite page.

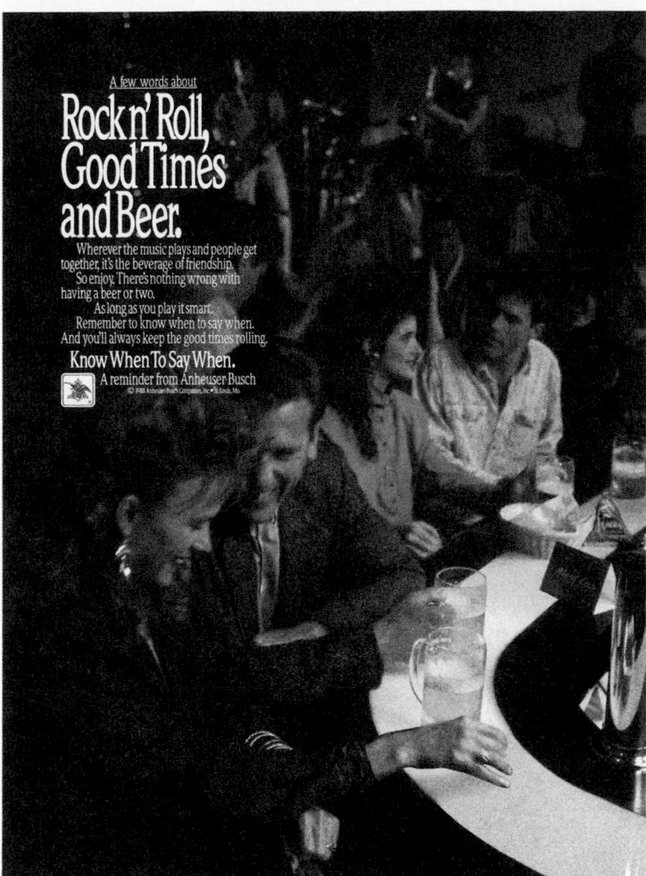

An advocacy advertisement about the responsible use of alcohol

2. *Pioneering institutional* advertisements, like the form of pioneering ads for products discussed above, are used for a new announcement about what a company is, what it can do, or where it is located.
3. *Competitive institutional* advertisements promote the advantages of one product class over another and are used in markets where different product classes compete for the same buyers. The dairy farmers' association runs ads to show milk is an "every time of the day drink" and not just for kids. The goal of these ads is to increase demand for milk as it competes against other beverages.
4. *Reminder institutional* advertisements, like the product form, simply bring the company's name to the attention of the target market again.

CONCEPT CHECK

1 **What is the difference between pioneering and competitive ads?**

2 **What is the purpose of institutional advertisements?**

DEVELOPING THE ADVERTISING PROGRAM

Because media costs are high, advertising decisions must be made carefully, using a systematic approach. Paralleling the planning, implementation, and control steps described in the strategic marketing process (Chapter 2), the advertising decision process is divided into (1) developing, (2) executing, and (3) evaluating the advertising program (Figure 17-1). Development of the advertising program focuses on the four *W*'s:

- *Who* is the target audience?
- *What* are (1) the advertising objectives, (2) the amounts of money that can be budgeted for the advertising program, and (3) the kinds of copy to use?
- *When* should the advertisements be run?
- *Where* should the advertisements be run?

FIGURE 17-1
The advertising decision process

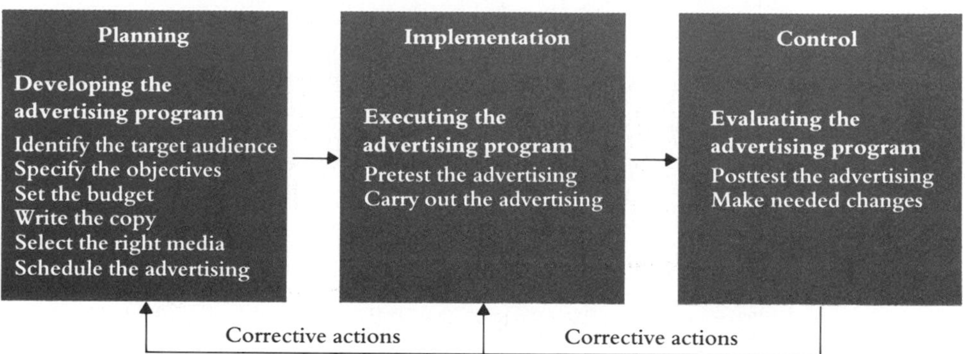

IDENTIFYING THE TARGET AUDIENCE

The first decision in developing the advertising program is identifying the *target audience,* the group of prospective buyers toward which an advertising program is directed. To the extent that time and money permit, the target audience for the advertising program is the target market for the firm's product, which is identified from marketing research and market segmentation studies. The more a firm knows about its target audience's profile—including their life-style, attitudes, and values—the easier it is to make an advertising decision. If a firm wanted to reach you with its ad, it would need to know what TV shows you watch and what magazines you read. Companies also recognize that consumers receive communications and accept ideas and products at different times.

SPECIFYING ADVERTISING OBJECTIVES

After the target audience is identified, a decision must be reached on what the advertising campaign is to accomplish. Consumers can be said to respond in terms of a **hierarchy of effects,** which is the sequence of stages a prospective buyer goes through from initial awareness of a product to eventual action (either trial or adoption of it).[10]

- Awareness: the consumer's ability to recognize and remember the product or brand name
- Interest: An increase in the consumer's desire to learn about some of the features of the product or brand
- Evaluation: the consumer's appraisal of how he or she feels about the product or brand
- Trial: the consumer's actual first purchase and use of the product or brand
- Adoption: through a favorable experience on the first trial, the consumer's repeated purchase and use of the product or brand

For a totally new product the sequence applies to the entire product category, but for a new brand competing in an established product category it applies to the brand itself. These steps can serve as guidelines for developing advertising objectives.

Although sometimes an objective for an advertising program involves several steps in the hierarchy of effects, it often stresses one main step. No matter what the specific objective might be, from building awareness to increasing repeat purchases, advertising objectives should possess three important qualities. They should (1) be designed for a well-defined target audience, (2) be measurable, and (3) cover a specified time period.

SETTING THE ADVERTISING BUDGET

You might not remember (?) who advertised during the 1973 Super Bowl, but it cost the company $207,000 a minute. By 1988 the cost of 1 minute during Super Bowl XIX was $1.35 million (Figure 17-2). The reason for the escalating costs is the growing numbers of viewers: an estimated 100 million people tune in for at least a few minutes of the game.[11]

From Figure 17-3, it is clear that the advertising expenditures needed to reach U.S. households are enormous. Note that three companies—P&G, Philip Morris, and Sears—each spend more than a billion dollars annually on advertising.

After setting the advertising objectives, a company must decide on how much to spend. Determining the ideal amount for the budget is difficult because there is no precise way to measure the exact results of spending advertising dollars. However, there are several methods used to set the advertising budget.

Percent of Sales In the **percent of sales budgeting** approach, funds are allocated to advertising as a percentage of past or anticipated sales, in terms of either dollars or units sold. A common budgeting method,[12] this approach is often stated in terms such as, "Our ad budget for this year is 3 percent of last year's gross sales." The advantage of this approach is obvious: it's simple and provides a financial safeguard whereby the advertising budget is tied to sales. However, there is a major fallacy in this approach, which implies that sales cause advertising, whereas the relationship should be reversed. Using this method, a company may reduce its advertising budget when it needs it the most because of a downturn in past sales or a forecast downturn in future ones.

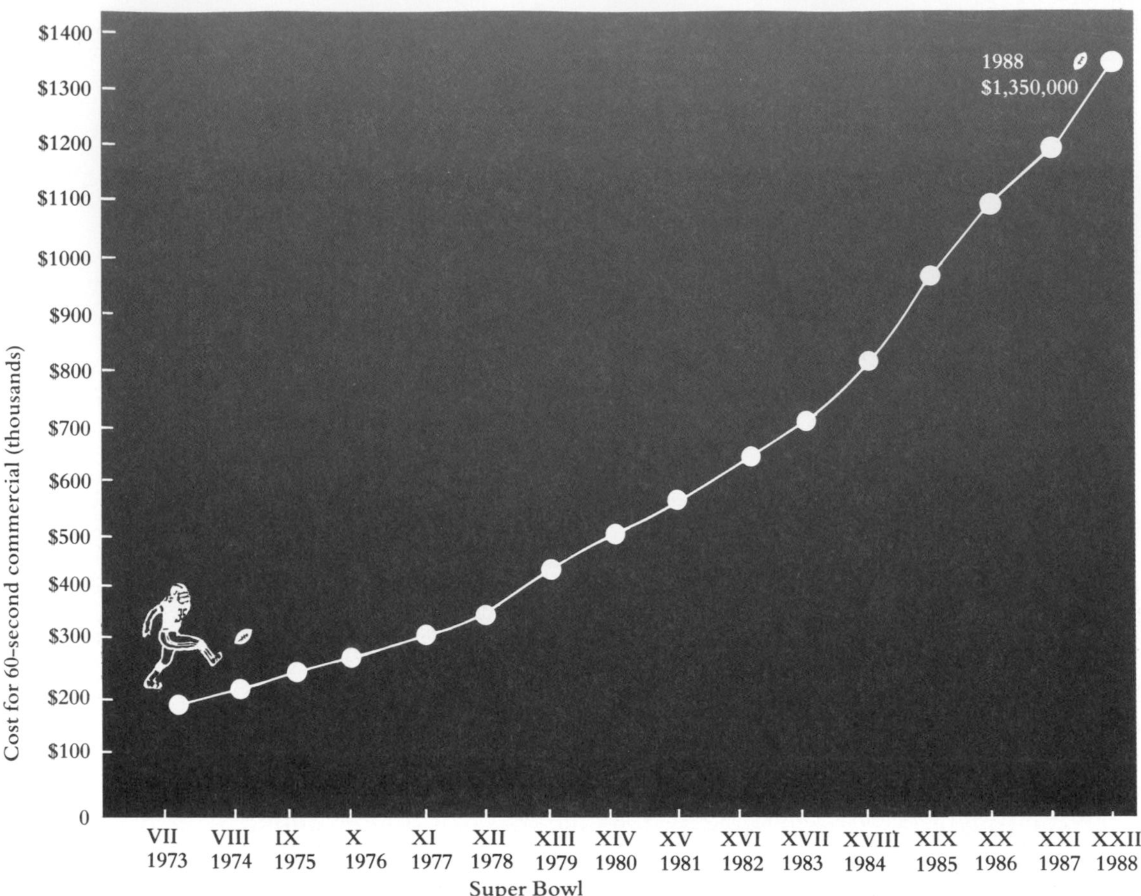

FIGURE 17-2
Rising media costs: Super Bowl, super dollars

Competitive Parity A second common approach, **competitive parity budgeting,** is matching the competitor's absolute level of spending or the proportion per point of market share a competitor has. This approach has also been referred to as *matching competitors* or *share of market*. It is important to consider the competition in budgeting. Consumer responses to ads are in the context of competing ads, so if a competitor runs 30 radio ads a week, it may be difficult for a firm to get its message across with only 5 messages.[13] The competitor's budget level, however, should not be the determinant in setting a company's budget. The competition might have very different advertising objectives, which require a different level of advertising expenditures.

All You Can Afford Common to many small businesses is **all you can afford budgeting** in which money is allocated to advertising only after all other budget items are covered. As one company executive said in reference to this budgeting process, "Why, it's simple. First, I go upstairs to the controller and ask how much they can afford to give us this year. He says a million and a half. Later, the boss comes to me and asks how much we should spend, and I say 'Oh, about a million and a half.' Then we have our advertising appropriation."[14]

Fiscally conservative, this approach has little else to offer. Using this bud-

RANK	COMPANY	ADVERTISING EXPENDITURES (MILLIONS)
1	Procter & Gamble Co.	$1,435
2	Philip Morris Co.	1,364
3	Sears, Roebuck & Co.	1,004
4	RJR Nabisco	935
5	General Motors Corp.	839
6	Ford Motor Co.	648
7	Anheuser-Busch Co.	643
8	McDonald's Corp.	592
9	K Mart Corp.	590
10	PepsiCo Inc.	581
11	General Mills	551
12	Warner-Lambert Co.	548
13	BCI Holdings	535
14	Unilever N.V.	517
15	J.C. Penney Co.	496

Source: R. Craig Endicott, "Ad Growth Edges Up," *Advertising Age* (September 24, 1987), p. 1. Reprinted with permission of *Advertising Age*. Copyright Crain Communications, Inc.

FIGURE 17-3
Advertising expenditures by companies in 1986

geting philosophy, a company acts as though it doesn't know anything about an advertising-sales relationship or what its advertising objectives are.

Objective and Task The best approach to budgeting is **objective and task budgeting,** whereby the company (1) determines its advertising objectives, (2) outlines the tasks to accomplish these objectives, and (3) determines the advertising cost of performing these tasks.[15]

This method takes into account what the company wants to accomplish and requires that the objectives be specified.[16] Strengths of the other budgeting

OBJECTIVE

To increase awareness among college students for the new CD-player cleaning kit. Awareness at the end of 1 semester should be 20 percent of all students from the existing 0 percent today.

TASKS	COSTS
Advertisements once a week for a semester in 500 college papers	$280,000
Advertisements weekly for a semester on the nationally syndicated Wolfman Jack radio show	25,000
Three monthly, full-page ads in *Audio* magazine	9,000
TOTAL BUDGET	$314,000

FIGURE 17-4
The objective and task approach

methods are integrated into this approach because each previous method's strength is tied to the objectives. For example, if the costs are beyond what the company can afford, objectives are reworked and the tasks revised. The difficulty with this method is the judgment required to determine the tasks needed to accomplish objectives. Would two or four insertions in *Time* magazine be needed to achieve a specific awareness level? Figure 17-4 shows a sample media plan with objectives, tasks, and budget outlined. The total amount to be budgeted is $314,000. If the company can only afford $200,000, the objectives must be reworked, tasks redefined, and the total amount recalculated.

WRITING THE COPY

The central element of an advertising program is the *advertising copy,* the messages that the target audience is intended to see (as in magazines, newspapers, and TV) or hear (as in radio and TV). This usually involves identifying the key benefits of the product that are deemed important to a prospective buyer in making trial and adoption decisions.

Message Content Every advertising message is made up of both informational and persuasional elements. These two elements, in fact, are so intertwined that it is sometimes difficult to tell them apart. For example, basic information contained in many ads such as the product name, benefits, features, and price are presented in a way that tries to attract attention and encourage purchase. On the other hand, even the most persuasive advertisements have to contain at least some basic information to be successful.

Information and persuasive content can be combined in the form of an appeal to provide a basic reason for the consumer to act. Although the marketer can use many different types of appeals, common advertising appeals include fear appeals, sex appeals, and humorous appeals.

Fear appeals suggest to the consumer that he or she can avoid some negative experience through the purchase and use of the product. Life insurance companies often try to show the negative effects of premature death on the relatives of those who don't carry enough life insurance. The famous advertising slogan of "ring around the collar" shows that others will be repelled if they observe a person with a stained collar. When using fear appeals, the advertiser must be sure that the appeal is strong enough to get the audience's attention and concern but not so strong that it will lead them to "tune out" the message.

In contrast, *sex appeals* suggest to the audience that the product will increase the attractiveness of the user. Sex appeals can be found in almost any product category from automobiles to toothpaste. Unfortunately, many commercials that use sex appeals are only successful at gaining the attention of the audience; they have little impact on how consumers think, feel, or act. Some advertising experts even argue that such appeals get in the way of successful communication by distracting the audience from the purpose of the ad.

Humorous appeals imply either directly or more subtly that the product is more fun or exciting than competitors' offerings. As with fear and sex appeals, the use of humor is widespread in advertising and can be found in many product categories. Unfortunately for the advertiser, humor tends to wear out quickly, thus boring the consumer. Bartles and Jaymes, featuring the Frank and Ed characters, frequently changes the television commercials for its wine coolers to avoid this advertising "wearout."

Creating the Actual Message The "creative people," or copywriters, in an advertising agency have the responsibility to turn appeals and features such as quality, style, dependability, economy, and service into attention-getting, believable advertising copy. This often relies on creative use of fear, sex, humor, sound, or visual effects.

A relatively new upstart among advertising agencies, Fallon, McElligott, Inc. (FM), was designated as *Advertising Age* magazine's 1983 Agency of the Year by using wit, irreverence, and shock in its advertising copy. Its basic premise: with the hundreds of advertising impressions most of us see every day, use creative ads—not bombardment—to get the target audience's attention.

FM's newspaper ad for ITT Life Insurance Corporation, promoting term over whole-life insurance policies, proclaimed, "Your whole life is a mistake." For newspaper and TV ads for the *Wall Street Journal,* FM came up with the theme line, "The daily diary of the American dream." Its magazine ad for Lee jeans—situated among the many four-color ads in consumer magazines—is a snapshot picture of a second in the life of a Lee jeans wearer and is shown in striking black and white, except for the tiny Lee logo in the corner.[17]

Translating the copywriter's ideas into an actual advertisement is also a complex process. Performing quality artwork, layout, and production for the advertisements is costly and time consuming. High-quality TV commercials typically cost about $125,000 to produce a 30-second ad, a task done by about 2,000 small commercial production companies across the United States. High-visibility commercials can be even more expensive: two 15-second Rolaids commercials involved $500,000 and 75 people over a 6-month period. About 70 "takes" are necessary, and typical, to get things "right!"[18]

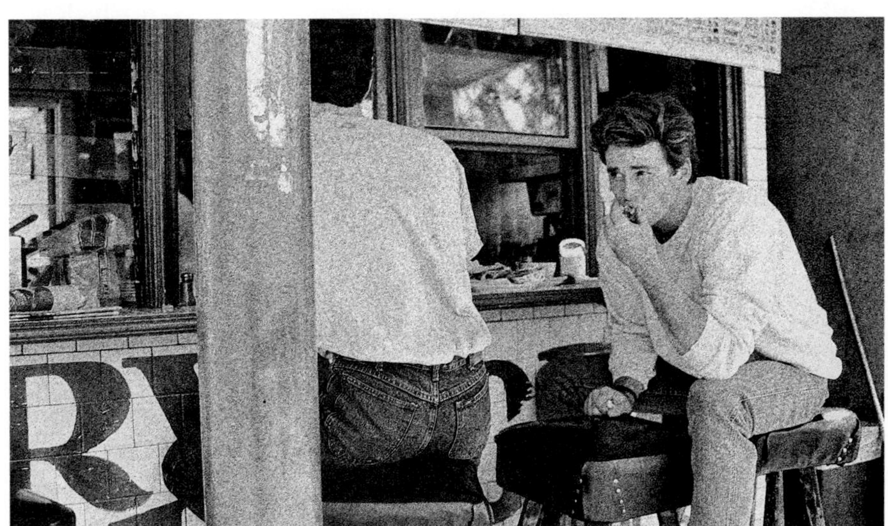
2 in the afternoon. Breakfast. Lee jeans.

Lee

A creative, attention-getting advertisement for Lee jeans

CONCEPT CHECK

1 What is the weakness of the percent of sales budgeting approach?

2 What are characteristics of good advertising objectives?

SELECTING THE RIGHT MEDIA

Every advertiser must decide where to place the advertisements. The alternatives are the *advertising media,* the means by which the message is communicated to the target audience. Newspapers, magazines, radio, and TV are examples of advertising media. This "media selection" decision is related to the target audience, type of product, nature of the message, campaign objectives, available budget, and the costs of the alternative media. Figure 17-5 shows expenditures on alternative major advertising media and indicates that expenditures more than doubled from 1980 to 1987 to about $110 billion.[19]

Choosing a Medium and a Vehicle Within that Medium In deciding where to place advertisements, a company has several media to choose from and a number of alternatives, or vehicles, within each medium. Often advertisers use a mix of media forms and vehicles to maximize the exposure of the message to the target audience while at the same time minimizing costs. These two conflicting goals of (1) maximizing exposure and (2) minimizing costs are of central importance to media planning.

Basic Terms Media buyers speak a language of their own. So every advertiser involved in selecting the right media for their campaigns must be familiar with some common terms used in the advertising industry. Figure 17-6 shows the most common terms used in media decisions.

Because advertisers try to maximize the number of individuals in the target market exposed to the message, they must be concerned with reach. **Reach** is the number of different people exposed to the message.

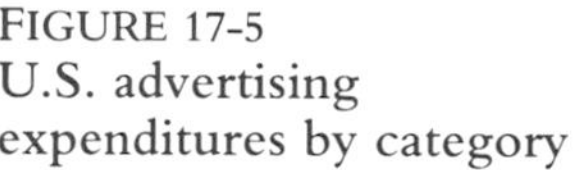

FIGURE 17-5
U.S. advertising expenditures by category

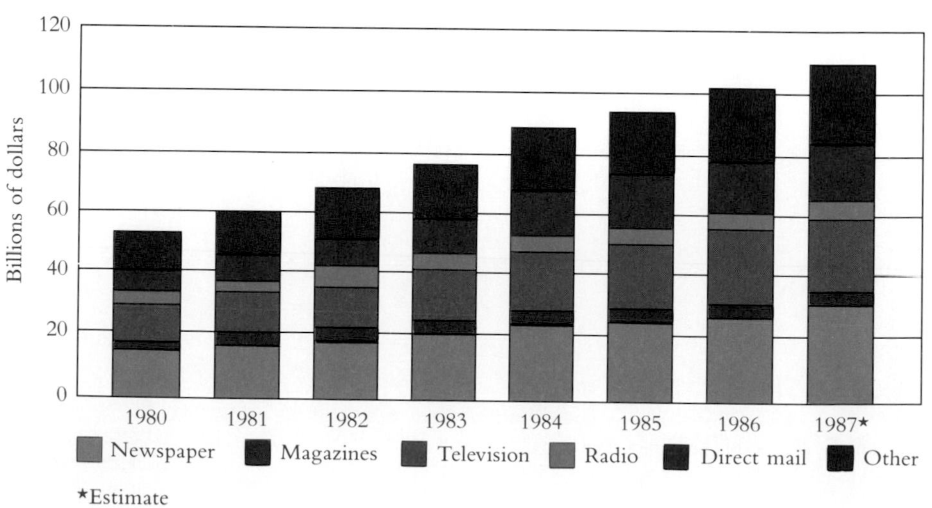

TERM	WHAT IT MEANS
Reach	• The number of different people exposed to an advertising message.
Rating	• The percentage of households in a market watching or listening to a broadcast.
Share	• The percentage of households with their sets turned on (radio or TV) who are tuned to a particular program.
Frequency	• The average number of times an individual is exposed to a series of advertisements.
Gross rating points (GRPs)	• Reach multiplied by frequency for a series of ads.
Cost per thousand (CPM)	• The cost of advertising divided by the number of thousands of individuals or households who are exposed.

FIGURE 17-6
The language of the media buyer

The exact definition of reach sometimes varies among alternative media. Newspapers often use reach to describe their total circulation or the number of different households that buy the paper. Television and radio stations, in contrast, describe their audience using the term **rating**—the percentage of households in a market that are tuned to a particular TV show or radio station. In general, advertisers try to maximize reach in their target market at the lowest cost.

Although reach is important, advertisers are also interested in exposing their message to the target audience more than once. This is because consumers often do not pay close attention to advertising messages, some of which contain large amounts of relatively complex information. When advertisers want to reach the same audience more than once, they are concerned with **frequency,** the average number of times a person in the target audience is exposed to a message or advertisement.

For example, if an advertiser places a full-page ad in your local newspaper on each of the five weekdays, some individuals will be exposed to none of the ads, others will see one of them, still others two, and so on. Frequency tells you the average number of times individuals in the target audience were exposed to these five ads. Like reach, greater frequency is desirable. But because of the cost, the media planner often must balance reach and frequency. **Cost per thousand** (CPM) refers to the cost of reaching 1,000 individuals or households with the advertising message in a given medium (*M* is the Roman numeral for 1,000).

DIFFERENT MEDIA ALTERNATIVES

Figure 17-7 summarizes the advantages and disadvantages of the important advertising media, which are described in more detail below.

Television Television is a valuable medium because it communicates with both sight and sound. Print advertisements could never give you the sense of the

FIGURE 17-7
Advantages and disadvantages of major advertising media

MEDIUM	ADVANTAGES	DISADVANTAGES
Television	Reaches extremely large audience; uses picture, print, sound, and motion for effect; can target specific audiences	High cost to prepare and run ads; short exposure time and perishable message; difficult to convey complex information
Radio	Low cost; can target specific audiences; ads can be placed quickly; can use sound, humor, intimacy effectively	No visual excitement; short exposure time and perishable message; difficult to convey complex information
Magazines	Can target specific audiences; high-quality color; long life of ad; ads can be clipped and saved; can convey complex information	Long time needed to place ad; limited control of ad position; relatively high cost; competes for attention with other magazine features
Newspapers	Excellent coverage of local markets; ads can be placed and changed quickly; ads can be saved; quick consumer response; low cost	Ads compete for attention with other newspaper features; can't control ad position on page; short life span; can't target specific audiences
Direct mail	Best for targeting specific audiences; very flexible (3-D, pop-up ads); ad can be saved; measurable	Relatively high cost; audience often sees it as "junk mail"; no competition with editorial matter
Billboard (outdoor)	Low cost; local market focus; high visibility; opportunity for repeat exposures	Message must be short and simple; low selectivity of audience; criticized as a traffic hazard, eyesore

Source: Courtland L. Bovée and William F. Arens, *Contemporary Advertising*, 2nd ed. (Homewood, Ill.: Richard D. Irwin, 1986), pp. 382-383; William G. Nickels, *Understanding Business* (St. Louis: Times Mirror/Mosby College Publishing, 1987), p. 204.

Mazda RX-7 sports car cornering at the speed of sound. In addition, network television is the only medium that can reach 95 percent of the homes in the United States.[20]

Television's major disadvantage is cost: the cost of a prime-time 30-second network spot is now as much as $400,000. Because of these high charges, there has been a growing trend toward reducing the length of the standard commercial from 30 seconds to 15 seconds. This practice, referred to as *splitting 30's,* reduces costs but severely restricts the amount of information that can be conveyed.[21] These 15-second ads now represent a third of all network commercials. Another problem with television is the likelihood of *wasted coverage*—having people outside the market for the product see the advertisement. In recent years the cost and wasted coverage problems of TV have been reduced through the in-

TV storyboards lead to action commercials

"DEEPER UNDERSTANDING-RX-7"

troduction of cable TV, whose advertising time is often less expensive than the prime time on major networks. This often allows far greater control over who sees the advertisement.

NATURAL SFX
ANNCR: (VO) When you first see the Mazda RX-7.
you begin to understand why it has become a legend among today's sports cars.
Because beyond its classic styling
you soon discover the orthopedic perfection of its bucket seats.
You feel the preciseness of its 5-speed overdrive
and experience its comprehensive instrumentation.
MAZDA RX-7 $10,945
Those things alone help
MAZDA RX-7 $10,945
make it an exceptional value.
But to gain an even deeper understanding of the Mazda RX-7.
you're going to have
to experience roads like these for yourself.
mazda
ANNCR: (VO) Mazda RX 7. Experience it.

Radio There are seven times as many radio stations as television stations in the United States. The major advantage of radio is it's a segmented medium. There are the Farm Radio Network, the Physician's Network, all-talk shows, and punk rock stations, all listened to by different market segments. The average college student is a surprisingly heavy radio listener and spends more time during the day listening to radio than watching television—1 hour 56 minutes versus 1 hour 20 minutes (Figure 17-8). So advertisers with college students as their target market must consider radio.

The disadvantage of radio is that it has limited use for products that must be seen. Another problem is the ease with which consumers can tune out a commercial by switching stations. Radio is a medium that competes for people's attention as they do other activities such as driving, working, or relaxing. Peak radio listening time is during the drive times (6 to 10 AM and 4 to 7 PM).

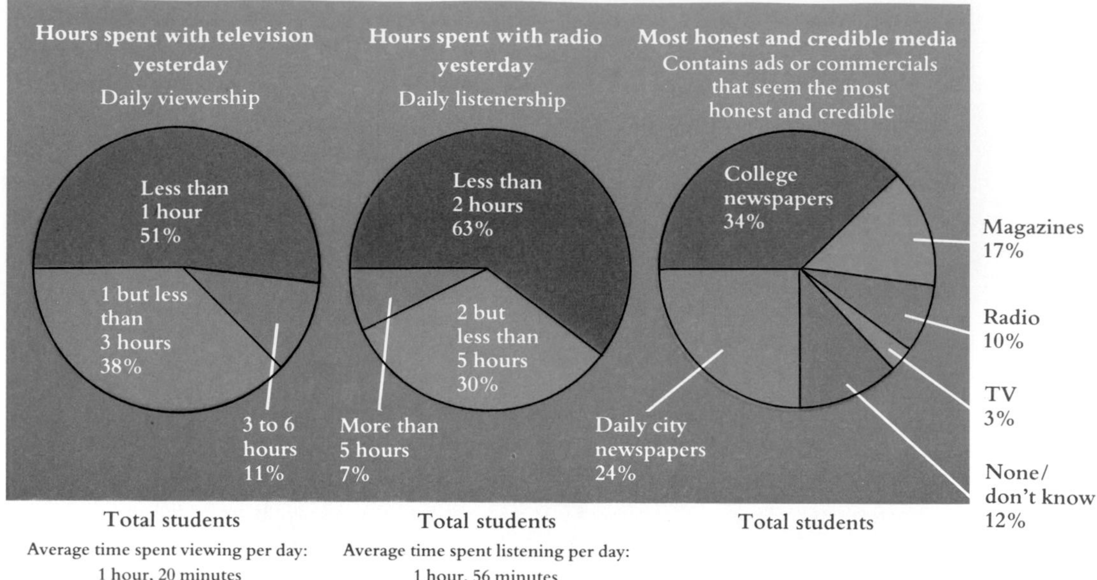

FIGURE 17-8
Media usage by college students

Source: Redrawn from B.G. Yovovich, "A Game of Hide-and-Seek," *Advertising Age* (August 2, 1982), p. M6. Reprinted with permission of *Advertising Age*. Copyright Crain Communications, Inc. Based on data from National Study by Belden Associates, Dallas, for CASS Student Advertising, Inc.

Magazines One of the fastest-growing media in the United States is magazines. The marketing advantage of this medium is the great number of special interest publications that appeal to defined segments. Runners read *Running,* sailors buy *Sail,* gardeners peruse *Organic Gardening,* and craftspeople subscribe to *Woodworking*. Over 200 publications cater to the computer industry, and high-tech companies filled about one-fourth of the ad pages in *Fortune, Forbes, Business Week,* and *Dun's*.[22] Each magazine's readers often represent a unique profile, such as the profile in Figure 17-9 of the *Rolling Stone* reader, who tends to travel, backpack, and ski more than most people. So a manufacturer of ski equipment that places an ad in *Rolling Stone* may be reaching the desired target audience. In addition to the distinct audience profiles of magazines, good color production is an advantage.

Who is the target audience? In what type of magazine should it be run? What action is it supposed to trigger? For the answers, see the text.

Reality.
If your idea of a Rolling Stone reader looks like a holdout from the 60's, welcome to the 80's.
Rolling Stone ranks number one in reaching concentrations of 18-34 readers with household incomes exceeding $25,000. When you buy Rolling Stone, you buy an audience that sets the trends and shapes the buying patterns for the most affluent consumers in America. That's the kind of reality you can take to the bank.
Rolling Stone

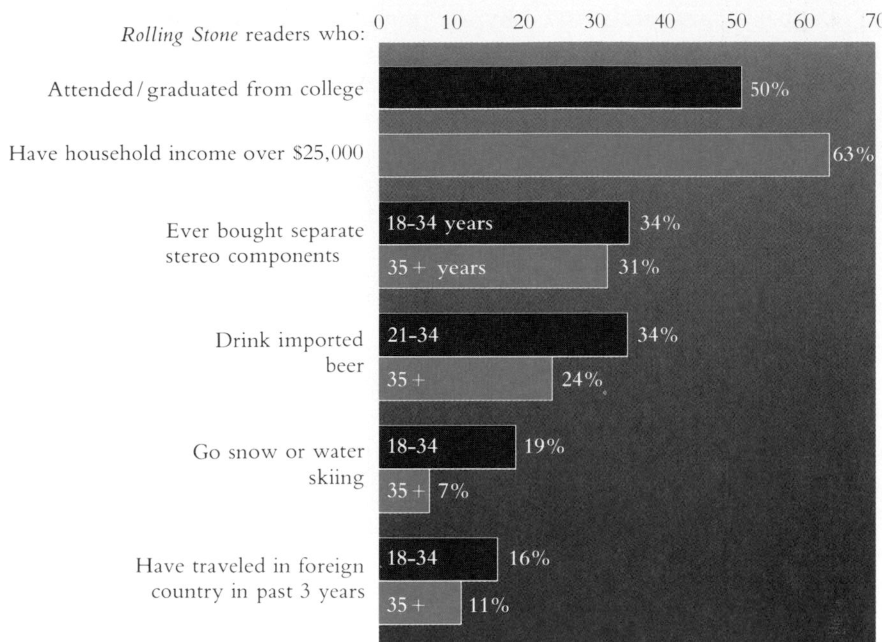

FIGURE 17-9
Some characteristics of the *Rolling Stone* reader

Source: *Rolling Stone Media Marketing Facts* (New York: Rolling Stone, 1988); 1987 Simmons Market Research Bureau.

Rolling Stone has had a perception problem: many prospective advertisers in the magazine saw it as a magazine read only by 1960's-era hippies. To alter this misperception, it developed a series of "Perception-Reality" ads targeted at its prospective advertisers and ran them in magazines such as *Advertising Age,* which media buyers read. The advertising succeeded in increasing the number of pages of advertising sold in *Rolling Stone.*

The cost of national magazines is a disadvantage compared with radio, but many national publications publish regional and even metro editions, which reduce the absolute cost and wasted coverage. *Time* publishes well over 100 different editions, ranging from a special edition for college students to a version for the area around Austin, Texas. In addition to cost, a limitation to magazines is their infrequency. At best, magazines are printed on a weekly basis, with many specialized publications appearing only monthly or less often.

High technology is arriving in magazine ads. Cardboard pop-up ads have been used by Dodge trucks and Disney World. Toyota introduced its 1988 Corolla with a pair of 3-D glasses inserted in *Time, People,* and *Cosmopolitan* magazines. Revlon offered actual samples of eyeshadow in fashion magazines, and if you read *Architectural Digest,* you could even smell a Rolls Royce leather interior using a special scent strip. What's on the horizon? Probably a music-and-blinking-light IBM PC magazine ad made possible by a computer microchip—an ad that has already run in France.[23]

Newspapers Newspapers are an important local medium with excellent reach potential. Because of the daily publication of most papers, they allow advertisements directed to immediate consumer actions such as "sale today only." Usually local retailers use newspapers as almost their sole medium.

Newspapers are rarely saved by the purchaser, so companies are generally limited to ads that call for an immediate customer response. But customers can clip and save ads they want. Companies also cannot depend on newspapers for color reproduction as good as that in most magazines.

National companies rarely use this medium except in conjunction with local distributors of their products. In these instances both parties often share the advertising costs using a cooperative advertising program, which was described in Chapter 16.

Direct Mail Direct mail allows the greatest degree of audience selectivity. Direct mail companies can provide advertisers with a mailing list of their market, such as students who live within 2 miles of the store, product managers in Texas, or people who own mobile homes. Direct mail has an advantage in providing complete product information, compared with that provided in 30-second or 60-second television or radio spots.

One disadvantage of direct mail is that rising postal costs are making it more expensive. The major limitation is that people view direct mail as junk, and the challenge is to get them to open a letter. Look at Figure 17-10 to see

FIGURE 17-10
Are you an expert? Which of the three envelopes did best? The text gives the answer and the reasons.

Source: Based on Jim Powell, "The Lucrative Trade of Crafting Junk Mail," *New York Times* (June 20, 1982), p. F7.

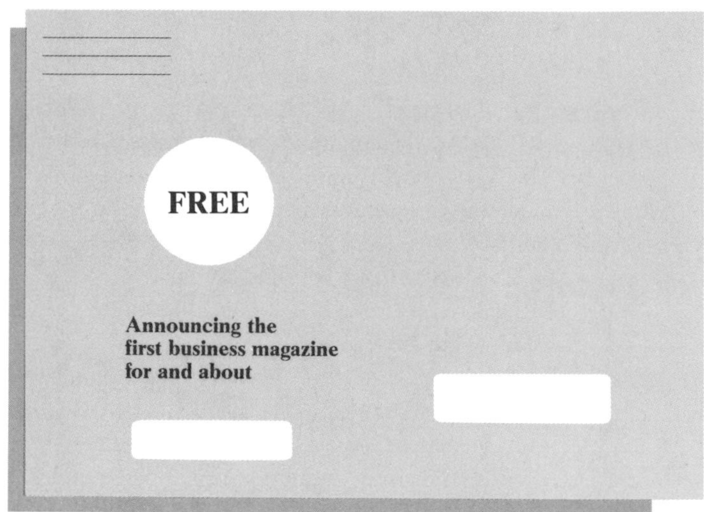

which envelope you think was most successful in overcoming the junk-mail hurdle.

If you picked the one with the simple word *Free,* in a white circle, pass "go," collect $200, and think about becoming a direct mail consultant. This envelope stands out because of its size. It also gives the impression of a strong offer by prominently displaying the word *free*—a key word in direct mail. This package generated 48 percent more subscription orders than the other two pieces combined. The second best response was obtained with the "mousetrap" appeal. The splashy graphic with the bright orange circle helped, and again the magic word *free* is displayed. The piece generated 56 percent more promotions than the third offer. No strong offer is provided with the "Preferred Subscription Invitation," and the envelope is standard size with little enticement to the reader to open it.[24] In this industry, a 1 percent to 2 percent response rate to a mailer is considered good.

Billboards A very effective medium for reminder advertising is outdoor billboards, such as the eye-catching sign by Sunrise Preschool shown on the next page. These signs often result in good reach and frequency when reinforcing a message originally communicated in other media. The visibility of this medium is good supplemental reinforcement for well-known products, and it is a relatively low-cost, flexible alternative. A company can buy space just in the desired geographical market.

A disadvantage to billboards is that no opportunity exists for lengthy advertising copy, and thus it is restricted to well-known products. Also, a good billboard site depends on traffic patterns and sight lines. In many areas environmental laws have limited the use of this medium.

Transit If you attend a metropolitan campus, chances are you might have seen some transit advertising. This medium includes messages on the interior and exterior of buses, subway cars, and taxis. As use of mass transit grows, transit advertising may become increasingly important. Selectivity is available to advertisers, who can buy space by neighborhood or bus route. To some extent, once inside the bus, the riders are captured readers.

One disadvantage to this medium is that the heavy travel times, when the audiences are the largest, are not conducive to reading advertising copy. People are standing shoulder to shoulder on the subway, hoping not to miss their stop, and little attention is paid to the advertising. Also, the demographic profile of the transit user is heavily weighted to middle-class and lower middle-class people with average incomes and educational profiles.

Other Media A variety of other media exist, ranging from the hot air balloons mentioned earlier to skywriting and theater advertising—where ads are shown on the screen before the movies are shown. Although you might expect to see advertisements *before* the movie in your local theater, do you expect to see them *in* the movie itself? Called *product placement,* the brand-name products used in a movie may be there because their manufacturer paid for the privilege. For example, Domino's Pizza paid $25,000 for its pizza to sit on the kitchen table between Tom Selleck and Ted Danson in the movie *Three Men and a Baby*. Ads

A unique billboard ad

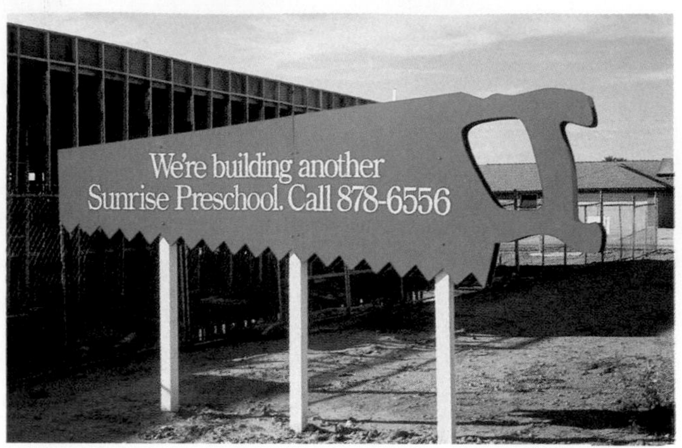
We're building another
Sunrise Preschool. Call 878-6556

are even starting to appear on the protective boxes covering rental VCR movies and at the start of the movies themselves—and would you believe?—on toilet stall doors![25]

Selection Criteria Choosing between these alternative media is difficult and hinges on several factors. First, knowing the media habits of the target audience is essential to deciding between the alternatives. Second, occasionally product attributes necessitate that certain media be used. For example, if color is a major aspect of product appeal, radio is excluded. Newspapers allow advertising for quick actions to confront competitors, and magazines are more appropriate for complicated messages because the reader can spend more time reading the message. The final factor in selecting an alternative medium is cost. When possible, alternative media are compared using a common denominator that reflects both reach and cost—a measure such as CPM.

SCHEDULING THE ADVERTISING

There is no correct schedule to advertise a product, but three factors must be considered. First is the issue of *buyer turnover,* which is how often new buyers enter the market to buy the product. The higher the buyer turnover, the greater is the amount of advertising required. A second issue in scheduling is the *purchase frequency;* the more frequently the product is purchased, the less repetition is required. Finally, companies must consider the *forgetting rate,* the speed with which buyers forget the brand if advertising is not seen.

Setting schedules requires an understanding of how the market behaves. Most companies tend to follow one of two basic approaches:

1. *Steady ("drip") schedule.* When demand and seasonal factors are unimportant, advertising is run at a steady or regular schedule throughout the year.
2. *Pulse ("burst") schedule.* Advertising is distributed unevenly throughout the year because of seasonal demand, heavy periods of promotion, or introduction of a new product.

For example, products such as dry breakfast cereals have a stable demand throughout the year and would typically use a steady schedule of advertising.

In contrast, products such as toys, snow blowers, and suntan lotions have seasonal demands and receive heavier, pulse-schedule advertising during the heavy demand season.

CONCEPT CHECK

1 **What is the weakness with a percent of sales budgeting approach?**

2 **You see the same ad in *Time* and *Fortune* and on billboards and TV. Is this an example of reach or frequency?**

3 **What is the most selective medium available?**

EXECUTING THE ADVERTISING PROGRAM

As shown earlier in Figure 17-1, executing the advertising program involves pretesting the advertising copy and actually carrying out the advertising program. John Wanamaker, the founder of Wanamaker's Department Store in Philadelphia, remarked, "I know half my advertising is wasted, but I don't know what half." The purpose of evaluating advertising efforts is to try to ensure that the advertising is not wasted. Evaluation is done usually at two separate times: before and after the advertisements are run in the actual campaign. Several methods used in the evaluation process at the stages of idea formulation and copy development are discussed below. Posttesting methods are reviewed in the section on evaluation.

PRETESTING ADVERTISING

To determine whether the advertisement communicates the intended message or to select between alternative versions of the advertisement, **pretests** are conducted before the advertisements are placed in any medium.

Portfolio Tests Portfolio tests are used to test copy alternatives. The test ad is placed in a portfolio with several other ads and stories, and consumers are asked to read through the portfolio. Afterward subjects are often asked for their impressions of the ads on several evaluative scales, such as from "very informative" to "not very informative."

Jury Tests Jury tests involve showing the ad copy to a panel of consumers and having them rate how they liked it, how much it drew their attention, and how attractive they thought it was. This approach is similar to the portfolio test in that consumer reactions are obtained. However, unlike the portfolio test, a test advertisement is not hidden within other ads.

Theater Tests Theater testing is the most sophisticated form of pretesting. Consumers are invited to view new television shows or movies in which test commercials are also shown. Viewers register their feelings about the advertisements either on hand-held electronic recording devices used during the viewing or on questionnaires afterward.

Carrying Out the Advertising Program

The responsibility for actually carrying out the advertising program can be handled in one of three ways, as shown in Figure 17-11. The **full-service agency** provides the most complete range of services, although some companies, such as retailers, have found in-house agencies to be very cost efficient. Agencies that assist a client by both developing and placing advertisements are compensated by receiving 15 percent of media costs. **Limited-service agencies** specialize in one aspect of the advertising process such as providing creative services to develop the advertising copy or buying previously unpurchased media space. Limited-service agencies that deal in creative work are compensated by a contractual agreement for the services performed. Finally, **in-house agencies** made up of the company's own staff may provide full services or a limited range of services.

Evaluating the Advertising Program

The advertising decision process does not stop with executing the advertising program. The advertisements must be posttested to determine whether they are achieving their intended objectives, and results may indicate necessary changes that must be made in the advertising program.

Posttesting Advertising

An advertisement may go through **posttests** after it has been shown to the target audience to determine whether it accomplished its intended purpose. Five approaches common in posttesting are[26]:

Aided Recall (Recognition-Readership) After being shown an ad, respondents are asked whether their previous exposure to it was through reading, viewing, or listening. The Starch test shown at right uses aided recall to determine the percentage (1) who remember seeing a specific magazine ad *(noted),* (2) who saw or read any part of the ad identifying the product or brand *(seen-associated),* and (3) who read at least half of the ad *(read most)*. Elements of the ad are then tagged with the results, as shown in the picture.

FIGURE 17-11
Alternative structures of advertising agencies used to carry out the advertising program

TYPE OF AGENCY	SERVICES PROVIDED
FULL-SERVICE AGENCY	Does research, selects media, develops copy, and produces artwork
LIMITED-SERVICE AGENCY	Specializes in one aspect of creative process
Creative boutique	Usually provides creative production work
Independent buying service	Buys previously unpurchased media space
IN-HOUSE AGENCY	Provides range of services, depending on company needs

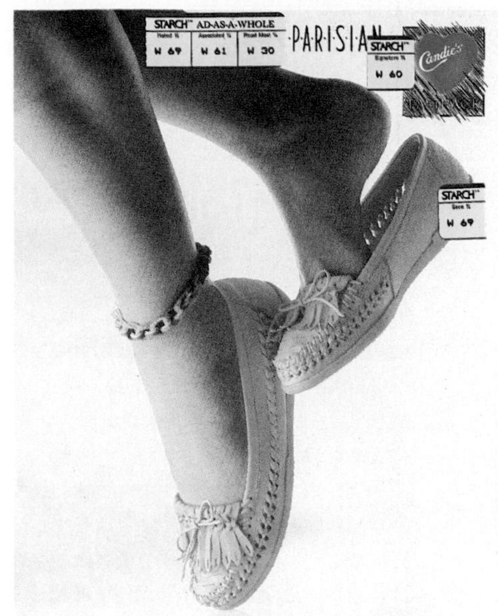

Starch scores an advertisement

Unaided Recall A question such as, "What ads do you remember seeing yesterday?" is asked of respondents without any prompting to determine whether they saw or heard advertising messages.

Attitude Tests Respondents are asked questions to measure changes in their attitudes after an advertising campaign, such as whether they have a more favorable attitude toward the product advertised.

Inquiry Tests Additional product information, product samples, or premiums are offered to an ad's readers or viewers. Ads generating the most inquiries are presumed to be the most effective.

Sales Tests Sales tests involve studies such as controlled experiments (for example, using radio ads in one market and newspaper ads in another and comparing the results) and consumer purchase tests (measuring retail sales that result from a given advertising campaign).

MAKING NEEDED CHANGES

Results of posttesting the advertising copy are used to reach decisions about changes in the advertising program. If the posttest results show that an advertisement is doing poorly in terms of awareness or cost efficiency, it may be dropped and other ads run in its place in the future. On the other hand, sometimes an advertisement may be so successful it is run repeatedly or used as the basis of a larger advertising program, as with Coca-Cola's Max Headroom and the California raisins ads in which animated clay raisins dance to a Motown beat.[27]

Concept Check

1 **Explain the difference between pretesting and posttesting advertising copy.**

2 **What is the difference between aided and unaided recall posttests?**

Summary

1 Advertising may be classified as either product or institutional. Product advertising can be pioneering, competitive, or reminder oriented. Institutional ads are one of these three or advocacy.

2 Advertising decisions center on determining who is the target audience, what to say, when to say it, and where the message should be said. The advertising decision process involves developing, executing, and evaluating the advertising program.

3 Setting advertising objectives, the *what* component, is based on the hierarchy of effects. Objectives should be measurable, have a specified time period, and state the target audience. Knowing these objectives and key competitive features of the product, creative people write the advertising copy—the message sent to the target audience.

4 Advertising budgets are based on the objectives set and tasks required. Budgeting methods often used are percent of sales, competitive parity, and the all you can afford approaches.

5 In selecting the right medium, there are distinct trade-offs between television, radio, magazines, newspapers, direct mail, billboards, transit, and other media. The decision is based on media habits of the target audience, product characteristics, and message requirements.

6 In determining advertising schedules, a balance must be made between reach and frequency. Scheduling must take into account buyer turnover, purchase frequency, and the rate at which consumers forget.

7 Advertising effectiveness is evaluated before and after the ad is run. Pretesting can be done with portfolio, jury, or theater tests. Posttesting is done on the basis of aided recall, unaided recall, attitude tests, inquiry tests, and sales tests.

8 To execute an advertising program, companies can use agencies outside the firm. These firms can provide a full range of services or specialize in creative or placement activities. Some firms use their own in-house agency.

Key Terms and Concepts

advertising p. 465
product advertisements p. 465
institutional advertisements p. 466
hierarchy of effects p. 468
percent of sales budgeting p. 469
competitive parity budgeting p. 470
all you can afford budgeting p. 470
objective and task budgeting p. 471
reach p. 474
rating p. 475
frequency p. 475
cost per thousand p. 475
pretests p. 483
full-service agency p. 484
limited-service agencies p. 484
in-house agencies p. 484
posttests p. 484

CHAPTER PROBLEMS AND APPLICATIONS

1 Suppose you are the advertising manager for a new line of children's fragrances. Which major form of media would you use for this new product?

2 How does competitive product advertising differ from competitive institutional advertising?

3 You have recently been promoted to be director of advertising for the Timkin Tool Company. In your first meeting with Mr. Timkin, he says, "Advertising is a waste! We've been advertising for 6 months now and sales haven't increased. Tell me why we should continue." Give your answer to Mr. Timkin.

4 A major life insurance company has decided to switch from using a strong fear appeal to using a humorous approach. What are the strengths and weaknesses of such a change in message strategy?

5 Some major national advertisers have found that they can have more impact with their advertising by running a large number of ads for a period and then running no ads at all for a period. Why might such a pulsing strategy be more effective than a steady schedule?

6 Which medium has the lowest cost per thousand?

MEDIUM	COST	AUDIENCE
TV show	$5000	25,000
Magazine	2200	6,000
Newspaper	4800	7,200
FM radio	420	1,600

7 Federated Banks has just developed two versions of an advertisement to encourage senior citizens to directly deposit their Social Security checks with the bank. Direct deposit means the government sends the funds directly to the bank, so that the consumer does not have to go and deposit the check. Suggest how the bank can determine the better ad.

8 The Toro Company has a broad product line. What timing approach would you recommend for the advertising of (1) the lawn mower line and (2) the new line of lawn and garden furniture?

9 What do you see as one or two major advantages and disadvantages of the five advertising posttests described in the chapter?

SUGGESTED READINGS

Dennis Kneal, "'Zapping' of TV Ads Appears Pervasive," *The Wall Street Journal* (April 25, 1988), p. 21. *This article gives a profile of who the TV zappers are and why there is so much concern about the problem.*

Charles H. Patti and Vincent Blanko, "Budgeting Practices of Big Advertisers," *Journal of Advertising Research,* Vol. 21 (December 1981), pp. 23-30. *This is an interesting study on how the budgeting practices of major companies have changed between the 1970's and 1980's.*

John Pfeiffer, "Six Months and Half a Million Dollars, All for 15 Seconds," *Smithsonian* (October 1987), pp. 134-145. *This article gives an inside look at how 75 people worked over 6 months and spent $500,000 to develop two 15-second TV commercials.*

"Print Ads that Make You Stop, Look—and Listen," *Business Week* (November 23, 1987), p. 38. *The article describes the sometimes zany high-tech magazine ads we can probably look forward to in the 1990's.*

18

Personal Selling and Sales Management

After reading this chapter you should be able to:

Recognize different types of personal selling.

•

Describe the stages in the personal selling process.

•

Specify the functions and tasks in the sales management process.

•

Determine whether a firm should use manufacturer's representatives or a company sales force.

•

Calculate the number of people needed in a company's sales force.

•

Understand how firms recruit, select, train, motivate, compensate, and evaluate salespeople.

A New Breed of Salespeople

What images come to mind when you hear the word *sales* mentioned as a career? Do you think of fast-talking, yarn-spinning people who travel a lot and are only interested in peddling their products or services? If you do, then you should talk with Wanda Truxillo of IBM. She epitomizes the new breed of professional salespeople who list sincerity, customer service, attention to customer needs before and after a sale, and good listening as the ingredients for successful selling.

Mrs. Truxillo will quickly tell you that "Knowing your customer's business and the products or service you are selling should be second nature. What really sets you apart from your competition is how responsive, knowledgeable, and good-natured you are when interfacing with your customer. Customer satisfaction is at the core of any successful business."

Wanda Truxillo has been bringing solutions to IBM customers for over 12 years. Her career path illustrates many of the topics described in this chapter. Wanda joined IBM at the age of 23. After training for a year, she became a marketing representative selling office products. Her principal style of selling, emphasizing a close, trusting relationship with customers, soon made her one of the top salespersons in her area. By age 28, she was the specialist for communications products supporting the Southern U.S. region. Within a year, Mrs. Truxillo was promoted to marketing manager in a major southern city. In this capacity, she recruited, trained, motivated, and evaluated a large marketing team responsible for establishing new accounts.

In 1985, Mrs. Truxillo became assistant to the president of IBM's National Marketing Division after completing a short assignment in strategy and plan management. In March, 1988, she was promoted to manager, mid-range marketing, responsible for marketing assistance to all of IBM's U.S. marketing and services locations.[1]

Recruiting, selecting, training, directing, and compensating salespeople such as Wanda Truxillo fall under the sales management function in the firm. Talented salespeople combined with effective sales management practices are essential for successful marketing. For example, besides her own personal talents, Wanda Truxillo benefits from IBM's unequalled training program, one that spends more than $1 billion a year on employee and customer training—an amount higher than Harvard University's annual budget.[2]

This chapter examines the scope and significance of personal selling and sales management in marketing. It highlights the many forms of personal selling and outlines the selling process. Finally, the functions of sales management are described.

Scope and Significance of Personal Selling and Sales Management

Chapter 16 described personal selling and management of the sales effort as being part of the firm's promotional mix. Although it is important to recognize that personal selling is a useful vehicle for communicating with present and potential buyers, it is much more. Take a moment to answer the questions in the personal selling and sales management quiz in Figure 18-1. As you read on, compare your answers with those in the text.

Nature of Personal Selling and Sales Management

Personal selling involves the two-way flow of communication between a buyer and seller, often in a face-to-face encounter, designed to influence a person's or group's purchase decision. However, with advances in telecommunications, personal selling also takes place over the telephone, through video teleconferencing, and through interactive computer links between buyers and sellers. For example, industrial customers today can often enter purchase orders into their computer, have it contact their supplier's computer, and find out when the product can be shipped.

FIGURE 18-1
Personal selling and sales management quiz

1. How attractive do you think each of the following rewards would be to the average salesperson? Rank them, with 1 being "most attractive" and 7 being "least attractive."

REWARDS	RANK
More pay	______
Sense of accomplishment	______
Opportunities for personal growth	______
Promotion	______
Liking and respect by peers	______
Security	______
Recognition	______

2. "A salesperson's job is finished when a sale is made." True or false? (Circle one)
3. "The primary job of all salespeople is to sell to the user." True or false? (Circle one)
4. About how much is the average cost of making a single sales call by an industrial product salesperson? (Check one)
   $100 ______ $150 ______ $200 ______
   $125 ______ $175 ______ $225 ______
5. "Sales training typically focuses on developing selling skills and gaining product knowledge." True or false? (Circle one)

Personal selling remains a highly human-intensive activity despite the use of technology. Accordingly, the people involved must be managed. **Sales management** involves planning the selling program and implementing and controlling the personal selling effort of the firm. Numerous tasks are involved in managing personal selling, including setting objectives, organizing the sales force, recruiting, selecting, training, and compensating salespeople, and evaluating the performance of individual salespeople.

PERVASIVENESS OF SELLING

"Everyone lives by selling something," wrote author Robert Louis Stevenson a century ago. His observation still holds true today. The Bureau of Labor Statistics reports that about 11 million people are employed in sales positions in the United States. Included in this number are manufacturing sales personnel, real estate brokers, stockbrokers, and sales clerks who work in retail stores. In reality, however, virtually every occupation that involves customer contact has an element of personal selling. For example, attorneys, accountants, bankers, and company personnel recruiters perform sales-related activities, whether or not they acknowledge it.

Many executives in major companies have held sales positions at some time in their careers. For example, the president of IBM has historically come from the sales department rather than engineering as one might expect. W.W. Clements, chairman of Dr Pepper, started his career in sales. Lee Iacocca, the

Personal selling occurs in many settings

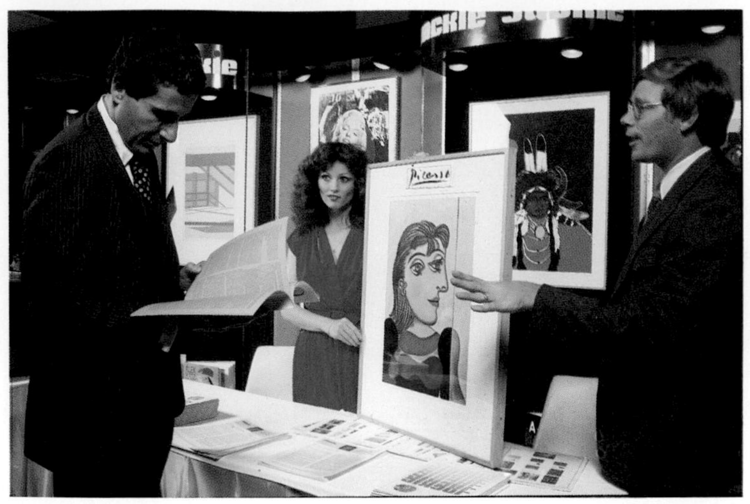

flamboyant chairman of the board of Chrysler Corporation, previously held a sales position at Ford Motor Company. It might be said that Iacocca is Chrysler's principal salesperson today. It is no accident that these individuals rose from sales and marketing positions to top management. Almost 30 percent of the chief executive officers in the 1,000 largest U.S. corporations have significant sales and marketing experience in their work history.[3] Thus selling often serves as a stepping-stone to top management, as well as being a career path in itself.

PERSONAL SELLING IN MARKETING

Personal selling serves three major roles in a firm's overall marketing effort. First, salespeople are the critical link between the firm and its customers. This role requires that salespeople match company interests with customer needs to satisfy both parties in the exchange process. Second, salespeople *are* the company in a consumer's eyes. They represent what a company is or attempts to be and are often the only personal contact a customer has with the company. For example, IBM takes pride in the image its salespeople like Wanda Truxillo convey to buyers. The "look" projected by salespeople for Avon Products, Inc., is an important factor in communicating the benefits of the company's cosmetic line. Third, personal selling may play a dominant role in a firm's marketing program. This situation typically arises when a firm uses a push marketing strategy, described in Chapter 16. Avon, for example, pays almost 40 percent of its total sales dollars for selling expenses.[4] Pharmaceutical firms and office and educational equipment manufacturers also rely heavily on personal selling in the marketing of their products.

CONCEPT CHECK

1 **What is personal selling?**

2 **What is involved in sales management?**

The Many Forms of Personal Selling

Personal selling assumes many forms based on the amount of selling done and the amount of creativity required to perform the sales task. Broadly speaking, three types of personal selling exist: order taking, order getting, and sales support activities. While some firms use only one of these types of personal selling, others use a combination of all three.

Order Taking

Typically an **order taker** processes routine orders or reorders for products that were already sold by the company. The primary responsibility of order takers is to preserve an ongoing relationship with existing customers and maintain sales. Two types of order takers exist. Outside order takers visit customers and replenish inventory stocks of resellers, such as retailers or wholesalers. For example, Frito-Lay salespeople call on supermarkets, neighborhood grocery stores, and other establishments to ensure that the company's line of salty snack products (such as Doritos and Tostitos) is in adequate supply. In addition, outside order takers typically provide assistance in arranging displays. Inside order takers, also called sales or order clerks, typically answer simple questions, take orders, and complete transactions with customers. Many retail clerks are inside order takers, as are people who take orders from buyers by telephone. In industrial settings, order taking arises in straight rebuy situations. For instance, stationery supply firms have inside order takers. Order takers, for the most part, do little selling in a conventional sense and engage in little problem solving with customers. They often represent simple products that have few options, such as confectionery items, magazine subscriptions, and highly standardized industrial products.

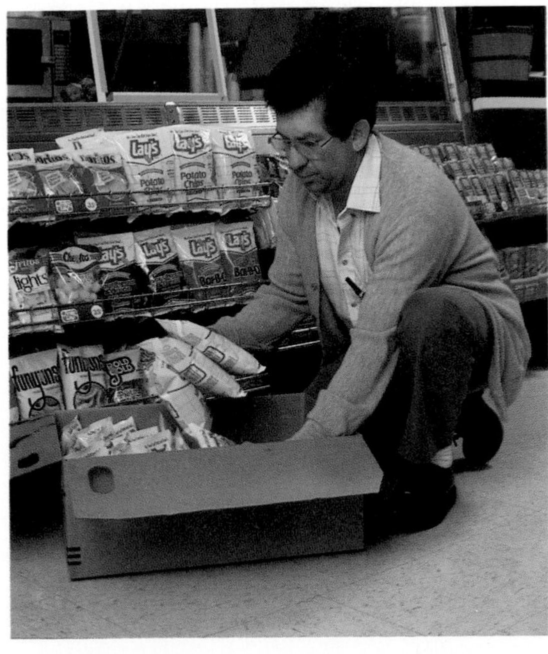

A Frito-Lay salesperson is an order taker

ORDER GETTING

An **order getter** sells in a conventional sense and identifies prospective customers, provides customers with information, persuades customers to buy, closes sales, and follows up on customers' use of a product or service. Like order takers, order getters can be inside (an automobile salesperson) or outside (an

MARKETING·ACTION·MEMO

TURNING SALESPEOPLE INSIDE OUT TO GET—NOT TAKE—ORDERS

Transforming order takers into order getters is no easy task. Order takers and order getters have a very different sales orientation (see below).

Interest in creating order getters transcends industries. Banks train officers to pursue accounts rather than waiting for customers to visit their offices. Miller Brewing Company now emphasizes "persuasive marketing" whereby its salespeople are taught to look for selling opportunities rather than just delivering beer. Deregulation of the communications industry prompted AT&T to recruit and train an entire order-getting sales force!

Changes in the marketing of personal computers—from home to business use—have forced computer retailers to transform their sales forces from in-store order takers to outside order getters—a double challenge. Some have met the challenge. MicroAge and CompuShop now generate over 80 percent of their revenues from outside sales to business. Tandy Corporation has yet to make this transition, despite repeated attempts. Recruiting and training efforts have failed to attract and retain outside order getters. John V. Roach, Tandy's chairman of the board, concedes that "the outbound sales program isn't growing as quickly as we would like it." He adds, "We need outbound sales. We will have outbound sales." Yes, turning salespeople inside out to get—not take—orders is a tough, challenging job.

Source: Based on "Tandy Finds a Cold, Hard World Outside the Radio Shack," *Business Week* (August 31, 1987), pp. 68-70; "AT&T's Instant Sales Force," *Sales and Marketing Management* (June 1987), p. 47; Linda Segall, "Turning Order-Takers Into Salesmen," *Training and Development Journal* (January 1986), pp. 72-73; Jim Mitchell, "Outbound Selling Replacing Retailers," *Dallas Morning News* (August 22, 1987), p. H2.

BASIS OF COMPARISON	ORDER TAKERS	ORDER GETTERS
Objective	Handle routine product orders or reorders	Identify new customers and sales opportunities
Purchase situation	Focus on straight rebuy purchase situations	Focus on new buy and modified rebuy purchase situations
Activity	Perform order processing functions	Act as creative problem solvers
Training	Require significant clerical training	Require significant sales training
Source of sales	Maintain sales volume	Create new sales volume

IBM salesperson like Wanda Truxillo). Order getting involves a high degree of creativity and customer empathy and typically is required for selling complex or technical products with many options. So considerable product knowledge and sales training are necessary. In modified rebuy or new buy purchase situations in industrial selling, an order getter acts as a problem solver who identifies how a particular product may satisfy a customer's need. Similarly, in the purchase of a service, such as insurance, an insurance agent can provide a mix of plans to satisfy a buyer's needs depending on income, stage of the family's life cycle, and investment objectives.

Increasingly, companies are transforming their sales forces into order getters through recruiting and training. The Marketing Action Memo illustrates this effort for a variety of firms.

Order getting is an expensive process.[5] It is estimated that the average direct cost of a single sales call for an industrial product is $207.21, a consumer product, $151.51, and a service, $193.18. (What amount did you check for Question 4 in Figure 18-1?) The direct annual cost for a salesperson, including compensation and field expenses (including travel, entertainment, food, and lodging) is $83,500 for industrial products, $65,000 for consumer products, and $79,000 for services. These costs illustrate why telephone selling, with a significantly lower cost per call and little or no field expenses, is so popular today.

SALES SUPPORT PERSONNEL

Sales support personnel augment the selling effort of order getters by performing a variety of services. For example, **missionary salespeople** do not directly solicit orders but rather concentrate on performing promotional activities and introducing new products. They are used extensively in the pharmaceutical industry, where they persuade physicians to prescribe a firm's product. Actual sales are made through wholesalers or directly to pharmacists who fill prescriptions. A **sales engineer** is a salesperson who specializes in identifying, analyzing, and

"Tarzan no want computer."

solving customer problems and brings know-how and technical expertise to the selling situation, but often does not actually sell products and services. Sales engineers are popular in selling industrial products such as chemicals and heavy equipment. In short, not all salespeople sell to the actual user. (What was your answer to Question 3 in the quiz?)

In many situations firms engage in **team selling,** the practice of using an entire team of professionals in selling to and servicing major customers.[5] Team selling is used when specialized knowledge is needed to satisfy the different interests of individuals in a customer's buying center. For example, a selling team might consist of a salesperson, a sales engineer, a service representative, and a financial executive, each of whom would deal with a counterpart in the customer's firm. Xerox Corporation emphasizes this approach in working with prospective buyers.

Xerox Corporation advertisement featuring team selling

CONCEPT CHECK

1 **What is the principal difference between an order taker and an order getter?**

2 **What is team selling?**

THE PERSONAL SELLING PROCESS

Selling, and particularly order getting, is a complicated activity. Although the salesperson-customer interaction is essential to personal selling, much of a salesperson's work occurs before this meeting and continues after the sale itself. The **personal selling process** consists of six stages: (1) prospecting, (2) pre-

STAGE	OBJECTIVE	COMMENTS
Prospecting	Search for and qualify prospects.	Start of the selling process; prospects produced through advertising, referrals, and cold canvassing.
Preapproach	Gather information and decide how to approach the prospect.	Information sources include personal observation, other customers, and own salespeople.
Approach	Gain prospect's attention, stimulate interest, and make transition to the presentation.	First impression is critical; gain attention and interest through reference to common acquaintances, a referral, or product demonstration.
Presentation	Begin converting a prospect into a customer by creating a desire for the product or service.	Different presentation formats are possible; however, involving the customer in the product or service through attention to particular needs is critical; important to deal professionally with prospect skepticism, indifference, or objections.
Close	Obtain a purchase commitment from the prospect and create a customer.	Salesperson asks for the purchase; different approaches include the trial close and assumptive close.
Follow-up	Ensure the customer is satisfied with the product or service.	Resolve any problems faced by the customer to ensure customer satisfaction and future sales possibilities.

FIGURE 18-2
Stages and objectives of the personal selling process

approach, (3) approach, (4) presentation, (5) close, and (6) follow-up (Figure 18-2).

PROSPECTING

Personal selling begins with *prospecting*—the search for and qualification of potential customers. For some products that are one-time purchases such as encyclopedias, continual prospecting is necessary to maintain sales. There are three types of prospects. A *lead* is the name of a person who may be a possible customer. A *prospect* is a customer who wants or needs the product. If an individual wants the product, can afford to buy it, and is the decision maker, this individual is a *qualified prospect*.

Leads and prospects are generated using several sources. For example, advertising may contain a coupon or a toll-free number to generate leads, as shown in the AT&T advertisement on p. 498. Some companies use exhibits at trade fairs, professional meetings, and conferences to generate leads or prospects.

An AT&T prospecting advertisement for its direct marketing service

Staffed by salespeople, these exhibits are used to attract attention of prospective buyers and disseminate information. Another approach for generating leads is through *cold canvassing* in person or by telephone.[6] This approach simply means that a salesperson may open a telephone directory, pick a name, and visit or call that individual. Although the refusal rate is high with cold canvassing, this approach can be successful. For example, Ford Motor Company used a telephone campaign involving 20 million telephone calls, which produced enough leads to keep its 34,000 salespeople busy making presentations for 30 days.[7]

PREAPPROACH

Once a salesperson has identified a qualified prospect, preparation for the sale begins with the preapproach. The *preapproach* stage involves obtaining further information on the prospect and deciding on the best method of approach. Activities in this stage include finding information on who the prospect is, how the prospect prefers to be approached, and what the prospect is looking for in a product or service. For example, a stockbroker will need information on a prospect's discretionary income, investment objectives, and preference for discussing brokerage services over the telephone or in person. For industrial products the preapproach involves identifying the buying role of a prospect (for example, influencer or decision maker), important buying criteria, and the prospect's receptivity to a formal or informal presentation.

APPROACH

The *approach* stage involves the initial meeting between the salesperson and prospect where the objectives are to gain the prospect's attention, stimulate interest, and build the foundation for the sales presentation itself. The first impression is critical at this stage, and it is common for salespeople to begin the conversation with a reference to common acquaintances, a referral, or even the product or service itself. Which tactic is taken will depend on the information obtained in the prospecting and preapproach stages.

PRESENTATION

The *presentation* is at the core of the order-getting selling process, and its objective is to convert a prospect into a customer by creating a desire for the product or service. Three major presentation formats exist: (1) stimulus-response format, (2) formula selling format, and (3) need-satisfaction format.

Stimulus-Response Format The **stimulus-response presentation** format assumes that given the appropriate stimulus by a salesperson, the prospect will buy. With this format the salesperson tries one appeal after another, hoping to "hit the right button." A counter clerk at McDonald's is using this approach when she asks whether you'd like an order of french fries or a dessert with your meal. The counter clerk is engaging in what is called *suggestive selling*. Although useful in this setting, the stimulus-response format is not always appropriate, and for many products a more formalized format is necessary.

Formula Selling Format A more formalized presentation, the **formula selling presentation** format, is based on the view that a presentation consists of information that must be provided in an accurate, thorough, and step-by-step manner to persuade the prospect to buy. A popular version of this format is the *canned sales presentation,* which is a memorized, standardized message conveyed to every

A counter clerk often uses a stimulus-response presentation, whereas a door-to-door salesperson often uses a formula selling presentation

prospect.[8] Used frequently by firms in telephone and door-to-door selling of consumer products (for example, Fuller Brush Company and Encyclopaedia Britannica), this approach treats every prospect the same regardless of differences in needs or preference for certain kinds of information. Canned sales presentations can be advantageous when the differences between prospects are unknown or with novice salespeople who are less knowledgeable about the product and selling process than experienced salespeople. Although it guarantees a comprehensive presentation, it lacks flexibility and spontaneity and, more important, does not provide for feedback from the prospective buyer—a critical component in the communication process.

Need-Satisfaction Format The stimulus-response and formula selling formats share a common characteristic: the salesperson dominates the conversation. By comparison, the **need-satisfaction presentation** format emphasizes probing and listening by the salesperson to identify needs and interests of prospective buyers.[9] Once these are identified, the salesperson tailors the presentation to the prospect and highlights product benefits that satisfy the prospect. The need-satisfaction

MARKETING·ACTION·MEMO

SELLING BY LISTENING—IT WORKS!

Listening, not talking, is a key ingredient in making successful sales presentations, according to professional sales training companies. Sales training today emphasizes that a salesperson be a good listener and questioner, sensitive to the needs of prospective customers, and a knowledgeable adviser on products and services—rather than the stereotypical hustler of the past. According to Curtis R. Berrien, an executive with Forum Corporation, a major Boston-based sales training firm, a bad salesperson has "an inability to listen, to care, to get off his agenda and onto the customer's agenda, to be patient. He's pushy, talks all the time, goes in with preconceived notions, shoots down objections, drops a client after he makes a sale." A good salesperson is the opposite of this description. The salesperson's primary tool is the probing question, not the quick sales pitch. Probing allows the salesperson to uncover a sales opportunity. Further questions convert the sales opportunity into a need for a product and ultimately the prospect into a customer. Does this presentation format work? About 200,000 salespeople are taught this approach each year by three major sales training firms: Xerox Learning Systems, Wilson Learning Corporation, and Forum Corporation. Commerce Clearing House, Inc., a publisher of tax information, observed a big improvement in the salespeople who were exposed to this type of sales training. In one of its divisions where salespeople were trained in this manner, they increased their billings by an average of 33.7 percent. In another division, without training, billings increased by only 2.5 percent.

Source: Based on "Sales Training," *Training,* Special Issue (February 1988); Monci Jo Williams, "America's Best Salesmen," *Fortune* (October 26, 1987), pp. 122-134; Jeremy Main, "How to Sell by Listening," *Fortune* (February 4, 1985), pp. 52-54.

format, which emphasizes problem solving, is the most consistent with the marketing concept, so many firms have adopted this approach, as described in the Marketing Action Memo. This format is used extensively for industrial products such as computers and heavy equipment. Many consumer service firms such as brokerage and insurance firms and consumer product firms like AT&T and Gillette also subscribe to this approach.

Handling Objections A critical concern in the presentation stage is handling objections. *Objections* are excuses for not making a purchase commitment or decision. Some objections are valid and are based on the characteristics of the product or service or price. However, many objections reflect prospect skepticism or indifference. Whether valid or not, experienced salespeople know that objections do not put an end to the presentation. Rather, techniques can be used to deal with objections in a courteous and professional manner. The following six techniques are the most common[10]:

1 *Acknowledge and convert the objection.* This technique involves using the objection as a reason for buying. For example, a prospect might say, "The price is too high." The reply: "Yes, the price is high because we use the finest materials. Let me show you . . ."
2 *Postpone.* The postpone technique is used when the objection will be dealt with later in the presentation: "I'm going to address that point shortly. I think my answer would make better sense then."
3 *Agree and neutralize.* Here a salesperson agrees with the objection, then shows that it is unimportant. A salesperson would say: "That's true and others have said the same. However, they concluded that issue was outweighed by the other benefits."
4 *Accept the objection.* Sometimes the objection is valid. Let the prospect express such views, probe for the reason behind it, and attempt to stimulate further discussion on the objection.
5 *Denial.* When a prospect's objection is clearly untrue based on misinformation, it is wise to meet the objection head on with a firm denial.
6 *Ignore the objection.* This technique is used when it appears that the objection is a stalling mechanism or is clearly not important to the prospect.

Each of these techniques requires a calm, professional interaction with the prospect, and is most effective when objections are anticipated in the preapproach stage. Handling objections is a skill requiring a sense of timing, appreciation for the prospect's state-of-mind, and adeptness in communication.

CLOSE

The *closing* stage in the selling process involves obtaining a purchase commitment from the prospect. This stage is the most important and the most difficult because the salesperson must determine when the prospect is ready to buy. Telltale signals indicating a readiness to buy include body language (prospect re-examines the product or contract closely), statements ("This equipment should reduce our maintenance costs"), and questions ("When could we expect delivery?"). The close itself can take several forms. Three closing techniques are used when a salesperson believes a buyer is about ready to make a purchase: (1) trial close, (2) assumptive close, and (3) urgency close. A *trial close* involves asking the prospect to make a decision on some aspect of the purchase: "Would you prefer the blue or gray model?" An *assumptive close* entails asking the prospect to make choices concerning delivery, warranty, or financing terms under the assumption that a sale has been finalized. An *urgency close* is used to commit the prospect quickly by making reference to the timeliness of the purchase: "The low interest financing ends next week," or, "That is the last model we have in stock." When a prospect is clearly ready to buy, the final close is used and a salesperson asks for the order.

FOLLOW-UP

The selling process does not end with the closing of a sale. Rather, contemporary selling requires customer follow-up. One marketing authority equated the follow-up with courtship and marriage.[11] He observed ". . . the sale merely consummates the courtship. Then the marriage begins. How good the marriage is depends on how well the relationship is managed." The *follow-up* stage includes making certain the customer's purchase has been properly delivered and installed and difficulties experienced with the use of the item are addressed. Attention to this stage of the selling process solidifies the buyer-seller relationship. In short, today's satisfied customers become tomorrow's qualified prospects or referrals. (What was your answer to Question 2 in the quiz?)

CONCEPT CHECK

1 **What are the six stages in the personal selling process?**

2 **What is the distinction between a lead and a qualified prospect?**

3 **Which presentation format is most consistent with the marketing concept? Why?**

SALES MANAGEMENT PROCESS

Selling must be managed if it is going to contribute to a firm's overall objectives. Although firms differ in the specifics of how salespeople and the selling effort are managed, the sales management process is similar across firms. Sales management consists of three interrelated functions: (1) sales plan formulation, (2) sales plan implementation, and (3) evaluation of the sales force (Figure 18-3).

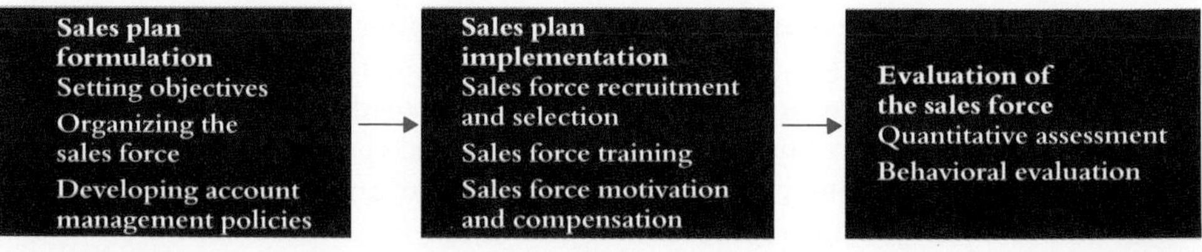

FIGURE 18-3
Sales management process

Source: Based on Gilbert A. Churchill, Jr., Neil M. Ford, and Orville C. Walker, Jr., *Sales Force Management*, 2nd ed. (Homewood, Ill.: Richard D. Irwin, Inc., 1985), pp. 19-28.

SALES PLAN FORMULATION

Formulating the sales plan is the most basic of the three sales management functions. According to the vice president of the Harris Corporation, a manufacturer of electronics products, "If a company hopes to implement its marketing strategy, it really needs a detailed sales planning process."[12] The **sales plan** is a statement describing what is to be achieved and where and how the selling effort of salespeople is to be deployed. Formulating the sales plan involves three tasks: (1) setting objectives, (2) organizing the sales force, and (3) developing account management policies.

Setting Objectives Setting objectives is central to sales management because this task specifies what is to be achieved. In practice, objectives are set for the total sales force and for each salesperson. Selling objectives can be output related and focus on dollar or unit sales volume, number of new customers added, and profit. Alternatively, they can be input related and emphasize the number of sales calls and selling expenses. Output- and input-related objectives are used for the sales force as a whole and for each salesperson. A third type of objective that is behaviorally related is typically specific for each salesperson and includes his or her product knowledge, customer service, and selling and communication skills. Increasingly, firms are also emphasizing knowledge of competition as an objective, since salespeople are calling on customers and should see what competitors are doing.[13]

Whatever objectives are set, they should be precise and measurable and specify the time period over which they are to be achieved. Once established, these objectives serve as performance standards for the evaluation of the sales force—the third function of sales management.

Organizing the Sales Force Establishing a selling organization is the second task in formulating the sales plan. Three questions are related to organization. First, should the company use its own sales force, or should it use independent agents such as manufacturer's representatives? Second, if the decision is made to employ company salespeople, then should they be organized according to geography, customer type, or product or service? Third, how many company salespeople should be employed?

The decision to use company salespeople or independent agents is made infrequently.[14] However, Apple Computer recently switched from using agents to its own sales force. Metropolitan Life Insurance replaced its sales force with independent insurance agents. The Optoelectronics Division of Honeywell, Inc., has switched back and forth between agents and its own sales force over the last 25 years. The decision is based on an analysis of economic and behavioral factors. An economic analysis examines the costs of using both types of salespeople and is a form of break-even analysis.

Consider a situation in which independent agents would receive a 5 percent commission on sales, and company salespeople would receive a 3 percent commission, salaries, and benefits. In addition, with company salespeople, sales administration costs would be incurred for a total fixed cost of $500,000 per year. At what sales level would independent or company salespeople be less costly? This question can be answered by setting the costs of the two options equal to each other and solving for the sales level amount, as shown in the equation below:

$$\frac{\text{Total cost of company salespeople}}{0.03(X) + \$500{,}000} = \frac{\text{Total cost of independent agents}}{0.05(X)}$$

where X = sales volume. Solving for X, sales volume equals $25 million, indicating that below $25 million in sales independent agents would be cheaper, but above $25 million a company sales force would be cheaper.

Economics alone does not answer this question, however. A behavioral analysis is also necessary and should focus on issues related to the control, flexibility, effort, and availability of independent and company salespeople.[15] Figure 18-4 shows the common behavioral arguments for independent agents versus a company sales force. An individual firm must weigh the pros and cons of the economic and behavioral considerations before making this decision.

If a company elects to employ its own salespeople, then it must choose an organizational structure based on (1) geography, (2) customer, or (3) product (Figure 18-5). A geographical structure is the simplest organization, where the United States, or indeed the globe, is first divided into regions and each region is divided into districts or territories. Salespeople are assigned to each district with defined geographical boundaries and call on all customers and represent all products sold by the company. The principal advantage of this structure is that it can minimize travel time and expenses and duplication of selling effort. However, if a firm's products or customers require specialized knowledge, then a geographical structure is not suitable.

FIGURE 18-4
The case for using company salespeople versus independent agents

CRITERIA	CASE FOR COMPANY SALES FORCE	CASE FOR INDEPENDENT AGENTS
Control	Company selects, trains, supervises, and can use multiple rewards to direct salespeople.	Agents are equally well selected, trained, and supervised by the representative organization.
Flexibility	Company can transfer salespeople, change customer selling practices, and otherwise direct its own sales force.	Little fixed cost is present with agents; mostly there are variable costs; therefore firm is not burdened with overhead.
Effort	Sales effort is enhanced because salespeople represent one firm, not several; firm loyalty is present; there is better customer service because salespeople receive salary as well as commission.	Agents might work harder than salespeople because compensation is based solely on commissions; customer service is good, since it builds repeat business.
Availability	Knowledgeable agents might not be available where and when needed.	Entrepreneurial spirit of agents will make them available where a marketing opportunity exists.

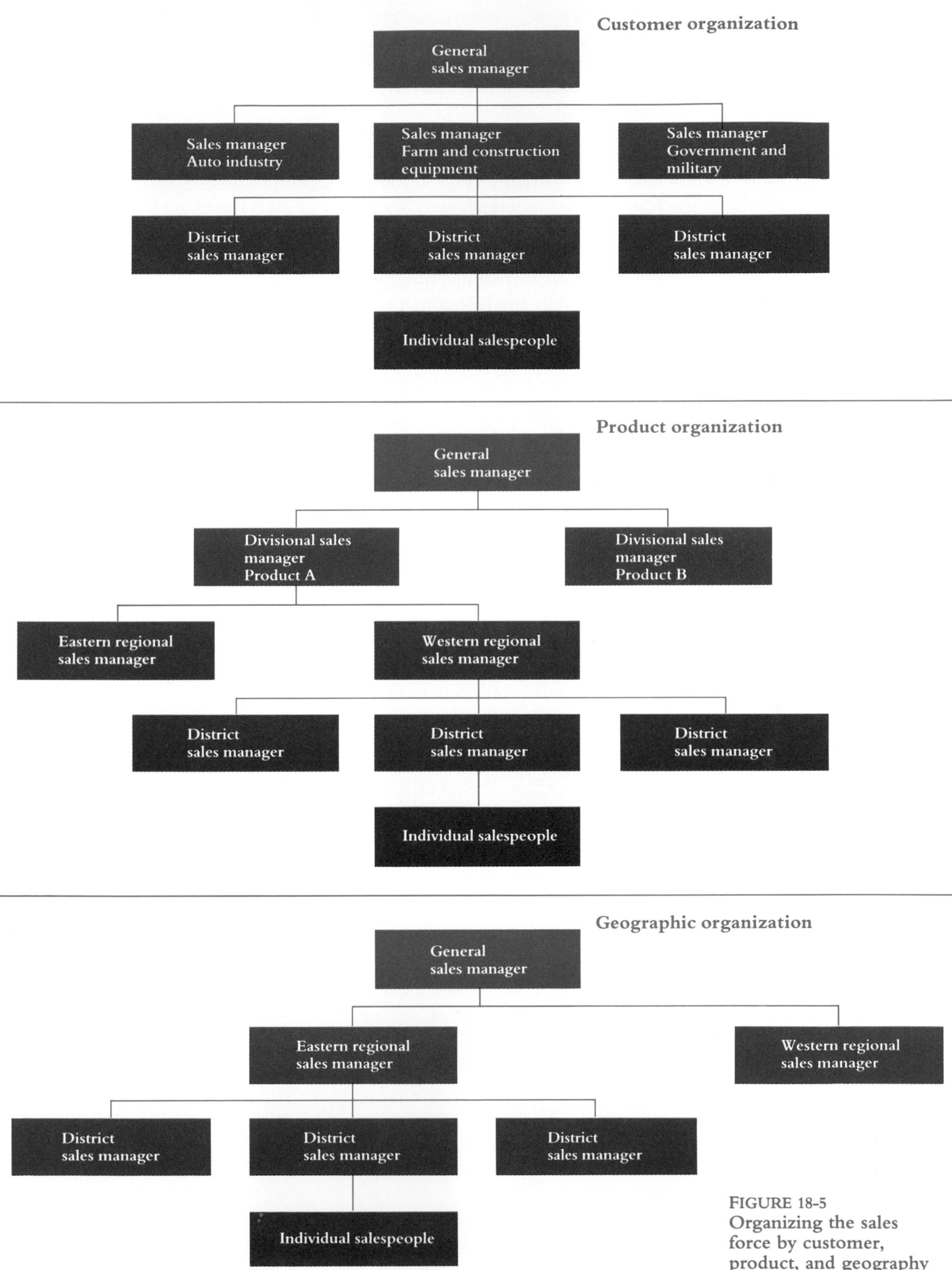

FIGURE 18-5
Organizing the sales force by customer, product, and geography

When different types of buyers have different needs, a customer sales organizational structure is used. In practice this means that a different sales force calls on each separate type of buyer. For example, Firestone Tire & Rubber has one sales force that calls on its own dealers and another that calls on independent dealers, such as gasoline stations. The rationale for this approach is that more effective, specialized customer support and knowledge is provided to buyers. However, this structure often leads to higher administrative costs and some duplication of selling effort, since two separate sales forces are used to represent the same products.

When specific knowledge is required to sell certain types of products, then a product sales organization is used. For example, Procter & Gamble has a sales force that sells household cleaning products and another that sells food products. The primary advantage of this structure is that salespeople can develop expertise with technical characteristics, applications, and selling methods associated with a particular product or family of products. However, this structure also produces high administrative costs and duplication of selling effort, since two company salespeople call on the same customer.

In short, there is no one best sales organization for all companies in all situations. Rather the organization of the sales force should reflect the marketing strategy of the firm. In 1987, 10 percent of U.S. firms changed their sales organizations to implement new marketing strategies.[16]

The third question related to sales force organization involves determining the size of the sales force. For example, why does Keebler have over 1,300 salespeople who call on supermarkets and grocery stores to sell snack foods, whereas Frito-Lay, Inc., has about 10,000 salespeople? The answer lies in the difference between these firms in terms of the number of accounts (customers) served, the frequency of calls on accounts, the length of an average call, and the amount of time a salesperson can devote to selling.

A common approach for determining the size of a sales force is the **work-load method**.[17] This formula-based method integrates the number of customers served, call frequency, call length, and available selling time to arrive at a figure for the sales force size. For example, Frito-Lay needs about 10,000 salespeople according to the work-load method formula:

$$NS = \frac{NC \times CF \times CL}{AST}$$

where:

NS = number of salespeople
NC = number of customers
CF = call frequency necessary to service a customer each year
CL = length of an average call
AST = average amount of selling time available per year

Frito-Lay sells its products to 315,000 supermarkets, grocery stores, and other establishments. Salespeople should call on these accounts at least once a week, or 52 times a year. The average sales call lasts 54 minutes (0.90 hour). An average salesperson works 2,000 hours a year (50 weeks × 40 hours a week), but 10 hours a week are devoted to nonselling activities such as travel, leaving 1,500 hours a year. Using these guidelines, Frito-Lay would need:

$$NS = \frac{315{,}000 \times 52 \times 0.90}{1{,}500} = 9984 \text{ salespeople}$$

The value of this formula is apparent in its flexibility, since a change in any one of the variables will affect the number of salespeople needed. Changes are determined, in part, by the firm's account management policies.

Developing Account Management Policies The third task in formulating a sales plan involves developing **account management policies** specifying whom salespeople should contact, what kinds of selling and customer service activities should be engaged in, and how these activities should be carried out.[18] These policies might state which individuals in a buying organization should be contacted, the amount of sales and service effort that different customers should receive, and the kinds of information salespeople should collect before or during a sales call.

An example of an account management policy in Figure 18-6 shows how different accounts or customers can be grouped according to level of opportunity

FIGURE 18-6
Account management policy grid

	COMPETITIVE POSITION OF SALES ORGANIZATION	
	High	Low
High	1 *Attractiveness.* Accounts offer good opportunity, since they have high potential and sales organization has a strong position. *Account management policy.* Accounts should receive high level of sales calls and service to retain and possibly build accounts.	3 *Attractiveness.* Accounts may offer good opportunity if sales organization can overcome its weak position. *Account management policy.* It should emphasize a heavy sales and service effort to build sales organization position or shift resources to other accounts if stronger sales organization position impossible.
Low	2 *Attractiveness.* Accounts are somewhat attractive, since sales organization has a strong position, but future opportunity is limited. *Account management policy.* Accounts should receive moderate level of sales and service to maintain current position of sales organization.	4 *Attractiveness.* Accounts offer little or no opportunity, and sales organization position is weak. *Account management policy.* Accounts should receive minimal level of sales and service effort by replacing personal calls with telephone sales or direct mail. Consider dropping account.

Source: Adapted from David W. Cravens and Raymond W. LaForge, "Sales Force Deployment," in Arch G. Woodside, ed., *Advances in Business Marketing* (Greenwich, Conn.: JAI Press, Inc., 1986), pp. 67-112; Raymond W. LaForge and Clifford E. Young, "A Portfolio Model for Planning Sales Call Coverage of Accounts," *Business*, Vol. 35, 1985, pp. 10-16; Alan Dubinsky and Thomas Ingram, "A Portfolio Approach to Account Profitability," *Industrial Marketing Management*, Vol. 13, 1984, pp. 33-41.

and the firm's competitive sales position. When specific account names are placed in each cell, salespeople clearly see which accounts should be contacted, with what level of selling and service activity, and how to deal with them. For example, accounts in Cells 1 and 2 might have high frequencies of sales calls and increased time spent on a call. Cell 3 accounts will have lower call frequencies, and Cell 4 accounts might be contacted by telephone rather than in person.

SALES PLAN IMPLEMENTATION

The sales plan is put into practice through the tasks associated with sales plan implementation. Whereas sales plan formulation focuses on "doing the right things," implementation emphasizes "doing things right." The three major tasks involved in implementing a sales plan are (1) sales force recruitment and selection, (2) sales force training, and (3) sales force motivation and compensation.

FIGURE 18-7
Job analysis for an order-getting salesperson

JOB FACTOR	ACTIVITIES
Assisting and working with district management	Assisting district sales management in market surveys, new product evaluations, etc.
	Preparing reports on territorial sales expenses
	Managing a sales territory within the sales expense budget
	Using district management to make joint sales calls on customers
Customer service	Arranging credit adjustments on incorrect invoicing, shipping, and order shortages
	Informing customers of supply conditions on company products
	Assisting customers and prospects in providing credit information to the company
Personal integrity and selling ethics	Representing company products at their true value
	Working within the merchandising plans and policies established by the company
	Investigating and reporting customer complaints
Direct selling	Knowing correct applications and installations of company products
	Making sales presentations that communicate product benefits
	Handling sales presentations
Developing relationships with customers	Maintaining a friendly, personal relationship with customers
	Using equipment to strengthen the business relationship with customers
	Providing customers with technical information on company products
Keeping abreast of market conditions	Keeping customers informed of market conditions that affect their businesses
	Keeping the company informed of market conditions
Meeting sales objectives	Identifying the person with authority to make the purchasing decision
	Closing the sale and obtaining the order
	Selling company products at a volume which meets or exceeds expectations
Maintaining complete customer records	Maintaining customer records that are complete and up to date
	Checking customers' inventory and recommending orders

Source: Lawrence M. Lamont and William J. Lundstrom, "Defining Industrial Sales Behavior: A Factor Analytic Study," *1974 Combined Proceedings* (Chicago: American Marketing Association, 1974), pp. 493–498; by permission of the American Marketing Association.

Sales Force Recruitment and Selection Effective recruitment and selection of salespeople is one of the most crucial tasks of sales management.[19] It entails finding people who match the type of sales position required by a firm. Recruitment and selection practices would differ greatly between order-taking and order-getting sales positions, given the differences in the demands of these two jobs. Therefore recruitment and selection begin with a carefully crafted job analysis.

A **job analysis** is a written description of what a salesperson is expected to do, and therefore it differs between firms. Figure 18-7 shows a job analysis for building material salespeople—an order-getting sales position. This analysis identifies eight major job factors and describes important activities associated with each.

Determining what makes a good salesperson is tricky, and the list of characteristics is endless. However, a recent study that asked sales executives to differentiate between successful and unsuccessful salespeople concerning 24 personal characteristics identified the profiles shown in Figure 18-8. Clearly, a pattern emerges that is consistent with the description of successful selling behaviors discussed in the beginning of this chapter.

Firms use a variety of methods for evaluating prospective salespeople. Personal interviews, reference checks, and background information provided on application blanks are the most frequently used methods.[20] However, a number of firms use psychological tests to complement these methods, as described in the Marketing Action Memo.

FIGURE 18-8
Characteristics of successful and unsuccessful salespeople

Source: Redrawn from Bradley D. Lockman and John H. Hallaq, "Who Are Your Successful Salespeople?" *Journal of the Academy of Marketing Science* (Fall 1982), p. 466.

MARKETING · ACTION · MEMO

PROBING THE PSYCHE OF THE SUCCESSFUL SALESPERSON

How would you answer the following two questions?

1. If performing the following activities paid the same compensation and carried equal status, which would you choose? (a) Representing clients in court, (b) performing as a concert pianist, (c) commanding a ship, or (d) advising clients on electronic problems.
2. Among these statements, which best describes you? (a) I don't need to be the focus of attention at parties, (b) I have a better understanding of what politicians are up to than most of my associates, or (c) I don't delay making decisions that are unpleasant.

Your answers, when considered with answers to 179 other questions, could offer insight into your potential as a salesperson, according to Herbert Greenberg, president of Personality Dynamics, Inc. (PDI), a management consulting and testing firm. Greenberg, along with other behavioral scientists, believes that personality may have more to do with successful selling than a person's experience, age, education, or sex.

Although training is important, behavioral scientists point out that the basic raw material must be there to work with. Testing allows sales managers to look beyond the employment interview and résumé and examine fundamental behavioral characteristics, including personal drive, a desire to persuade others, resiliency, and empathy for others.

Are such tests useful? One company gave the PDI test to 20 salespeople, including a group of top performers and those who were soon to be fired. The test identified both groups perfectly.

However, the value of psychological testing remains a hotly debated issue. About 25 percent of U.S. companies use these tests in the salesperson selection process.

Source: Based on Richard Nelson, "Maybe It's Time to Take Another Look at Tests as a Sales Selection Tool?" *Journal of Personal Selling & Sales Management* (August 1987), pp. 33-38; Sara Delano, "Improving the Odds for Hiring Success." Reprinted with permission, *Inc.* magazine (June 1983). Copyright © 1983 by *Inc.* Publishing Company, 38 Commercial Wharf, Boston, MA 02110.

Sales Force Training Whereas recruitment and selection of salespeople is a one-time event, sales force training is an ongoing process affecting both new hirees and seasoned salespeople. Sales training typically focuses on two issues: (1) selling skills and (2) product knowledge. (What was your answer to Question 5 on the quiz?) For the new salesperson, familiarity with company policy and procedures is also emphasized.

Training new salespeople is expensive and time-consuming.[21] The average cost of training a new industrial product salesperson (including salary) is $27,569, and takes 22 weeks. Training a new consumer product salesperson costs $22,500 and covers 22 weeks, and training new salespeople in service industries costs $30,000 and takes 27 weeks. Training occurs in a variety of locations, including formal classes at the firm's home office, field office, regional office, and central training facilities, and on-the-job training by a senior salesperson or manager.

Sales Force Motivation and Compensation A sales plan cannot be successfully implemented without motivated salespeople. Research on salesperson motivation suggests that (1) a clear job description, (2) effective sales management practices, (3) a sense of achievement, and (4) proper incentives or rewards will produce a motivated salesperson.[22] A study on the attractiveness of different rewards given to salespeople by companies indicates that more pay was most preferred, followed in order by opportunities for personal growth, a personal sense of accomplishment, promotion, liking and respect for peers, job security, and recognition.[23] (How did you answer Question 1 on the quiz?)

The importance of more pay as a motivating factor means that close attention must be given to how salespeople are financially rewarded for their efforts. Salespeople are paid using one of three plans: (1) straight salary, (2) straight commission, or (3) a combination of salary and commission. Under a **straight salary compensation plan** a salesperson is paid a fixed fee per week, month, or year. With a **straight commission compensation plan** a salesperson's earnings are directly tied to the sales or profit generated. For example, an insurance agent might receive a 2 percent commission of $2,000 for selling a

FIGURE 18-9
Comparison of different compensation plans

	STRAIGHT SALARY	STRAIGHT COMMISSION	COMBINATION
Frequency of use	18%	9%	73%
Especially useful	When compensating new salespersons; when firm moves into new sales territories that require developmental work; when salespersons need to perform many nonselling activities	When highly aggressive selling is required; when nonselling tasks are minimized; when company cannot closely control sales force activities	When sales territories have relatively similar sales potentials; when firm wishes to provide incentive but still control sales force activities
Advantages	Provides salesperson with maximum amount of security; gives sales manager large amount of control over salespersons; easy to administer; yields more predictable selling expenses	Provides maximum amount of incentive; by increasing commission rate, sales managers can encourage salespersons to sell certain items; selling expenses related directly to sales resources	Provides certain level of financial security; provides some incentive; selling expenses fluctuate with sales revenue; sales manager has some control over salesperson's nonselling activities
Disadvantages	Provides no incentive; necessitates closer supervision of salespersons' activities; during sales declines, selling expenses remain at same level	Salespersons have little financial security; sales manager has minimum control over sales force; may cause salespeople to provide inadequate service to smaller accounts; selling costs less predictable	Selling expenses less predictable; may be difficult to administer

Source: Gilbert A. Churchill, Jr., Neil M. Ford, and Orville C. Walker, Jr., *Sales Force Management: Planning, Implementation, and Control,* 2nd ed. (Homewood, Ill.: Richard D. Irwin, Inc., 1985), p. 472; "Sales Pay Survey: Figures and Methods," *Management Briefing—Marketing* (New York: The Conference Board, Inc., October 1986), pp. 4-5.

$100,000 life insurance policy. A **combination compensation plan** contains a specified salary plus a commission on sales or profit generated. Obviously each plan has its advantages and disadvantages and is particularly suited to certain situations (Figure 18-9).

Of course, nonmonetary rewards are also given to salespeople for meeting or exceeding objectives. These rewards include trips, honor societies (such as the Xerox President's Club), distinguished salesperson awards, and letters of commendation. Some unconventional rewards include the new pink Cadillacs, fur coats, and jewelry given by Mary Kay Cosmetics to outstanding salespeople.

SALES FORCE EVALUATION

The final function in the sales management process involves evaluating the sales force. It is at this point that salespeople are assessed as to whether sales objectives were met and account management policies were followed. Both quantitative and behavioral measures are used.

Quantitative Assessments Quantitative assessments are based on input- and output-related objectives set forth in the sales plan. Input-related measures focus on the actual activities performed by salespeople such as those involving sales calls, selling expenses, and account management policies. The number of sales calls made, selling expense related to sales made, and the number of reports submitted to superiors are the most frequently used input measures.

Output measures focus on the results obtained and include sales produced, accounts generated, profit achieved, and orders produced compared with calls made. Dollar sales volume, last year/current year sales ratio, the number of new accounts, and sales of specific products are the most frequently used measures when evaluating salesperson output.[24]

Behavioral Evaluation Less quantitative, behavioral measures are also used to evaluate salespeople. These include subjective and often informal assessments of a salesperson's attitude, product knowledge, selling and communication skills, appearance, and demeanor. Even though these assessments are highly subjective, they are frequently considered, and in fact inevitable, in salesperson evaluation.[25] Moreover, these factors are often important determinants of quantitative outcomes.

CONCEPT CHECK

1 **What are the three types of selling objectives?**

2 **What three factors are used to structure sales organizations?**

3 **Sales training typically focuses on what two sales-related issues?**

SUMMARY

1 Personal selling involves the two-way flow of communication between a buyer and a seller, often in a face-to-face encounter, designed to influence a person's or group's purchase decision. Sales management involves planning the sales program and implementing and controlling the personal selling effort of the firm.

2 Personal selling is pervasive in the U.S. economy, since virtually every occupation that involves customer contact has an element of selling attached to it.

3 Personal selling plays a major role in a firm's marketing effort. Salespeople occupy a boundary position between buyers and sellers; they *are* the company to many buyers and account for a major cost of marketing in a variety of industries.

4 Three types of personal selling exist: order-taking, order-getting, and sales support activities. Each type differs from the others in terms of actual selling done and the amount of creativity required to perform the job.

5 The personal selling process, particularly for order getters, is a complex activity involving six stages: (1) prospecting, (2) preapproach, (3) approach, (4) presentation, (5) close, and (6) follow-up.

6 The sales management process consists of three interrelated functions: (1) sales plan formulation, (2) sales plan implementations, and (3) evaluation of the sales force.

7 A sales plan is a statement describing what is to be achieved and where and how the selling effort of salespeople is to be deployed. Sales planning involves setting objectives, organizing the sales force, and developing account management policies.

8 Effective sales force recruitment and selection efforts, sales training that emphasizes selling skills and product knowledge, and motivation and compensation practices are necessary to successfully implement a sales plan.

9 Salespeople are evaluated using quantitative and behavioral measures that are linked to selling objectives and account management policies.

KEY TERMS AND CONCEPTS

personal selling p. 490
sales management p. 491
order taker p. 493
order getter p. 494
missionary salespeople p. 495
sales engineer p. 495
team selling p. 496
personal selling process p. 496
stimulus-response presentation p. 499
formula selling presentation p. 499
need-satisfaction presentation p. 500
sales plan p. 503
work-load method p. 506
account management policies p. 507
job analysis p. 509
straight salary compensation plan p. 511
straight commission compensation plan p. 511
combination compensation plan p. 512

CHAPTER PROBLEMS AND APPLICATIONS

1 Jane Dawson is a new sales representative for Charles Schwab brokerage firm. In searching for clients, Jane purchased a mailing list of *Wall Street Journal* subscribers and called them all regarding their interest in discount brokerage services. She asked if they have any stocks and if they have a regular broker. Those people without a regular broker were asked their investment needs. Two days later Jane called back with investment advice and asked if they would like to open an account. Identify each of Jane Dawson's actions in terms of the steps of selling.

2 For the first 50 years of business the Johnson Carpet Company produced carpets for residential use. The sales force was structured geographically. In the past 5 years a large percentage of carpet sales has been to industrial users, hospitals, schools, and architects. The company also has broadened its product line to include area rugs, Oriental carpets, and wall-to-wall carpeting. Is the present sales force structure appropriate, or would you recommend an alternative?

3 Where would you place each of the following sales jobs on the order taker/order getter continuum shown below? (a) Burger King counter clerk, (b) automobile insurance salesperson, (c) IBM computer salesperson, (d) life insurance salesperson, and (e) shoe salesperson.

Order taker ———————————————— **Order getter**

4 Listed below are three different firms. Which compensation plan would you recommend for each firm, and what reasons would you give for your recommendations? (a) A newly formed company that sells lawn care equipment on a door-to-door basis directly to consumers, (b) the Nabisco Company, which sells heavily advertised products in supermarkets by having the sales force call on these stores and arrange shelves, set up displays, and make presentations to store buying committees, and (c) the Wang word processing division, which makes word processing system presentations to company buying committees consisting of purchasing agents and future users.

5 The TDK tape company services 1,000 audio stores throughout the United States. Each store is called on 12 times a year, and the average sales call lasts 30 minutes. Assuming a salesperson works 40 hours a week, 50 weeks a year, and devotes 75 percent of the time to actual selling, how many salespeople does TDK need?

6 A furniture manufacturer is currently using manufacturer's representatives to sell its line of living room furniture. These representatives receive an 8 percent commission. The company is considering hiring its own salespeople and has estimated that the fixed cost of managing and paying their salaries would be $1 million annually. The salespeople would also receive a 4 percent commission on sales. The company has sales of $25 million dollars, and sales are expected to grow by 15 percent next year. Would you recommend that the company switch to its own sales force? Why or why not?

7 Suppose someone said to you, "The only real measure of a salesperson is the amount of sales produced." How might you respond?

8 Which input and output salesperson evaluation measures might be best suited for the order-getting salesperson described in the job analysis in Figure 18-7?

9 Which type of personal selling—order getting, order taking, or support—is the most likely to be taken over by interactive computer links between buyers and sellers? Why?

10 How might a company personnel recruiter use the six-stage selling process when recruiting you during a campus interview?

SUGGESTED READINGS

Ronald D. Balsley and E. Patricia Birsner, *Selling: Marketing Personified* (Chicago: The Dryden Press, 1987). *This book covers the personal selling process in detail from a behavioral perspective.*

F. Robert Dwyer, Paul H. Schurr, and Sejo Oh, "Developing Buyer-Seller Relationships," *Journal of Marketing* (April 1987), pp. 11-27. *This article examines issues in relational marketing with particular relevance to personal selling and sales management.*

Walter Kiechel III, "How to Manage Salespeople," *Fortune* (March 14, 1988), pp. 179-180. *This short article describes the many approaches for motivating and directing salespeople.*

Jerry McAdams, "Rewarding Sales and Marketing Performance," *Management Review* (April 1987), pp. 33-38. *This article describes salesperson compensation plans, including financial and nonfinancial rewards.*

Sales and Marketing Management's Survey of Selling Costs (February 1988). *This special issue published annually by* Sales and Marketing Management *magazine provides a thorough summary of selling and sales management practices and costs. This special issue is typically published every February.*

PART FIVE

MANAGING THE MARKETING PROCESS

The Olive Garden
ITALIAN
RESTAURANT
the Olive Garden
ITALIAN RESTAURANT

19

The Strategic Marketing Process: The Planning Phase

After reading this chapter you should be able to:

Describe how the three key aspects of planning—situation analysis, goal setting, and the marketing program—relate to the strategic marketing process.

•

Explain how sales response functions help a marketing manager allocate the firm's marketing effort.

•

List the generic strategies available to increase profit.

•

Describe the characteristics of a good marketing plan.

•

Explain how marketing managers can use the growth-share matrix and the market-product grid to help plan strategy.

Mixing Cheerios, Pudding Roll-Ups, and Olive Gardens

"It was," said one restaurant patron, "just awful" and "tasted like glue."[1]

The "it" was fettucine eaten at The Olive Garden, an experimental Italian restaurant being tested in 1982 by General Mills. Unfortunately the patron for that meal was General Mills' chairman and chief executive officer, H. Brewster Atwater.

The scene shifts to General Mills' 1987 annual meeting with its shareholders. It is now 5 years, $130 million of investment, and 58 Olive Garden restaurants after Atwater's disastrous fettucine experience. After extensive marketing research, General Mills now believes it has the right concept for The Olive Garden, an Italian restaurant with many menu items. About half of them include pasta, which is made in a highly answers to the question. "How much is it worth to us to try to increase our market share by another 1 [or 2, or 5, or 10] percentage point?"

This also enables higher level managers to make resource allocation trade-offs between different kinds of businesses owned by the company, such as between breakfast cereals, Red Lobster restaurants, and Betty Crocker cake mixes. To make these resource allocation decisions, marketing managers must estimate (1) the market share for the product, (2) the revenues associated with each point of market share (it may be $50 million for breakfast cereals, $10 million for seafood restaurants, and $5 million for cake mixes), and (3) the contribution to overhead profit (or gross margin) of each share point.

When sales of its fashion and toy divisions nosedived, General Mills "spun-off" (set up as independent companies) these two divisions. It then restructured its remaining organization to redirect resources into its "core businesses" of consumer foods and restaurants. It also took a careful look at where it should allocate these resources to give the greatest returns. Here are some of the decisions it made in 1987 and 1988 for its 2 core businesses:

- Consumer foods. Introduce Total oatmeal (General Mills' first hot cereal), new lines of dry adult cereals (Oatmeal Raisin Crisp) and children cereals (Ice Cream Cones and Citrus Fun), Microwave Crunchy line of Gorton's fish sticks, Betty Crocker brand ice cream novelties, and two dozen other new products.
- Restaurants. Finish refurbishing the Red Lobster restaurants and complete their shift from a fried to a fresh menu and expand in Canada and Japan; add new units of The Olive Garden restaurants. Sell its chain of Leeann Chin Chinese carryout restaurants back to Leeann Chin, the entrepreneur who had successfully started the chain in the upper Midwest.

These decisions reflect General Mills' assessment of what actions will best prepare it for the 1988 to 1990 period and beyond. For example, the company sold five specialty retail chains, including its Talbots and Eddie Bauer units, because they couldn't meet company targets and because General Mills wanted to focus on its two core businesses. Also, it decided against expanding its cereal business into Europe because the expected returns would not justify the investment risks.[4]

CONCEPT CHECK

1 **What is the significance of the S-shape of the sales response function in Figure 19-1?**

2 **What is the purpose of resource allocation in an organization?**

THE PLANNING PHASE OF THE STRATEGIC MARKETING PROCESS

After clarifying some basic terms, we will analyze the three steps of the planning phase of the strategic marketing process: situation analysis, goal setting, and marketing program.

ROLE OF THE STRATEGIC MARKETING PROCESS

To understand the role of the strategic marketing process in a firm, it's important to recognize some basic terms, annual and long-range marketing plans, and the activities and information present.

Key Terms The strategic marketing process varies from organization to organization, and so do the terms used to describe various aspects of this process. However, the purpose of the strategic marketing process and all planning activities is very clear: to allocate the organization's resources most efficiently. For clarity, let's summarize pertinent terms, some of which are defined in Chapter 2:

FIGURE 19-2
Steps a large consumer package goods firm takes in developing its annual marketing plan

STEPS IN ANNUAL MARKETING PLANNING PROCESS	WEEKS BEFORE APPROVAL OF PLAN					
	50	40	30	20	10	0
1. Obtain up-to-date marketing information from marketing research study of product users.						
2. Brainstorm alternatives to consider in next year's plan with own marketing research and outside advertising agency personnel.						
3. Meet with internal media specialists to set long-run guidelines in purchase of media.						
4. Obtain sales and profit results from last fiscal year, which ended 16 weeks earlier.						
5. Identify key issues (problems and opportunities) to address in next year's plan by talks with marketing researchers, advertising agency, other personnel.						
6. Hold key issues meeting with marketing director; form task force of line managers if significant product, package, or size change is considered.						
7. Write and circulate key issues memo; initiate necessary marketing research to reduce uncertainty.						
8. Review marketing mix elements and competitors' behavior with key managers, keeping marketing director informed.						
9. Draft marketing plan, review with marketing director, and revise as necessary.						
10. Present plan to marketing director, advertising agency, division controller, and heads of responsible line departments (product, packaging, sales, etc.), and make necessary changes.						
11. Present marketing plan to division general manager for approval, 10 weeks before start of fiscal year.						

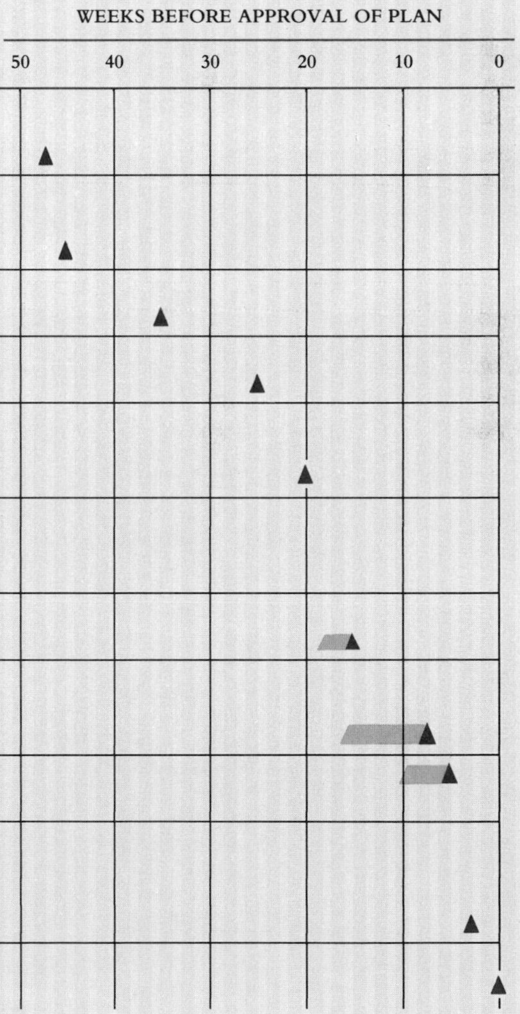

Source: Adapted from Stanley F. Stasch and Patricia Langtree, "Can Your Marketing Planning Procedures Be Improved?" *Journal of Marketing* (Summer 1980), p. 82; by permission of the American Marketing Association.

- **Strategic marketing process.** Continuing efforts by an organization to allocate its marketing mix resources to reach its target market; involves phases of (1) planning, (2) implementation, and (3) control
- **Goals** (or objectives). Precise statement of results sought, quantified in time and magnitude, where possible
- **Marketing strategies** (or marketing actions). Means by which the goals are to be achieved
- **Marketing program** (or marketing plan). Written document approved by higher management that a marketing manager uses to record and communicate the result of planning (the goals and marketing strategies) so marketing personnel can implement it
- **Industry.** Group of firms producing products that are close substitutes for each other

Annual and Long-Range Marketing Plans A marketing plan is the heart of a firm's business plan. Stated broadly, marketing plans, or marketing programs, fall into two categories. **Annual marketing plans** deal with the marketing goals and strategies for a product, product line, or entire firm for a single year, whereas **long-range plans** cover from 2 to 5 years. Except for firms in industries like autos, steel, or forest products, marketing plans rarely go beyond 5 years into the future because the tremendous number of uncertainties present make the benefits of planning less than the effort expended.

FIGURE 19-3
The strategic marketing process; actions and information

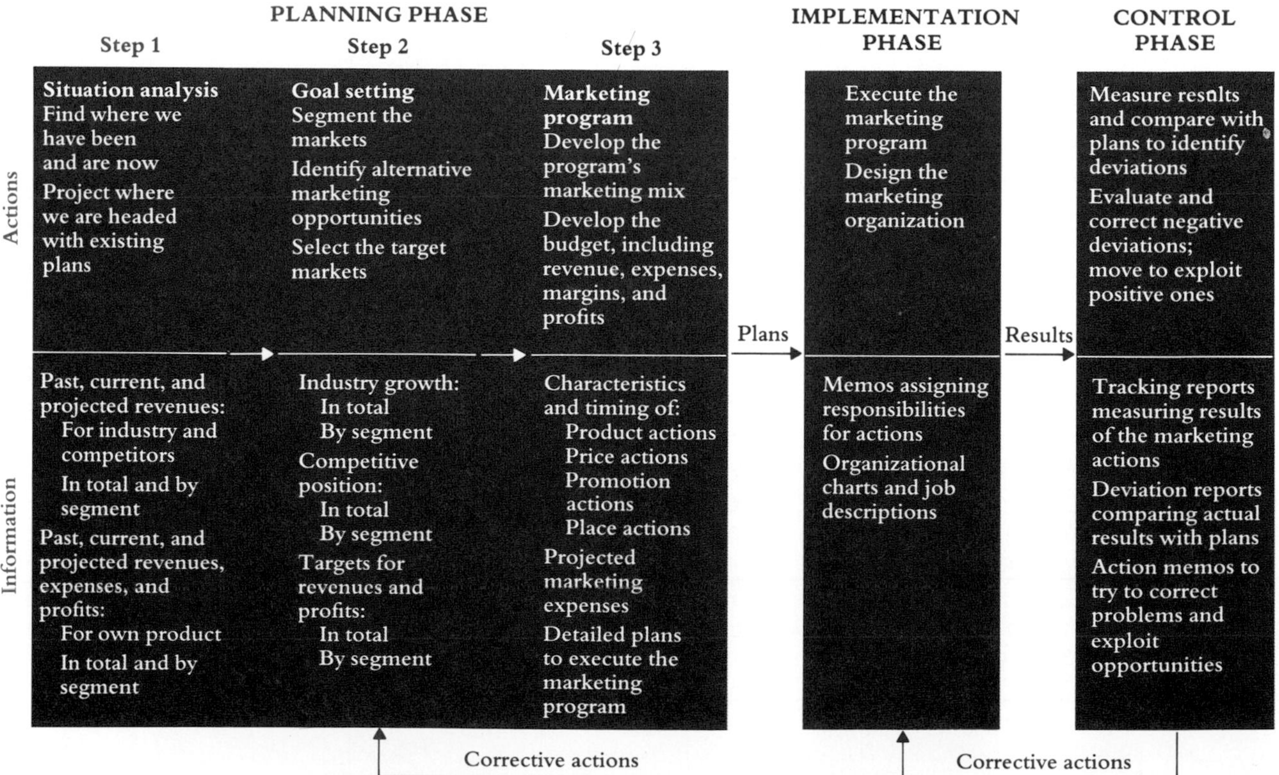

The steps a consumer package goods firm (such as food, health, and beauty products) takes in developing its annual marketing plan are shown in Figure 19-2. This annual planning cycle starts with a detailed marketing research study of present users and ends after 48 weeks with the approval of the plan by the division general manager—10 weeks before the fiscal year starts. In between these points there are continuing efforts to uncover new ideas through brainstorming and key-issues sessions with specialists both inside and outside the firm. The plan is fine-tuned through a series of often excruciating reviews by several levels of management, which leaves few surprises and little to chance.

Actions and Information Figure 19-3 summarizes the strategic marketing process introduced in Chapter 2, along with the actions and information that compose it. The upper half of each box highlights the actions involved in that part of the strategic marketing process, and the lower half summarizes the information and reports used. Note that each phase has an output report:

PHASE	OUTPUT REPORT
Planning	Plans (or programs) that define goals and the marketing mix strategies to achieve them
Implementation	Results (memos or computer outputs) that summarize the outcomes of implementing the plans
Control	Corrective action memos, triggered by comparing results with plans, that (1) correct problems and (2) exploit opportunities

STEP 1 IN PLANNING: SITUATION ANALYSIS

To find out where a firm has been, is now, and is headed with present plans in the situation analysis requires very detailed information. This includes past, current, and projected information about revenues, expenses, and profits for the entire industry and the firm's own products (and ideally competitors' products), in total and by individual segments. This is a big order, but it makes possible goal setting, the second step in the planning phase of the strategic marketing process. Additional information is needed to develop the marketing mix actions, timing, and budgets for the marketing program to complete the planning phase. Finally, the results must be measured during the marketing implementation phase so that corrective actions can be taken in the control phase.

The survey of 176 product managers summarized in Figure 19-4 shows the actual information they use in developing their marketing plans. At least 70 percent of the product managers made forecasts of their own product's sales, direct costs, and direct contribution (gross margin). At least half also used forecasts of industry sales, projections of their own product's market share, and projected profitability statements for their own product. Shaded rows in Figure 19-4 show data used by more than half of those surveyed.

Of these six kinds of information, only one deals with something other than the product manager's own product: forecasts of industry sales. In most situation analyses two principal ingredients are the size of the industry market now and its growth rate in the near future. This tells the product manager what the size of the total pie is and the amount by which it is growing annually, and runs from 0 to 20 percent, although in practice it might run even higher. The axis has arbitrarily been divided at 10 percent into high-growth and low-growth areas.

The horizontal axis is the **relative market share**, defined as the sales of the SBU divided by those of the largest firm in the industry. A relative market share of 10× (at the left end of the scale) means that the SBU has 10 times the share of its largest competitor, whereas a share 0.1× (at the right end of the scale) means it has only 10 percent of the sales of its largest competitor. The scale is logarithmic and is arbitrarily divided into high and low relative market shares at a value of 1×.

BCG has given specific names and descriptions to the four resulting quadrants in its growth-share matrix based on the amount of cash they generate for the firm or require from it:

- Cash cows (lower left quadrant) are SBUs that typically generate large amounts of cash, far more than they can invest profitably in their own product line. They have a dominant share of a slow-growth market and provide cash to pay large amounts of company overhead and to invest in other SBUs.
- Stars (upper left quadrant) are SBUs with a high share of high-growth markets that may not generate enough cash to support their own demanding needs for future growth. When their growth slows, they are likely to become cash cows.
- Question marks or problem children (upper right quadrant) are SBUs with a low share of high-growth markets. They require large injections of cash just to maintain their market share, much less increase it. Their name implies management's dilemma for these SBUs: finding the right ones to bet on and phasing out the rest.
- Dogs (lower right quadrant) are SBUs with a low share of low-growth markets. Although they may generate enough cash to sustain them-

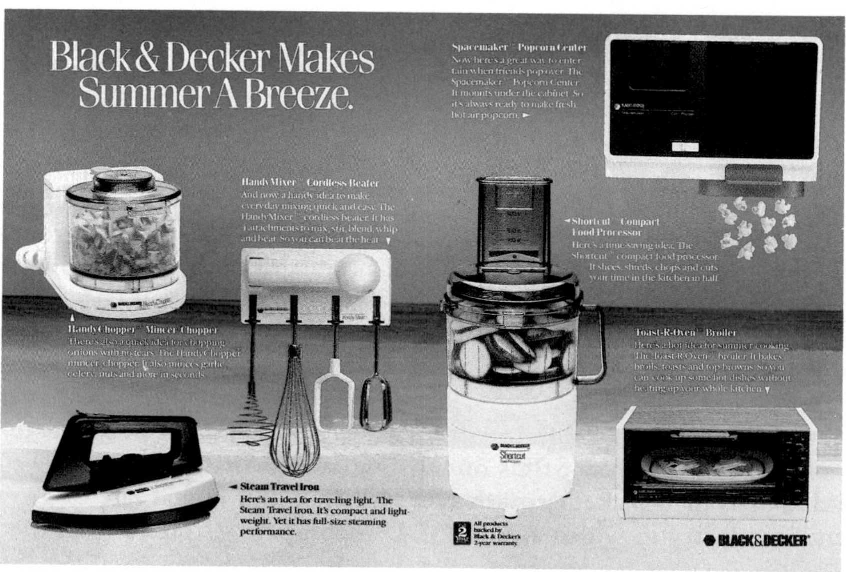

GE's "divest" strategy was the start of Black & Decker's small appliance line selves, they do not hold the promise of ever becoming real winners for the firm.

The hollow circles in Figure 19-6 show the location of the SBUs in a strong, diversified firm. The area of each hollow circle is proportional to that SBU's annual sales revenue.

Use in Marketing Planning The portfolio in Figure 19-6 is a strong and diversified one because over half the SBUs have high relative market shares, there are many stars, the cash cows are strong and numerous enough to feed the needs of the question marks, and even most of the question marks and dogs have high market shares. Most firms are unable to influence the market growth rate—the factor shown on the vertical axis; an exception is a firm whose product is strong enough to stimulate primary demand for the entire product class. If a firm cannot affect market growth, its main planning alternative using business portfolio analysis is to try to change the relative market share, the factor on the horizontal axis. This is done mainly through a conscious management decision to either inject or withdraw cash from a specific SBU.

A firm must determine what role to assign each SBU in trying to assemble its ideal future portfolio.[14] BCG identifies four alternative objectives for an SBU. Ranked from most to least cash infused into an SBU, these four alternatives are described below and pictured in Figure 19-6.

1. Build. Increase the SBU's market share through injections of cash, even foregoing short-term profits to do so. This is often an appropriate strategy for question marks that need large amounts of cash to become stars. By injecting cash into SBU A in Figure 19-6, a firm hopes to move it from its present question mark position to a star (solid circle). Starting in 1980, through aggressive new product and marketing efforts, Colgate has succeeded in challenging Procter & Gamble's Crest for first place in the toothpaste market.
2. Hold. Maintain the SBU's market share, without appreciably altering the cash it uses. SBU B is typical of a holding strategy often applied to cash cows that are generating large amounts of cash and are intended to retain that same position in the future. The Dayton Hudson retail chain is using a holding strategy for its department stores that are in a slow-growth segment of the retail market.
3. Harvest. Increase the SBU's short-term cash output, even if this results in a loss of market share. This strategy can be used with question marks, dogs, or cash cows; an example of the latter is shown as SBU C. The resulting cash can then be pumped into stars or question marks. When General Mills marketing research showed that the decor and menu in Red Lobster restaurants were losing customer appeal, it pumped money out of its profitable consumer food divisions to cover the refurbishing cost of $200,000 per restaurant.

4. Divest. Sell the SBU to put its cash, physical, and human resources to use elsewhere in the firm. Question marks and dogs (such as SBU D) that require too much cash are candidates for divestiture. General Electric's sale of its small appliance division to Black & Decker provided it with cash that it put into new high-technology and service businesses.

Just as most products have life cycles, so do most SBUs. An SBU often starts out as a question mark and then moves counterclockwise around the growth-share matrix—question mark to star to cash cow to dog—as industry competition increases. This means a firm's portfolio of SBUs and their positions are changing continuously, and the firm must always be on the lookout for new products and business opportunities to become the stars and cash cows in its future portfolio.

Strengths and Weaknesses Primary strengths of business portfolio analysis include (1) forcing a firm to assess each of its SBUs in terms of its relative market share and industry market growth rate, which in turn (2) requires the firm to forecast which SBUs will be cash producers and cash needers in the future. Weaknesses are that (1) it is often difficult to get the information needed to locate each SBU on the growth-share matrix, (2) there are other important factors missing from the analysis such as possible synergies among the SBUs when they use the same sales force or research and development facilities, and (3) there are problems in motivating people in an SBU that has been labeled a dog or even a cash cow and is unlikely to get new resources from the firm to grow and provide opportunities for promotion.[15]

Underlying the BCG analysis is the assumption about the importance of the firm's absolute market share and, in turn, relative market share. Many early analyses suggested that if a firm could gain an increase in market share, then a sizeable increase in ROI would automatically follow, a conclusion about which there is increasing debate.[16]

MARKET-PRODUCT GRID

A marketing manager responsible for an individual SBU can use the market-product grid to identify specific product opportunities or market niches that might be pursued.

Information Needed As summarized in Chapter 8, the process of segmenting a market first necessitates finding characteristics to form market segments and then product clusters. Displaying these in a table forms a market-product grid. The use of this grid in the strategic marketing process is based on the kind of detailed information shown in Figure 19-3: (1) past, current, and projected information, (2) about revenues, expenses, and profits, (3) for the entire industry and the firm's own products, (4) in total and by individual market segments and product clusters.

Use in Marketing Planning The market-product grid facilitates trade-offs in the strategic marketing process. Suppose you are a product manager for Great States Corporation's line of nonpowered lawn mowers sold to the consumer market. You are looking for new product and new market opportunities to increase your revenues and profits.

You conduct a market segmentation study and develop a market-product grid to analyze future opportunities. You identify three major segments in the consumer market based on geography: (1) city, (2) suburban, and (3) rural areas.

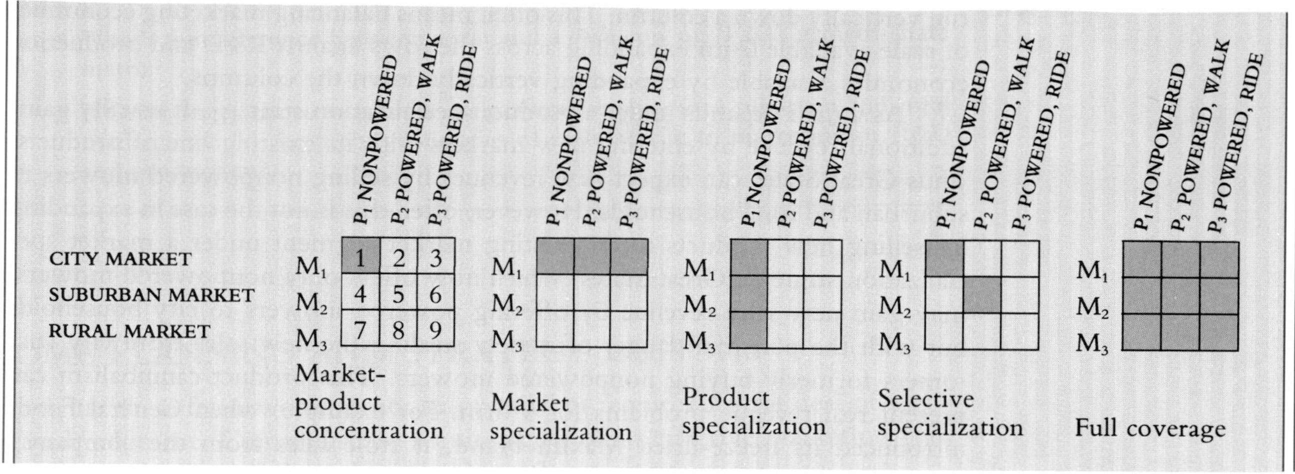

FIGURE 19-7
Market-product grid of alternative strategies for a lawn-mower manufacturer

These segments relate to the size of lawn a consumer must mow. The product clusters are (1) nonpowered, (2) powered walking, and (3) powered riding mowers.

Five alternative marketing strategies are shown in market-product grids in Figure 19-7[17]:

- Market-product concentration. Great States' initial strategy focused its efforts on one market segment (city households with small lawns) with a single product line (nonpowered mowers).
- Market specialization. This entails retaining the focus on a single market segment (city households) but adding two new product lines (powered walking and powered riding mowers). The strategic problem is developing and manufacturing two product lines new to Great States.
- Product specialization. This involves retaining Great States' focus on a single product line (nonpowered mowers) but marketing it to two unknown markets (suburban and rural households). The potential danger is entering two markets in which a producer may have no marketing experience or distribution outlets.
- Selective specialization. This involves targeting separate product lines for separate segments: nonpowered mowers for city households and powered walking mowers for suburban dwellers. The difficulty is the lack of scale economies available in the two previous strategies.
- Full coverage. With this strategy Great States will offer all three product lines in all three market segments.

The five grids in Figure 19-7 highlight some trade-offs that marketing managers face in designing strategies. For example, marketing economies of scale run horizontally across the rows: adding new products for a given market segment represents few new marketing expenses but sizeable new R&D and production expenses. The reverse is true for R&D and production economies of scale: these

FIRM	STRATEGY	RESULT
PLANS THAT DID WORK		
Digital Equipment Corporation	Sell large computer networks to nontechnical users (a new market), double size of salesforce and train it about user's needs	Increased revenues 25 percent per year during 1980's, succeeding in beating IBM in some market segments
Liz Claiborne	Develop stylish clothes for professional women, have salesforce sell retailers only what is needed—thereby reducing markdowns	Achieved a 5-year sales growth rate of 47 percent per year—about 6 times the industry average
Merck	Develop important drugs (such as cholesterol-reducing Meracor) and give salesforce unequaled training on technical, presentation, and customer-service details	Ranked #1 on *Fortune*'s list of most admired corporations and had 5-year sales growth twice the industry average
PLANS THAT DIDN'T WORK		
Pratt & Whitney (Division of United Aircraft)	Diversify into new businesses and invest billions of dollars to develop three completely new jet engines to power new aircraft of the 1980's	Overestimated the demand for its new large engines and lost large market share to GE's jet engines
Western Union	Go beyond the telegraph business to become full-service in telecommunications after deregulation occurred	Failed to recognize intensity of competition and time needed to become profitable, and ran out of money
People Express	Shore up lagging revenues by targeting low-cost, no-frills air service to business travelers	Failed to win business travelers, and airline was absorbed by Texas Air

Sources: William M. Bulkeley, "A 'Tekkie' on the Inside Track at Digital," *The Wall Street Journal* (September 1, 1987), p. 31; Edward C. Baig, "America's Most Admired Corporations," *Fortune* (January 19, 1987), pp. 18-31; Bro Uttal, Companies that Serve You Best," *Fortune* (December 7, 1987), pp. 98-116; "Pratt & Whitney's Stall Is Turning Into a Tailspin," *Business Week* (December 14, 1987), p. 37; "The Sad Saga of Western Union's Decline," *Business Week* (December 14, 1987), pp. 108-114.

FIGURE 19-8
Results of strategic marketing plans

mix factors and incorporated the key ones in the marketing plan. Marketing resources must be adequate to make the plan feasible.

Controllable and Flexible Plans Few plans are carried to completion without a hitch. Results of marketing actions are compared with the measurable, targeted goals to discern problem areas that trigger new, corrective actions. Marketing plans must provide for this control, which in turn allows replanning—the flexibility to update the original plans.

PROBLEMS IN MARKETING PLANNING AND STRATEGY

From postmortems on company plans that did work and also on those that did not work, a picture emerges as to where problems occur in the planning phase of a firm's strategic marketing process. The following list explores these problems:

1. Corporate plans may be based on very poor assumptions about environmental factors, especially changing economic conditions and competitors' actions. As shown in Figure 19-8, Western Union's plan failed because it didn't reflect the impact of deregulation and competitors' actions on business.
2. Planners and their plans may have lost sight of their customers' needs. People Express airline failed to realize that low-cost air fares did not have the appeal to business customers they did for tourists. But Figure 19-8 shows that Digital Equipment, Liz Claiborne, and Merck had marketing strategies that succeeded because of customer-oriented products and sales forces.
3. Too much time and effort may be spent on collection and analysis of data required for the plans. The result is that line managers have their focus diverted from developing and implementing creative strategies. Westinghouse has cut its planning instructions for operating units "that looked like an auto repair manual" to five or six pages.
4. Responsibility for planning and strategy development may be assigned to the planners so that line operating managers feel no sense of ownership in implementing the plans. This is the refrain running throughout today's blue-ribbon American firms, including General Electric, General Motors, U.S. Steel, and Rockwell International. The solution is to assign more planning activities to line operating managers.

WHERE PLANNING AND STRATEGY ARE HEADED

The focus of this chapter is on marketing planning and strategy to compete with products offered by other businesses. However, in today's corporate environment, the head of a corporation competes in another market as well: the market for corporate control. His or her goal is to run the various divisions and strategic business units so that they are more valuable together than standing alone. If this is not possible, the corporation may be purchased by outsiders, who sell off the divisions one by one with the goal of receiving a bigger collective amount for the pieces than they paid to buy the entire corporation.

In this form of planning, a firm's value is the value of its future cash flows discounted back to their present value. *Value-based planning* combines marketing planning ideas discussed in this chapter and financial planning techniques to assess how much a division or SBU contributes to the price of a company's stock (or shareholder wealth).[21] Although the topic is beyond the main topics of this book, it promises to influence marketing planning and strategy significantly.

CONCEPT CHECK

1 **What is a measurable goal?**

2 **Why is it important to be able to replan?**

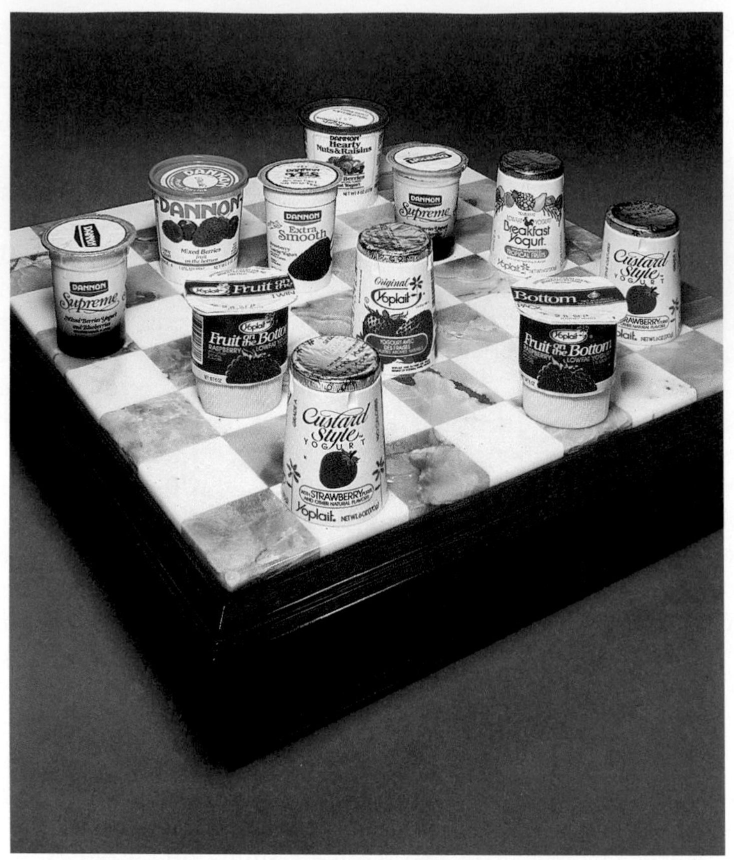

Yoplait's products face-off against competitive ones

YOPLAIT YOGURT: THE PLANNING PHASE OF THE STRATEGIC MARKETING PROCESS

To illustrate these planning concepts, let's follow the strategic marketing process of an actual new product introduction and describe how Yoplait USA, a subsidiary of General Mills, introduced its yogurt.[22] In the next chapter we'll see the implementation and control phases of Yoplait.

CORPORATE MISSION STATEMENT OF GENERAL MILLS

General Mills has a stated mission: "To be competitively excellent in everything it decides to undertake." Its corporate goal is one of consistent growth in sales and earnings, which General Mills defines as achieving a return on equity in the upper 25 percent of larger American companies—about 15 percent to 19 percent in a typical year. To achieve this, it has set some broad corporate strategies[23]:

- Balance its diversification in the industry groups in which it competes
- Undertake aggressive consumer marketing that can lead to strong brands that outperform competitive brands, ideally becoming first or second in market share in their product category
- Enter industry growth segments early, starting with small commitments

and then investing heavily in opportunities that promise substantial growth
- Achieve the internal financial goal of 25 percent ROI

These guide business units in General Mills in developing their strategic marketing plans.

SITUATION ANALYSIS

In 1977 a General Mills team including Steven Rothschild investigated the yogurt business—a dairy business that is new to General Mills, whose experience is in its traditional grocery products such as breakfast cereals and cake mixes. The team conducted a detailed situation analysis that revealed information on yogurt's history, current types of yogurt, consumer use and preferences, and the industry and competition.

History Yogurt, a cultured milk product, has been around for centuries. It is widely consumed in the Middle East and parts of Europe. Yogurt first came to the United States in the 1930's but didn't have much consumer appeal until the 1960's. Then in the late 1970's yogurt became one of the fastest-growing food products in the country.

Types of Yogurt Rothschild and the team discovered that about 95 percent of the yogurt consumed in the United States is mixed with fruit or flavoring and about 5 percent is plain. About 95 percent is consumed in 8-ounce cups. The team also found that there are four basic types of yogurt available in the United States today in addition to plain yogurt:

- Sundae style: fruit on bottom of cup
- Swiss style: fruit blended throughout using stabilizers to keep it from settling
- Western style: fruit on bottom and flavored syrup on top
- Frozen style: ice cream or soft custard form

Other research showed that yogurt is available in 20 different flavors and a wide range of textures. When refrigerated, it has a shelf life of 21 to 60 days, depending on whether preservatives are added.

Consumer Preferences and Use Rothschild found the U.S. annual per capita consumption of yogurt was low (5 cups per person) compared with consumption in European countries (27 cups per person a year in France). Research data showed that 25 percent of U.S. households had eaten yogurt in the past month; 30 percent had eaten it but less frequently; and 45 percent had never bought or eaten it.

When asked why they eat yogurt, about 48 percent of yogurt consumers said, "It tastes good," and another 18 percent said, "For weight watching." Almost two thirds ate it as a between-meal snack. The heaviest monthly consumption was from April to September.

Indexes were developed to identify where yogurt consumption is concentrated, using an index of 100 as average. These indexes showed heavy use by households with over $20,000 annual income (index 166), 18- to 34-year-old women (index 121), and 12- to 17-year-old girls (index 118). In geographic consumption West Coast households consumed the most yogurt (index 162), followed by those in New England (index 156) and the Middle Atlantic states (index 139).

Industry and Competition Steven Rothschild estimated that industry sales of yogurt in the United States for 1978 would be about $350 million, with unit sales of 80 million 12-pack cases of single-serving cups. Unit sales of yogurt averaged 18 percent annual growth from 1970 to 1977. Strong continued growth was anticipated.

There is no national brand of yogurt, but there are about a half dozen premium-quality regional brands, including Dannon in the East and Midwest and Knudsen on the West Coast. About three fourths of U.S. dairies offer private label, local brands to customers.

GOAL SETTING

Rothschild and the team recommended that General Mills enter the yogurt market. In doing so, it committed the yogurt venture to the following goals set for new products at General Mills:

1. Fit with General Mills' strengths: "products with high value-added distributed through supermarkets"
2. Achieve 20 percent share of the yogurt market in 5 years
3. Achieve $100 million in sales in 5 years—double the minimum required by General Mills
4. Meet internal financial goals of 25 percent ROI in 5 years
5. Become a multiproduct business

A yogurt product also met some other brand goals for a new product at General Mills: (1) a high-turnover branded item that allows a significant profit margin, (2) a product for which the firm's skills in positioning, advertising, packaging, and promotion will provide an advantage over competition, and (3) a business that will capitalize on trends resulting from long-term changes in consumer behavior.

MARKETING PROGRAM

Rothschild was convinced that General Mills must move quickly and decisively into the yogurt market if it were to succeed. He concluded the company didn't have time to develop its own yogurt in its own laboratories, so he moved to acquire a high-quality yogurt and then devise a marketing mix strategy.

Yogurt Acquisition In October 1977 General Mills acquired the right to market Yoplait Yogurt in the United States from Sodima, a large French cooperative. It named Steven Rothschild to head the team of people in its new subsidiary, Yoplait USA. At that time Yoplait was the best-selling yogurt in France and was being distributed in less than 10 percent of the United States. Rothschild estimated the acquisition would save General Mills 3 years compared with developing and marketing its own brand from scratch.

Positioning Strategy Rothschild and his team decided to try to position Yoplait as a French yogurt that would appeal to the typical American consumer.

Product Strategy The team saw some significant product benefits in Yoplait Yogurt:

- One hundred percent natural yogurt with active yogurt cultures without artificial sweeteners and preservatives
- Creamy French-style yogurt with real fruit mixed throughout
- Outstanding taste as measured by marketing research

The team decided to market Yoplait in a convenient, attention-getting package.

Pricing Strategy Their strategy was to set a price that would provide margins for retailers comparable to those of major regional brands. This margin should provide enough profit in this high-velocity consumer product (at 2.6 stockturns per week) for retailers to advertise and promote Yoplait in their local market.

Promotional Strategy The advertising would be designed to inform consumers about Yoplait's outstanding taste and unique texture while reminding them of its French heritage. Television, print media, and sampling would be used to introduce consumers to Yoplait.

Place Strategy National distribution was needed as soon as possible. Because of fast turnover, a plan was made to avoid running out of stock by a carefully scheduled inventory program tied to delivery frequency and sales level of the store. Because Yoplait is best when consumed within 30 days of manufacture, each package would be marked with a 30-day "use by" date. Inventory on the shelf beyond that date would be destroyed, the reasons investigated, and recurrence prevented.

How Steven Rothschild has implemented and controlled Yoplait's strategy is described at the end of Chapter 20.

SUMMARY

1. Marketing managers using the strategic marketing process search continuously for differential advantages in the markets they serve and the products they offer.
2. They exploit these differential advantages by allocating their resources as effectively as possible. Sales response functions help them assess what the market's response will be to additional marketing effort.

3 With so much at risk from bad decisions, the strategic marketing process often requires an enormous amount of detailed information that includes (a) past, current, and projected information, (b) about revenues, expenses, and profits, (c) for the entire industry, the firm, and competitors, (d) in total and by individual segments.

4 Generic strategies for a firm to increase its profits are (a) increasing revenues, (b) decreasing expenses, and (c) a combination of both.

5 BCG's growth-share matrix enables a firm to position its strategic business units (SBUs) on a two-dimensional graph whose axes are (a) annual market (industry) growth rate and (b) the SBU's relative market share (firm's sales divided by those of the largest competitor).

6 The market-product grid displays an SBU's market segments and product clusters in a table to identify opportunity niches; assess economies of scale in marketing, R&D, and production; and project possible lost revenues if new products steal sales from existing products.

7 An effective marketing plan has measurable, achievable objectives; uses facts and valid assumptions; is simple, clear, and specific; is complete and feasible; and is controllable and flexible.

KEY TERMS AND CONCEPTS

sustainable competitive advantage p. 520
sales response function p. 520
share points p. 521
strategic marketing process p. 524
goals p. 524
marketing strategies p. 524
marketing program p. 524
industry p. 524
annual marketing plans p. 524
long-range plans p. 524
generic marketing strategy p. 527
strategic business units p. 531
business portfolio analysis p. 531
market growth rate p. 531
relative market share p. 532

CHAPTER PROBLEMS AND APPLICATIONS

1 Assume a firm faces an S-shaped sales response function. What happens to the ratio of incremental sales revenue to incremental marketing effort at the (a) bottom, (b) middle, and (c) top of this curve?

2 What happens to the ratio of incremental sales revenue to incremental marketing effort when the sales response function is an upward-sloping straight line?

3 Does the S-shaped (Question 1) or upward-sloping straight line (Question 2) sales response function best describe the typical situation facing a firm?

4 From 1988 to 1990 General Mills plans to invest $1.6 billion in expanding its two core businesses of consumer foods and restaurants (such as Red Lobster). In deciding how to allocate this money between these two businesses, what information would General Mills like to have?
5 Campbell Soup now has 60 percent of the canned soup business. Write a specific marketing goal for Campbell Soup.
6 In early 1985 General Mills' product portfolio included Bisquick, Wheaties, Red Lobster restaurants, Eddie Bauer retail stores, Izod sportswear, and Parker Brothers video games. From the chapter and what you know, categorize these products in terms of the BCG matrix. What does this tell you about why General Mills got out of the sportswear and video game businesses?
7 Explain why a product often starts as a question mark and then moves counterclockwise around BCG's growth-share matrix.
8 Suppose Apple Computer wants to increase its profits through increasing its revenues. Use its market-product grid shown in the Marketing Action Memo in Chapter 8 to identify an action it might take for each of the four generic strategies for increasing revenues.
9 In Figure 19-8, which generic strategies for increasing revenues seem to have been followed by (a) Digital Equipment, (b) Pratt & Whitney, (c) Western Union, and (d) People Express.

SUGGESTED READINGS

"America's Leanest and Meanest," *Business Week* (October 5, 1987), pp. 78-84. *This article identifies 14 U.S. companies and the strategies they are using to meet the challenges of worldwide competition.*

George S. Day, *Analysis for Strategic Marketing Decisions* (St. Paul, Minn.: West Publishing Co., 1987). *This book gives a practical summary of marketing strategies and how planning techniques relate to them.*

Walter Kiechel, III, "Corporate Strategy for the 1990s," *Fortune* (February 29, 1988), pp. 34-42. *This article gives a view of value-based planning and what it means for American businesses in the 1990's.*

Bill Saporito, "Cutting Costs Without Cutting People," *Fortune* (May 25, 1987), pp. 26-32. *While many firms have reduced costs by massive layoffs, this article describes alternative strategies for reducing a firm's costs and increasing its competitiveness.*

Bro Uttal, "Companies that Serve You Best," *Fortune* (December 7, 1987), pp. 98-112. *This article describes the success many U.S. firms have found in customer "coddling"—providing great customer service.*

DOMINO'S
PIZZA
DOMINO'S
PIZZA

20

THE STRATEGIC MARKETING PROCESS: IMPLEMENTATION AND CONTROL PHASES

After reading this chapter you should be able to:

Relate the implementation and control phases to the strategic marketing process.

•

Describe the alternatives for organizing marketing activities and the role of a product manager in a marketing department.

•

List the key activities needed to ensure that a marketing program is implemented effectively.

•

Schedule a series of tasks to meet a deadline using a Gantt chart.

•

Understand how sales and profitability analyses and marketing audits are used to evaluate and control marketing programs.

Eleven Years to Get It Right: Tasty, Hot, Home-Delivered Pizzas in 30 Minutes

Thomas S. Monaghan tried to succeed in two parts of the pizza business: sit-down and delivery. He finally realized that doing both was one too many things to implement and control. So he focused on delivery, which resulted in the most successful home delivered–meal business in the United States.

The focus for his better idea: delivering tasty, hot, custom-made pizzas to consumers' homes within 30 minutes of receiving their telephone order. What could be simpler? It only took Monaghan 11 years and a near bankruptcy to implement and control that 1 idea.[1]

In 1960 Monaghan scraped together $500 to buy a tiny Italian restaurant near Eastern Michigan University, hoping to make enough money to finance his architecture degree. On the theory that tasteless dormitory food generates demand for pizza near college campuses, less than 1 year later he opened outlets near the University of Michigan and Central Michigan University. By 1965 he was thousands of dollars in debt, so he crossed out every entrée on the menu except pizza, threw out the tables and chairs, and concentrated on pizza delivery.

Searching for the Better Idea Monaghan started franchising the outlets, found he couldn't fulfill the promises he made to the franchisees, and saw his headquarters burn down. "We just went too far, too fast, without being ready," he reflects. Finding himself $1 million in debt when franchisees and creditors filed 150 lawsuits, Monaghan watched a bank take over his restaurants.

Monaghan went back to working in his restaurants, paid off his debts, and regained control of the business in 1971. He observes, "I began rebuilding by staking out a business niche—free delivery—and doing it better and faster than anyone else." In fact, his stores also offer carry-out service but target the delivery segment, which explains why 90 percent of sales are home delivery. He called his firm Domino's Pizza, Inc., and by 1980 had 398 outlets, mostly franchised, and $98 million in sales.[2]

Precise Implementation: One Key to Success Monaghan decided he had to reduce his dependence on colleges and try to penetrate the lucrative residential market. Research showed that taste and prompt delivery are the key buying criteria for both the main (ages 18 to 34) and secondary (age 35 and over) target markets of Domino's. This helped him select and emphasize Domino's unique appeal: delivery of a hot pizza to a customer's home within 30 minutes from the phone order, or a $3 discount for the customer. In addition, the company has a product guarantee.

Monaghan's actions are a textbook example of the precise, effective implementation and control phases of a marketing program. His strategy includes an acute attention to quality and detail (see the Marketing Action Memo). For example, the cheese is half the cost of a pizza. Unlike competitors who have cut quality, Monaghan insists on using an expensive, 100% real cheese.[3]

Employee motivation is also critical. The big carrot for good performance as a driver and in the store is—surprise!—a Domino's Pizza franchise. With no franchises available on the open market, the only way to get one is to earn it by starting out in the store, often as a driver, then working on the "make-line," and successfully completing the manager-in-training program. After accomplishing this, the employee has the opportunity to franchise. This ensures quality of the product and of store operations.

Future Goals By 1989 Domino's had more than 4,700 outlets. Tom Monaghan has announced his new goal: 10,000 outlets by 1992.

Domino's success is testimony to the notion that great marketing ideas are usually clear, simple, and workable. Also, they must be capable of being im-

MARKETING·ACTION·MEMO

What Implementation Involves at Domino's Pizza

The implementation actions at Domino's Pizza involve an acute level of detail.

SIMPLE, FLEXIBLE MENU

Domino's offers only two sizes of thin-crust pizza (12 inch and 16 inch) and one beverage (cola).

PRECISE ORDERING INSTRUCTIONS FOR CUSTOMERS

Domino's puts five instructions on its menu to facilitate prompt delivery:

1. Know what you want before ordering (size of pizza, toppings, beverages).
2. Know the phone number and address of the residence from which you are calling.
3. When placing an order, let us know if you have large-denomination bills.
4. Remain by the phone after ordering. We may call back to confirm the order.
5. Turn on your porch light.

On this list Item 3 is intended to protect the driver, and Item 4 discourages crank calls.

DETAILED ORDER-PROCESSING AND DELIVERY PROCEDURES

When a customer phones in an order, a dispatcher records it and locates the customer's house on a blown-up map of the surrounding community. Employees on the "make-line" assemble the pizza by adding ingredients in order from the bottom up: dough, sauce, cheese, and toppings. Ideally, after 7 minutes (1 to make and 6 to bake) the hot pizzas are put in rigid corrugated boxes in racks earmarked for specific delivery routes.

CONTINUING CUSTOMER FEEDBACK

A questionnaire often accompanies each pizza delivered asking about factors such as the courteousness of telephone and delivery personnel, pizza quality, and delivery time. Survey results are turned over to regional offices, which then correct problems in individual stores.

This concern for effective implementation should help Domino's fend off dozens of new competitors featuring home-delivered meals.

Source: Bernie Whalen, "'People-Oriented' Marketing Delivers a Lot of Dough for Domino's," *Marketing News* (March 15, 1984), p. 4ff.; Kevin T. Higgins, "Home Delivery Is Helping Pizza to Battle Burgers," *Marketing News* (August 1, 1986), pp. 1, 6.

plemented and controlled—the phases of the strategic marketing process covered in this chapter—by ordinary people, not geniuses (Figure 20-1).

The Implementation Phase of the Strategic Marketing Process

The Monday morning diagnosis of a losing football coach often runs something like, "We had an excellent game plan: we just didn't execute it."

Is Planning or Implementation the Problem?

The planning-versus-execution issue applies to the strategic marketing process as well: a difficulty when a marketing plan fails is determining whether it results

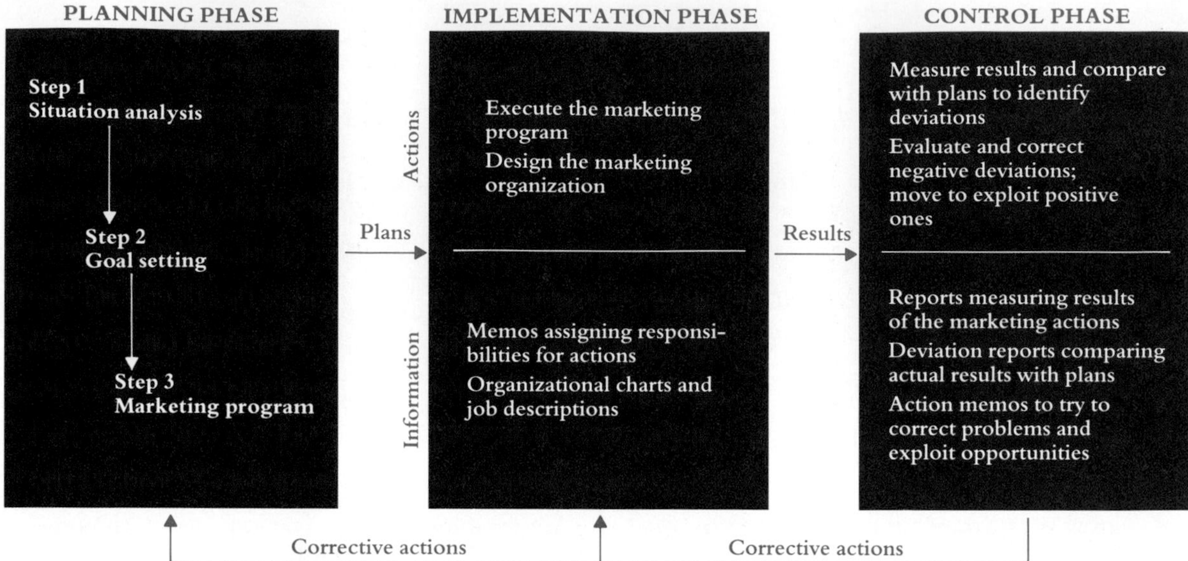

FIGURE 20-1
The strategic marketing process: actions and information in the implementation and control phases

primarily from a poor plan or poor implementation. Figure 20-2 shows the outcomes of (1) good and bad marketing planning and (2) good and bad marketing implementation. Good planning and good implementation in Cell 1 spell success, as with IBM's entry into the PC business with a strong product coupled with excellent advertising, distribution, and pricing. Atari fell into the "bad-bad" Cell 4 when its inability to see the shift in consumer tastes from video games to home computers, combined with both bad planning and implementation, led to failure and a $650 million loss.

Cells 2 and 3 indicate trouble because either the marketing planning *or* marketing implementation—not both—is bad. A firm or product does not stay

FIGURE 20-2
Results of good and bad market planning and implementation

MARKETING IMPLEMENTATION	MARKETING PLANNING AND STRATEGY	
	Good (appropriate)	Bad (inappropriate)
Good (effective)	1 Success: Marketing program achieves its objectives.	2 Trouble: Solution lies in recognizing that only the strategy is at fault and correcting it.
Bad (ineffective)	3 Trouble: Solution lies in recognizing that only implementation is at fault and correcting it.	4 Failure: Marketing program flounders and fails to achieve its objectives.

Source: Reprinted by permission of the *Harvard Business Review*. An exhibit from "Making Your Marketing Strategy Work" by Thomas V. Bonoma (March/April 1984). Copyright © 1984 by the President and Fellows of Harvard College; all rights reserved.

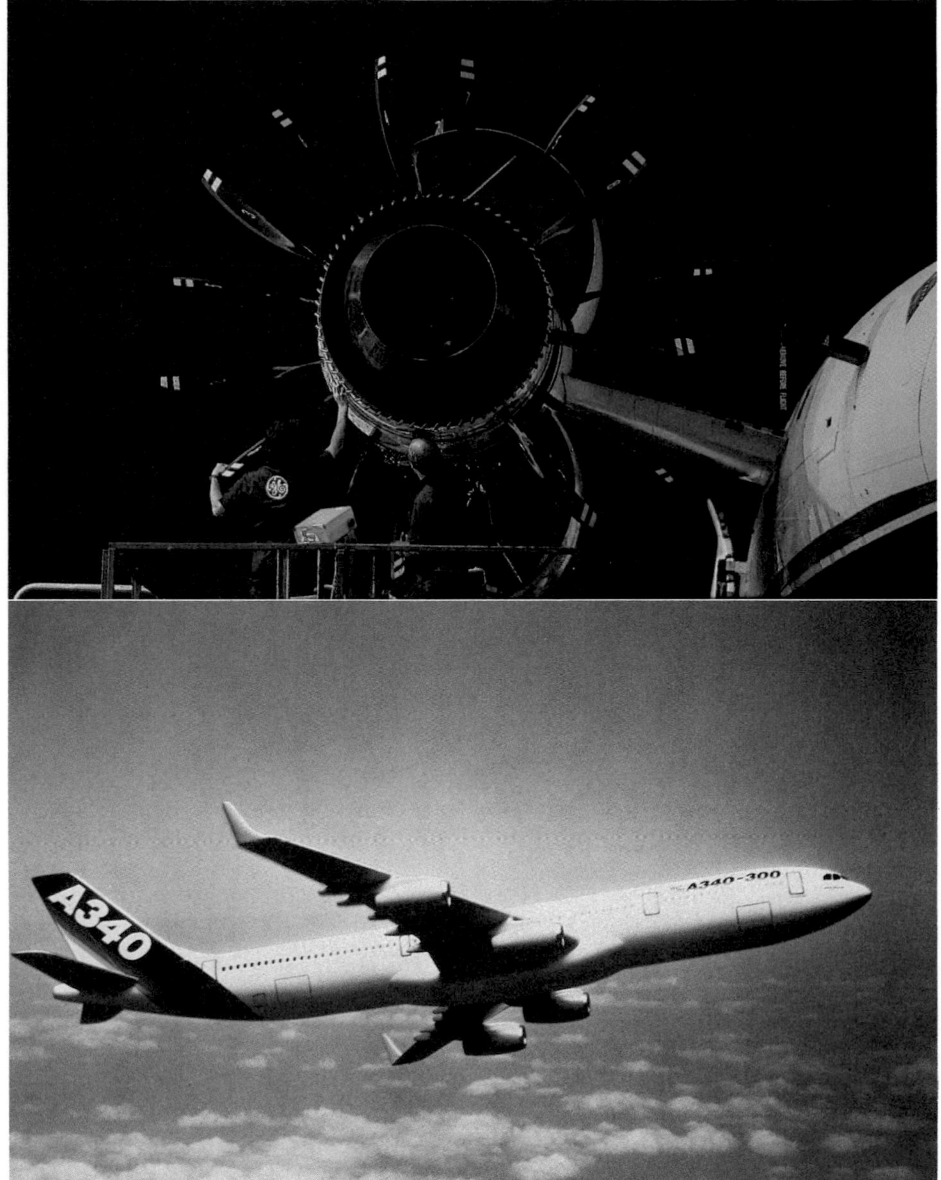

To see how GE's *not* having strategic planners helped it put its engine in this commercial jet and what it means for many U.S. firms, see the text

permanently in Cell 2 or 3. If the problem is solved, the result can be success (Cell 1); if not, it is failure (Cell 4).[4]

In 1965 Domino's Pizza looked like a total failure (Cell 4). But when Tom Monaghan regained control of the company, minor changes in plans and major efforts in implementation made it today's success. P&G lost millions on its soft-cookie line. Although the implementation appeared strong in terms of its promotion and distribution, the question of basic consumer demand, a fundamental planning and strategy issue, probably placed the product in Cell 2. In 1987 the product line was failing (Cell 4), so P&G dropped it.

INCREASING EMPHASIS ON MARKETING IMPLEMENTATION

In the 1980's, the great importance of the role of the implementation phase of the strategic marketing process has emerged in American corporations. What often happened in the past was that the firm's strategic planners from its corporate staff designed plans that were imposed on the firm's line managers and personnel to implement. The predictable result was near disaster for many firms in the "us versus them" confrontations—staff planners versus line operating personnel.

Like many restructured and downsized American corporations, GE has done away with hundreds of planning jobs. Although planners had some successes at GE, chairman John F. Welch, Jr., is trying to make line managers both planners and doers (see the Marketing Action Memo). In fact, the head of GE's aircraft engine business says that the quick development of a more powerful fan to upgrade a midsize jet engine was possible only because of a reduction in the

MARKETING·ACTION·MEMO

GENERAL ELECTRIC'S MANAGER OF THE 1990'S: IMPLEMENT A VISION IN A LEAN ORGANIZATION

Because GE is the most diversified company in America, it has a significant effect on American management style. In fact, as GE's management techniques change in one decade, so do those in corporate America a few years later. GE decentralized into profit centers in the 1950's and installed a huge staff of corporate strategic planners in the early 1970's. Thousands of American companies followed suit.

GE Appliance Group planners correctly predicted the large-scale entry of Japanese appliances into U.S. markets in the 1980's. But GE planners misread the 1970's energy crunch and sent GE into a crash program to improve refrigerator insulation when it should have redesigned its refrigerator compressors—a far better way than insulation to improve energy efficiency.

When John F. Welch, Jr., was named chairman of GE, he drastically reduced the size of the corporate strategic planning units because they were too costly, spent too much time "meddling" and "nitpicking," and demanded reports that didn't lead to making and marketing better products. GE's line managers now do much of the strategic thinking and planning, with an emphasis on studying consumers and competitors.

What about the future? Welch is moving decision making and authority lower in the organization by making line managers both planners and doers and is promoting teamwork through candor and trust. According to *Business Week* magazine, Welch knows what he wants in a future GE manager. He or she must be able to develop a vision of what their unit is to become, gain an acceptance of the vision through effective communication, and then "relentlessly drive implementation of that vision to a successful conclusion."

Many experts think this GE strategy, which emphasizes implementation, will become standard in American companies of the 1990's.

Sources: "Jack Welch: How Good a Manager?" *Business Week* (December 14, 1987), pp. 92-103; Thomas Moore, "Goodbye, Corporate Staff," *Fortune* (December 21, 1987), pp. 65-76; "The New Breed of Strategic Planner," *Business Week* (September 17, 1984), pp. 62-68.

number of staff planners, which eliminated multiple layers of review; this enabled GE to beat out an international consortium led by Pratt & Whitney and win $1 billion in new orders, including those for the Airbus 340 wide-body commercial jet.[5]

IMPROVING IMPLEMENTATION OF MARKETING PROGRAMS

No magic formula exists to guarantee effective implementation of marketing plans. In fact, the answer seems to be equal parts of good management, moving decisions as far down the organization as possible, attention to detail, and plain common sense. However, some guidelines can be identified.

Communicate Goals and the Means of Achieving Them to the Doers Those called on to implement plans need to understand both the goals sought and how they are to be accomplished. Everyone in Domino's Pizza—from Tom Monaghan to telephone order takers, make-line people, and drivers—is clear on what the firm's goal is: to deliver tasty, hot pizzas within 30 minutes to homes of customers who order them by telephone. All Domino's personnel are trained in detail to perform their respective jobs to help achieve that goal.

Have a Responsible Program Champion Willing to Act Successful high-technology programs, such as IBM's PC and Cray Research's supercomputers, almost always have a **product or program champion** who is able and willing to cut red tape and move the program forward. Such people often have the uncanny ability to move back and forth between big-picture strategy questions and specific details when the situation calls for it. This program champion idea applies to the successful implementation of marketing plans, but the title varies with the firm and position. For Domino's Pizza this person in day-to-day operations is the franchise owner who is running the restaurant, whereas for Sara Lee Corporation it might be the product manager responsible for Chef Pierre pies. Diffused responsibility in marketing programs at best can mean important delays and at worst can result in disaster when team members don't know who is responsible for decisions.

Have Doers Benefit Personally from Successful Program Implementation People work best when they have a clear goal. When the organization's goal and their own personal goal are consistent or the same, they have maximum incentive to see a program implemented successfully because they have personal ownership and a stake in that success. This also means employees are more willing to jump into critical situations and perform tasks that are "below" them or not in their job descriptions. Drivers delivering Domino's pizza take their job seriously—because it may lead directly to their owning a franchise in a few years.

Take Action and Avoid "Paralysis by Analysis" In their book *In Search of Excellence,* Thomas J. Peters and Robert H. Waterman, Jr., warn against paralysis by analysis, the tendency to excessively analyze a problem instead of taking action. To overcome this pitfall, they call for a "bias for action" and recommend a "do it, fix it, try it" approach.[6] They conclude that perfectionists finish last, so getting 90 percent perfection and letting the marketplace help in the fine tuning makes good sense in implementation.

Lockheed Aircraft's Skunk Works got its name from the comic strip *L'il Abner* and its legendary reputation from achieving superhuman technical feats with a low budget, ridiculously short deadlines, and only 7 percent to 25 percent of the people used on comparable aircraft industry programs. Under the leadership of Kelly Johnson, in 35 years the Skunk Works has turned out the first American jet airplane (the P-80), the highest flying reconnaissance plane (the U-2), and today's fastest jet (the SR-71). Called out of retirement to work on the nation's most invisible aircraft (the Stealth), Johnson restated two of his basic tenets: (1) make decisions promptly and (2) avoid paralysis by analysis. In fact, one U.S. Air Force audit showed that Johnson's Skunk Works could carry out a program on schedule with 126 people, whereas a competitor on a comparable program was behind schedule with 3,750 people.[7]

Program champions are notoriously brash in overcoming organizational hurdles. The U.S. Navy's Admiral Grace Murray Hopper not only gave the world the COBOL computer language but also the word "bug"—meaning any glitch in a computer or computer program. Probably more important is this program champion's famous advice for moving decisions to actions by cutting through an organization's red tape: "Better to ask forgiveness than permission." Using this strategy, 3M's Art Fry championed Post-it notes to success, an idea he got while looking for a simple way to mark his hymnal while singing in his church choir.

Foster Open Communication to Surface the Problems Bugs and glitches aren't limited to computer programs. Both technical and marketing programs have them too, but success often lies in fostering a work environment that is open enough so doers are willing to speak out when they see problems without fear of recrimination. The focus is placed on trying to solve the problem as a group rather than finding someone to blame. Solutions are solicited from anyone who has a creative idea to suggest—from the janitor to the president—without regard to status or rank in the organization.

Two more Kelly Johnson axioms from Lockheed's Skunk Works apply here: (1) when trouble develops, surface the problem immediately, and (2) get help; don't keep the problem to yourself. This latter point is important even if it means getting ideas from competitors.

Ford's Taurus and Sable models were 2 of the rare successes of American car producers in the 1980's. Ford put $3 billion into this new car project and decided to throw out its old idea of running the project in sequence from design to engineering to manufacturing and so on. Instead, Ford formed a team composed of all the groups, which worked together simultaneously to come up with the design. Ideas used came from detailed surveys filled out by people ranging from consumers (they suggested having a net in the trunk to hold grocery bags upright) to production workers (they suggested that all bolts used have the same size head so workers wouldn't have to hunt to find the right wrench). Ford employees suggested more than 1,400 improvements[8] (see Chapter 9). This team approach broke down communication barriers and speeded up problem recognition and decisions. It also used a system "borrowed" from Japanese car

FORD'S NEW DESIGN PHILOSOPHY:
TO ANSWER YOUR NEEDS
BY LISTENING TO
WHAT YOU WANT.
FORD TAURUS.
THE GOAL WAS TO BE BEST IN CLASS.
Even as the first designer or engineer began work, over 400 specific objectives were being established for Taurus.
The list was based on how you drive an automobile...what you want from it...what you need from it. The list included: How comfortable the seat belts are to wear; the effort required to open and close the doors; the ease with which the heater controls should work; the convenience of checking the oil.
The idea was this: If we design each part, assembly and feature to make the car better to use, then we will have designed a better vehicle overall.
THE RESULT IS TAURUS. MOTOR TREND CAR OF THE YEAR.
Motor Trend's Car of the Year award offers proof that Taurus' philosophy works. It is a front-wheel-drive sedan that is responsive and rewarding to drive. A unique sedan where design and engineering come together in one functional unit.
CONSIDER THE SHAPE.
Even the shape of Taurus is designed to help it work better. The shape manages the flow of air to help press the tires to the pavement for positive road holding. The flush-fitting side windows not only contribute to the overall integrity of the design, but reduce wind noise as well.
Taurus. Even the shape is part of its dedication to function. So you can judge it not only by how good it looks, but how well it works.
Ford

For the unusual way Ford developed its winning Taurus, see the text

manufacturers, showing that Ford has tried to avoid the "NIH syndrome"—the reluctance to accept ideas "not invented here," or not originated inside one's own firm.[9]

Schedule Precise Tasks, Responsibilities, and Deadlines Successful implementation requires that people know the tasks for which they are responsible and the deadline for completing them. With Domino's Pizza's drivers, their task (deliver a hot pizza) and deadline (within 30 minutes from the telephone order) are very clear.

To implement the thousands of tasks on an orbiting satellite, GE's Aerospace Group typically holds weekly program meetings. The outcome of each of these meetings is an **action item list** that has three columns: (1) the task, (2) the name of the person responsible for accomplishing that task, and (3) the date by which the task is to be finished. Within hours of completing a program meeting, the action item list is circulated to those attending. This then serves as the starting agenda for the next meeting. Meeting minutes are viewed as secondary and backward looking. Action item lists are forward looking, clarify the targets, and put strong pressure on people to achieve their designated tasks by the deadline.

Related to the action item lists are formal *program schedules,* which show the relationships through time of the various program tasks. Starting with the design of the Polaris submarines in the 1950's, computer-based scheduling techniques such as PERT (Program Evaluation and Review Technique) developed in defense programs became very complex. However, simplified software programs based on these techniques are now available for PCs.

Scheduling an action program involves (1) identifying the main tasks, (2) determining the time required to complete each, (3) arranging the activities to meet the deadline, and (4) assigning responsibilities to complete each task.

Suppose, for example, that you and two friends are asked to do a term project on the problem, "How can the college increase attendance at its performing arts concerts?"[10] And suppose further that the instructor limits the project in the following ways:

1. The project must involve a mail survey of the attitudes of a sample of students.
2. The term paper with the survey results must be submitted by the end of the 11-week quarter.

To begin the assignment, you need to identify all the project tasks and then estimate the time you can reasonably allot to each one. As shown in Figure 20-3, it would take 15 weeks to complete the project if you did all the tasks sequentially; so to complete it in 11 weeks, your team must work on different parts at the same time, and some activities must be independent enough to overlap. This requires specialization and cooperation. Suppose that of the three of you (A, B, and C), only Student C can type. Then you (Student A) might assume the task of constructing the questionnaire and selecting samples, and Student B might tabulate the data. This division of labor allows each student to concentrate on and become expert in one area, but you should also cooperate. Student C might help A and B in the beginning, and A and B might help C later on.

You must also figure out which activities can be done concurrently to save time. In Figure 20-3 you can see that Task 2 must be completed before Task 4. However, Task 3 might easily be done before, at the same time as, or after Task 2. Task 3 is independent of Task 2.

Scheduling production and marketing activities—from a term project to a new product rollout to a manned space launch—can be done efficiently with

FIGURE 20-3
Tasks in completing a term project

Shown below are the tasks you might face as a member of a student team to complete a marketing research study using a mail questionnaire. Elapsed time to complete all the tasks is 15 weeks. How do you finish the project in an 11-week quarter? For an answer, see the text.

TASK	TIME (WEEKS)
1. Construct and test a rough-draft questionnaire for clarity (in person, not by mail) on friends.	2
2. Type and mimeograph a final questionnaire.	2
3. Randomly select the names of 200 students from the school directory.	1
4. Address and stamp envelopes; mail questionnaires.	1
5. Collect returned questionnaires.	3
6. Tabulate and analyze data from returned questionnaires.	2
7. Write final report.	3
8. Type and submit final report.	1
TOTAL TIME NECESSARY TO COMPLETE ALL ACTIVITIES	15

Source: Adapted from William Rudelius and W. Bruce Erickson, *An Introduction to Contemporary Business*, 4th ed. (New York: Harcourt Brace Jovanovich, Inc., 1985), p. 94.

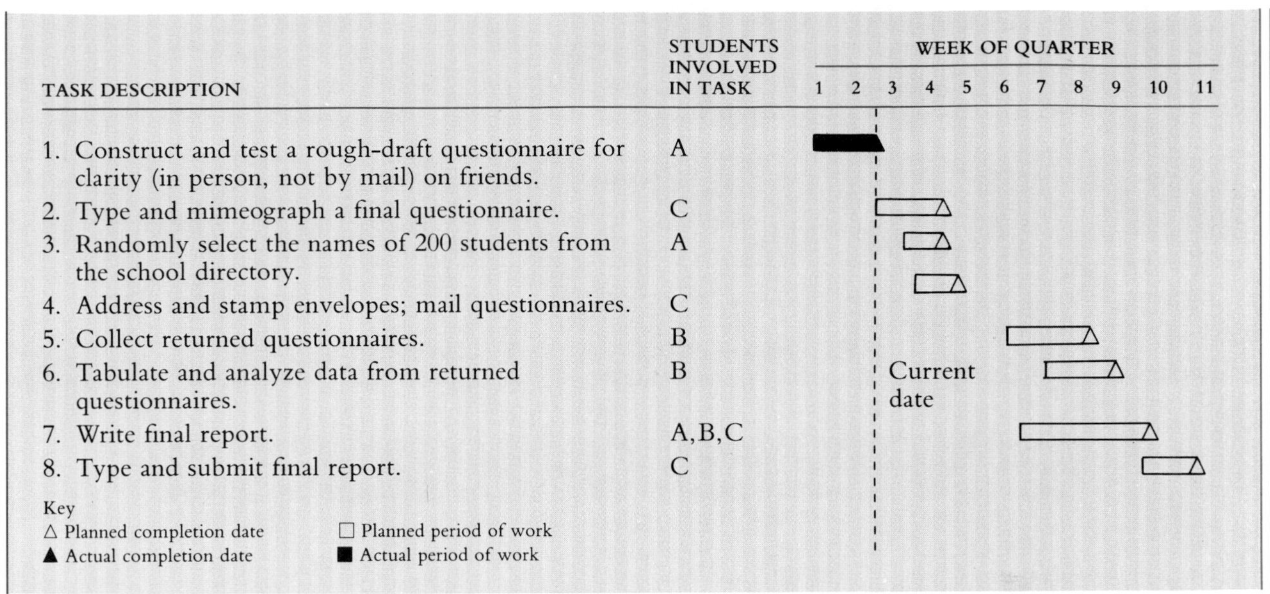

Source: Adapted from William Rudelius and W. Bruce Erickson, *An Introduction to Contemporary Business,* 4th ed. (New York: Harcourt Brace Jovanovich, Inc., 1985), p. 95.

FIGURE 20-4
Gantt chart for scheduling the term project

Gantt charts. Figure 20-4 shows one variation of a Gantt chart used to schedule the class project, demonstrating how the concurrent work on several tasks enables the students to finish the project on time. Developed by Henry L. Gantt, this method is the basis for the scheduling techniques used today, including elaborate computerized methods. The key to all scheduling techniques is to distinguish tasks that *must* be done sequentially from those which *can* be done concurrently. As in the case of the term project, scheduling tasks concurrently often reduces the total time required for a project. Also, as in the case of Ford's Taurus discussed earlier in the chapter, Ford revolutionized its development of a new design by concurrently—rather than sequentially—involving the different groups needing to be involved. This not only reduced development time but also avoided problems by improving communications.

Scheduling any action program (1) translates plans into specific, understandable tasks, (2) forces planners to distinguish sequential from concurrent tasks, reducing the time to implement the program, and (3) forces people to take responsibility for specific tasks and allot time to them. Otherwise, they tend to concentrate on the tasks they prefer and neglect the others.

CONCEPT CHECK

1 **Why does GE want the "doers" to do its planning?**

2 **What is the meaning and importance of a program champion?**

3 **What is the difference in scheduling sequential versus concurrent tasks?**

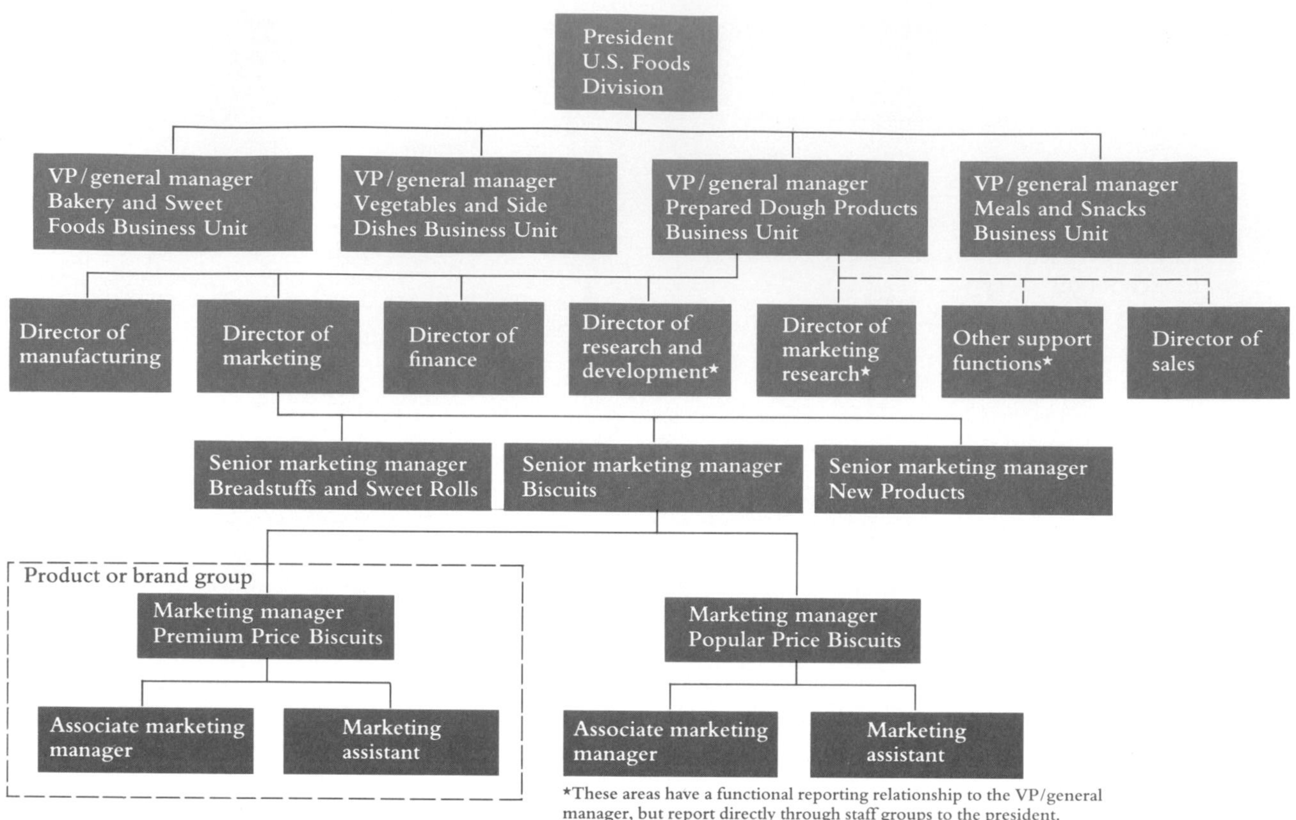

FIGURE 20-5
Organization of the Pillsbury Company's U.S. Foods Division

ORGANIZING FOR MARKETING

A marketing organization is needed to implement the firm's marketing plans. Basic issues in today's marketing organizations include understanding (1) how line versus staff positions and divisional groupings interrelate to form a cohesive marketing organization and (2) the role of the product manager.

Line versus Staff and Divisional Groupings Although simplified, Figure 20-5 shows the organization of Pillsbury's Prepared Dough Products Business Unit in detail and highlights the distinction between line and staff positions in marketing. People in **line positions,** such as group marketing managers, have the authority and responsibility to issue orders to the people who report to them, such as marketing managers. In this organizational chart, line positions are connected with solid lines. Those in **staff positions** (shown by dotted lines) have the authority and responsibility to advise people in line positions but cannot issue direct orders to them. For example, the directors of R&D, marketing research, and sales advise the vice-president/general manager of the Prepared Dough Products Business Unit but do not report directly to him or her. Instead, they report directly to other vice-presidents (not shown in this organizational chart) who issue them orders.

Products from Pillsbury's line of prepared dough products

Most marketing organizations use divisional groupings—such as product line, functional, and geographical—to implement plans and achieve their organizational objectives (discussed in Chapter 18). All appear in some form in Pillsbury's organizational chart in Figure 20-5. At the top of its organization, Pillsbury organizes by **product line groupings,** in which a unit is subdivided according to offerings for which it is responsible. For example, the entire company is first divided into four broad product line groupings. In addition to the U.S. Foods Division shown in Figure 20-5 are three other divisions not shown: Restaurant (including Burger King, Bennigan's, and Steak & Ale), International, and Growth and Technology. Heads of these four divisions, which are divided by product line groupings, report to Pillsbury's chief executive officer (not shown in Figure 20-5).

The U.S. Foods Division in turn has four main product lines: Bakery & Sweet Foods; Vegetables & Side Dishes; Prepared Dough Products; and Meals & Snacks. These product line groupings reflect a 1985 Pillsbury reorganization that grouped products by the way consumers think about them, rather than by the previously used sales-oriented distribution systems (Dry Grocery; Frozen; and Refrigerated Foods).

The Prepared Dough Products Business Unit is organized by **functional groupings** such as manufacturing, marketing, and finance, which are the different business activities within a firm.

Pillsbury uses **geographical groupings** for its more than 500 field sales representatives throughout the United States. Each director of sales has several regional sales managers reporting to him or her, such as Western, Southern, and so on. These, in turn, have district managers reporting to them (although for simplicity these are not shown in the chart).

Role of the Product Manager The key person in the product or brand group shown in Figure 20-5 is the manager who heads it. As mentioned in Chapter 10, this person is often called the *product manager* or *brand manager,* but in Pillsbury he or she carries the title *marketing manager.* This person and the assistants in the product group are the basic building blocks in the marketing department of most consumer and industrial product firms. The function of a product manager is to plan, implement, and control the annual and long-range plans for the products for which he or she is responsible. This responsibility includes six primary tasks[11]:

1. Developing long-range competitive strategies for the product that will achieve target sales, profit, and market share objectives
2. Preparing annual marketing plans, sales forecasts, and budgets
3. Working with advertising agencies to develop advertising appeals, copy, and campaigns
4. Developing support for the product from the firm's salesforce and distributors
5. Gathering continuous marketing research information on customers, noncustomers, dealers, competitors, the product's performance, and new opportunities and problems
6. Finding ways to improve the existing products and create new ones

Although these six functions are common to both consumer product and industrial product managers, some important differences exist. Consumer product managers are typically responsible for fewer products and spend more time working with marketing people inside their firm (marketing research, packaging design, and sales) and outside it (advertising agencies and distributors). In contrast, industrial product managers like those in Intel who are responsible for integrated circuit chips usually have more products and spend more time working with technical personnel in the firm's engineering, production, and R&D departments and in talking directly to sales representatives and important customers.[12]

There are both benefits and dangers to the product manager system used by many consumer product and industrial product companies. On the positive side, product managers become strong advocates for the assigned products. This means they (1) can react quickly to problems or changes in the marketplace and cut red tape to work with people in various functions both inside and outside the organization (Figure 20-6); (2) can orchestrate and balance both marketing and nonmarketing activities; and (3) can assume profit-and-loss responsibility for the performance of the product line.

Balanced against these benefits are some potential dangers that all relate to one factor: even though product managers have major responsibilities, they have relatively little direct authority. Product managers, responsible for one or more products, typically have two people reporting to them at most—often less in industrial product manager positions. However, all the other groups and func-

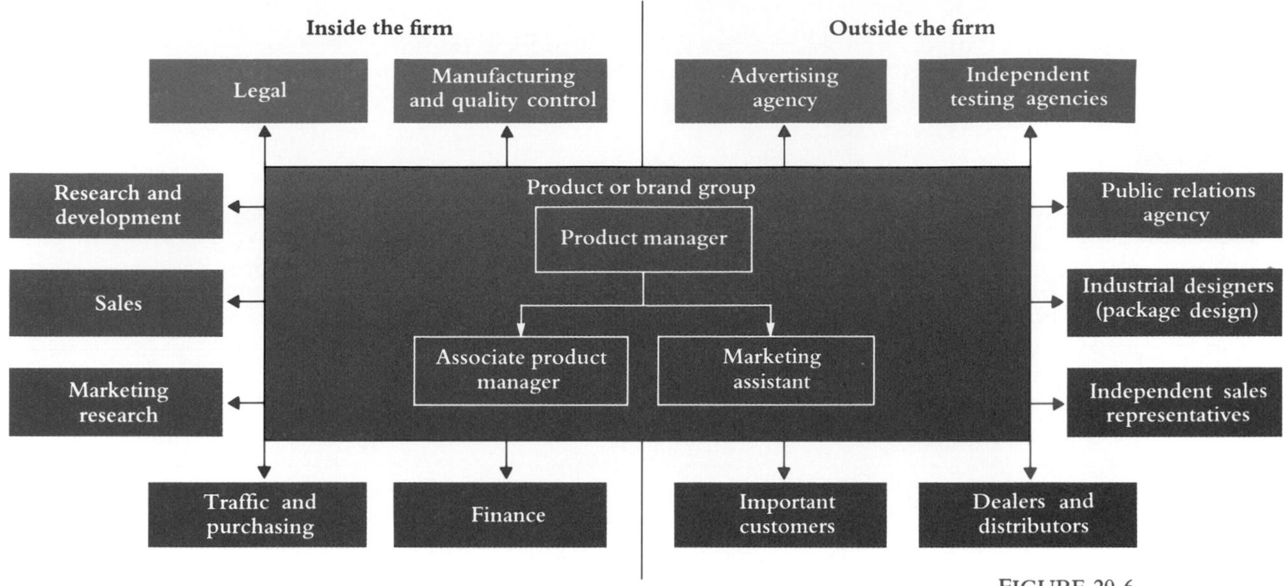

FIGURE 20-6
Units with which the product manager and product group work

tions shown in Figure 20-6 must be coordinated and used to meet the product's goals.

To accomplish this coordination, product managers must use persuasion rather than orders and often become concerned with immediate results rather than long-term performance of their products because promotions or transfers to other products may take place after a couple of years on the job.[13]

CONCEPT CHECK

1 What is the difference between a line and a staff position in a marketing organization?

2 What are three groupings used within a typical marketing organization?

THE CONTROL PHASE OF THE STRATEGIC MARKETING PROCESS

The essence of control, the final phase of the strategic marketing process, is comparing results with planned goals for the marketing program and taking necessary actions.

THE MARKETING CONTROL PROCESS

Ideally, quantified goals come into the control phase from the marketing plans developed in the planning phase and meet the measured results of the marketing

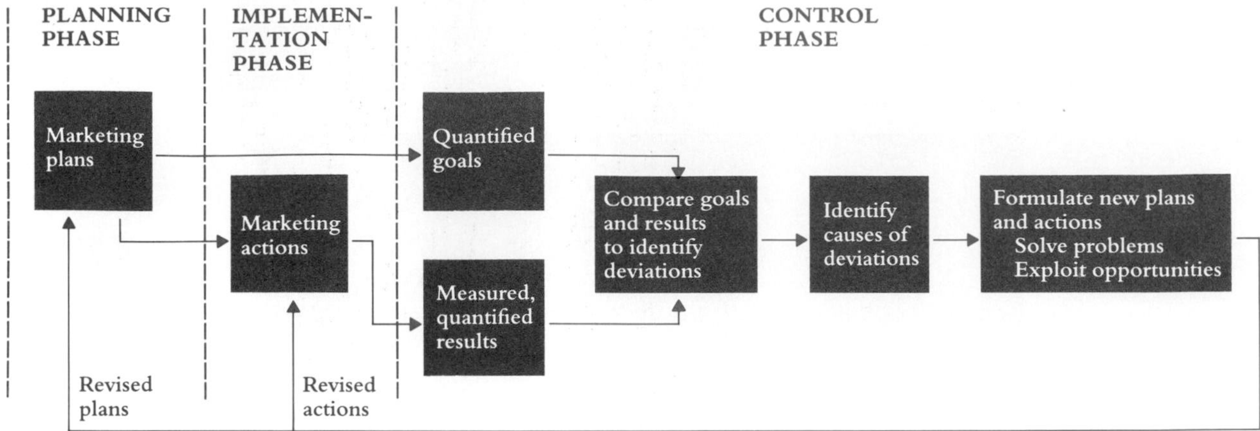

FIGURE 20-7
The control phase of the strategic marketing process

actions taken in the implementation phase (Figure 20-7). A marketing manager then uses *management by exception,* which means identifying results that deviate from plans to diagnose their causes and take new actions. Often results fall short of plans, and a corrective action is needed. At other times the comparison shows that performance is far better than anticipated, in which case the marketing manager tries to identify the reason and move quickly to exploit the unexpected opportunity.

Marketing control is an especially difficult and important problem in today's corporations with many divisions carrying diverse products and services among which scarce resources must be deployed. Sometimes controls are inadequate, and divisions are sold off. This was the case with Allegis Corporation—which sought to become a full-service travel company by combining Hilton International and Westin premium hotel chains, Hertz Car Rental, and United Airlines. However, the concept was never controlled adequately, all but United Airlines were sold off, and the company was renamed UAL Corporation in mid-1988.

Measuring Results Without some quantitative goal, no benchmark exists with which to compare actual results. Manufacturers of both consumer and industrial products are increasingly trying to develop marketing programs that have not only specific action programs but also specific procedures for monitoring and measuring them. For example, computer analysis of scanner data from UPC markings now enables a retailer to recognise "hot" sales items quickly.[14]

Taking Marketing Actions When results deviate significantly from plans, some kind of action is essential. Levi Strauss discovered that consumer tastes in the 1980's were shifting from jeans to more fashionable clothes. As a result, it took decisive actions: it increased its local advertising budgets dramatically, offered retailers volume discounts for the first time in history, sold through Sears and J.C. Penney (thereby alienating some of its smaller retailers, who dropped the Levi's line), and closed nine plants. To stay in touch with retail trends, Levi Strauss affixes UPC-bar-code labels to each product at its factory, which enables it to spot new sales trends quickly.[15]

SALES ANALYSIS

For controlling marketing programs, **sales analysis**—using the firm's sales records to compare actual results with sales goals and identify areas of strength and weakness—is critical. All the variables that might be used in the market segmentation may be broken down in sales component analysis. **Sales component analysis,** also called microsales analysis, traces sales revenues to their sources such as specific products, sales territories, or customers. Common breakdowns include:

- Customer characteristics: demographics. Standard Industrial Classification, size, reason for purchase, and type of reseller (retailer or wholesaler)
- Product characteristics: model, package size, and color
- Geographical region: sales territory, city, state, and region
- Order size
- Price or discount class
- Commission to the sales representative

Today's computers can easily produce these breakdowns, provided the input data contain these classifications. Therefore it is critical that marketing managers request the breakdowns they require from accounting and information systems departments.

The danger is that marketing managers or chief executive officers are so overwhelmed by the volume of computerized reports that they can't spot the key performance numbers in the report needed for control and subsequent action. Each Tuesday, Ken Iverson, sitting in a small town in South Carolina, carefully inputs into the computer numbers on the tons of steel each of Nucor's divisions produced the previous week. What makes the situation unique is that Iverson is chief executive officer of Nucor, whose efficient "minimills" have revolutionized American steel production and distribution. Although Nucor's "no frills" operation is lean (17 people, counting secretaries, in the corporate headquarters of an $800-million-a-year company), saving money is *not* the reason he does his own computer inputting. His explanation, "By keying in the numbers, you're forced to look at every figure for every week. That's the value."[16]

PROFITABILITY ANALYSIS

To their surprise, marketing managers often discover the 80/20 principle (see Chapter 14) the hard way, on the job. **Profitability analysis** enables the manager to measure the profitability of the firm's products, customer groups, sales territories, channels of distribution, and even order sizes. This leads to decisions to expand, maintain, reduce, or eliminate specific products, customer groups, or channels.[17]

For example, following the 80/20 principle, a marketing manager will try to find the common characteristics among the 20 percent of the customers (or products, brands, sales districts, salespeople, or kinds of orders) that are generating 80 percent (or the bulk) of revenues and profits to find more like them to exploit competitive advantages. Conversely, the 80 percent of customers, products, brands, and so on that are generating few revenues and profits may need to be reduced or even dropped entirely unless a way is found to make them profitable.

	E. MARTIN		J. TAYLOR		W. JONES		DISTRICT TOTALS	
	DOLLARS (THOUSANDS)	PERCENT	DOLLARS (THOUSANDS)	PERCENT	DOLLARS (THOUSANDS)	PERCENT	DOLLARS (THOUSANDS)	PERCENT
Sales	$ 2200	100%	$ 2500	100%	$ 2000	100%	$ 6700	100%
Cost of goods sold	1721	78.23	1887	75.48	1543	77.15	5151	76.88
Contribution margin	479	21.77	613	24.52	457	22.85	1549	23.12
Account costs								
Freight	63	2.86	65	2.60	60	3.00	188	2.80
Inventory	44	2.00	30	1.20	39	1.95	113	1.69
Accounts receivable	64	2.91	75	3.00	59	2.95	198	2.96
Technical services	18	0.82	18	0.72	17	0.85	53	0.79
Advertising and promotion	21	0.96	35	1.40	18	0.90	74	1.10
TOTAL CUSTOMER COSTS	$ 210	9.55%	$ 223	8.92%	$ 193	9.65%	$ 626	9.34%
Personal selling costs								
Compensation	$ 31.50	1.43%	$ 33.00	1.32%	$ 29.90	1.50%	$ 94.40	1.41%
Transportation	6.00	0.27	5.00	0.20	7.00	0.35	18.00	0.27
Lodging, meals	3.50	0.16	3.50	0.14	4.00	0.20	11.00	0.16
Telephone	1.35	0.06	1.70	0.07	1.20	0.06	4.25	0.06
Entertainment	3.00	0.14	1.00	0.04	2.50	0.12	6.50	0.10
Samples, brochures	2.00	0.09	2.00	0.08	1.50	0.07	5.50	0.08
Miscellaneous	0.50	0.02	0.50	0.02	0.30	0.02	1.30	0.02
TOTAL PERSONAL SELLING COSTS	$ 47.85	2.17%	$ 46.70	1.87%	$ 46.40	2.32%	$140.95	2.10%
Net territory contribution	$221.15	10.05%	$343.30	13.73%	$217.60	10.88%	$782.05	11.67%

Source: Reprinted by permission of the *Harvard Business Review*. An exhibit from "Computerized Sales Management" by G. David Hughes (March/April 1983).

FIGURE 20-8
Comparative income statement for three sales representatives and the total sales district

Profitability analysis provides the basis for such decisions. The type of profitability analysis discussed here is **contribution margin analysis,** which spotlights the behavior of controllable costs and indicates the contribution to profit of a specific marketing factor.

Figure 20-8 is an example of a contribution margin analysis of the comparative sales performance of three sales representatives who make up a sales district. The report, provided by a microcomputer, breaks the sales revenue, contribution margin, and personal selling costs down by sales territory to show the net contribution of each sales representative.

The separate costs for each sales representative are expressed as an **expense-to-sales ratio,** a form of ratio analysis in which a specific cost or expense is expressed as a percentage of sales revenue. This ratio reveals important deviations from the average for the total district. Sales representative Taylor clearly contributes the most to the district because sales revenues are higher and costs such as inventory, advertising, promotion, and entertainment are lower.[18]

THE MARKETING AUDIT

Both sales and profitability analyses like those just discussed have great value in the control phase of the strategic marketing process, but the focus on such analyses is usually quite narrow, such as monthly, quarterly, or annual deviations that address a specific product, customer segment, sales territory, or order size.

Often a broader marketing perspective is needed, one that covers a longer time horizon and relates the marketing mix factors to environmental, consumer, competitive, and industry variables. This is the role of a **marketing audit,** which is a comprehensive, unbiased, periodic review of the strategic marketing process of a firm or strategic business unit (SBU). The purpose of the marketing audit, which serves as both a planning and control technique, is to identify new problems and opportunities that warrant an action plan to improve performance.[19]

Most firms undertaking a marketing audit use a checklist such as that shown in Figure 20-9. Before deciding where the firm or SBU should go (the goal-setting step in the planning phase), the firm must determine where it is now through a situation analysis. The checklist used covers factors ranging from the marketing mix factors and customer profiles to markets and competitors.

For a meaningful, comprehensive marketing audit, the individual or team conducting the audit must have a free rein to talk to managers, employees, salespeople, distributors, and customers, as well as have access to all pertinent internal and external reports and memoranda. They need to involve top management and the doers in the process to ensure that resulting action recommendations have their support.

CONCEPT CHECK

1 **What two marketing variables are compared to control a marketing program?**

2 **What is the difference between a sales analysis and a profitability analysis?**

3 **What is a marketing audit?**

YOPLAIT YOGURT: IMPLEMENTATION AND CONTROL PHASES OF THE STRATEGIC MARKETING PROCESS

Having seen the planning phase of Yoplait Yogurt in Chapter 19, let's now look at its implementation and control phases.[20]

IMPLEMENTATION PHASE

After developing the marketing plans and strategies described in Chapter 19, Yoplait USA then had to implement them in detail. These details ranged from fine-tuning the target market and positioning to devising production capacity to mesh with the execution of marketing mix strategies.

Target Market Present and prospective yogurt eaters tend to be urban, upscale, and better educated. The Yoplait product manager went one step beyond

PRODUCTS/SERVICES: THE REASON FOR EXISTENCE

1. Is the product/service free from deadwood?
2. What is the life cycle stage?
3. How will user demands or trends affect you?
4. Are you a leader in new product innovation?
5. Are inexpensive methods used to estimate new product potentials before considerable amounts are spent on R&D and market introduction?
6. Do you have different quality levels for different markets?
7. Are packages/brochures effective salesmen for the products/services they present?
8. Do you present products/services in the most appealing colors (formats) for markets being served?
9. Are there features or benefits to exploit?
10. Is the level of customer service adequate?
11. How are quality and reliability viewed by customers?

CUSTOMER: USER PROFILES

1. Who is the current and potential customer?
2. Are there geographic aspects of use: regional, rural, urban?
3. Why do people buy the product/service; what motivates their preferences?
4. Who makes buying decisions; when, where?
5. What is the frequency and quantity of use?

MARKETS: WHERE PRODUCTS/SERVICES ARE SOLD

1. Have you identified and measured major segments?
2. Are small, potential market segments overlooked in trying to satisfy the majority?
3. Are the markets for the products/services expanding or declining?
4. Should different segments be developed; gaps in penetration?

COMPETITORS: THEIR INFLUENCE

1. Who are the principal competitors, how are they positioned, and where are they headed?
2. What are their market shares?
3. What features of competitors' products/services stand out?
4. Is the market easily entered or dominated?

PRICING: PROFITABILITY PLANNING

1. What are the objectives of current pricing policy: acquiring, defending, or expanding?
2. Are price policies set to produce volume or profit?
3. How does pricing compare with competition in similar levels of quality?
4. Does cost information show profitability of each item?
5. What is the history of price deals, discounts, and promotions?

FIGURE 20-9
Marketing audit questions

these demographics to cover psychographic segmentation as well, targeting early adopters who try new products and influence others.

Product Positioning The product team built on Yoplait's personality and its French origin to stress its differences and position it as a unique, high-quality product with fresh fruit. The team tried to generate consumer awareness and trial by differentiating Yoplait from its American competitors, which are mainly sundae style with fruit preserves on the bottom that have to be stirred up.

Manufacturing There was no sense promoting Yoplait if manufacturing couldn't produce enough to fill the distribution channels and get the product on supermarket shelves. General Mills has no other refrigerated products, so it had no applicable experience in producing and distributing a product such as yogurt. It started initial production in two plants.

Product Actions The team took maximum advantage of Yoplait's unique creamy texture, its popular taste, the fruit spread throughout the yogurt, and

6. Are middlemen making money from the line?
7. Can the product/service support advertising or promotion programs?
8. Will the manufacturing process require more volume?

MARKETING CHANNELS: SELLING PATHS
1. Does the system offer the best access to all target markets?
2. Do product/service characteristics require specials?
3. What is the most profitable type of presentation for each market: direct vs. reps, master distributors or dealers, etc.?
4. What are the trends in distribution methods?

SALES ADMINISTRATION: SELLING EFFICIENCY
1. Are customers getting coverage in proportion to their potential?
2. Are sales costs planned and controlled?
3. Does the compensation plan provide optimum incentive and security to reasonable cost?
4. Is performance measured against potential?
5. Are selling expenses proportionate to results and potentials within markets or territories?
6. Are there deficiencies in recruitment, selection, training, motivation, supervision, performance, promotion, or compensation?
7. Are effective selling aids and sales tools provided?

ADVERTISING: MEDIA PROGRAM
1. Are media objectives and strategies linked to the marketing plan?
2. What are the objectives of the ad program?
3. How is media effectiveness measured?
4. Is advertising integrated with promotion and sales activity?
5. Is the ad agency's effectiveness periodically evaluated?
6. Do you dictate copy theme and content to the agency?
7. Are you spending realistically, in relation to budget?

SALES PROMOTION: SALES INDUCEMENT
1. Does the sales promotion support a marketing objective?
2. Is it integrated with advertising and selling activity?
3. How is it measured for results?
4. Are slogans, trademarks, logos, and brands being used effectively?
5. Is point-of-sale material cost-effective?
6. Are you effectively using couponing, tie-ins, incentives, sampling, stuffers, combination offers?
7. How do you evaluate trade shows for effectiveness?

Source: Adapted from Hal W. Goetsch, "Conduct a Comprehensive Marketing Audit to Improve Marketing Planning," *Marketing News* (March 18, 1983), p. 14; by permission of the American Marketing Association.

its "100 percent natural" ingredients with no artificial sweeteners or preservatives. The team wanted to maintain its unique package shape and use 6-ounce containers (compared with 8 ounces from competitors) because research showed that 6 ounces is a good amount to eat at one sitting. It also used image-reinforcing packaging that stressed the product's origin with some French words.

Pricing Actions It was decided to set distributor margins to achieve a 41-cent price at the retail level.

Promotional Actions The Yoplait team initially used independent food brokers to sell its product. Gradually, it then augmented the regular General Mills grocery product salesforce to represent Yoplait.

The team developed advertising to enhance the image-building copy on its package. It positioned Yoplait as the yogurt of France, with the copy execution using Americans as presenters: TV personalities Jack Klugman and Loretta Swit and Los Angeles Dodgers manager Tommy Lasorda. (General Mills legend has

Yoplait Yogurt's product line, including the recently introduced Yoplait 150 and snack packs

it that Tommy Lasorda's TV commercial involved 37 takes—during which time he ate 37 cups of Yoplait.)

The media plan—directed at upscale early adopters—relied on nighttime television plus unconventional print vehicles: city magazines, *The Dial* (the Public Broadcasting System publication), *Psychology Today,* and *Cosmopolitan.* The pictures of the celebrities were carried into the print campaign for the product.

The Yoplait team was convinced that if it could get people to try Yoplait once, the product would sell itself. It devised a unique strategy to give away free samples to build both primary and selective demand and to gain free publicity. The team hired a fleet of refrigerated vans, dressed the servers in French outfits, and gave away free Yoplait packages downtown at noon on weekdays and at the beach on weekends. It had a French balloonist take reporters on a free balloon ride and give them free Yoplait samples, which resulted in tremendous amounts of publicity. The brand group devised the "50-kilometer bicycle challenge" and gave a semitrailer full of Yoplait away at the finish line to both participants and spectators.

Place Actions The salesforce worked closely with distributors to ensure Yoplait was profitable for them so it could achieve a stock turnover in supermarkets of 2.6 times a week. In terms of shelf position, the salesforce sought 4 feet in the dairy sections (25 percent of that normally allotted to yogurt), the second or third shelf in horizontal sections, and a position near other premium brands.

Marketing Organization The initial marketing organization was a bare-bones product management team containing only five people: President Steven Rothschild, a marketing vice-president, and a brand group consisting of a product manager, an assistant product manager, and a marketing assistant.

CONTROL PHASE

Implementation activity is one thing and market performance another. Did the execution work?

Measured Results After only 3 years, Yoplait was in national distribution, had a 13.2 percent market share, and was the second best-selling yogurt, behind Dannon. After 6 years it had a 21.7 percent market share of retail sales and $135 million in annual sales—exceeding its original goals. Yoplait also achieved its 25 percent ROI target.

Resulting Actions The Yoplait team concluded that after 3 years it had attracted new consumers to yogurt and had contributed substantially to growth of the entire product class. It created an entirely new yogurt segment, the creamy French style. To continue growth, it introduced new flavors and an 18-ounce package.

One of the original objectives was to become a multiproduct business. Soon after Yoplait was acquired, the team set up a new business group that screened over 100 new product ideas. Looking at market segmentation, the group realized that it had created the creamy segment, but that four fifths of the market was still the thick yogurt—sundae and Swiss style—segments. By 1984 Yoplait carefully developed new products targeted at two other bases of segmentation:

1. Texture segmentation. Yoplait introduced custard-style yogurt to compete with thick yogurts.
2. Texture and usage segmentation. Yoplait added its Breakfast Yogurt, creamy yogurt with nuts, fruit, and grains.

In the process Yoplait grew rapidly to four brand groups.

Yoplait Yogurt Today Buoyed by Yoplait's success, new people added to the team apparently watched as national brands (such as Dannon and Kraft) and regional brands attacked. Although number 2 nationally, Yoplait's market share and profit fell. Its Fruit-on-the-Bottom line failed. Steven Rothschild, promoted now to president of General Mills' Convenience and International Food Group, commented, "Our offering wasn't unique enough, and implementation wasn't up to standards." He pulled Fruit-on-the-Bottom off the market in 1986. In response to extensive marketing research studies, a revitalized Yoplait took some important corrective actions in 1986 and 1987[21]:

1. Reformulated the entire Original Yoplait yogurt line to give it a thicker creamier texture

2. Introduced new Yoplait 150, a low-calorie fruit yogurt targeted at the health-conscious and weight-conscious segments
3. Developed a bold new advertising campaign ("Yoplait—taste how good yogurt should be") that featured TV personalities like Allyce Beasley ("Moonlighting") and Phylicia Rashad ("The Cosby Show")

By the end of 1987, sales, profit, and market share were significantly better. Yoplait Yogurt appeared under control again.

SUMMARY

1 The implementation phase of the strategic marketing process is concerned with executing the marketing program developed in the planning phase. Successful marketing programs require both effective planning and effective implementation.

2 Today successful marketing implementation has high priority in many firms. Keys to this include communicating both goals and means to doers: finding a program champion; having doers benefit from success; acting rather than overanalyzing; fostering open communications to surface problems; and scheduling precise tasks, responsibilities, and deadlines.

3 Essential to good scheduling is separating tasks that can be done concurrently from those which must be done sequentially. Gantt charts are a simple, effective means of scheduling.

4 Organizing marketing activities necessitates recognition of two different aspects of an organization: (1) line and staff positions and (2) product line, functional, and geographical groupings.

5 The product manager performs a vital marketing role in both consumer and industrial product firms, interacting with numerous people and groups both inside and outside the firm.

6 In many consumer product organizations the product manager heads up a product or brand group. A product manager has important responsibilities in being an advocate for the product line but often suffers from a lack of direct authority to get things done.

7 The control phase of the strategic marketing process involves measuring the results of the actions from the implementation phase and comparing them with goals set in the planning phase. Deviations are identified, and necessary actions are taken to correct deficiencies and exploit opportunities.

8 To control marketing programs, sales analyses, profitability analyses, and marketing audits are used.

Key Terms and Concepts

product or program champion p. 553
action item list p. 555
line positions p. 558
staff positions p. 558
product line groupings p. 559
functional groupings p. 559
geographical groupings p. 559
sales analysis p. 563
sales component analysis p. 563
profitability analysis p. 563
contribution margin analysis p. 564
expense-to-sales ratio p. 564
marketing audit p. 565

Chapter Problems and Applications

1 After first selecting sites for his Domino's Pizza restaurants near college campuses, Tom Monaghan also located them near military bases. Why? What implementation problems are (a) similar and (b) different for restaurants near a college campus versus a military base?
2 What is the "offering" to a Domino's Pizza customer? What needs to be measured to see the offering is satisfactory to customers and under control?
3 A common theme among managers who succeed repeatedly in program implementation is fostering open communication. Why is this so important?
4 Parts of Tasks 6 and 7 in Figure 20-4 are done *both* concurrently and sequentially. How can this be? How does it help the students meet the term paper deadline?
5 In Pillsbury's organizational chart in Figure 20-5, where do product line, functional, and geographical groupings occur?
6 In what way can a product manager in a grocery products firm have *both* (a) great responsibility and (b) limited authority?
7 Why are quantified goals in the planning phase of the strategic marketing process important for the control phase?
8 In Figure 20-8, which sales representative makes the least net territory contribution to the sales district? Why?
9 Before Pillsbury's 1985 reorganization, shown in Figure 20-5, the four units headed by vice-presidents / general managers were vegetables, refrigerated business, entrées business, and frozen vegetables business. Where would Totino's Pizza, Green Giant canned corn, Green Giant frozen peas, and Van de Kamp's frozen dinners fit in the old and new organizations? What are the advantages and disadvantages of the old and new organizations?

Suggested Readings

Thomas J. Peters and Robert H. Waterman, Jr., *In Search of Excellence: Lessons from America's Best-Run Companies* (New York: Harper & Row, Publishers, Inc., 1982). *The best-selling management book of the 1980's gives numerous examples of what well-managed American firms do to get that way.*

Arthur Rock, "Strategy vs. Tactics from a Venture Capitalist," *Harvard Business Review* (November-December, 1987), pp. 63-67. *In this article the man who provided early funding for firms such as Apple Computer and Intel says "good ideas and good products are a dime a dozen" and that "good execution and good management . . . are rare."*

Ellen Schultz, "America's Most Admired Corporations," *Fortune* (January 18, 1988), pp. 32-52. *Based on a poll of more than 8,000 top executives, the article describes leading firms in many industries and how many of them got there.*

Orville C. Walker, Jr. and Robert W. Ruekert, "Marketing's Role in the Implementation of Business Strategies: A Critical Review and Conceptual Framework," *Journal of Marketing* (July 1987), pp. 15-33. *This article gives ideas about the form of organizations and processes best suited to implement three different types of business unit strategies.*

PART SIX

EXPANDING MARKETING SETTINGS

Kellogg's
CORN
FLAKES
...avec le coq!
Le bon réflexe

21

International Marketing

After reading this chapter you should be able to:

Describe why U.S. firms are undertaking international marketing.

•

Contrast global and customized approaches to international marketing.

•

Understand the importance of environmental factors (political and legal, economic and cultural) in successful international marketing.

•

Identify alternative modes of entering international marketing operations.

•

Explain how and why U.S. firms may have to adapt their marketing mix when entering the international arena.

Kellogg's French Connection: Marketing Cold Corn Flakes Against Hot Croissants

Although Americans often eat some form of French croissants at almost any meal, the Kellogg Company has almost the reverse problem: selling its corn flakes and other cold cereals to French households for breakfast.

Kellogg's French subsidiary, Kellogg's P.A., is working hard to overcome long-time habits of French consumers. In marketing Kellogg Corn Flakes to the French, three problems are especially severe: (1) over 30 percent of French adults skip breakfast entirely, (2) most of the rest have a cup of café au lait and bread at home or a croissant and coffee standing up at a bar on the way to work, and (3) many French adults still view corn, which first arrived on French farms after World War II, as only fit for chickens and pigs to eat.

Kellogg's P.A. marketing strategy for selling breakfast cereals in France is similar to that of many American firms taking a familiar domestic product abroad that is exotic to foreign tastes—and for foreign firms selling their products in the United States. As described by the *Wall Street Journal,* this strategy involves great patience, advertising budgets far out of line with sales, and a thorough understanding of what is required for success in gaining sales for the export product.[1] For example, marketing research shows that 40 percent of French consumers eating cereal for breakfast pour on *warm* milk. So Kellogg's TV ads carefully show milk poured on its corn flakes from a transparent glass pitcher—traditionally used in France for cold milk—and not the opaque porcelain one that holds the hot milk used for café au lait.

After defining exactly what international marketing is and why firms such as Kellogg assume great risks to do it, this chapter discusses the importance of environmental factors in successful international marketing, describes alternative means of entering the international market, and explains how successful marketing programs in the United States often have to be modified for use abroad.

THE SCOPE OF INTERNATIONAL MARKETING

Why would a successful U.S. company like Kellogg want to enter the international market, when domestic marketing seems so much easier? Indeed, with the potential problems of foreign languages, different currencies, volatile political and legal arenas, and different consumer needs and expectations, why get involved in international marketing at all?

WHAT INTERNATIONAL MARKETING IS

International marketing is simply marketing across national boundaries. Since the end of World War II, improved travel, communications, and technology have made the world smaller and fostered trade between nations.

The General Agreement on Tariffs and Trade (GATT) is an international agreement drafted in 1947 that seeks to reduce tariffs around the world and create more favorable conditions for world trade. Some countries have developed economic "communities," such as the Common Market (or European Economic Community), to reduce tariffs and prices while increasing investment and employment.

WHY FIRMS UNDERTAKE INTERNATIONAL MARKETING

The main reason for companies to do international marketing is to exploit a better business opportunity in terms of increased sales and profits. Either firms are limited in their home country or their opportunities are great in the foreign countries.

Many companies find themselves with little room for growth in their domestic market. Competition may increase and leave a smaller portion of the pie to enjoy, or demand may shift to a newer, better product. The economic environment in the home country may be undesirable because of higher taxes

1. To counter adverse demographic or economic factors in the home market.
2. To extend a product's life cycle.
3. To reduce or avoid competition.
4. To enhance economies of scale in production and marketing.
5. To dispose of inventories.
6. To export (and import) new technology.

FIGURE 21-1
Key reasons U.S. firms "go international"

or a recession. It would seem logical to turn to other markets in any of these cases, as Japan's Honda has done (see the ad below).

So foreign markets may offer an opportunity for growth. A product that is mature at home and thus facing dwindling sales may be new and exciting elsewhere. For example, France's Sodima, whose Yoplait yogurt was in a mature phase of its product life cycle at home, was happy to license its product to General Mills for sale in the United States, where yogurt sales were growing rapidly (see Chapters 19 and 20). Similarly, Kellogg hopes that its Corn Flakes will catch hold in France, where the product is at an early stage in its product life cycle and competition in the ready-to-eat cereal market is less intense than in the United States. Foreign trade may offer favorable tax and trade options. Even with the costs of transportation and tariffs, a profit can be made. Figure 21-1 summarizes the main reasons U.S. companies consider entering international markets.

Honda searches for markets outside Japan

THE DIFFICULTIES IN INTERNATIONAL MARKETING

Is international marketing easy? Not at all. Many companies have tried and failed. International marketing is an attractive alternative, yet it requires serious efforts. Although it involves the same principles of domestic marketing discussed throughout this book, those principles must be applied with care.

Campbell Soup, the company with a 60 percent market share in the U.S. wet soups category, lost $30 million in Great Britain. The problem was that Campbell's didn't clearly communicate that the soup was condensed, and consumers saw it as a poor value compared with the larger cans stocked next to it.

Americans recognize the brand names of foreign products that have been introduced successfully here: Honda and BMW cars, Sony TV sets, Nestlé candy bars, and Shell gasoline and oil products. Although this chapter will describe foreign successes in the United States, it will also identify the American firms that have been successful abroad—from consumer products from companies such as Gillette, McDonald's, and Kellogg to industrial products such as IBM and Apple computers, GE locomotives, and Boeing aircraft. We shall also try to discover how successful firms overcome difficulties in marketing their products abroad.[2]

THE IMPORTANCE OF INTERNATIONAL MARKETING

The dollar volume of U.S. exports and imports indicates the importance of international marketing and why it affects virtually every American today. A nation's **balance of trade** is the difference between the monetary value of its exports and imports. When its exports exceed its imports, it has incurred a *surplus* in its balance of trade. When imports exceed exports, a *deficit* has occurred. In the 25 years after World War II ended in 1945, European countries and Japan were rebuilding their shattered economies. They had limited money to import products, and what money they had was often used to import U.S. construction equipment and machine tools to rebuild their cities and factories.

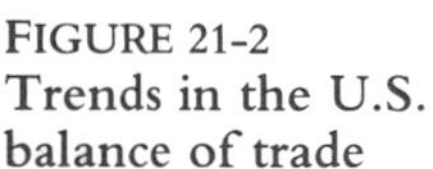
FIGURE 21-2
Trends in the U.S. balance of trade

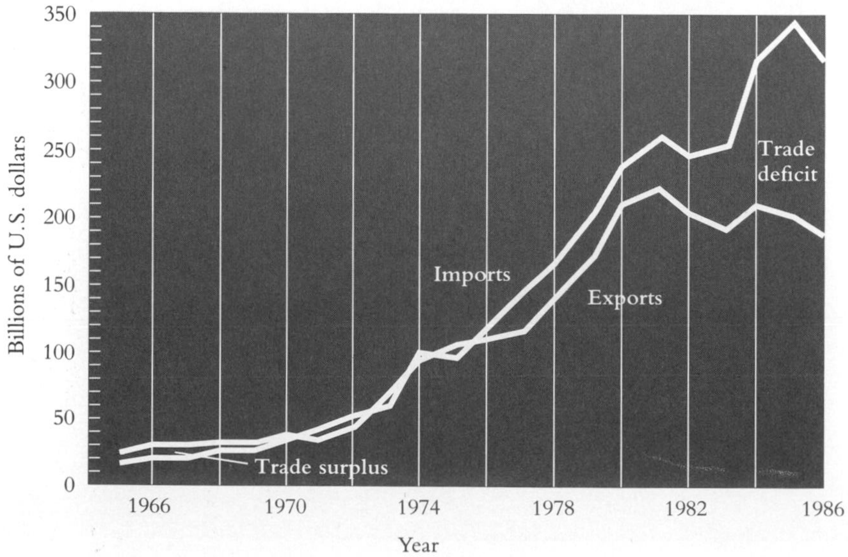

So, as shown in Figure 21-2, because of the long-range economic effects of World War II, the United States ran a surplus in its balance of trade until 1970.

Figure 21-2 also shows that since 1970 two important things have happened in U.S. exports and imports. First, with a few exceptions, imports have significantly exceeded exports each year, indicating that the United States is running a continuing balance of trade deficit. Second, the volume of both exports and imports is about 10 to 15 times what it was in 1965—showing why almost every American is significantly affected. The effect varies from the products they buy (TV sets from Japan, wool suits from Great Britain, wine from France) to those they sell (GM's cars to Europe, DuPont's chemicals to the Far East, and Allied-Signal's automobile turbochargers to Japanese and Swedish car producers) and the additional jobs and improved standard of living that result.[3]

SOME LEADING U.S. AND FOREIGN TRANSNATIONALS

A **transnational corporation** is one that has a global orientation to marketing its products. The phrase *transnational corporation* is replacing *multinational corporation* because the latter has developed an unpleasant, predatory connotation. A transnational corporation runs its business and makes its decisions based on all

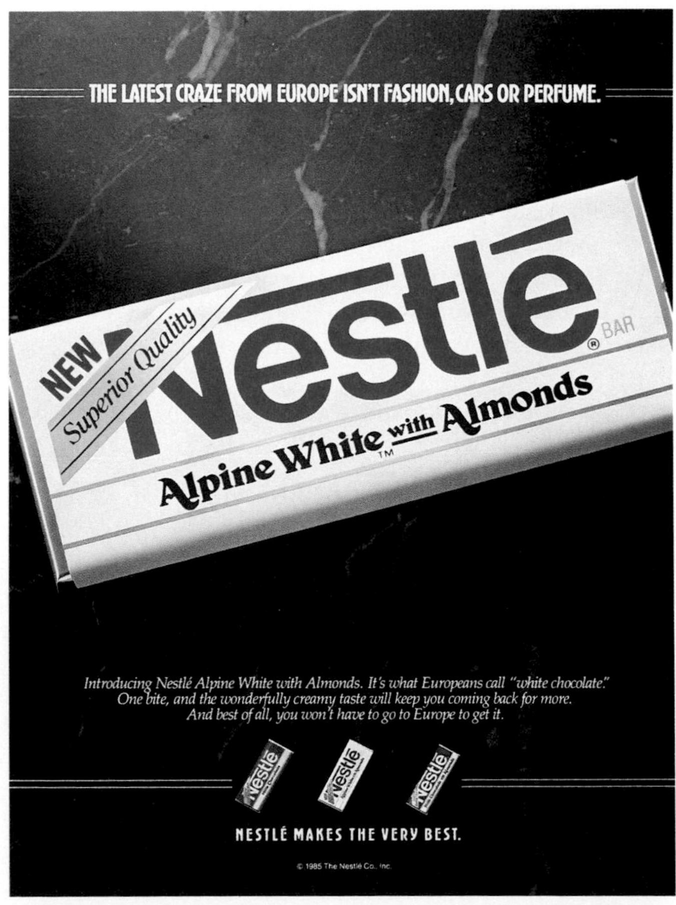

THE LATEST CRAZE FROM EUROPE ISN'T FASHION, CARS OR PERFUME.
NEW
Superior Quality
Nestlé
BAR
Alpine White with Almonds
Introducing Nestlé Alpine White with Almonds. It's what Europeans call "white chocolate."
One bite, and the wonderfully creamy taste will keep you coming back for more.
And best of all, you won't have to go to Europe to get it.
NESTLÉ MAKES THE VERY BEST.
© 1985 The Nestlé Co., Inc.

Is Nestlé an American firm?

COMPANY	FOREIGN REVENUE (BILLIONS)	TOTAL REVENUE (BILLIONS)	FOREIGN REVENUE AS PERCENT OF TOTAL	FOREIGN OPERATING PROFIT (BILLIONS)	TOTAL OPERATING PROFIT (BILLIONS)	FOREIGN OPERATING PROFIT AS PERCENT OF TOTAL	FOREIGN ASSETS (BILLIONS)	TOTAL ASSETS (BILLIONS)	FOREIGN ASSETS AS PERCENT OF TOTAL
1. Exxon	50	70	72	3.9	5.2	75	31	69	44
2. Mobil	27[1]	46[1]	60	1.9[2]	1.4[2]	132	18	37	47
3. IBM	26	51	51	3.2[2]	4.8[2]	67	28	58	48
4. Ford Motor	20	63	32	.8[2]	3.3[2]	25	19	38	50
5. General Motors	20	103	19	−.2[2]	2.9[2]	D-P	16	72	22
6. Texaco	15	32	49	1.2	1.2	99	10	35	29
7. Citicorp	11	23	47	.5[2]	1.1[2]	49	86[3]	184[3]	47
8. E.I. du Pont	10[4]	27	37	.6	1.8[5]	36	8	27	30
9. Dow Chemical	6	11	54	.7	1.3	53	6	12	49
10. Chevron	6	24	23	.8[6]	1.1[6]	77	8	35	23

[1]Includes other income.
[2]Net income.
[3]Average assets.
[4]Includes excise taxes.
[5]Operating income after taxes.
[6]Net income before corporate expenses.
D-P, Deficit over profit.

Source: "The 100 Largest U.S. Multinationals," *Forbes* (July 27, 1987), p. 152. © Forbes, Inc., 1987.

FIGURE 21-3
The 10 largest U.S. transnationals

the possible choices in the world, not simply favoring domestic options because they are convenient.

There is no one accepted meaning of transnational corporation. Some definitions include:

- Not only exporting products but also conducting R&D, employing foreign personnel, and manufacturing in foreign countries
- Having foreign sales that exceed 10 percent of total sales
- Having a global or worldwide products division rather than an international division in the company (that is, operating with a "home country" perspective)
- Having a mixture of nationalities represented in the company's management

Regardless of the definition, some U.S. companies generally considered to be transnational corporations include Pan American Airlines, Citicorp, Mobil, IBM, Coca-Cola, and Xerox. These are well-known because they sell consumer and industrial products and services. However, among the 10 largest U.S. transnationals, as Figure 21-3 shows, most are petrochemical and automobile firms.

There are some companies whose makes are so well-known to Americans that we assume they are based in the United States, although in fact their headquarters are abroad. Examples are Howard Johnson's, Norelco, Shell Oil (Royal Dutch/Shell), Baskin-Robbins, Nestlé, and Timex. The top three foreign transnationals in the world are Royal Dutch/Shell, Mitsui & Company, Ltd., and the Mitsubishi Corporation.

Importantly, it's not necessary to be a huge company to engage in international marketing. There are numerous small businesses involved in foreign trade—many of them very successfully. A surprising example is Lakewood

For the way a small U.S. envelope firm exchanges ideas with foreign companies to be more competitive, see the text

Industries, a small Midwestern firm that has succeeded in exporting millions of chopsticks—to Japan. Lakewood Industries has two competitive advantages: (1) aspen logs that make white chopsticks that are prized in Japan, and (2) automated equipment that can produce 1.8 billion pairs of chopsticks a year—still less than 10 percent of the 20 billion pairs a year the Japanese use.[4]

In fact, in one unusual respect a small regional American firm has an advantage over its huge transnational rivals in the international arena. That is when it can trade product technology and marketing ideas with foreign firms with whom it does not compete directly. Minnesota Color Envelopes is a small firm that produces a variety of specialized packaging for photofinishers (shown in the picture above). By exchanging information with regional European printers, it is able to obtain information on new printing equipment, inks, running speeds, and printing plates that give high-quality printing—thereby gaining advantage over its American competitors. It in turn provides ideas to the European printers, so the exchange benefits both parties.[5]

GLOBAL VERSUS CUSTOMIZED PRODUCTS

As international marketing grows, firms selling both consumer and industrial products in foreign countries face a dilemma: should they use a global or customized strategy in the products they sell?

A **global approach** assumes that the way the product is used and the needs it satisfies are universal and therefore the marketing mix need not be adjusted for each country. A **customized approach** entails designing a different marketing plan for each nation based on different needs, values, customs, languages, and purchasing power. The global approach to international marketing is less common but has been successful for a few firms.

U.S. firms, as discussed later, have often encountered problems when they simply took American products and marketing programs into foreign countries with almost no change (a global approach). Other U.S. firms watched these errors and shifted to a customized strategy. An example is Kodak's European launch of its Ektaprint copier-duplication line. It had watched Xerox take a successful U.S. copier into Great Britain, only to discover it didn't fit through narrower British doorways. When Kodak introduced its European copier into Europe, the design included language keys on the control panel that are tailored to individual countries and a variable reduction capability for different page sizes, since there is no standard paper size in Europe comparable to the American 8½ × 11 inch.[6]

Professor Theodore Levitt, however, argues that a firm can overreact and carry customized marketing too far in trying to respond to wants of consumers and that a global strategy is needed.[7] When a global strategy succeeds, huge savings are possible in manufacturing, packaging, and advertising costs. For example, when Colgate-Palmolive introduced its Colgate tartar-control toothpaste in over 40 countries, its marketing executives in these countries received only 2 TV ads from which to choose. The ads were translated to the local language and were a success. Colgate-Palmolive estimates that it saves $1 million to $2 million in TV production costs for every country that runs the same TV commercial. It has also saved millions of dollars by standardizing the packaging of many of its brands and consolidating production in fewer factories.[8]

But when a globalization strategy doesn't work, it can be a disaster. Parker Pen, Ltd., is an example. In 1982, it was making about 500 styles of pens and letting local marketing managers in about 150 countries create their own ads and packaging. Using a globalization strategy, by 1984 it had reduced the number of styles of pens to about 100 and offered only a single ad campaign—one that could be translated into local languages. The strategy backfired because local marketing managers resented the standardization of ads and advertising agencies. The company almost went bankrupt until it returned to its customized strategy and let each country develop its own ads.[9]

McDonald's: use a global or customized strategy overseas?

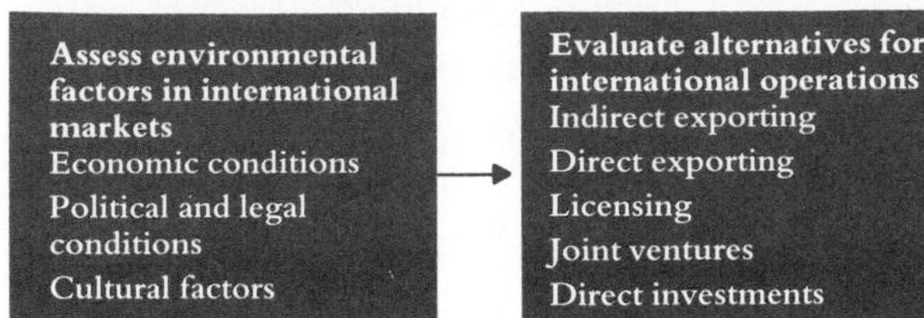

FIGURE 21-4
Sequence of decisions in entering international markets

McDonald's—the undisputed world hamburger king—seems to have achieved the ideal hybrid between a global and customized strategy. Although it has standardized much of its menu, it gives a degree of flexibility to franchises to allow for local customer preferences in their countries. McDonald's in Germany and France have beer on their menu, and those in Japan offer saki. In the Philippines, where noodle houses are popular, its customers can find—what else?—McSpaghetti!

Companies such as Kodak, Colgate-Palmolive, and McDonald's had to make a series of decisions when they entered international markets. These decisions, outlined in Figure 21-4, are discussed in more detail throughout the remainder of the chapter.

CONCEPT CHECK

1 **Given the risks involved, what are several reasons a firm might undertake international marketing?**

2 **What is a transnational corporation?**

ASSESSING ENVIRONMENTAL FACTORS

The uncontrollable environmental variables—including economic factors, political and legal concerns, and cultural differences—that affect international marketing are strikingly different from those in domestic markets. This is why many transnational firms considering marketing efforts in a new country undertake serious marketing research—ranging from using published data to personal interviews with end users and distributors in the country.[10]

ECONOMIC CONDITIONS

There are several important rules to international marketing in light of a country's economic conditions: the product must fit the needs of the country's consumers and the product must be sold where there is the income to buy it and effective means of distributing, using, and servicing it. Four aspects of these considerations are (1) the country's stage of economic development, (2) its economic infrastructure, (3) consumer income, and (4) currency exchange rates.

Stage of Economic Development There are over 200 countries in the world today, each of which is at a slightly different point in terms of its stage of economic development. However, they can be classified into two major groupings that will help the international marketer better understand their needs:

- *Developed* countries have somewhat mixed economies. Private enterprise dominates, although they have substantial public sectors as well. The United States, Canada, Japan, and most of Western Europe can be considered developed.
- *Developing* countries are in the process of moving from an agricultural to an industrial economy. There are two subgroups within the developing category: (1) those which have already made the move and (2) those which remain locked in the preindustrial economy. Countries such as Australia, Israel, Venezuela, and South Africa fall into the first group. In the second group are Pakistan, Sri Lanka, Tanzania, and Chad, where living standards are low and show little promise of improvement. One third of the world's population is in this second group.

Communist countries, because of political and legal barriers, have been barely tapped by the United States. One third of the world's population lives in these countries, which include Eastern Europe, Russia, Cuba, and China. Opportunities appear bright for more international trade between capitalist and communist countries. One example is Russian General Secretary Mikhail S. Gorbachev's *perestroika* (economic reform) policy to encourage more free market incentives. The policy was launched in January, 1988, and should increase international trade with Russia. A joint venture (explained later in the chapter) between the United States' Combustion Engineering and the Russian state-owned oil company to manufacture controls to upgrade Russian petrochemical plants is the first time since the 1920's that an American firm has been allowed to own a part of a Russian operation. In addition, McDonald's now has a go-ahead to open 20 outlets in Moscow.[11]

Economic Infrastructure A country's **economic infrastructure**—its communication, transportation, financial, and distribution systems—is a critical consideration in determining whether to try to market to a country's consumers and organizations. This is why American appliance makers have generally avoided China. But sales of industrial products is a different matter. GE has sold its locomotives, and Boeing its 747 commercial jet aircraft, to China in conjunction with programs to train Chinese engineers and technicians to maintain and service these products.

Consumer Income An international marketer selling consumer goods also must consider what the average per capita income is among a nation's consumers and how the income is distributed. Per capita income is less than $200 annually in some of the developing countries. However, a country's distribution of income is important, too. India, for example, has a per capita income of about $300, but there are 60 to 100 million upper and middle class consumers who are a market for transnational companies.[12]

Currency Exchange Rates Fluctuations in exchange rates among the world's currencies are of critical importance in international marketing. Such fluctuations

MCDONALD'S MENU ITEM		PRICE IN FRANCS, EARLY 1988	PRICE IN DOLLARS	
IN FRANCE	IN THE U.S.		EARLY 1988*	MID-1985†
Hamburger	Hamburger	7.20f	$1.35	$0.67
Big Mac	Big Mac	17.50	3.27	1.64
Chicken McNuggets (6 morceaux)	6 Chicken McNuggets	17.10	3.20	1.60
Chocolate Shake	Chocolate Shake	7.60	1.42	.71
Biere	Beer on Tap	7.90	1.48	.74
Frites (grand)	French Fries (large)	9.10	1.70	.85
Coca-Cola (moyen)	Coca-Cola (medium)	8.40	1.57	.79

*At $1.00 = 5.35 French Francs
†At $1.00 = 10.70 French Francs

FIGURE 21-5
Price variations in a French McDonald's restaurant caused by currency exchange fluctuations

affect everyone—from international vacationers to transnational corporations.

The strength of the U.S. dollar against foreign currencies in 1985 and 1986 was a stroke of good fortune to Americans traveling abroad. Some luxury goods such as Zeiss binoculars and Gucci handbags were priced 30 percent to 70 percent less in Europe than in the United States. By early 1988, the value of dollar against foreign currencies had plummeted. For example, in mid-1985, one American dollar could be exchanged for 10.7 French francs, but in early 1988 a dollar only bought 5.35 francs—exactly half its value 2½ years earlier.

Figure 21-5 shows the impact of these swings in the dollar-franc exchange rate on the prices in a French McDonald's restaurant. The highlighted rows show that in early 1988, a Big Mac, French fries, and medium Coke would cost $6.54 in France—twice its cost in dollars in mid-1985. Figure 21-5 also shows the identical names used on the French menu for many of McDonald's items (a global strategy) although tap beer or "biere" also appears (a degree of customized strategy). McDonald's opens more than 200 new outlets outside the United States each year. As mentioned earlier in the chapter, McDonald's "tight-loose" strategy is what many international marketers are seeking. Although McDonald's extensive procedures manual (19 steps to cook the perfect French fries described in the Marketing Action Memo) is legendary and enables tight controls on quality and cleanliness, it allows flexibility—or "looseness"—to let outlets in foreign countries adapt to local conditions.[13]

In seeking to protect their investments, transnational corporations face even more frantic currency exchange problems than individual tourists. For example, all these transnational corporations have foreign currency traders whose job goes on 24 hours a day. Currency fluctuations can wipe out a firm's profits from regular operations, so decisions on when to buy and sell foreign currencies are critical. For example, in four years in the early 1980's Kodak lost about $500 million because the strong dollar made its foreign receivables less valuable when converted to dollars.[14] The chief foreign exchange trader for New York's Manufacturers Hanover Trust Company—like many others in this business—sleeps

MARKETING · ACTION · MEMO

Homework in International Marketing: McDonald's Search for the Perfect—Polish—French Fries

Those French fried potatoes that we wolf down at our local McDonald's restaurant aren't made from just any potato. McDonald's has spent thousands of dollars finding the *right* potato, slicing it into the *right* thickness, and dipping it in the *right* cooking oil for the *right* length of time.

McDonald's potatoes illustrate the special problems in international marketing. Only one potato meets McDonald's exacting standards: the Russet Burbank that is grown mainly in Idaho. It uses millions of pounds of French fries in western European restaurants. But they aren't quite up to McDonald's standards because they aren't Russet Burbank, which aren't grown in Europe and are too costly to ship from Idaho.

Enter Poland. The job of growing the right potatoes was entrusted to Mr. Marian Dobrowolski, who was born in Poland but now works in Illinois at McDonald's headquarters and the site of its Hamburger University. Poles produce more than 36 million tons of potatoes annually, but Dobrowolski discovered that these potatoes didn't meet McDonald's taste standards. He asked Polish farmers to grow the Russet Burbank potatoes he had shipped in from Idaho. The problem: the Polish farmers weren't about to pamper these potatoes to the degree needed, and they didn't grow.

So Dobrowolski asked Polish food scientists at the Guzow Vegetable Experiment Station to grow 15 acres of the needed potatoes. In 1986 a sample of these potatoes was harvested, cut to shape, French fried, and served to Dobrowolski for the critical taste test. Dobrowolski pronounced them "OK" and he and the food scientists toasted each other.

"To the golden orchards," toasts one scientist.

"Arches," says Dobrowolski. And raising his glass, he toasts, "to Poland."

So after 6 years of work, Polish-grown Russet Burbank potatoes will cross international borders to McDonald's Golden Arches restaurants across western Europe.

Source: Barry Newman, "Its Eye on Fries, Poland Pursues Potato Parity," *The Wall Street Journal* (October 9, 1986), pp. 1, 28.

at night with a computer turned on next to him. If he has a large investment in a currency, he often programs the computer to wake him up every 15 minutes through the night to buy and sell currencies.[15]

Political and Legal Conditions

The difficulties in assessing the political and legal condition of a country lie not only in identifying the current condition but also in estimating exactly how long that condition will last. Some transnational companies use analyses ranging from computer projections to intuition and lost-horse forecasts (see Chapter 7) to assess a country's condition. The dimensions being evaluated include the government attitude toward foreign marketers, the stability and financial policies of the country, and government bureaucracy.

Government Attitude Some countries invite foreign investment through offering investment incentives, helping in site location, and providing other services. Mexico is one such country that realizes foreign investment can mean an improved economy and jobs for its citizens. On the other hand, some countries are interested in hosting foreign investors only on their own terms. Coca-Cola discontinued business in India rather than give up majority control and reveal its "secret formula," which is kept in an Atlanta bank vault. Tiny Double-Cola from Tennessee beat out giant Pepsi-Cola in gaining government permission to build bottling plants in India and sell its soft drink there.[16]

Stability and Financial Policies Millions of dollars have been lost in the Middle East as a result of war and changes in governments. Holiday Inn has been badly hurt during the war in Lebanon. Oil drilling firms have lost vast sums throughout the Iran-Iraq war. Losses like these encourage careful selection of stable countries not likely to be suddenly at war.

When instability is suspected, companies do everything they can to protect themselves against losses. Companies will limit their trade to exporting products into the country, minimizing investments in new plants in the foreign economy. Currency will be converted as soon as possible.

Even friendly countries can change their policies toward international marketing. **Quotas** can be revised or set, currency can be blocked, duties can be imposed, and in extreme cases companies can be expropriated. Quotas are limits placed on the amount of products allowed to enter the country. **Blocked currency** means that a government will not allow it to be converted into other currencies. **Duties** are special taxes on imports. **Expropriation** occurs when a company or its assets are taken over by the host country.

Bureaucracy Even though a law degree isn't essential, it certainly is advantageous when engaging in international trade. Governments can bog down any business transaction with restrictions in a number of forms: tariffs, quotas, boycotts, barriers to entry, and state ownership. These restrictions can apply to an industry, a company, or even a specific product. **Tariffs** are duties imposed by a government on imported (and sometimes even exported) goods. **Boycotts** are a refusal to deal with a country—usually to express disapproval or enforce certain conditions.

One way to measure a country's attitude toward active encouragement of international trade is to examine the restraints put on it. If tariffs and quotas are plentiful and restrictive, chances are the country is not very receptive to foreign involvement in its economy.

CULTURAL FACTORS

Understanding a foreign nation's society and its **culture** is of vital importance. The culture of a country will influence what needs consumers have and how they go about satisfying them.

Language An international marketer not only should know the native tongue of a country but also the nuances and idioms of a language. This can spell the

difference between success and failure in a marketing program. Not doing so may trigger classic mistakes like these:

- Those who speak Spanish might wonder why Chevrolet sells a car with the name Nova—which to them means "It won't go."
- 3M seemed a little silly to the Japanese when it said its Scotch tape "sticks like crazy," which to the Japanese means it sticks foolishly.
- In Taiwan the ad slogan "Come Alive With Pepsi" was translated too literally and read in Chinese "Pepsi brings your ancestors back from the grave."

International marketers should test and retest their communications in a foreign country to verify that they are saying, in fact, what they want to be saying. Often this is very difficult. Mars Candy has successfully introduced its M & M's across Europe. But it had a special problem in France making the name pronounceable because neither the ampersand nor the apostrophe *s* plural exists. The solution: explain to the French that M & M's should be pronounced "aimainaimze!"[17]

Customs **Customs**—the way people have of doing things—are different for each country. Did you know that mothers in Tanzania don't serve their children eggs? They believe that eggs cause both baldness and impotence. Some Northern European countries consider both cold and hot cereals a delicious dessert. Other customs unusual to Americans include[18]:

- In France men wear more than twice the number of cosmetics that women do.
- In Italy a favorite snack is a candy bar eaten between two slices of bread.
- Business people in South America prefer to negotiate within inches of their colleagues; Americans who find this difficult can offend their potential associates and ruin a possible agreement.

New firms are springing up to counsel expatriates-to-be on the business practices, social customs, and life-styles they will encounter in their new country of residence.[19]

Values A nation's **values** reflect the religious or moral beliefs of its people. Understanding and working with these aspects of a society are also factors in successful international marketing. For example:

- A door-to-door salesman would find selling in Italy impossible because it is improper for a man to call on a woman if she is home alone.
- McDonald's and other hamburger restaurants would not have a chance in India, where the cow is considered sacred.
- The British don't believe marketing is quite respectable, a factor contributing to their loss of markets in which they had the technological lead.[20]

German exporters such as BMW (cars) and Stihl (chain saws) probably are the most sophisticated in understanding the values of the customers of the nation's to which they sell products. In 1986 Germany (*not* Japan) passed the United States as the world's largest exporter through a strategy that stresses high quality products sold to specific market segments by a strong network of dealers.[21]

CONCEPT CHECK

1 Why is analysis of the international marketing environment so important?

2 When a firm is considering another country as a potential market, why is that country's per capita income important?

3 How might the religious beliefs of a nation affect international marketing to that country?

EVALUATING ALTERNATIVES FOR INTERNATIONAL OPERATIONS

Once a company has decided to enter the international marketplace, a means of entry must be selected. The option chosen depends on its willingness and ability to commit financial, physical, and managerial resources. As Figure 21-6 demonstrates, the relative difficulty of entry increases as the firm moves from exporting to direct investments.

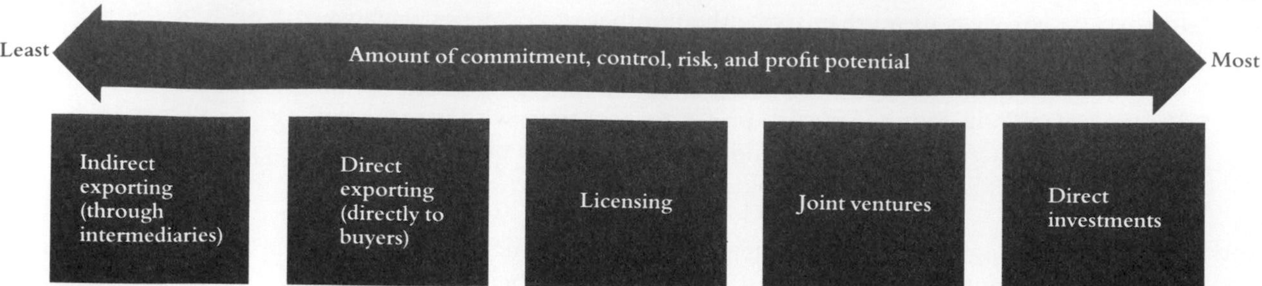

FIGURE 21-6
Modes of entry into international markets

INDIRECT EXPORTING (THROUGH INTERMEDIARIES)

Having another firm sell products in a foreign country is **exporting.** This entry option allows a company to make the least number of changes in terms of its product, its organization, and even its corporate goals.

Indirect exporting, or marketing through an intermediary, involves the least amount of commitment and risk but will probably return the least profit. This kind of exporting is ideal for the company that has no overseas contacts but wants to market abroad. The intermediary has the international marketing know-how and the resources necessary for the effort to succeed.

DIRECT EXPORTING (DIRECTLY TO BUYERS)

When a company handles its own exports directly, without intermediaries, this is **direct exporting.** Most companies become involved in direct exporting when they are approached by buyers or when their exporting becomes sufficiently large to merit more explicit attention within the company. This increases the risk that the company is taking but also opens the door to increased profits.

LICENSING

Under **licensing** a company offers the right to a trademark, patent, trade secret, or other similarly valued items of intellectual property in return for a royalty or a fee. The advantages to the company granting the license are low-risk and a capital-free entry into the international market. The licensee gains some piece of information that allows it to start at a point beyond the beginning. Yoplait Yogurt is licensed from Sodima, a French cooperative, by General Mills for sales in the United States.

There are some serious drawbacks to this mode of entry, however. The licensor foregoes control of its product and reduces the potential profits gained from it. In addition, while the relationship lasts, the licensor may be creating its own competition. Some licensees are able to modify the product somehow and enter the market with product and marketing knowledge gained at the expense of the company that got them started. To offset this disadvantage, many companies strive to stay innovative so that the licensee remains dependent on them for improvements and successful operation. Finally, should the licensee prove to be a poor choice, the name or reputation of the company may be harmed.

Two variations on licensing, contract manufacturing and foreign assembly, represent an alternative way to produce a product within the foreign country. **Contract manufacturing** is considered the next step up from licensing. U.S. companies may contract with a foreign firm to manufacture products according to certain specifications. The product is then sold in the foreign country or exported to the United States. **Foreign assembly,** the next step from contract manufacturing, involves using foreign labor to assemble (not manufacture) parts and components that have been shipped to that country. The advantage to the foreign country is the employment of its people, and the U.S. firm benefits because import tariffs are lower on parts than they are on finished products. U.S. firms also take advantage of cheaper labor forces when products are assembled overseas.

JOINT VENTURES

When a foreign company and a local concern invest together to create a local business, it is called a **joint venture.** These two companies share ownership, control, and profits of the new company. Investment may be made by having either of the companies buy shares in the other or by creating a third and separate entity.

To understand how Ericsson used a joint venture to beat AT&T and win a large French contract, see the text

The advantages of this option are twofold. First, one company may not have the necessary financial, physical, or managerial resources to enter a foreign market alone. The joint venture between Ericsson, a Swedish telecommunications firm, and CGCT, an ailing French switch maker, enabled them together to beat out AT&T for a $100 million French contract. Ericsson's money and technology combined with CGCT's knowledge of the French market helped them to win the contract that neither of them could have won alone. Second, a government may require or strongly encourage a joint venture before it allows a company to enter its market. This was exactly the condition set down by the French government in the award of its large contract to Ericsson.[22]

Japanese car manufacturers have formed joint ventures with GM, Ford, and Chrysler to produce subcompacts for U.S. consumers—to such a degree that by 1990 all U.S. subcompacts will bear a foreign stamp.[23] And in 1987 McDonnell Douglas built its first commercial jet aircraft in China in a joint venture with a government-owned aircraft manufacturer.[24]

The disadvantages arise when the two companies disagree about policies or courses of action. For example, U.S. firms place a high priority on marketing a product, whereas foreign companies rely more heavily on selling. It is also common for U.S. companies to reinvest earnings gained, whereas some foreign companies may want to spend those earnings.

DIRECT INVESTMENTS

The biggest commitment a company can make when entering the international market is by **direct investment,** which entails actually investing in an assembly or manufacturing plant located in a foreign country. For example, Honda's Marysville, Ohio, plant produces Civics and Accords, and Nissan's Smyrna, Tennessee, plant produces pickup trucks. Honda's initial success in direct investment in the United States has been so great that it is building a second car-production plant in Ohio.[25] The decline of the dollar against foreign currencies led to $200 billion of direct foreign investment in the United States in 1986, causing concern by some American businesses.[26] Many U.S. transnational corporations are also switching to this mode of entry. McDonald's chose this alternative in Great Britain and built a plant to produce 2 million rolls a week when no local bakers would make them to McDonald's specifications.[27]

Just as some Americans are concerned with the volume of foreign direct investment in the United States and possible loss of domestic control of our industries, many foreign countries have the same concern with U.S. transnationals. For example, some Canadians are increasingly concerned over the "Americanization" of its industries.[28]

The advantages to direct investment include cost savings, better understanding of local market conditions, and fewer local restrictions.

CONCEPT CHECK

1 **What mode of entry could a company follow if it has no previous experience in international marketing?**

2 **How does licensing differ from joint ventures?**

Avon targets Latin American markets

TAILORING MARKETING PROGRAMS TO THE COUNTRY

Marketing programs must be adapted to the international scene, not simply be duplicates of those at home. Three basic steps in adapting a marketing program for foreign marketing are (1) selecting a country for entry, (2) establishing the most effective organization for marketing on an international level, and (3) designing the marketing program to fit the market's needs.

SELECTING A COUNTRY FOR ENTRY

In choosing a country for its international marketing efforts, a company must evaluate many factors, following these steps.

Specify the marketing objectives. These objectives should be achievable yet challenging. Profit levels, return on investment (ROI), sales, and competitive positions are all areas for which objectives are delineated.

Choose a single- or multiple-country strategy. Choosing to enter a single country or several countries in a region is based on the product or products being sold and the sales potential. If several adjacent countries all want the same size or style of product, the marketing and production economies of scale may suggest a multiple-country strategy.

Specify the candidate countries or regions to consider. Alternative countries or regions that meet both the stated objectives for international marketing and the economic profile needed for success should be listed as potential candidates.

Estimate the ROI for each of the candidates. To estimate the ROI, a company must project the size of the market, the expected revenues, the expenses, and the profits for each candidate country or region.

Select the one or more countries or regions to enter. The preceding analysis screens the candidates to provide a list of the one or more countries or regions that appear most likely to achieve the firm's objectives for its international marketing program.

Granted, these are all estimates and include some room for error. However, they will provide the necessary framework to enable the firm to make a knowledgeable choice between countries and regions.

ESTABLISHING A MARKETING ORGANIZATION

After selecting a country for entry, an appropriate marketing organization must be established. Its goal is to respond to the different needs of international marketing, yet take advantage of the experience and knowledge of domestic marketers. Some alternative marketing organizations are discussed below.

Export Department When a company is simply exporting its goods, this is typically done through an export department. Made up of a manager and perhaps several assistants, this group handles the necessary paperwork.

Foreign Subsidiary A wholly owned foreign subsidiary commonly has its own head of operations who reports directly to the company president. Sales of Apple's Macintosh computer in Japan were slow until it established a subsidiary there in 1983. Sales started rising when the subsidiary developed a Japanese-language operating system for the Macintosh and announced that much of its software would use the new system.[29]

International Division When international sales become substantial or when modes of entry other than simple exporting are added, a company usually expands to include an international division. This division can be either geographically based or product based. All international marketing—the movement of products and also their marketing—is then handled by this group.

Coca-Cola, the world's best-known brand name

Worldwide Products Division A worldwide products division is used when a company decides that it is no longer a company conducting international marketing, but a transnational firm marketing throughout the world. Like an international division, this structure can be divided by regions, with each division responsible for all products within a region, or it can be divided by products, with each division responsible for all markets where its product is sold. Most likely this structure is accompanied by a management base recruited from around the world.

DESIGNING A MARKETING PROGRAM

An international marketer goes through the same steps in designing a marketing program as a domestic marketer. However, the international marketer must decide whether to use a global or customized approach. Many firms are discovering that they need elements of both. Gillette is seeking ways to develop some global brands in its marketing strategy that includes 800 products. To do this it is trying to find one name for a product that can then be marketed in many countries (see the Marketing Action Memo). Black & Decker bought General Electric's small appliance department in 1984, which it plans to integrate with its household power tool business. The Black & Decker name is better known in some European countries than in the United States. It is trying a globalization strategy but wonders how far it can be carried: will American

MARKETING·ACTION·MEMO

GILLETTE: THE SEARCH FOR GLOBAL BRANDS

The Gillette Company currently manufactures and sells over 800 products in more than 200 countries. Gillette is a transnational company in the truest sense of the word.

Recognizing this, Gillette is striving to create a global marketing organization. The problem? Most of its 800 products are sold under different names.

In 1985, a U.S. traveller interested in purchasing a twin-blade disposable Trac II razor would have to ask for Gillette Desechable in Spain, Radi & Getta in Italy, and Blue II in Great Britain. Equally confusing, Gillette's Silkience shampoo and conditioner is known as Soyance in France, Sientel in Italy, and Silience in Germany. Whatever spillover the brands got in advertising across borders was completely lost, since there was no common denominator.

By 1988, many of these brand names—but not the products—were disappearing as Gillette moved to a global advertising strategy to reach consumers in all Western European countries with exactly the same video part of its TV ads. Its razor became simply "Blue II" across Europe. Dubbed in 10 languages, the audio part of the TV ads invited shavers to "step into the blue" and buy Blue II.

Source: Based on "Gillette Finds World-Brand Image Elusive," *Advertising Age* (June 25, 1984), p. 50; Shawn Tully, "U.S.-Style TV Turns on Europe," *Fortune* (April 13, 1987), pp. 96-98.

consumers buy Black & Decker toasters and waffle irons—a problem it doesn't face in Europe?[30]

Careful marketing research is essential in an international marketing program. There are many sources of secondary information. Some of the most readily available include U.S. government publications, the United Nations, the International Monetary Fund, the host country's government, and foreign publications. However, this information must be carefully evaluated for timeliness, completeness, accuracy, and compatibility with needs.

Primary research must also be undertaken within the foreign market to establish the buyers' needs and preferences. This is not as easy as doing research in the United States because even in some industrialized countries, only a third of the population has phones. Telephone surveys are not representative.

Whatever the problems, research must help the international marketer decide whether to modify or maintain domestic product, price, promotion, and place strategies.

Product The product may be sold internationally in one of three ways: (1) in the same form as in the domestic market, (2) with some adaptations, or (3) as a totally new product.

- *Extension*. Selling the same product in other countries is an extension strategy. It works well for products like Coca-Cola, Wrigley's gum, General Motors cars, and Levi's jeans. However, it didn't work for Jell-O (a more solid gelatin was preferred to the powder in England) or for Duncan Hines (which was seen as too moist and crumbly to eat with tea in England).
- *Adaptation*. Changing a product in some way to make it more appropriate for a country's climate or preferences is an adaptation strategy. Heinz baby food offers strained lamb brains for Australians and strained brown beans in the Netherlands. Exxon sells different gasoline blends based on each country's climate.
- *Invention*. Designing a product to meet the unmet needs of a foreign nation is an invention strategy. This is probably the strategy with the most potential, since there are so many unmet needs, yet it is actually the least used. National Cash Register has followed a reverse invention strategy by introducing crank-operated cash registers in some developing nations that have unreliable or inaccessible electric power.

In international markets—as in domestic ones—nothing succeeds like quality products that satisfy consumer needs and wants at reasonable prices. Honda motorcycles, Caterpillar construction equipment, Canon cameras, and Black & Decker power tools are examples.

Price Most foreign countries use a cost-plus pricing strategy. For international firms this can mean their products are priced higher than the local goods. Why? International products must include not only the cost of production and selling but also tariffs, transportation and storage costs, and higher payments to intermediaries.

Surprisingly, many products are sold internationally below their normal

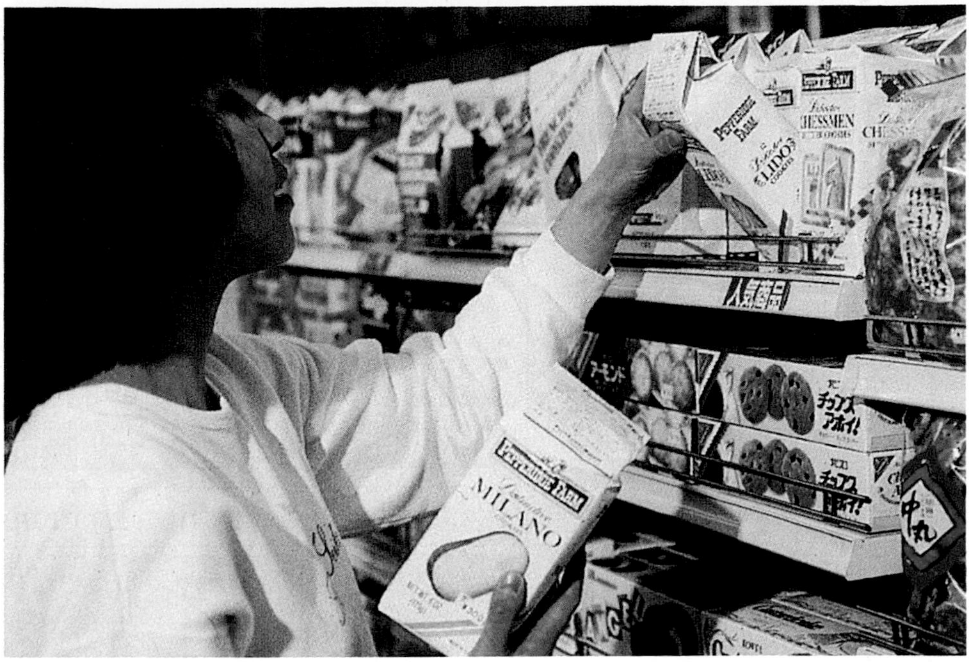

Quality products: essential for entering foreign markets

price in the country of origin. Called **dumping,** this is most often done to build a share of the market by pricing at a competitive level. Another reason is that the products being sold may be surplus that cannot be sold domestically and are therefore already a burden to the company. The firm may be glad to sell them at any price.

Some U.S. pharmaceutical firms have sold penicillin, for example, at a lower price in foreign countries than at home. They justify this by saying that R&D costs are not included in foreign prices. Japan has been accused of following a dumping strategy for some of its products in the United States. Its response is that the volume sold here allows economies of scale, the savings of which are passed on to U.S. consumers.

An unusual pricing dimension of international marketing is **countertrade,** using barter rather than money in making international sales. Although countertrade accounts for only about 9 percent of the U.S. international trade, it represents about 25 percent of the world's trade. An example for an American firm is when McDonnell Douglas sold airplanes to Yugoslavia in exchange for canned hams and tools.[31]

An unpleasant aspect of pricing is bribery, a common practice used in many countries to reduce red tape and make sales. Although in many countries bribery is an accepted business practice in some international sales, it is officially illegal in all countries. Under the Foreign Corrupt Practices Act of 1977 such a practice is illegal for U.S. companies. Even if a U.S. firm labels the bribe a sales commission and includes it on its books, in the United States this is now a federal offense punishable by fines for the company and prison terms for the individuals responsible.

Promotion Two aspects of promotion may have to be changed to reflect the differences in foreign markets. The first is the creative aspect. Because values differ substantially from country to country, a product that is a luxury in one country may be a necessity in another. Creative messages must then be designed to directly address the peculiarities within each market.

Western Europeans, however, are becoming more similar in the TV programs they watch and the products they can buy. In 1987, massive changes in TV came to Western Europe, significantly affecting the TV programs these 320 million consumers watch and the TV ads they see. Spain and Italy can see private and cable TV rather than state-run TV. The effect has been a tremendous increase in advertising and stress on global brands that can be advertised across Europe. When the Common Market (European Economic Community) eliminates a number of national standards and local regulations on December 31, 1992, 320 million consumers can be reached with essentially the same TV ads and products.[32]

Where there is a common language, many TV and print ads can be used both domestically and in a common-language country. For example, New Zealand markets vacations to the United States while America markets winter trips to New Zealanders—both often using domestic ad campaigns in the other country as well.

A common language helps New Zealand market itself to U.S. tourists

FIGURE 21-7
International marketing channel of distribution

Place An international marketer must establish a channel of distribution to meet the goals it has set. Figure 21-7 outlines the normal channel through which a product must travel to reach its destination in international markets. The first step involves the seller; its headquarters is the starting point and is responsible for the successful distribution to the ultimate consumer.

The next step is the channel between the two nations, moving the product from the domestic market to the foreign market. There are three types of intermediaries that can handle this responsibility:

- *A resident buyer in the foreign country* works for foreign companies and resides in the destination country.
- *An overseas representative for foreign firms* is a wholesaler who also works for foreign companies but resides in the exporter's country.
- *An independent intermediary* can be a merchant wholesaler, who buys and sells the products, or an agent, who brings buyers and sellers together.

Once the product is in the foreign nation, that country's distribution channels take over. Foreign channels can be very long or surprisingly short, depending on the product line. In Japan fresh fish go through three intermediaries before getting to a retail outlet. Conversely, shoes only go through one middleman. In other cases the channel does not even involve the host country. P&G sells its soap door to door in the Philippines because there are no other alternatives in many parts of that country.

The sophistication of the distribution channel increases with the economic development of the country. Supermarkets facilitate selling products in many nations, but they are not popular or available in many others where low incomes, culture, and lack of refrigeration dictate shopping on a daily rather than weekly basis. In addition, because preservatives are not common, consumers in these developing countries are suspicious of packaged goods—they fear that the box may contain something spoiled. The result is that refrigerated products and large package sizes are almost nonexistent in many developing countries.

CONCEPT CHECK

1. **What steps should a company follow to select appropriate international markets to enter?**
2. **What are the three international marketing product strategies, and when might each be used?**
3. **What is countertrade?**

SUMMARY

1 International marketing, or trade between nations, is filled with risks and problems but promises profits to those who undertake it. The size of international marketing is large and growing: over 12 percent of the U.S. GNP.

2 Although international and domestic marketing are based on the same marketing principles, many underlying assumptions must be reevaluated when a firm moves into international operations. Environmental variables such as economic conditions, political and legal conditions, and cultural factors must be carefully assessed to achieve successful operations.

3 International markets should be selected on the basis of their size, consumer income, potential market growth, cost of doing business in that country, competitive advantage that would be realized, and risk involved in entering them.

4 Five basic modes of entry into international marketing are indirect exporting, direct exporting, licensing, joint ventures, and direct investment. The relative difficulty of international marketing, as well as the amount of commitment, control, and risk, increases in moving from indirect exporting to direct investments.

5 An organizational structure for international marketing should respond to the unique needs of international marketing, while still taking advantage of the experience and know-how of the domestic marketers. Examples include an export department, foreign subsidiary, international division, and global products division.

6 Because foreign countries have different languages, customs, values, purchasing power, needs, and levels of economic development, a firm must take great care in deciding whether to use a global or customized strategy.

7 Product, price, promotion, and place strategies can all be modified or adapted to reflect these differences and improve the chances of success in international markets.

KEY TERMS AND CONCEPTS

international marketing p. 576
balance of trade p. 578
transnational corporation p. 579
global approach p. 581
customized approach p. 581
economic infrastructure p. 584
quotas p. 587
blocked currency p. 587
duties p. 587
expropriation p. 587
tariffs p. 587
boycotts p. 587
culture p. 587
customs p. 588
values p. 589
exporting p. 590
indirect exporting p. 590
direct exporting p. 590
licensing p. 590
contract manufacturing p. 591
foreign assembly p. 591
joint venture p. 591
direct investment p. 592
dumping p. 597
countertrade p. 597

CHAPTER PROBLEMS AND APPLICATIONS

1 Campbell Soup Company introduced its products in England to considerably less than rave reviews because it used a global approach in their introduction. What are the advantages and disadvantages of the global approach? If Campbell had pursued a customized approach, what dimensions, in addition to the size of the can, might it have explored?

2 In 1988 the British pound was worth $1.81 in the United States; in 1985 it was worth about $1.05. In which year would you choose to travel to Great Britain? In which year should a U.S. firm market internationally? Why?

3 A manufacturer of shoes has decided to enter the international market. As a point of entry, he has selected India. His assumption is that with such a large population, a lot of shoes can be sold. Why might India be a good or bad market opportunity? What steps should the manufacturer follow to select the appropriate market?

4 What steps do some countries take to discourage trade? Why might they do this?

5 As a novice in international marketing, which type of operations would you select to get your feet wet? Why? What other alternatives do you have for market entry?

6 What are the three product strategies a marketer can use in foreign market introductions? Which strategy has the most potential? Why? Can you think of any reverse inventions that might be successful?

7 Knowing that owning Western goods is a status symbol in Russia, what goods might you want to sell to that market? How would the type of economic system in the U.S.S.R. affect your decision to enter this market?

8 If the same domestic principles of marketing are used internationally, why did Kentucky Fried Chicken and McDonald's, both successful companies, fail in some of their attempts to enter foreign markets?

9 Because English is the official language in Australia, many U.S. companies might select this market as an easy one to expand to internationally. Others, however, believe that this similarity in language could make it even harder to successfully engage in foreign trade. Who's right? Why?

10 Coca-Cola is sold worldwide. In some countries Coca-Cola owns the manufacturing facilities; in others it has signed contracts with licensees. When selecting a licensee in each country, what factors should Coca-Cola consider?

SUGGESTED READINGS

Andrew Kupfer, "How to Be a Global Manager," *Fortune* (March 14, 1988), pp. 52-58. *Companies that have succeeded in reaching worldwide markets provide lessons on both the opportunities and problems.*

Theodore Levitt, "The Globalization of Markets," *Harvard Business Review* (May-June 1983), pp. 92-102. *This article summarizes Levitt's argument that customized strategies can be taken too far in international marketing.*

Joanne Lipman, "Marketers Turn Sour on Global Sales Pitch Harvard Guru Makes," *The Wall Street Journal* (May 12, 1988), pp. 1, 10. *The article is a rebuttal to Levitt's* Harvard Business Review *article (above) and cites examples of why customized international strategy still makes sense.*

Shawn Tully, "Europe Gets Ready for 1992," *Fortune* (February 1, 1988), pp. 81-84. *The 12 countries in the Common Market will strike down thousands of regulations and standards by December 31, 1992, which will give a "vast unified market of 320 million consumers."*

22

MARKETING OF SERVICES

After reading this chapter you should be able to:

Explain the differences between goods and services.

•

Recognize how various services differ and how they can be classified.

•

Understand the way in which consumers view and judge services.

•

Develop a customer contact audit to identify service advantages.

•

Understand the important role of internal marketing in service organizations.

•

Explain the role of the 4 *P*'s in the services marketing mix.

A Happy Fable: In Which Mickey Mouse and Snow White Keep Their Home

In 1984 all was not well in the land of Mickey Mouse, Thumper, Pinocchio, Dumbo, Bambi, Snow White, and all their friends. Corporate takeover specialists wanted to buy their "home"—the Walt Disney Company—and then break it up, selling the various pieces to the highest bidders.

Their "home" in 1984 included a huge range of service-related businesses—from the California Disneyland and Florida Disney World theme parks to TV programs, cartoons, and full-length movies. By 1984, the theme parks were accused of lacking new attractions and the TV and movie units were producing duds. The big problem: after Walt Disney's death in 1966, no one had a real vision for the company. Michael Eisner—shown at left with a Disney friend—brought that new vision to the company.

Since Eisner was named to head the company in 1984, he has given it a direction that has turned the company toward incredible growth, expected to carry it into the 1990's. For example, by 1988, the company:

- Broke ground for a $2 billion Euro Disneyland near Paris scheduled to open in 1992, with the expectation it will be as successful as the Tokyo Disneyland
- Spent lavishly to add new rides in its U.S. theme parks, such as a Star Tours space ride and Splash Mountain—a ride in a hollowed-out log past 101 robotic characters from Disney films
- Announced plans for a $375 million hotel next to Disney World
- Hit the right buttons with the movies *Down and Out in Beverly Hills, Ruthless People,* and *Outrageous Fortune* and with *Captain EO*—a 3-D music video starring Michael Jackson
- Launched TV and movie efforts featuring new fantasy characters such as Gummi Bears and Webbigail VanderQuack—many of whom will eventually star on the Disney TV Channel

Eisner and his Walt Disney Company have even found success in China, where the most popular children's TV program (seen by almost 200 million viewers each Sunday night!) is the Mickey and Donald Show.[1]

As the Walt Disney Company illustrates, the marketing of services offers great challenges. In this chapter we discuss how services differ from traditional physical products (goods), how consumers make service purchase decisions, and the ways in which the marketing mix is used.

THE UNIQUENESS OF SERVICES

As noted in Chapter 1, **services** are intangible items such as airline trips, financial advice, or telephone calls that an organization provides to consumers. To obtain these services, consumers exchange money or something else of value such as their own time.

Services are receiving increasing attention as the U.S. economy becomes increasingly service-based.[2] In fact, about 90 percent of 36 million new jobs created in the past 2 decades are in the service sector.

The U.S. Department of Commerce has developed its own list of service businesses: hotels and other lodging places; establishments involving personal, business, repair, amusement and recreation, health, legal, and educational services; social services and membership organizations; and other professional services.[3] As shown in Figure 22-1, services on this list accounted for $639 billion dollars in 1985, which was 16 percent of the gross national product (GNP). If retail and wholesale trade are included as part of services (which many studies do), the total dollar value increases to about $1.3 billion or one-third of the GNP. Services also represent a large export business—the $48 billion of services exports in 1986 is expected to grow by 60 percent in 1990.[4]

New services are also becoming popular. Lois Barnett, the founder of Personalized Services in Chicago, says, "We'll find it, we'll do it, we'll wait for

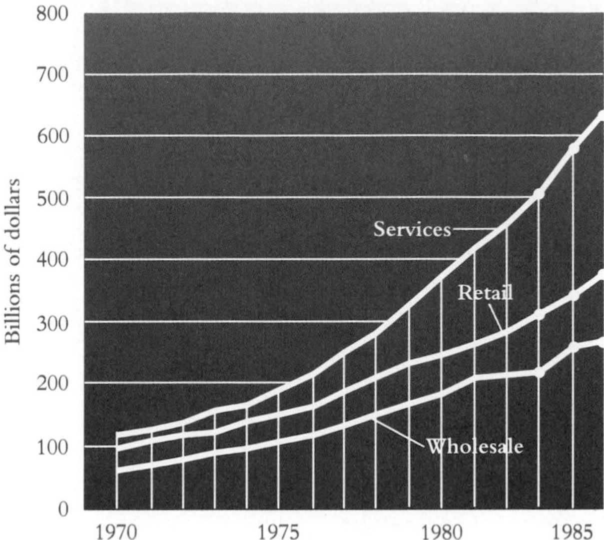

FIGURE 22-1
Importance of services in the U.S. Gross National Product (GNP)

it."[5] Her service will do just about anything that is legal, including walking the dog, picking up the kids, or waiting in line for tickets. Other new service firms include Comp-U-Card International Inc., an electronic catalog shopping service; Molly Maid, Inc., a home cleaning service with franchises in 25 states; and Jiffy Lube, the franchiser of fast oil-change and lube shops. These firms and many others like them are examples of the revolutionary role services will play in our economy in the future.

THE FOUR *I*'S OF SERVICES

There are four unique elements to services: intangibility, inconsistency, inseparability, and inventory. These four elements are referred to as the **four *I*'s of services.**

Intangibility Services are intangible; that is, they can't be held, touched, or seen before the purchase decision. In contrast, before purchasing a traditional product, a consumer can touch a box of laundry detergent, kick the tire of an automobile, or sample a new breakfast cereal. A major marketing need for services is to make them tangible or show the benefits of using the service.[6] So a Norwegian Cruise Line advertisement shows happy vacationers enjoying themselves on an island beach, American Express emphasizes the year-end summary of charges they send you, and a leading insurance company says, "You're in Good Hands With Allstate."

Inconsistency Marketing services is challenging because the quality of a service is often inconsistent. Because services depend on the people who provide them, their quality varies because people have different capabilities and also vary in their job performance from day to day. Inconsistency in services is much more of a problem than it is in physical product marketing. These products can be

LIVING IN AN IMPERFECT WORLD MAY BE NECESSARY. VACATIONING IN ONE IS NOT.
Imagine a vacation where you travel thousands of miles and never worry about reserving rooms, hunting for restaurants, or repacking a suitcase more than once.
Imagine a hotel where, as you sip daiquiris by the pool or work on your golf swing, an ocean floats gently by. A hotel that's so dedicated to serving you, there's actually one staff member for every two guests.
Imagine, if you will, a world so cosmopolitan, you can spend the day visiting a Dutch fort, a French village, or a British colony. And then spend the night seeing a Broadway play or a Las Vegas revue.
Imagine a resort that doesn't simply schedule activities, but plans adventures. So instead of just some things to do, you can do some things that perhaps you've never done. Like climbing a tropical waterfall. Exploring the ruins of an ancient civilization. Or simply playing the day away on a private island reserved exclusively for you.
Imagine a tropical getaway that's so romantic, almost every day has a classic Hollywood ending as you, literally, sail off into the sunset together.
Finally, imagine a vacation so easy to plan, you can arrange it all by making one call, to your travel agent, and asking for an NCL cruise. And soon, instead of just imagining the perfect vacation, you can start living it.
NORWEGIAN CRUISE LINE.

Services must emphasize their benefits

good or bad in terms of quality, but with modern production lines the quality will at least be consistent. On the other hand, one day the Philadelphia Phillies baseball team may have great hitting and pitching and look like a pennant winner, but lose by 10 runs the very next day. Or a soprano at New York's Metropolitan Opera may have a bad cold and give a less-than-perfect performance. Whether the service involves tax assistance at Arthur Andersen or guest relations at the Hyatt Regency, organizations attempt to reduce inconsistency through standardization and training.[7]

Inseparability A third difference between services and goods, related to problems of consistency, is inseparability. In most cases the consumer cannot (and does not) separate the service from the deliverer of the service or the setting in which the service occurs. For example, to receive an education, a person may attend a university. The quality of the education may be high, but if the student has difficulty parking, finds counseling services poor, or sees little opportunity for extracurricular activity, he or she may not be satisfied with the educational experience.

Inventory Inventory of services is different from that of goods. Inventory problems exist with goods because many items are perishable and, as noted in Chapter 14, there are costs associated with handling inventory. With services, inventory carrying costs are more subjective and are related to **idle production capacity,** which is when the service provider is available but there is no demand. The inventory cost of a service is the cost of reimbursing the person used to provide the service along with any needed equipment. If a physician is paid to

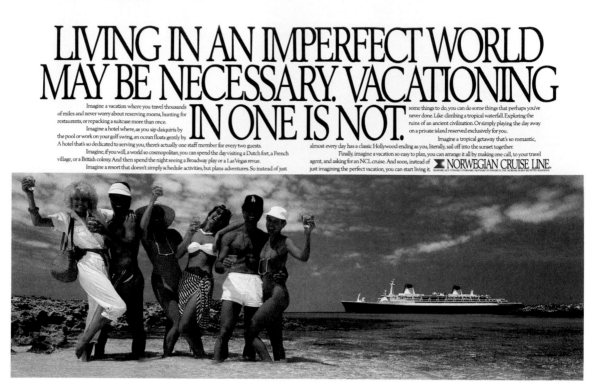

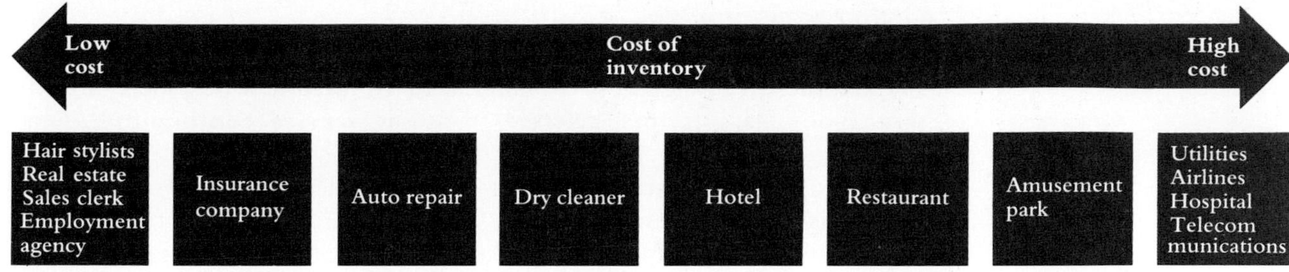

FIGURE 22-2
Inventory carrying costs in services

see patients but no one schedules an appointment, the fixed cost of the idle physician's salary is a high inventory carrying cost. In some service businesses, however, the provider of the service is on commission (the Merrill Lynch stockbroker) or is a part-time employee (a counterperson at McDonald's). Inventory carrying costs can be significantly lower or nonexistent because the idle production capacity can be cut back by reducing hours or having no salary to pay because of the commission compensation system. Figure 22-2 shows a sliding scale of inventory carrying costs represented on the high side by airlines and hospitals and on the low end by real estate agents and hair stylists. The inventory carrying costs of airlines is high because of high-salaried pilots and very expensive equipment. In contrast, real estate agents and hair stylists work on commission and need little expensive equipment to conduct business.

THE SERVICE CONTINUUM

The four *I*'s differentiate services from goods in most cases, but many companies are not clearly service-based or good-based organizations. Is Wang a computer

Services are people

company or service business? Does Dow Jones provide only goods in the sense of publishing *The Wall Street Journal,* or does it consider itself a service in terms of up-to-date business information? As companies look at what they bring to the market, there is a range from the tangible to the intangible or good-dominant to service-dominant factors, referred to as the **service continuum** (Figure 22-3).

Teaching, nursing, and the theater are intangible, service-dominant activities, and inseparability, inconsistency, inventory, and intangibility are major concerns in their marketing. Salt, neckties, and dog food are tangible goods, and the problems represented by the four *I*'s are not relevant in their marketing. However, some businesses are a mix of intangible service and tangible good factors. A clothing tailor provides a service but also a good, the finished suit. How pleasant, courteous, and attentive the tailor is to the customer is an important component of the service, and how well the clothes fit is an important part of the product. As shown in Figure 22-3, a fast-food restaurant is about half tangible goods (the food) and half intangible services (courtesy, cleanliness, speed, convenience).

CLASSIFYING SERVICES

Throughout this book, marketing organizations, techniques, and concepts have been classified to show the differences and similarities in an organized framework. Services can also be classified in several ways, according to (1) whether they are delivered by people or equipment, (2) whether they are profit or nonprofit, or (3) whether or not they are government sponsored.

Delivery by People or Equipment As seen in Figure 22-4, companies offering services provided by people include management consulting firms such as Booz,

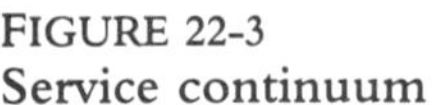
FIGURE 22-3
Service continuum

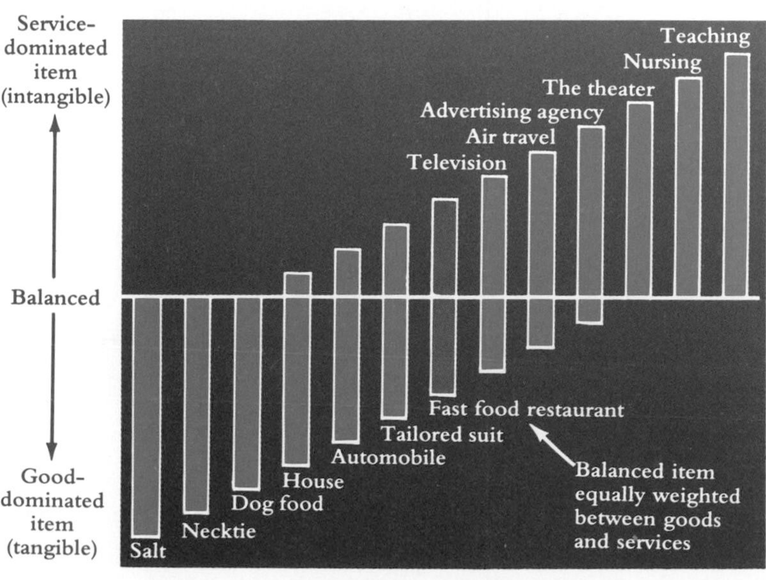

Allen & Hamilton and executive recruitment companies such as the Physicians Executive Management Center in Tampa. Unskilled labor such as that used by Brinks store security forces is also a service provided by people.

Equipment-based services do not have the marketing concerns of inconsistency because people are removed from provision of the service. Bally's video game equipment provides entertainment without relying on people except to service the machines.

Profit or Nonprofit Organizations Many organizations involved in services also distinguish themselves by their tax status as profit or nonprofit organizations. In contrast to *profit organizations, nonprofit organizations'* excesses in revenue over expenses are not taxed or distributed to shareholders. When excess revenue exists, the money goes back into the organization's treasury to allow continuation of the service. Based on the corporate structure of the nonprofit organization, it may pay tax on revenue-generating holdings not directly related to its core mission.

The American Red Cross, United Way, Greenpeace, St. Mary's Health Center in St. Louis, and the University of New Mexico are nonprofit organizations. Such organizations historically have not used marketing tactics in the belief that they were inappropriate. In recent years, however, competitive pressures have forced these organizations to reevaluate their strategies. The Mar-

FIGURE 22-4
Service classifications

Source: Reprinted by permission of the *Harvard Business Review*. An exhibit from "Strategy Is Different in Service Businesses" by Dan R.E. Thomas (July/August 1978). Copyright © 1978 by the President and Fellows of Harvard College; all rights reserved.

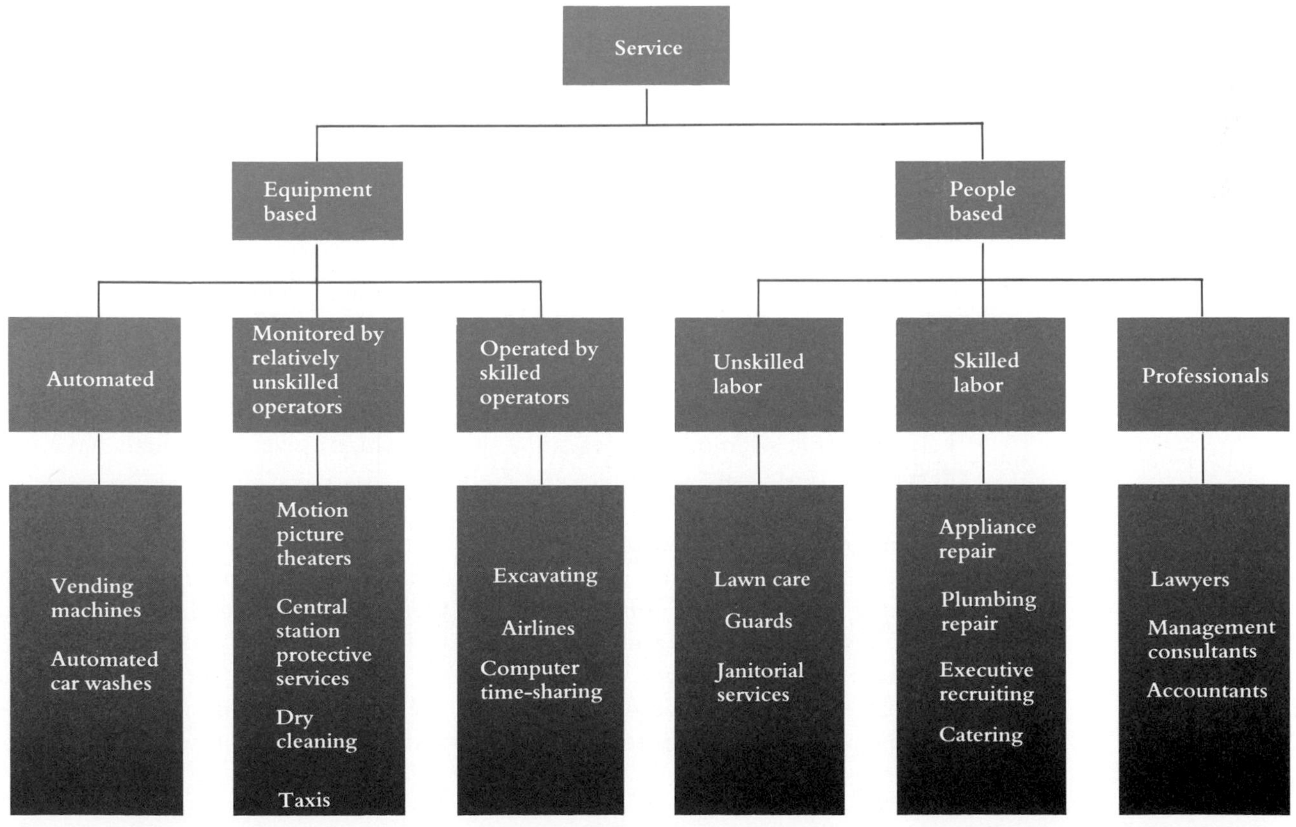

MARKETING · ACTION · MEMO

Marketing Medicine: Reduced Demand Develops Competitive Skills

What is your image of a hospital? A complex, impersonal place with masked medical people too busy to spend much time with patients?

The health care industry wants to change your mind. Today marketing is used by hospitals and other health-care organizations to focus on serving patients better. One reason is that they face a declining demand because of fewer patients and shorter stays. As Linda Bogue, an administrator at San Francisco's Mount Zion Hospital and Medical Center, explains, "Hospitals are struggling to learn all the competitive skills that businesses have known and applied for a long time."

One of the biggest changes has been in promotion. Advertising expenditures were $726 million in 1987, up from only $50 million in 1983. And messages like these are designed to give you new perceptions:

- To gain a reputation as a warm and soothing place, Mount Sinai Medical Center in Miami Beach promotes its own brand of chicken soup.
- Swedish American Hospital in Rockford, Illinois, offers expectant fathers electronic beepers so they can be paged when mothers go into labor.
- New kidney stone equipment at Saint Joseph Medical Center in Burbank, California, is advertised with the theme "Kidney Stones? Who Ya Gotta Call—Stonebusters!"

Special clinics are devoted to problems of unique market niches, such as eating disorders, sleeping disorders, hearing loss, sports injuries, and Alzheimer's disease. Toll-free crisis lines, newsletters, and roving mammography vans have also helped to create a more personalized experience for patients. Today, consumers know they have choices, and they no longer simply go where their doctor is located. But hospitals know doctors are important, too. Some are even using marketing programs to attract and retain physicians.

Source: Based on Stephen Koepp, "Hospitals Learn the Hard Sell," *Time* (January 12, 1987), p. 56; "Hospital Use Down Since Payment Methods Changed," *Marketing News* (October 9, 1987), p. 5; Hospitals Need New Attitude to Succeed in '88," *Marketing News* (October 9, 1987), p. 4.

keting Action Memo describes some of the changes several hospitals have undertaken.

Government Sponsored or Not A third way to classify services is based on whether they are government sponsored. Although there is no direct ownership and they are nonprofit organizations, governments at the federal, state, and local levels provide a broad range of services. The U.S. Army, for example, has adopted many marketing activities. Their "Be All You Can Be" campaign has succeeded at emphasizing adventure and opportunity. In addition, education benefits provide up to $25,200 for college as an incentive for Army enlistment.

Dear Dad,
Remember the time you told me that real courage is putting your fear aside and doing the job?
I thought about that a lot this morning. You see Dad, here in the Army, everything you taught me really means something.

The Army can teach you a lot. Because the Army gives you an education you can't get anywhere else.
In the Army, you'll learn a valuable skill. You'll learn to work as part of a team.
And you'll learn about confidence. Determination. Self-discipline. And character.
Plus, the Montgomery GI Bill and Army College Fund give you the opportunity to learn even more. If you qualify, you can earn as much as $25,200 to help pay for your college education. To find out more, call toll-free 1-800-USA-ARMY.
With your college diploma and your Army experience, you'll have something that most other young people don't: an edge on life.
ARMY. BE ALL YOU CAN BE.

Nonprofit and government services often advertise

CONCEPT CHECK

1 What are the four *I*'s of services?

2 Inventory carrying costs for an accounting firm with certified public accountants would be (a) high, (b) low, or (c) nonexistent?

3 To eliminate service inconsistencies, companies rely on __________ and __________.

HOW CONSUMERS PURCHASE SERVICES

Colleges, hospitals, hotels, and even charities are facing an increasingly competitive environment. Successful service organizations, like successful product-oriented firms, must understand how the consumer views a service and in what ways a company can present a differential advantage relative to competing offerings.

THE PURCHASE PROCESS

The intangible and inseparable aspects of services affect the consumer's evaluation of the purchase. Because services cannot be displayed, demonstrated, or illustrated, consumers cannot make a prepurchase evaluation of all the characteristics of services.[8] Similarly, because services are produced and consumed simultaneously, the buyer must participate in producing the service and that participation can affect the evaluation of the service. Figure 22-5 portrays how different types of goods and services are evaluated by consumers. Tangible goods such as clothing, jewelry, and furniture have *search* qualities, such as color, size, and style, which can be determined before purchase. Services such as restaurants and child care have *experience* qualities, which can only be discerned after purchase or during consumption. Finally, services provided by specialized professionals such as medical diagnoses and legal services have *credence* qualities, or characteristics which the consumer may find impossible to evaluate even after purchase and consumption. Some services, such as those of the banks described in the Marketing Research Report, may have all three qualities!

FIGURE 22-5
How consumers evaluate goods and services

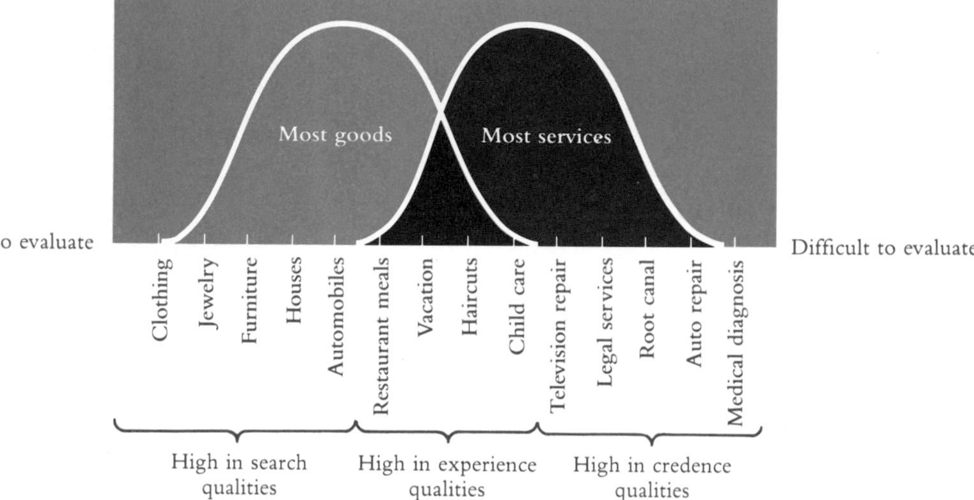

PURCHASE EVALUATION

Once a customer tries a service, what dimensions are evaluated? Two basic dimensions—complexity and divergence—play an important role in the evaluation.[9] *Complexity* is the number and intricacy of the steps required for the service. Plumbing, for example, is more complex than lawn mowing. *Divergence* is the amount of latitude possible in the execution of the service. So standardized services such as hotels have low divergence as compared with the customized services of architects.

CUSTOMER CONTACT AUDIT

Consumers judge services on the tangible aspects of their experience and on their interaction with the service provider. To focus on these experiences, a firm can develop a **customer contact audit**—a flow chart of the points of interaction between consumer and service provider.[10] This is particularly important in high-contact services such as hotels, educational institutions, and automobile rental agencies.[11] Figure 22-6 is a consumer contact audit for renting a car from Hertz. Look carefully at the sequence.

MARKETING · RESEARCH · REPORT

HOW DO YOU SELECT A BANK?

Selecting a bank requires potential customers to evaluate many aspects of the service. Bank managers, faced with the issue of attracting and retaining customers, have attempted to understand how people make the decision to use one bank instead of another.

A study of consumer bank selection was designed to help understand this decision. In the first phase, focus groups discussed the attributes they evaluated when selecting a bank. In the second phase, 1,300 questionnaires were mailed from 3 types of banks (city, college, and rural) to persons who had opened a new account during the past 6 months. Respondents (307) rated the importance of 12 characteristics of financial institutions. The results are shown at right.

There are significant differences in the characteristics used to select a bank that depend on the type of community in which it is located. City people ranked pricing, reputation, and location convenience highest. The customers of the college community bank ranked time convenience, ownership, and employee expertise highest. And the rural community placed pricing, employee attitudes, and return on investment highest. So bank service marketers must be sensitive not only to the various characteristics that may be evaluated but also to the unique needs of potential customers in different communities.

Rank Order of Bank Characteristics

CHARACTERISTIC	TYPE OF BANK		
	CITY	COLLEGE	RURAL
Pricing of services	1	6	1
Reputation	2	8	7
Services offered	5	4.5	9
Time convenience	2	1	10
Location convenience	3	10	6
Employee expertise	7	3	4
Employee attitudes	6	4.5	2
Ownership of institution	9	2	5
Return on investments	10	7	3
Security of deposits	12	11	8
Physical appearance	8	9	12
Promotion efforts	11	12	11

Source: Based on Gene W. Murdock and Robert G. Roe, "Consumer Bank Selection: Attributes of Choice," in Terence A. Shimp et al., eds., *AMA Educator's Proceedings* (Chicago: American Marketing Association, 1986), pp. 12-17.

A Customer's Car Rental Activities A customer decides to rent a car and (1) makes a telephone reservation (see Figure 22-6). An operator answers and receives the information (2) and checks the availability of the car at the desired location (3). When the customer arrives at the rental site (4) the reservation system is again accessed, and the customer provides information regarding payment, address, and driver's license (5). A car is assigned to the customer (6), who proceeds by bus to the car pickup (7). On return to the rental location (8), the car is parked and the customer checks in, providing information on mileage, gas consumption, and damages (9). A bill is subsequently prepared (10).

Each of the steps numbered 1 to 10 is a customer contact point where the tangible aspects of Hertz service are seen by the customer. Figure 22-6, however,

FIGURE 22-6
Customer contact in car rental (shaded boxes)

1 Customer telephones reservation
2 Receive customer information
3 Access reservation system
4 Customer arrives
5 Receive customer information
6 Assign car
7 Customer gets bus to car and departs
8 Customer returns car to receiving lot
A Preliminary inspection
9 Customer checks in and gives information
B Secondary inspection
C Perform periodic maintenance
Update car status in computer
D Preparation and park in ready lot
10 Prepare and present billing
E Update car status with computer

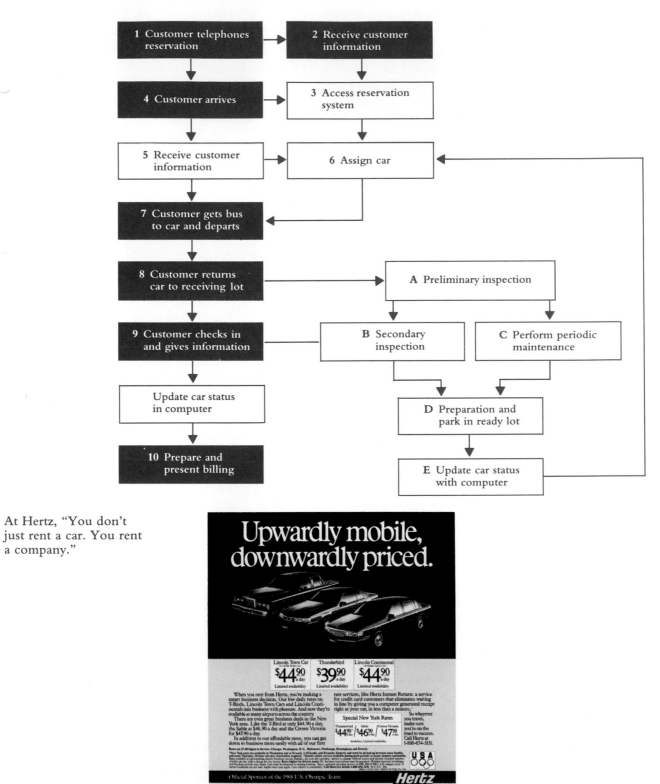

At Hertz, "You don't just rent a car. You rent a company."

also shows a series of steps lettered A to F that involve two levels of inspections on the automobile. These steps are essential in providing a car that runs, but they are not points of customer interaction. To create a service advantage, Hertz must create a competitive advantage in the sequence of interactions with the customer.

CONCEPT CHECK

1 **What is the difference between search and experience qualities?**

2 **Hertz created its differential advantage at the points of ___________.**

MANAGING THE MARKETING OF SERVICES

Just as the unique aspects of services necessitate changes in the consumer's purchase process, the marketing management process requires special adaptation. As emphasized earlier in the chapter, in services marketing the employee plays a central role in attracting, building, and maintaining relationships with customers.[12] This aspect of services marketing has led to a new concept—internal marketing.[13]

Internal marketing is based on the notion that a service organization must focus on its employees, or internal market, before successful programs can be directed at customers.[14] The internal marketing concept holds that an organization's employees (its "internal market") will be influenced to develop a market orientation by applying marketing-like activities to them. This idea suggests that employees and employee development through recruitment, training, communication, and administration are critical to the success of service organizations.[15]

Let's use the four *P*'s framework of the text for discussing the marketing mix for services.

PRODUCT (SERVICE)

To a large extent, the concepts of the product component of the marketing mix discussed in Chapters 9 and 10 apply equally well to Cheerios (a good) and to American Express (a service). Yet there are three aspects of the product/service element of the mix that warrant special attention: exclusivity, brand name, and capacity management.

Exclusivity Chapter 9 pointed out that one favorable dimension in a new product is its ability to be patented. Remember that a patent gives the manufacturer of a product exclusive rights to its production for 17 years. A major difference between products and services is that services cannot be patented. So the creator of a successful fast-food hamburger chain could quickly discover the concept being copied by others. Domino's Pizza now sees competitors copy its quick delivery advantage, which has propelled the company to the success discussed in Chapter 20.

Logos create service identities

Branding An important aspect in marketing goods is the branding strategy used. However, because services are intangible, the brand name or identifying logo of the organization is particularly important in consumer decisions because it is more difficult to describe what is being provided.[16] Take a look at the figures above to determine how successful some companies have been in branding their service by name, logo, or symbol.

Capacity Management A key distinction between goods and services is the inseparability of services. To buy and simultaneously use the service, the customer must be present at the service delivery site. For example, a patient must be in a hospital to "buy" an appendectomy, and a guest must be in a hotel to "buy" an accommodation. So the product/service component of the mix must be made available to the consumer by managing demand. This is referred to as **capacity management.**

Service organizations must manage the availability of the offering to (1) smooth demand over time so that demand matches capacity and (2) ensure that the organization's assets are used in ways that will maximize the return on investment (ROI).[17] Figure 22-7 shows how a hotel tries to manage its capacity during the high and low seasons. Differing price structures are assigned to each

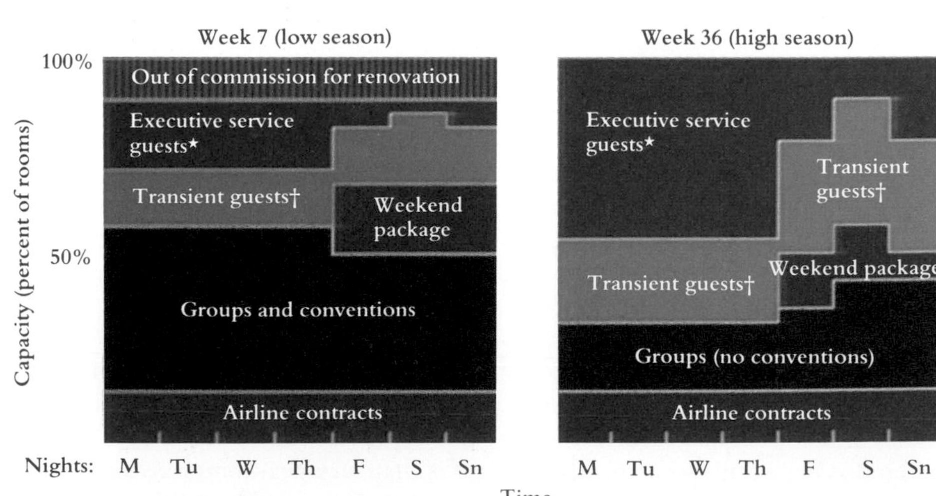

FIGURE 22-7
Balancing capacity management

Source: Redrawn from Christopher H. Lovelock, *Services Marketing*, © 1984, p. 205. Reprinted by permission of Prentice-Hall, Inc., Englewood Cliffs, New Jersey.

*Employees of corporations called upon by sales force (pay full price and book rooms through special reservations line).

†Individual customers paying full price but reserving rooms via publicized telephone number or by just "walking in."

Hotels manage capacity with deals

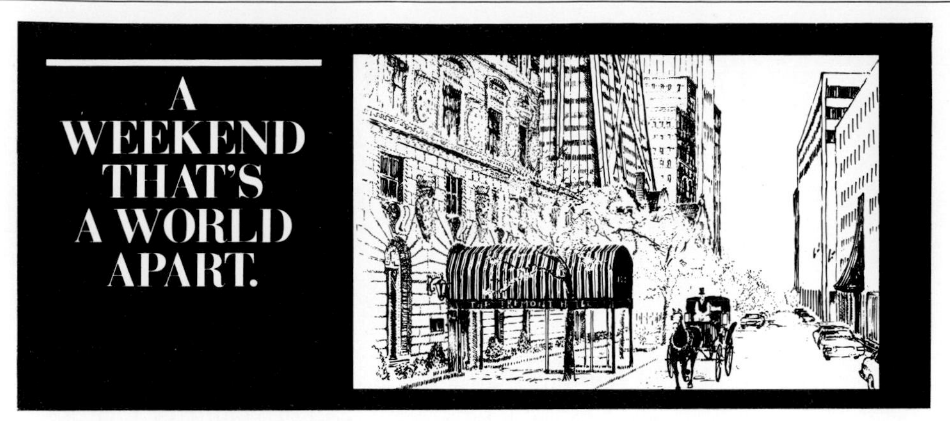

ONE MAGNIFICENT HOLIDAY

- Guest room accommodations for two nights
- Continental Breakfast each morning
- Chilled bottle of champagne
- Complimentary valet parking
- Exclusive Michigan Avenue gift certificates
- Fresh rose for the lady
- Available for a Friday or Saturday arrival
- Upgrade to suite for $100 extra per night
- Taxes and gratuities included
- $269 per couple

FIVE DIAMOND HOLIDAY

- Penthouse suite accommodations for two nights
- Limousine service from your residence (greater Chicago area) or from airport to hotel
- Chilled bottle of Taittinger Blanc de Blanc and beluga caviar served during the trip to the hotel
- Two dozen fresh roses for the lady
- Dinner served in the privacy of the penthouse suite from a special menu
- Breakfast in bed Saturday morning
- Limousine tour of galleries, shops and other sights during the day on Saturday
- Exclusive Michigan Avenue gift certificates
- Gourmet picnic lunch served from the limousine anywhere in Chicago
- Dinner at Cricket's
- A "special event" chosen personally by our concierge
- A very special gift before retiring: a crystal decanter of one of the world's best brandies and imported chocolates
- Brunch Sunday morning at Cricket's
- Limousine service to residence or airport
- Taxes and gratuities included
- $2,500 per couple—this weekend is so personalized, only one will be sold per weekend, per hotel

John B. Coleman Hotels/Chicago

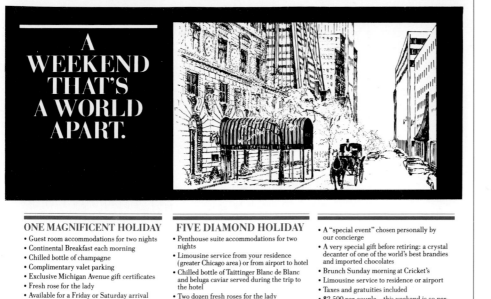

segment of consumers to help moderate or adjust demand for the service. Airline contracts fill a fixed number of rooms throughout the year. In the low season, when more rooms are available, tour packages at appealing prices are used to attract groups or conventions, such as an offer for 7 nights in Orlando at a reduced price. Weekend packages are also offered to buyers. In the high-demand season groups are less desirable because guests who will pay top dollar travel to Florida on their own.

PRICING

In the service industries, *price* is often referred to in various ways. Hospitals refer to charges; consultants, lawyers, physicians, and accountants to fees; airlines to fares; and hotels to rates.

Setting Prices Two common methods of pricing services are cost plus percentage-of-cost and target ROI pricing.

Cost plus percentage-of-cost pricing, discussed in Chapter 12, entails charging a customer for the cost of providing the service plus an additional fixed percentage. Professional service organizations such as accounting firms charge a fee based on a billable rate. The billable rate is the cost of the accountant (salary, benefits, training, and overhead) plus a markup. This pricing is common to most professional service organizations such as law, medicine, and consulting.

In *target ROI pricing* the price for the service allows a targeted rate of ROI.

Price influences perceptions of services

This method of setting price is common in capital-intensive services such as airlines or public utilities.

Role of Pricing Pricing services plays two essential roles: (1) to affect consumer perceptions and (2) to be used in capacity management. Because of the intangible nature of services, price can indicate the quality of the service. Would you be willing to risk a $100 surgery? Or a $50 divorce lawyer? Studies have shown that when there are few well-known cues by which to judge a product, consumers use price.[18] Look at the ad above. Would you have concerns about a $795 delivery or think it's good value for the money?

The capacity management role of price is also important to movie theaters, hair stylists, restaurants, and hotels. Many service businesses use **off-peak pricing,** which consists of charging different prices as a function of the variations in service demand during different times of the day or days of the week. Restaurants offer luncheon specials, and movie theaters offer matinee prices. Sunrise Hospital in Las Vegas offered a 5¼ percent rebate on the total hospital bill to patients admitted on a Friday or Saturday so it could level out the demand for surgical suites.[19]

PLACE (DISTRIBUTION)

Place or distribution is a major factor in developing service marketing strategy because of the inseparability of services from the producer. Rarely are intermediaries involved in the distribution of a service; the distribution site and service deliverer are the tangible components of the service.

Historically in professional services marketing, little attention was paid to distribution. But as competition grows, the value of convenient distribution is being recognized. Dental chains such as Omnidentix,[20] legal firms such as the Hyatt chain, and accounting firms such as Arthur Young all use multiple locations for the distribution of services. For several years banks have offered automatic teller services to their customers. Today customers of participating banks using the Cirrus system can access any one of thousands of automatic teller systems throughout the United States.

PROMOTION

The value of promotion, specifically advertising, for many services is to show the benefits of purchasing the service, such as the outcome of using United Airlines. It is valuable to stress consistent quality and efficient, courteous service.[21] In most cases promotional concerns of services are similar to those of products. For example, sales promotions such as the all-expense paid trip to Jamaica described in the Marketing Action Memo can be used to encourage trial. However, publicity is a more common tool in the promotion of services.[22]

Publicity Publicity has played a major role in the promotional strategy of nonprofit services and some professional organizations. Nonprofit organizations such as public school districts, the Chicago Symphony, religious organizations, and hospitals have used publicity to disseminate their messages. Because of the heavy reliance on publicity, many services use public service announcements (PSAs). Because PSAs are free, nonprofit groups have tended to rely on them

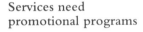

Services need promotional programs

MARKETING·ACTION·MEMO

THE NEW COLLEGIANS: A TARGET FOR CABLE TV

Does an all-expense-paid trip to Jamaica with rock group Bon Jovi sound appealing to you?

If you are a college student, programming service Music Television (MTV) hopes it will. According to vice president of marketing Bob Friedman, "We want our promotions to be unlike anything else. They must be something fantasy-like, a dream we can give away." The dreams are those of students like you, who represent $20 billion in annual discretionary purchasing power. The promotion is intended to capture your entertainment interest.

Cable TV is considered a "mature" industry where success requires that programming meet the needs of a well-defined market segment. New services such as The Fashion Channel, Gospel Music Network, Movietime, and The Travel Channel are products designed to fill special needs. MTV and New York–based Campus Network's National College Television (NCTV) are targeted specifically to the 12.5 million college students in the United States.

College life is changing. Several years ago, a TV and a stereo were luxuries at college. Today, students may have stereo systems, VCRs, PCs, CD players, and cable-ready color TVs. To purchase and maintain these entertainment centers, students spend more than 80 percent of their disposable income. They also have primary interest in music and movies—two types of entertainment that cable TV can provide.

For example, in response to the findings of studies of their viewing audience, NCTV offers 2 hours of video music called "Audiophila," a 60-minute concert, and a progressive video program called "New Grooves." Bradley I. Siegel of NCTV explains, "We found that the college student does not always want to watch what the networks and independent stations offer during prime time." Another system, Video Center Events (VCE), will offer live concerts, political/social issue debates, and Broadway shows to college auditoriums via satellite. So the alternatives for college student TV watchers are increasing dramatically, as is the competition for your time.

See you in Jamaica!

Source: Based on Christopher Colletti, "Dormitories Wired for Success," *Advertising Age* (February 2, 1987), pp. S1, S16; Marilyn Adler and Geralyn Wiener, "Student Buying Rates High Interest," *Advertising Age* (February 2, 1987), p. S1; Wayne Walley, "New Services Need to Channel Resources," *Advertising Age* (December 7, 1987), pp. 514-515.

as the foundation of their media plan.[23] However, as discussed in Chapter 16 on promotion, the timing and location of a PSA are under the control of the medium, not the organization. So the nonprofit service group cannot control who sees the message or when the message is given.

Negative Attitudes In the past, advertising has been viewed negatively by many nonprofit and professional service organizations. In fact, professional groups such as law, dentistry, and medicine had previously barred their members from advertising by their respective professional codes of conduct. A Supreme Court case in 1976, however, struck down this constraint on professional services advertising.[24] In recent years these associations have set up ethical guidelines on the use of promotion.

FIGURE 22-8
Key events in deregulating the services industries

YEAR	DEVELOPMENT
1969	The Federal Communications Commission gives MCI the right to hook its long-distance network into local phone systems
1970	The Federal Reserve Board frees interest rates on bank deposits over $100,000 with maturities of less than 6 months
1975	The Securities and Exchange Commission orders brokers to cease fixing commissions on stock sales
1977	Congress passes the "Federal Express" bill, deregulating the air freight industry
1977	Merrill Lynch offers the Cash Management Account, competing more closely with commercial banks
1978	Congress deregulates the passenger airline industry
1979	The Federal Communications Commission allows AT&T to sell nonregulated services, such as data processing
1980	The Federal Reserve System allows banks to pay interest on checking accounts
1980	Congress deregulates the trucking and railroad industries
1981	Sears becomes the first one-stop financial supermarket, offering insurance, banking, brokerage, and real estate services
1982	Congress deregulates the intercity bus industry
1984	AT&T agrees to divest its local phone companies; receives permission to compete in other computing and communications activities

Source: Adapted from James L. Heskett, *Managing in the Service Economy* (Boston, Mass.: Harvard Business School Press, 1986), p. 156.

Although opposition to advertising remains strong in some professional groups, the barriers to promotion are being broken down. In recent years, advertising has been used by religious groups; legal, medical, and dental services; educational institutions; and many other service organizations. As shown in the cartoon, even political candidates are using marketing and promotion techniques.

SERVICES IN THE FUTURE

What can we expect from the services industry in the future? Two factors that will have a major effect are the deregulation of the services industries and technological development.[25]

Deregulation is partially the result of the technological innovation that has introduced many new forms of competition into many "old" industries. As Figure 22-8 illustrates, one by one, transportation, communications, financial institutions, professional services, and others have gone through some kind of regulatory changes. The changes have generally led to a greater variety of services and the recognition that services require management of all functions, including marketing.

CONCEPT CHECK

1. **How does a movie theater use off-peak pricing?**
2. **Smoothing demand is the focus of __________ management.**
3. **Does a lawyer use cost plus percentage-of-cost or target return on investment pricing?**

SUMMARY

1. Services differ from goods in that they are intangible and inseparable. Intangible means advertising is needed to present the service benefits. Inseparable means that service deliverers represent the service quality.
2. Because services are inseparable from the producer, they are often inconsistent. Service companies rely on standardization and training to reduce service delivery inconsistencies.
3. Inventory concerns differ between goods and services. In people-based services, costs of inventory can be high if the service provider is on a fixed salary.
4. Services can be classified in several ways. The primary distinction is whether they are provided by people or equipment. Other distinctions of services are in terms of tax status (profit versus nonprofit) or whether the service is provided by a government agency.
5. Consumers can evaluate three aspects of goods or services: search qualities, experience qualities, and credence qualities.
6. A customer contact audit is a flow chart of the points of interaction between a service provider and its customers, where competitive differential advantages should be created.
7. Internal marketing, which focuses on an organization's employees, is critical to the success of a service organization.
8. In new service development a difficulty for organizations is that patent rights protecting the developer's exclusivity are not awarded. Therefore brands and logos (which can be protected) are particularly important to help distinguish between competing service providers.
9. Because of the inseparability of production and consumption of services, capacity management is important in the service element of the mix. This process involves smoothing demand to meet capacity.
10. The intangible nature of services makes price an important cue to indicate service quality to the consumer.
11. Inseparability of production and consumption in services eliminates intermediaries in most service marketing. Distribution is important as a tangible component of a service offering.
12. Historically, promotion has not been viewed favorably by many nonprofit and professional service organizations. In recent years this attitude has changed, and traditional reliance on publicity is waning. Service organizations are seeking greater control of their promotional programs.

KEY TERMS AND CONCEPTS

services p. 604
four I's of services p. 605
idle production capacity p. 606
service continuum p. 608
customer contact audit p. 612
internal marketing p. 615
capacity management p. 616
off-peak pricing p. 618

CHAPTER PROBLEMS AND APPLICATIONS

1 Explain how the four I's of services would apply to a branch office of the Bank of America.
2 Idle production capacity may be related to inventory or capacity management. How would the pricing component of the mix reduce idle production capacity for (a) a car wash, (b) a stage theater group, and (c) a university?
3 What are the search, experience, and credence qualities of an airline for the business traveler and pleasure traveler? What qualities are most important to each group?
4 Outline the customer contact audit for the typical deposit you make at your neighborhood bank.
5 The text suggests that internal marketing is necessary before a successful marketing program can be directed at consumers. Why is this particularly true for service organizations?
6 Outline the capacity management strategies that an airline must consider.
7 Draw the channel of distribution for the following services: (a) a restaurant, (b) a hospital, and (c) a hotel.
8 How does off-peak pricing differ from the target return on investment or cost plus percentage-of-cost approach?
9 In recent years many service businesses have begun to provide their employees with uniforms. Explain the rationale behind this strategy in terms of the concepts discussed in this chapter.
10 Look back at the service continuum in Figure 22-3. Explain how the following points in the continuum differ in terms of consistency: (a) salt, (b) automobile, (c) advertising agency, and (d) teaching.

SUGGESTED READINGS

"Do You Believe in Magic?" *Time* (April 25, 1988), pp. 66-76. *This article describes the miraculous changes in the Walt Disney Company in its theme park, movie, and television service offerings in the past 5 years.*

James L. Heskett, "Lessons in the Service Sector," *Harvard Business Review* (March-April 1987), pp. 118-126. *This article describes the common themes and practices of successful service companies.*

Christopher H. Lovelock, *Managing Services* (Englewood Cliffs, N.J.: Prentice-Hall, Inc., 1988). *This book provides a collection of articles and cases on services management and marketing.*

"Presto! The Convenience Industry: Making Life a Little Simpler," *Business Week* (April 27, 1987), pp. 86-94. *This article describes some new services designed to provide convenience.*

APPENDIX B

CAREER PLANNING IN MARKETING

Getting a Job: The Process of Marketing Yourself

Getting a job is usually a lengthy process, and it is exactly that—a *process* that involves careful planning, implementation, and control. You may have everything going for you: a respectable grade point average (GPA), relevant work experience, several extracurricular activities, superior interpersonal and communication skills, and demonstrated leadership qualities. Despite these, you still need to market yourself systematically and aggressively; after all, even the best products lie dormant on the retailer's shelves unless marketed effectively.

The process of getting a job involves the same activities marketing managers use to develop and introduce products into the marketplace. The only difference is you are marketing yourself, not a new product. You need to conduct marketing research by analyzing your personal qualities (performing a self-audit) and by identifying job opportunities. Based on your research results, select a target market—those job opportunities which are compatible with your interests, goals, skills, and abilities—and design a marketing mix around that target market. *You* are the "product"; you must decide how to "position" yourself in the job market. The price component of the marketing mix is the salary range and job benefits (such as health and life insurance, vacation time, and retirement benefits) that you hope to receive. Promotion involves communicating your product message to prospective employers through written correspondence (advertising) and job interviews (personal selling). The place element focuses on how to reach prospective employers, such as job interviews at the campus placement center or direct contact by letters or in person.

This appendix will assist you in career planning by (1) providing information about careers in marketing and (2) outlining a job search process.

CAREERS IN MARKETING

The diversity of marketing opportunities is reflected in the many types of marketing jobs, ranging from purchasing to marketing research to public relations to product management. The growing concern with marketing in many nontraditional organizations—such as hospitals, financial institutions, the perform-

ing arts, and government—has added to the numerous opportunities offered by traditional employers such as manufacturers, retailers, consulting firms, and advertising agencies. Most of these marketing careers offer the chance to work with interesting people on stimulating and rewarding problems. Comments one product manager, "I love marketing as a career because there are different challenges every day."[1]

Recent studies of career paths and salaries suggest that marketing careers can also provide an excellent opportunity for advancement and substantial pay. For example, a survey of chief executive officers (CEOs) of the nation's 500 largest industrial corporations and 500 largest service corporations revealed that CEOs were more likely to have backgrounds in marketing than in any other field.[2] Similarly, reports of average starting salaries of college graduates indicate that salaries in marketing compare favorably with those in many other fields. The average monthly starting salary of marketing undergraduates in 1987 was $1,686, compared with $1,876 for accounting majors and $1,831 for students with degrees in business administration.[3] The future is likely to be even better. *Business Week's Guide to Careers* suggests that 3 of the top 12 entry-level positions (in terms of ultimate salary potential and number of openings expected) in business in the coming decade will be in marketing and sales.[4] Two of these positions—retail buying and international marketing—will have the highest salaries of the 12.

Figure B-1 describes marketing occupations in six major categories: product management and physical distribution, advertising, retailing, sales, marketing research, and nonprofit marketing. One of these may be right for you! (Additional sources of marketing career information are provided at the end of this appendix.)

PRODUCT MANAGEMENT AND PHYSICAL DISTRIBUTION

Many organizations assign one manager the responsibility for a particular product or group of products. For example, P&G has separate managers for Tide, Cheer, Gain, and Bold. Product or brand managers are involved in all aspects

PRODUCT MANAGEMENT AND PHYSICAL DISTRIBUTION

Product manager for consumer goods develops new products that can cost millions of dollars, with advice and consent of management—a job with great responsibility.

Administrative manager oversees the organization within a company that transports products to consumers and handles customer service.

Operations manager supervises warehousing and other physical distribution functions and often is directly involved in moving goods on the warehouse floor.

Traffic and transportation manager evaluates the costs and benefits of different types of transportation.

Inventory control manager forecasts demand for stockpiled goods, coordinates production with plant managers, and keeps track of current levels of shipments to keep customers supplied.

Administrative analyst performs cost analyses of physical distribution systems.

Customer service manager maintains good relations with customers by coordinating sales staffs, marketing management, and physical distribution management.

Physical distribution consultant is an expert in the transportation and distribution of goods.

ADVERTISING

Account executive maintains contact with clients while coordinating the creative work among artists and copywriters. In full-service ad agencies, account executives are considered partners with the client in promoting the product and helping to develop marketing strategy.

Media buyer deals with media sales representatives in selecting advertising media and analyzes the value of media being purchased.

Copywriter works with art director in conceptualizing advertisements and writes the text of print or radio ads or the storyboards of television ads.

Art director handles the visual component of advertisements.

Sales promotion manager designs promotions for consumer products and works at an ad agency or a sales promotion agency.

Public relations manager develops written or filmed messages for the public and handles contacts with the press.

Specialty advertising manager develops advertising for the sales staff and customers or distributors.

RETAILING

Buyer selects products a store sells, surveys consumer trends, and evaluates the past performance of products and suppliers.

Store manager oversees the staff and services at a store.

SALES

Direct salesperson (door-to-door) calls on consumers in their homes to make sales.

Trade salesperson calls on retailers or wholesalers to sell products for manufacturers.

Industrial or semitechnical salesperson sells supplies and services to businesses.

Complex or professional salesperson sells complicated or custom-designed products to business. This requires understanding of the technology of a product.

MARKETING RESEARCH

Project manager for the supplier coordinates and oversees the market studies for a client.

Account executive for the supplier serves as a liaison between client and market research firm, like an advertising agency account executive.

In-house project director acts as project manager (see above) for the market studies conducted by the firm for which he or she works.

Marketing research specialist for an advertising agency performs or contracts for market studies for agency clients.

NONPROFIT MARKETING

Marketing manager for nonprofit organizations develops and directs mail campaigns, fund raising, and public relations.

FIGURE B-1
Twenty-six marketing occupations

Source: David W. Rosenthal and Michael A. Powell, *Careers in Marketing*, © 1984, pp. 352-354. Adapted by permission of Prentice-Hall, Englewood Cliffs, N.J.

of a product's marketing program, such as marketing research, sales, sales promotion, advertising, and pricing, as well as manufacturing.[5]

College graduates with bachelor's and master's degrees—often in marketing and business—enter P&G as brand assistants, the only starting position in its product or brand group. Each year over 1,000 students from 200 campuses accept positions with P&G.[6] As brand assistants, their responsibilities consist primarily of selling and sales training.

After 1 to 2 years of good performance, the brand assistant is promoted to assistant brand manager and after about the same period to brand (product) manager. These promotions often involve several brand groups. For example, a new employee might start as brand assistant for P&G's soap products, be promoted to assistant brand manager for Crest toothpaste, and subsequently become brand manager for Folger's coffee, Charmin, or Pampers.

Several other jobs related to product management (Figure B-1) deal with physical distribution issues such as storing the manufactured product (inventory), moving the product from the firm to the customers (transportation), maintaining good relations with customers (customer service), and engaging in many other aspects of the manufacture and sale of goods. Prospects for these jobs are likely to increase dramatically in the 1990's as more firms adopt a marketing orientation and attempt to become more adept at meeting customers' needs.

ADVERTISING

Although we may see hundreds of advertisements in a day, what we can't see easily is the fascinating and complex advertising profession. The 1,500 to 3,000 starting positions filled every year include jobs with a variety of firms.[7] Advertising professionals often remark that they find their jobs appealing because the days are not routine and involve creative activities with many interesting people.

Advertising positions are available in three kinds of organizations: advertisers, media, and agencies. Advertisers include manufacturers, retail stores, service firms, and many other types of companies. Often they have an advertising department responsible for preparing and placing their own ads. Advertising careers are also possible with the media: television, radio stations, magazines, and newspapers. Finally, advertising agencies offer job opportunities through their use of account management, research, media, and creative services.

Most starting positions in advertising are as a media buyer—the person who chooses and buys the media that will carry the ad—or as a copywriter—the person responsible for the message, or copy, in an ad. From these positions, promotion to assistant account executive, who acts as a liaison between the client and the agency's creative department, may come quickly. Students interested in advertising should develop good communications skills and try to gain advertising experience through summer employment or internships.

RETAILING

There are two separate career paths in retailing: merchandise management and store management (Figure B-2). The key position in merchandising is that of a buyer, who is responsible for selecting merchandise, guiding the promotion of the merchandise, setting prices, bargaining with wholesalers, training the salesforce, and monitoring the competitive environment. The buyer must also be able to organize and coordinate many critical activities under severe time

FIGURE B-2
Typical retailing career paths

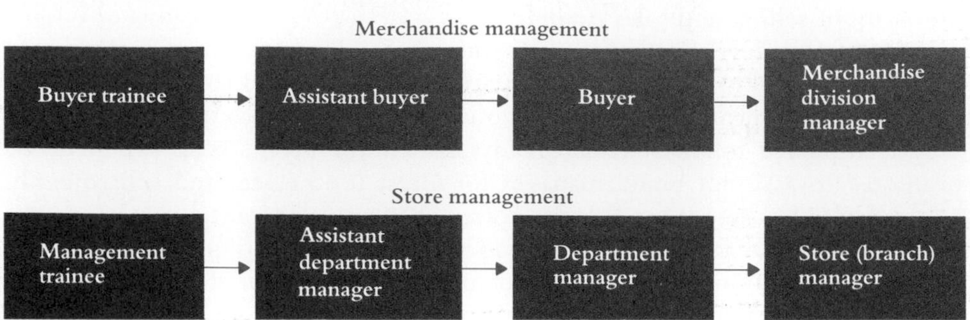

constraints. In contrast, store management involves the supervision of personnel in all departments and the general management of all facilities, equipment, and merchandise displays. In addition, store managers are responsible for the financial performance of each department and for the store as a whole.

Most starting jobs in retailing are trainee positions. A trainee is usually placed in a management training program and then given a position as an assistant buyer or assistant department manager. Advancement and responsibility can be achieved quickly because there is a shortage of qualified personnel in retailing and because superior performance of an individual is quickly reflected in sales and profits—two visible measures of success.

SALES

Over a third of new marketing jobs in 1987 were sales positions.[8] College graduates from many disciplines are attracted to these positions because of the increasingly professional nature of selling jobs and the many opportunities they can provide. A selling career offers benefits that are hard to match in any other field: (1) the opportunity for rapid advancement (into management or to new territories and accounts), (2) the potential for extremely attractive compensation, (3) the development of personal satisfaction, feelings of accomplishment, and increased self-confidence, and (4) independence; salespeople often have almost complete control over their time and activities.

Employment opportunities in sales occupations are found in a wide variety of organizations, including insurance agencies, retailers, and financial service firms (Figure B-3). Activities in sales jobs include *selling duties,* such as prospecting for customers, demonstrating the product, or quoting prices; *sales-support duties,* such as handling complaints and helping solve technical problems; and *nonselling duties,* such as preparing reports, attending sales meetings, and monitoring competitive activities. Given the many sales organizations and activities, there are more job openings in sales than in any other area in marketing.

MARKETING RESEARCH

Marketing researchers play important roles in many organizations today. They are responsible for obtaining, analyzing, and interpreting data to facilitate making marketing decisions. This means marketing researchers are basically problem solvers. Success in the area requires not only an understanding of statistics and computers but also knowledge of consumer behavior and an ability to communicate with management. Individuals who are inquisitive, methodical, analytical, and solution oriented find the field particularly rewarding.

More than 30,000 men and women are currently working in the market research industry.[9] Their responsibilities include defining the marketing problem, designing the questionnaire, selecting the sample, collecting and analyzing the data, and, finally, reporting the results of the research. These jobs are available in three kinds of organizations. *Marketing research consulting firms* contract with large companies to provide research about their products or services. *Advertising agencies* may provide research services to help clients with questions related to advertising and promotional problems. Finally, some companies have an *in-house research staff* to design and execute their research projects.

Although marketing researchers may start as assistants performing routine tasks, the potential for learning is enormous. Survey design, interviewing, report writing, and all aspects of the research process are challenging learning tasks and useful skills. In addition, research projects deal with very diverse problems such as consumer motivation, pricing, forecasting, and competition. The field of marketing research offers almost limitless opportunity for creative and challenging work.

THE JOB SEARCH PROCESS

Activities you should consider during your job search process include assessing yourself, identifying job opportunities, preparing your résumé and related correspondence, and going on job interviews.

ASSESSING YOURSELF

You must know your product—you—so that you can market yourself effectively to prospective employers. Consequently a critical first step in your job search is conducting a self-analysis, which involves critically examining yourself on the following dimensions: interests, abilities, education, experience, person-

FIGURE B-3
Employment opportunities in selected sales occupations (1986 to 2000)

OCCUPATION	1986 EMPLOYMENT	2000 EMPLOYMENT	PERCENT CHANGE 1986-2000	AVERAGE ANNUAL GROWTH
Insurance sales workers	463,000	565,000	+22	7,300
Retail sales workers	3,579,000	4,780,000	+34	85,800
Securities and financial services sales workers	197,000	279,000	+42	5,900
Real estate agents and brokers	376,000	542,000	+44	11,900
Travel agents	105,000	154,000	+46	3,500

Source: *Monthly Labor Review* (Washington, D.C.: U.S. Department of Labor, Bureau of Labor Statistics, September, 1987), p. 52.

ality, desired job environment, and personal goals.[10] The importance of performing this assessment was stressed by a management consultant[11]:

> Many graduates enter the world of work without even understanding the fact that they are specific somebodies, much less knowing the kinds of competencies and motivations with which they have been endowed. . . . The tragedy of not knowing is awesome. Ignorant of who they are, most graduates are doomed to spend too much of their lives in work for which they are poorly suited. . . . Self-knowledge is critical to effectively managing your career.

Asking Key Questions A self-analysis, in part, entails asking yourself some very important and difficult questions (Figure B-4). It is critical that you respond to the questions honestly because your answers ultimately will be used as a guide in your job selection. A less-than-candid appraisal of yourself might result in a job mismatch.

FIGURE B-4
Questions to ask in your self-analysis

INTERESTS

How do I like to spend my time?

Do I enjoy being with people?

Do I like working with mechanical things?

Do I enjoy working with numbers?

Am I a member of many organizations?

Do I enjoy physical activities?

Do I like to read?

ABILITIES

Am I adept at working with numbers?

Am I adept at working with mechanical things?

Do I have good verbal and written communication skills?

What special talents do I have?

In which abilities do I wish I were more adept?

EDUCATION

How have my courses and extracurricular activities prepared me for a specific job?

Which were my best subjects? My worst? The most fun? The least?

Is my GPA an accurate picture of my academic ability? Why?

Do I aspire to a graduate degree? Before beginning my job?

Why did I choose my major?

EXPERIENCE

What previous jobs have I held? What were my responsibilities in each?

Were any of my jobs applicable to positions I may be seeking? How?

What did I like the most about my previous jobs? Like the least?

Why did I work in the jobs I did?

If I had it to do over again, would I work in these jobs? Why?

PERSONALITY

What are my good and bad traits?

Am I competitive?

Do I work well with others?

Am I outspoken?

Am I a leader or a follower?

Do I work well under pressure?

Do I work quickly, or am I methodical?

Do I get along well with others?

Am I ambitious?

Do I work well independently of others?

DESIRED JOB ENVIRONMENT

Am I willing to relocate? Why?

Do I have a geographical preference? Why?

Would I mind traveling in my job?

Do I have to work for a large, nationally known firm to be satisfied?

Must the job I assume offer rapid promotion opportunities?

If I could design my own job, what characteristics would it have?

How important is high initial salary to me?

PERSONAL GOALS

What are my short-term and long-term goals? Why?

Am I career oriented, or do I have broader interests?

What are my career goals?

What jobs are likely to help me achieve my goals?

What do I hope to be doing in 5 years? In 10 years?

What do I want out of life?

STRENGTHS	WEAKNESSES
Enjoy being with people	Am not adept at working with numbers
Am an avid reader	Have minimal work experience
Have good communication skills	Have a mediocre GPA
Am involved in many extracurricular activities	Am sometimes impatient
Work well with others	Resent close supervision
Work well independently	Work methodically (slowly)
Am aggressive	Will not relocate
Am willing to travel in the job	Anger easily sometimes
Am goal oriented	
Have a good sense of humor	
Am a self-starter, have drive	

FIGURE B-5
Hypothetical list of job candidate's strengths and weaknesses

Identifying Strengths and Weaknesses After you have addressed the questions posed in Figure B-4, you are ready to identify your strengths and weaknesses. To do so, draw a vertical line down the middle of a sheet of paper and label one side of the paper "strengths" and the other side "weaknesses." Based on your answers to the questions, record your strong and weak points in their respective column. Ideally this cataloging should be done over a few days to give you adequate time to reflect on your attributes. In addition, you might seek input from others who know you well (such as parents, close relatives, friends, professors, or employers) and can offer more objective views. They might even evaluate you on the questions in Figure B-4, and you can compare the results with your own evaluation. A hypothetical list of strengths and weaknesses is shown in Figure B-5.

Additional information about yourself can be obtained by developing a list of the five experiences or activities you most enjoy and analyzing what they have in common. Don't be surprised if the common characteristics are related to your strengths and weaknesses!

Taking Job-Related Tests Personality and vocational interest tests, provided by many colleges and universities, can give you other ideas about yourself. After tests have been administered and scored, test takers meet with testing service counselors to discuss the results. Test results generally suggest jobs for which students have an inclination. If you have not already done so, you may wish to see whether your school offers testing services.[12]

IDENTIFYING YOUR JOB OPPORTUNITIES

To identify and analyze the job market, you must conduct some marketing research to determine what industries *and* companies offer promising job opportunities that relate to the results of your self-analysis. Several sources can help in your search. Figure B-6 presents the percentage of newly hired college graduates in 1985 to 1986 who obtained their jobs from various sources. A number of sources warrant special attention.

FIGURE B-6
Sources of jobs for newly hired college graduates

SOURCE OF JOB	PERCENT OF NEW EMPLOYEES
On-campus interviewing	43.4
Write-ins	10.5
Responses from want ads	8.7
Job listings with placement office	7.9
Current employee referrals	5.7
Walk-ins	4.5
Cooperative education programs	3.8
Internship programs	3.7
High-demand major programs	3.6
Summer employment	3.0
Part-time employment	2.5
Minority career programs	1.8
Referrals from campus organizations	1.8
Unsolicited referrals from placement	1.4
Women's career programs	0.5

Source: *Recruiting Trends 1986-87*, J.D. Shingleton and L.P. Scheetz, Michigan State University.

College Placement Office Your college placement office is an excellent source of job information. Personnel in that office can (1) inform you about which companies will be recruiting on campus, (2) alert you to unexpected job openings, (3) advise you about short-term and long-term career prospects, (4) offer advice on résumé construction, (5) assess your interviewing strengths and weaknesses, and (6) help you evaluate a job offer. In addition, the office usually contains a variety of written materials focusing on different industries and companies and tips on job hunting. One major publication available in most campus placement offices is the *Campus Placement Annual,* which contains a list of employers, kinds of job openings for college graduates, and whom to contact about jobs in those firms.

Library The public or college library can provide you with reference material that, among other things, describes successful firms and their operations, defines the content of various jobs, and forecasts job opportunities. For example, *Fortune* publishes lists of the 1,000 largest U.S. manufacturers and their respective sales and profits; Dun & Bradstreet publishes directories of all companies in the United States with a net worth of at least $500,000. *Careers in Marketing,* a publication of the American Marketing Association, presents career opportunities in marketing. The *Occupational Outlook Handbook* is an annual publication of the U.S. Department of Labor that provides projections for specific job prospects, as well as information pertaining to those jobs. The librarian can indicate reference materials that will be most pertinent to *your* job search.

Advertisements Help-wanted advertisements provide an overview of what is happening in the job market. Local (particularly Sunday editions) and college newspapers, trade press (such as *Marketing News* or *Advertising Age*), and business magazines (such as *Sales and Marketing Management*) contain classified advertisement sections that generally have job opening announcements, often for entry-level positions. Reviewing the want ads can help you identify what kinds of positions are available and their requirements and job titles, which firms offer certain kinds of jobs, and levels of compensation.

Employment Agencies An employment agency can make you aware of several job opportunities very quickly because of its large number of job listings available through computer data bases. Many agencies specialize in a particular field (such as sales and marketing). The advantages of using an agency include that it (1) reduces the cost of a job search by bringing applicants and employers together, (2) often has exclusive job listings available only by working through the agency, (3) performs much of the job search for you, and (4) tries to find a job that is compatible with your qualifications and interests.[13] Employment agencies are much maligned because some engage in questionable business practices, so check with the Better Business Bureau or your business contacts to determine the quality of the various agencies.

Personal Contacts An important source of job information that students often overlook is their personal contacts. People you know often may know of job opportunities, so you should advise them that you're looking for a job. Relatives and friends might aid your job search. Instructors you know well and business contacts can provide a wealth of information about potential jobs and even help arrange an interview with a prospective employer. They may also help arrange "informational interviews" with employers who do not have immediate openings. These interviews allow you to collect information about an industry or an employer and give you an advantage if a position does become available. It is a good idea to leave your résumé with all your personal contacts so they can pass it along to those who might be in need of your services. Student organizations (such as the student chapter of the American Marketing Association and Pi Sigma Epsilon, the professional sales fraternity) may be sources of job opportunities, particularly if they are involved with the business community. Local chapters of professional business organizations (such as the American Marketing Association and Sales and Marketing Executives International) also can provide job information; contacting their chapter presidents is a first step in seeking assistance from these organizations.

State Employment Office State employment offices have listings of job opportunities in their state and counselors to help arrange a job interview for you. Although state employment offices perform functions similar to employment agencies, they differ in listing only job opportunities in their state and providing their services free.

Direct Contact Another means of obtaining job information is direct contact—personally communicating to prospective employers (either by mail or in person) that you would be interested in pursuing job opportunities with them. Often you may not even know whether jobs are available in these firms. If you correspond with the companies in writing, a letter of introduction and an attached résumé should serve as your initial form of communication. Your major goal in direct contact is ultimately to arrange a job interview.

WRITING YOUR RÉSUMÉ

A résumé is a document that communicates to prospective employers who you are. An employer reading a résumé focuses on two key questions: (1) What is the candidate like? and (2) What can the candidate do for me?[14] It is imperative that you design a résumé that addresses these two questions and presents you in a favorable light. Personnel in your campus placement office can provide assistance in designing résumés.

The Résumé Itself A well-constructed résumé generally contains up to nine major sections: (1) identification (name, address, and telephone number), (2) job or career objective, (3) educational background, (4) extracurricular activities, (5) work experience or history, (6) skills or capabilities (that pertain to a particular kind of job for which you may be interviewing), (7) accomplishments or achievements, (8) personal interests, and (9) personal references.[15] There is no universally accepted format for a résumé, but three are more frequently used: chronological, functional, and targeted. A *chronological* format presents your work experience and education according to the time sequence in which they occurred (that is, in chronological order). If you have had several jobs or attended several schools, this approach is useful to highlight what you have done. With a *functional* format, you group your experience into skill categories that emphasize your strengths. This option is particularly appropriate if you have no experience or only minimal experience related to your chosen field. A *targeted* format focuses on the capabilities you have for a specific job. This alternative is desirable if you know what job you want and are qualified for it.[16] In any of the formats, if possible, you should include quantitative information about your accomplishments and experience, such as "increased sales revenue by 20 percent" for the year you managed a retail clothing store. A résumé that illustrates the chronological format is shown in Figure B-7.

Letter Accompanying a Résumé The letter accompanying a résumé, or cover letter, serves as the job candidate's introduction. As a result, it must gain the attention and interest of the reader or it will fail to give the incentive to examine the résumé carefully. In designing a letter to accompany your résumé, address the following issues:

- Identify the position for which you are applying and how you heard of it.
- Indicate why you are applying for the position.
- Summarize your main qualifications.
- Refer the reader to the enclosed résumé.
- Request a personal interview.

A sample letter comprising these five factors is presented in Figure B-8.

INTERVIEWING FOR YOUR JOB

The job interview is a conversation between a prospective employer and a job candidate that focuses on determining whether the employer's needs can be satisfied by the candidate's qualifications. The interview is a "make or break" situation: if the interview goes well, you have increased your chances of receiving a job offer; if it goes poorly, you probably will be eliminated from further consideration.

Preparing for a Job Interview To be successful in a job interview, you must prepare for it so you can exhibit professionalism and indicate to a prospective employer that you are serious about the job. When preparing for the interview, several critical activities need to be performed.

Before the interview, gather facts about the industry, the prospective employer, and the job. Relevant information might include the general description for the occupation; the firm's products or services; the firm's size, number of employees, and financial and competitive position; the requirements of the position; and the name and personality of the interviewer.[17] Obtaining this infor-

SALLY WINTER

Campus address (until 6/1/89)	Home address
Elm Street Apartments #2B	123 Front Street
College Town, Ohio 44042	Teaneck, NJ 07666
Phone: (614) 424-1648	Phone: (201) 836-4995

EDUCATION

B.S. in Business Administration, Ohio State University, 1989 Cum laude—3.3 overall GPA—3.6 GPA in major

WORK EXPERIENCE

Paid for 70 percent of my college expenses through the following part-time and summer jobs:
Legal Secretary, Smith, Lee & Jones, Attorneys at Law, New York, NY—summer, 1988

- Took dictation and transcribed tapes of legal proceedings
- Typed contracts and other legal documents
- Reorganized client files for easier access
- Answered the phone and screened calls for the partners

Sales clerk, College Varsity Shop, College Town, Ohio—1986-1988 academic years

- Helped customers with buying decisions
- Arranged stock and helped with window displays
- Assisted in year-end inventories
- Took over responsibilities of store manager when she was on vacation or ill

Assistant Manager, Treasure Place Gift Shop, Teaneck, NJ—summers and Christmas vacations—1985-1988

- Supervised two sales clerks
- Helped select merchandise at trade shows
- Handled daily accounting
- Worked comfortably under pressure during busy seasons

CAMPUS ACTIVITIES

- Elected captain of the women's varsity tennis team for 2 years
- Worked as a reporter and night editor on campus newspaper for 2 years
- Elected historian for Mortar Board chapter, a senior women's honorary

PERSONAL INTERESTS

- Collecting antique clocks, listening to jazz, swimming

REFERENCES AVAILABLE ON REQUEST

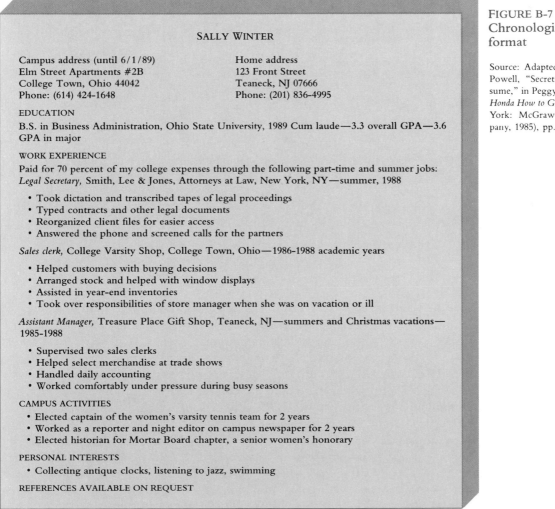

FIGURE B-7
Chronological résumé format

Source: Adapted from C. Randall Powell, "Secrets of Selling a Resume," in Peggy Schmidt, ed., *The Honda How to Get a Job Guide* (New York: McGraw-Hill Book Company, 1985), pp. 4-9.

FIGURE B-8
Sample letter accompanying a résumé

Sally Winter
Elm Street Apartments #2B
College Town, Ohio 44042
January 31, 1989

Mr. J.B. Jones
Sales Manager
Hilltop Manufacturing Company
Minneapolis, MN 55406

Dear Mr. Jones:

Dr. William Johnson, Professor of Business Administration at the Ohio State University, recently suggested that I write to you concerning your opening and my interest in a sales position. With a B.S. degree in business administration and courses in personal selling and sales management, I am confident that I could make a positive contribution to your firm.

During the past 4 years I have been a sales clerk in a clothing store and an assistant manager in a gift shop. These two positions required my performing a variety of duties including selling, purchasing, stocking, and supervising. As a result, I have developed an appreciation for the viewpoints of the customer, salesperson, and management. Given my background and high energy level, I feel that I am particularly well qualified to assume a sales position in your company.

My enclosed résumé better highlights my education and experience. My extracurricular activities should strengthen and support my abilities to serve as a sales representative.

I am eager to talk with you because I feel I can demonstrate to you why I am a strong candidate for the position. I have friends in Minneapolis with whom I could stay on weekends, so Fridays or Mondays would be ideal for an appointment. I will call you in a week to see if we can arrange a mutually convenient time for a meeting. I am hopeful that your schedule will allow this.

Thank you for your kind consideration. If you would like some additional information, please feel free to contact me. I look forward to talking with you.

Sincerely,

Sally Winter

enclosure

mation will provide you with additional insight into the firm and help you formulate questions to ask the interviewer. The above information might be gleaned, for example, from corporate annual reports, *The Wall Street Journal,* Moody's manuals, Standard and Poor's *Register of Corporations, Directors, and Executives,* selected issues of *Business Week,* or trade publications. If information is not readily available, you could call the company and indicate that you wish to obtain some information about the firm before your interview.

Preparation for the job interview should also involve role playing, or pretending that you are in the "hot seat" being interviewed. Before role playing, anticipate questions interviewers may pose and how you might address them (Figure B-9). Do not memorize your answers, though, because you want to appear spontaneous, yet logical and intelligent. Nonetheless it is helpful to practice how you might respond to the questions. In addition, develop questions

INTERVIEWER QUESTIONS

1. What can you tell me about yourself?
2. What are your strengths? Weaknesses?
3. What do you consider to be your most significant accomplishment to date?
4. What do you see yourself doing in 5 years? In 10 years?
5. Are you a leader? Explain.
6. What do you really want out of life?
7. How would you describe yourself?
8. Why did you choose your college major?
9. In which extracurricular activities did you participate? Why?
10. What jobs have you enjoyed the most? The least? Why?
11. How has your previous work experience prepared you for a job?
12. Why do you want to work for our company?
13. What qualifications do you think a person needs to be successful in a company like ours?
14. What do you know about our company?
15. What criteria are you using to evaluate the company for which you hope to work?
16. In what kind of city would you prefer to live?
17. What can I tell you about our company?
18. Are you willing to relocate?
19. Are you willing to spend at least 6 months as a trainee? Why?
20. Why should we hire you?

FIGURE B-9
Questions frequently asked by interviewers

that you might ask the interviewer that are important and of concern to you (Figure B-10).

When role playing, you and someone with whom you feel comfortable should engage in a mock interview. Afterward ask the stand-in interviewer to appraise candidly your interview content and style. You may wish to videotape the mock interview; ask the personnel in your campus placement office where videotaping equipment can be obtained for this purpose.

FIGURE B-10
Questions frequently asked by interviewees

INTERVIEWEE QUESTIONS

1. Why would a job candidate want to work for your firm?
2. What makes your firm different from competitors?
3. What is the company's promotion policy?
4. Describe the typical first-year assignment for this job.
5. How is an employee evaluated?
6. What are the opportunities for personal growth?
7. Do you have a training program?
8. What are the company's plans for future growth?
9. What is the retention rate of people in the position for which I am interviewing?
10. How can you use my skills?
11. Does the company have development programs?
12. What kind of image does the firm have in the community?
13. Why do you enjoy working for your firm?
14. How much responsibility would I have in this job?
15. What is the corporate culture in your firm?

Before the job interview you should attend to several details. Know the exact time and place of the interview; write them down—do not rely on your memory. Get the full company name straight. Find out what the interviewer's name is and how to pronounce it. Bring a note pad and pen along on the interview in case you need to record anything. Make certain that your appearance is clean, neat, professional, and conservative. And be punctual; being tardy to a job interview gives you an appearance of being unreliable.

Succeeding in Your Job Interview You have done your homework, and at last the moment arrives and it is time for the interview. Although you may experience some apprehension, view the interview as a conversation between the prospective employer and you. Both of you are in the interview to look over the other party, to see whether there might be a good match. You know your subject matter (you); furthermore, because you did not have a job with the firm when you walked into the interview, you really have nothing to lose if you don't get it—so relax.[18]

When you meet the interviewer, greet him or her by name, be cheerful, smile, and maintain good eye contact. Take your lead from the interviewer at the outset. Sit down after the interviewer has offered you a seat. Do not smoke. Sit up straight in your chair and look alert and interested at all times. Appear relaxed, not tense. And be enthusiastic.

During the interview, be yourself. If you try to behave in a manner that is different from the "real" you, your attempt may be transparent to the interviewer or you may ultimately get the job but discover that you aren't suited for it.

As the interview comes to a close, leave it on a positive note. Thank the interviewer for his or her time and the opportunity to discuss employment opportunities. If you are still interested in the job, express this to the interviewer. The interviewer will normally tell you what the employer's next step is. Rarely will a job offer be made at the end of the initial interview. If it is and you want the job, accept the offer; if there is any doubt in your mind about the job, however, ask for time to consider the offer.

Following Up on Your Job Interview After your interview, send a thank-you note to the interviewer and indicate whether you are still interested in the job. If you want to continue pursuing the job, "polite persistence" may help you get it. According to one expert, "Many job hunters make the mistake of thinking that their career fate is totally in the hands of the interviewer once the job interview is finished."[19] You *can* have an impact on the interviewer *after* the interview is over.

The thank-you note is a gesture of appreciation and a way of maintaining visibility with the interviewer. (Remember the adage, "Out of sight, out of mind.") Even if the interview did not go well, the thank-you note may impress the interviewer so much that his or her opinion of you changes. After you have sent your thank-you note, you may wish to call the prospective employer to determine the status of the hiring decision. If the interviewer told you when you would hear from the employer, make your telephone call *after* this date (assuming, of course, that you have not yet heard from the employer); if the interviewer did not tell you when you would be contacted, make your telephone call a week or so after you have sent your thank-you note.

As you conduct your follow-up, be persistent but polite. If you are too eager, one of two things could happen to prevent you from getting the job. The employer might feel that you are a nuisance and would exhibit such behavior on the job, or the employer may perceive that you are desperate for the job and thus are not a viable candidate.

Handling Rejection You have put your best efforts into your job search. You developed a well-designed résumé and prepared carefully for the job interview. Even the interview appears to have gone well. Nevertheless a prospective employer may send you a rejection letter. ("We are sorry that our needs and your superb qualifications don't match.") Although you will probably be disappointed, not all interviews lead to a job offer because there normally are more candidates than there are positions available.

If you receive a rejection letter, you should think back through the interview. What appeared to go right? What went wrong? Perhaps personnel from your campus placement office can shed light on the problem, particularly if they are in the custom of having interviewers rate each interviewee. Try to learn lessons to apply in future interviews. Keep interviewing and gaining interview experience; your persistence will eventually pay off.

SELECTED SOURCES OF MARKETING CAREER INFORMATION

The following is a selected list of marketing information sources that you should find useful during your academic studies and professional career.

BUSINESS AND MARKETING REFERENCE PUBLICATIONS

Stewart H. Britt and Norman F. Guess, eds., *The Dartnell Marketing Manager's Handbook,* 2nd ed. (Chicago: Dartnell Corporation, 1983). This handbook contains 76 chapters on many important marketing topics, including organization and staffing, establishing objectives, marketing research, developing a marketing plan, putting the plan into action, promoting products and services, international marketing, and program appraisal.

Victor P. Buell, ed., *Handbook of Modern Marketing,* 2nd ed. (New York: McGraw-Hill, 1986). This handbook was designed to provide a single authoritative source of information on marketing and marketing-related subjects. Sections and chapters contain conceptual background material to aid the reader in overall understanding followed by "how-to" information.

Business Periodicals Index (BPI) (New York: H.W. Wilson Company). This is a monthly (except July) index of almost 300 periodicals from all fields of business and management.

Chase Cochrane, *Marketing Problem Solver,* 2nd ed. (Radnor, Penn.: Chilton Book Company, 1977). A good reference for "how to" problems, this handbook contains chapters on marketing research, marketing planning, product planning, pricing, advertising, trade shows, sales promotion, legal aspects of marketing, and other topics.

Lorna M. Daniells, *Business Information Sources,* rev. ed. (Berkeley, Calif.: University of California Press, 1985). This comprehensive guide to selected business books and reference sources is useful for business students, as well as the practicing businessperson.

Doran Howitt and Marvin I. Weinberger, *Databasics: Your Guide to Online Business Information* (New York: Garland Publishing, Inc., 1984). Databasics is a comprehensive reference for finding and using information contained in online data bases.

Jerry M. Rosenberg, *Dictionary of Business and Management,* 2nd ed. (New York: John Wiley & Sons, Inc., 1983). This dictionary contains over 10,000 concise definitions of business and management terms.

Jean L. Sears, *Using Government Publications* (Phoenix: Oryx Press, 1985). An easy-to-use manual arranged by topics such as consumer expenditures, business and industry statistics, economic indicators, and projections. Each chapter contains a search strategy, a checklist of sources, and a narrative description of the sources. Volume 1: Searching by Subjects and Agencies. Volume 2: Finding Statistics and Using Special Techniques.

Irving J. Shapiro, *Dictionary of Marketing Terms,* 4th ed. (Totowa, N.J.: Littlefield, Adams & Company, 1981). This dictionary contains definitions of over 5,000 marketing terms.

Richard H. Stansfield, *The Dartnell Advertising Managers Handbook,* 3rd ed. (Chicago: Dartnell, 1982). This handbook provides a practical review of advertising planning and practice. Topics include advertising department organization, campaign planning, agency selection, copywriting, media, and research.

CAREER PLANNING PUBLICATIONS

Richard N. Bolles, *What Color Is Your Parachute? A Practical Manual for Job Hunters and Career Changers* (Berkeley, Calif.: Ten Speed Press, 1987).

William A. Charland, Jr., *Life Work: Meaningful Employment in an Age of Limits* (New York: Continuum Publishing Company, 1986).

Harold W. Dickhut, *Executive Resume Handbook* (New York: Prentice-Hall Press, 1987).

Judith A. Katz, *The Ad Game* (New York: Harper & Row, Publishers, Inc., 1984).

William Lewis and Carol Milano, *Profitable Careers in Non-Profit* (New York: John Wiley & Sons, Inc., 1987).

William Lewis and Nancy Schuman, *Fast-Track Careers: A Guide to the Highest-Paying Jobs* (New York: John Wiley & Sons, Inc., 1987).

H. Anthony Medley, *Sweaty Palms: The Neglected Art of Being Interviewed* (Berkeley, Calif.: Ten Speed Press, 1984).

David W. Rosenthal and Michael A. Powell, *Careers in Marketing* (Englewood Cliffs, N.J.: Prentice-Hall, Inc., 1984).

Peggy J. Schmidt, *Making It on Your First Job: When You're Young, Inexperienced, and Ambitious* (New York: Avon Books, 1985).

Lila B. Stair, *Careers in Business: Selecting and Planning Your Career Path* (Homewood, Ill.: Richard D. Irwin, Inc., 1980).

David Win, *International Careers: An Insiders Guide* (Charlotte, Ver.: Williamson Publishing Co., 1987).

SELECTED PERIODICALS

Advertising Age, Crain Communications, Inc. (semi-weekly). Write to 740 N. Rush St., Chicago, IL 60611 (subscription rate: $55).

Business Horizons, Indiana University (bi-monthly). Write to Indiana University, School of Business, Bloomington, IN 47405 (subscription rate: $24).

Business Week, McGraw-Hill (weekly). Write to 1221 Avenue of the Americas, New York, NY 10020 (subscription rate: $39.95).

Fortune, Time, Inc. (bi-weekly). Write to Time, Inc., 541 N. Fairbanks Court, Chicago, IL 60611 (subscription rate: $39).

Harvard Business Review, Harvard University (bi-monthly). Write to Harvard University, Graduate School of Business Administration, Soldiers Field Road, Boston, MA 02163 (subscription rate: $30).

Industrial Marketing Management, Elsevier Science Publishing Co., Inc. (quarterly). Write to 52 Vanderbilt Ave., New York, NY 10017 (subscription rate: $48 for individuals, $45 for students).

Journal of the Academy of Marketing Science, The Academy of Marketing Science (quarterly). Write to University of Miami, School of Business Administration, P.O. Box 248505, Coral Gables, FL 33124 (subscription rate: $35).

Journal of Advertising Research, Advertising Research Foundation (bi-monthly). Write to 3 E. 54th St., New York, NY, 10022 (subscription rate: $75).

Journal of Business and Industrial Marketing, Marketing Journal Publishing Co. (quarterly). Write to Box 3000, Dept. P, Denville, NJ 07834 (subscription rate: $60).

Journal of Consumer Marketing (quarterly). Write to 108 Loma Media Rd., Santa Barbara, CA 93103-2152 (subscription rate: $60).

Journal of Consumer Research, Journal of Consumer Research, Inc. (quarterly). Write to P.O. Box 70787, Pasadena, CA 91107 (subscription rate: $66 for nonmembers, $33 for members).

Journal of Health Care Marketing, American Marketing Association (quarterly). Write to 250 S. Wacker Dr., Suite 200, Chicago, IL 60606 (subscription rate: $35 for nonmembers, $25 for members).

Journal of Marketing, American Marketing Association (quarterly). Write to 250 S. Wacker Dr., Suite 200, Chicago, IL 60606 (subscription rate: $50 for nonmembers, $25 for members).

Journal of Marketing Education, University of Colorado (three per year). Write to University of Colorado, Graduate School of Business Administration, Campus Box 420, Boulder, CO 80309 (subscription rate: $16).

Journal of Marketing Research, American Marketing Association (quarterly). Write to 250 S. Wacker Dr., Suite 200, Chicago, IL 60606 (subscription rate: $50 for nonmembers, $25 for members).

Journal of Personal Selling and Sales Management, Pi Sigma Epsilon (tri-annually). Write to 155 E. Capitol Drive, Hartland, WI 53029 (subscription rate: $30).

Journal of Retailing, Institute of Retail Management (quarterly). Write to New York University, 202 Tisch Bldg., Washington Square, New York, NY 10003 (subscription rate: $20).

Marketing Communications, Media Horizons, Inc. (monthly). Write to 50 W. 23rd St., New York, NY 10010 (subscription rate: $40).

Marketing and Media Decisions, Decisions Publications, Inc. (monthly). Write to 1140 Avenue of the Americas, New York, NY 10036 (subscription rate: $40).

Marketing News, American Marketing Association (bi-weekly). Write to 250 S. Wacker Dr., Suite 200, Chicago, IL 60606 (subscription rate: $40 for nonmembers, $20 for members).

Sales and Marketing Management, Bill Publications, Inc. (16 per year). Write to Box 1024, Southeastern, PA 19398-9974 (subscription rate: $38).

Stores, National Retail Merchants Association (monthly). Write to 100 W. 31st St., New York, NY 10001 (subscription rate: $9).

PROFESSIONAL AND TRADE ASSOCIATIONS

American Advertising Federation
1400 K St. N.W., Suite 1000
Washington, DC 20005
(202) 898-0089

American Marketing Association
250 S. Wacker Dr., Suite 200
Chicago, IL 60606
(312) 648-0536

American Society of Transportation and Logistics
P.O. Box 33095
Louisville, KY 40232
(502) 451-8150

Bank Marketing Association
309 W. Washington St.
Chicago, IL 60606
(312) 782-1442

Business/Professional Advertising Association
205 E. 42nd St.
New York, NY 10017
(212) 661-0222

Direct Marketing Association
6 E. 43rd St.
New York, NY 10017
(212) 689-4977

International Franchise Association
1350 New York Ave., NW, Suite 900
Washington, DC 20005
(202) 628-8000

Life Insurance Marketing and Research Association
P.O. Box 208
Hartford, CT 06141
(203) 677-0033

Marketing Research Association
111 E. Wacker Dr., Suite 600
Chicago, IL 60601
(312) 644-6610

Marketing Science Institute
1000 Massachusetts Ave.
Cambridge, MA 02138
(617) 491-2060

National Association for Professional Saleswomen
P.O. Box 255708
Sacramento, CA 95865
(916) 484-1234

National Association of Purchasing Management
P.O. Box 418
496 Kinderamack Rd.
Oradell, NJ 07649
(201) 967-8585

National Association of Wholesaler-Distributors
1725 K St. N.W.
Washington, DC 20006
(202) 872-0885

National Retail Merchants Association
100 W. 31st St.
New York, NY 10001
(212) 244-8780

Public Relations Society of America
845 Third Ave.
New York, NY 10022
(212) 826-1750

Sales and Marketing Executives International
Statler Office Tower, #446
Cleveland, OH 44115
(216) 771-8072

Women in Advertising and Marketing
4200 Wisconsin Ave., N.W., Suite 106-238
Washington, DC 20016
(202) 279-9093

Cases

CASE 1

Quetzal Products Corporation

Quetzal Products Corporation is an importer and distributor of a wide variety of South American and African artifacts. It is also a major source of Southwestern Indian—especially Hopi and Navajo—authentic jewelry and pottery. The firm's headquarters are in Phoenix, and currently there are branch offices in Los Angeles, Miami, and Boston.

Quetzal (named after the national bird of Guatemala) originated as a trading post near Tucson in the early 1900's. Through a series of judicious decisions, the firm established itself as one of the more reputable dealers in authentic Southwestern jewelry and pottery. Over the years, Quetzal gradually expanded its product line to include pre-Columbian artifacts from Peru and Venezuela and tribal and burial artifacts from Africa. By carefully inspecting these artifacts for authenticity, Quetzal Products developed a national reputation as one of the most respected importers of South American and African artifacts.

In the early 1980's Quetzal further expanded its product line to include replicas of authentic artifacts. For example, African fertility gods and masks were made by craftsmen who took great pains so that only the truly knowledgeable buyer— a collector—would know the difference. At present Quetzal has native craftsmen in Central and South American, Africa, and the Southwestern United States who provide these items. Replicas accounted for a small portion of total Quetzal sales, and it only agreed to enter this business at the prodding of the firm's clients who desired an expanded line. These items found most favor among buyers of gifts and novelty items.

Quetzal gross sales were about $12 million and had increased at a constant rate of 20 percent per year over the last decade. Myron Rangard, the firm's national sales manager, attributed the sales increase to the popularity of its product line and the expanded distribution of South American and African artifacts:

> For some reason, our South American and African artifacts have been gaining greater acceptance. Two of our department store customers featured examples of our African line in their Christmas catalogs last year. I personally think consumer tastes are changing from the modern and abstract to the more concrete, like our products.

Quetzal distributes its products exclusively through specialty shops (including interior decorators), firm-sponsored showings, and a few very exclusive department stores. Often the company is the sole supplier to its clients. The reasons for this highly limited distribution were recently expressed by Rangard:

> Our limited distribution has been dictated to us because of the nature of our product line. As acceptance grew, we expanded our distribution to specialty shops and some exclusive department stores. Previously, we had to push our products through our own showings. Furthermore, we just didn't have the product. These South American artifacts aren't always easy to get and the political situation in Africa is limiting our supply. Our perennial supply problem has become even more critical in recent years for several reasons. Not only must we search harder for new products, but the competition for authentic artifacts has increased tenfold. On top of this, we must now contend with governments not allowing exportation of certain artifacts because of their "national significance." Increasingly, our people are feeling like Indiana Jones in the movie *Raiders of the Lost Ark* or the *Temple of Doom!*

The problem of supply has forced Quetzal to add 3 new buyers in the last 2 years. Whereas Quetzal identified five major competitors a decade ago, there are 11 today. "Our bargaining position has eroded," noted David Olsen, director of procurement. "We have watched our gross margin slip in recent years due to aggressive competitive bidding by others."

"And competition at the retail level has increased also," interjected Rangard. "Not only are some of our specialty and exclusive department store customers sending out their own buyers to deal directly with some of our Hopi and Navajo suppliers, but we are often faced with amateurs or fly-by-night competitors. These people move into a city and dump a bunch of inauthentic junk on the public at exorbitant prices. Such antics give the industry a bad name."

In recent years several mass-merchandise department store chains and a number of up-scale discount operations have begun to sell merchandise similar to that offered by Quetzal. Even though product quality was often mixed and most items were replicas, occasionally an authentic group of items was found in these stores, according to company sales representatives. Subsequent inquiries by both Rangard and Olsen revealed that other competing distributors had signed purchase contracts with these outlets. Moreover, the items were typically being sold at retail prices below those charged by Quetzal's dealers.

Late one spring morning Rangard was contacted by a mass-merchandise department store chain concerning the possibility of carrying a complete line of Quetzal products. The chain was currently selling a competitor's items but wished to move to a more exclusive product line. A tentative contract submitted by the chain stated that it would buy at 10 percent below Quetzal's existing prices and that the initial purchase would be for no less than $250,000. Depending on consumer acceptance, purchases were estimated to be at least $1 million annually. An important clause in the contract dealt with the supply of replicas. Inspection of this clause revealed that Quetzal would have to triple its replica production to satisfy the contractual obligation. Soon after executives of Quetzal Products began discussing the contract, the president mentioned that accepting the contract could have a dramatic effect on how Quetzal defined its business.

QUESTIONS

1 What might the product-market grid for Quetzal's products look like?
2 What is Quetzal Products' business definition? How might the contractual arrangement with the mass-merchandise department store chain change it?
3 What is Quetzal's distinctive competency?
4 Under what marketing conditions should Quetzal Products accept the contract?

CASE 2

GIRL SCOUTS OF AMERICA*

BE PREPARED. The motto of the Girl Scouts of America (GSA) has been the same since Mrs. Juliette Gordon Low founded the organization in 1912 with money from an inheritance and a divorce settlement. However, Girl Scout membership has declined from an all-time high of 3.9 million in 1969 to 2.8 million in the early 1980's. Had the principles underlying GSA become obsolete, or were there other forces operating that could explain declining membership? Furthermore, would the changes adopted by GSA in the early 1980's lead to success?

When Low founded the GSA, she wanted young girls to be self-reliant and independent and to uphold the highest standards of citizenship and moral character. The many activities of the GSA focused on young girls developing into wives and mothers, and merit badges were awarded for accomplishments such as dressmaking, homemaking, and being a hostess. The GSA also had focused on traditional family life and increasingly found itself following population migration to the suburbs and away from the cities. This meant that the GSA recruited many scouts from white, middle-class families.

However, the environment has changed in recent years. Divorce has fractured the traditional family, opportunities for women to work outside the home have expanded, more married women are working outside the home, fewer children are being born, and the technology affecting everyday living has become more complex. The racial and ethnic composition in the United States also has changed, with a growing number of blacks and Hispanics.

In addition to fewer girls becoming scouts, the GSA observed that girls who had become Girl Scouts as youngsters did not continue as they grew older. Many girls who had progressed from Brownies (the youngest group of 6- to 8-year-olds) to Juniors (ages 9 to 11) had dropped out before attaining the rank of Cadette at age 12 and never achieved the highest rank of Senior (ages 14 to 17). It seemed that the scout troop organizational structure had contributed to the loss of scouts as they grew older. The troop format required frequent meetings and was believed to be too confining as teenagers became involved in a

*Source: Based on Maria Shao, "The Girl Scouts Make Many Changes to Stay Viable in the 1980s," *The Wall Street Journal* (June 15, 1982), pp. 1, 22.

wider range of activities. Another disadvantage of the troop format was it demanded considerable time from the adult troop leader.

To counteract the forces in the environment, the GSA has adopted different approaches for attracting and retaining young people. For example, the GSA has focused attention on recruiting young girls, particularly blacks and Hispanics, in the city in addition to the suburbs. Emphasis has been placed on recruiting lower income and delinquent girls as well. The GSA has reached out to pregnant teenagers with a program dealing with career opportunities. GSA activities also have changed, as evidenced by the new merit badges. Today merit badges are awarded in categories such as "Aerospace," "Business-Wise," "Computer Fun," and "Ms. Fix-it," which recognizes skill in home repairs. An increasing emphasis on careers is also evident. The troop concept and requirement has been relaxed. Girls can now become scouts without joining a troop, provided they attend one official event per year. Once members, they are invited to participate in special interest projects that include field trips, guest speakers, and conferences.

QUESTIONS

1 Has the business definition of the GSA changed in the 1980's?
2 How has the product-market grid for the GSA changed, given environmental trends?
3 What is your prognosis for the GSA, given its response to the environment?

CASE 3

THE JOHNSONS BUY A FOOD PROCESSOR*

At 4:52 PM on Friday, January 15, 1988, Brock and Alisha Johnson bought a food processor. There was no doubt about it. Any observer would agree that the purchase took place at precisely that time. Or did it?

When questioned after the transaction, neither Brock nor Alisha could remember which of them at first noticed or suggested the idea of getting a food processor. They do recall that in the summer of 1986 they attended a dinner party given by a friend who specialized in French and Chinese cooking. The meal was scrumptious, and their friend Brad was very proud of the Cuisinart food processor he had used to make many of the dishes. The item was expensive, however—about $200.

The following summer, Alisha noticed a comparison study of food processors in *Better Homes and Gardens.* The performance of four different brands was compared. At about the same time, Brock noticed that *Consumer Reports* also compared a number of brands of food processors. In both instances, the Cuisinart brand came out on top.

Later that fall, new models of the Cuisinart were introduced and the old

*This case was written by Roy D. Adler, Associate Professor of Marketing at Pepperdine University/Malibu, as a basis for class discussion. Copyright © by Roy D. Adler. Reproduced by permission.

standard model went on sale in department stores at $140. The Johnsons searched occasionally for Cuisinarts in discount houses or in wholesale showroom catalogs, hoping to find an even lower price for the product. They were simply not offered there.

For Christmas 1987, the Johnsons traveled from Atlanta to the family home in Michigan. While there, the Johnsons received a gift of a Sunbeam Deluxe Mixer from a grandmother. While the mixer was beautiful, Alisha immediately thought how much more versatile a food processor would be. One private sentence to that effect brought immediate agreement from Brock. The box was (discreetly) not opened, although many thanks were expressed. The box remained unopened the entire time the Johnsons kept the item.

Back home in Atlanta in January, Alisha again saw the $140 Cuisinart advertised by Rich's, one of the two major full-service department stores in Atlanta. Brock and Alisha visited a branch location on a Saturday afternoon, and saw the item. The salesperson, however, was not knowledgeable about its features and not very helpful in explaining its attributes. The Johnsons left, disappointed.

Two days later, Alisha called the downtown location, where she talked to Mrs. Evans, a seemingly knowledgeable salesperson who claimed to own and love exactly the model the Johnsons had in mind. Furthermore, Mrs. Evans said that they did carry Sunbeam mixers and would make an exchange of the mixer, which had been received as a gift and for which no receipt was available.

On the following Friday morning, Brock put the mixer in his car trunk when he left for work downtown. That afternoon, Alisha and 6-month-old Brock, Jr., rode the bus downtown to meet Brock and to make the transaction. After meeting downtown, they drove through heavy rainy-day traffic to Rich's to meet Mrs. Evans, whom they liked as much in person as they did on the telephone. After a brief, dry-run demonstration of the use and operation of the attachments for all of the models, the Johnsons confirmed their initial decision to take the $140 basic item. They then asked about exchanging the Sunbeam mixer that they had brought with them. "No problem," said Mrs. Evans.

After making a quick phone call, Mrs. Evans returned with bad news. Rich's had not carried that particular model of mixer. This model mixer (i.e., I-73) was a single-color model that is usually carried at discount houses, catalog sales houses, and jewelry stores. The one carried by the better department stores, such as Rich's, was a two-tone model. Mrs. Evans was sorry she could not make the exchange, but suggested that other stores such as Davison's, Richway Discount, or American Jewelers might carry the item. She even offered to allow the Johnsons to use her phone to verify the availability of the item. The Johnsons did exactly that.

Alisha dialed several of the suggested stores, looking for a retailer who carried both the Cuisinart and the Sunbeam Model I-73, but she quickly learned that they were distributed through different types of retail stores. The young man who answered the phone at American Jewelers, however, seemed friendly and helpful, and Alisha was able to obtain his agreement to take the item as a return if she could get there that afternoon.

American Jewelers was about ½ mile away. Brock volunteered to babysit for Brock, Jr., at Rich's while Alisha returned the mixer. She took the downtown shoppers' bus to American Jewelers with the still unopened mixer box under her arm.

About an hour later, Alisha returned, cold and wet, with a $57 refund. Brock, having run out of ways to entertain a 6-month-old, was very happy to see her. Together they bought the Cuisinart at 4:52 PM and proudly took it home.

QUESTIONS

1 Which of the Johnsons decided to buy a food processor? The Cuisinart?
2 When was the decision to buy made?
3 What were the salient and determinant attributes in the evaluation of the Cuisinart brand?
4 Would you characterize the Johnsons' purchase decision process as exhibiting routine response behavior, limited problem solving, or extended problem solving? Why?

CASE 4

HASBRO, INC.*

In a recent board of directors meeting, Stephen Hassenfeld, president of Hasbro, Inc., exclaimed, "This is really getting to be fun." The reason for his statement? Hasbro, Inc., had recorded worldwide sales of $1.2 billion and $99 million in profits, and was the number one toy company in the world. Moreover, Hasbro, Inc. intended to double its U.S. market share and make similar gains in Europe in the next 5 years.

However, industry observers are not so optimistic. Toys tend to be fads and companies often must replace 60 percent of their toy volume each year with new products. Moreover, it is estimated that 80 percent of new toys introduced each year are failures. Mr. Hassenfeld believes Hasbro, Inc., can overcome these problems with deft product development.

HASBRO PRODUCT DEVELOPMENT AND MARKETING

Hasbro, Inc., looks for three qualities in new products: (1) lasting play value, (2) the ability to be shared with other children, and (3) the ability to stimulate a child's imagination. In addition, the company provides toys for stages of a child's development. Beginning with toys for infants and preschool children, it

*Source: Based on Andrea Stone, "Toy Fair No Picnic for Toy Industry," *USA Today* (February 8, 1988), pp. B1-B2; "Worlds of Wonder Files for Protection Under Chapter 11," *The Wall Street Journal* (December 27, 1987) p. 24; Ann Hagedorn, "Toy Firms Search for Next Blockbuster," *The Wall Street Journal* (September 12, 1986), p. 23; "How Hasbro Became King of the Toymakers," *Business Week* (September 22, 1986), pp. 90-92; Steve Weiner, "If a Toy Flops, It Can Be Tough Explaining Why," *The Wall Street Journal* (September 12, 1986), p. 23; Linda M. Watkins, "Tapping Hot Markets: Toys Aimed at Minority Children," *The Wall Street Journal* (September 12, 1986), p. 23; "Marketing," *The New Yorker* (February 23, 1987), pp. 28-29; Sara Steen, "Hasbro Follows Interactive Trend," *Advertising Age* (April 20, 1987), p. 24.

CATEGORY	PERCENT
Dolls and action figures	31.6
Games and puzzles	11.6
Preschool and infant toys	10.1
Activity toys	9.5
Toy vehicles	9.0
Riding toys	8.6
Stuffed toys	7.6
Arts and crafts	4.2
Other	7.8

Note: Children's books and video games not included.

FIGURE C4-1
Percentage of industry sales by toy category

Source: Ann Hagedorn, "Toy Firms Search for Next Blockbuster," *Wall Street Journal* (September 12, 1986), p. 23.

has toys and games for pre-adolescents of both sexes, and some adults (Scruples).

For example, preschool toys include Glo Worm and Teach Me Reader, young boys' toys include action figures like Transformers and G.I. Joe, and young girls have My Little Pony and Jem. In addition, Hasbro markets stuffed toys like Yakity Yaks and Watchimals and games and puzzles including Candyland and Bed Bugs. An element of the company's marketing strategy includes reaching mothers from the time of the child's birth for infant toys. As the child develops, toys such as G.I. Joe are promoted through Saturday morning cartoon shows where complementary toys (aircraft carriers) are advertised.

TOY INDUSTRY

The toy industry produced an estimated $12.75 billion in sales in 1988. This figure has remained largely unchanged in recent years. A percentage breakdown of volume by toy category is shown in Figure C4-l.

According to the editor of *Toy & Hobby World*, a trade publication, the toy industry is a "hit-driven business." Recent hits include Cabbage Patch Kids by Coleco which produced estimated sales of $600 million in 1986. It was estimated that sales would fall to $300 million in 1987. Teddy Ruxpin made by Worlds of Wonder, Inc., was the hit of 1986 and 1987. However, hits can quickly become disasters. For example, video games produced sales of $2.1 billion in 1983; 1984 sales were nearly zero. Worlds of Wonder, Inc., filed for bankruptcy in December 1987.

The search for hit products has resulted in the production of technologically advanced toys in recent years. These include Teddy Ruxpin–like "talking toys" and Lazer Tag, also produced by Worlds of Wonder, Inc., where opponents shoot at one another with infrared-light-emitting guns. Creating a hit also involves making large marketing expenditures. It is estimated that a full-scale introduction of a major toy requires $5 million to $10 million in advertising plus $12 million to $15 million to produce a cartoon show featuring the toy or character.

In recent years, some toy companies have focused on specific children. For example, some firms have recently produced black, Hispanic, and Asian dolls and action figures to reach previously untapped buyers. For example, Coleco has sold about 54 million black Cabbage Patch Kids since 1983, or 10 percent of the dolls' total volume. Olmec Corporation markets a line of black, Hispanic, and Asian action figures called Rulers of the Sun. Other firms have produced dolls for disabled children. Mattel, for example, markets the Hal's Pals line which includes a girl with leg braces and a cane and a boy in a wheelchair. The company donates the proceeds from Hal's Pals sales to disabled-children groups.

QUESTIONS

1 How do toy marketers, including Hasbro, apply concepts from consumer behavior in the marketing of toys?
2 What variables might be used to segment the toy market?
3 What might a product-market grid for Hasbro look like, and where are new product-market opportunities for Hasbro?
4 What are your thoughts on the subject of marketing Lazer Tag, ethnic dolls and action figures, and dolls for disabled children?

CASE 5

HONEYWELL, INC., OPTOELECTRONICS DIVISION

After several years of developing fiber optic technology for Department of Defense projects, executives in the Optoelectronics Division of Honeywell, Inc., decided to pursue commercial applications for their products and technology. The task would not be easy because fiber optics was a new technology that many firms would find unfamiliar. Fiber optics is the technology of transmitting light through long, thin, flexible fibers of glass, plastic, or other transparent materials. When it is used in a commercial application, a light source emits infrared light flashes corresponding to data. Millions of light flashes per second send streams through a transparent fiber. A light sensor at the other end of the fiber "reads" the data transmitted. It is estimated that sales of fiber optic technology could reach $1.9 billion in 1990. Almost half the dollar sales volume would come from telecommunications, about 25 percent from government or military purchases, and about 25 percent from commercial applications in computers, robotics, cable TV, and other products.

Interest in adapting fiber optic technology and products for commercial applications had prompted Honeywell executives to carefully review buying behavior associated with the adoption of a new technology. The buying process appeared to contain at least six phases: (1) need recognition, (2) identification of available products, (3) comparison with existing technology, (4) vendor or seller evaluation, (5) the decision itself, and (6) follow-up on technology performance. Moreover, there appeared to be several people within the buying organization who would play a role in the adoption of a new technology. For example, top management (such as the president and executive vice-presidents) would certainly be involved. Engineering and operations management (for example, vice-presidents of engineering and manufacturing) and design engineers (for example, persons who develop specifications for new products) would also play a major role. Purchasing personnel would have a say in such a decision and particularly in the vendor-evaluation process. The role played by each person in the buying organization was still unclear to Honeywell. It seemed that engineering management personnel could slow the adoption of fiber optics if they did not feel it was appropriate for the products made by the company. Design engineers, who would actually apply fiber optics in product design, might be favorably or unfavorably disposed to the technology depending on whether they knew how to use it. Top management personnel would participate in any final decisions to use fiber optics and could generate interest in the technology if stimulated to do so.

This review of buying behavior led to questions about how to penetrate a company's buying organization and have fiber optics used in the company's products. Although Honeywell was a large, well-known company with annual sales exceeding $5 billion, its fiber optic technology capability was much less familiar. Therefore the executives thought it was necessary to establish Honeywell's credibility in fiber optics. This was done, in part, through an advertising image campaign that featured Honeywell Optoelectronics as a leader in fiber optics.

QUESTIONS

1 What type of buying situation is involved in the purchase of fiber optics, and what will be important buying criteria used by companies considering using fiber optics in their products?
2 Describe the purchase decision process for adopting fiber optics, and state how members in the buying center for this technology might play a part in this process.
3 What effect will perceived risk have on a company's decision of whether to use fiber optics in its products?
4 What role does the image advertising campaign play in Honeywell Optoelectronics' efforts to market fiber optics?

CASE 6

BOOKWORMS, INC.*

Late one August morning, Nancy Klein, co-owner of Bookworms, Inc., sat at her desk near the back wall of a cluttered office. With some irritation, she had

*Source: This case was written by Professor James E. Nelson, University of Colorado at Boulder. Used with permission.

just concluded that her nearby calculator could help no more. "What we still need," she thought to herself, "are estimates of demand and market share . . . but at least we have 2 weeks to get them."

Klein's office was located in the rear of Bookworms, Inc., an 1800-square-foot bookstore specializing in quality paperbacks. The store carried over 10,000 titles and sold more than $520,000 worth of books in 1983. Titles were stocked in 18 categories, ranging from art, biography, and cooking to religion, sports, and travel.

Bookworms, Inc., was located in a small business district across the street from the boundary of Verdoon University (VU). VU currently enrolled about 12,000 undergraduate and graduate students majoring in the liberal arts, the sciences, and the professions. Despite national trends in enrollment, the VU admissions office had predicted that the number of entering students would grow at about 1 percent per year through the 1980's. The surrounding community, a city of about 350,000, was projected to grow at about twice that rate.

Bookworms, Inc., carried no texts even though many of its customers were VU students. Both Klein and her partner, Susan Berman, felt that the VU bookstore had simply too firm a grip on the textbook market in terms of price, location, and reputation. Bookworms also carried no classical records, as of 2 months ago. Klein recalled with discomfort the $15,000 or so they had lost on the venture. "Another mistake like that and the bank will be running Bookworms," she thought. "And, despite what Susan thinks, the copy service could just be that final mistake."

The idea for a copy service had come from Susan Berman. She had seen the candy store next door to Bookworms (under the same roof) go out of business in July. She had immediately asked the building's owner, Ed Anderson, about the future of the 800-square-foot space. Upon learning it was available, she had met with Klein to discuss her idea for the copy service. She had spoken excitedly about the opportunity: "It can't help but make money. I could work there parttime and the rest of the time we could hire students. We could call it 'Copycats' and even use a sign with the same kind of letters as we do in 'Bookworms.' I'm sure we could get Ed to knock the wall out between the two stores, if you think it would be a good idea. Probably we could rent most of the copying equipment, so there's not much risk."

Klein was not so sure. A conversation yesterday with Anderson had disclosed his desire for a 5-year lease (with an option to renew) at $1,000 per month. He had promised to hold the offer open for 2 weeks before attempting to lease the space to anyone else. Representatives from copying-equipment firms had estimated that charges would run between $200 and $2,000 per month, depending on equipment, service, and whether the equipment was bought or leased. The copy service would also have other fixed costs in terms of utility expenses, interest, insurance, and the inventory (and perhaps equipment). Klein concluded that the service would begin to make a profit at about 20,000 copies per month under the best-case assumptions, and at about 60,000 copies per month under worst-case assumptions.

Further informal investigation had identified two major competitors. One was the copy center located in the Krismann Library on the west side of the campus, a mile away. The other was a private firm, Kinko's, located on the south side of the campus, also 1 mile away. Both offered service while you wait, on several machines. The Library's price was about ½ cent per copy higher than Kinko's. Both offered collating, binding, color copying, and other services, all on a 7-day-a-week schedule.

Actually, investigation had discovered that a third major "competitor" consisted of the VU departmental machines scattered throughout the campus. Most faculty and administrative copying was done on these machines, but students were allowed the use of some, at cost. In addition, at least 20 self-service machines could be found in the Library and in nearby drugstores, grocery stores, and banks.

Moving aside a stack of books on her desk, Nancy Klein picked up the telephone and dialed her partner. When Berman answered, Klein asked, "Susan, have you any idea how many copies a student might make in a semester? I mean, according to my figures, we would break even somewhere between 20,000 and 60,000 copies per month. I don't know if this is half the market or what."

"You know, I have no idea," Berman answered. "I suppose when I was going to school I probably made 10 copies a month—for articles, class notes, old tests, and so on."

"Same here," Klein said. "But some graduate students must have done that many each week. You know, I think we ought to do some marketing research before we go much further on this. What do you think?"

"Sure. Only it can't take much time or money. What do you have in mind, Nancy?"

"Well, we could easily interview our customers as they leave the store and ask them how many copies they've made in the past week or so. Of course, we'd have to make sure they were students."

"What about a telephone survey?" Berman asked. "That way we can have a random sample. We would still ask about the number of copies, but now we would know for sure they would be students."

"Or what about interviewing students in the union cafeteria? There's always a good-sized line there around noon, as I remember, and this might be even quicker."

"Boy, I just don't know. Why don't I come in this afternoon and we can talk about it some more?"

"Good idea," Klein responded. "Between the two of us, we should be able to come up with something."

QUESTIONS

1 What sources of information should Klein and Berman use?
2 How should Klein and Berman gather data?
3 What questions should they ask?
4 How should they sample?

GENERAL MOTORS CORPORATION*

A beleaguered General Motors Corporation (GM) launched its 1988 model cars with great hopes. Net profit on sales had fallen in each of the past 3 years and the company's market share had approached post-World War II lows. Efforts to bolster sales, increase market share, and reduce car inventories through low interest financing in 1985, 1986, and 1987 had placed further downward pressure on profits. Other efforts to launch the Saturn project with state-of-the-art manufacturing and car styling had been slowed. Against this backdrop, GM had restructured itself and planned a new positioning strategy for its five divisions: Buick, Cadillac, Chevrolet, Oldsmobile, and Pontiac. These actions and plans, which were developed in 1984, were the basis for the high hopes for the 1988 model year. However, GM had its critics. In particular, GM was criticized for not differentiating its cars from competitors and between its five divisions. According to one critic: "It appears to me that GM doesn't have a long-term strategy to make its cars appealing to the market. They offer squarish, boxy cars, while the rest of the market is going to individual-looking autos. It smacks of not staying close to what the market wants. I've seen the 1988 models; they don't appear to have responded to that challenge very well."

GM STRATEGY

GM executives do not agree that the company lacks a long-term strategy to overcome its present sales and profit problems. Rather, these executives point out that efforts over the past four years have laid the foundation for the future growth and prosperity of GM.

A central element of the GM strategy was the massive reorganization of the company begun in 1984. The company divided itself into two groups—one for large cars and one for small cars (see Chapter 2). The large car group would be responsible for manufacturing and marketing Oldsmobile, Buick, and Cadillac. The small car group would be responsible for Chevrolet and Pontiac. This reorganization affected 300,000 of GM's 800,000 employees. These structural changes were deemed necessary to make GM more responsive to the market.

A second element of the GM strategy was the plan for positioning its divisions. Positioning the divisions, as reflected in how GM wished to project the image of each, had been of concern since the early 1980's. Moreover, GM

*Source: Based on Alex Taylor III, "Detroit vs. New Upscale Imports," *Fortune* (April 27, 1987, pp. 69-78; Bryan S. Moskal, "Is GM Getting A Bum Rap?" *Industry Week* (January 12, 1987), pp. 41-44; Jesse Snyder, "4 GM Car Divisions are Repositioned in Effort to Help Sales," *Automotive News* (September 15, 1986), pp. 1, 49; "General Motors: What Went Wrong," *Business Week* (March 16, 1987), pp. 102-110; "How Pontiac Pulled Away from the Pack," *Business Week* (August 25, 1986), pp. 56-57; John Koten, "Car Makers Use 'Image' Map as Tool to Position Products," *The Wall Street Journal* (March 22, 1984), p. 35; John Holuska, "G.M.'s Overhaul: A Return to Basics," *New York Times* (January 15, 1984), p. F1; "GM Is Offering New Incentives For Auto Sales," *The Wall Street Journal* (August 6, 1987), pp. 1, 17.

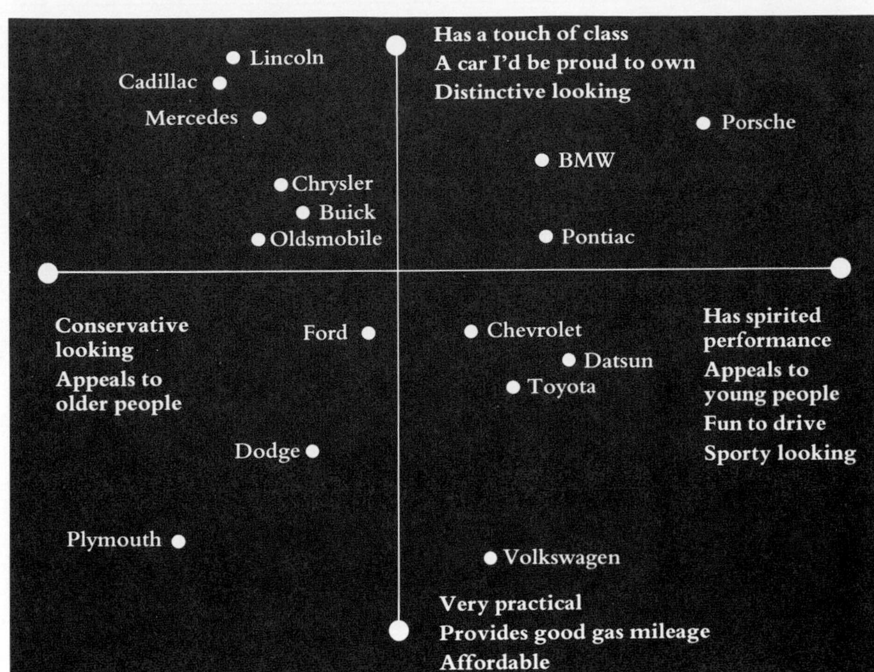

FIGURE C7-1
Perceptual map of U.S. and foreign automakers

competitors were also looking to position themselves in ways that would differentiate their automobiles from domestic and foreign car manufacturers. One example of such an effort was the research conducted by the Chrysler Corporation (Figure C7-1). The technique used by Chrysler produced a *perceptual map,* which is a variation of positioning by attributes or benefits sought by consumers. In practice, the technique involves asking owners of different brands to rate cars on a scale of 1 to 10 for qualities such as "youthfulness" and "luxury," and whether the car is "for older people" or "for younger people." For example, scales might look like those shown below:

	Plymouth is . . .	
For younger people	1 2 3 4 5 6 7 8 9 10	For older people
Sporty looking	1 2 3 4 5 6 7 8 9 10	Conservative looking

Responses indicated on each scale are then worked into a score for each car model and plotted on a graph called a perceptual map that shows which models are similar and which are different from each other. The location of each model on the map and the distance between models has strategic significance. For example, models clustered together probably will compete head-on against each other. Also, failure to have a model in a particular location on the map suggests a need for repositioning that model through changes in styling, price, or advertising.

GM plans for positioning its divisions were drafted in 1984 (see Chapter

FIGURE C7-2
GM's actual and planned positioning of its car divisions

Source: Jesse Snyder, "4 GM Car Divisions Are Repositioned in Effort to Help Sales," *Automotive News* (September 15, 1986), pp. 1, 49.

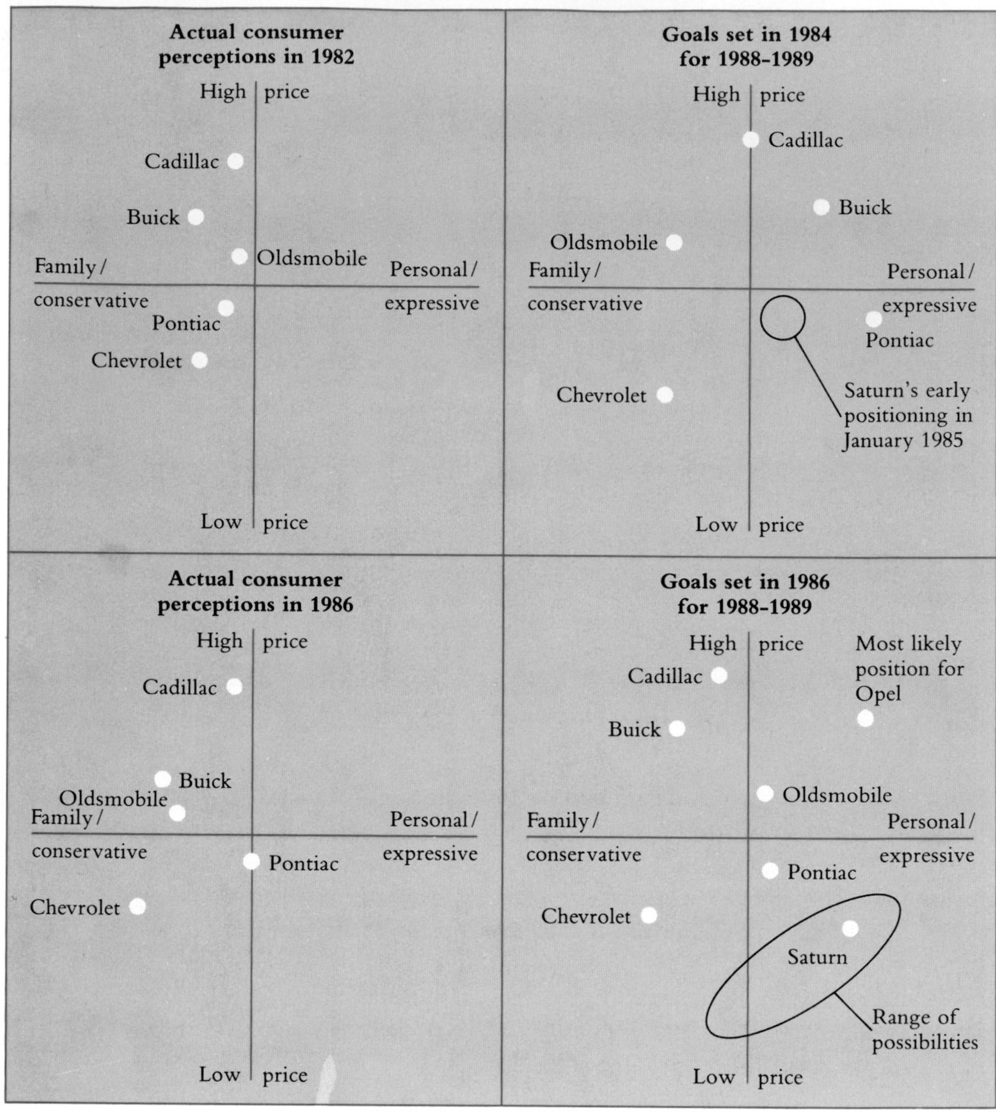

8). The company had traditionally positioned its divisions on price only. The lowest price cars were sold by Chevrolet with Pontiac, Oldsmobile, Buick, and Cadillac representing higher-priced cars in ascending order. For example, a Chevrolet Caprice Classic was priced at $12,000 while the Cadillac Allanté was priced at $54,700 with the models in other divisions priced between these price levels. However, GM departed from this one-dimensional positioning approach during planning efforts in 1984. At that time, GM developed a two-dimensional positioning approach featuring price on one dimension and a family-conservative/personal-expressive orientation on the other dimension. Figure C7-2 shows the evolution of GM's plans and actual positions in 1982 and 1986.

Figure C7-2 illustrates the repositioning evident in GM's strategy. Buick and Oldsmobile were to switch positions from the 1984 plan to the 1988-89 plan. Oldsmobile would become more personal-expressive while Buick would become more family-conservative. Pontiac and Saturn also changed positions. The Saturn, scheduled for introduction in 1991, was initially (1985) positioned as more expensive and less personal or expressive than Pontiac. However, GM's revised 1988-89 plan called for Saturn to be less expensive and more personal or expressive than Pontiac. Also, GM's Adam Opel subsidiary in West Germany was added to the positioning map as a higher-priced, personal-expressive car.

STRATEGY EXECUTION

Results of the GM planning effort were not expected to produce immediate results. However, early signals indicated that GM's efforts had an effect on the marketplace. The Pontiac Division had shown significant sales gains from repositioning. Styling changes coupled with its "We Build Excitement" advertising theme made Pontiac the fastest growing GM division. The Oldsmobile Division was the second fastest growing division given its styling and advertising theme: "Oldsmobile Quality. Feel It." On the other hand, Cadillac and Buick were the two slowest growing divisions. Chevrolet fell in the mid-range of sales gains for all GM divisions.

QUESTIONS

1 How might the "positions" of GM cars in Figure C7-1 and C7-2*A* be interpreted? What are the implications of these positions for GM?
2 What is your assessment of GM's 1984 repositioning goals shown in Figure C7-2*B* given 1984 consumer perceptions shown in Figure C7-1?
3 What are your thoughts on GM's 1984 positioning (Figure C7-2*B*) and its changed strategy for 1988-89 (Figure C7-2*D*)?
4 If you were to assign GM's divisions to a location on Figure C7-2, would you make any changes? What changes would you make and why?

CASE 8

BLACK & DECKER CORPORATION—HOUSEHOLD PRODUCTS GROUP (A)*

When Black & Decker (B&D) acquired General Electric's (GE) small appliance business in April 1984, B&D executives were forced to change brand names on one of the largest, most recognized line of consumer products, without losing market share. This challenge—a brand transition—was complicated further because GE would continue to advertise its brand on other GE product lines.

*This case was prepared by Scott Tonneslan, Managing Partner, Arcus, Minneapolis, MN. Based on marketing services provided to Black & Decker.

The potential for consumer confusion and retailer resistance was enormous, and the competition could not be happier.

Kenneth Homa, Vice President of Marketing for B&D's newly formed U.S. Household Products Group, would direct the planning and implementation of a successful transition. Acquisition terms permitted him to market products under the GE label for 3 years, until April 1987. During that time, B&D not only would be required to convert some 150 products in 14 separate categories, but B&D also had to absorb the organization it inherited from GE—management, sales, manufacturing, distribution, and service.

SMALL APPLIANCE MARKET

For years the best known name in small appliances, GE had long dominated the $8.3 billion industry. No competitor came close to equaling GE's consumer awareness: 92 percent of consumers surveyed named GE as a maker of small appliances, while only 41 percent mentioned Sunbeam—GE's closest rival. Nor could the competition match GE's broad product line or share of market.

Besides Sunbeam, Hamilton Beach, Norelco, and Proctor-Silex were major competitors. Many others, such as Rival, Toastmaster, and West Bend competed in fewer categories. Some, including Melitta, Mr. Coffee, and Cuisinart, specialized in a single category. And a number of foreign producers—Braun, Krups, and Matsushita (Panasonic)—had successfully entered the U.S. market.

GE held market share rankings of first or second in most categories in which it competed. Only in toasters, food processors, and hair care products did the company hold a lesser share. Irons constituted GE's most prized category, where it owned over 50 percent of the market. Approximately 25 percent of the division's revenues came from iron sales alone. GE's complete product line and major competition are shown below:

CATEGORY	MAJOR COMPETITION
Bathroom scales	Counselor / West Bend
Can openers	Rival / Sunbeam
Curling brushes and irons	Conair / Clairol
Coffee makers	Mr. Coffee / Norelco
Electric knives	Hamilton Beach
Electric skillets	West Bend
Food processors	Cuisinart / Hamilton Beach
Grills / griddles	Presto / Toastmaster
Hair dryers	Conair
Irons	Proctor-Silex / Sunbeam
Portable mixers	Sunbeam / Hamilton Beach
Toaster ovens	Toastmaster
Toasters	Toastmaster / Proctor-Silex
Smoke alarms	First Alert / Jameson

GE also produced the Spacemaker line of premium-priced, under-the-cabinet products—consisting of a drip coffeemaker, toaster oven, mixer, can opener, and electric knife. This product family—called a subbrand—cut across categories and was designed to encourage current appliance owners to "trade up" to new products, rather than delay purchases until their old appliances wore out. In addition, GE developed a new, highly innovative iron, the Automatic Shut-off iron, which shut itself off if accidentally left on.

Sales growth within the small appliance industry—beyond replacement sales and new household formation—was highly dependent upon new product development. However, competitors quickly copied the more successful new product introductions, which led to many similar products, with nearly identical features. Customers perceived little brand differentiation and had become highly sensitive to prices. As a result, they did not hesitate to switch brands should another offer a better price.

BLACK & DECKER CORPORATION

B&D was the foremost manufacturer and marketer of power tools and lawn care products prior to the acquisition (1983 sales of $1.17 billion). However, beginning in the late 1970's, the company experienced increased foreign competition and slower growth.

B&D executives identified the small appliance market as a possible area for expansion. Beginning in 1979, the firm developed and marketed three housewares products based on rechargeable, or cordless, technology. These products—the Dustbuster hand-held vacuum, the SpotLiter flashlight, and the Scrub Brusher scrubber—proved to be highly successful and produced pretax margins of about 10 percent. They were sold by B&D's power tools salesforce primarily to hardware buyers and were stocked within retailers' hardware departments. Future success, however, depended on access to housewares department shelf space, and thus housewares buyers.

When GE offered its Housewares Division—along with its 150-person salesforce—for sale, B&D saw an immediate opportunity to acquire relationships in all housewares distribution channels. Based on its initial experience in housewares, B&D believed GE's business could be made more profitable through streamlining and more aggressive marketing and sales programs.

With the elimination of the dominant brand in small appliances, B&D's new competition was provided an unexpected opportunity to increase sales. They responded with dramatically increased advertising budgets, reduced or delayed price hikes, accelerated new product development, and expanded retailer incentive programs. Norelco and Matsushita even entered the all-important U.S. iron market for the first time.

MARKETING CHALLENGE

B&D was now selling products in 14 categories under the GE brand, in three categories under the B&D name, and would begin marketing the 14 GE categories under the B&D label. Soon consumers would observe an increasing B&D brand presence over a broad range of categories on retail shelves. At times they would see identical products standing side by side—one B&D, the other GE.

Mr. Homa and his associates carefully studied various strategies for changing brands on its products. The process would be more complex than simply affixing new logos on products. Research suggested that consumer acceptance, and thus purchases, of B&D branded small appliances would differ by category. B&D was encouraged, however, by surveys revealing that consumers perceived B&D as a manufacturer of innovative and reliable products—to a greater degree than GE.

Ultimately, the sequence chosen would influence decisions regarding advertising and promotional programs, product redesigns and introductions, new trade deals and pricing, packaging changes, and factory retooling. At least five strategic options were possible:

1. Change all GE products to the B&D brand immediately.
2. Execute the transition category-by-category over the entire 3-year period. The specific order might be determined by a category's current sales and likely consumer acceptance of the B&D label.
3. Convert the products category-by-category, but set the order according to a new product program. Under this scenario, a category is transitioned only after a new product is introduced under the B&D brand to lead that category.
4. Switch brands on the most advanced, premium-priced GE products first, all others later. B&D could utilize innovative subbrands, such as Spacemaker, to establish "beachheads" in a range of categories.
5. Market the GE products under the GE name during the entire 3-year brand transition period. At the end of the period, convert the products to the B&D name.

QUESTIONS

1 What are the pros and cons of the brand transition strategies under consideration by Black & Decker?
2 Which strategy should Black & Decker employ? Why?

CASE 9

THE SOUTHLAND CORPORATION: 7-ELEVEN*

THANK HEAVEN FOR 7-ELEVEN. It is estimated that 8 million people visit a 7-Eleven convenience store every day. With almost 8,200 stores in 49 of 50 states, the District of Columbia, and 5 Canadian provinces, 7-Eleven is the 12th largest retailer in the United States and the world's largest operator and franchisor of convenience stores. However, in 1986, the company recorded its first drop in sales and profits in the past 17 years. Company officials attributed this decline to the economic slowdown in many southern and midwestern markets. However, competitive forces were operating as well. Convenience stores, in general, were being affected by the rise in the number of gasoline/mini-convenience stores (called "g-stores") and more competitive prices at large,

*Source: Monica Padovans, "7-Eleven's Ads Blaze New Trail in Pursuit of Customers," *Convenience Store News* (June 22-July 12, 1987), p. 92; Sally Bell, "7-Eleven Marketing Push Aimed at Changing Clientele," *Dallas Times Herald* (May 4, 1987), p. 6; Lisa Gubernick, "Thank Heaven for 7-Eleven," *Forbes* (March 23, 1987), pp. 52, 54; Lisa Gubernick, "Stores for Our Times," *Forbes* (November 3, 1986), pp. 40-42; "Jere Thompson Clears the Air," *Convenience Store News* (May 4-May 28, 1987), pp. 1ff.; *The Southland Corporation 1986 Annual Report; The Southland Corporation: A Company Profile, 1987.*

combination food and drug grocery stores. Moreover, these grocery stores had broad product assortments that often mirrored the products sold by convenience stores, remained open 24 hours per day, and provided express check-out lanes to serve the "fill-in" customer. 7-Eleven executives knew that the company would have to alter its marketing strategy in the months to come.

THE COMPANY

7-Eleven is the convenience store arm of The Southland Corporation. Other retail operations include High's Dairy Stores, Chief Auto Parts Stores, Quik Mart gasoline/convenience stores, and Super-7 self-service gasoline stations. Total company revenues were slightly over $8.6 billion and net earnings were $200.4 million.

Convenience store retailing, comprised mainly of 7-Eleven stores, accounted for 93.3 percent of total company sales. A breakdown of sales by merchandise category is shown below:

CATEGORY	PERCENT OF SALES
Gasoline	22.1
Tobacco products	15.8
Beer/wine	11.7
Soft drinks	10.9
Groceries	8.6
Food service	8.1
Non-foods	6.4
Dairy products	5.2
Candy	4.0
Baked goods	3.5
Health/beauty aids	2.6
Customer services	1.1
TOTAL	100.0%

Gross margins (sales less cost of goods sold) vary greatly by merchandise category. Industry sources estimate that the gross margin on gasoline was around 9 percent while customer services had a gross margin of about 50 percent. Representative gross margins on selected other product categories include 22 percent for tobacco products, 26 percent for beer and wine, 34 percent for soft drinks, 30 percent for baked goods, 19 percent for dairy items, and 29 percent for health and beauty aids. The average gross profit for food service, non-food items, groceries, and candy was an estimated 27.5 percent for each category. The Southland Corporation overall gross margin was approximately 23 percent.

Since its founding in 1927, 7-Eleven has been an innovative leader in convenience store retailing. It was the first convenience store chain to be open 24 hours (1963) and to use television advertising (1949). The company experimented with microwave-cooked fast-food products as early as 1959. Ongoing product search and development efforts have produced an ever-changing mix of products and services for 7-Eleven customers. Asked about the 7-Eleven store of the future, Jere Thompson, president and CEO, remarked that company stores are becoming increasingly electronic (ATMs, electronic cash registers, money orders, gasoline dispensing) and that banking and financial services will play a major role in the future.

MARKETING ENVIRONMENT

The convenience store industry produces $65 billion annually through 75,000 outlets. The four largest convenience store chain retailers, in order, are The Southland Corporation, Circle K, Convenient Food Mart, and Cumberland Farms. On average, a convenience store is visited by 654 customers each day. Based on these data, the average sale per customer per visit is about $3.60.

Convenience store chains have distinguished themselves with the wide assortment of merchandise and services they provide. At the same time, broadened assortments have brought convenience stores into competition with a variety of other retailers. Convenience stores compete with gasoline stations, fast-food outlets, grocery stores, and video rental businesses for customers. Recently, joint ventures have emerged. The Southland Corporation, for example, is now a Hardee's franchisee and has installed Hardee's units inside its 7-Eleven stores.

The convenience store customer is typically a male. For example, approximately 65 percent to 70 percent of 7-Eleven customers are men. However, with two-income and single-parent families becoming the norm, women have been identified as an important, but underdeveloped, customer segment for convenience stores. The reason for this growing interest in attracting women is the lack of time to shop grocery stores. While convenience stores have historically sold time savings for higher prices on merchandise, women have still not patronized convenience stores as frequently as men. Still, as time becomes an even more scarce commodity, convenience store operators believe women will find it necessary to become frequent customers.

7-ELEVEN MARKETING STRATEGY

The changing environment for convenience stores in general prompted 7-Eleven officials to draft a new marketing strategy. The objective of the strategy, according to the company officials was to position 7-Eleven as the "quality convenience store that features value and service to attract the price-sensitive shoppers, such as women and older people." Southland's vice-president of marketing added, "We are conducting a broad-based pursuit of customers who shop at supermarkets, other convenience stores, grocery stores, video rental stores, dairy stores, and at any other competing outlet."

The positioning statement represented a major departure from past marketing efforts. Historically, 7-Eleven emphasized speed of service and had targeted a male audience. The new thrust, however, would be communicated in an advertising campaign featuring the theme: "Where Good Things Come Easy." This advertising campaign was designed to change consumer perceptions of 7-Eleven from a place the customer *has* to go, to a place the customer *wants* to go.

A second major element of the strategy was a change in prices. The company would lower its prices on soft drinks, beer, and cigarettes (tobacco products) to make them competitive with supermarkets. This would help erase the perception that convenience stores charge significantly higher prices as the trade-off for convenience, noted one company official. The lower prices on selected items would be integrated into the "Where Good Things Come Easy" campaign with the copy line, "Now, even good prices come easy."

When 7-Eleven announced its new marketing strategy, some industry analysts expressed reservations about its likely success. According to one, "Convenience stores sell time savings. The real question is: Can you cut prices in an industry where location is tops? I'm not sure it can work."

QUESTIONS

1 How would *you* assess the marketing environment for convenience stores and implications for 7-Eleven, including why people patronize these stores?
2 How well does the new marketing strategy for 7-Eleven fit this environment and the company's competitive situation?
3 What is the likelihood of success for the new marketing strategy in terms of sales and profits if the percent of sales by product category remains unchanged? (Assume the gross margins on tobacco products, soft drinks, and the beer / wine category each drop by 5 percentage points given lower prices.)

CASE 10

HEALTH CRUISES, INC.*

Health Cruises, Inc., packages cruises to Caribbean islands such as Martinique and the Bahamas. Like conventional cruises, the packages are designed to be fun. But the cruise is structured to help participants become healthier by breaking old habits, such as smoking or overeating. The Miami-based firm was conceived by Susan Isom, 30, a self-styled innovator and entrepreneur. Prior to this venture, she had spent several years in North Carolina promoting a behavior-modification clinic.

Isom determined that many people were very concerned about developing good health habits; yet they seemed unable to break away from their old habits because of the pressures of day-to-day living. She reasoned that they might have a chance for much greater success in a pleasant and socially supportive environment, where good health habits were fostered. Accordingly, she established Health Cruises, Inc., hired 10 consulting psychologists and health specialists to develop a program, and chartered a ship. DeForrest Young, a Miami management consultant, became the chairperson of Health Cruises. Seven of Isom's business associates contributed an initial capital outlay totaling more than $250,000. Of this amount, $65,000 went for the initial advertising budget, $10,000 for other administrative expenses, and $220,000 for the ship rental and crew.

Mary Porter, an overweight Denver schoolteacher, has signed up to sail on a 2-week cruise to Nassau, departing December 19. She and her shipmates will be paying an average of $1,500 for the voyage. The most desirable staterooms cost $2,200.

Mary learned of the cruise by reading the travel section of her Sunday

*Source: Maurice Mandell, Larry J. Rosenberg, *Marketing*, 2nd ed., © 1981, pp. 365-366. Reprinted by permission of Prentice-Hall, Inc., Englewood Cliffs, N.J.

newspaper on October 16. On that date, Pittsford and LaRue Advertising Agency placed promotional notices for the cruise in several major metropolitan newspapers. Mary was fascinated by the idea of combining therapy sessions with swimming, movies, and an elegant atmosphere.

Pittsford and LaRue account executive Carolyn Sukhan originally estimated that 300 people would sign up for the cruise after reading the October 16 ads. But as of November 14, only 200 had done so. Isom and Health Cruises, Inc., faced an important decision.

"Here's the situation as I see it," explained a disturbed Ms. Isom at the Health Cruises board meeting. "We've already paid out more than a quarter of a million to get this cruise rolling. It's going to cost us roughly $200 per passenger for the 2 weeks, mostly for food. Pittsford and LaRue predicted that 300 people would respond to the advertising campaign, but we've only got 200.

"I see three basic options: (1) we cancel the cruise and take our losses; (2) we run the cruise with the 200 and a few more that will trickle in over the next month; or (3) we shell out some more money on advertising and hope that we can pull in more people.

"My recommendation to this board is that we try to recruit more passengers. There are simply too many empty rooms on that ship. Each one costs us a bundle."

At this point, Carolyn Sukhan addressed the board: "I've worked out two possible advertising campaigns for the November 20 papers. The first, the limited campaign, will cost $6,000. I estimate that it will bring in some 20 passengers. The more ambitious campaign, which I personally recommend, would cost $15,000. I believe this campaign will bring in a minimum of 40 passengers.

"I realize that our first attempt was somewhat disappointing. But we're dealing here with a new concept, and a follow-up ad might work with many newspaper readers who were curious and interested when they read our first notice.

"One thing is absolutely certain," Sukhan emphasized. "We must act immediately if there's any hope of getting more people on board. The deadline for the Sunday papers is in less than 48 hours. And if our ads don't appear by this weekend, you can forget it. No one signs up in early December for a December 18 sailing date."

Isom interrupted, shaking her head. "I just don't know what to say. I've looked over Carolyn's proposals, and they're excellent. Absolutely first-rate. But our problem, to be blunt, is money. Our funds are tight, and our investors are already nervous. I get more calls each day, asking me where the 300 passengers are. It won't be easy to squeeze another $6,000 out of these people. And to ask them for $15,000—well, I just don't know how we're going to be able to justify it."

QUESTIONS

1 What is the minimum number of passengers that Health Cruises must sign up by November 20 to break even with the cruise? (Show your calculations.)

2 Should Health Cruises go ahead with the cruise, since 200 passengers had signed up as of November 14?

3 Would it be worthwhile for Health Cruises to spend either $6,000 or $15,000 for advertising on November 20? If so, which figure would you recommend?
4 How realistic are Carolyn Sukhan's estimates of 20 more passengers for the $6,000 advertising campaign and 40 more passengers for the $15,000 campaign?
5 Should Health Cruises consider cutting its prices for this maiden voyage health cruise?

CASE 11

PORSCHE AG*

Peter Schultz seemed to have everything going his way. In the 3 years since he had become president of Porsche AG, the Porsche model 944 had become a resounding success in the United States and Europe and Porsche sales in the United States had more than doubled. Nevertheless Schultz had expressed concerns about Porsche's distribution effort in the United States and was contemplating a change.

Since 1969 Volkswagen of American (VWoA), a subsidiary of Volkswagenwerk AC, had handled all aspects of Porsche's U.S. automotive business, including importing, advertising, sales, and service. VWoA sold the Porsche line through 323 independent franchised dealers. These dealers also sold Audis, produced by a Volkswagen subsidiary, and sometimes Volkswagens as well. Dealers received a 16 percent to 18 percent margin on Porsche automobiles. It is estimated that Volkswagen made $40 million importing Porsches into the United States in 1983.

Porsche's contract with VWoA was due to expire in August 1984, and Schultz felt the time was right to make the "single most important decision in the company's entire history." The decision was whether to change the way Porsche sold, warehoused, and repaired its cars in the United States. Several factors led Schultz to consider a change. First, he had heard that successful dealers in need of cars often had to buy Porsches from other dealers at premium prices, which inflated the price paid by customers. Second, he thought a high-volume, low-priced car dealer that carried Volkswagens was the wrong outlet for his low-volume, high-priced cars (ranging from $21,400 to $44,000). Third, he believed the Japanese would soon enter the high-performance sports car market in the United States, and Porsche needed a distribution system that would enable it to compete against them. These factors led him to conclude that a new distribution arrangement was necessary to bring the Porsche factory closer to its customers. Furthermore he believed U.S. sales would increase if dealers could be ensured of getting cars more readily with the special features customers desired.

The new distribution plan envisioned by Schultz contained four major points. First, Porsche would withdraw from its contract with VWoA in August

*Source: Based on "Porsche Is Doing Great—So Changes Course," *Fortune* (March 5, 1984), p. 59; "Porsche to End Pact with VWoA," *Automotive News* (February 6, 1984), p. 3; "Porsche Forms Its Own U.S. Distribution Unit to Sell and Service Cars," *The Wall Street Journal* (February 16, 1984), p. 44; David Tinnin, "Porsche's Civil War with Its Dealers," *Fortune* (April 16, 1984), pp. 63-68.

1984 and stop selling its cars through the VWoA dealer network. Second, Porsche would recruit and use agents to sell its cars rather than dealers. These agents would not have to buy cars and inventory them at a fixed location like dealers. Therefore they would not have to tie up cash in a car inventory, incur interest costs on that inventory, and operate a dealership. Agents would receive an 8 percent commission on sales and order Porsches as they sold them. Third, Porsche would operate two warehouses in the United States, one in Reno, Nevada, and the other at an undetermined location on the East Coast. Fourth, 40 distribution and repair centers would be operated in the United States in areas where the population of Porsche buyers was highest. The 40 distribution centers would also sell Porsches. The distribution company would be called Porsche Cars North America. Porsche AG would have to invest $350 million to start the operation and hire at least 275 employees. Schultz planned to announce his plan to U.S. Porsche-Audi dealers on February 15, 1984, in Reno.

QUESTIONS

1 How would you characterize the relationship between VWoA and Porsche AG in terms of the type of conflict in the channel of distribution, channel leadership, and channel power?
2 How do you think present and potential Porsche customers will react to the plan envisioned by Schultz? How will Porsche-Audi dealers react?
3 Would you favor the plan Schultz has outlined? Why or why not?

CASE 12

MRS. FIELDS COOKIES*

At age 19 Debbi Fields decided to take cookies seriously. She completed community college and baked cookies for 6 months to find the ideal recipes. Then in 1977 she borrowed $50,000 from her husband, Randy, and opened her first Mrs. Fields store in Palo Alto, California. Within 8 months she opened a second store. By 1984 there were 160 Mrs. Fields outlets, mostly in 13 western states and Singapore, Hong Kong, and Australia. These stores produce over $30 million in sales annually.

THE COMPANY

Mrs. Fields' success in the cookie business was no accident. She insisted on offering the public a superior product, first tested on her family. Mixed and baked on the premises of each store, her cookies are sold fresh and warm. The

*Source: Based on Louis Weisberg, "All the Chips Fall into Place for Mrs. Fields," *Advertising Age* (April 2, 1984), p. M20; Kevin McManus, "The Cookie Wars," *Forbes* (November 7, 1983), pp. 150-152; "Chocolate Chip Cookies," *Consumer Reports* (February 1985), pp. 69-72; "A Tale of Two Companies," *Inc.* (July 1984), pp. 38-43.

shelf life of a Mrs. Fields cookie is 2 hours. If a cookie is not sold by then, it is called a "cookie orphan" and is given to the Red Cross for blood donors. A recent rating of Mrs. Fields cookies in *Consumer Reports* indicated her cookies are some of the best. Her cookies were rated as being crisp and chewy with a silky, syrupy chip texture and an excellent baked flavor.

On a visit to a Mrs. Fields outlet, one quickly sees that a hallmark of Debbi Fields' philosophy is to keep things simple. Besides cookies, the only items sold are coffee, milk, soft drinks, and three sizes of decorative cookie tins. Only seven kinds of cookies are available, and five of those are variations on a chocolate chip theme. Chocolate lovers also may buy brownies or a little tidbit called the FROSTBITE—a vanilla- or chocolate-glazed frozen mousse that sits on a base of crushed cookies. For those avoiding chocolate, there are oatmeal or coconut–macadamia nut cookies.

The outlets have a simple red and white decor. There is no place to sit while munching a Mrs. Fields cookie, so it is likely that a customer will stand and chat with the counterperson. The personal and friendly style expected of a Mrs. Fields counterperson has resulted in complaints of slow service, particularly in New York City. Debbi Fields, however, refused to ask her employees to speed up. Her attention to the customer is also evident in the fact that she frequently visits her outlets, bakes cookies, and waits on customers. In an article in *Inc.* magazine, Fields is quoted as saying, "We're a people company and what we're really selling a customer is a feel-good feeling."

The company organization also reflects the desire for simplicity and the focus on customers. The corporate staff consists of just 25 people, and everyone is involved in every aspect of the business from making batter, to running operations, to handling customer inquiries and complaints. Every employee, including secretaries, gets working experience in a cookie store.

THE INDUSTRY

Although estimates vary, the fresh-baked, soft and chewy, over-the-counter cookie industry is estimated to have had sales of $200 million in 1984 and $400 million in 1985. Although small, independent cookie stores still exist, there are five major chains listed in order of estimated sales volume:

- The Original Great American Chocolate Chip Cookie Company
- Mrs. Fields Cookies
- David's Cookies
- The Original Cookie Company
- The Famous Chocolate Chip Cookie Company

A sixth competitor—The Famous Amos Chocolate Chip Cookie Corporation—sells its cookies through 20,000 wholesalers and a handful of retail outlets. Wally ("Famous") Amos started the company in 1975, and his name is virtually synonymous with chocolate chip cookies.

The popularity of chocolate chip cookies has resulted in rapid expansion by the five major chains. However, some important differences exist among them in terms of how they have expanded. For example, The Original Great American Chocolate Chip Cookie Company and David's Cookies had begun franchising outlets in addition to opening company-owned stores. David's Cookies also sells its cookies in some department stores such as Macy's and has four stores in Japan that are operated with a joint venture partner. The Famous Chocolate Chip Cookie Company operates company-owned stores and also sells its batter to 85 independent owners. The Original Cookie Company, a division of Cole National Corporation, only operates company-owned stores, as does Mrs. Fields Cookies. Mrs. Fields also operates its own stores in Singapore, Hong Kong, and Australia. Recognizing the potential for cookie stores, the Famous Amos Chocolate Chip Cookie Corporation has established a franchise program to open 100 outlets within 2 years.

The consensus among competitors is that the industry's future is bright. Not only are sales expected to grow, but it also is estimated that the cookie competitors achieve a pretax profit of 10 percent to 20 percent of sales. However, as each firm expands, the likelihood of face-to-face competition increases. Competition will obviously revolve around which company makes the best cookie but will also arise in terms of finding good store locations and finding different ways to sell cookies, including direct marketing through mail and telephone. Mrs. Fields, too, must consider these issues. One important concern is the company's policy of only selling through company-owned stores and the speed with which the company can grow. At present a cookie outlet costs $150,000 to open, and Mrs. Fields Cookies recently borrowed $6 million from the Bank of California to finance store expansion. To date, Mrs. Fields has turned away inquiries from the 7-Eleven chain of convenience stores to carry its cookies. Also, Mrs. Fields recently declined a joint venture offer in Japan to open new stores and will handle its expansion into that country alone.

QUESTIONS

1 What is your opinion of Debbi Fields' approach to running her company?

2 Do you think Mrs. Fields should consider (a) direct marketing of cookies, (b) a franchise program, or (c) other outlets for its cookies such as 7-Eleven convenience stores? Why or why not?

CASE 13

RASTON FURNITURE COMPANY

Edward Meadows, president of Raston Furniture Company, met with representatives of Kelly, Astor, & Peters Advertising (KAP) and Andrew Reed, Raston's vice-president of marketing and sales, to discuss the company's advertising program for 1989. The KAP representatives recommended that Raston Furniture increase its advertising in shelter magazines (such as *Good Housekeeping* and *Better Homes and Gardens*, which feature home improvement ideas and new ideas in home decorating) by $250,000 and maintain the expenditures for other promotional efforts at a constant level during 1989. The rationale given for the increase in advertising was that Raston Furniture had low name recognition among prospective buyers of furniture and it intended to introduce new styles of living and dining room furniture. Reed, however, had a different opinion as to how Raston Furniture should spend the $250,000. He thought it was necessary to (1) hire additional salespeople to call on the 30 new retail stores to be added by the company in 1989, (2) increase the funds devoted to cooperative advertising, and (3) improve the selling aids given to retail stores and salespeople.

THE COMPANY

Raston Furniture is a medium-size manufacturer of medium- to high-priced living and dining room furniture. Sales in 1988 were $50 million. The company sells its furniture through 1,000 furniture specialty stores nationwide, but not all stores carry the company's entire line. This fact bothered Meadows because, in his words, "If they ain't got it, they can't sell it!" The company employs 10 full-time salespeople, who receive a $40,000 base salary annually and a small commission on sales. A company salesforce is atypical in the furniture industry, since most furniture manufacturers use selling agents or manufacturer's representatives who carry a wide assortment of noncompeting furniture lines and receive a commission on sales. "Having our own sales group is a policy my father established 30 years ago," noted Meadows, "and we've been quite successful having people who are committed to our company. Our people don't just take furniture orders. They are expected to motivate retail salespeople to sell our line, assist in setting up displays in stores, coordinate cooperative advertising plans, and give advice on a variety of matters to our retailers and their salespeople."

In 1988 Raston spent $2.45 million for total promotional expenditures, excluding the salary of the vice-president of marketing and sales. Promotional expenditures were categorized into four groups: (1) sales expense and administration, (2) cooperative advertising programs with retailers, (3) trade promotions, and (4) consumer advertising. Cooperative advertising allowances are usually spent on newspaper advertising in a retailer's city and are matched by the retailer's funds on a dollar-for-dollar basis. Trade promotion is directed toward retailers and takes the form of catalogs, trade magazine advertisements, booklets for consumers, and point-of-purchase materials such as displays for use in retail stores. Also included in this category is the expense of trade shows. Raston is represented at two trade shows a year. Consumer advertising is directed to potential consumers through shelter magazines. The typical format used in consumer advertising is to highlight new furniture and different living and dining room arrangements. Dollar allocation for each program in 1988 was as follows:

PROMOTIONAL PROGRAM	EXPENDITURE
Sales expense and administration	$ 612,500
Cooperative advertising	1,102,500
Trade advertising	306,250
Consumer advertising	428,750
TOTAL	$2,450,000

THE INDUSTRY

The household wooden furniture industry is composed of over 5,000 firms. Industry sales at manufacturers' prices were $10 billion. California, North Carolina, Virginia, New York, Tennessee, Pennsylvania, Illinois, and Indiana are the major U.S. furniture-producing areas. Although Ethan Allen, Bassett, Henredon, and Kroehler are the major furniture manufacturers, no one firm captured over 3 percent of the total household wooden furniture market.

The buying and selling of furniture to retail outlets centers around manufacturers' expositions at selected times and places around the country. At these marts, as they are called in the furniture industry, retail buyers view manufacturers' lines and often make buying commitments for their stores. However, Raston's experience has shown that sales efforts in the retail store by company representatives account for as much as half the company's sales in a given year. The major manufacturer expositions are held in High Point, North Carolina, in October and April. Regional expositions are also scheduled in June through August in locations such as Dallas, Los Angeles, New York, and Boston.

Company research on consumer furniture-buying behavior indicated that people visit several stores when shopping for furniture and the final decision is just made jointly by a husband and wife in about 90 percent of furniture purchases. Other noteworthy findings are:

- Eighty-four percent of buyers believe "the higher the price, the higher the quality" when buying home furnishings.
- Seventy-two percent of buyers browse or window shop in furniture stores even if they don't need furniture.
- Eighty-five percent read furniture ads before they actually need furniture.
- Ninety-nine percent agree with the statement, "When shopping for furniture and home furnishings, I like the salesperson to show me what alternatives are available, answer my questions, and let me alone so I can think about it and maybe browse around."
- Ninety-five percent get redecorating ideas from shelter magazines.
- Forty-one percent have written for a manufacturer's booklet.
- Sixty-three percent need decorating advice for "putting it all together."

BUDGETARY ISSUES

After the KAP Advertising representatives made their presentation, Reed again emphasized that the incremental $250,000 should not be spent for consumer advertising. He noted that Raston had set as an objective that each salesperson would make six calls per year at each store and spend at least 4 hours at each store on every call. "Given that our salespeople work a 40-hour week, 48 weeks per year, and devote only 80 percent of their time to selling due to travel time between stores, we already aren't doing the sales job," Reed added. Meadows agreed but reminded Reed that the $250,000 increment in the promotional budget was a maximum the company could spend, given other cost increases.

QUESTIONS

1 How might you describe furniture buying using the purchase decision process described in Chapter 4?

2 How might each of the elements of the promotional program influence each stage in the purchase decision process?
3 What should Raston's promotional objectives be?
4 How many salespeople does Raston need to adequately service its accounts?
5 Should Raston Furniture emphasize a push or pull promotional strategy? Why?

CASE 14

BLACK & DECKER CORPORATION—HOUSEHOLD PRODUCTS GROUP (B)*

In April 1984, Black & Decker (B&D) acquired General Electric's (GE) small appliance division. The GE business consisted of approximately 150 products in 14 separate categories. Consumer research indicated that 92 percent of consumers recognized GE as a manufacturer of small appliances, while only 12 percent knew B&D had entered the business. B&D faced a substantial consumer education challenge and would have to develop highly effective advertising strategies and promotional programs to successfully transition the products.

GE PRESENCE IN THE SMALL APPLIANCE MARKET

GE had long been the dominant firm in the $8.3 billion small appliance industry. The company held market share rankings of first or second in most of the 14 product categories in which it competed. Irons constituted GE's most prized category, where it captured over 50 percent of the market. GE's complete product line is shown below:

Bathroom scales	Grills / griddles
Can openers	Hair dryers
Curling brushes and irons	Irons
Coffee makers	Portable mixers
Electric knives	Toaster ovens
Electric skillets	Toasters
Food processors	Smoke alarms

DISTRIBUTION AND PRICING

GE enjoyed high market share in the volume, price-sensitive distribution channels—especially mass merchandisers and catalog showrooms. These accounts carried an average of 30 GE SKUs (stock-keeping units), individual items of product stocked on retail shelves. Additional product was sold through hardware dealers, drugstores, and military outlets. Department stores could not compete

*This case was prepared by Scott Tonneslan, Managing Partner, Arcus, Minneapolis, MN. Based on marketing services provided to Black & Decker. Copyright © Scott Tonneslan. Used with permission.

with the cutthroat pricing policies of mass merchandisers, and generally stocked premium-priced models.

Over the years—as manufacturers are prevented by law from setting retail prices—mass merchandisers pushed their prices down in competition with each other. As a result, they squeezed their own margins. These same merchandisers then pressured GE and other manufacturers to lower their list prices. GE found its retail prices under further pressure because its products often were used as traffic builders because of their strong brand franchise.

CONSUMER BEHAVIOR

The seasonality of retail sales, owing to gift giving, peaked during the November to December holiday season—over 40 percent of sales occurred in the fourth quarter—with a minor peak before Mother's Day. Twice each year, usually in January and May, housewares buyers determined which products they would carry—their "basics"—for the following 6 months.

Most customers had come to expect a price break on their purchase—two of three bought their last product on sale or with a rebate. Manufacturers, including GE, offered rebates on many products and softened most list price increases with rebates. Retailers featured rebates and sales not only in advertising, but also through point-of-purchase advertising consisting primarily of tags attached to displayed products.

PROMOTIONAL ACTIVITY

Small-appliance manufacturers competed fiercely for retail shelf space to defend market share. Because the products were not highly profitable to retailers, companies offered numerous trade incentives, or deals, to persuade retailers to stock their products.

Marketing strategies emphasized the design and continual adjustment of these trade incentives. GE had a reputation for providing a wealth of incentives, which included volume rebates, off-invoice purchase allowances, liberal dating terms, stock balancing, consumer rebates, and a generous cooperative advertising program.

GE provided cooperative advertising funds to subsidize the retailer's cost of local advertising—newspaper advertising, Sunday newspaper inserts, store flyers—that featured GE products. Such advertising emphasized price, and was considered essential in driving retail sales. One in four purchasers, for example, was found to carry an advertisement into the retail department. Relatively little national product advertising was employed by manufacturers—except in support of new product introductions—because of the lack of product differentiation.

DRAFTING ADVERTISING AND PROMOTION PROGRAMS

B&D faced a monumental consumer education challenge. Consumers did not associate the B&D brand name with small appliances and most had no idea GE had left the business. However, market research also revealed that consumers viewed B&D as a manufacturer of quality products, equal to those of GE. In fact, consumers perceived B&D, to a greater degree than GE, as a producer of innovative and reliable products.

These research findings would play a significant role in the design of B&D's national product advertising messages. B&D executives needed to decide how the old GE brand name should be utilized, if at all. One approach would attempt to transfer GE's strong customer franchise to the B&D name by references to GE in television and print advertising. A second scenario would omit all references to GE and highlight the B&D brand only.

In addition, B&D executives faced a complex set of retailer support concerns. Although B&D inherited the GE salesforce and its relationships with retailers, the company still faced the important challenge of gaining retailer confidence. Retailers wondered whether B&D would provide the generous merchandising and promotional programs formerly given by GE. They also had no way of gauging potential consumer reaction to the new B&D brand. On the other hand, B&D's short-term need to gain the confidence and support of its major retailers through expensive incentives conflicted, to a large degree, with its long-term objective to improve the profitability of the business.

Simply put, three strategies were possible. B&D could maintain GE's level of retailer promotional incentives, increase them, or limit them during the brand transition period. Later, depending on sales, the incentives could be adjusted further. But whatever level of support B&D chose to provide, the company had to develop a special retailer promotion early in the brand transition to motivate its retailers.

QUESTIONS

1 What are the pros and cons of using the GE name in B&D's national television advertising?
2 Should Black & Decker maintain GE's level of retailer incentives? Why?

CASE 15

WILKINSON SWORD USA*

In late 1984, Norman R. Proulx, president, and Ronald E. Mineo, vice-president of Sales for Wilkinson Sword USA, were faced with a decision of strategic

*Source: Based on "Wilkinson Sword Limited (A) and (B)" in T.J. McNichols, *Policy-Making and Executive Action*, 5th ed. (New York: McGraw-Hill Book Co., 1977); R. Skolnik, "The Birth of a Sales Force," *Sales & Marketing Management* (March 10, 1986), pp. 42-44; Donald B. Thompson, "Can Close Shaves Cut Off Slump for Allegheny Unit?" *Industry Week* (September 16, 1985), p. 24; "Gillette: When Being No. 1 Just Isn't Enough," *Business Week* (August 13, 1984), pp. 126, 131; "100 Leaders Advertising as a Percent of Sales," *Advertising Age* (September 8, 1983), p. 166; "Daisy (A): The Women's Shaving Marketing," HBS #9-582-152; Allegheny International 10-K Reports; and Kevin Higgins, "Japanese Buyout Fuels Scripto's Campaign for Dominance in Lighter, Writing Instrument Markets," *Marketing News* (February 15, 1985), pp. 1, 15.

importance. They had to decide whether or not Wilkinson Sword USA should establish its own salesforce or continue to use manufacturers' representatives, brokers, and/or the salesforces of other companies to represent the Wilkinson Sword's line of razors and blades. If they decided to form a dedicated salesforce for Wilkinson Sword USA, they would reverse a policy that had existed for 30 years dating back to the creation of the U.S. arm of the London, England-based Wilkinson Sword Ltd.

WET-SHAVE MARKET

The shaving market broadly divides into two segments: (1) dry-shave (electric) market, and (2) wet-shave (razor) market. The wet-shave market accounts for the majority of sales volume. The wet-shave market for razors and blades is variously estimated at $450 million to $500 million at manufacturer's prices. The Gillette Company is the worldwide leader in the production and marketing of razors and blades. Furthermore, it is estimated that six out of ten American men and women who shave use Gillette products.

Four other companies are major competitors in the wet-shave market. They are Schick, American Safety Razor, Wilkinson Sword, and BIC, which is the leader in the disposable razor segment. These four competitors, coupled with private (store) brand sales, capture 40 percent of the wet-shave market.

Razors and blades are sold primarily through supermarkets, drugstores, and mass (discount) merchandisers. Although the dollar volume sold through each type of retail outlet varies over time, it is estimated that supermarkets account for 45 percent of sales, drugstores account for 30 percent of sales, and mass merchandisers account for 25 percent of sales of razors and blades. Catalog and department stores also account for a small percentage of razor and blade sales in any given year.

Advertising and consumer promotions play an important role in the marketing of razors and blades. For example, in 1983, Gillette was reported to have spent $205 million for advertising. While this amount was for all company products, since razor and blade sales account for almost 80 percent of Gillette total sales, a sizeable percentage was presumably earmarked for these products. Consumer promotions typically take the form of premium offers, coupons, cent-off deals, and on-package premiums such as a free razor with a cartridge of blades.

Similarly, personal selling is important in the marketing of razors and blades. Salespeople typically call on retail buyers responsible for purchasing items for the health and beauty aid sections of supermarket, drug, and mass merchandise stores. Their job is to introduce new products and special promotions and generally work with buyers to gain shelf space and display, including advertising. In addition, some firms, like Gillette, also employ retail merchandisers who make sure store displays are adequately stocked. How the selling function is performed differs between firms. For example, Gillette, American Safety Razor, BIC, and Schick have their own salesforces; Wilkinson Sword has relied upon manufacturers' agents, brokers, and salesforces of other companies.

THE COMPANY

The Wilkinson Sword Company, Limited, traced its origins to 1772. At that time, the company was a major producer of guns and bayonets. In 1820, the company began manufacturing swords. At the close of the 19th century, Wilkinson Sword production of cavalry swords was between 30,000 and 60,000 annually.

The company produced its first straight-edged razor in 1890 and the first safety razor in 1898. In 1956, Wilkinson Sword introduced its first stainless steel razor blade. Then, in 1961, the company introduced its Teflon-coated Wilkinson Sword Blade. Consumer response to this innovation was phenomenal. The company's market share in Great Britain increased from 20 percent in 1962 to 45 percent in 1966. During the same period in the United States, Wilkinson Sword's market share increased from 2 to 3 percent to 15 percent.

Wilkinson Sword's competitive position in the United States during the late 1960's and early 1970's was continually buffeted by product innovation and aggressive marketing efforts by Gillette, American Safety Razor, Schick, and BIC. Nevertheless, Wilkinson's market share in the United States remained at a respectable percent in 1974. However, by the end of 1984, Wilkinson Sword's market share had fallen to 0.7 percent. Three factors contributed to this decline. First, Wilkinson Sword elected to stop advertising in the United States in 1974 and focus promotional efforts on European markets. Second, product innovation had not kept pace with U.S.-based competitors. A third factor was the lack of a company salesforce. In the late 1960's and early 1970's, Wilkinson Sword's product line was sold by the Colgate-Palmolive salesforce, a large Fortune 500 manufacturer and marketer of personal care products. Wilkinson Sword parted with Colgate-Palmolive in the mid-1970's. In its place, Wilkinson Sword used manufacturers' agents to call on and service drugstores and brokers for supermarkets.

In late 1980, Wilkinson Sword was acquired by Allegheny International Holdings, Inc., a wholly-owned subsidiary of Allegheny International, a Pittsburgh, Pennsylvania-based conglomerate. Allegheny International also owned or had major equity positions in such well-known consumer products firms as Scripto, Inc., and Sunbeam Appliance Company. Scripto, Inc., was engaged in the production and marketing of writing instruments and components and the marketing of disposable lighters. Sunbeam Appliance Company manufactured and marketed a broad line of portable electric products. Sunbeam Personal Products Company manufactured and marketed a wide line of products including hair dryers, curling irons, and electric razors, among other items.

In the early 1980's, Wilkinson Sword's sales, marketing, and administrative functions in the United States were integrated into Scripto, Inc. This action, however, failed to arrest the decline in Wilkinson Sword's market share in the United States. Then, in 1984, Allegheny International sold Scripto, Inc., to Tokai Seiki Company, Ltd., a Japanese lighter manufacturer. This action left Wilkinson Sword without the sales, marketing, and administrative support it had benefited from with Scripto, Inc.

At the time of the Scripto, Inc., acquisition by Tokai Seiki Company, Ltd., Norman R. Proulx was vice-president and general manager of Scripto, Inc.

When it became apparent that he was not going to stay with Scripto, Inc., top management at Allegheny International offered him the presidency of Wilkinson Sword USA. He accepted and offered Ronald E. Mineo, vice-president of sales for Scripto, Inc., the same position at Wilkinson Sword USA.

SALES FORCE DECISION

One of the major issues facing Proulx and Mineo was whether or not Wilkinson Sword should change its sales program in the United States. Wilkinson Sword had relied upon manufacturers' agents, brokers, or the sales forces of other companies to represent its product line in the United States for 30 years. To recruit, train, organize, and manage its own sales force would be a major undertaking. Furthermore, the decision had a time dimension to it. The Scripto, Inc., salesforce would continue to represent Wilkinson Sword for 2 months following the acquisition for a fee. After that, Wilkinson Sword USA would assume the responsibility for its own sales and marketing functions.

If Proulx and Mineo decided to create a Wilkinson Sword USA salesforce, then a sales plan would be necessary. This plan would include the policies and procedures for staffing, training, organizing, and managing a salesforce. The first step in the process would involve account identification. Mineo identified 25 key accounts from among the supermarkets, drug stores, and mass merchandisers that carried razors and blades. In addition, 400 other accounts were identified. The 25 key accounts would be managed from its Atlanta, Georgia, headquarters. The other accounts would be handled by the salesforce, including sales managers.

The sales organization would include two key account managers to handle the 25 key accounts. Three field sales managers would be needed, or one for each of three sales divisions: west, central, and east. Geographical sales territories would be identified within each division.

Alternatively, Proulx and Mineo could seek out manufacturers' agents, brokers, and/or another company's salesforce to represent the Wilkinson Sword USA product line. This approach would be consistent with past policies.

QUESTIONS

1 What are the advantages and disadvantages to Wilkinson Sword USA's using agents, brokers, and/or other company salesforces to represent its product line?

2 What are the advantages and disadvantages to Wilkinson Sword USA's creating its own dedicated salesforce?

3 Given the following assumptions and information provided in the case, how many salespeople will Wilkinson Sword USA need to hire, not including the two key account managers and sales managers?

Assumptions

a. Average amount of selling time available per year = 1,500 hours

b. Length of an average call = 1 hour

c. Call frequency necessary to service a customer each year = 52 times

4 Given the following assumptions, your answer to Question 3 above, and information provided in the case, should Wilkinson Sword USA use independent agents and/or brokers, or its own salesforce? What other factors should be considered?

Assumptions

a. Experienced Salesperson Salary = $35,000
b. Agent/Broker Commission on Sales = 10 percent
c. Experienced Sales Manager Salary = $50,000
d. Salesperson Commission = 5 percent
e. Key Account Manager Salary = $35,000
f. Key Account Manager Commission on Sales = 5 percent

CASE 16

AMHURST COMPUTER, INC.*

Jay Allen is a sales representative for Amhurst Computer, Inc., a large manufacturer of computer hardware and software. The computer systems Allen sells are used primarily for accounting purposes (e.g., use in payroll, accounts receivable, or accounts payable processing). Allen specializes in selling to physicians owning partnerships in medical clinics.

In January (the beginning of the current fiscal year), Allen's sales manager assigned him a sales quota (goal) of $200,000 for the year. In mid-December (2 weeks before the end of the current fiscal year), Allen was $25,000 short of his quota. If he did not reach his quota within 2 weeks, he would not receive his annual bonus of $5,000. He was very discouraged about the prospects of achieving his goal.

As Allen was contemplating how to attain his quota, the office manager from the Uptown Clinic, Eloise Jones, called and told him that the five doctors from the Uptown Clinic had decided that their practice was large enough to justify the purchase of a computer system. She also stated that the doctors wanted to purchase a computer before the first of the year for tax reasons. To help the doctors with their purchase decision, Jones told Allen that they had engaged the services of an independent business consultant, Edward Seawell. She asked Allen if he could meet with Seawell and her the next morning at 9, to which he agreed. As Allen said good-bye to Jones, he was ecstatic; he still had a chance to achieve his sales quota.

The next morning at 9 Allen met with Jones and Seawell at the Uptown Clinic and discussed the clinic's accounting problems and how those problems could conceivably be solved with a computer system. After a lengthy and detailed discussion, Allen told Jones and Seawell that he wanted to take the information he had obtained from them and develop a sales proposal that would describe the results of his analysis and offer his recommendations regarding the most appropriate Amhurst computer system for the clinic. The three of them agreed to meet the following day at 4 PM to discuss Allen's proposal.

When Allen returned to his office, he reviewed his notes about the Uptown Clinic's accounting needs. After careful consideration, he decided that the com-

*Source: Professor Alan J. Dubinsky, St. Cloud State University.

puter that would be appropriate for the clinic was Amhurst Computer's Z600, a newly released model. The cost of the Z600 was $30,000. If he sold the Uptown Clinic the Z600, he would surpass his quota by $5,000.

As Allen was thinking about his chances for achieving his sales quota, he knew that there was another Amhurst computer that could satisfy the Uptown Clinic's accounting needs, the X300. The X300 had just been replaced in the product line by the Z600. The X300 was quite comparable to the Z600 but lacked certain features found in the Z600. None of these features, however, was needed by the Uptown Clinic, although they *might* be of use in the *future* if the clinic's accounting needs changed. Because the X300 was a discontinued model, Amhurst management had reduced its price to $10,000.

Allen was now in a quandary. He had to decide whether he should recommend the X300 or the Z600. Allen knew that if he proposed and sold the Z600 to the clinic, he would achieve his sales quota. If, however, he recommended and sold the X300 to the clinic, he would not reach his sales quota. After contemplating the dilemma, he decided to go ahead and recommend the Z600.

At 4 PM the following day, Allen met with Jones and Seawell and presented his proposal. After reviewing the proposal, Jones and Seawell told Allen that they would discuss the proposal with the clinic's physicians and would have a decision for him hopefully within 3 days.

Three days later Jones called Allen and told him that the doctors felt that $30,000 was too much to spend on a computer. They had instructed Seawell and her to seek out sales proposals from other computer manufacturers in hopes of finding one that was less expensive than the Z600. Jones thanked Allen for his time and efforts and said good-bye.

As he put down the telephone receiver, Allen was upset. Not only had he lost his chance to achieve his sales quota (by not selling the Z600) but had also lost an opportunity to come closer to achieving his quota (by failing to recommend and sell the X300).

Allen began to ponder how he might salvage the sale with the Uptown Clinic and at last arrived at what he thought was a good solution. He would tell Jones and Seawell that a computer, which would serve the Uptown Clinic's needs, had been recently discontinued by Amhurst. Because it had been discontinued, management had *just* reduced its price to $10,000—a real value for the money. He would strongly encourage their considering this alternative, particularly since it was $20,000 less than the Z600.

After thinking through his solution, Allen called Jones. He told her that some "new developments" had just taken place at Amhurst Computer, Inc., that should be of interest to the Uptown Clinic and that he would like to discuss them with Seawell and her. Jones said that Seawell and she would be willing to meet with Allen the next afternoon at 1.

Allen arrived at the Uptown Clinic at 1 PM the next day and was greeted by Jones and Seawell. Allen explained the "new developments" at Amhurst Computer, Inc. After he told his "story," both Jones and Seawell seemed irritated. They told Allen that it appeared that he had initially tried to "price gouge" the Uptown Clinic by recommending a more expensive model of computer. And now that the clinic's doctors had decided to purchase a computer that was less expensive than the Z600, Allen was trying to salvage the sale by proposing the very product that he should have recommended in the first place (the X300). Allen attempted to assure them that only recently had the price of the X300 been reduced to $10,000, so it was not until now that he was in a position to propose it. Moreover, he said, in no way had he tried to "price gouge" the clinic by recommending the Z600 to them for purchase.

Before Allen left the clinic, Seawell asked him to send a one-page proposal describing the merits of the X300 to Jones. Jones and Seawell would present the new proposal to the clinic's physicians.

When Allen got back to his office, he was disgruntled. His "story" had not gone over smoothly with Jones and Seawell. In addition, he felt that since Jones and Seawell thought he had tried to "price gouge" the clinic, they might be unwilling to tell the doctors about the X300.

After he prepared the one-page proposal, Allen decided that he would send the proposal to Jones, as Seawell had requested, and also to the doctors at their homes without notifying Jones or Seawell. He felt that by sending the proposal to the physicians' homes, they would be certain to see it and be more likely to act on it than if he were to have Jones and Seawell continue to be his intermediaries with the doctors.

Two days later at 9 at night Seawell called Allen at his home. They had the following conversation:

Seawell: Allen, this is Edward Seawell.

Allen: Hello Ed! How are you?

Seawell: Let's dispense with the courtesies, Allen, because you deserve none. Tell me, Allen, do you normally do business at customers' homes? Is that a typical practice of yours?

Allen: No, Ed. Why do you ask?

Seawell: Don't get cute with me by saying why do I ask. You sent the X300 proposal to Eloise as well as to the homes of the clinic's doctors without even seeking our approval. Eloise feels very hurt by your action. She thinks that you don't trust her or me to convey information to the doctors.

Allen: I'm really very sorry, Ed. I wasn't trying to offend or hurt anyone. I just wanted to distribute the information to the doctors. I'm sorry that I've caused a problem.

Seawell: Yes, I'm sorry too, and I'm madder than heck about it. To show you how upset I am over your behavior, I am going to persuade the doctors not to do business with you or your company. There is no way the Uptown Clinic will purchase a Z600, X300, or any other Amhurst computer. Your conduct has been reprehensible, and you don't deserve our business or respect. Good night!

QUESTIONS

1 What mistakes did Allen make?
2 Instead of making these mistakes, what should Allen have done?
3 What could Amhurst Computer management do to prevent similar situations from happening in the future?

MANOR HILL HOSPITAL MEDICAL EMERGENCY CLINIC

"We've been open for 11 months and have yet to break even in any 1 month," mulled Heather Waite as she scanned last month's revenue and expense summary for the Medical Emergency Clinic (MEC) operated by Manor Hill Hospital. As the administrator for MEC, Waite knew that something had to change. Even though Manor Hill was a nonprofit hospital, the charter for MEC stipulated that it had to be self-supporting in its second year of operation.

MEC was established to serve the health care needs of people who work in the central business district. The specific services offered by MEC included (1) preventive health care (such as physical examinations), (2) minor emergencies, (3) specialized employer services (such as preemployment examinations and worker's compensation injuries), and (4) primary health care services (for personal illnesses). A breakdown of average monthly service usage and the average charge for each service was as follows:

SERVICE	PERCENT OF VISITS	AVERAGE CHARGE
Personal illness	39%	$25
Physical examinations	14	25
Worker's compensation	25	39
Employment or insurance examinations	19	47
Emergency	3	67

The weighted average charge per visit was $33.94, and the weighted average variable cost per visit was $5.67. Fixed costs per month averaged $17,500. The average number of visits per month was 590.

Since its opening, MEC had surveyed patients to find out how it might better serve their needs. Patient concerns fell into two categories: service hours and waiting time. To date, MEC had been open from 8 AM to 5 PM, Monday through Friday. However, patients had requested extended hours with an opening time of 7 AM and a closing time at 7 PM. A second concern was waiting time, particularly during lunch hours (11 AM to 2 PM). A check of MEC records indicated that 70 percent of patient visits occurred during this period, and most of these visits were for personal illnesses and examinations for various reasons. Further checking revealed that people actually left MEC because of congestion and did not return at a later date. Waite believed these concerns could be dealt with if MEC increased its personnel. Her plan was to add another physician and support personnel to create two staffs. One staff could work from 7 AM to 3 PM, and a second staff could work from 11 AM to 7 PM. By using paramedical personnel and part-time medical assistants, she estimated that average monthly fixed costs would increase by 25 percent even with a raise in personnel salaries next year. The staff overlap at lunchtime would alleviate some of the congestion.

Still, Waite felt that something had to be done about the uneven demand for MEC's services during operating hours. She knew that personal physical examinations and employment and insurance examinations could be handled by appointment. Moreover these services might be provided before or after normal working hours (before 8 AM or after 5 PM). Her interviews with employers and insurance companies revealed that they would schedule employment and insurance examinations during this period. Based on her interviews, she estimated that MEC could significantly modify its visit mix and number of patients in an average month. Specifically, she believed MEC would have an average of 749 patient visits per month if the hours were expanded. Almost all the additional visits would be for employment and insurance examinations. In addition, Waite had received approval to increase the prices of MEC's major services. The new prices, which would become effective at the beginning of the second year of operation, and the forecast mix of patient visits were as follows:

SERVICE	PERCENT OF VISITS	AVERAGE CHARGE
Personal illness	31%	$27
Physical examinations	11	37
Worker's compensation	20	41
Employment or insurance examinations	36	50
Emergency	2	70

Waite believed that the average variable cost per patient visit would be $6 next year, regardless of the mix of patient visits.

As she prepared her recommendation to the Manor Hill Hospital administrator, she identified at least two options to enable MEC to break even. She could simply institute the price increase, or she could increase prices and expand hours and incur higher fixed costs. Whatever she recommended, she knew she would have to support her argument from both a profit and service perspective.

QUESTIONS

1 How many visits below the break-even point is MEC at the present time?
2 Can MEC break even when the price increases are put into effect, assuming fixed costs remain unchanged, the visit mix is the same, but variable costs become $6 per visit?
3 Can MEC expand its hours, thereby increasing fixed cost, and break even given a price increase, the increased variable cost per visit, and the new patient visit mix expected by Waite?

CASE 18

INTERNATIONAL PLAYTEX, INC.*

Will a single advertising campaign work in 12 separate countries? Executives at International Playtex, Inc., believe it will, at least for the Playtex WOW-brand brassiere.

*Source: Based on "Maintaining Modesty in Bra Commercials is a Snap," *Ad Week* (May 4, 1987), p. 23; "Playtex Kicks Off a One-Ad-Fits-All Campaign," *Business Week* (December 16, 1985), pp. 48–49; Pat Sloan, "Smilow Moves to Keep Playtex in Top Position," *Advertising Age* (March 30, 1987), p. 3ff.

International Playtex, Inc., is one of the world's largest manufacturers of women's intimate apparel and personal care products. Company sales were $1.2 billion of which intimate apparel accounted for $375 million. It is estimated that the company captures between 16 and 17 percent of the brassiere segment of the intimate apparel-undergarment category of women's clothing. Fully one half of the company's sales of intimate apparel came from overseas markets.

Playtex is the leading advertiser of brassieres in the world. It accounts for 40 percent of the total media expenditures spent in the brassiere segment of the intimate apparel-undergarment category.

Coordinating an international advertising program for Playtex is not an easy task. In the past, Playtex managers and advertising agencies developed and executed advertising campaigns for individual countries. At one point, Playtex had 43 separate and distinct advertising campaigns running throughout the world at the same time. This practice proved to be costly. Moreover, as Playtex moved to streamline its international operations, it consolidated its advertising agency roster and awarded its worldwide advertising account to Grey Advertising, Inc., one of the world's largest advertising agencies. The WOW-brand brassiere campaign would be the first global campaign assigned to Grey Advertising.

The WOW-brand was the product of 3 years of research and development. The brand contained a new plastic that replaced wires that were used for support and shape. This feature would become the centerpiece of the global campaign because comfort, support, and shape had universal appeal to all women, according to one Grey Advertising executive.

The first step in developing the global campaign was selecting female models with universal appeal. After viewing dozens of models, three were selected—one blonde and two brunettes. These three models would be featured in commercials shown around the world.

Campaign implementation would involve dealing with a variety of specific circumstances. First, Playtex would have to overcome language differences. For example, the WOW-brand would be called Traumbügel (dream wire) in German and Alas (wings) in Spanish. Addressing unique preferences of women would also have to be considered in presenting the brand. French women prefer lacy brassieres; American women prefer plain opaque styles. Adapting to governmental regulations and TV commercial standards in different countries would be a third hurdle. For instance, the commercial for Australia had to be produced in Australia since Australian TV would show only locally produced commercials. In South Africa, TV standards precluded women from modeling bras; therefore fully clothed models would have to simply hold the item. Production constraints would be present as well. Again as a result of country differences, some commercials could be 30 seconds while others would be limited to 20 seconds. In addition, some countries required 1 second of no sound at the beginning of a commercial and others did not.

QUESTIONS

1 Where would you place the WOW-brand marketing strategy on a continuum from a pure globalization approach to a pure customized approach? Why?

2 Which environmental factors described in Chapter 22 would help or hinder a global marketing strategy for women's intimate apparel like that sold by Playtex?
3 What is the likelihood for success of the WOW-brand marketing strategy? Why?

CASE 19

GENERAL MILLS, INC.

General Mills, a diversified Fortune 500 company with corporate headquarters in Minneapolis, is constantly seeking new product concepts to add to its line of consumer products. One such product concept was a fruit-flavored concentrate that could be sprayed into a glass of water to produce a fruit-flavored beverage. This product concept had emerged from a study of the beverage market indicating that tremendous potential existed for a new product entry. However, a major unresolved question was how to make the product—tentatively named Jet 24—a commercial success. The product manager in charge of Jet 24 had commissioned extensive research to address this broad question.

PRODUCT DEVELOPMENT AND MARKETING RESEARCH

Product development efforts had produced a pressurized can that would contain enough concentrate to provide 24 8-ounce drinks, or the equivalent of one case of soft drinks. The pressurization, which would squirt the concentrate, coupled with the 24-drink capability in each can led to the name Jet 24. Preliminary work on flavors indicated that five or six flavors were possible: orange, grape, cherry, lemon-lime, strawberry or raspberry, and punch. Furthermore Jet 24 would have a "light carbonated" feel in the mouth even though no carbonation was added.

Marketing research on the product concept had focused on the inherent characteristics of Jet 24 and its position in the marketplace. Several different studies were conducted. In one study focus group interviews were held with female heads of households and their children in New Orleans. The results of this study were summarized by the researcher as follows:

- Jet 24 is perceived first as a kid's drink, but also secondarily as a drink for the whole family because of its excellent quality.
- After mixing their drinks and before tasting, about half the respondents said they would buy Jet 24 and half would not. Those who had said they would buy the product were even more favorably disposed toward Jet 24 after tasting the product than before tasting it.
- Jet 24 appears to be perceived as a high-grade Kool-Aid for day-to-day use, especially in the summer, rather than as a soft drink.
- Consumers believe the can may cause problems because it may clog up, kids may make a mess with it, and parents won't know how much is left.
- The present flavors of Jet 24 concentrate taste excellent with little after-

taste. Further taste testing will be required to optimize the quality of the drinks.

- Consumers recognize that the drink produced from the Jet 24 concentrate is slightly carbonated.
- The need for a vitamin C additive in fruit-based drinks, and thus in Jet 24, is recognized by all consumers.
- Users, especially children, enjoy squirting Jet 24 into a glass of water.
- Although 24 servings for 69 cents is considered a fair price, there is some doubt about whether the can would actually produce 24 servings.
- The possible use of Jet 24 for Popsicles, ice cream toppings, and other cooking needs should be pursued.

In a second study four focus group interviews were held with female heads of households with at least one child between 3 and 14 years of age. This study's findings reported by the researchers were:

- Two groups had negative reaction to Jet 24, and two groups offered a positive response. The latter two said they would buy it for their children as a special treat, but not necessarily as a regular item.
- The operation of the can was a mildly pleasant surprise to the respondents. It had a "fun element" for many. However, continued use indicated that Jet 24 was a children's product, one that would likely be bought only with children in mind.
- With initial trial of this product, there would be tremendous variations in the amount of concentrate used, use of ice, and the need to stir. The wide range of colors in the final beverage indicates that consumers will be drinking very different drinks, depending on concentrate usage.
- From the interviews, three distinct categories of beverages are evident: juices, carbonated pops, and Kool-Aid. Jet 24 falls into the Kool-Aid category. In comparison to Kool-Aid, Jet 24 wins on two points—more fun to use and a tastier drink—and loses on three points—expense (24 servings is not believed), lack of food value, and messiness.
- The addition of vitamin C is almost expected today in a fruit drink. If the product is a fruit drink, it should have nutritive goodies; if it's a pop, this isn't expected.
- There are two areas of concern regarding the concept of Jet 24.
  a. The emphasis on the "presweetened" nature of Jet 24 produced an image of "aftertaste" and "too sweet." A large percentage of people who drink diet pop are drinking it in spite of this image, however. The term *presweetened* certainly grabs many women today because of its low-calorie implications, but simultaneously it tends to raise questions about flavor and also about "stickiness," which is a bad word in connection with any fruity beverage.
  b. The claim of 24 servings arouses skepticism.

A third study involving in-home tests under actual usage conditions indicated that Jet 24 was favored over Kool-Aid for orange, grape, and lemon-lime flavors. However, the punch flavor did not compare favorably with Hawaiian Punch. Jet 24 lost on features such as taste, color, and aftertaste. This research also revealed that most consumers (60 percent) thought Jet 24 was most similar to carbonated soft drinks, while 21 percent said it was more like a fruit drink and 19 percent thought it was like a powdered (Kool-Aid) drink.

About this time research was also under way to determine the potential sales volume for Jet 24. According to an independent research firm retained by General Mills, the pattern of acceptance for similar products indicated that 15 percent to 20 percent of the 58 million households with children in the United States would try the product at least once. Of those households that tried the product, 25 percent to 40 percent would make a repeat purchase. The firm estimated the average consumption of each trier to be one can and additional sales for each repeat buyer household to be three cans. The trial rate would depend, in part, on amount of funds devoted to advertising and quality of the advertising copy.

INTRODUCTORY PROGRAM CONSIDERATIONS

The Jet 24 product manager was also considering how the product would be introduced. Discussions with the firm's advertising agency had resulted in two options. One option was that advertising for Jet 24 would focus on children and feature commercials on Saturday morning cartoon shows and advertisements in Sunday comic strips. This annual expenditure level was $3,855,000. A second option was to focus on the family, including adults, and feature TV commercials during prime-time evening hours. Annual expenditure level for this option was $7,862,000. In addition, coupons applied to the purchase of Jet 24 would be inserted into "Big G" cereals and in Sunday comic strips under both options.

Distribution would be through over 50,000 food stores where General Mills had well-established working relationships. The company would sell Jet 24 to supermarkets for $12 per case of 24 cans, or 50 cents per can. Consumers would pay 69 cents per can, or 2.9 cents per 8-ounce drink. This figure for an 8-ounce serving was slightly lower than the price of powdered drinks and significantly lower than the price of soft drinks and fruit drinks.

Since General Mills had contracted with another firm to produce the cans and the concentrate, the company would have no investment in equipment. The cost of a case of Jet 24 provided a gross profit of $4.75 per case to General Mills. Other estimated variable costs were 25 cents per case.

QUESTIONS

1 How would you describe the roles of mothers and children in a purchase of this type?
2 Should Jet 24 be positioned as a powdered (Kool-Aid), carbonated, or fruit drink? Why?
3 How would you describe Jet 24's proposed distribution intensity, new product pricing strategy, and promotional strategy given its emphasis on heavy consumer advertising?
4 What would be your forecast of revenue for Jet 24?
5 What estimate(s) of profitability is (are) possible given the data provided?
6 Would you recommend introducing Jet 24? Why or why not?

GLOSSARY

above-, at-, or below-market pricing pricing based on what the market price is.

accelerated development the second stage of the retail life cycle, characterized by rapid increases in market share and profitability.

accessory equipment a type of support good that includes tools and office equipment; usually purchased in small order sizes by many buyers.

account management policies policies that specify whom salespeople should contact, what kinds of selling and customer service activities should be engaged in, and how these activities should be carried out; in an advertising agency, refers to policies used by an account executive in dealing with clients.

action item list an aid to implementing a marketing plan, consisting of three columns: (1) the task, (2) the name of the person responsible for completing the task, and (3) the date by which the task is to be finished.

administered vertical marketing system a channel arrangement in which the stages of production and distribution are determined by the size and influence of one channel member.

advertising any paid form of nonpersonal communication about an organization, product, or service by an identified sponsor.

advocacy advertisements institutional advertisements that state the position of a company on an issue.

affective component dimension of an attitude that refers to how one feels about an object or product.

all you can afford budgeting allocating funds to advertising only after all other budget items are covered.

allowances reductions in the original purchase price of an item granted to customers who retain ownership of it.

alternatives the factors over which the decision maker has control.

anchor stores well-known national or regional stores that are located in regional shopping centers.

annual marketing plans plans that deal with the marketing goals and strategies for a product, product line, or entire firm for a single year.

approach stage in the personal selling process, the initial meeting between the salesperson and prospect where the objectives are to gain the prospect's attention, stimulate interest, and build the foundation for the sales presentation.

assumptions conjectures about factors or situations that simplify the problem enough to allow it to be solved within stated constraints.

atmosphere a store's ambiance or setting.

attitudes learned predispositions to respond to an object or class of objects in a consistent manner.

automated warehouse a warehouse with computer-controlled technologies that replace people with machines.

average revenue the average amount of money received for selling one unit of a product.

baby boomers the generation of children born between 1946 and 1964.

bait-and-switch advertising an advertising practice in which a company shows a product that it has no intention of selling to lure the customer into the store and sell him a higher-priced item.

balance of trade the difference between the monetary value of its exports and imports.

barriers to entry business practices or conditions that make it difficult for a new firm to enter the market.

basing-point pricing selecting one or more geographical locations (basing point) from which the list price for products plus freight expenses are charged to the buyers.

behavioral component dimension of an attitude that refers to one's intention regarding an object or product, such as the likelihood of purchase.

beliefs a consumer's subjective perception of how well a product or brand performs on different attributes; these are based on personal experience, advertising, and discussions with other people.

bidders list a list of firms believed to be qualified to supply a given item.

blanket branding *see* multiproduct branding.

blended family two families from prior marriages merged into a single household as spouses remarry.

blocked currency currency that a government will not allow to be converted into other currencies.

bonded warehouse a specialized public warehouse that allows a firm to defer taxes on stored items until they are released.

boycott in international trade, the refusal by the government of one country to have dealings with another country.

brand name any word or device (design, shape, sound, or color) that is used to distinguish one company's products from a competitor's.

brand loyalty a favorable attitude toward and consistent purchase of a single brand over time.

brand manager *see* product manager.

brand mark the part of a brand that is a symbol or design and cannot be vocalized.

branding activity in which an organization uses a name, phrase, design, or symbols or a combination of these to identify its products and distinguish them from those of a competitor.

breadth of line the relative variety of different items a store, wholesaler, or manufacturer carries.

break-even analysis an analysis of the relationship between total revenue and total cost to determine profitability at various levels of output.

break-even chart a graphic presentation of a break-even analysis.

break-even point (BEP) quantity at which total revenue and total cost are equal and beyond which profit occurs.

brokers channel intermediaries that do not take title to merchandise and make their profits from commissions and fees by negotiating contracts or deals between buyers and sellers.

buildup approach a sales forecasting technique that sums the sales forecasts of each of the components to arrive at a total forecast.

bundle pricing the marketing of two or more products in a single "package" price.

business *see* mission.

business analysis stage Step 4 of the new product process, which involves specifying the product features and marketing strategy and making necessary financial projections to commercialize a product.

business ethics guidelines that indicate how to act rightly and justly in a business situation.

business firm an organization that carries on economic activity to earn a profit.

business logistics coordination of the physical movement and storage of parts, raw materials, and finished goods to minimize total cost for a given service level.

business portfolio analysis analysis of a firm's strategic business units (SBUs) as though they were a collection of separate investments.

buy classes groups of three specific buying situations organizations face: new buy, straight rebuy, and modified rebuy.

buyer turnover the frequency with which new buyers enter the market.

buying center the group of persons within an organization who participate in the buying process and share common goals, risks, and knowledge important to that process.

buying criteria the factors buying organizations use when evaluating a potential supplier and what it wants to sell.

buying objectives goals set by the participants in the buying process to help them achieve their organization's goals.

cannibalization a situation where a company's new brand steals market share or sales from its existing brands.

capacity management managing the demand for a service so that it is available to consumers.

cash allowance a trade sales promotion in which a discount is given on each case ordered during a specific time period.

cash and carry wholesaler a limited-service merchant wholesaler that takes title to merchandise but sells only to buyers who call on it and pay cash for and transport their own merchandise.

cash discounts a reduction in price awarded retailers if they pay their bills quickly.

cause-related marketing (CRM) tying the charitable contributions of a firm directly to the customer revenues produced through the promotion of one of its products.

cease and desist order action by the FTC in which it orders a company to stop a practice that it considers unfair.

cells boxes in a table or cross tabulation.

central business district the oldest retail setting; the community's downtown area.

channel captain a marketing channel member that coordinates, directs, and supports other channel members; may be a manufacturer, wholesaler, or retailer.

Child Protection Act (1960) a law that bans the sale of hazardous toys and articles used by children.

Clayton Act (1914) a law that forbids certain types of tie-in sales, exclusive dealing arrangements, and acquisitions whose effect might be to lessen competition or help create a monopoly.

closed-end question *see fixed* alternative question.

closing stage the stage in the personal selling process that involves getting a purchase commitment from a prospect.

cognitive component dimension of an attitude that refers to the way one thinks about an object or product.

cognitive dissonance the feeling of postpurchase psychological tension or anxiety a consumer often experiences.

combination compensation plan a compensation plan whereby a salesperson is paid a specified salary plus a commission based on sales or profit generated.

commercialization stage the final phase of the new product process in which the product is positioned and launched into full-scale production and sale.

communication the sharing of meaning, which requires five elements: source, message, receiver, and the processes of encoding and decoding.

community shopping center a retail site location that typically has one primary store and a relatively large number of smaller outlets and serves a population base of about 100,000.

company forecast *see* sales forecast.

comparative advertisements advertisements that show one brand's strengths relative to those of competitors.

competition the set of alternative firms that could provide a product to satisfy a specific market's needs.

competitive advantage a firm's strength relative to competitors' strengths in the markets they serve and the products they offer.

competitive advertisements advertisements that promote a specific brand's features and benefits.

competitive institutional advertising institutional advertising that promotes the advantages of one product class over another; used in markets where different product classes compete for the same buyers.

competitive parity budgeting allocating funds to advertising to match the competitors' level of spending.

computer-assisted retailing a retailing method whereby customers order products over computer linkups from their home.

concept tests external evaluations of a product idea that consist of preliminary testing of the new product idea (rather than the actual product) with consumers.

consolidated metropolitan statistical area (CMSA) the largest designation in terms of geographical area and market size, made up of several primary metropolitan statistical areas (PMSAs).

constraints the restrictions, such as time and money, placed on potential solutions by the nature and importance of the problem.

consumer behavior actions of a person to purchase and use goods and services.

consumer cooperative a retail outlet owned by consumers who also manage, operate, and shop at the store.

consumer goods products purchased by the ultimate consumer.

Consumer Product Safety Act (1972) a law that established the Consumer Product Safety Commission to monitor product safety and establish uniform product safety standards.

consumer socialization the process by which people acquire consumer skills, knowledge, and attitudes.

consumerism a movement started in the 1960's when consumers sought to obtain a greater say in the quality of products they buy and the information they receive from sellers to increase their influence, power, and rights in dealing with institutions.

consumer-oriented sales promotions sales tools used to support a company's advertising and personal selling efforts directed to ultimate consumers; examples include coupons, sweepstakes, and trading stamps.

contest a sales promotion in which consumers apply their analytical or creative thinking to win a prize.

continuous innovations products that require no new learning to use.

contract manufacturing agreeing to have another firm manufacture products according to certain specifications; if the manufacturing firm is foreign, the products may then be sold in the foreign country or exported back to the home country.

contracting a strategy used during the decline stage of the product life cycle in which a company contracts the manufacturing or marketing of a product to another firm.

contractual vertical marketing system a channel arrangement whereby independent production and distribution firms integrate their efforts on a contractual basis to obtain greater economies and marketing impact.

contribution margin analysis a form of profitability analysis that spotlights the behavior of controllable costs and indicates how much a specific marketing factor adds to profit.

control group a group not exposed to the experimental variable in an experiment.

controllable factor the marketing mix element (product, price, promotion, or place) a manager can act on to solve a marketing problem.

controlled distribution minimarkets test markets run in smaller test areas that electronically monitor product purchases at checkout counters for more careful testing at reduced costs.

convenience goods items that the consumer purchases frequently and with a minimum of shopping effort.

cooperative advertising advertising in which a national company shares the cost with local distributors.

corporate chain a type of retail ownership in which a single firm owns multiple outlets.

corporate takeover the purchase of a firm by outsiders.

corporate vertical marketing system a channel arrangement whereby successive stages of production and distribution are combined under a single owner.

corrective advertising FTC action requiring a company to spend money on advertising to correct prior misleading ads.

cost of goods sold total value of the products sold during a specified time period.

cost per thousand (CPM) a formula to compare the cost of alternative media; CPM equals the price of the medium times 1,000, divided by the circulation or delivered audience.

cost plus fixed-fee pricing a pricing method where a supplier is reimbursed for all costs, regardless of what they may be, plus a fixed percentage of the production or construction costs.

cost plus percentage-of-cost pricing setting the price of a product or service by adding a fixed percentage to the production or construction costs.

countertrade using barter rather than money in making international sales.

coupons sales promotions that usually offer a discounted price to consumers.

creative boutiques advertising agencies specializing in creative and production work.

creative lateral leap a belief that in pursuing one idea, people often identify a different, significant opportunity.

cross tabulation method of presenting and relating data on two or more variables to display summary data and discover relationships in the data.

culture the sets of values, ideas, and attitudes of a homogeneous group of people that are transmitted from one generation to the next.

cumulative quantity discounts price reductions based on the accumulation of purchases of a product over a given time period.

customary pricing a method of pricing based on a product's tradition, standardized channel of distribution, or other competitive factors.

customer contact audit a flow chart of the points of intervention between a consumer and a service provider.

customer service the actions of a logistics system to satisfy users in terms of time, dependability, communication, and convenience.

customized approach (to global marketing) an international marketing method that entails designing a different marketing plan for each nation, recognizing their different needs, values, customs, languages, and purchasing power.

customs norms and expectations about the way people do things in a particular country.

data the facts and figures pertinent to the problem, composed of primary and secondary data.

deal a sales promotion that offers a short-term price reduction.

deceptive pricing a practice by which prices are artificially inflated and then marked down under the guise of a sale.

decision a conscious choice from among two or more alternatives.

decision factors the different sets of variables—the alternatives and uncertainties—that combine to give the outcome of a decision.

decision making the act of consciously choosing from alternatives.

decision-making unit (DMU) the people in a household or an organization's buying center who are involved in the decision to buy a product.

decline stage the fourth and last stage of the product life cycle when sales and profitability decline.

decoding the process by which a receiver translates and interprets a message in the communication process.

deletion a strategy of dropping a product from the product line, usually in the decline stage of the product life cycle.

delivered pricing a pricing method where the price the seller quotes includes all transportation costs.

Delphi method a survey in which a group of experts gives anonymous forecasts of sales or of the probability of some future event; estimates are summarized and reported back to them, and they may revise them for several rounds.

demand curve the summation of points representing the maximum quantity of a product consumers will buy at different price levels.

demand factors factors that determine the strength of consumers' willingness and ability to pay for goods and services.

demand-backward pricing setting a price by estimating the price consumers would be willing to pay, then working backward through margins for retailers and wholesalers to determine the price a manufacturer should charge wholesalers.

demographics distribution of a population on selected characteristics such as where people live, their numbers, and who they are in terms of age, sex, income, and occupation.

dependent variable the factor of interest in an experiment that may be affected by the change in an independent variable.

depth of line the assortment of each item a store, wholesaler, or retailer carries.

derived demand the demand for industrial products is driven by, or derived from, demand for consumer products.

desk jobber *see* drop shipper.

determinant attributes those brand characteristics which are most important to a consumer in making a purchase.

development stage phase of the new product process in which the idea on paper is turned into a prototype; includes manufacturing and laboratory and consumer tests.

dichotomous question a fixed alternative question that allows only a "yes" or "no" response.

differentiation positioning positioning a product in a smaller market niche that is less competitive.

diffusion of innovation the process by which people receive new information and accept new ideas and products.

direct channel a marketing channel where a producer and ultimate consumer interact directly with each other.

direct exporting a company handling its own exports directly, without intermediaries.

direct forecast an estimate of the value to be forecast without the use of intervening steps.

direct investment an investment in an assembly or manufacturing plant located in a foreign country.

direct marketing selling products by having consumers interact with various advertising media without a face-to-face meeting with a salesperson.

discontinuous innovations products that require totally new consumption patterns.

discounts reductions from list price that a seller gives a buyer as a reward for some buyer activity favorable to the seller.

discretionary income the money that remains after taxes and necessities have been paid for.

disposable income the money a consumer has left after taxes to use for food, shelter, and clothing.

distinctive competency an organization's principal competitive strengths and advantages in terms of marketing, technological, and financial resources.

distribution center a privately owned warehouse that focuses on the rapid movement of goods through the warehouse.

diversification a strategy of developing new products and selling them in new markets.

downsizing a packaging trend in which a product is reduced in package size; with reference to corporations, *see* restructuring.

drive a stimulus that moves an individual to action.

drop shipper a merchant wholesaler that owns the merchandise it sells but does not physically handle, stock, or deliver; also called a desk jobber.

dual distribution an arrangement by which a firm reaches buyers by employing two or more different types of channels for the same basic product.

dumping the practice of selling products internationally below their domestic prices.

durable good an item that lasts over an extended number of uses.

duties special taxes on imports.

dynamically continuous innovations products that disrupt the consumer's normal routine but do not require learning totally new behaviors.

early adopters the 13.5 percent of the population who act as an information source on new products for other people.

early growth the first stage of the retail life cycle, when a new outlet emerges as a sharp departure from competitive forms.

early majority the 34 percent of the population who rely on personal sources for information about new products.

ecology the relationship of physical resources in the environment.

economic forces a society's income, expenditures, and resources that affect the cost of running a business and household.

economic infrastructure a nation's communication, transportation, financial, and distribution networks.

80/20 rule the principle that 80 percent of the sales (and costs) are generated by 20 percent of the items or customers, and vice versa, thus suggesting priorities.

elastic demand a situation where a percentage decrease in price produces a larger percentage increase in quantity demanded, thereby actually increasing sales revenue.

elements of the marketing mix *see* marketing mix.

encoding the process by which a source develops a message in the communication process.

environmental factor *see* uncontrollable factor.

environmental scanning acquiring information on events occurring outside the company and interpreting potential trends.

evaluative criteria both the objective attributes and subjective factors important to consumers when making a purchase decision.

evoked set the subset of brands that a consumer would consider buying out of the set of brands in the product class of which he or she is aware.

exchange the trade of things of value between buyer and seller so that each is better off after the trade.

exclusive dealing an arrangement a manufacturer makes with a reseller to handle only its products and not those of competitors.

exclusive distribution a distribution strategy whereby a producer sells its products or services in only one retail outlet in a specific geographical area.

expense-to-sales ratio a form of ratio analysis in which a specific cost or expense is expressed as a percentage of sales revenue.

experience curve pricing a method of pricing where price often falls following the reduction of costs associated with the firm's experience in producing or selling a product.

experiment method of obtaining data by manipulating factors under tightly controlled conditions to test cause and effect.

experimental group a group exposed to the experimental variable in an experiment.

experimental variable *see* independent variable.

exporting selling products in a foreign country.

express warranties written statements of a manufacturer's liabilities for product deficiencies.

expropriation the situation where a foreign company or its assets are taken over by the host country.

external secondary data published data from outside the firm or organization.

extraneous independent variable (extraneous variable) outside factors that the experimenter cannot control but that might change the behavior of what is studied.

facilitators intermediaries that assist in the physical distribution channel by moving, storing, financing, or insuring products.

fad a product whose life cycle has two stages consisting of rapid introduction and equally quick decline.

Fair Packaging and Labeling Act (1966) a law that requires manufacturers to state on the package the ingredients, volume, and identity of the manufacturer.

family branding *see* multiproduct branding.

family life cycle the concept that each family progresses through a number of distinct phases, each of which is associated with identifiable purchasing behaviors.

fashion product a product whose life cycle curve may decline, then return through another life cycle.

feedback the communication flow from a receiver back to the source, which indicates how the message was decoded.

field of experience a person's understanding and knowledge; to communicate effectively, a sender and receiver must have a mutually shared field of experience.

field experiment a test of marketing variables in actual store or buying settings.

field warehouse a specialized public warehouse that takes possession of a firm's goods and issues a receipt that can be used as collateral for a loan.

finance allowance a trade sales promotion in which retailers are paid for financing costs or losses associated with consumer sales promotions.

fixed alternative question a question in which the respondent merely checks an answer from predetermined choices.

fixed cost an expense of the firm that is stable and does not change with the quantity of product that is produced and sold.

flexible-price policy offering the same product and quantities to similar customers, but at different prices.

FOB (free on board) refers to the point at which the seller stops paying transportation costs.

FOB with freight-allowed pricing a method of pricing that allows the buyer to deduct freight expenses from the list price of the product sold; also called freight absorption pricing.

FOB origin pricing a method of pricing where the title of goods passes to the buyer at the point of loading.

focus group an informal session of 6 to 10 current or potential users of a product in which a discussion leader seeks their opinions on the firm's or a competitor's products.

follow-up stage the phase of the personal selling process that entails making certain that the customer's purchase has been properly delivered and installed and that any difficulties in using the product are promptly and satisfactorily addressed.

Food, Drug, and Cosmetic Act (1938) a law that prevents the adulteration or misbranding of these three categories of products.

foreign assembly using foreign labor to assemble parts and components that have been shipped to that country.

form of ownership who owns a retail outlet. Alternatives are independent, corporate chain, cooperative, or franchise.

form utility the value to consumers that comes from production of a good or service.

formula selling presentation a selling format that consists of providing information in an accurate, thorough, and step-by-step manner to persuade the prospect to buy.

four *I's* of services the elements that make services unique in relation to products; the four *I's* are intangibility, inconsistency, inseparability, and inventory.

four *P's* *see* marketing mix.

franchising the contractual agreement between a parent company and an individual or firm that allows the franchisee to operate a certain type of business under an established name and according to specific rules.

freight forwarders firms that accumulate small shipments into larger lots, then hire a carrier to move them, usually at reduced rates.

frequency how often the same people see an advertisement.

FTC Act (1914) a law that established the Federal Trade Commission (FTC) to monitor deceptive or misleading advertising and unfair business practices.

full warranty a statement of liability by a manufacturer that has no limits of noncoverage.

full-service agency an advertising agency providing a broad range of market research services, media selection, copy development, artwork, and production for clients.

full-service retailer a retailer that provides a wide range of services to customers.

functional groupings organizational divisions based on areas such as marketing, finance, and R&D.

general merchandise stores outlets that carry a broad product line with limited depth.

general merchandise wholesaler a full-service merchant wholesaler that carries a broad assortment of merchandise and performs all channel functions.

generic a term applied to a nonproprietary product name; that is, the name applies to the entire product class and cannot be protected by trademark.

generic brands products given no identifying names other than a description of the contents.

generic marketing strategy a strategy that can be adopted by any firm, regardless of the product or industry involved.

geographical groupings organizational divisions based on geographical location.

global approach an international marketing method which assumes that product use and the needs it satisfies are universal and need not be adjusted for each country.

goal setting setting measurable marketing objectives to be achieved.

goals (or objectives) precise statements of results sought, quantified in time and magnitude, where possible.

government units federal, state, and local agencies that buy goods and services for the constituents they serve.

gross income the total amount of money earned in 1 year by a person, family, or household.

gross margin (gross profit) net sales minus the cost of goods sold; also called maintained markup in retail stores.

gross sales the total amount a firm bills to customers during a specific period.

growth stage the second stage of the product life cycle characterized by rapid increases in sales and by the appearance of competitors.

harvesting a strategy used during the decline stage of the product life cycle in which a company continues to offer a product but reduces support costs.

head-to-head positioning competing directly with competitors on similar product attributes in the same target market.

hierarchy of effects the stages from a consumer's initial awareness of a product to interest, evaluation, trial, and adoption.

high learning product a product that has a long introductory phase to its life cycle because significant education is required for consumers to use the item or appreciate its benefits.

horizontal conflict disagreements between intermediaries at the same level in a marketing channel.

hypermarket a large store (over 100,000 square feet) offering a mix of food and general merchandise items.

hypothesis an educated guess about the relationship of two or more factors or what might happen in the future.

hypothesis evaluation research to test ideas generated earlier to assist in making recommendations for marketing actions.

hypothesis generation a search for a list of ideas (hypotheses) that can be evaluated in later research.

idea generation stage a phase of the new product process, in which a firm develops a pool of concepts as candidates for new products.

idle production capacity a situation where a service provider is available but there is no demand.

implied warranties warranties assigning responsibility for product deficiencies to a manufacturer even though the item was sold by a retailer.

inconsistency a unique element of services; variation in service quality existing because services are delivered by people.

independent retailer a retail outlet for which there is an individual owner.

independent variable the causal condition in an experiment; a factor that is expected to cause a change in the dependent variable; also called experimental variable.

indirect channel a marketing channel where intermediaries are situated between the producer and consumers.

indirect exporting exporting through an intermediary, which often has the knowledge and means to succeed in selling a firm's product abroad.

individual interviews a situation where a single researcher asks questions of one respondent.

industrial distributor a specific type of intermediary between producers and consumers that generally sells, stocks, and delivers a full product assortment.

industrial firm an organizational buyer that in some way reprocesses a good or service it buys before selling it again.

industrial goods products used in the production of other items for ultimate consumers.

industry a group of firms offering products that are close substitutes for each other.

industry potential *see* market potential.

inelastic demand a situation where a small percentage decrease in price produces a smaller percentage increase in quantity demanded.

in-home retailing a retailing operation in which representatives offer goods to customers in their homes.

in-house agency a company's own group of advertising people who are included on the company payroll.

innovators the 2.5 percent of the population who are the first to adopt a new product.

inseparability a unique element of services; the fact that a service cannot be separated from the deliverer of the service.

installations a type of support good consisting of buildings and fixed equipment.

institutional advertisement advertisements designed to build goodwill or an image for an organization, rather than promote a specific product or service.

intangibility a unique element of services; the fact that they cannot be held, touched, or seen before the purchase decision.

intensive distribution a distribution strategy whereby a producer sells products or services in as many outlets as possible in a geographical area.

intermodal transportation coordination or combination of different transportation modes to get the best features of each, while minimizing the shortcomings.

internal marketing the notion that a service organization must focus on its employees, or internal market, before successful programs can be directed at customers.

internal secondary data data that have already been collected and exist inside a business firm or organization.

international marketing marketing across national boundaries.

intertype competition competition between dissimilar retail outlets brought about by scrambled merchandising.

introductory phase the first stage of the product life cycle in which sales grow slowly and profit is low.

inventory physical material purchased from suppliers, which may or may not be reworked and is available for sale to customers.

involvement the personal and economic significance of the purchase to the consumer.

job analysis a written description of what a salesperson is expected to do.

joint venture an arrangement in which two companies, sometimes a foreign company and a local concern, invest together to create a local business; the two companies share ownership, control, and profits of the new company.

jury of executive opinion a survey of knowledgeable executives inside a firm and a combination of their opinions to obtain a sales forecast.

jury test a pretest in which a panel of consumers is shown an advertisement and asked to rate its attractiveness, how much they like it, and how much it draws their attention.

just-in-time (JIT) concept a strategy for reducing inventory by using suppliers that can guarantee fast, reliable delivery of supplies to prevent a production shutdown.

laboratory experiment a simulation of marketing-related activity in a highly controlled setting.
laggards the 16 percent of the market who accept ideas and products only after they have been long established in the market.
Lanham Act (1946) a law that allows a company to register a trademark (symbol or word) for its exclusive use.
late majority the 34 percent of the population who rely less on advertising and personal selling for information than do innovators or early adopters.
lead time the lag from ordering an item until it is received in stock.
learning the process of gaining experiences and storing them in memory, which in turn influences future attitudes and behaviors.
level of service the degree of service provided by a retailer: self, limited, or full.
licensing a contractual agreement by which a company allows someone else to use its brand name.
life-style mode of living identified by an individual's activities, interests, and opinions.
Likert scale a fixed alternative question in which the respondent indicates the extent to which he agrees or disagrees with a statement.
limited-coverage warranty a manufacturer's statement indicating the bounds of coverage and noncoverage for any product deficiencies.
limited-line store a retail outlet such as a sporting goods store that offers considerable assortment, or depth, of a related line of items.
limited-service agency an advertising agency that specializes in one aspect of the advertising process.
limited-service retailer a retailer that provides selected services to customers.
line position one held by people in an organization who have the authority and responsibility to issue orders to people who report to them.
linear trend extrapolation forecasting by extending data observed from a past trend along a straight line on a graph into the future.
logical incrementalism a strategy of entering new businesses in which a company can capitalize on its existing strength or expertise.
long-range marketing plan a marketing plan that deals with the marketing goals and strategies for a product, product line, or entire firm and covers from 2 to 5 years.
loss-leader pricing deliberately pricing a product below its customary price to attract attention to it.
lost-horse forecasting making a projection by starting with the last known value of an item, identifying positive and negative factors that might affect it, and estimating where it might end up.
low learning product a product that has an immediate gain in sales in the introductory phase because the benefits are easily observed by consumers and little education is required to use it.

macromarketing the study of the aggregate flow of a nation's goods and services to benefit society.
Magnuson-Moss Warranty/FTC Improvement Act (1975) an act that regulates the content of consumer warranties and also has strengthened consumer rights with regard to warranties.
mail order retailer a retailing operation in which merchandise is offered to customers by mail.
maintained markup the difference between the final selling price and retailer cost; also called gross margin.
make-buy decision an evaluation of whether a product or its parts will be purchased from outside suppliers or built by the firm.
management by exception a tool used by a marketing manager that involves identifying results that deviate from plans, diagnosing their causes, making appropriate new plans, and taking new actions.
manufacturer branding a branding strategy in which the brand name for a product is designated by the producer, using either a multiproduct or multibranding approach.
manufacturer's agents individuals or firms that work for several producers and carry noncompetitive, complementary merchandise in an exclusive territory; also called manufacturer's representatives.
manufacturer's branch office a wholly owned extension of a producer that performs channel functions, including carrying inventory, generally performed by a full-service merchant wholesaler.
manufacturer's sales office a wholly owned extension of a producer that typically performs only sales functions.
marginal analysis principle of allocating resources that balances incremental revenues of an action against incremental costs.
marginal cost the change in total cost that results from producing and marketing one additional unit.
marginal revenue the change in total revenue obtained by selling one additional unit.
markdown reduction in a retail price, usually expressed as a percentage equal to the amount reduced, divided by the original price, and multiplied by 100.
market people with the desire and ability to buy a specific product.
market development a strategy of selling existing products to new target markets.
market growth rate the annual rate of growth of a specific market or industry; often used as the vertical axis in business portfolio analysis.
market penetration a strategy of increasing sales of present products in their existing markets.
market potential maximum total sales of a product by all firms to a segment under specified environmental conditions and marketing efforts; also called industry potential.

market segmentation the process of forming submarkets, or market segments, by either aggregating individual potential buyers or subdividing large markets.

market segments the groups that result from the process of market segmentation; these groups ideally (1) have common needs and (2) will respond similarly to a marketing action.

market share the ratio of sales revenue of the firm to the total sales revenue of all firms in the industry, including the firm itself.

market testing stage a phase of the new product process, in which prospective consumers are exposed to actual products under realistic purchase conditions to see if they will buy.

marketing the process of planning and executing the conception, pricing, promotion, and distribution of ideas, goods, and services to create exchanges that satisfy individual and organizational objectives.

marketing audit a comprehensive, unbiased, periodic review of a firm's or SBU's strategic marketing process.

marketing channel people and firms involved in the process of making a product or service available for use or consumption by consumers or industrial users.

marketing concept the idea that an organization should seek to satisfy the wants of customers while also trying to achieve the organization's goals.

marketing concept era current period of American business history that is consumer oriented so organizations strive to produce products that meet consumer wants while achieving organizational objectives.

marketing decision support system (MDSS) a computerized method of providing timely, accurate information to improve marketing decisions.

marketing mix a marketing manager's controllable factors: product, price, promotion, and place.

marketing modifications attempts to increase product usage by creating new use situations, finding new customers, or altering the marketing mix.

marketing plan a written statement identifying the target market, specific marketing goals, the budget, and timing for the marketing program.

marketing program a plan that integrates the marketing mix to provide a product, service, or idea to consumers.

marketing research the process of defining a marketing problem and then systematically collecting and analyzing information to recommend actions to improve an organization's marketing activities.

marketing strategy actions characterized by a specified target and a marketing program to reach it.

marketing tactics the detailed day-to-day operational decisions essential to the overall success of marketing strategies.

market-product grid framework for relating market segments to products offered or potential marketing actions by a firm.

markup the amount added to the cost of goods sold to arrive at a selling price, expressed in dollar or percentage terms.

materials handling the movement of small amounts of goods over short distances in support of warehouse operations.

mature households households headed by people over age 50.

maturity phase the third stage of the product or retail life cycle in which market share levels off and profitability declines.

measures of success criteria or standards used in evaluating proposed solutions to the problem.

Meat Inspection Act (1906) an act that strengthened federal inspection of meat packing plants.

mechanical observational data data collected by electronic or other impersonal means, such as meters connected to television sets in viewers' homes.

merchandise allowance a trade sales promotion in which a retailer is reimbursed for extra in-store support or special featuring of the brand.

merchandise line the number of different types of products and the assortment a store carries.

message the information component of communication, sent by a source to a receiver.

method of operation how and where a retailer provides services; the alternative approaches are an in-store or nonstore format (mail, in home, vending, or computer-assisted).

methods the approaches a researcher or decision maker can use to solve all or part of a problem.

metropolitan statistical area (MSA) an area within (1) a city having a population of at least 50,000 or (2) an urbanized area with a population in excess of 50,000 with a total population of at least 100,000.

micromarketing the marketing activities of an individual organization.

minitrain a short train that runs frequently, often used in implementing just-in-time inventory systems.

mission a statement about the type of customer an organization wishes to serve, the specific needs of these customers, and the means or technology by which it will serve these needs.

missionary salespeople sales support personnel who do not directly solicit orders but rather concentrate on performing promotional activities and introducing new products.

mixed branding a branding strategy in which the company may follow both manufacturer and reseller branding approaches for products in its line.

modified rebuy a buying situation in which the users, influencers, or deciders change the product specifications, price, delivery schedule, or supplier.

monopolistic competition a competitive setting in which a large number of sellers offer unique but substitutable products.

monopoly a competitive setting in which there is a single seller of a good or service.

motivation a force that leads a person to act in a particular way in response to a need.

multibranding a manufacturer's branding strategy in which a distinct name is given to each of its products.

multinational corporation *see* transnational corporation.

multiple-zone pricing pricing products the same when delivered within one of several specified zones or geographical areas, but with different prices for each zone depending on demand, competition, and distance; also called zone-delivered pricing.

multiproduct branding a branding strategy in which a company uses one name for all products; also referred to as blanket or family branding.

need that which occurs when a person feels deprived of food, clothing, or shelter.

need-satisfaction presentation a selling formula that emphasizes probing and listening by the salesperson to identify needs and interests of prospective buyers.

new buy the first-time purchase of a product or service, characterized by greater potential risk.

new product concept a tentative description of a product or service that a firm might offer for sale.

new product process seven steps followed in the commercialization of a new product: new product strategy, idea generation, screening and evaluation, business analysis, development, testing, and commercialization.

new product strategy development stage the phase of the new product process in which a firm defines the role of new products in terms of overall corporate objectives.

news conference a publicity tool consisting of an informational meeting with representatives of the media who receive advance materials on the meeting content.

noise extraneous factors that can distort a message or feedback in the communication process.

noncumulative quantity discounts price reductions based on the size of an individual purchase order.

nondurable good an item consumed in one or a few uses.

nonprobability sampling the selection of a sample using arbitrary judgments so the chance of selecting a particular element may be unknown or 0.

nonprofit organization an organization that carries on economic activity to serve the needs of special segments of the public.

nonrepetitive decisions those decisions unique to a particular time and situation.

objective and task budgeting allocating funds to advertising according to the desired objectives and the tasks necessary to accomplish these objectives.

objectives *see* goals.

observational data data collected by watching how people actually behave.

odd-even pricing setting prices a few dollars or cents under an even number, such as $19.95.

off-peak pricing setting prices that vary with fluctuations in service demand, such as seasonal hotel rates.

off-price retailing selling brand name merchandise at lower than regular prices.

oligopoly a competitive setting in which a few large companies account for a large amount of an industry's sales.

one-price policy setting the same price for similar customers who buy the same product and quantities under the same conditions.

one-price store a form of off-price retailing in which all items in the store are sold at one low price.

open-end question a question that a respondent can answer in his or her own words.

opinion leaders individuals who exert direct or indirect social influence over others.

order cycle time from the seller's viewpoint, the time required to transmit, process, prepare, and ship an order.

order getter a salesperson who sells in a conventional sense and engages in identifying prospective customers, providing customers with information, persuading customers to buy, closing sales, and following up on customer experience with a product or service.

order taker a salesperson who processes routine orders and reorders for products that have already been sold by the company.

organizational buyers business firms and nonprofit establishments that buy goods and services and then resell them, with or without reprocessing, to other organizations or ultimate consumers.

organizational buying behavior the decision-making process that organizations use to establish the need for products and identify, evaluate, and choose among alternative brands and suppliers.

organizational goals specific objectives a business or nonprofit unit seeks to achieve and by which it can measure its performance.

original markup the difference between retailer cost and initial selling price.

outsourcing contracting work that formerly was done in-house by employees such as those in marketing research, advertising, and public relations departments to small, outside firms.

packaging the container in which a product is offered for sale and on which information is communicated.

panel a sample of consumers or stores from which researchers take a series of measurements periodically.

parallel development an approach to new product development in which multidisciplinary teams of people from throughout a firm simultaneously work together on a new product from conception through production.

patent exclusive rights to the manufacture of a product or related technology granted to a company for 17 years.

penetration pricing setting a low initial price to discourage new competitors and build market share.

per se illegality an action that by itself is illegal.

perceived risk the anxieties felt because the consumer cannot anticipate the outcome but sees that there might be negative consequences.

percent of sales budgeting allocating funds to advertising as a percentage of past sales, anticipated unit sales, or anticipated total sales.

perception the process by which an individual selects, organizes, and interprets information inputs.

perceptual map a graph displaying consumers' perceptions of product attributes across two or more dimensions.

personal selling the two-way flow of communication between buyer and seller that often occurs face-to-face but may take place over the telephone, through video teleconferencing, or through interactive computer links.

personal selling process sales activities occurring before and after the sale itself, consisting of six stages: (1) prospecting, (2) preapproach, (3) approach, (4) presentation, (5) close, and (6) follow-up.

personality a person's enduring or consistent psychological traits, such as extroversion, aggression, or compliance.

physical distribution management a narrow view of the distribution process that focuses on the flow of finished goods to the consumer but does not include procuring or moving raw materials.

piggyback franchising a variation of franchising in which stores operated by one chain sell the products or services of another franchised firm.

pioneering advertisements advertisements that tell what a product is, what it can do, and where it can be found.

pioneering institutional advertisements institutional advertisements about what a company is or can do or where it is located.

place utility the value to consumers of having a good or service available where needed.

planning gap the difference between the projection of a new goal and the projection of the results of a plan already in place.

point-of-purchase displays displays located in high-traffic areas in retail stores, often next to checkout counters.

population the universe of all people, stores, or salespeople about which researchers wish to generalize.

portfolio test a pretest in which a test ad is placed in a portfolio with other ads and consumers are questioned on their impressions of the test ad.

possession utility the value to consumers of getting a good or service to them so they can use it.

posttesting tests conducted after an advertisement is run in a medium to assess whether it accomplished its intended purpose.

preapproach stage the stage of the personal selling process that involves obtaining further information about a prospect and deciding on the best method of approach.

predatory pricing selling products at a low price to injure or eliminate a competitor.

premium a sales promotion that consists of offering merchandise free or at significant savings over retail.

presentation stage the core of the personal selling process in which the salesperson tries to convert the prospect into a customer by creating a desire for the product or service.

prestige pricing setting a high price so that status-conscious consumers will be attracted to the product.

pretests tests conducted before an advertisement is placed to determine whether it communicates the intended message or to select between alternative versions of an advertisement.

price the money or other considerations exchanged for the purchase or use of a product, idea, or service.

price discrimination the practice of charging different prices to different buyers for goods of like grade and quality; the Clayton Act as amended by the Robinson-Patman Act prohibits this action.

price elasticity of demand the percentage change in quantity demanded relative to a percentage change in price.

price fixing a conspiracy among firms to set prices for a product.

price lining setting the price of a line of products at a number of different specific pricing points.

pricing constraints factors that limit a firm's latitude in the price it may set.

pricing objectives goals that specify the role of price in an organization's marketing and strategic plans.

primary data those facts and figures which are new and are collected for the first time for the project at hand.

primary demand desire for a product class rather than for a specific brand.

primary metropolitan statistical area (PMSA) an area that is part of a larger consolidated statistical metropolitan area with a total population of 1 million or more.

prime rate the rate of interest banks charge their largest customers.

private branding when a company manufactures products that are sold under the name of a wholesaler or retailer.

proactive strategies new product strategies that involve an aggressive allocation of resources to identify opportunities for product development.

probability sampling the selection of a sample using precise rules such that each element of the population has a specific known chance of being selected.

product a good, service, or idea consisting of a bundle of tangible and intangible attributes that satisfies consumers and is received in exchange for money or other unit of value.

product advertisements advertisements that focus on selling a product or service and take three forms: (1) pioneering, (2) competitive, and (3) reminder.

product cannibalization *see* cannibalization.

product (program) champion a person within a firm whose job it is to cut red tape and move a product or program forward.

product class an entire product category or industry.

product development a strategy of selling a new product to existing markets.

product differentiation a strategy that has come to have different but related meanings; it involves a firm's using different marketing mix activities, such as product featuring and advertising, to help consumers perceive the product as being different and better than competing products.

product form variations of a product within a product class.

product item a specific product noted by a unique brand, size, and price.

product life cycle the life of a product over four stages: introduction, growth, maturity, and decline.

product line a group of products closely related because they satisfy a class of needs, are used together, are sold to the same customer group, are distributed through the same outlets, or fall within a given price range.

product line groupings organizational divisions based on product type.

product manager a person who manages the marketing efforts for a closely related family of products or brands.

product mix the number of product lines offered by a company.

product modifications strategies of altering a product characteristic, such as quality, performance, or appearance.

product positioning the place an offering occupies in a consumer's mind with regard to important attributes relative to competitive offerings.

product repositioning changing the place an offering occupies in a consumer's mind relative to competitive offerings.

product semantics a belief that a product's design should communicate its function.

production era period of American business history when goods were scarce so it was assumed they would sell themselves.

production goods products used in the manufacturing of other items that become part of the final product.

profit a business firm's reward for the risk it undertakes in offering a product for sale; the amount of revenues in excess of expenses.

profit equation Profit = Total revenue − Total cost.

profitability analysis a means of measuring the profitability of the firm's products, customer groups, sales territories and regions, channels of distribution, and order sizes.

program schedule a formal time-line chart showing the relationships through time of the various program tasks.

promotional allowance the cash payment or extra amount of "free goods" awarded sellers in the channel of distribution for undertaking certain advertising or selling activities to promote a product.

promotional mix the combination of actions that a company takes to communicate with consumers about its products; alternatives include advertising, personal selling, publicity, and sales promotion.

prospecting stage in the personal selling process, the search for and qualification of potential customers.

protocol in the new product development process, an early statement that identifies a well-defined target market; specifies customers' needs, wants, and preferences; and states what the product will be and do.

psychographic variables consumer activities, interests, and opinions.

psychographics characteristics represented by personality and life-style traits (activities, interests, and opinions).

public service announcement (PSA) a publicity tool that uses free space or time donated by the media.

public warehouse a facility that rents space and miscellaneous services to more than one firm.

publicity a nonpersonal, indirectly paid presentation of an organization, good, or service.

publicity tools methods used to get a nonpersonal, indirectly paid presentation of a company or its products; examples are news releases, news conferences, and public service announcements.

pull strategy directing the promotional mix to ultimate consumers in an attempt to get them to ask the retailer for the product.

pulse schedule distributing advertising unevenly throughout the year because of seasonal demand, heavy periods of promotion, or introduction of a new product; sometimes called "burst" scheduling.

purchase decision process steps or stages a buyer passes through in making choices about which products to buy.

purchase frequency the number and rate of purchases for a specific item.

pure competition a competitive setting in which a large number of sellers produce similar products.

push strategy directing the promotional mix to channel members or intermediaries to gain their cooperation in ordering and stocking a product.

quantity discounts reductions in unit costs for a larger order quantity.

questionnaire a method of obtaining data by asking people about their attitudes, awareness, intentions, and behaviors.

quota in international trade, a legal limit placed on the amount of a product allowed to leave or enter a country.

rack jobber a merchant wholesaler that furnishes racks or shelves to display merchandise in retail stores, performs all channel functions, and sells on consignment to retailers.

rating (TV or radio) the percentage of households in a market that are tuned to a particular TV show or radio station.

reach the number of different people exposed to an advertisement.
reactive strategies new product strategies that involve developing new products in response to competitors' new items.
reasonable range the perceived level of acceptable service quality.
rebate a sales promotion in which money is returned to the consumer based on proof of purchase.
receivers the people who read, hear, or see the message sent by a source in the communication process.
reciprocity an industrial buying practice in which two organizations agree to purchase products from each other.
reference group people to whom a person turns as a standard of self-appraisal or source of personal standards.
regional centers suburban malls with up to 100 stores that typically draw customers from a 5- to 10-mile radius, usually containing one or two anchor stores.
regional marketing strategy involving developing marketing plans to reflect specific geographical differences of consumers in terms of taste preferences or perceived needs.
regional rollout introduction of a product sequentially into geographical areas of a country, enabling a gradual buildup of production and marketing levels.
regulation the laws placed on business with regard to the conduct of its activities.
reinforcement a reward that tends to strengthen a response.
relative market share the sales of any firm divided by that of the largest firm in the industry; often used as the horizontal axis in business portfolio analysis.
reminder advertisements advertisements used to reinforce prior knowledge of a product.
repeat purchase purchase of a product again after satisfactory trial.
repetitive decisions decisions repeated at standard intervals during the work year.
replenishment time the time required to transmit, process, prepare, and ship an order, from the buyer's viewpoint.
repositioning changing a product's or brand's image in consumers' minds.
requirements contract a contract that requires a buyer to meet all or part of its needs for a product from one seller for a period of time.
reseller a wholesaler or retailer that buys physical products and resells them again without any processing.
response action taken by a person to satisfy a drive.
restructuring (downsizing or streamlining) striving for more efficient corporations that can compete globally by selling off unsatisfactory product lines and divisions, closing down unprofitable plants, and laying off employees.
retail life cycle a concept that describes a retail operation over four stages: early growth, accelerated development, maturity, and decline.
retail positioning matrix a framework for positioning retail outlets in terms of breadth of product line and value added.
retailing all the activities that are involved in selling, renting, and providing services to ultimate consumers for personal, nonhousehold use.
retailing mix the strategic components that a retailer offers, including goods and services, physical distribution, and communication tactics.
retail-sponsored cooperative a wholesale facility run cooperatively by small, independent retailers to concentrate buying power and plan joint promotional and pricing activities.
return on investment (ROI) the ratio of after-tax net profit to the investment used to earn that profit.
returns refunds or credit granted a customer for an item returned to the seller.
Robinson-Patman Act (1936) a regulation that makes it unlawful to discriminate in prices charged to different purchasers of the same product where the result is to substantially lessen competition or help create a monopoly.
run-through train a train that carries more than one commodity but makes no stops between the points of origin and destination.

sales analysis a tool used for controlling marketing programs where actual sales records are compared with sales goals to identify strengths and weaknesses.
sales component analysis tracing sales revenues back to their sources such as specific products, sales territories, or customers.
sales engineer a salesperson who specializes in identifying, analyzing, and solving customer problems and brings technical expertise to the selling situation, but does not actually sell goods and services.
sales era period of American business history when firms could produce more than they could sell and the focus was on hiring more salespeople to find new markets and customers.
sales force survey a method of forecasting sales using estimates by a firm's salespeople of expected sales during a coming period.
sales forecast the amount a firm expects to sell during a time period under specified conditions for the controllable and uncontrollable factors affecting the forecast.
sales management planning, implementing, and controlling the personal selling effort of the firm.
sales plan a statement describing what is to be achieved and where and how the selling effort of salespeople is to be deployed.
sales promotion short-term inducements of value offered to arouse interest in buying a product.
sales response function the relationship between the dollars of marketing effort expended and the market results of interest, such as sales revenue, profit, units sold, or level of awareness.

salient attributes characteristics that the consumer deems important in evaluating brands.
sample (1) some elements taken from the population or universe, or (2) a sales promotion consisting of offering a product free or at a greatly reduced price.
sampling (1) the process of selecting elements from a population, or (2) the process manufacturers use of giving away free samples to introduce a new product.
scrambled merchandising offering several unrelated product lines in a single retail store.
screening and evaluation stage the phase of the new product process in which a firm uses internal and external evaluations to eliminate ideas that warrant no further development effort.
sealed-bid pricing a method of pricing whereby prospective firms submit price bids for a contract to the buying agency at a specific time and place with the contract awarded to the qualified bidder with the lowest price.
seasonal discounts price reductions granted buyers for purchasing products and stocking them at a time when they are not wanted by customers.
secondary data data that have already been recorded.
selective comprehension interpreting information to make it consistent with one's attitudes and beliefs.
selective demand demand for a specific brand within a product class.
selective distribution a distribution strategy whereby a producer sells its products in a few retail outlets in a specific geographical area.
selective exposure the tendency to seek out and pay attention to messages consistent with one's attitudes and beliefs and to ignore messages inconsistent with them.
selective perception the tendency for humans to filter or choose information from a complex environment so they can make sense of the world.
selective retention the tendency to remember only part of all the information one sees, hears, or reads.
self-concept the way people see themselves and the way they believe others see them.
self-liquidating premium a sales promotion offering merchandise at a significant cost savings to the customer, its price covering the cost of the premium for the company.
self-regulation an industry policing itself rather than relying on government controls.
selling agent a person or firm that represents a single producer and is responsible for all marketing functions of that producer.
semantic differential scale a seven-point scale in which the opposite ends have one- or two-word adjectives with opposite meanings.
sensitivity analysis an analysis of marketing problems to assess how different levels of a factor such as price, product features, or trends affect a decision.
service continuum a range of products and services in terms of the degree of tangibility involved.
services intangible activities, benefits, or satisfactions provided by an organization to consumers in exchange for money or some other value.
share points percentage points of market share; often used as the common basis of comparison to allocate resources among marketing programs.
shelf life the time a product can be stored before it spoils.
Sherman Anti-Trust Act (1890) a law that forbids (1) contracts, combinations, or conspiracies in restraint of trade and (2) actual monopolies or attempts to monopolize any part of trade or commerce.
shippers' associations cooperative freight forwarders formed by several shippers to take advantage of reduced costs and better service.
shopping goods products for which the consumer will compare several alternatives on various criteria.
shrinkage a term used by retailers to describe theft of merchandise.
single-line store a store that offers tremendous depth in one primary line of merchandise; for example, a running shoe store.
single-source data information offered by a single firm that includes secondary data on consumer demographics and primary data such as consumer purchases in response to TV ads or free samples.
single-zone pricing pricing policy in which all buyers pay the same delivered product price, regardless of their distance from the seller; also known as uniform delivered pricing or postage stamp pricing.
situation analysis taking stock of where the firm or product has been recently, where it is now, and where it is likely to end up using present plans.
situational influence a situation's effect on the nature and scope of the purchase decision process.
skimming pricing setting a high initial price for a product to recover development costs and capitalize on the price insensitivity of early buyers.
social classes the divisions in a society of people or families sharing similar values, life-styles, interests, and behavior.
social forces the characteristics of the population, its income, and its values in a particular environment.
societal marketing concept the view that an organization should assess and satisfy the needs of its customers in a way that also provides for society's well-being.
solution the best alternative identified.
source a company or person who sends a message; an essential element in communication.
specialty goods products that a consumer will make a special effort to search out and buy.
specialty merchandise wholesaler a full-service merchant wholesaler that offers a relatively narrow range of products but has an extensive assortment within the product lines carried.
splitting 30s reducing the length of a standard commercial from 30 seconds to 15 seconds.

Chapter Notes

CHAPTER ONE

1 "Microwave Popcorn: The Heat Is On," *Business Week* (July 6, 1987), p. 52.
2 "Pop Secrets," *Twin Cities* (July 1987), pp. 40-42.
3 "Sales Poppin'," *Dallas Times Herald* (August 13, 1986), pp. 1B, 3B.
4 "Pop Secrets" (reference cited), p. 42.
5 "Microwaves' Prevalence Opening New Avenues for Food Marketers," *Marketing News* (June 5, 1987), p. 17.
6 "AMA Board Approves New Marketing Definition," *Marketing News* (March 1, 1985), p. 1.
7 Robert W. Ruekert and Orville C. Walker, Jr., "Marketing's Interaction with Other Functional Units: A Conceptual Framework and Empirical Evidence," *Journal of Marketing* (January 1987), pp. 1-19.
8 Richard P. Bagozzi, "Marketing as Exchange," *Journal of Marketing* (October 1975), pp. 32-39.
9 D.J. Tice, "Toy Wars," *Twin Cities* (December 1983), pp. 96-107.
10 E. Jerome McCarthy, *Basic Marketing: A Managerial Approach* (Homewood, Ill.: Richard D. Irwin, Inc., 1960).
11 Bernie Whalen, "Kotler: Rethink the Marketing Concept," *Marketing News* (September 14, 1984), p. 1.
12 Carl P. Zeithaml and Valarie A. Zeithaml, "Environmental Management: Revising the Marketing Perspective," *Journal of Marketing* (Spring 1984), pp. 46-53.
13 *1986 Annual Report* (Edina, Minn.: Golden Valley Microwave Foods, Inc., 1987), pp. 1-6.
14 *1986 Annual Report* (reference cited), p. 2; "Golden Valley Announces New Microwave French Fry Product," (Edina, Minn.: *Golden Valley Microwave Foods, Inc., News* (March 10, 1988), p. 1; Kevin G. Salwena, "Short Sellers Betting Golden Valley Microwave Can't Repeat Success in Popcorn with Fries," *The Wall Street Journal* (April 13, 1988), p. 49; Julie Liesse Erickson, "New Pop in Popcorn Market," *Advertising Age* (April 11, 1988), p. 77.
15 "Pop Secrets" (reference cited), p. 41.
16 For a contrary view, see Ronald A. Fullerton, "How Modern Is Modern Marketing? Marketing's Evolution and the Myth of the 'Production Era'," *Journal of Marketing* (January 1988), pp. 108-125.
17 Robert F. Keith, "The Marketing Revolution," *Journal of Marketing* (January 1960), pp. 35-38.
18 *1952 Annual Report* (New York: General Electric Company, 1952), p. 21.
19 Alan J. Resnik and Robert J. Harmon, "Consumer Complaints and Managerial Response: A Holistic Approach," *Journal of Marketing* (Winter 1983), pp. 86-97.
20 Donald P. Robin and R. Eric Reidenbach, "Social Responsibility, Ethics, and Marketing Strategy: Closing the Gap Between Concept and Application," *Journal of Marketing* (January 1987), pp. 44-58.
21 Shelby D. Hunt and John J. Burnett, "The Macromarketing/Micromarketing Dichotomy: A Taxonomical Model," *Journal of Marketing* (Summer 1982), pp. 9-26.
22 Philip Kotler and Sidney I. Levy, "Broadening the Concept of Marketing," *Journal of Marketing* (January 1969), pp. 10-15.

CHAPTER TWO

1 Carol J. Loomis, "IBM's Big Blues: A Legend Tries to Remake Itself," *Fortune* (January 19, 1987), pp. 34-54; "Big Blue Still Has a Case of the Blahs," *Business Week* (January 25, 1987), p. 39; "The PC Wars: IBM vs. the Clones," *Business Week* (July 28, 1986), pp. 62-67; Janice Steinberg, "Technology Drives Industry Down a New Path," *Advertising Age* (April 6, 1987), pp. S1-S12.
2 Dennis Kneale, "IBM Is Trailing Digital in Getting Computers to Talk to Each Other," *The Wall Street Journal* (October 3, 1986), pp. 1, 16.
3 Philip Kotler, *Marketing Management,* 5th ed. (Englewood Cliffs, N.J.: Prentice-Hall, Inc., 1984), pp. 60-64.
4 Theodore Levitt, "Marketing Myopia," *Harvard Business Review* (July-August 1960), pp. 45-56.
5 Kenichi Ohmae, *The Mind of the Strategist* (New York: McGraw-Hill Book Company, 1982), p. 91.
6 Robert A. Bennett, "Toughing It Out at Dean Witter," *The New York Times* (October 5, 1986), Section 3, pp. 1, 30; Bill Saporito, "Are IBM and Sears Crazy? Or Canny?" *Fortune* (September 28, 1987), pp. 74-80; Judith Graham, "Linkup," *Advertising Age* (May 23, 1988), pp. 1, 93.
7 Jeff Bailey, "Sears Is Discovering Discover Credit Card Isn't Hitting Pay Dirt," *The Wall Street Journal* (February 10, 1988), pp. 1, 12.
8 Roger A. Kerin and Robert A. Peterson, *Strategic Marketing Problems* (Boston: Allyn & Bacon, Inc., 1987), pp. 5-6; Derek F. Abell, *Defining the Business* (Englewood Cliffs, N.J.: Prentice-Hall, Inc., 1980), p. 18.
9 Arthur A. Thompson, Jr., and A.J. Strickland III, *Strategic Management* (Plano, Tex.: Business Publications, Inc., 1984), pp. 178-179.
10 "General Electric Is Stalking Big Game Again," *Business Week* (March 10, 1987), pp. 112-113.
11 Peter Petre, "What Welch Has Wrought at GE," *Fortune* (July 7, 1986), pp. 43-47; "Can Jack Welch Reinvent GE?," *Business Week* (June 30, 1986), pp. 62-67.

12 "Overnight, Thomson Has the Stuff to Take on the Titans," *Business Week* (August 10, 1987), pp. 36-37; Laura Landro and Douglas R. Sease, "General Electric to Sell Consumer Electronics Lines to Thomson SA for Its Medical Gear Business, Cash," *The Wall Street Journal* (July 23, 1987), pp. 3, 6.

13 "Jumping Jack Strikes Again," *Time* (August 3, 1987), p. 44.

14 H. Igor Ansoff, "Strategies for Diversification," *Harvard Business Review* (September-October 1957), pp. 113-124.

15 Timothy K. Smith and George Anders, "Coca-Cola Plans to Sell 51% of Bottling Group Publicly for $1.5 Billion," *The Wall Street Journal* (October 15, 1986), pp. 1, 10; Betsy Morris, "Coca-Cola's Corporate Strategy Is Divide and Conquer," *The Wall Street Journal* (October 8, 1987), p. 6.

16 Timothy K. Smith and Laura Landro, "Profoundly Changed, Coca-Cola Co. Strives to Keep on Bubbling," *The Wall Street Journal* (April 24, 1986), pp. 1, 22.

17 John Bussey, "P&G's New Disposable Diaper Intensifies Marketing Battle with Kimberly-Clark," *The Wall Street Journal* (January 4, 1985), p. 33; Steven Greenhouse, "Innovation Key to Diaper War," *The New York Times* (November 25, 1986), pp. 29, 35.

18 Cynthia F. Mitchell, "How Kimberly-Clark Wraps Its Bottom Line in Disposable Huggies," *The Wall Street Journal* (July 23, 1987), pp. 1, 20.

19 Loomis (reference cited).

20 "Introducing the IBM Personal System/2," a 24-page advertisement (Armonk, N.Y.: IBM Corporation, 1987).

21 "IBM Unveils Family of New PCs, Fueling Competition in Industry," *The Wall Street Journal* (April 3, 1987), pp. 2, 6.

22 "Into the Wild Blue Yonder," *Time* (April 13, 1987), p. 68.

23 "IBM Unveils Family of New PCs, Fueling Competition in the Industry" (reference cited).

24 Michael W. Miller, "IBM Gets Defensive Over New PCs," *The Wall Street Journal* (August 24, 1987), p. 6; Michael W. Miller, "IBM Computer Buyers Are Bewildered by PCs with Secret Ingredient," *The Wall Street Journal* (March 22, 1988), pp. 1, 17; "If the PS/2 Is a Winner, Why Is IBM So Frustrated?" *Business Week* (April 11, 1988), pp. 82-83.

25 Cleveland Horton, "M★A★S★H Stars Enjoy Reunion," *Advertising Age* (April 20, 1987), p. 78.

26 Jesse Snyder, "4 GM Car Divisions Are Repositioned in Effort to Help Sales," *Automotive News* (September 25, 1986), pp. 1, 49.

27 Alex Taylor III, "Bumps Ahead for a Car Guy," *Fortune* (September 28, 1987), pp. 105-109.

28 "General Motors: What Went Wrong," *Business Week* (March 16, 1987), pp. 102-110; Raymond Serafin, "How GM Is Shifting Gears," *Advertising Age* (January 4, 1988), pp. 1, 42; Jacob M. Schlesinger, "GM Seeks Revival of Buick and Olds," *The Wall Street Journal* (April 12, 1988), p. 39.

29 "Why Kodak Is Starting to Click Again," *Business Week* (February 23, 1987), pp. 134-138; Clare Ansberry, "Kodak vs. Fuji: Latest Battle Is Throwaways," *The Wall Street Journal* (February 20, 1987), p. 19; Clare Ansberry, "Eastman Kodak Co. Has Arduous Struggle to Regain Lost Edge," *The Wall Street Journal* (April 2, 1987), pp. 1, 12.

CHAPTER THREE

1 "Toddlers in $90 Suits? You Gotta Be Kidding," *Business Week* (September 21, 1987), pp. 52-54; Geoffrey Colvin, "What the Baby Boomers Will Buy Next?" *Fortune* (October 15, 1984), pp. 28-34.

2 Janice Castro, "In Fashion, Bigger Is Beautiful," *Time* (May 4, 1987), pp. 74-77; Barry Tarshis, *The "Average" American Book* (New York: Atheneum Publishers, 1979).

3 "Population Update," *Population Today* (February 1988), p. 9.

4 James Jorgensen, "The Greying of America" (New York: Dial Press, 1980).

5 "Last Year It Was the Yuppies—This Year It's Their Parents," *Business Week* (March 10, 1986), pp. 68, 72, 74.

6 Colvin (reference cited).

7 Thomas G. Exter, "Baby Boom Incomes," *American Demographics* (November 1987), p. 62.

8 Paul Glick, "How American Families Are Changing," *American Demographics* (January 1984), pp. 21-25; Daniel Yankelovich, *New Rules* (New York: Random House, Inc., 1981).

9 Jeff Rosenfeld, "Demographics and Interior Design," *American Demographics* (February 1984), pp. 28-33.

10 "Shifting Population," *The Wall Street Journal* (February 9, 1988), p. 41.

11 "Marketing's New Look," *Business Week* (January 26, 1987), pp. 64-69.

12 Alex M. Freedman, "National Firms Find that Selling to Local Tastes Is Costly, Complex," *The Wall Street Journal* (February 9, 1987), p. 21.

13 Daphne Spain and Suzanne M. Bianchi, "How Women Have Changed," *American Demographics* (May 1983), pp. 19-25; "Women at Work," *Business Week* (January 28, 1985), pp. 80-87.

14 Betsy Sharkey, "The Invisible Woman," *Ad Week* (July 6, 1987), pp. wr4-wr8.

15 Basia Helwig, "How Working Women Have Changed America," *Working Woman* (November 1986), pp. 129-146.

16 Nancy Giges, "More Men Food Shopping," *Advertising Age* (February 6, 1984), p. 12.

17 "Procter & Gamble Goes on a Health Kick," *Business Week* (June 29, 1987), pp. 90-92.

18 Thomas G. Exter, "Where the Money Is," *American Demographics* (March 1987), pp. 26-31.

19 "How Consumers Spend," *American Demographics* (October 1983), pp. 17-21.

20 Fabian Linden, Gordon W. Green, Jr., and John F. Coder, *A Marketer's Guide to Discretionary Income* (Washington, D.C.: U.S. Government Printing Office, 1984).

21 William Lazer, "How Rising Affluence Will Reshape Markets," *American Demographics* (February 1984), pp. 17-21; Thomas J. Stanley and George Moschis, "America's Affluent," *American Demographics* (March 1984), pp. 28-33.

22 "America 2000," *Battelle* (May 3, 1983).

23 Lawrence Strauss, *Electronic Marketing* (White Plains, N.Y.: Knowledge Industry Publications, Inc., 1983); "The Home Information Revolution," *Business Week* (June 29, 1981), pp. 74-83.

24 Stuart Gannes, "The Big Boys Are Joining the Biotech Party," *Fortune* (June 22, 1987), pp. 114-118; Gene Bylinsky,

"The High Tech Race: Who's Ahead?" *Fortune* (October 13, 1986), pp. 26-44; Gene Bylinsky, "Genentech Has a Golden Goose," *Fortune* (May 9, 1988), pp. 52-62; "Merck's Medicine Man," *Time* (February 22, 1988), pp. 44-45; "The Best of 1987," *Business Week* (January 11, 1988), p. 156.

25 Anthony Ramirez, "Superconductors Get into Business," *Fortune* (June 22, 1987), pp. 114-118; Gene Bylinsky, "The High Tech Race: Who's Ahead?" (reference cited).

26 "Garbage: It Isn't the Other Guy's Problem Anymore," *Business Week* (May 25, 1987), pp. 150-154; Amal Kumar Naj, "Can $100 Billion Have 'No Material Effect' on Balance Sheets?" *The Wall Street Journal* (May 11, 1988), pp. 1, 8.

27 "Plastic that Won't Clutter the Countryside," *Fortune* (September 1, 1986), p. 48.

28 Stuart Gannes, "A Down-to-Earth Job: Saving the Sky," *Fortune* (March 14, 1988), pp. 134-141; "The Heat Is On," *Time* (October 19, 1987), pp. 58-67.

29 Kenneth Labich, "Winners in the Air Wars," *Fortune* (May 11, 1987), pp. 68-79.

30 Michael Porter, *Competitive Strategy* (New York: Free Press, 1980).

31 Roger Rowand, "Car-Truck Sales Smash Record in Busy Year," *Automotive News* (January 12, 1987), pp. 42-43.

32 Johnnie L. Roberts, "By Concentrating on Marketing, Stride Rite Does Well Despite Slump for Shoemakers," *Wall Street Journal* (February 22, 1983), p. 31.

33 Myron Maguet, "Restructuring Really Works," *Fortune* (March 2, 1987), pp. 38-46; "Rebuilding to Survive," *Time* (February 16, 1987), pp. 44-47.

34 Anne B. Fisher, "The Downside of Downsizing," *Fortune* (May 23, 1988), pp. 42-52.

35 "The Best of 1987," *Business Week* (January 11, 1988), p. 153.

36 Amanda Bennett, "As Big Firms Continue to Trim Their Staffs, 2-Tier Setup Emerges," *The Wall Street Journal* (May 4, 1987), pp. 1, 14.

37 David L. Birch, "Down, But Not Out," *Inc.* (May 1988), pp. 20-21.

38 "Dictating Product Safety," *Business Week* (May 18, 1974), pp. 56-62.

39 United States v. Trans-Missouri Freight Association, 166 U.S. 290 (1897).

40 This conceptual framework of distribution controls was developed by Marshall Howard, *Legal Aspects in Marketing* (New York: McGraw-Hill Book Company, 1964).

41 International Business Machines Corporation v. United States, 298 U.S. 131 (1936).

42 Joanne Lipman, "Double Standards for Kids' TV Ads," *The Wall Street Journal* (June 10, 1988), p. 21.

CHAPTER FOUR

1 These examples were drawn from "Marketing's New Look," *Business Week* (January 26, 1987), pp. 64-69; "Southland Redefines Convenience," *Advertising Age* (April 20, 1987), p. 97; "You Aren't Paranoid If You Feel Someone Eyes You Constantly," *The Wall Street Journal* (March 29, 1985), p. lff; "Women Carry Clout," *Dallas Times Herald* (April 1, 1986), p. 1B.

2 James F. Engel, Roger D. Blackwell, and Paul Miniard, *Consumer Behavior*, 5th ed. (Chicago: Dryden Press, 1986), p. 43.

3 For an extended discussion of problem definition, see Gordon C. Bruner III and Richard J. Pomazal, "Problem Recognition: The Crucial First Stage of the Consumer Decision Process," *Journal of Consumer Marketing* (Winter 1988), pp. 53-63.

4 Mita Sujan, "Consumer Knowledge: Effects on Evaluation Strategies Mediating Consumer Judgments," *Journal of Consumer Research*, Vol. 11 (1985), pp. 31-46.

5 Joseph W. Alba and J. Wesley Hutchinson, "Dimensions of Consumer Expertise," *Journal of Consumer Research*, Vol. 14 (1987), pp. 411-454.

6 Thomas S. Robertson, Joan Zielinski, and Scott Ward, *Consumer Behavior* (Glenview, Ill.: Scott, Foresman & Company, 1984), pp. 84-87.

7 Engel, Blackwell, and Miniard (reference cited), pp. 93-96.

8 John A. Howard, *Consumer Behavior: Applications of Theory* (New York: McGraw-Hill Book Company, 1977), p. 32.

9 See, for example, William Cummings and M. Venkatesan, "Cognitive Dissonance and Consumer Behavior: A Review of the Evidence," *Journal of Marketing Research* (August 1976), pp. 303-308; Pradeep Korgaonkor and George Mochis, "An Experimental Study of Cognitive Dissonance, Product Involvement, Expectations, Performance and Consumer Judgment of Product Performance," *Journal of Advertising*, Vol. 11 (1982), pp. 32-43.

10 For a review of selected research on involvement, see Mark Slama and Armen Tashchian, "Selected Socioeconomic and Demographic Characteristics Associated with Purchasing Involvement," *Journal of Marketing* (Winter 1985), pp. 72-82; Gilles Laurent and Jean-Noel Kapferer, "Measuring Consumer Involvement Profiles," *Journal of Marketing Research* (February 1985), pp. 41-53; Sharon E. Beatty and Scott M. Smith, "External Search Effort: An Investigation Across Several Product Categories," *Journal of Consumer Research*, Vol. 14 (1987), pp. 83-95.

11 Robertson, Zielinski, and Ward (reference cited), pp. 119-122.

12 John L. Lastovicka and David M. Gardner, "Components of Involvement," in John C. Maloney and Bernard Silverman, eds., *Attitude Research Plays for High Stakes* (Chicago: American Marketing Association, 1979), pp. 119-122.

13 J. Paul Peter and Jerry C. Olson, *Consumer Behavior: Marketing Strategy Perspectives* (Homewood, Ill.: Richard D. Irwin, 1987), pp. 259-265.

14 Russell W. Belk, "Situational Variables and Consumer Behavior," *Journal of Consumer Research*, Vol. 2 (1975), pp. 157-164.

15 Ronald E. Milliman, "Using Background Music to Affect the Behavior of Supermarket Shoppers," *Journal of Marketing* (Summer 1982), pp. 86-91. See also Ronald E. Milliman, "The Influence of Background Music on the Behavior of Restaurant Patrons," *Journal of Consumer Research*, Vol. 13 (1986), pp. 286-289.

16 This perspective on motivational and personality factors is drawn from Del I. Hawkins, Roger J. Best, and Kenneth A. Coney, *Consumer Behavior: Implications for Marketing Strategy*, 3rd ed. (Plano, Tex.: Business Publications, Inc., 1987), p. 379.

17 K.H. Chung, *Motivational Theories and Practices* (Columbus, Ohio: Grid Publishing, Inc., 1977). See also A.H. Maslow, *Motivation and Personality* (New York: Harper & Row, 1970).

18 Arthur Koponen, "The Personality Characteristics of Purchases," *Journal of Advertising Research* (September 1960), pp. 89-92.

19 Joel B. Cohen, "An Interpersonal Orientation to the Study of Consumer Behavior," *Journal of Marketing Research* (August 1967), pp. 270-278.

20 J. Neher, "Toro Cutting a Wide Swath in Outdoor Appliances Marketing," *Advertising Age* (February 25, 1979), p. 21.

21 Ronald Alsop, "Color Grows More Important in Catching Consumers' Eyes," *The Wall Street Journal* (November 19, 1984), p. 35.

22 Adapted from Robertson, Zielinski, and Ward (reference cited), p. 186. For a review of the perceived risk literature, see G.R. Dowling, "Perceived Risk: The Concept and Its Management," *Psychology and Marketing* (Fall 1986), pp. 193-210.

23 This description of learning principles is based on Hawkins, Best, and Coney (reference cited), pp. 350-354, and David Loudon and Albert J. Della Bitta, *Consumer Behavior*, 3rd. ed. (New York: McGraw-Hill, Inc., 1988), pp. 437-474.

24 Gordon Allport, "Attitudes," in Martin Fishbein, ed., *Readings in Attitude Theory and Measurement* (New York: John Wiley & Sons, Inc., 1968), p. 3.

25 Milton J. Rokeach, *The Nature of Human Values* (New York: Free Press, 1973).

26 Engel, Blackwell, and Miniard (reference cited), p. 104.

27 Peter and Olson (reference cited), pp. 209-211. See also Richard J. Lutz, "Changing Brand Attitudes Through Modification of Cognitive Structure," *Journal of Consumer Research*, Vol. 2 (1975), pp. 49-59; Michael Gershman, "If at First You Don't Succeed, Remarket," *Management Review* (April 1987), pp. 28-32.

28 Henry Assael, *Consumer Behavior and Marketing Action,* 3rd ed. (Boston: Kent Publishing Company, 1987), p. 260.

29 For an extended discussion of self-concept, see M. Joseph Sirgy, "Self-Concept in Consumer Behavior: A Critical Review," *Journal of Consumer Research*, Vol. 9 (1982), pp. 287-300.

30 For a description of the VALS Program and examples of purchasing behavior, see Arnold Mitchell, *The Nine American Lifestyles: Who Are We & Where Are We Going* (New York: Macmillan Publishing Company, 1983); Michael Hedges, "Radio's Lifestyles," *American Demographics* (February 1986); pp. 32-35; Beckley Townsend, "Psychographic Glitter," *Across the Board* (March 1986), pp. 41-46; "Mass Appeal: An Advertising Edsel?" *Dallas Times Herald* (August 25, 1987), pp. C1, C5; "Singles Boom Now . . . But Bust Later," *Marketing & Media Decisions* (December 1982), pp. 70-74.

31 See, for example, Lawrence F. Feick and Linda Price, "The Market Maven: A Diffuser of Marketplace Information," *Journal of Marketing* (January 1987), pp. 83-97; Peter H. Block, "The Product Enthusiast: Implications for Marketing Strategy," *Journal of Consumer Marketing* (Summer 1986), pp. 51-61.

32 Meg Cox, "Ford Pushing Thunderbird with VIP Plan," *The Wall Street Journal* (October 17, 1983), p. 37.

33 "Importance of Image," *The Wall Street Journal* (August 12, 1985), p. 19.

34 Damon Darlin, "Although U.S. Cars Are Improved, Imports Still Win Quality Survey," *The Wall Street Journal* (December 12, 1985), p. 27; "The Best Kind of Advertising," *Forbes* (April 20, 1987), pp. 91-92.

35 Representative recent work on positive and negative word-of-mouth can be found in Vijay Majahan, Eitan Muller, and Roger A. Kerin, "Introduction Strategy for New Products with Positive and Negative Word-of-Mouth," *Management Science* (December 1984), pp. 1389-1404; Marc G. Weinberger, "Products as Targets of Negative Information: Some Recent Findings," *European Journal of Marketing*, Vol. 20, (Nb. 3/4, 1986); Barry L. Bayers, "Word of Mouth: The Indirect Effects of Marketing Efforts," *Journal of Advertising Research* (June-July 1985), pp. 31-39; Marsha L. Richins, "Negative Word of Mouth by Dissatisfied Consumers: A Pilot Study," *Journal of Marketing* (Winter 1983), pp. 68-78.

36 William O. Bearden and Michael J. Etzel, "Reference Group Influence on Product and Brand Purchase Decisions," *The Journal of Consumer Research,* Vol. 8 (1982), pp. 183-194.

37 Grady Hauser, "How Teenagers Spend the Family Dollar," *American Demographics* (December 1986), pp. 38-41; Ellen Graham, "As Kids Gain Power of Purse, Marketing Takes Aim at Them," *The Wall Street Journal* (January 19, 1988), pp. 1, 8; Joe Agnew, "Children Come of Age as Consumers," *Marketing News* (December 4, 1987), p. 8.

38 This definition and ensuing discussion is adapted from Patrick E. Murphy and William A. Staples, "A Modernized Family Life Cycle," *Journal of Consumer Research*, Vol. 6 (1979), pp. 12-22.

39 A third decision-making style for households is automatic in which an equal number of purchase decisions is made by each spouse. For example, see Harry L. Davis and Benny P. Rigaux, "Perceptions of Marital Roles in Decision Processes," *Journal of Consumer Research*, Vol. 1 (1974), pp. 51-62. Also see Robert Green et al., "Societal Development and Family Purchasing Roles, *Journal of Consumer Research,* Vol. 11 (1984), pp. 38-48.

40 "Doing Business with Mr. Mom," *Forbes* (January 13, 1986), p. 281; "Women Carrying Clout," *Dallas Times Herald* (April 2, 1986), p. 1B.

41 The following examples are found in Hauser (reference cited).

42 An extended discussion of social class influence on purchase behavior is found in Hawkins, Best, and Coney (reference cited); Engel, Blackwell, and Miniard (reference cited). See also McKinley L. Blackburn and David E. Bloom, "What's Happening to the Middle Class?" *American Demographics* (January 1985), pp. 19-25.

43 For further insight into subcultural influences on behavior, see William O'Hare, "Blacks and Whites: One Market or Two?" *American Demographics* (March 1987), pp. 44-48; Leon F. Bouvier and Anthony J. Agresta, "The Fastest Growing Minority," *American Demographics* (May 1985), p. 31ff; Bryant Robey, "America's Asians," *American Demographics* (May 1985), pp. 22ff; Brad Edmondson, "From Dixie to Detroit," *American Demographics* (January 1987), pp. 26-31ff.

CHAPTER FIVE

1 Based on personal interview with Joe Alvité and "Limping Along in Robot Land," *Time* (July 13, 1987), pp. 46-47.

2 Michael D. Hutt and Thomas W. Speh, *Industrial Marketing Management,* 2nd ed. (Chicago: Dryden Press, 1985), p. 4.

3 *Standard Industrial Classification Manual* (Washington, D.C.: U.S. Government Printing Office, 1982).

4 An argument that consumer buying and organizational buying do not have important differences is found in Edward F. Fern and James R. Brown, "The Industrial/Consumer Marketing Dichotomy: A Case of Insufficient Justification," *Journal of Marketing* (Spring 1984), pp. 68-77. However, most writers on the subject do draw distinctions between the two types of buying. See, for example, Robert R. Reeder, Edward G. Brierty, and Betty H. Reeder, *Industrial Marketing: Analysis, Planning, and Control* (Englewood Cliffs, N.J.: Prentice-Hall, Inc., 1987), and Hutt and Speh (reference cited).

5 Implications of derived demand for marketing management can be found in William S. Bishop, John L. Graham, and Michael H. Jones, "Volatility of Derived Demand in Industrial Markets and Its Management Implications," *Journal of Marketing* (Fall 1984), pp. 95-103.

6 Gary W. Dickson, "An Analysis of Vendor Selection Systems and Decisions," *Journal of Purchasing* (February 1966), pp. 5-17.

7 Norm Alister, "Supplying to IBM: The Obligations of Victory," *Electronic Business Magazine* (October 15, 1985), pp. 92ff.

8 See, for example, Barbara C. Perdue, Ralph L. Day, and Ronald E. Michaels, "Negotiation Styles of Industrial Buyers," *Industrial Marketing Management* (August 1986), pp. 171-176.

9 "Where Three Sales a Year Make You a Superstar," *Business Week* (February 17, 1986), pp. 76-77.

10 Carl McDaniel, Jr., and Willam R. Darden, *Marketing* (Boston: Allyn & Bacon, Inc., 1987), p. 167.

11 "McDonnell Douglas Grabs a Piece of China's Sky," *Business Week* (August 17, 1987), p. 35.

12 Thomas V. Bonoma, "Major Sales: Who Really Does the Buying?" *Harvard Business Review* (May-June 1982), pp. 111-119. See also Lowell F. Crow and Jay D. Lindquist, "Impact of Organizational and Buyer Characteristics on the Buying Center," *Industrial Marketing Management* (February 1985), pp. 49-58; Susan Lynn, "Identifying Buying Influences for a Professional Service: Implications for Marketing Efforts," *Industrial Marketing Management* (May 1987), pp. 119-130.

13 These definitions are adapted from Frederick E. Webster, Jr., and Yoram Wind, *Organizational Buying Behavior* (Englewood Cliffs, N.J.: Prentice-Hall, Inc., 1972), p. 6.

14 For insights into buying industrial services, see James R. Stock and Paul H. Zinszer, "The Industrial Purchase Decision for Professional Services," *Journal of Business Research* (February 1987) pp. 1-16.

15 Patrick J. Robinson, Charles W. Faris, and Yoram Wind, *Industrial Buying and Creative Marketing* (Boston: Allyn & Bacon, Inc., 1967).

16 Recent studies on the buy-class framework which document its usefulness include: Erin Anderson, Wujin Chu, and Barton Weitz, "Industrial Purchasing: An Empirical Exploration of the Buyclass Framework," *Journal of Marketing* (July 1987), pp. 71-86; Morry Ghingold, "Testing the 'Buygrid' Buying Process Model," *Journal of Purchasing and Materials Management* (Winter 1986), pp. 30-36; P. Matthyssens and W. Faes, "OEM Buying Process for New Components: Purchasing and Marketing Implications," *Industrial Marketing Management* (August 1985), pp. 145-157; Thomas W. Leigh and Arno J. Rethaus, "A Script-Theoretic Analysis of Industrial Purchasing Behavior," *Journal of Marketing* (Fall 1984), pp. 22-32. Studies not supporting the buy-class framework include Joseph A. Bellizi and Philip McVey, "How Valid Is the Buy-Grid Model?" *Industrial Marketing Management* (February 1983), pp. 57-62; Donald W. Jackson, Janey E. Keith, and Richard K. Burdick, "Purchasing Agents' Perceptions of Industrial Buying Center Influences: A Situational Approach," *Journal of Marketing* (Fall 1984), pp. 75-83.

17 See, for example, Gary L. Lilien and Anthony Wong, "An Exploratory Investigation of the Structure of the Buying Center in the Metal Working Industry," *Journal of Marketing Research* (February 1984), pp. 1-11; Wesley J. Johnston and Thomas V. Bonoma, "The Buying Center: Structure and Interaction Patterns," *Journal of Marketing* (Summer 1981), pp. 143-156. See also Christopher P. Puto, Wesley E. Patton III, and Ronald H. King, "Risk Handling Strategies in Industrial Vendor Selection Decisions," *Journal of Marketing* (Winter 1985), pp. 89-98.

18 William Rudelius, "Selling to the Government," in Victor Buehl, ed., *Handbook of Modern Marketing,* 2nd ed. (New York: McGraw-Hill Book Company, 1985).

19 C. William Verity, Jr., "Unleashing America's Space Entrepreneurs," *Across the Board* (April 1988), pp. 23-27.

20 Annette Kornblum, "How to Waste $12 Million," *Inc.* (December 1981), p. 95.

21 Gregory Stricharchuk, "Smokestack Industries Adopt Sophisticated Sales Approach," *The Wall Street Journal* (March 15, 1984), p. 31.

22 Richard M. Hill, "Suppliers Need to Supply Reliably, in Volume, with Value Engineering Analysis, Market Data," *Marketing News* (April 4, 1980), p. 7.

23 Niren Vyas and Arch Woodside, "An Inductive Model of Industrial Supplier Choice Processes," *Journal of Marketing* (Winter 1984), pp. 30-45; see also Ronald P. LeBlanc, "Insights into Organizational Buying," *Journal of Business & Industrial Marketing* (Spring 1987), pp. 5-10; Robert E. Krapfel, Jr., "An Advocacy Model of Organizational Buyers' Vendor Choice," *Journal of Marketing* (Fall 1985), pp. 51-54.

24 Jackson, Keith, and Burdick (reference cited).

25 Kevin Higgins, "Searle Plots a Dual Marketing Strategy for NutraSweet Brand," *Marketing News* (August 3, 1984), p. 1.

CHAPTER SIX

1 Thomas More, "He Put the Kick Back into Coke," *Fortune* (October 26, 1987), pp. 46-56; Betsy Morris, "Coke vs. Pepsi: Cola War Marches On," *The Wall Street Journal* (June 3, 1987), p. 29.

2 "New Marketing Research Definition Approved," *Marketing News* (January 2, 1987), pp. 1, 14.

3 Rohit Deshpande, "The Organizational Context of Market

Research Use," *Journal of Marketing* (Fall 1982), pp. 91-101; John G. Myers, Stephen A. Greyser, and William F. Massy, "The Effectiveness of Marketing's 'R&D' for Marketing Management: An Assessment," *Journal of Marketing* (January 1979), pp. 17-29.

4 "Who'll Buy a Drink in a Box?" *Marketing and Media Decisions* (April 1982), p. 74ff.

5 Ronald Alsop, "Firms Promote Aseptic Packs as More Than a Fad for Kids," *The Wall Street Journal* (October 31, 1985), p. 31.

6 Jim Hyatt, "At One Toy Company the Guys in Research Are 3 and 4 Years Old," *The Wall Street Journal* (December 20, 1971), p. 1.

7 The dot and match problems are from Martin Scheerer, "Problem Solving," *Scientific American* (April 1963), pp. 118-128.

8 John H. Dessauer, *My Years with Xerox* (New York: Doubleday & Company, Inc., 1971), pp. 45-48.

9 The bubble gum and hair dye examples are adapted from Roger Ricklefs, "Success Comes Hard in the Tricky Business of Creating Products," *The Wall Street Journal* (August 23, 1978), p. 1.

10 For example, see Gilbert A. Churchill, Jr., *Marketing Research: Methodological Foundations,* 4th ed. (New York: Dryden Press, 1987).

11 Felix Kessler, "High-Tech Shocks in Ad Research," *Fortune* (July 7, 1986), pp. 58-62.

12 "The Networks' Big Headache," *Business Week* (July 6, 1987), pp. 26-28; Verne Gay, "Networks Zap Debut of Meters," *Advertising Age* (September 7, 1987), pp. 1, 56; Verne Gay, "TV's Ratings Gap Lessens," *Advertising Age* (September 14, 1987), pp. 3, 113.

13 Dennis Kneale, "As TV Season Ends, Ratings Show Networks Lost Millions of Viewers," *The Wall Street Journal* (April 18, 1988), p. 34.

14 Ronald Alsop, "People Watchers Seek Clues to Consumers' True Behavior," *The Wall Street Journal* (September 4, 1986), p. 25.

15 Susan Feyder, "It Took Tinkering by Twin Cities Firms to Save Some 'Sure Bets,' " *Minneapolis Star and Tribune* (June 9, 1982), p. 11A.

16 Jeffrey A. Trachtenberg, "Listening, the Old-Fashioned Way," *Forbes* (October 5, 1987), pp. 202-204.

17 The impact on answers of subtle differences in question wording to political surveys is described in Harper W. Boyd, Jr., Ralph Westfall, and Stanley F. Stasch, *Marketing Research,* 6th ed. (Homewood, Ill.: Richard D. Irwin, Inc., 1985), pp. 265-266.

18 Johny K. Johansson and Ikujiro Nonaka, "Market Research the Japanese Way," *Harvard Business Review* (May-June 1987), pp. 16-22.

19 O.C. Ferrell and Steven J. Skinner, "Ethical Behavior and Bureaucratic Structure in Marketing Research Organizations," *Journal of Marketing Research* (February 1988), pp. 103-109.

20 John Koten and Scott Kilman, "How Coke's Decision to Offer 2 Colas Undid 4½ Years of Planning," *The Wall Street Journal* (July 15, 1985), pp. 1, 13; Ronald Alsop, "Coke's Flip-Flop Underscores Risks of Consumer Taste Tests," *The Wall Street Journal* (July 18, 1985), p. 23; Anne B. Fisher, "Coke's Brand Loyalty Lesson," *Fortune* (August 5, 1985), pp. 44-46; Betsy D. Gelb and Gabriel M. Gelb, "New Coke's Fizzle—Lessons for the Rest of Us," *Sloan Management Review* (Fall 1986), pp. 71-76.

CHAPTER SEVEN

1 John Koten, "How the Marketers Perform a Vital Role in a Movie's Success," *The Wall Street Journal* (December 14, 1984), p. 1.

2 Charles Champlin, "Audience's Opinions Make Final Cut," *Dallas Times Herald* (May 12, 1986), p. 30.

3 "Killer!" *Time* (November 16, 1987), pp. 72-79.

4 "How Paramount Keeps Churning Out Winners," *Business Week* (June 11, 1984), pp. 148-151; Laura Landro, "Frank Maruso's Marketing Savvy Paves Way for Paramount Hits," *The Wall Street Journal* (June 27, 1984), p. 27.

5 Koten (reference cited), p. 1; Jeffrey A. Trachtenberg, "Listening, the Old-Fashioned Way," *Forbes* (October 5, 1987), p. 204.

6 "A Case of Malpractice—In Market Research?" *Business Week* (August 10, 1987), pp. 28-29.

7 "Merchandising Plays Effective? Scanners Know," *Marketing News* (January 4, 1985), p. 17.

8 "Analyzing Promotions: The Free-Standing Insert Coupon," *Nielsen Researcher,* No. 4 (1982), pp. 16-20.

9 Bernice Kanner, "How a New Gizmo 'Plays' in Peoria Often Foretells Its 'Flyability' in 'Buyoria,'" *Minneapolis Star and Tribune* (June 9, 1982), p. 11A.

10 Eric N. Berkowitz, Roger A. Kerin, and William Rudelius, *Marketing* (St. Louis: Times Mirror/Mosby College Publishing, 1986), pp. 3-4, 14-16.

11 Dick Youngblood, "Prosperity Awaits the Inventor of Simple Blood-Sugar Tester," *Minneapolis Star and Tribune* (February 15, 1987), pp. 1D, 3D.

12 Leslie Brennan, "Test Marketing Put to the Test: Ocean Spray Mauna La'i Hawaiian Guava Drink," *Sales and Marketing Management* (March 1987), p. 68.

13 George M. Zinkhan, Erich A. Joachimsthaler, and Thomas C. Kinnear, "Individual Differences and Marketing Decision Support System Usage and Satisfaction," *Journal of Marketing Research* (May 1987), pp. 208-214.

14 Thayer C. Taylor, "The Computer in Sales and Marketing: Software Juices Up Ocean Spray Promotions," *Sales and Marketing Management* (May 1986), pp. 74-75.

CHAPTER EIGHT

1 Jean Sherman, "No Pain, No Gain," *Working Woman* (May 1987), p. 92; "Can Reebok Sprint Even Faster?" *Business Week* (October 6, 1986), pp. 74-75.

2 Mary Rowland, "Keep on Walking," *Working Woman* (May 1987), pp. 87-92; "Reebok's Recent Blisters Seem to Be Healing," *Business Week* (August 3, 1987), p. 62; "Sneakers that Don't Specialize," *Business Week* (June 6, 1988), p. 146.

3 Peter R. Dickson and James L. Ginter, "Market Segmentation, Product Differentiation, and Marketing Strategy," *Journal of Marketing* (April 1987), pp. 1-10.

4 Jean Sherman (reference cited).

5 "How Paramount Keeps Churning Out Winners," *Business Week* (June 11, 1984), pp. 148-151; John Koten, "How the

Marketers Perform a Vital Role in a Movie's Success," *The Wall Street Journal* (December 14, 1984), p. 1.

6 James Cook, "Where's the Niche?" *Forbes* (September 24, 1984), pp. 54-55; John Koten, "Giving Buyers Wider Choice May Be Hurting Auto Makers," *The Wall Street Journal* (December 15, 1983), p. 33; Jacob M. Schlesinger and Joseph B. White, "The New-Model GM Will Be More Compact But More Profitable," *The Wall Street Journal* (June 6, 1988), pp. 1, 8.

7 *1988 Ford Thunderbird* (Dearborn, Mich.: Ford Motor Company, October 1987), pp. 18-21; *1988 Model Thunderbird Ordering Guide* (Dearborn, Michigan: Ford Motor Company, February 29, 1988), pp. 1-6; Jacob M. Schlesinger and Joseph B. White, "The New-Model GM Will Be More Compact But More Profitable," *The Wall Street Journal* (June 6, 1988), pp. 1, 8.

8 "Segmentation: Is It Real or Just a 'Research Event'?" *Marketing News* (August 28, 1987), pp. 37-40; "Segmentation Won't Work Until It's Strategic," *Marketing News* (August 28, 1987), pp. 40-41.

9 Issues in using market segmentation studies are described in William Rudelius, John R. Walton, and James C. Cross, "Improving the Managerial Relevance of Market Segmentation Studies," in Michael J. Houston, ed., *1987 Review of Marketing* (Chicago: American Marketing Association, 1987), pp. 385-404.

10 Larry Carpenter, "How to Market to Regions," *American Demographics* (November 1987), pp. 44-45; "Marketing's New Look," *Business Week* (January 26, 1987), pp. 64-69.

11 "GE Is Pulling Out the Stops at Home," *Business Week* (November 2, 1987), p. 94; "On the Verge of World War in White Goods," *Business Week* (November 2, 1987), pp. 91-98.

12 Russell I. Haley, "Benefit Segmentation: A Decision-Oriented Research Tool," *Journal of Marketing* (July 1968), pp. 30-35.

13 "Wendy's Tries Warming Up the Basic Burger," *Business Week* (May 18, 1987), p. 51.

14 Robert Metz, "Apple Now a Strong Investment," *Minneapolis Star and Tribune* (October 1, 1987), p. 2M.

15 Brian O'Reilly, "Growing Apple Anew for the Business Market," *Fortune* (January 4, 1988), pp. 36-37; "Linking Up Olsen's DEC and Sculley's Apple," *Fortune* (February 15, 1988), p. 8.

16 "How Two Pioneers Brought Publishing to the Desktop," *Business Week* (October 1, 1987), p. 61.

17 Anthony Ramirez, "America's Super Minority," *Fortune* (November 25, 1986), pp. 148-162.

18 Stuart Gannes, "The Riches in Market Niches," *Fortune* (April 27, 1987), pp. 227-230.

19 Advantages and disadvantages of cross tabulations are adapted from Roseann Maguire and Terry C. Wilson, "Banners or Cross Tabs? Before Deciding, Weigh Data—Format, Pros, Cons," *Marketing News* (May 13, 1983), pp. 10-11.

20 Regis McKenna, "Playing for Position," *Inc.* (April 1985), pp. 92-97.

21 Michael G. Harvey and Roger A. Kerin, "Diagnosis and Management of the Product Cannibalization Syndrome," *University of Michigan Business Review* (November 1979), pp. 18-21.

22 "Positioning Is Key to Marketing Says Trout; Yes, But It's Perceptual Positioning, Says Davis," in Patrick Dunne and Susan Oberhouse, eds. *Product Management* (Chicago: American Marketing Association, 1980), pp. 105-107.

23 Jesse Snyder, "4 GM Car Divisions Are Repositioned in Effort to Help Sales," *Automotive News* (September 15, 1986), pp. 1, 49.

24 Schlesinger and White (reference cited).

CHAPTER NINE

1 The "smart car" material is based on "Smart Cars," *Business Week* (June 13, 1988), pp. 68-77.

2 Definitions within this classification are from Committee on Definitions, *Marketing Definitions: A Glossary of Marketing Terms* (Chicago: American Marketing Association, 1960).

3 Committee on Definitions (reference cited).

4 Ed Fitch, "Life in the Food Chain Becomes Predatory," *Advertising Age* (May 9, 1988), p. S-2.

5 David S. Hopkins, *New Product Winners and Losers,* Conference Board Study Report no. 773 (New York: Conference Board, 1980).

6 "Marketing Briefs," *Business Week* (April 22, 1967), p. 120.

7 Thomas Robertson, "The Process of Innovation and Diffusion of Innovation," *Journal of Marketing* (January 1967), p. 15.

8 R.G. Cooper and U. deBrentani, "Criteria for Screening Industrial Products," *Industrial Marketing Management,* Vol. 13 (1984), pp. 149-156; C.M. Crawford, "New Product Failure Rates—Facts and Fallacies," *Research Management* (September 1979), pp. 9-13.

9 Arthur Buckler, "Holly Farms' Marketing Error: The Chicken that Laid an Egg," *The Wall Street Journal* (February 9, 1988), p. 36.

10 R.G. Cooper and E.J. Kleinschmidt, "New Products—What Separates Winners from Losers?" *Journal of Product Innovation Management* (September 1987), pp. 169-184.

11 "Canon Finally Challenges Minolta's Mighty Maxxum," *Business Week* (March 2, 1987), pp. 89-90.

12 *New Products Management for the 1980's* (Booz, Allen & Hamilton, Inc., 1982).

13 Glen L. Urban, John R. Hauser, and Nikhilesh Dholakia, *Essentials of New Product Management* (Englewood Cliffs, N.J.: Prentice-Hall, Inc., 1987), pp. 15-17.

14 Susan Fraker, "High-Speed Management for the High-Tech Age," *Fortune* (March 5, 1984), pp. 62-68; Kevin Higgins, "Meticulous Planning Pays Dividends at Stouffers," *Marketing News* (October 28, 1983), pp. 1, 20.

15 Edward M. Tauber, "Discovering New Product Opportunities with Problem Inventory Analysis," *Journal of Marketing* (January 1975).

16 "The Burning Question at RJR: Now What?" *Business Week* (September 28, 1987), pp. 28-29.

17 Louis Therrien, "Bausch & Lomb Is Correcting Its Vision of Research," *Business Week* (March 30, 1987), p. 9.

18 Lee Smith, "A Miracle in Search of a Market," *Fortune* (December 1, 1981), pp. 92-98; Laurie Hays, "DuPont's Difficulties in Selling KEVLAR Show Hurdles of Innovation," *The Wall Street Journal* (September 27, 1987), pp. 1, 23; Diane Beulke, "Activitrax Set the Pace for Medtronic," *City Business* (June 17, 1987), pp. 1, 14, 15.

19 "How Ford Hit the Bull's-Eye with Taurus," *Business Week* (June 30, 1986), pp. 69-70.
20 Lee Adler, "Before Plunging into the Market, Try a Little Concept Testing," *Sales and Marketing Management* (January 16, 1984), pp. 98-103.
21 "Airwick's Discovery of New Markets Pays Off," *Business Week* (June 16, 1980), pp. 139-401.
22 Thayer C. Taylor, "A Strategy for Every New Product," *Sales and Marketing Management* (May 17, 1982), pp. 52-55.
23 J. Quincy Hunsicker, "Misinnovation: How to Guard Against Investing in Systems that Won't Work," *Management Review* (April 1984), pp. 16-18.
24 Paul Ingrassia, "Industry Is Shopping Abroad for Good Ideas to Apply to Products," *The Wall Street Journal* (April 29, 1985), p. 1.
25 Michael J. Baker and Ronald McTavish, *Product Policy and Management* (London: Macmillan Press, Ltd., 1976), p. 146.
26 J. Hugh Davidson, "Why Most New Consumer Brands Fail," *Harvard Business Review* (March-April 1976), p. 117.
27 Jay Klopmaker, David Hughes, and R. Haley, "Test Marketing in New Product Development," *Harvard Business Review* (May-June 1976).
28 Mary Huhn, "Not-So-Hot-After-All Products," *Adweek* (November 2, 1987), pp. HP22-27.
29 Liz Murphy, "Beer Drinkers Put Coors to the Test!" *Sales and Marketing Management* (March 12, 1984), pp. 93-100.
30 Ronald Alsop, "Companies Get on the Fast Track to Roll Out Hot New Brands," *The Wall Street Journal* (July 10, 1986), p. 27.
31 Glen L. Urban and John R. Hauser, *Design and Marketing of New Products* (Englewood Cliffs, N.J.: Prentice-Hall, Inc., 1980), p. 74.
32 Urban and Hauser (reference cited).
33 Bro Uttal, "Speeding New Ideas to Market," *Fortune* (March 2, 1987), pp. 62-66; John Bussey and Douglas R. Sease, "Manufacturers Strive to Slice Time Needed to Develop Products," *The Wall Street Journal* (February 23, 1988), pp. 1, 13; Hirotaka Takeuchi and Ikujiro Nonaka, "The New New Product Development Game," *Harvard Business Review* (January-February 1986), pp. 137-146.
34 *New Products Management for the 1980's* (reference cited).

CHAPTER TEN

1 Ann Hughey, "Sales of Home Movie Equipment Falling as Firms Abandon Market, Video Grows," *The Wall Street Journal* (March 17, 1982), p. 25; "Is There Room for 8-mm Video?" *Business Week* (December 24, 1984), pp. 64-65.
2 Several early studies in marketing have reported this general curve: Robert D. Buzzell and V. Cook, *Product Life Cycles* (Cambridge, Mass.: Marketing Science Institute, 1969), pp. 29-35; F.J. Kovac and M.F. Daque, "Forecasting by Product Life Cycle Analysis," *Research Management* (July 1972); M.T. Cunningham, "The Application of Product Life Cycles to Corporate Strategy: Some Research Findings," *British Journal of Marketing* (Spring 1969), pp. 32-44; A. Patton, "Top Management's Stake in the Product Life Cycle," *Management Review* (June 1959), pp. 9-14.
3 Barbara Rudolph, "Hot Growth in a Cold Market," *Time* (June 29, 1987), p. 47.
4 Carl R. Anderson and Carl P. Zeithaml, "Stage of the Product Life Cycle, Business Strategy, and Business Performance," *Academy of Management Journal* (March 1984), pp. 5-24.
5 George J. Avlonitis, "Ethics and Product Elimination," *Management Decision*, Vol. 21, No. 2 (1983), pp. 37-45; R.T. Hise and M.A. McGinnis, "Product Elimination: Practices, Policies, and Ethics," *Business Horizons* (June 1975), pp. 25-32.
6 David R. Rink and John E. Swan, "Product Life Cycle Research: A Literature Review," *Journal of Business Research* (September 1979), pp. 218-242.
7 David R. Rink and John E. Swan, "Fitting Marketing Strategy to Varying Product Life Cycles," *Business Horizons* (January-February 1982), pp. 72-76.
8 Martha Nolan, "The Sound of the Future," *Madison Avenue* (March 1984), pp. 28-32.
9 The terms *high* and *low learning life cycles* were developed by Chester R. Wasson, *Dynamic Competitive Strategies and Product Life Cycles* (Austin, Tex.: Austin Press, 1978).
10 "If It's Friday, It Must Be Goofy Videocassette Day," *Advertising Age* (February 22, 1988), pp. 44, 45.
11 Lester A. Neidell, "Don't Forget the Product Life Cycle for Strategic Planning," *Business* (April-June 1983), pp. 30-35.
12 Jennifer Lawrence, "Nautilus Pumps Iron in Home Gym Market," *Advertising Age* (December 1987), p. 22; Jeffrey A. Tannenbaum, "Video Games Revive—and Makers Hope This Time the Fad Will Last," *The Wall Street Journal* (March 8, 1988), p. 33.
13 "Living-Room Cinema Deluxe," *Time* (February 28, 1988), pp. 88-90.
14 Paul Duke, Jr., and Karen Blumenthal, "CD Recorder Poses Upset for Industry," *The Wall Street Journal* (April 26, 1988), p. 6.
15 Bob Geiger, "Liquid Yogurts Pour into the U.S.," *Advertising Age* (June 1, 1987), pp. 3, 62.
16 Pat Sloan, "Suncare Marketers Raise Their Screens," *Advertising Age* (May 25, 1987), pp. 1, 66.
17 Raymond Serafin, "BMW Races Mercedes on High End of Market," *Advertising Age* (December 7, 1987), p. 4; Raymond Serafin, "BMW Boosts Ad Budget to Pace Mercedes Sales," *Advertising Age* (March 2, 1987), p. 24.
18 "The Squeeze on Product Mix," *Business Week* (January 6, 1974), pp. 50-57.
19 Lori Kesler, "Extensions Leave Brands in New Areas," *Advertising Age* (June 1, 1987), pp. s-1, s-2; Hal Lancaster, "Sports Leagues Increasingly Put Retail Licensing on Starting Lineup," *The Wall Street Journal* (May 17, 1988), p. 29.
20 J. McNeal and L. Zeren, "Brand Name Selection for Consumer Products," *MSU Business Topics* (Spring 1981).
21 Robert Mainis, "Name-Calling," *Inc.* (July 1984), pp. 67-74.
22 Scott Hume, "Court Orders Hyatt Legal Name Change," *Advertising Age* (June 18, 1984), p. 10.
23 Ronald Alsop, "Firms Unveil More Products Associated with Brand Names," *The Wall Street Journal* (December 13, 1984), p. 33.
24 Walter J. Salmon and Karen A. Cmar, "Private Labels Are Back in Fashion," *Harvard Business Review* (May-June 1987), pp. 99-106.
25 A. Ken Granzin, "An Investigation of the Market for Generic Products," *Journal of Retailing* (Winter 1981), pp. 39-55; Julie

Franz, "Ten Years May Be a Generic Lifetime," *Advertising Age* (March 23, 1987), p. 76; Brian F. Harris and Roger A. Strang, "Marketing Strategies in the Age of Generics," *Journal of Marketing* (Fall 1985), pp. 70-81.

26 Patrick E. Murphy and Gene R. Lackniak, "Generic Supermarket Items: A Product and Consumer Analysis," *Journal of Retailing* (Summer 1979), pp. 1-14; Robert H. Ross and Frederic B. Kraft, "Creating Low Product Expectations," *Journal of Business Research,* Vol. 11 (March 1983), pp. 1-9.

27 Kathleen Day, "Designers Go for a Package Deal," *Dallas Times Herald* (March 19, 1985), p. C1.

28 Walter McQuade, "Packages Bear Up Under a Bundle of Regulations," *Fortune* (May 7, 1979), p. 179.

29 Yoram S. Wind, *Product Policy* (Reading, Mass.: Addison-Wesley Publishing Company, Inc., 1982), pp. 355-356.

30 In recent years there has been significant debate over the value of government-required grade labeling. See John A. Miller, *Labeling Research: The State of the Art,* Report No. 78-115 (Cambridge, Mass.: Marketing Science Institute, 1978).

31 Amy Dunkin, "Want to Wake Up a Tired Old Product? Repackage It," *Business Week* (July 15, 1985), pp. 130, 134; "Solution for Soggy Cereal," *Time* (July 27, 1987), p. 70.

32 Michael Hiestand and Stephen Battaglio, "The Clothes Make The Brand," *Marketing Week* (August 17, 1987), pp. 1, 4.

33 "A Coke and a Style," *Advertising Age* (December 1987), p. 4.

34 Carl McDaniel and R.C. Baker, "Convenience Food Packaging and the Perception of Product Quality," *Journal of Marketing* (October 1977), pp. 57-58.

35 Ronald Alsop, "Color Grows More Important in Catching Consumers' Eyes," *The Wall Street Journal* (November 28, 1984), p. 37.

36 Fred Feucht, "Which Hue Is Best? Test Your Color I.Q.," *Advertising Age* (September 14, 1987), pp. 18, 20.

37 Martin Friedman, "New Packaging for Old Standbys," *Marketing Week* (August 24, 1987), p. 32.

38 Dan Schneidman, "Plastic: Progress and Peril," *Marketing News* (December 18, 1987), pp. 1, 6, 7; Amal Kumar Naj, "Big Chemical Concerns Hasten to Develop Biodegradable Plastics," *The Wall Street Journal* (July 21, 1988), pp. 1, 11.

39 Robert E. Wilkes and James B. Wilcox, "Limited Versus Full Warranties: The Retail Perspective," *Journal of Retailing* (Spring 1981), pp. 65-77.

CHAPTER ELEVEN

1 This example is based on Cara S. Trager, "Right Price Reflects a Magazine's Health Goals," *Advertising Age* (March 9, 1987), pp. 5-8, 9, 12; Julie L. Erickson, "Industry Racks Up New Ideas to Build Circulation," *Advertising Age* (March 9, 1987), pp. S1, S20; Frank Bruni, "Price of Newsweek? It Depends," *Dallas Times Herald* (August 14, 1986), pp. 1D, 5D; Ron Scott, "The Economics of Cover Pricing," *Folio: The Magazine for Magazine Management* (March 1985), pp. 127-128.

2 Jack G. Kaikati, "Marketing Without Exchange of Money," *Harvard Business Review* (November-December 1982), pp. 72-74.

3 Kent B. Monroe, *Pricing: Making Profitable Decisions* (New York: McGraw-Hill Book Company, 1979), p. 38. See also Fabian Linden, "Value of the Dolls," *Across the Board* (December 1985), pp. 54-57, 60; David J. Curry, "Measuring Price and Quality Competition," *Journal of Marketing* (Spring 1985), pp. 106-117.

4 Damon Darlin, "Although U.S. Cars Are Improved, Imports Still Win Quality Survey," *The Wall Street Journal* (December 12, 1985), p. 27.

5 Numerous studies have examined the price-quality-value relationship. See, for example, J. Jacoby and J. Olsen, eds. *Perceived Quality* (Lexington, Mass.: Lexington Books, 1985); Akshay R. Rao and Kent B. Monroe, "The Moderating Effect of Prior Knowledge on Cue Utilization in Product Evaluations," *Journal of Consumer Research* (in press); Kent B. Monroe and William B. Dodds, "A Research Program for Establishing the Validity of the Price-Quality Relationship," *Journal of the Academy of Marketing Science* (in press).

6 These examples from Roger A. Kerin and Robert A. Peterson, *Morgantown, Inc., (A), Strategic Marketing Problems: Cases and Comments* (Boston: Allyn & Bacon, Inc., 1987), pp. 314-325; "Software Economics 101," *Forbes* (January 28, 1985), p. 88.

7 Thomas T. Nagle, *The Strategy & Tactics of Pricing* (Englewood Cliffs, N.J.: Prentice-Hall, Inc., 1987), p. 107.

8 For a thorough review of the price-quality-value relationship, see Valarie A. Ziethaml, "Consumer Perceptions of Price, Quality, and Value," *Journal of Marketing* (July 1988), pp. 2-22.

9 Saeed Samiee, "Pricing in Marketing Strategies of U.S.- and Foreign-Based Companies," *Journal of Business Research* (February 1987), pp. 1-16.

10 "MGM Grand Air, About to Take Off, Has Some Skeptics," *The Wall Street Journal* (May 28, 1987), p. 15.

11 "Why TI May Well Return to Home Computers," *Business Week* (November 14, 1983), pp. 48-49; "A Fast-Moving Target," *Dallas Times Herald* (June 19, 1983), p. M1.

12 "Bausch & Lomb: Hardball Pricing Helps It Regain Its Grip on Contact Lenses," *Business Week* (March 5, 1984), pp. 104-106.

13 GM Is Acting as if There's No Tomorrow," *Business Week* (March 5, 1984), pp. 104-106.

14 "Should Water Supplies Go Down the Drain?" *Business Week* (March 5, 1984), pp. 104-106.

15 John R. Nevin, "Laboratory Experiments for Estimating Consumer Demand: A Validation Study," *Journal of Marketing Research* (August 1974), pp. 261-268; Gerald J. Eskin and Penny H. Baron, "Effects of Price and Advertising in Test-Market Experiments," *Journal of Marketing Research* (November 1977), pp. 499-508.

16 Ronald C. Curhan, "The Effects of Merchandising and Temporary Promotional Activities on the Sales of Fresh Fruits and Vegetables in Supermarkets," *Journal of Marketing Research* (August 1974), pp. 286-294.

17 Scott A. Neslin and Robert W. Shoemaker, "Using a Natural Experiment to Estimate Price Elasticity: The 1974 Sugar Shortage and the Ready-to-Eat Cereal Market," *Journal of Marketing* (Winter 1983), pp. 44-57.

18 Monroe (reference cited), p. 20.

19 For illustrations of break-even analysis that document its use and versatility, see Thomas L. Powers, "Break-Even Analysis with Semifixed Costs," *Industrial Marketing Management* (February 1987), pp. 35-41; "Break-Even Analysis," *Small Business Report* (August 1986), pp. 22-24.

CHAPTER TWELVE

1 Based on Bob Davis and Janet Guyon, "AT&T Ordered to Trim Rates 3.5% Annually," *The Wall Street Journal* (January 4, 1988), p. 3; Janet Guyon, "FCC Hopes New Regulations Will Cut Phone Rates—But Others Aren't Sure," *The Wall Street Journal* (August 6, 1987), p. 27; "A Marketing Blitz to Sell Long-Distance Service," *Business Week* (July 2, 1984), p. 86; and Stuart Gannes, "The Phone Fights Frenzied Finale," *Fortune* (April 14, 1986), pp. 52-60.

2 Contemporary perspectives on pricing that review aspects of setting the final price can be found in Gerard J. Tellis, "Beyond the Many Faces of Price: An Integration of Pricing Strategies," *Journal of Marketing* (October 1986), pp. 146-160; and Vithala Rao, "Pricing Research in Marketing: The State of the Art," *Journal of Business* (January 1984), pp. 39-60.

3 Alan G. Sawyer, Parker M. Worthing, and Paul E. Sendak, "The Role of Laboratory Experiments to Test Marketing Strategies," *Journal of Marketing* (Summer 1979), pp. 60-67.

4 For an extended treatment of skimming and penetration pricing, see Joel Dean, "Pricing Policies for New Products," *Harvard Business Review* (November-December 1976), pp. 141-153.

5 Jeffrey H. Birnbaum, "Pricing of Products Is Still an Art, Often Having Little Link to Costs," *The Wall Street Journal* (November 25, 1981), p. 25.

6 "Strategic Mix of Odd, Even Pricing Can Lead to Increased Retail Profits," *Marketing News* (March 7, 1980), p. 24.

7 For an excellent review of bundle pricing, see Joseph P. Guiltinan, "The Price Bundling of Services: A Normative Framework," *Journal of Marketing* (April 1987), pp. 74-85; and Thomas T. Nagle, *The Strategy & Tactics of Pricing* (Englewood Cliffs, N.J.: Prentice-Hall, Inc., 1987), pp. 170-172, 257-258.

8 Douglas R. Sease, "You Can Buy a Car at $49 Over Invoice, But It Will Take Time," *The Wall Street Journal* (September 21, 1983), p. 1.

9 George S. Day and David B. Montgomery, "Diagnosing the Experience Curve," *Journal of Marketing* (Spring 1983), pp. 44-58; and Pankaj Ghemawat, "Building Strategy on the Experience Curve," *Harvard Business Review* (March-April 1985), pp. 143-149.

10 "As Answering Machines Proliferate, Nature of Telephone Use Changes," *The Wall Street Journal* (May 20, 1987), p. 33; and "Compact-Disc Players," *Consumer Reports* (May 1987), pp. 284-285.

11 "One Word for One Price: Success," *Business Week* (May 23, 1988), p. 123.

12 "Pechin's Mart Breaks Many Rules, But Not the One on Pricing," *The Wall Street Journal* (March 5, 1984), p. 1.

13 "Why TI May Well Return to Home Computers," *Business Week* (November 14, 1983), pp. 48-49.

14 Pat Baldwin, "Smart Pricing Pays in Profits," *Dallas, Inc* (March 21-March 27, 1988), p. 17.

15 For a review of quantity discounts, see George S. Day and Adrian B. Ryans, "Using Price Discounts for a Competitive Advantage," *Industrial Marketing Management* (February 1988), pp. 1-14; and James B. Wilcox, Roy D. Howell, Paul Kuzdrall, and Robert Britney, "Price Quantity Discounts: Some Implications for Buyers and Sellers," *Journal of Marketing* (July 1987), pp. 60-70.

16 Michael Levy and Charles Ingene, "Retailers: Head Off Credit Cards with Cash Discounts," *Harvard Business Review* (May-June 1983), pp. 18-22.

17 Ronald C. Curhan and Robert J. Kopp, "Obtaining Retailer Support for Trade Deals: Key Success Factors," *Journal of Advertising Research* (December-January, 1987/1988), pp. 51-60; and Michael Levy, John Webster, and Roger A. Kerin, "Formulating Push Marketing Strategies: A Method and Application," *Journal of Marketing* (Winter 1983), pp. 25-34.

18 For additional insights into price fixing, see "Cola Sellers May Have Bottled Up Their Competition," *The Wall Street Journal* (December 9, 1987), p. 6; and Mary Jane Sheffet and Debra L. Scammon, "Resale Price Maintenance: Is It Safe to Suggest Retail Prices?" *Journal of Marketing* (Fall 1985), pp. 82-91.

19 "Saks, I. Magnin Hit on Pricing," *Chain Store Age Executive* (June 1979), p. 4.

20 For an overview on price discrimination practices and perspectives, see Norton E. Marks and Neely S. Inlow, "Price Discrimination and Its Impact on Small Business," *Journal of Consumer Marketing* (Winter 1988), pp. 31-38; Michael H. Morris, "Separate Prices as a Marketing Tool," *Industrial Marketing Management* (May 1987), pp. 79-86; and James C. Johnson and Kenneth C. Schneider, "Those Who Can, Do—Those Who Can't . . . Marketing Professors and the Robinson-Patman Act," *Journal of the Academy of Marketing Science*, Vol. 12 (1984), pp. 123-128.

21 See, for example, "Laws Against 'Predatory Pricing' by Firms and Being Relaxed in Many Court Rulings," *The Wall Street Journal* (July 14, 1982), p. 46; and "GF Wins in Coffee Price Suit," *Advertising Age* (April 30, 1984), pp. 1, 78.

CHAPTER THIRTEEN

1 "Saturn Widens Traditional Rings of Auto Distribution," *Marketing News* (July 17, 1987), p. 1; "Japanese Automakers Look Toward Luxury Car Market," *Dallas Times Herald* (August 23, 1987), p. L3; "Auto Makers Want to Ensure That You Don't Identify New Cars with the Old," *The Wall Street Journal* (January 18, 1985), p. 19; "Detroit's New Goal: Putting Yuppies in the Driver's Seat," *Business Week* (September 3, 1984), pp. 16-17; "Toyota Takes Aim at Luxury Market," *Dallas Times Herald* (July 29, 1987), p. 5D; "Honda Hits Early Snags in Effort to Enter the Luxury Car Market," *The Wall Street Journal* (September 24, 1986), p. 31.

2 "Computer Retailers: Things Have Gone from Worse to Bad," *Business Week* (June 8, 1987), pp. 104-105; "Computer Battle for Shelf Space," *Dun's Business Month* (August 1983), pp. 72-73.

3 "Porsche Is Doing Great—So Changes Course," *Fortune* (March 1984), p. 30.

4 Michael D. Hutt and Thomas W. Speh, *Industrial Marketing Management*, 3rd ed. (Chicago: Dryden Press, 1985), pp. 314-315.

5 James D. Hlavacek and Tommy J. McCuistion, "Industrial Distributors—When, Who, and How?" *Harvard Business Review* (March-April 1983), pp. 96-101.

6 For an extended discussion on dual distribution, see John A. Quelch, "Why Not Exploit Dual Marketing?" *Business Horizons* (January-February 1987), pp. 52-60; Robert E. Weigand, "Fit Products and Channels to Your Market," *Harvard Business Review* (January-February 1977), pp. 95-105.

7 For an extended treatment of direct marketing, see Herbert Katzenstein and William S. Sachs, *Direct Marketing* (Columbus, Ohio: C.E. Merrill Publishing Company, 1986).
8 "Food Giants Take to the Mails to Push Fancy Product Lines," *The Wall Street Journal* (February 28, 1985), p. 35.
9 For estimates on the size and growth of direct marketing, see "Direct Response Billings by Nine Categories," *Advertising Age* (March 26, 1987), p. 53; Robert M. Sabloff, "The Future of Canadian Direct Response: Vast Opportunities," *Direct Marketing* (October 1984), pp. 76-88.
10 Stanley D. Sibly and R. Kenneth Teas, "The Manufacturer's Agent in Industrial Distribution," *Industrial Marketing Management* (November 1979), pp. 286-292.
11 Nancy Giges, "Grocers 'Middleman' Step to the Forefront," *Advertising Age* (October 11, 1982), pp. M18, M19ff.
12 Donald J. Jackson, Robert F. Krampf, and Leonard J. Konopa, "Factors that Influence the Length of Industrial Channels," *Industrial Marketing Management* (October 1982), pp. 263-268.
13 Louis W. Stern and Adel I. El-Ansary, *Marketing Channels*, 3rd ed. (Englewood Cliffs, N.J.: Prentice-Hall, Inc., 1988), p. 316.
14 See "Portrait of a Franchise," *Inc.* (April 1988), pp. 125-126; *Statistical Abstract of the United States,* 107th ed. (Washington, D.C.: U.S. Department of Commerce, 1987).
15 This description of franchise arrangements is adapted from J. Barry Mason and Morris L. Mayer, *Modern Retailing,* 4th ed. (Plano, Tex.: Business Publications, Inc., 1987), pp. 773-776.
16 "Coke's New Program to Placate Bottlers," *Business Week* (October 12, 1981), p. 48.
17 "Fuller Brush Hopes to Clean Up by Expanding to Retail Stores," *Dallas Times Herald* (September 15, 1987), pp. C1, C5.
18 "Merrill Lynch's Big Dilemma," *Business Week* (January 16, 1984), pp. 60-67.
19 Toby Levin, "Flower Power," *SKY* (February 1987), pp. 11-16.
20 "Distributors: No Endangered Species," *Industry Week* (January 24, 1983), pp. 47-52.
21 "Liquid Paper Corporation," in Roger A. Kerin and Robert A. Peterson, *Strategic Marketing Problems: Cases and Comments,* 4th ed. (Boston: Allyn & Bacon, Inc., 1987), pp. 394-413.
22 Richard Green, "A Boutique in Your Living Room," *Forbes* (May 7, 1984), pp. 86-94.
23 Milton P. Brown, Richard N. Cardozo, Scott M. Cunningham, Walter J. Salmon, and Ralph G.M. Sultan, *Problems in Marketing,* 4th ed. (New York: McGraw-Hill Book Company, 1968), pp. 293-294.
24 "Auto Makers Want to Ensure that You Don't Identify New Cars with the Old," *The Wall Street Journal* (January 18, 1985), p. 19.
25 For recent examples of channel conflict, see Allan J. Magrath and Kenneth G. Hardy, "Avoiding the Pitfalls in Managing Distribution Channels," *Business Horizons* (September-October 1987), pp. 29-33.
26 Kenneth G. Hardy and Allan J. Magrath, *Marketing Channel Management* (Glenview, Ill.: Scott, Foresman & Company, 1988), pp. 102-109.
27 "Heinz Struggles to Stay at the Top of the Stack," *Business Week* (March 11, 1985), p. 49.
28 Rogert W. Little, "The Marketing Channel: Who Should Lead This Extracorporate Organization?" *Journal of Marketing* (January 1970), pp. 31-39.
29 Recent studies that explore the dimensions and use of power and influence in marketing channels include: Gul Butaney and Lawrence H. Wortzel, "Distributor Power Versus Manufacturer Power: The Customer Role," *Journal of Marketing* (January 1988), pp. 52-63; Kenneth A. Hunt, John T. Mentzer, and Jeffrey E. Danes, "The Effect of Power Sources on Compliance in a Channel of Distribution: A Causal Model," *Journal of Business Research* (October 1987), pp. 377-398; John F. Gaski, "Interrelations Among a Channel Entity's Power Sources: Impact of the Exercise of Reward and Coercion on Expert, Referent, and Legitimate Power Sources," *Journal of Marketing Research* (February 1986), pp. 62-67; Gary Frazier and John O. Summers, "Interfirm Influence Strategies and Their Application Within Distribution Channels," *Journal of Marketing* (Summer 1984), pp. 43-55; Sudhir Kale, "Dealer Perceptions of Manufacturer Power and Influence Strategies in a Developing Country," *Journal of Marketing Research* (November 1986), pp. 387-393; George H. Lucus and Larry G. Gresham, "Power, Conflict, Control, and the Application of Contingency Theory in Channels of Distribution," *Journal of the Academy of Marketing Science* (Summer 1985), pp. 27-37.
30 Portions of this discussion are based on Bert Rosenbloom, *Marketing Channels: A Management View,* 3rd ed. (Chicago: Dryden Press, 1987), pp. 91-99; Hardy and Magrath (reference cited), pp. 492-500; Stern and El-Ansary (reference cited), pp. 370-409.

CHAPTER FOURTEEN

1 James C. Johnson and Donald F. Wood, *Contemporary Physical Distribution and Logistics,* 3rd ed. (New York: Macmillan Publishing Company, 1986), pp. 7-8.
2 Adapted from Donald V. Harper, *Transportation in America,* 2nd ed. (Englewood Cliffs, N.J.: Prentice-Hall, Inc., 1982), p. 97.
3 Roy D. Shapiro, "Get Leverage from Logistics," *Harvard Business Review* (May-June 1984), p. 124.
4 Johnson and Wood (reference cited), p. 3.
5 Bernard J. LaLonde and Paul H. Zinszer, *Customer Service: Meaning and Measurement* (Chicago: National Council of Physical Distribution Management, 1976).
6 "'Superwarehouses' Chomp into the Food Business," *Business Week* (April 16, 1984), p. 72.
7 Philip B. Schary, *Logistics Decisions* (Chicago: Dryden Press, 1984), pp. 358-359.
8 John J. Coyle and Edward J. Bardi, *The Management of Business Logistics,* 3rd ed. (St. Paul, Minn.: West Publishing Company, 1984), pp. 96-101.
9 Donald B. Thompson, "Customer Service Nears Center Stage," *Industry Week* (September 5, 1983), pp. 59-61.
10 Coyle and Bardi (reference cited), p. 95.
11 "Why Federal Express Has Overnight Anxiety," *Business Week* (November 9, 1987), pp. 62-66.
12 "The Basic Problem: Skyrocketing Costs," *Purchasing Week* (October 25, 1971), p. 18.

13 R.H. Ballou, *Business Logistics Management* (Englewood Cliffs, N.J.: Prentice-Hall, Inc., 1973), p. 106.

14 John G. Smale and John E. Pepper, "Letter to Shareholders," (Cincinnati: Procter & Gamble Company, June 11, 1987).

15 Hank Gilman, "Rural Retailing Chains Prosper by Combining Service, Sophistication," *The Wall Street Journal* (July 2, 1984), p. 1.

16 "Wal-Mart Credits Deep Discounts to Hub-and-Spoke Planning," *Marketing News* (June 20, 1986), p. 18.

17 Bernard J. LaLonde and Douglas M. Lambert, "A Methodology for Determining Inventory Carrying Costs: Two Case Studies," in James Robeson and John Grabner, eds., *Proceedings of the Fifth Annual Transportation and Logistics Educators' Conference* (October 1975), p. 47.

18 A. Ansari and Jim Heckel, "JIT Purchasing: Impact of Freight and Inventory Costs," *Journal of Purchasing and Materials Management* (Summer 1987), pp. 24-28.

CHAPTER FIFTEEN

1 William Dunn, "Edmonton's Eighth Wonder of the World," *American Demographics* (February 1986), p. 20; William Severini Kowinski, "Endless Summer at the World's Biggest Shopping Wonderland," *Smithsonian* (December 1986), pp. 35-43.

2 *Statistical Abstract of the United States,* 107th ed. (Washington, D.C.: U.S. Department of Commerce, Bureau of Census, 1987), p. 759.

3 Joel Dryfuss, "More Power to the PC Chains," *Fortune* (May 1, 1984), pp. 83-88.

4 Based on estimates from the *Co-op Directory,* 8th ed. (Albuquerque, N.M.: Co-op Directory, 1980); A.C. Nielsen Company, "Review of Retail Grocery Store Trends," *Chain Store Age / Supermarkets* (October 1980), pp. 45-76.

5 Jack Craig, *Multinational Cooperatives: An Alternative for Development* (Saskatoon, Canada: Western Producer Prairie, 1976).

6 Ronald C. Curhan and Edward G. Wertheim, "Consumer Food Buy Cooperatives—A Market Examined," *Journal of Retailing,* Vol. 48 (1972-1973), pp. 29-39; Ann Able Hoyt, "An Analysis of a Consumer Food Buying Cooperative," Master's thesis (Davis: University of California, 1973); Robert Sommer, William E. Hohn, and Jason Tybu, "Motivation of Food Cooperative Members: Reply to Curhan and Wertheim," *Journal of Retailing,* Vol. 57 (Winter 1981), pp. 114-117.

7 Janice Castro, "Franchising Fever," *Time* (August 31, 1987), pp. 36-38.

8 Anthony Ramirez, "Department Stores Shape Up," *Fortune* (September 1, 1986), pp. 50-52.

9 "Wal-Mart Launches Hypermarket U.S.A.," *Discount Store News* (January 18, 1988), pp. 1, 4, 11; Thomas C. Hayes, "The Hypermarket: 5 Acres of Store," *The New York Times* (February 4, 1988), pp. D1, D2; Susan Zimmerman, "Wal-Mart Opens First Supermarket," *Supermarket News* (March 7, 1988), pp. 1, 8.

10 "Hypermarkets: Successful at Last?" *Chain Store Age Executive* (January 1988), pp. 15-18.

11 Ann Hagedorn, "'Tis Already the Season for Catalog Firms," *The New York Times* (November 24, 1987), p. 16.

12 "Catalogue Fallout," *Fortune* (January 20, 1986), pp. 63, 64; "Catalogs Extending Reach via New Distribution Outlets," *Marketing News* (February 3, 1987), p. 12.

13 Joel Schwartz, "The Evolution of Retailing," *American Demographics* (December 1986), pp. 30-37.

14 William Church, "Shopping at Home," *American Way* (March 19, 1985), pp. 27, 29.

15 "25% of Homes to Get Videotex by '90: Delphi Panel," *Marketing News* (November 9, 1984), p. 1.

16 *Prestel Magazine,* "Prestel and Telecard Launch New Service," 1st ed. (1986), p. 1.

17 "CDN Joins Growing List of Failed Teleshoppers," *Discount Store News* (January 4, 1988), pp. 3, 66; "Teleshopping Seminars: Industry Entering Battle for Survival Phase," *Discount Store News* (January 4, 1988), pp. 3, 66.

18 The following discussion is adapted from William T. Gregor and Eileen M. Friars, "Money Merchandising: Retail Revolution in Consumer Financial Services" (Cambridge, Mass.: Management Analysis Center, Inc., 1982).

19 William Lazer and Eugene J. Kelley, "The Retailing Mix: Planning and Management," *Journal of Retailing* (Spring 1961), pp. 34-41.

20 "Where the Buyers Are," *World* (January-February 1986), pp. 38-42; "The Mad Rush to Join the Warehouse Club," *Fortune* (January 6, 1986), pp. 59-61.

21 Joseph H. Ellis, "The Warehouse Club Industry: Summary and Update," research report by Goldman Sachs & Co. (New York: July 25, 1986).

22 Kenneth M. Chanko, "One-Price Apparel Stores Carve Niche Below Off-Price Chains," *Discount Store News* (March 14, 1988), pp. 3, 32.

23 Pierre Martineau, "The Personality of the Retail Store," *Harvard Business Review,* Vol. 36 (January-February 1958), p. 47.

24 See, for example, the special issue on store image, *Journal of Retailing,* Vol. 50 (Winter 1974-1975); Ronald B. Marks, "Operationalizing the Concept of Store Image," *Journal of Retailing,* Vol. 52 (Fall 1970), pp. 37-46; Leon G. Schiffman, Joseph F. Dash, and William R. Dillon, "The Contribution of Store Image Characteristics to Store-Type Choice," *Journal of Retailing* (Summer 1977), pp. 3-14; Robert A. Hansen and Terry Deutscher, "An Empirical Investigation of Attribute Importance in Retail Store Selection," *Journal of Retailing,* Vol. 53 (Winter 1977-1978), pp. 59-72.

25 Hal Lancaster, "Trendy Men's Store Finds Locking Door Is a Key to Its Success," *The Wall Street Journal* (January 22, 1981), p. 1.

26 Scott Kilman, "Retailers Change Their Stores and Goods, Looking to Cash In on New Buying Habits," *The Wall Street Journal* (September 8, 1986), p. 21.

27 Philip Kotler, "Atmosphere as a Marketing Tool," *Journal of Retailing,* Vol. 49 (Winter 1973-1974), p. 61.

28 The wheel of retailing theory was originally proposed by Malcolm P. McNair, "Significant Trends and Development in the Postwar Period," in A.B. Smith, ed., *Competitive Distribution in a Free, High-Level Economy and Its Implications for the University* (Pittsburgh: University of Pittsburgh Press, 1958), pp. 1-25; see also Stanley C. Hollander, "The Wheel of Retailing," *Journal of Marketing* (July 1960), pp. 37-42; "Will the Wheel of Retailing Stop Turning?" *Akron Business and Economic Review* (Summer 1978), pp. 26-29; Malcolm P. McNair and Eleanor May, "The Next Revolution of the

Retailing Wheel," *Harvard Business Review* (September-October 1978), pp. 81-91.

29 Stephen P. Galante, "Some Hamburger Restaurants See Their Future in the 1950's," *The Wall Street Journal* (September 8, 1986), p. 29.

30 William R. Davidson, Albert D. Bates, and Stephen J. Bass, "Retail Life Cycle," *Harvard Business Review* (November-December 1976), pp. 89-96.

31 "At Today's Supermarket, the Computer Is Doing It All," *Business Week* (August 11, 1986), pp. 64-65.

32 Ramirez (reference cited).

33 J. Barry Mason and Morris J. Mayer, "Retail Merchandise Information Systems for the 1980's," *Journal of Retailing*, Vol. 56 (Spring 1980), pp. 56-76; Richard K. Robinson and Frederick W. Langehr, "Consumers' Evaluation of Selected Aspects of Supermarket Scanners," in Neil Beckwith, Michael Houston, Robert Mittlestaedt, Kent B. Monroe, and Scott Ward, eds., *1979 Educator's Conference Proceedings* (Chicago: American Marketing Association, 1979), pp. 389-391; "Scanning 1½ Years Later," *Chain Store Age Executive*, Vol. 52 (February 1976), pp. 16-17; Michael D. Pommer, Eric N. Berkowitz, and John R. Walton, "UPC Scanning: An Assessment of Shopper Response to Technological Change," *Journal of Retailing*, Vol. 56 (Summer 1980), pp. 25-44.

34 James M. Sinkula, "Status of Company Usage of Scanner Based Research," *Journal of the Academy of Marketing Science* (Spring 1986), pp. 63-71.

35 "More than One Way to Catch a Thief," *Chain Store Age Executive* (April 1982), p. 39.

36 "Athlete's Foot Steps on Theft," *Chain Store Age Executive* (July 1987), pp. 103-106.

CHAPTER SIXTEEN

1 Patricia Sellers, "How Busch Wins in a Doggy Market," *Fortune*, June 22, 1987, pp. 99-111; "How Do You Follow an Act Like Bud?" *Business Week* (May 2, 1988), pp. 118-119.

2 Ronald Alsop, "In TV Viewers' Favorite 1987 Ads, Offbeat Characters Were the Stars," *The Wall Street Journal* (March 3, 1988) p. 19; "The 10 Favorite TV Campaigns," *Adweek's Marketing Week* (March 7, 1988), p. F.C. 7.

3 Wilbur Schramm, "How Communication Works," in Wilbur Schramm, ed., *The Process and Effects of Mass Communication* (Urbana, Ill.: University of Illinois Press, 1955), pp. 3-26.

4 E. Cooper and M. Jahoda, "The Evasion of Propaganda," *Journal of Psychology*, Vol. 22 (1947), pp. 15-25; H. Hyman and P. Sheatsley, "Some Reasons Why Information Campaigns Fail," *Public Opinion Quarterly*, Vol. 11 (1947), pp. 412-423; J.T. Klapper, *The Effects of Mass Communication* (New York: Free Press, 1960), Chapter VII.

5 David A. Ricks, Jeffrey S. Arpan, and Marilyn Y. Fu, "Pitfalls in Advertising Overseas," *Journal of Advertising Research*, Vol. 14 (December 1974), pp. 47-51.

6 B.C. Cotton and Emerson M. Babb, "Consumer Response to Promotional Deals," *Journal of Marketing*, Vol. 42 (July 1978), pp. 109-113.

7 Robert George Brown, "Sales Response to Promotions and Advertising," *Journal of Advertising Research*, Vol. 14 (August 1974), pp. 33-40.

8 Dunn Sunnoo and Lynn Y.S. Lin, "Sales Effects of Promotion and Advertising," *Journal of Advertising Research*, Vol. 18 (October 1978), pp. 37-42.

9 J. Ronald Carey, Stephen A. Clique, Barbara A. Leighton, and Frank Milton, "A Test of Positive Reinforcement of Customers," *Journal of Marketing*, Vol. 40 (October 1976), pp. 98-100.

10 Sellers (reference cited).

11 "Promotional Practices Survey," *Adweek's Marketing Week* (March 14, 1988), pp. 10-11.

12 *Consumer Promotion Report* (monograph) (New York: Dancer, Fitzgerald, Sample, 1982).

13 Felix Kessler, "The Costly Coupon Craze," *Fortune* (July 9, 1986), pp. 83-84.

14 Roger A. Strang, "Sales Promotion—Fast Growth, Faulty Management," *Harvard Business Review*, Vol. 54 (July-August 1976), pp. 115-124; Ronald W. Ward and James E. Davis, "Coupon Redemption," *Journal of Advertising Research*, Vol. 18 (August 1978), pp. 51-58; similar results on favorable mail-distributed coupons were reported by Alvin Schwartz, "The Influence of Media Characteristics on Coupon Redemption," *Journal of Marketing*, Vol. 30 (January 1966), pp. 41-46.

15 Michael deCourcy Hinds, "Rebates Can Be Both a Blessing and a Curse, But Manufacturers Often Lose Business Without Them," *Star and Tribune* (April 24, 1988), pp. 1E, 6E.

16 Scott Hume, "Burger King Drinks to the 'Jedi,'" *Advertising Age* (August 22, 1983), pp. M10, M11.

17 "Ralston-Purina Offers Adult Incentive in Kids' Cereal Boxes," *Marketing News* (April 25, 1988), p. 1.

18 William A. Robinson, *Best Sales Promotions of 1977-78* (Chicago: Crain Books, 1979), p. 93.

19 Don A. Schultz and William A. Robinson, *Sales Promotion Essentials* (Chicago: Crain Books, 1982).

20 Fred C. Allvine, Richard D. Teach, and John Connelly, Jr., "The Demise of Promotional Games," *Journal of Advertising Research*, Vol. 16 (October 1976), pp. 79-84.

21 "P&G Tests Bleach-Added Tide," *Advertising Age* (February 1, 1988), p. 1.

22 "New Handy Snack Display Is Dandy," *Marketing News* (October 9, 1987), p. 15.

23 "Coming to a Shopping Cart near You: TV Commercials," *Business Week* (May 30, 1988), p. 61; "VideOcart Shopping Cart with Computer Screen Creates New Ad Medium that Also Gathers Data," *Marketing News* (May 9, 1988), pp. 1-2.

24 Marvin A. Jolson, Joshua L. Wiener, and Richard B. Rosecky, "Correlates of Rebate Proneness," *Journal of Advertising Research* (February-March 1987), pp. 33-43.

25 This discussion is drawn primarily from John A. Quelch, *Trade Promotions by Grocery Manufacturers: A Management Perspective* (Cambridge, Mass.: Marketing Science Institute, August 1982).

26 Michael Chevalier and Ronald C. Curhan, "Retail Promotions as a Function of Trade Promotions: A Descriptive Analysis," *Sloan Management Review*, Vol. 18 (Fall 1976), pp. 19-32.

27 Robert S. Mason, "What's a PR Director for Anyway?" *Harvard Business Review*, Vol. 52 (September-October 1974), pp.

120-126; Jack Bernstein, "Kroll, Roman Discuss Role of PR," *Advertising Age* (April 11, 1988), pp. 42-43.

28 "Behind the Scenes Look at Cabbage Patch PR," *Advertising Age* (December 26, 1983), pp. 2, 18; Steven Flax, "The Christmas Zing in Zapless Toys," *Fortune,* Vol. 108 (December 26, 1983), pp. 98-103.

29 P. Rajan Varadarajan and Anil Menon, "Cause-Related Marketing: A Coalignment of Marketing Strategy and Corporate Philanthropy," *Journal of Marketing* (July 1988), pp. 58-74; Kathleen K. Wiegner, "A Cause on Every Carton?" *Forbes* (November 18, 1985), p. 248; Martin Gottlieb, "Cashing In on a Higher Cause," *The New York Times* (July 6, 1986); Monci Jo Williams, "How to Cash In on Do-Good Pitches," *Fortune* (June 9, 1986), pp. 71-76.

30 Jonathan Dahl, "Fare Play: States Target Airlines over Ads and Frequent-Flier Plans," *The Wall Street Journal* (August 31, 1987), p. 19.

31 Courtland L. Bovée and William F. Arens, *Contemporary Advertising* 2nd ed. (Homewood, Ill.: Richard D. Irwin, Inc., 1986), pp. 59-66.

32 Rita Weisskoff, "Current Trends in Children's Advertising," *Journal of Advertising Research* (February-March 1985), pp. RC-12-14.

33 Robert E. Hite and Randy Eck, "Advertising to Children: Attitudes of Business vs. Consumers," *Journal of Advertising Research* (October-November 1987), pp. 40-53.

34 "FCC Loses in Ruling on Children's TV Program," *Marketing News* (October 23, 1987), p. 1; Bob Davis, "Ruling Reopens Issue of Regulation of Children's TV," *The Wall Street Journal* (June 29, 1987), p. 26.

35 Thomas W. Leigh, Arno J. Rethans, and Tamatha Reichenbach Whitney, "Role Portrayals of Women In Advertising: Cognitive Responses and Advertising Effectiveness," *Journal of Advertising Research* (October-November 1987), pp. 54-63.

CHAPTER SEVENTEEN

1 Dennis Kneale, "'Zapping' of TV Ads Appears Pervasive," *The Wall Street Journal* (April 25, 1988), p. 21.

2 Ronald Alsop, "Can Scooter Ads Get Any More Offbeat Than This?" *The Wall Street Journal* (June 4, 1987), p. 27.

3 Kneale (reference cited).

4 David A. Aaker and Donald Norris, "Characteristics of TV Commercials Perceived as Informative," *Journal of Advertising Research,* Vol. 22, No. 2 (April-May 1982), pp. 61-70.

5 William Wilkie and Paul W. Farris, "Comparison Advertising: Problems and Potentials," *Journal of Marketing,* Vol. 39, No. 4 (October 1975), pp. 7-15.

6 Bill Abrams, "Comparative Ads Are Getting More Popular, Hard Hitting," *The Wall Street Journal* (March 11, 1982), p. 25.

7 Dorothy Cohen, "The FTC's Advertising Substantiation Program," *Journal of Marketing* (Winter 1980), pp. 26-35; Michael Etger and Stephen A. Goodwin, "Planning for Comparative Advertising Requires Special Attention," *Journal of Advertising,* Vol. 8, No. 1 (Winter 1979), pp. 26-32.

8 Joe Agnew, "Hot-Air Balloons Rise in Popularity as High-Visibility Promotion Device," *Marketing News* (April 11, 1988), pp. 1-2.

9 Robert Selwitz, "The Selling of an Image," *Madison Avenue* (February 1985), pp. 61-69.

10 Robert J. Lavidge and Gary A. Steiner, "A Model for Predictive Measurements of Advertising Effectiveness," *Journal of Marketing* (October 1961), p. 61.

11 Patrick McGeehan and Verne Gay, "Super Bowl-Buster," *Advertising Age* (December 7, 1987), pp. 1, 76.

12 Charles H. Patti and Vincent Blanko, "Budgeting Practices of Big Advertisers," *Journal of Advertising Research,* Vol. 21 (December 1981), pp. 23-30.

13 Jeffrey A. Lowenhar and John L. Stanton, "Forecasting Competitive Advertising Expenditures," *Journal of Advertising Research,* Vol. 16, No. 2 (April 1976), pp. 37-44.

14 Daniel Seligman, "How Much for Advertising?" *Fortune* (December 1956), p. 123.

15 Patti and Blanko (reference cited).

16 Jimmy D. Barnes, Brenda J. Muscove, and Javad Rassouli, "An Objective and Task Media Selection Decision Model and Advertising Cost Formula to Determine International Advertising Budgets," *Journal of Advertising,* Vol. 11, No. 4 (1982), pp. 68-75.

17 Scott Hume, "Tom McElligott: The Engine that Powers FMR's Creative Machine," *Advertising Age* (June 20, 1985), pp. 5-9; Eleanor Johnson Tracy, "Envy of Madison Avenue: A Minneapolis Ad Agency," *Fortune* (March 4, 1985), p. 89; Mike Meyers, "Fallon McElligott Changing 2 Images," *Star and Tribune* (October 12, 1987), pp. 1M, 7M.

18 John Pfeiffer, "Six Months and a Half a Million Dollars, All for 15 Seconds," *Smithsonian* (October 1987), pp. 134-135; Alex Ben Block, "Where the Money Goes," *Forbes* (September 21, 1987), pp. 178-180.

19 Joanne Lipman, "Ad Industry's Health Draws Mixed Prognoses," *The Wall Street Journal* (September 23, 1987), pp. 33, 41.

20 Katherine Barrett, "Taking a Closer Look," *Madison Avenue* (August 1984), pp. 106-109.

21 Gupta Udayan, "A House Divided," *Madison Avenue* (October 1984), pp. 62-64.

22 "Clutter Bucks," *Fortune* (October 29, 1984), pp. 78-79.

23 "Print Ads that Make You Stop, Look—and Listen," *Business Week* (November 23, 1987), p. 38.

24 Erik Larson, "In Direct-Mail Biz, Envelopes Are What Are Run Up Flagpole," *The Wall Street Journal* (May 5, 1986), pp. 1, 15; Jim Powell, "The Lucrative Trade of Creating Junk Mail," *The New York Times* (June 20, 1982), p. F7.

25 Wayne Walley, "Ads Spread to Video Covers," *Advertising Age* (September 14, 1988), p. 21; Dan Wascoe, Jr., "What's New on Restroom Walls? Ads, That's What," *Star and Tribune* (May 9, 1988), p. 30.

26 The discussion of posttesting is based on Courtland L. Boveé and William F. Arens, *Contemporary Advertising,* 2nd ed. (Homewood, Ill.: Richard D. Irwin, Inc., 1988), p. 209.

27 Ronald Alsop, "In TV Viewers' Favorite 1987 Ads, Offbeat Characters Were the Stars," *The Wall Street Journal* (March 3, 1988), p. 19; Ron Gales, "Fateful Attractions: Rollicking Raisins and Manic Noid," *Adweek* (October 12, 1987), pp. 54-59.

CHAPTER EIGHTEEN

1 Personal communication from Wanda Truxillo, April 1, 1988.

2 Patricia Sellers, "How IBM Teaches Techies to Sell," *Fortune* (June 6, 1988), pp. 141-142.

3 *Chief Executive Officer* (Chicago: Heidrick and Struggles, 1987), p. 7.
4 Paul S. Busch and Michael J. Houston, *Marketing: Strategic Foundations* (Homewood, Ill.: Richard D. Irwin, Inc., 1985), p. 706.
5 *Sales and Marketing Management's 1988 Survey of Selling Costs* (February 22, 1988).
6 Marvin A. Jolson, "Prospecting by Telephone Prenotification: An Application of the Foot-In-The-Door Technique," *Journal of Personal Selling and Sales Management* (August 1986), pp. 39-42.
7 G. Scott Osborne, *Electronic Direct Marketing* (Englewood Cliffs, N.J.: Prentice-Hall, Inc., 1984), p. 120.
8 See Marvin A. Jolson, "The Underestimated Potential of the Canned Sales Presentation," *Journal of Marketing* (January 1975), pp. 75-78; James Reed, "Comments on the Underestimated Potential of the Canned Sales Presentation," *Journal of Marketing* (January 1976), pp. 67-68.
9 See "Sales Training," *Training,* Special Issue (February 1988); Michael Belch and Robert W. Haas, "Using Buyer's Needs to Improve Industrial Sales," *Business* (September-October 1979), pp. 8-14; Dennis McDermott and Charles N. Sweitzer, "Product vs. Customer Focus in Industrial Selling," *Industrial Marketing Management,* Vol. 9 (1980), pp. 151-157; Robert Saxe and Barton A. Weitz, "The Soco Scale: A Measure of the Customer Orientation of Salespeople," *Journal of Marketing Research* (August 1983), pp. 343-351.
10 Based on Ronald D. Balsley and E. Patricia Birsner, *Selling: Marketing Personified* (Chicago: Dryden Press, 1987), pp. 261-263.
11 Theodore Levitt, *The Marketing Imagination* (New York: Free Press, 1983), p. 111. See also Monci Jo Williams, "America's Best Salesmen," *Fortune* (October 26, 1987), pp. 122-134; F. Robert Dwyer, Paul H. Schurr, and Sejo Oh, "Developing Buyer-Seller Relationships," *Journal of Marketing* (April 1987), pp. 11-27; Robert E. Spekman and Wesley J. Johnston, "Relationship Management: Managing the Selling and Buying Interface," *Journal of Business Research,* Vol. 14 (1986), pp. 519-531.
12 *Management Briefing: Marketing* (New York: The Conference Board, October 1986), pp. 3-4.
13 See, for example, Troy A. Festervand, Stephen J. Grove, and Eric Reidenbach, "The Sales Force as a Marketing Intelligence System," *Journal of Business & Industrial Marketing* (Winter 1988), pp. 53-60.
14 For a discussion on managing independent agents, see Joseph A. Bellizzi and Christine Glacken, "Building a More Successful Rep Organization," *Industrial Marketing Management* (August 1986), pp. 207-213.
15 Benson Shapiro, *Sales Program Management: Formulation and Implementation* (New York: McGraw-Hill Book Company, 1977), pp. 250-255.
16 Louis A. Wallis, *Marketing Priorities* (New York: The Conference Board, 1987), p. 6.
17 Walter J. Talley, "How to Design Sales Territories," *Journal of Marketing* (January 1961), pp. 7-13.
18 Gilbert A. Churchill, Jr., Neil M. Ford, and Orville C. Walker, Jr., *Sales Force Management: Planning, Implementation, and Control* (Homewood, Ill.: Richard D. Irwin, Inc., 1985), p. 72.
19 William J. Stanton and Richard H. Buskirk, *Management of the Sales Force,* 7th ed. (Homewood, Ill.: Richard D. Irwin, Inc., 1987), p. 97.
20 Alan J. Dubinsky and Thomas E. Barry, "A Survey of Sales Management Practices," *Industrial Marketing Management,* Vol. 11 (1980), pp. 130-140.
21 *Sales and Marketing Management's 1988 Survey of Selling Costs* (reference cited).
22 See, for example, Walter Kiechel III, "How to Manage Salespeople," *Fortune* (March 14, 1988), pp. 179-180; Richard C. Beckerer, Fred Morgan, and Lawrence Richard, "The Job Characteristics of Industrial Salespersons: Relationship to Motivation and Satisfaction," *Journal of Marketing* (Fall 1982), pp. 125-135; Thomas Ingram and Danny N. Bellenger, "Motivational Segments in the Sales Force," *California Management Review* (Spring 1982), pp. 81-88.
23 Gilbert A. Churchill, Jr., Neil M. Ford, and Orville C. Walker, Jr., "Personal Characteristics of Salespeople and the Attractiveness of Alternative Rewards," *Journal of Business Research,* Vol. 7 (1979), pp. 25-50.
24 Donald W. Jackson, Jr., Janet E. Keith, and John Schlacter, "Evaluation of Selling Performance: A Study of Current Practice," *Journal of Personal Selling and Sales Management* (November 1983), pp. 43-51.
25 Jerry McAdams, "Rewarding Sales and Marketing Performance," *Management Review* (April 1987), pp. 33-38. See also Gilbert A. Churchill, Jr., Neil M. Ford, Steven W. Hartley, and Orville C. Walker, Jr., "The Determinants of Salesperson Performance: A Meta-Analysis," *Journal of Marketing Research* (May 1985), pp. 103-118.

CHAPTER NINETEEN

1 Robert Johnson, "General Mills Risks Millions Starting Chain of Italian Restaurants," *The Wall Street Journal* (September 21, 1987), pp. 1, 15.
2 *General Mills Review, First Quarter, 1988* (Minneapolis: General Mills, 1988), p. 7; *General Mills Review, Second Quarter, 1988* (Minneapolis: General Mills, 1988), pp. 11-13.
3 David A. Aaker, *Developing Business Strategies* (New York: John Wiley & Sons, Inc., 1984), pp. 5-9; Victor J. Cook, Jr., "Marketing Strategy and Differential Advantage," *Journal of Marketing* (Spring 1983), pp. 68-75; Pankaj Ghemawat, "Sustainable Advantage," *Harvard Business Review* (September-October 1986), pp. 53-58; Michael E. Porter, *Competitive Advantage* (New York: Free Press, 1985).
4 *General Mills Review, First Quarter, 1988* (reference cited), pp. 4-15; Francine Schwadel and Richard Gibson, "General Mills to Sell Last Retail Units, Talbot's and Bauer, for $585 Million," *The Wall Street Journal* (May 19, 1988), p. 4.
5 Johnson (reference cited), pp. 1, 15.
6 Stanley F. Stasch and Patricia Langtree, "Can Your Marketing Planning Procedures Be Improved?" *Journal of Marketing* (Summer 1980), pp. 79-90; David S. Hopkins, *The Marketing Plan* (New York: The Conference Board, 1981), p. 24.
7 Hopkins (reference cited), p. 24.
8 Michael E. Porter, *Competitive Strategies: Techniques for Analyzing Industries and Competitors* (New York: Free Press, 1980); George S. Day, *Strategic Market Planning* (St. Paul, Minn.: West Publishing Company, 1984), pp. 101-128; William K. Hall, "Survival Strategies in a Hostile Environment," *Harvard Business Review* (September-October 1980), pp. 75-85.

9 "Hershey: A Hefty Ad Budget Has Profits Flying High," *Business Week* (February 13, 1984), p. 88; Michael E. Porter, "How to Attack the Industry Leader," *Fortune* (April 29, 1985), pp. 153-166.
10 Joseph A. Lawton, "Kodak Penetrates the European Copier Market with Customized Marketing Strategy and Product Changes," *Marketing News* (August 3, 1984), p. 1.
11 Steve Gross, "3M Holds Share in Competitive Videotape Sales," *Minneapolis Star and Tribune* (July 19, 1987), pp. 10, 6D.
12 "Culture Shock at Xerox," *Business Week* (June 22, 1987), pp. 106-110; Maggie McComas, "Cutting Costs Without Killing the Business," *Fortune* (October 13, 1986), pp. 70-78.
13 Philip Kotler, *Marketing Management,* 6th ed. (Englewood Cliffs, N.J.: Prentice-Hall, Inc., 1988), pp. 38-40.
14 George S. Day, "Diagnosing the Product Portfolio," *Journal of Marketing* (April 1977), pp. 29-38.
15 Strengths and weaknesses of the BCG technique are based largely on Derek F. Abell and John S. Hammond, *Strategic Market Planning: Problem and Analytic Approaches* (Englewood Cliffs, N.J.: Prentice-Hall, Inc., 1979); Yoram Wind, Vijay Mahajan, and Donald Swire, "An Empirical Comparison of Standardized Portfolio Models," *Journal of Marketing* (Spring 1983), pp. 89-99.
16 Robert D. Buzzell, Bradley T. Gale, and Ralph G.M. Sultan, "Market Share—A Key to Profitability," *Harvard Business Review* (January-February 1975), pp. 97-106; Carolyn Y. Woo and Arnold C. Cooper, "The Surprising Case for Low Market Share," *Harvard Business Review* (November-December 1982), pp. 106-113; Robert Jacobson and David A. Aaker, "Is Market Share All that It's Cracked Up to Be?" *Journal of Marketing* (Fall 1985), pp. 11-22.
17 Derek F. Abell, *Defining the Business: The Starting Point of Strategic Planning* (Englewood Cliffs, N.J.: Prentice-Hall, Inc., 1980), Chapter 8.
18 Michael G. Harvey and Roger A. Kerin, "Diagnosis and Management of the Product Cannibalism Syndrome," *University of Michigan Business Review* (November 1979), pp. 18-24.
19 Thomas J. Peters and Robert H. Waterman, Jr., *In Search of Excellence: Lessons from America's Best-Run Companies* (New York: Harper & Row, Publishers, Inc., 1982); Michael E. Porter, "From Competitive Advantage to Corporate Strategy," *Harvard Business Review* (May-June 1987), pp. 43-59.
20 George S. Yip, "Gateways to Entry," *Harvard Business Review* (September-October 1980), pp. 85-92.
21 Walter Kiechel III, "Corporate Strategy for the 1990s," *Fortune* (February 29, 1988), pp. 34-42; Enrique R. Arzac, "Do Your Business Units Create Shareholder Value?" *Harvard Business Review* (January-February 1986), pp. 121-126; Alfred Rappaport, "Selecting Strategies that Create Shareholder Value," *Harvard Business Review* (May-June 1981), pp. 139-149.
22 General Mills, "The Yogurt Market" (April 4, 1977); General Mills, "Growth Through Acquisition" (1984) (company documents).
23 *General Mills: 1983 Annual Report* (August 19, 1983).

CHAPTER TWENTY

1 J.A. Dunnigan, "Hard Work, Hot Delivery Put Domino's on the Map," *Entrepreneur* (April 1985), pp. 52-55.
2 Much of the Domino's Pizza material is taken from Bernie Whalen, "'People-Oriented' Marketing Delivers a Lot of Dough for Domino's," *Marketing News* (March 15, 1984), p. 4ff; by permission of the American Marketing Association.
3 Kevin T. Hoggins, "Home Delivery Is Helping Pizza to Battle Burgers," *Marketing News* (August 1, 1986), pp. 1, 6; "A Saucy Fight for a Slice of the Pie," *Time* (April 18, 1988), p. 60.
4 Thomas V. Bonoma, "Making Your Marketing Strategy Work," *Harvard Business Review* (March-April 1984), pp. 69-76.
5 "Jack Welch, How Good a Manager?" *Business Week* (December 14, 1987), p. 95.
6 Thomas J. Peters and Robert H. Waterman, Jr., *In Search of Excellence: Lessons from America's Best-Run Companies* (New York: Harper & Row, Publishers, Inc., 1982).
7 Roy J. Harris, Jr., "The Skunk Works: Hush-Hush Projects Often Emerge There," *The Wall Street Journal* (October 13, 1980), p. 1; Tom Peters, "Winners Do Hundreds of Percent Over Norm," *Minneapolis Star and Tribune* (January 8, 1985), p. 5B.
8 "How the Best Get Better," *Business Week* (September 14, 1987), pp. 98-120.
9 "How Ford Hit the Bull's Eye with Taurus," *Business Week* (June 30, 1986), pp. 69-70.
10 The scheduling example is adapted from William Rudelius and W. Bruce Erickson, *An Introduction to Contemporary Business,* 4th ed. (New York: Harcourt Brace Jovanovich, Inc., 1985), pp. 94-95.
11 Philip Kotler, *Marketing Management,* 6th ed. (Englewood Cliffs, N.J.: Prentice-Hall, Inc., 1988), p. 709.
12 Robert W. Ruekert and Orville W. Walker, Jr., "Marketing's Interaction with Other Functional Units: A Conceptural Framework and Empirical Evidence," *Journal of Marketing* (January 1987), pp. 1-19.
13 John A. Quelch, Paul W. Farris, and James Olver, "The Product Management Audit: Design and Survey Findings," *The Journal of Consumer Marketing* (Summer 1987), pp. 45-58.
14 "Power Retailers," *Business Week* (December 21, 1987), pp. 86-92.
15 "A Kick in the Pants for Levi's," *Business Week* (June 11, 1984), p. 47; "How Levi Strauss Is Getting the Lead Out of Its Pipeline," *Business Week* (December 21, 1987), p. 92.
16 John Grossman, "Ken Iverson: Simply the Best," *American Way* (August 1, 1987), pp. 23-25; Thomas Moore, "Goodbye, Corporate Staff," *Fortune* (December 21, 1987), pp. 65-76.
17 Stanley J. Shapiro and V.H. Kirpalani, *Marketing Effectiveness: Insights from Accounting and Finance* (Boston: Allyn & Bacon, Inc., 1984); Leland L. Biek and Stephen L. Busby, "Profitability Analysis by Market Segments," *Journal of Marketing* (July 1973), pp. 48-53; V.H. Kirpalani and Stanley J. Shapiro, "Financial Dimensions of Marketing Management," *Journal of Marketing* (July 1973), pp. 40-47; Paul Fischer and W.J.E. Crissy, "New Approaches to Analyzing Marketing Profitability," *Journal of Marketing* (April 1974), pp. 43-48.
18 G. David Hughes, "Computerized Sales Management," *Harvard Business Review* (March-April 1983), pp. 102-112.
19 Philip Kotler, William Gregor, and William Rogers, "The

Marketing Audit Comes of Age," *Sloan Management Review* (Winter 1977), pp. 25-43.

20 General Mills, "The Yogurt Market" (April 4, 1977); General Mills, "Growth Through Acquisition" (1984); General Mills, *Review* (Third Quarter, 1987), General Mills, *1986 Annual Report* (1986); General Mills, *1987 Annual Report* (1987).

21 Neal St. Anthony, "General Mills Rebounds," *Minneapolis Star and Tribune* (October 19, 1987), pp. 1M, 11M.

CHAPTER TWENTY-ONE

1 Philip Revzin, "While Americans Take to Croissants, Kellogg Pushes Cornflakes on France," *The Wall Street Journal* (November 11, 1986), p. 36.

2 Kenneth Labich, "America's International Winners," *Fortune* (April 14, 1986), pp. 34-46.

3 Alan Farnham, "America's Leading Exporters," *Fortune* (July 20, 1987), pp. 72-73.

4 Mark Gill, "The Great American Chopstick Master," *American Way* (August 1, 1987), pp. 34-36, 78-79.

5 Edward P. Johnson, "U.S. Firms Can Benefit from European Contacts," *Photo Marketing* (March 1987), p. 60.

6 Joseph A. Lawton, "Kodak Penetrates the European Copier Market with Customized Marketing Strategy and Product Changes," *Marketing News* (August 3, 1984), p. 1.

7 Theodore Levitt, "The Globalization of Markets," *Harvard Business Review* (May-June 1983), pp. 92-102; Theodore Levitt, "The Pluralization of Consumption," *Harvard Business Review* (May-June 1988), pp. 7-8.

8 Joanne Lipman, "Marketers Turn Sour on Global Sales Pitch Harvard Guru Makes," *The Wall Street Journal* (May 12, 1988), pp. 1, 10.

9 Lipman (reference cited).

10 S. Tamer Cavusgil, "Guidelines for Export Market Research," *Business Horizons* (November-December 1985), pp. 27-33.

11 "Ivan Starts Learning the Capitalist Ropes," *Business Week* (November 2, 1987), p. 154.

12 Anthony Spaeth, "A Thriving Middle Class is Changing the Face of India," *The Wall Street Journal* (May 19, 1988), p. 22.

13 "McWorld," *Business Week* (October 13, 1986), pp. 78-86; Frederick Katayama, "Japan's Big Mac," *Fortune* (September 15, 1986), pp. 114-120.

14 Michael R. Sesit, "Avoiding Losses," *The Wall Street Journal* (March 5, 1984), pp. 1, 24.

15 Steve Coll and David A. Vise, "Trader's Night Watch: A Computer by the Bed," *International Herald Tribune* (January 18, 1988), pp. 1, 6.

16 "The Mouse that Roared at Pepsi," *Business Week* (September 7, 1987), p. 42.

17 Laurel Wentz, "M & M Continues Global Roll," *Advertising Age* (September 14, 1987), p. 90.

18 Letitia Baldwin, "Genetic Product Sales Enjoy Mexican Windfall," *Advertising Age* (July 9, 1984), p. 36.

19 "Innocents Abroad," *Inc.* (June 1984), p. 19.

20 John Marcom, Jr., "British Industry Suffers from Failure to Heed Basics of Marketing," *The Wall Street Journal* (January 14, 1987), pp. 1, 12.

21 Thomas F. O'Boyle, "German Firms Stress Top Quality, Niches to Keep Exports High," *The Wall Street Journal* (December 10, 1987), pp. 1, 15; Louis S. Richman, "Lessons from German Managers," *Fortune* (April 27, 1987), pp. 267-268.

22 "The Swedes Give AT&T, and the U.S., Painful Black Eyes," *Business Week* (May 4, 1987), pp. 44-45.

23 "GM Moves into a New Era," *Business Week* (July 16, 1984), pp. 48-54.

24 "McDonnell Douglas Grabs a Piece of China's Sky," *Business Week* (August 17, 1987), p. 35.

25 "Honda Is Turning Red, White, and Blue," *Business Week* (October 5, 1987), p. 38; "The Americanization of Honda," *Business Week* (April 25, 1988), pp. 90-96; Alex Taylor III, "Japan's Carmakers Take on the World," *Fortune* (June 20, 1988), pp. 66-76.

26 Peter Gumbel and Douglas R. Sease, "Foreign Firms Build More U.S. Factories, Vex American Rivals," *The Wall Street Journal* (July 24, 1987), pp. 1, 6.

27 Carla Rapoport, "Seasoning for the World's Palate," *Boston Sunday Globe* (October 21, 1984), pp. A9-A10.

28 John Urquhart and Peggy Berkowitz, "Canada Worries Anew over Loss of Identity to Its Big Neighbor," *The Wall Street Journal* (September 22, 1987), pp. 1, 24.

29 Joel Dreyfuss, "How to Beat the Japanese at Home," *Fortune* (August 31, 1987), pp. 80-83.

30 Bill Saporito, "Black & Decker's Gamble on 'Globalization,'" *Fortune* (May 14, 1984), pp. 40-48.

31 Demos Vardiabasis, "Countertrade: New Ways of Doing Business," *Business To Business* (December 1985), pp. 67-71.

32 Shawn Tully, "U.S.-Style TV Turns On Europe," *Fortune* (April 13, 1987), pp. 96-98; John Marcom, Jr., "Cable and Satellites Are Opening Europe to TV Commercials," *The Wall Street Journal* (December 22, 1987), pp. 1, 11; "Toward Real Community," *Time* (April 18, 1988), pp. 54-55.

CHAPTER TWENTY-TWO

1 "Do You Believe in Magic?" *Time* (April 25, 1988), pp. 66-76; "Disney's Magic," *Business Week* (March 9, 1987), pp. 62-69.

2 P.E. Eigher, E. Langeard, Christopher Lovelock, J.E.G. Bateson, and R.F. Young, *Marketing Consumer Services: New Insights* (Cambridge, Mass.: Marketing Science Institute, 1977); John M. Rathmell, *Marketing in the Service Sector* (Cambridge, Mass.: Winthrop Publishers, 1974); G.L. Shostack, "Breaking Free from Product-Marketing," *Journal of Marketing* (April 1977), pp. 73-80; James L. Heskett, "Thank Heaven for the Service Sector," *Business Week* (January 26, 1987), p. 22.

3 *Statistical Abstract of the United States,* 107th ed. (Washington, D.C.: U.S. Department of Commerce, 1987), p. 752.

4 Richard I. Kirkland, Jr., "The Bright Future of Service Exports," *Fortune* (June 8, 1987), pp. 31-36.

5 "Presto! The Convenience Industry: Making Life a Little Simpler," *Business Week* (April 27, 1987), pp. 86-94.

6 Leonard Berry, "Big Ideas in Services Marketing," *Journal of Consumer Marketing,* Vol. 3 (Spring 1986), pp. 47-51.

7 "Standardized Services Run Gamut from Mufflers to Wills," *Marketing News,* Vol. 21 (April 10, 1987), pp. 17, 43; Valerie

A. Zeithaml, Leonard L. Berry, and A. Parasuraman, "Communication and Control in the Delivery of Service Quality," *Journal of Marketing* (April 1988), pp. 35-48.

8 Valarie A. Zeithaml, "How Consumer Evaluation Processes Differ Between Goods and Services," in James H. Donnelly and William R. George, eds., *Marketing of Services* (Chicago: American Marketing Association, 1981).

9 G. Lynn Stostack, "Service Positioning Through Structural Change," *Journal of Marketing,* Vol. 51 (January 1987), pp. 34-43.

10 W. Earl Sasser, R. Paul Olsen, and D. Daryl Wyckoff, *Management of Service Operations* (Boston: Allyn & Bacon, Inc., 1978).

11 "Services Marketers Must Balance Customer Satisfaction Against Their Operational Needs," *Marketing News,* Vol. 20 (October 10, 1986), pp. 1, 14.

12 Patriya Tansuhaj, Donna Randall, and Jim McCullough, "A Services Marketing Management Model: Integrating Internal and External Marketing Functions," *Journal of Services Marketing,* Vol. 2 (Winter 1988), pp. 31-38.

13 Christian Gronroos, "Internal Marketing Theory and Practice," in Tim Bloch, G.D. Upah, and V.A. Zeithaml, eds., *Services Marketing in a Changing Environment* (Chicago: American Marketing Association, 1984).

14 Gronroos (reference cited).

15 James L. Heskett, "Lessons in the Service Sector," *Harvard Business Review* (March/April 1987), pp. 118-126; Leonard Berry, "Big Ideas in Services Marketing," *Journal of Consumer Marketing,* Vol. 3 (Spring 1986), pp. 47-51; Ray Lewis, "Whose Job Is Service Marketing?" *Advertising Age* (August 3, 1987), pp. 18, 20.

16 Dan R.E. Thomas, "Strategy Is Different in Service Businesses," *Harvard Business Review* (July-August 1978), pp. 158-165.

17 Christopher Lovelock, *Services Marketing* (Englewood Cliffs, N.J.: Prentice-Hall, Inc., 1984), pp. 201-207.

18 Kent B. Monroe, "Buyer's Subjective Perceptions of Price," *Journal of Marketing Research* (February 1973), pp. 70-80; Jerry Olson, "Price as an Informational Cue: Effects on Product Evaluation," in A.G. Woodside, J.N. Sheth, and P.D. Bennett, eds., *Consumer and Industrial Buying Behavior* (New York: Elsevier North-Holland, Inc., 1977), pp. 267-286.

19 B.D. Colen, "Hospitals Turn to Advertising," *Washington Post* (June 25, 1979), pp. 1, 6A.

20 "Moving the Dentist's Chair to Retail Stores," *Business Week* (January 19, 1981), p. 56.

21 William R. George and Leonard L. Berry, "Guidelines for the Advertising of Services," *Business Horizons* (July-August 1981), pp. 52-56; Eugene M. Johnson, Eberhard E. Scheuing, and Kathleen A. Gaida, *Profitable Service Marketing* (Homewood, Ill.: Dow-Jones-Irwin, 1986).

22 William A. Mindak and Seymour Fine, "A Fifth P: Public Relations," in James H. Donnelly and William R. George, eds., *Marketing of Services* (Chicago: American Marketing Association, 1981), pp. 71-73.

23 Joe Adams, "Why Public Service Advertising Doesn't Work," *Ad Week* (November 17, 1980), p. 72.

24 Bates and O'Sheen vs. State of Arizona, 433 U.S. 350, 391-395 (1977); "Supreme Court Opens Way for Lawyers to Advertise Prices for Routine Services," *The Wall Street Journal* (June 28, 1977), p. 4.

25 James L. Heskett, *Managing in the Service Economy* (Boston: Harvard Business School Press, 1986), pp. 153-173; James Brian Quinn and Christopher E. Gagnon, "Will Services Follow Manufacturing into Decline?" *Harvard Business Review,* Vol. 64 (November-December 1986), pp. 95-105.

APPENDIX B

1 Nicholas Basta, "The Wide World of Marketing," *Business Week's Guide to Careers* (February-March 1984), pp. 70-72.

2 Maggie McComas, "Atop the Fortune 500: A Survey of the C.E.O.s," *Fortune* (April 28, 1986), pp. 26-31.

3 Victor R. Lindquist, *Northwestern Endicott-Lindquist Report* (Evanston, Ill.: Northwestern University, The Placement Center, 1987), p. 7.

4 Steven S. Ross, "Entry-Level Jobs with a Future," *Business Week's Guide to Careers* (February-March 1984), pp. 35-37, 78.

5 Sandy Gillis, "On the Job: Product Manager," *Business Week's Guide to Careers* (April/May 1988), pp. 63-66; Richard Koenig, "P & G Creates New Posts in Latest Step to Alter How Firm Manages Its Brands," *The Wall Street Journal* (October 12, 1987), p. 23.

6 Phil Moss, "What It's Like to Work for Procter & Gamble," *Business Week's Guide to Careers* (March/April 1987), pp. 18-20.

7 Janine Linden, "The Exciting World of Advertising," *Business Week's Guide to Careers* (Spring/Summer 1984), pp. 33-34, 36.

8 "Demand for Sales, Marketing Execs Rises 7% in Last Six Months of '87," *Marketing News* (February 1, 1988), p. 2.

9 Judith George, "Market Researcher," *Business Week's Guide to Careers* (October 1987), p. 10.

10 Ronald B. Marks, *Personal Selling* (Boston: Allyn & Bacon, Inc., 1985), pp. 451-452.

11 Arthur F. Miller, "Discover Your Design," in *1984-1985 CPC Annual,* Vol. 1 (Bethlehem, Penn.: College Placement Council, Inc., 1984), p. 2.

12 For an alternative approach to conducting a self analysis, see Miller (reference cited), pp. 2-8.

13 Marks (reference cited), pp. 461-462.

14 John L. Munschauer, "How to Find a Customer for Your Capabilities," in *1984-1985 CPC Annual,* Vol. 1 (Bethlehem, Penn.: College Placement Council, Inc., 1984), p. 24.

15 C. Randall Powell, "Secrets of Selling a Resume," in Peggy Schmidt, ed., *The Honda How to Get a Job Guide* (New York: McGraw-Hill Book Co., 1985), pp. 4-9.

16 Powell (reference cited), p. 4.

17 Julie Griffin Levitt, *Your Career: How to Make It Happen* (Cincinnati: South-Western Publishing Co., 1985).

18 Marks (reference cited), p. 469.

19 Bob Weinstein, "What Employers Look For," in Peggy Schmidt, ed., *The Honda How to Get a Job Guide* (New York: McGraw-Hill Book Co., 1985), p. 10.

INDEXES

Author Index

Y

Z

Company and Product Index

General Index

D

Q

R

S

Credits

Table of Contents

pg. xv, Courtesy of Black & Decker; pg. xvi, Courtesy of 3M; pg. xviii, Courtesy of Simmons, Durham & Associates, St. Louis; pg. xx, Photography by John S. Abbott; pg. xxi, Photography by Ray Marklin; pg. xxii, Reprinted Courtesy of Eastman Kodak Company; pg. xxv, Courtesy of AIG.

Chapter 1

pg. 2, © Mitch Kezar; pg. 6, Courtesy of the Xerox Corporation; pg. 9, Tanker cartoon, drawing by Richter, © 1988 The New Yorker Magazine, Inc.; pg. 9, diet Coke, photography by Ray Marklin; pg. 11, RCA Selectavision player, Courtesy of RCA; pg. 11, Strawberry Shortcake, Courtesy of General Mills, by permission of American Greetings; pg. 12, Carebears, Courtesy of General Mills; pg. 12, X-wing fighter, Courtesy of General Mills, by permission of Lucasfilm, Ltd.; pg. 12, Playdoh, photography by Voyles; pg. 16, Reprinted with permission of General Mills Inc.; pg. 17, Courtesy of Golden Valley Microwave Foods, Inc.; pg. 22, Courtesy of The Cleveland Clinic Foundation.

Chapter 2

pg. 28, Courtesy of International Business Machines; pg. 32, Courtesy of Prodigy Services Company; pg. 33, Photography by Voyles; pg. 35, Joseph McNally Photography, Courtesy of General Electric; pg. 40, Photography by Peter Freed; pg. 41, Courtesy of Hush Puppies Shoes, a Division of Wolverine World Wide, Inc.; pg. 43, Courtesy of The Coca-Cola Company and Arthur Meyerson Photography; pg. 45, Photography by Ray Marklin; pg. 47, Courtesy of International Business Machines; pg. 49, Courtesy of International Business Machines; pg. 52, Reprinted Courtesy of Eastman Kodak Company.

Chapter 3

pg. 56, Photography by Ray Marklin, Formalwear Courtesy of Castelli Tuxedo Rental and Sales; pg. 62, Courtesy of Clairol Inc.; pg. 64, Photography by Greg Wolff; pg. 65, Courtesy of Mosley; pg. 67, Photography by Greg Wolff; pg. 70, Advertisement courtesy of British Airways; pg. 71, Courtesy of Consumers Digest; pg. 72, Courtesy of NewVector Communications; pg. 73, John Ficara/Newsweek; pg. 75, Photography by Greg Wolff; pg. 77, Photography by Ray Marklin; pg. 81, Photography by Voyles.

Chapter 4

pg. 88, Photography by Andrew J. Thacker, Courtesy of The Southland Corporation; pg. 92, Compliments of Pioneer Electronics, Saatchi and Saatchi/DFS—Richard Noble, photographer; pg. 97, Michelin Tires, used with permission of Michelin Tire Corporation. All rights reserved; pg. 97, Mutual of America, Courtesy of Mutual of America; pg. 98, Good Housekeeping Seal reprinted by permission of the Hearst Corporation, publishers of Good Housekeeping; pg. 99, Passion Perfume counter, photography by Greg Wolff, Courtesy of Dillard's Department Stores; pg. 99, Duncan Hines Free Trial, Courtesy of Proctor & Gamble Company; pg. 99, Clairol Hair Color, photography by Voyles; pg. 101, Photography by Ray Marklin; pg. 104, Reprinted Courtesy of General Mills; pg. 105, Photography by Ray Marklin; pg. 108, Courtesy of McDonald's Corporation.

Chapter 5

pg. 112, Courtesy of General Motors; pg. 114, Courtesy of J. Alvite, Mecanotron Corporation, St. Paul, MN; pg. 115, Courtesy of Domtar Gypsum; pg. 119, Courtesy of Weyerhaeuser; pg. 120, Courtesy of GTE Products Corp.; pg. 123, Courtesy of Loctite; pg. 128, Photography by Voyles, Courtesy of Emerson Electric Company; pg. 130, Science Source/Photo Researchers Inc.; pg. 134, © 1988 The NutraSweet Company, reprinted with permission.

Chapter 6

pg. 140, Photography by Voyles; pg. 142, Philip Amdal/Time Magazine; pg. 143, Photography by Voyles; pg. 146, Courtesy of Fisher Price, Division of the Quaker Oats Company; pg. 149, Courtesy of Duds 'N Suds; pg. 152, Photography by Voyles; pg. 156, Courtesy of Nielsen Media Research; pg. 158, Photography by Voyles; pg. 164, Drawing by Ziegler, © 1988 The New Yorker Magazine, Inc.

Chapter 7

pg. 168, Photography by Ray Marklin; pg. 171, Photography by Voyles; pg. 172, Photography by Ray Marklin; pg. 173, Reprinted with permission of Warner-Lambert Company; pg. 176, Courtesy of Garid, Inc.; pg. 178, Courtesy of Garid, Inc.; pg. 180, Courtesy of Safeway, Inc.; pg. 181, Photography by Ray Marklin; pg. 184, Photography by Ray Marklin.

Chapter 8

pg. 194, Photography by Ray Marklin, Shoes Courtesy of The Foot Locker; pg. 196, Photography by Ray Marklin; pg. 199, Courtesy of The Conde Nast Publications, Inc.; pg. 203, Great Starts Breakfast, photography by Ray Marklin; pg. 203, GE Refrigerator, furnished by G.E. Appliances, Louisville, Kentucky; pg. 207, Photography by Ray Marklin; pg. 209, Photography by Ray Marklin; pg. 211, Photography by Ray Marklin; pg. 213, Photography by Greg Wolff, Courtesy of Advant Computers; pg. 216, Courtesy of Volvo North America Corporation.

Chapter 9

pg. 225, Courtesy of Pontiac Division-General Motors Corporation; pg. 227, Courtesy of Adidas USA; pg. 228, Courtesy of Geers Gross Advertising, Inc. for G.H. Bass & Co.; pg. 230, Courtesy of Rolex Watch USA; pg. 233, Photography by Ray Marklin; pg. 234, Photography by Ray Marklin; pg. 236, Photography by Ray Marklin; pg. 240, Lean Cuisine, photography by Ray Marklin; pg. 240, Speak & Math, Courtesy of Texas Instruments; pg. 246, Courtesy of Proctor & Gamble; pg. 248, Courtesy of Adolph Coors Company.

Chapter 10

pg. 254, Photography by Voyles; pg. 258, Courtesy National Potato Promotion Board; pg. 260, Sony CD player, Courtesy of Sony Corporation of America; pg. 260, Tonka Gobots, photography by Voyles; pg. 260, Swatch Watches, Courtesy of Swatch Watches U.S.A.; pg. 263, Courtesy of Jolt; pg. 267, Courtesy of Oscar Mayer Foods Corporation; pg. 270, Photography by Ray Marklin; pg. 272, Photography by Greg Wolff; pg. 274, Photography by Ray Marklin; pg. 276, Photography by Ray Marklin.

Chapter 11

pg. 282, Photography by Greg Wolff; pg. 286, Courtesy of BMW of North America, Inc.; pg. 292, Courtesy of the Pontiac Division—General Motors Corporation; pg. 297, Courtesy of Trojan Yacht; pg. 298, Snack aisle, photography by Voyles; pg. 298, Vegetable aisle, Randy Matusow/Archive Pictures, Inc.; pg. 304, Reproduced Courtesy of General Motors Corporation.

Chapter 12

pg. 310, Courtesy of NW Ayer Advertising on Behalf of AT&T Co. Inc., © 1985; pg. 314, Courtesy of Horn Abbott, Ltd.; pg. 316, Courtesy of Jean Patou; pg. 318, Courtesy of Krug Champagne; pg. 319, Photography by Andrew J. Thacker; pg. 321, Photography by Ray Marklin; pg. 325, Courtesy Christian Dior Monsieur, a Hartmarx brand; pg. 331, Copyright © The Toro Company, 1986; pg. 333, Photography by Voyles; pg. 334, Courtesy of Fortune Magazine; pg. 336, Courtesy of Pearle Vision Centers.

Chapter 13

pg. 348, Photography by Andrew J. Thacker; pg. 352, Logos, Courtesy of IBM, Courtesy of Apple Computer Inc., Courtesy of COMPAQ Computer Center, Courtesy of AT&T; pg. 353, Gas station, Owen Franken/Stock Boston; pg. 353, Tailoring, photography by Voyles, Courtesy of Boyd's Department Store; pg. 353, Travel Car, Courtesy of Ask Mr. Foster; pg. 361, Photography by Voyles; pg. 363, Western Auto, Courtesy of Western Auto Supply Company; pg. 364, Courtesy of H&R Block; pg. 366, Courtesy of The Kroger Company; pg. 368, Photography by Andrew J. Thacker; pg. 369, Courtesy of the Organization of Manufacturing Representatives.

Chapter 14

pg. 376, Courtesy of Wal-Mart Stores, Inc.; pg. 379, Courtesy of Brod Dugan; pg. 381, Photography by Voyles, Courtesy of Wetterau, Inc.; pg. 390, Courtesy of Conrail Railways; pg. 392, Trucks, Hank Lebo/Jeroboam, Inc.; pg. 392, Pipeline, Courtesy of Alyeska; pg. 392, Barge, Courtesy of CSX Corporation; pg. 392, Ships, Chris Brown/Stock Boston; pg. 394, The photograph is reprinted with the permission of Federal Express Corporation. All rights reserved; pg. 395, Tom Tracy/The Stock Shop; pg. 396, Photography by Voyles, Courtesy of Wetterau, Inc.; pg. 398, Courtesy of Lear Siegler, Inc.; pg. 399, Advertisement Courtesy of Leaseway Transportation Corporation.

Chapter 15

pg. 404, Courtesy of West Edmonton Mall; pg. 405, Copyright © 1985 Marvel Entertainment Group, Inc. All rights reserved; pg. 408, Courtesy of West Edmonton Mall; pg. 413, Courtesy of Tenneco Automotive, Lincolnshire, Illinois; pg. 416, © The Sharper Image; pg. 424, bijan's, Courtesy of bijan's; pg. 424, Quincy Market, Ulrike Welson/Stock Boston; pg. 427, Tom Tracy/The Stock Shop.

Chapter 16

pg. 432, Courtesy of Anheuser-Busch Companies, Inc.; pg. 435, Courtesy of Jaguar Cars; pg. 438, OREO is a registered trademark of Nabisco Inc. Advertisement reprinted with permission of Nabisco; pg. 439, Photography by Voyles; pg. 440, Courtesy of Carey-McFall Corporation; pg. 441, Courtesy of Communication Channels, Inc.; pg. 443, Photography by Greg Wolff; pg. 450, The Triumphs of Black Women, "A Century of Empowerment," © Varnette P. Honeywood, 1985. Reprinted by permission of The Gillette Company and Essence Magazine; pg. 450, Snoopy glasses, photography by Voyles; pg. 452, Gravity feed bin, photography by Ray Marklin; pg. 452, VideOcart Michael Abramson/Woodsin Camp and Associates, Inc.; pg. 454, Courtesy of Chrysler Plymouth; pg. 457, Neil Leifer/Time Magazine.

Chapter 17

pg. 426, Dave Hogan/Lynn Goldsmith, Inc.; pg. 464, Courtesy of Waterford Wedgewood USA, Inc.; pg. 464, Courtesy of Max Factor; pg. 464, Courtesy of Northwestern Mutual Life; pg. 466, Photography by Greg Wolff; pg. 467, Courtesy of Anheuser-Busch Companies, Inc.; pg. 473, Courtesy Lee Apparel Company; pg. 477, Courtesy of Mazda Motors; pg. 478, From Rolling Stone Magazine By Straight Arrow Publishers, Inc., © 1986. All rights reserved. Reprinted by permission; pg. 482, Courtesy of Richardson or Richardson; pg. 485, Courtesy of Starch, Inra Hooper.

Chapter 18

pg. 488, Courtesy of International Business Machines Corporation; pg. 492, Steve Hansen/Stock Boston; pg. 493, Courtesy of Frito-Lay, Inc.; pg. 495, Drawing by Woodman, © 1987 The New Yorker Magazine, Inc.; pg. 496, Courtesy of Needham Harper Worldwide, Inc.; pg. 498, Courtesy of Husk Jennings Overman for AT&T American Transtech; pg. 499, Counter clerk, photography by Voyles, Courtesy of Naugles, Inc.; pg. 499, Door-to-door sales, Courtesy of Fuller Brush Company; pg. 512, Courtesy of Mary Kay Cosmetics, photography by Ted Munger.

Chapter 19

pg. 518, Courtesy of General Mills Corporation; pg. 527, Courtesy of General Mills Corporation; pg. 529, Courtesy of 3M; pg. 532, Courtesy of Black & Decker, Inc., Howard Menken and David Zimmerman photographers; pg. 533, Courtesy of General Mills Corporation; pg. 540, Photography by Voyles.

Chapter 20

pg. 546, Photography by Voyles; pg. 548, Photography by Ray Marklin; pg. 551, GE Jet Engine, Alan Bergman Photography; pg. 551, Airplane, Courtesy of Airbus Industrie of North America, Inc.; pg. 555, Courtesy of the Ford Motor Company; pg. 559, Courtesy of Pillsbury Corporation; pg. 568, Photography by Greg Wolff.

Chapter 21

pg. 574, Photography by Ray Marklin; pg. 577, Photography by Greg Wolff; pg. 579, Courtesy of the Nestle Company, Inc.; pg. 582, Courtesy of McDonald's Corporation; pg. 588, Drawing by Leo Cullum; pg. 591, Courtesy of Ericsson Industries; pg. 593, Courtesy of Avon; pg. 594, Courtesy of the Coca-Cola Company; pg. 597, Courtesy of Skai Shinota; pg. 598, Courtesy of the New Zealand Tourist Board.

Chapter 22

pg. 602, Courtesy of The Walt Disney Company; pg. 606, Courtesy of Norwegian Cruise Lines; pg. 607, Courtesy of the Hyatt Corporation; pg. 611, © Greenpeace; pg. 611, Army photographs courtesy U.S. government, as represented by the Secretary of the Army; pg. 614, Courtesy of The Hertz Corporation; pg. 616, Courtesy of Club Relations Director, Courtesy of McDonald's Corporation, Courtesy of AT&T, and Courtesy of the United Way; pg. 617, Courtesy of Whitehall and Tremont Hotel; pg. 618, Courtesy of Inter-County Leader, Frederic, Wisconsin; pg. 619, Courtesy of the New Haven Symphony Orchestra.

Appendix B

pg. 625, Reprinted by permission of the Boston Herald.

DISCOVER WHAT "MAKING THE GRADE" IS ALL ABOUT

STUDY GUIDE
by
Erica S. Michaels

Prepare for your exams with the study guide that accompanies your textbook! It will help you:

- master key concepts;
- match definitions with key terms;
- apply important ideas to real-world applications;
- test yourself with quick recall questions;
- check your answers against those provided at the end of every chapter.

Contact your bookstore manager for availability, or call toll-free 800-323-4560. *Ask for* the Michaels study guide (0-256-07514-X).